The Economics of Barter and Countertrade

The International Library of Critical Writings in Economics

Series Editor: Mark Blaug

Professor Emeritus, University of London, UK
Professor Emeritus, University of Buckingham, UK
Visiting Professor, University of Amsterdam, The Netherlands
Visiting Professor, Erasmus University of Rotterdam, The Netherlands

This series is an essential reference source for students, researchers and lecturers in economics. It presents by theme a selection of the most important articles across the entire spectrum of economics. Each volume has been prepared by a leading specialist who has written an authoritative introduction to the literature included.

A full list of published and future titles in this series is printed at the end of this volume.

Wherever possible, the articles in these volumes have been reproduced as originally published using facsimile reproduction, inclusive of footnotes and pagination to facilitate ease of reference.

For a list of all Edward Elgar published titles visit our site on the World Wide Web at http://www.e-elgar.co.uk

The Economics of Barter and Countertrade

Edited by

Rolf Mirus

Professor of International Business
University of Alberta, Canada

and

Bernard Yeung

Abraham Krasnoff Professor in Global Business and Professor of Economics
New York University, USA
and Area Research Director
William Davidson Institute, University of Michigan, USA

THE INTERNATIONAL LIBRARY OF CRITICAL WRITINGS IN ECONOMICS

An Elgar Reference Collection
Cheltenham, UK • Northampton, MA, USA

Published by
Edward Elgar Publishing Limited
Glensanda House
Montpellier Parade
Cheltenham
Glos GL50 1UA
UK

Edward Elgar Publishing, Inc.
136 West Street, Suite 202
Northampton
Massachusetts 01060
USA

A catalogue record for this book is available from the British Library.

Library of Congress Cataloguing in Publication Data

The economics of barter and countertrade / edited by Rolf Mirus and Bernard Yeung.
p. cm. — (The international library of critical writings in economics ; 138 (An Elgar reference collection)
Includes bibliographical references and index.
1. Countertrade. 2. Barter. 3. International trade. I. Mirus, Rolf, 1940– II. Yeung, Bernard, 1953– III. Series. IV. Series: An Elgar reference collection

HF1414.3 .E26 2002
382—dc21 2001040454

ISBN 1 84064 438 9

Printed and bound in Great Britain by MPG Books Ltd, Bodmin, Cornwall

Contents

Acknowledgements

The editors and publishers wish to thank the authors and the following publishers who have kindly given permission for the use of copyright material.

American Economic Association for articles: Steve Williamson and Randall Wright (1994), 'Barter and Monetary Exchange Under Private Information', *American Economic Review*, **84** (1), March, 104–23; Joseph A. Ritter (1995), 'The Transition from Barter to Fiat Money', *American Economic Review*, **85** (1), March, 134–49; Dalia Marin and Monika Schnitzer (1995), 'Tying Trade Flows: A Theory of Countertrade with Evidence', *American Economic Review*, **85** (5), December, 1047–64.

Asian Journal of Economics and Social Studies for article: Abla M. Abdel-Latif and Jeffrey B. Nugent (1993), 'Countertrade, Licensing and Direct Foreign Investment: Comparative Effects on LDCs and MNEs', *Asian Journal of Economics and Social Studies*, **12** (2), April, 81–96.

Blackwell Publishers Ltd for articles: Richard E. Caves and Dalia Marin (1992), 'Countertrade Transactions: Theory and Evidence', *Economic Journal*, **102**, September, 1171–83; Erwin Amann and Dalia Marin (1994), 'Risk-sharing in International Trade: An Analysis of Countertrade', *Journal of Industrial Economics*, **XLII** (1), March, 63–77.

Business Horizons for article: Robert E. Weigand (1980), 'Barters and Buy-backs: Let Western Firms Beware!', *Business Horizons*, **23** (1–3), June, 54–61.

Canadian Journal of Administrative Sciences for article: Rolf Mirus and Bernard Yeung (1989), 'Buy-back and Technology Transfer – Some Theoretical Considerations', *Canadian Journal of Administrative Sciences*, **6** (3), September, 31–6.

Elsevier Science for articles: Raissa Chan and Michael Hoy (1991), 'East–West Joint Ventures and Buyback Contracts', *Journal of International Economics*, **30** (3/4), May, 331–43; Chong J. Choi and Daniel Maldoom (1992), 'A Simple Model of Buybacks', *Economics Letters*, **40**, 77–82; Tore Ellingsen and Lars A. Stole (1996), 'Mandated Countertrade as a Strategic Commitment', *Journal of International Economics*, **40**, 67–84; Dalia Marin and Monika Schnitzer (1998), 'Economic Incentives and International Trade', *European Economic Review*, **42**, 705–16.

Journal of International Business Studies for articles: Bruce Kogut (1986), 'On Designing Contracts to Guarantee Enforceability: Theory and Evidence from East–West Trade', *Journal of International Business Studies*, **17** (1), Spring, 47–61; Rolf Mirus and Bernard Yeung (1986), 'Economic Incentives for Countertrade', *Journal of International Business Studies*, **17** (3),

Fall, 27–39; Jean-François Hennart (1990), excerpt from 'Some Empirical Dimensions of Countertrade', *Journal of International Business Studies*, **21** (2), Second Quarter, 243–6, 254–63, 264–5, 267–70.

Kiel Institute of World Economics for article: Rolf Mirus and Bernard Yeung (1987), 'Countertrade and Foreign Exchange Shortages: A Preliminary Assessment', *Weltwirtschaftliches Archiv*, **123** (3), 535–44.

Macmillan Ltd for excerpt: Richard E. Caves (1974), 'The Economics of Reciprocity: Theory and Evidence on Bilateral Trading Arrangements', in Willy Sellekaerts (ed.), *International Trade and Finance: Essays in Honour of Jan Tinbergen*, Chapter 1, 17–54.

Oxford University Press for articles: Peter Murrell (1982), 'Product Quality, Market Signaling and the Development of East–West Trade', *Economic Inquiry*, **XX** (4), October, 589–603; Ellen Magenheim and Peter Murrell (1988), 'How to Haggle and to Stay Firm: Barter as Hidden Price Discrimination', *Economic Inquiry*, **XXVI** (1), January, 449–59; Jean-François Hennart (1989), 'The Transaction-cost Rationale for Countertrade', *Journal of Law, Economics, and Organization*, **5** (1), Spring, 127–53; Abla M. Abdel-Latif and Jeffrey B. Nugent (1994), 'Countertrade as Trade Creation and Trade Diversion', *Contemporary Economic Policy*, **XII** (1), January, 1–11.

Taylor and Francis, Inc. for article: Rolf Mirus and Bernard Yeung (1993), 'Why Countertrade? An Economic Perspective', *International Trade Journal*, **VII** (4), Summer, 409–33.

Westburn Publishers Ltd for article: C.W. Neale, D. Shipley and P. Sercu (1992), 'Motives for and the Management of Countertrade in Domestic Markets', *Journal of Marketing Management*, **8** (4), October, 335–49.

Every effort has been made to trace all the copyright holders but if any have been inadvertently overlooked the publishers will be pleased to make the necessary arrangement at the first opportunity.

In addition the publishers wish to thank the Library of the London School of Economics and Political Science, the Marshall Library of Economics, Cambridge University and the Library of Indiana University at Bloomington, USA for their assistance in obtaining these articles.

Introduction

Rolf Mirus and Bernard Yeung

In the post-war era, the world economy was segmented into groups of developed, developing, and centrally planned economies. Many developing countries engaged in import substitution programmes, and inward foreign direct investment was stifled by restrictions, or even explicitly prohibited. International trade and investment between centrally planned economies and the rest of the world were, respectively, very limited or nonexistent.

In the 1980s, the world changed. First, technological progress in transportation, communication, and organization fostered scale economies in operations, increasing the need and the ability to conduct trade internationally and pursue foreign direct investment (FDI).

Second, the growth experience of trade-oriented countries effectively appeared to have changed the stance of many public policy makers. 'Export promotion' replaced 'import substitution'. Trade liberalization took place, in part due to the genuine acceptance of the free-trade principle, and partly as disguised mercantilism. Membership in the original General Agreement on Tariffs and Trade (GATT) (and later the World Trade Organization (WTO)) increased, and many of the current free-trade areas are the result of the negotiations and agreements of the 1980s.

Third, even the previously closed communist economies changed. After years of unsuccessful experiments in central planning, many command economies were more or less close to collapse. These economies turned to economic liberalization, which included acceptance of imports and adoption of foreign technologies. Some countries, such as those in Eastern Europe, abandoned communism in their national politics and embraced the market system for their economy. Others, like China, while preserving their political system, experimented selectively with free(r) markets and later explicitly aimed to develop a market economy.

The outcome was heightened economic interaction, in the form of trade and direct investment, between the developed economies, newly liberalizing command economies, and some of the previously closed economies in developing countries. For many of the not yet developed economies importing and inward foreign direct investment were new experiences. They were without the institutional and market environment that characterizes the 'West', and many of them still are. Their regulatory framework was 'restrictive', and their market infrastructure was either absent or at a very basic level. As a result, their prices conveyed little economic information. Indeed, the information processing capability of these markets was very limited. Neither the infrastructure, nor the legal code to protect property rights were well developed. Because the rule of law was at an early stage of development, Western firms and local companies found the writing and subsequent enforcement of contracts a daunting task. Into this context countertrade was born. It was the outcome of early and tentative economic interactions between firms from advanced market economies and firms operating in the aforementioned environment.

Countertrade can be viewed as an awkward form of transaction. Some would describe it as in-kind exchange of goods and services, some would describe it as bundling of transactions. The literature has generally distinguished three types of countertrade:

1. *Barter*: The direct exchange of goods and services, completed nearly simultaneously.
2. *Counterpurchase*: The assumption by an exporter of a transferable obligation through a separate but linked contract to accept as full or partial payment goods and services from the importer or importing country. The contract usually stipulates a period during which the counterpurchase is to be completed, and the goods and services received in return are prespecified, subject to availability and to changes made by the importing country. In essence, counterpurchase represents an intertemporal exchange of goods and services or the bundling of two transactions, namely current buying and future selling.
3. *Buyback*: An agreement by an exporter of plant and equipment to take back in the future part of the output produced by these exports in full or partial payment. The distinguishing feature here is the vertical link between the current and the future exchanges. Another important difference from counterpurchase is that buybacks usually stretch over a longer period of time, possibly as long as 15–20 years.

Early work focused on drawing analysts' attention to the fact that these transactions appear to be very different from the money-based transactions prevalent in mature market economies. Initial conventional wisdom was that countertrade represented a backward and inefficient form of transaction forced upon 'Western' firms by governments of developing countries that wanted to promote exports or deal with balance of payments difficulties.

Analysts, however, very quickly discovered that the complicated features typical of countertrade transactions serve important economic functions, given the environment within which these transactions take place. Their research identified the difficulties of transacting in an environment replete with 'market' inadequacies, such as lack of means to hedge risks, unreliable price signals, poor property rights protection linked to weak rule of law, and excessive regulation. Researchers began to argue that the complicated governance and transaction features of countertrade contracts provide solutions to market inadequacies. The logical basis for the functional features of these complicated countertrade agreements is found in well-known economic concepts: signalling, precommitment, and incentive compatibility. At the outset, the ideas were advanced in the form of verbal arguments, the intended audience consisting mostly of nontechnical economists. Later, the ideas were presented in more formal ways and began to appear in mainstream economic journals.

Countertrade research therefore has advanced our understanding of the relationship between efficiency and transactional governance arrangements. It also has deepened our appreciation of the usefulness of basic concepts in the economics of information and organization. This literature provides the insight that at the microeconomic level efficiency in international trade and direct investment transactions is intricately tied to contractual and governance features. In that sense, countertrade research has made an important contribution to what is now an established component of organization economics.

While 25 years is a small span in the development of economic analysis, the contribution of the countertrade literature has been significant: it shows that it is vitally important how transactions are arranged! The microeconomic structure of transactions matters, and countertrade can serve to enhance efficiency. These issues, which were not addressed by the theories of comparative advantage and factor mobility, result in substantial additional insights. It therefore seems an appropriate and opportune time to trace out the roots of this literature by assembling a collection of the key (published) papers that document its intellectual development.

Our introduction aims, as do the major divisions of the collection's contents, to review the early attempts to analyse the countertrade phenomenon, to highlight the subsequent refinements of its theoretical underpinnings, and to touch upon the managerial and policy issues raised by this literature.

The Rise, and Rejection, of Conventional Wisdom

By the mid to late 1970s, articles had begun to appear in the business and professional press that reported, and warned of, special contractual arrangements in East–West and North–South trade. The observed practices were referred to as 'barter' and 'countertrade', with the terms 'counterpurchase', 'compensation trade' and 'buyback' denoting particular forms of countertrade.

Barter, said to derive from the old French 'barater', to cheat, in this context meant moneyless, simultaneous market exchange. Countertrade was the generic term for transactions that were reciprocal in nature. It likely was the direct translation of the term 'Gegengeschäft', which was used to describe the bilateral clearing arrangements that Germany relied upon to sustain raw material imports from the Balkans during the protectionist years prior to the Second World War. These arrangements were set up between the Reichsbank and particular countries and allowed settlement of net positions once a year. Officially these kinds of trade transactions were referred to as 'Kompensationsgeschäft' or compensation trade.

Exchanges in kind are not uncommon. In developed economies exchanges in kind have been carried out for the purpose of tax avoidance, for example. Exchanges in kind are more prevalent, however, when the currency and financial markets are in disarray. When a currency is not trustworthy, people resort to exchanges denominated in a foreign currency or to exchanges in kind, like paying workers with their products. In the immediate post-war years, when financial markets were in disarray, Britain and Western Europe relied on similar clearing systems, and the emerging communist countries used their own versions of exchanges in kind among themselves and neighbouring countries like Finland. Conceptually, these practices were based on the establishment of trade credit accounts among trading partners for the exchange of unrelated goods.

Countertrade transactions observed in the 1970s and 1980s were different, yet similarities remained. The partners were not necessarily familiar with each other, and the goods exchanged, on occasion, were vertically related. Characteristically, the observed practices involved companies from developed market economies in interaction with companies from command or transition economies. It was noteworthy of many such countertrade transactions that they involved two separate contracts and used actual money.

At first glance, then, countertrade is a puzzling form of transaction: it is cumbersome to pay for goods and services with goods and services, and the arrangement reminds observers of exchanges in kind during periods of either hyperinflation or other currency turmoil. This similarity, however, is more apparent than real. The older barter transactions were carried out in an environment where no credible fiat monies existed or where the use of foreign monies was politically unacceptable. Countertrade transactions observed in the 1970s and 1980s, however, were mediated by highly credible hard currencies. In any event, early observers were warning practitioners about the pitfalls of countertrade. An example is 'Barter and Buy-backs: Let Western Firms Beware!' (Weigand, Chapter 1, this volume).

The conventional wisdom at the time seemed to be that, while inefficient and cumbersome, countertrade could bring benefits to developing countries, benefits such as improved terms of trade, a better trade balance, and access to credit.

The conventional wisdom was challenged by Banks (1984) and Mirus and Yeung (Chapter 2). To the best of our knowledge Banks (1984) was the first to voice disagreement with what were alleged to be policy objectives of countertrading countries. According to Banks, most centrally planned and less developed economies are too small to have a significant degree of market power. They are more likely to be price takers in world markets and, were they to have market power, they would be better off exploiting it by means of a tariff than by using the cumbersome and complex practice of countertrade, which does not generate revenue directly as a tariff would. For that reason, Banks argued, countertrade cannot be a policy to address foreign exchange shortages or credit constraints.

We hasten to add that this view can be disputed. Caves (Chapter 13) argues that for a firm from a developing country countertrade can be a means to bargain down high prices charged by a dominant firm from a developed economy. We shall return to this point in a subsequent section. Also, for expositional convenience, we shall refer to the former firm as 'East' and the latter as 'West'.

Using Banks' doubt as a point of departure, Mirus and Yeung, in Chapter 2, offer a systematic analysis of the conventional wisdom in the context of commonly accepted economic identities. They argue that if countertrade is indeed a response to foreign exchange shortages, it is because it improves economic efficiency. Were it an inefficient practice, it would exacerbate the country's shortage of hard currency. They essentially derive their argument from the identity that the current account balance is equal to savings minus investment. Another way to put the point is that the change in money demand minus the change in money supply is equal to the balance of payments and is positively associated with the change in currency strength. (Or the change in currency demand is positively associated with an economy's income performance.) Hence, the two arguments that countertrade (a) creates inefficiency and (b) alleviates balance of payments deficits or currency weakness, are not compatible.

Mirus and Yeung do admit in Chapter 2 that the conventional wisdom may imply that barter can be a means to increase imports. Having incurred too much debt, a country may be forced to impose austerity measures including the curtailment of imports. Barter can then be seen as a means to bypass austerity measures, but it will be successful only if the bartered exports escape the creditors' attention or audit.

Hennart (Chapter 3) makes a useful contribution by taking a tally of observed countertrade practices. In addition to its informative classification of countertrade (Hennart's Figure 1), Chapter 3 adduces evidence on the relative frequency of barter, buyback and counterpurchase from transactions reported during 1983 to 1986 in *Countertrade Outlook*, a newsletter for industry professionals. The chapter reveals that countertrade is essentially a practice adopted in trade among developing countries and trade between developing and developed countries. His finding validates the contention raised in our introduction, namely that countertrade is the result of the emergence of economic interactions between firms in countries with a poor institutional infrastructure and firms from advanced market economies.

Hennart also shows that the propensity to barter is indeed higher in countries with low credit ratings, whereas the propensities to, respectively, engage in buyback and counterpurchase do not correlate closely with a country's creditworthiness. These findings validate the contention that 'credit constraint' is only a partial explanation for the emergence of countertrade.

The growth of countertrade observed in the late 1970s and early 1980s, coupled with projections from that time that this practice would soon comprise 30 per cent of world trade, served to attract the attention of scholars. As a result a number of analytical contributions appeared by the mid 1980s.

Countertrade as a Solution to Difficulties in Transacting: New Analytical Approaches

Not surprisingly, from the outset analysts focused their attention on the economic implications of the contractual features of countertrade and the institutional environment within which it takes place. Their research draws attention to the economic meaning of contractual arrangements and governance features in the institutional environment in which the trade and investment transactions are implemented.

Tschoegl (1985) referred to the obvious possibility that barter and counterpurchase can be means to bypass price controls and avoid taxes, and that buyback has the property of a performance bond. Yet, since creative accounting and long-term contracts could also achieve these ends, the question remained why they were not chosen. Students of the phenomenon thus began to surmise that the contractual features and the governance of countertrade might be based on a more sophisticated economic foundation and linked to the environment in which these transactions occurred.

In 'Product Quality, Market Signaling and the Development of East–West Trade' (Chapter 4) Murrell hypothesizes countertrade as a 'signal' of quality. 'West's' commitment to buy back goods that have been produced with the technology it transfers to 'East' is a signal of the quality and reliability of its transfer. Murrell's idea is part of the overall argument that contractual features are devised to overcome transactional difficulties stemming from information asymmetry. He anticipates Kogut's focus on enforcement when he says: 'By placing themselves in a position of mutual dependence, the two parties are signaling the reliability of their future conduct.' (p. 591). His hypotheses regarding buyback as a quality signal are, by and large, corroborated by the data.

In Chapter 5 'On Designing Contracts to Guarantee Enforceability: Theory and Evidence from East–West Trade', Kogut raises the importance of the issue of contract enforceability as a means for understanding countertrade. 'West' needs enforceability in contracts and relationship governance and can offer superior managerial and risk-shifting services. Managerial services pertain to information gathering and processing, to marketing, distribution, and the like. Risk-shifting ability refers to 'West' having shareholders with low risk aversion and to institutional arrangements that result in sharing or shifting of risks. Such situations call for self-enforcing contracts, that is, the contract terms are devised in such a way that it will be in the contracting party's interest to honor the contract. For Kogut the prevalence of coproduction agreements and buyback in East–West trade had a microeconomic underpinning: they are means to address bilateral hostage exposure so that the contract is incentive-compatible.

Taken together, Murrell's emphasis of the signalling aspect and Kogut's focus on the enforceability of contracts prepare the ground for a more comprehensive analysis of the countertrade phenomenon.

Mirus and Yeung's Chapter 6 searches for the economic rationale for countertrade arrangements and ends up offering an encompassing analysis of the observed practices. Their rationale is that some countertrade partners, especially the 'Western' firms, have access to ordinary market transactions in the global market place. To engage in a countertrade deal, the partners must each have an economic incentive to forgo these ordinary economic opportunities. Like Kogut, the authors emphasize that the environment in which countertrade deals take place is often characterized by tight regulatory control/interference, lack of either private, or especially, foreign ownership rights, lack of such information as is provided by a competitive price system, and generally underdeveloped markets. In this context, they enumerate 'transaction' difficulties and show how countertrade arrangements may alleviate these, to the extent that gains from countertrade can exceed the opportunity gains available in normal global market practices.

Mirus and Yeung divide their discussion of countertrade in Chapter 6 into examinations of contemporaneous and intertemporal exchanges. Their analysis essentially focuses on the exchange of (1) related goods and services (here technology and capital inputs linked with output) and (2) unrelated goods and services. In countertrade of unrelated goods and services, they argue that barter is a bundled transaction: 'West' sells not only goods (denoted as W) to 'East', but also its marketing services to push 'East's' goods (denoted as E) onto the global market. The marketing services may include the hiring of another company to do the job. 'West' is presumably more able than 'East' at identifying markets and selling E (either directly or by hiring a third company to do so). The bundled transaction provides several efficiency gains. First, assigning 'West' to push 'East's' goods economizes on search and transactions costs. Second, the arrangement is equivalent to making available to 'West' a 'commodity' hedge to reduce foreign exchange risks in its sales of W to 'East'.

The bundled transaction implies an 'incentive compatibility' condition. 'West' fully appropriates the revenues generated from selling E. Thus, it will act in a profit-maximizing manner. The consequence is that 'West' will have reason to attach the highest possible value to the 'marketing services' component of a barter or a counterpurchase deal. This will mean that 'East' would have a better chance to extract a higher consumer surplus from its consumption of 'West's' goods (W). As an illustration, consider the following simple case. 'East's' surplus in the countertrade transaction is the difference between the utility in consuming W and the cost of producing E. 'West's' surplus in the countertrade deal is the sum of the surplus in selling E (revenues less the cost in the marketing effort) minus the cost of producing W. The joint surplus is then the sum of (1) 'East's' willingness to pay for W less 'West's' cost of producing W and (2) 'West's' surplus in selling E less 'East's' cost of producing E. As the contract induces 'West' to maximize its surplus in selling E, the joint surplus of 'East' and 'West' increases. This makes possible that both 'East' and 'West' benefit.

Mirus and Yeung in Chapter 6 recognize that intertemporal countertrade often involves the transfer of technology and sale of future output. The key insight in this second section is that these transactions normally involve information-based assets, such as skills, technology, quality, or effort. Such transactions face intrinsic difficulties that stem from information asymmetry, moral hazard, and inconsistency in the timing of decisions. Countertrade is shown to serve as a contractual resolution of these problems. In the articles to follow, many of these issues will be taken up for refinement, and so it seems appropriate to provide a listing here of those features of countertrade that represent solutions to contracting problems.

In intertemporal countertrade, such as the delivery of a technology package in return for its output, Mirus and Yeung (p. 29) show that this arrangement addresses the buyer's relative lack of knowledge about the quality and performance of technology that often tends to involve highly specialized assets (information asymmetry). By tying the supplier to the output, buyback elicits his continuous efforts to service the technology. Mirus and Yeung point out that the divergence of interests of supplier and buyer derives from the prohibition against or high cost of foreign ownership and can be overcome by the buyback feature. Without these problems, full integration of buyer and seller would solve the transaction difficulties, the result being wholly owned foreign direct investment.

Mirus and Yeung (Chapter 6) caution that a carefully devised profit sharing contract may also deliver the same result (see also Chan and Hoy, Chapter 10). However, given the difficulties in contract enforcement and the lack of reliable accounting information, a buyback contract may have the advantage of operational convenience. The additional advantage of buyback is that it is equivalent to a continuous forward sale that lessens the risk for the technology buyer. This idea is subsequently developed by Amann and Marin (Chapter 12).

In addition, Mirus and Yeung point out that in an ordinary sharing contract the buyer has little control over the quality of the technology transferred. In particular the technology transferred may maximize the value of the transfer package but may not satisfy the buyer's desire for more sophisticated technology. If there is a monotonic relationship between the sophistication of technology transferred and the per unit value of the resultant output, stipulating the quantity of output to be taken back as compensation for the technology transfer is shown to give the buyer influence over the type of technology transferred.

A double moral hazard arises when the output is to be used as a component in further production by the technology supplier. Fewer such deals are likely to be concluded because of the asset specificity and resulting problems. Once the plant is built and prices for the buyback have been agreed upon, a mutual hostage situation exists. *Ex post* the technology supplier could try to renegotiate the price downward, and the buyer could try to do the same in the opposite direction. Buyback represents an incentive-compatible contract for both parties in this situation: both have an incentive to put forth their best efforts (Mirus and Yeung, Chapter 6, p. 33). In fact, without countertrade, there may be no market solution in this case! These notions are proposed but not formally established in Chapter 6. The argument is formally established in Marin and Schnitzer (Chapters 8 and 9) and Choi and Maldoom (Chapter 11).

Hennart (Chapter 7) essentially uses the arguments and economic concepts developed in Mirus and Yeung (Chapter 6), namely that countertrade is a solution for the transactional difficulties that fully integrated ownership can alleviate. He thus suggests that countertrade is a substitute for hierarchical coordination when such choice is not permitted, as Mirus and Yeung had posited. The empirical evidence he adduces indicates that countries with a high frequency of involvement in countertrade are also countries with severe FDI restrictions.

The Literature of the Nineties: Double Moral Hazard, Hostage Exchange, and Quantity Stipulation

As the research effort continued into the 1990s, the notion that countertrade arrangements solve transactional difficulties was presented in more formal models. A formal analysis of counterpurchase is found in Marin and Schnitzer (Chapter 8). They recognize that counterpurchase is equivalent to a mutual hostage exchange capable of mitigating the double moral hazard problem described below.

Their model consists of two parties from two different environments (again, we call them 'West' and 'East' here) facing a double moral hazard problem. 'West' exports a turnkey factory to 'East'; 'West's' efforts in the turnkey transfer have a positive effect on the value of the output from the factory. However, 'West's' efforts are unobservable and cannot be easily stipulated by a contract. 'East' has a credit constraint and can only pay 'West' for the turnkey project in the future. (As such, 'West' extends a credit to 'East'.) Yet, given the environment in which 'East' operates, 'West' cannot force 'East' to pay up in the future.

A counterpurchase arrangement can solve the double moral hazard problem. The arrangement commits 'East' to sell a good G to 'West' in the future at a given price. It is assumed that if 'East' has produced G, the contract is effective in forcing 'East' to first sell it to 'West'. It is further assumed that 'East' can afford to produce G if 'West' transfers good technology (thus increases 'East's' cash flow). The prices in the counterpurchase contract can be such that 'East' will be interested to produce G when it can afford to. Note, that whenever G is produced, 'West' will get it. Thus, if 'East' does not pay back its loan from 'West', 'West' can refuse to fully pay for G. The end result is that the mutual hostage exchange induces 'West' to perform in the turnkey project and later motivates 'East' to fully repay the loan it obtained from 'West'.

Based on a unique data set of 230 countertrade observations they assembled from Viennese countertrade specialists and containing detailed information on each transaction as well as the specialists' perceptions of the trade, Marin and Schnitzer's empirical evidence corroborates that the contract form chosen varies in accordance with the incentive to undersupply quality (as proxied by the complexity of the product exported).

In Chapter 9 Marin and Schnitzer utilize the same model and data set to show how economic incentives can drive countertrade arrangements. In the face of a credit constraint 'West' may be inclined to accept goods as payment for exports. These goods assume the role of collateral; hence homogeneous goods that can easily be liquidated are more desirable than differentiated goods. In countries where restrictions on FDI make efficient technology transfer a particular concern, countertrade can help elicit effort by both parties, especially if differentiated consumer goods have to be marketed by 'West' in return for the exported technology. In Marin and Schnitzer's sample the more severely credit-constrained less-developed country (LDC) importers indeed supplied relatively more homogeneous products in 'payment', while importers from the East, facing less of a credit constraint but more severe restrictions on foreign ownership, offered differentiated consumer and investment goods in their deals. These findings therefore corroborate the hypothesis that the nature of the underlying transactional issue, be it creditworthiness or efficiency of technology transfer, dictates the type of arrangement agreed upon.

Chan and Hoy (Chapter 10) focus on buybacks. They model the case where output is a function of inputs from a multinational corporation (MNC) and a host country enterprise (HCE) in a socialist environment. The authors implicitly assume that the quality of the inputs is not easily verifiable so that there is a double moral hazard problem. The first best outcome is one where HCE and MNC supply the 'quality' that maximizes the joint profits of HCE and MNC. The first best is presumably the outcome under fully integrated ownership. The authors show that under a sharing rule both sides still do not fully appropriate the returns to their effort and so will undersupply their quality inputs. The authors further argue that a minimum quality standard requirement (in exchange for monetary compensation) may lead to an outcome closer to the first best outcome than under the sharing rule. In addition, they show that if one side supplies more than one input, then combining a sharing rule and a 'minimum quality requirement' may generate a joint profit that is higher than under a pure sharing rule and under a pure minimum quality requirement rule.

Strictly speaking, the 'combined minimum quality requirement and sharing rule' does not exactly resemble buyback arrangements. Moreover, one may question the logic that assumes 'quality' as unobservable and at the same time a 'minimum quality requirement' as enforceable. Still, Chan and Hoy contribute to the idea that contractual features in joint ventures between 'East' and 'West' have important efficiency-enhancing functions. In particular, given that full integration is prohibited, using sharing rules may not be sufficient to fully alleviate transactional difficulties.

Choi and Maldoom's Chapter 11 presupposes the absence of any legally enforceable mechanism for contracts conditional on the quality of an input or an output. While output quality may be observable, it is not contractible in their model. They consider two alternatives: (1) a prespecified division of output between selling in 'East's' and 'West's' market, and (2) a market allocation mechanism. Under the market allocation mechanism, a middleman observes the quality of the output and allocates output optimally between 'East's' and 'West's' markets. In both alternatives, 'East' and 'West' share the sum of the revenues from selling in the two markets. The authors show that prespecified quantity division in selling to 'East's' and 'West's' market can be superior to the market allocation mechanism. Again, the contractual arrangement in alternative (1) is not very similar to buyback contracts we are familiar with. However, the authors contribute to an important idea: for a quantity split the decline in revenue is greater, given the same drop in effort, than for the market-allocated division of output. Thus, quantity stipulation can elicit effort. Essentially, this is the idea Mirus and Yeung (Chapter 6) similarly proposed when they argued that quantity buyback (sending a fixed output quantity from 'East' to 'West' as compensation for 'West's' original input) elicits 'West's' contribution of quality in the technology transfer.

Risk Sharing and Risk Shifting

Earlier commentators also suggest that countertrade is motivated by the lack of means to hedge currency and price risks in general (e.g. Kogut (Chapter 5) and Mirus and Yeung (Chapter 6)). Amann and Marin (Chapter 12) argue that countertrade is a form of risk sharing between 'West' and 'East'. They assume the absence of futures markets. Relying on a straightforward two-parameter (risk and return) utility function, they show that it is rational for 'East' to sell its product forward via counterpurchase; indeed, risk sharing is a Nash bargaining solution and can be Pareto optimal when no other means of reducing risk are available. They tacitly assume that 'West's' good exhibits no price volatility. Hence, they imply, as Kogut (Chapter 5) has argued, that 'West' has better risk reduction capability, with the result that the risk sharing is evidenced by 'West's' forward purchases of some of 'East's' output.

Countertrade as Hidden Price Discrimination

Countertrade could also be motivated by attempts at price discrimination. This issue is raised by Caves in Chapter 13. Having observed barter and a variety of other reciprocal agreements, some of them involving shopping lists as in counterpurchase, Caves hypothesizes that these practices might represent price discrimination in action. He cites as indirect evidence for this the complaints about resales by some of the LDC exporters. As well, the lower terms of trade offered by less developed countries to centrally planned economies might reflect attempts by the former to correct for overvalued exchange rates. Thus Caves proposes that bilateral arrangements, such as barter and counterpurchase, may also represent price discrimination as a competitive tool 'to offset inefficient trade interferences or to cheat on collusive prices' (p. 39).

Other efforts that focus on countertrade as a device to practice price discrimination are those of Caves and Marin (Chapter 15) and Magenheim and Murrell (Chapter 14). In Chapter 15 Caves and Marin follow up on price discrimination as a motivation for countertrade. 'West' exports a heterogeneous good and possesses some market power. 'East' uses countertrade as a means to extract back some of 'West's' rent. Caves and Marin then adduce empirical evidence that the implicit price in countertrade reflects the bargaining power of the two trading partners. Their work, though, begs two questions: can 'East' extract back some of 'West's' monopoly rent via other means? And why is countertrade chosen over these other means?

In Chapter 14 Magenheim and Murrell pursue two firms, each with market power, that can use each other's output as an input in their production process. Open price discrimination can lead to haggling and hence loss of future market power. Thus there is an attraction to hiding discounts. As net prices in barter cannot easily be observed, the undesirable consequences of open price discrimination can be avoided, yet its benefits can be reaped. One implication of this finding is that since the necessary double coincidence of wants is rare, barter exchanges can be expected to develop in order to facilitate the practice.

Policy Implications

The above literature referred to the policy impact of countertrade only by implication. The analytical literature we have reviewed so far implies that countertrade is efficiency creating. It is perhaps needless to point out that caution is warranted. A series of papers by Abdel-Latif and Nugent (Chapters 16 and 17) provides theoretical and empirical insights regarding barter and counterpurchase programmes practiced during the 1980s by Egypt.

In Chapter 16 Abdel-Latif and Nugent emphasize that countertrade may create trade but it may also have trade distortion effects. Consider that there are tariffs and other trade barriers. 'East' conducts countertrade with 'West', and the deal allows 'West' exclusive access to 'East's' home country market. It also allows 'East' to bypass tariffs and trade barriers in 'West's' home market. The result is trade creation that allows 'East's' country to gain consumer surplus.

Also, there will be a transfer of wealth from other firms in 'East's' country and forgone tariff revenue will accrue to 'East' itself. There is, however, trade diversion if partner 'West' is not the most efficient supplier. Inasmuch as more efficient firms are likely to have better market opportunities, this cautionary note is particularly appropriate: such firms are more inclined to reject requests for countertrade because their opportunity costs of engaging in it are higher.

If trade barriers are based on high transactions cost, and if countertrade indeed reduces transactions costs, the gain to the country is more likely to be positive. The authors articulate a series of complicated cost and benefit considerations, assessing the effects of an Egyptian company's countertrade with Japan's NEC, a firm that is unlikely to be the lowest cost supplier. They find that the programme benefited the Egyptian company, but that it yielded disappointingly low realized barter exports compared to the level planned for. Moreover, the exports were obtained at significant costs in terms of the implied exchange rate subsidy. Factors that may have contributed to the low ratio of realized to planned deals are the lengthy approval process, a bias in favour of large requests, the concurrent decline of Eastern Europe, general trade liberalization elsewhere, and the absence of data on private transactions.

Chapter 17 by Abdel-Latif and Nugent also applies partial equilibrium analysis to compare direct investment, licensing and licensing coupled with countertrade from the perspective of 'East' and 'West'. Based on consumer surplus and producer profit, buyback emerges as a possible bargaining solution when direct investment is ruled out, whereas counterpurchase proves inferior to even simple licensing due to the extra costs of disposing the goods.

Another policy suggestion is that social welfare can be improved by government-mandated countertrade. Ellingsen and Stole (Chapter 18) point to this as a possibility in circumstances where foreign buyers value domestic goods highly and the direct cost of mandating the practice is low. Their starting point can be interpreted to be that international trade is not frictionless due to the existence of information barriers. Information asymmetry between buyers and sellers leaves extractable surpluses. The intuition underlying their argument is that mandated countertrade allows domestic firms to extract more consumer's surplus in their international transactions, similar to the idea of countertrade as a means to practice price discrimination. Mandated countertrade, however, clearly has a strategic aspect when the frictions it causes are not overwhelming. Ellingsen and Stole's work therefore gives credence to the early conventional wisdom, which had led to complaints about the practice by Western firms.

Managerial Implications

Obviously, the key contribution of the economics of barter and countertrade, namely that the way in which transactions are arranged is vitally important for their success, has significant implications for managers. Surprisingly, there are relatively few scholarly papers that directly address the managerial dimension, at least in comparison to the number of sophisticated analytical and empirical contributions just described.

Neale, Shipley and Sercu (Chapter 19) survey countertrade practices within the national markets of Canada and the UK. This chapter sheds light on the perceptions of participants and points to implications of the practice of countertrade for a firm's marketing strategy and planning. Reactive versus proactive strategies, effective organization of countertrade, negotiating team composition, as well as effective evaluation and control mechanisms are some of the issues this paper alerts readers to. Survey respondents also corroborate that hidden price reductions and short-term credit problems are major motives for domestic countertrade.

In Chapter 20 Mirus and Yeung approach the managerial dimension from the point of view of a Western firm engaging in the export of capital equipment to an emerging economy. A stylized case study is used to motivate the derivation of a number of hypotheses that formalize what had been reported by management, namely that the buyback agreement helped speed up negotiations by avoiding delays from foreign exchange approvals, that the plant design was better adapted to accommodate the quality of local feed-stocks, and that some of the best employees were sent for assembly, supervision and start-up training. The managerial benefits of buyback as a monitoring device and as a signal of quality are thus re-emphasized. The major contribution of this chapter lies in the conjectures it presents on the managerial implications, based on the analytical foundations of countertrade.

While the literature focusing on the managerial implications could be considered somewhat sparse, it is not obvious that this is a serious shortcoming, because the analytical literature discussed previously has already advanced the notion of countertrade as an efficiency enhancing governance arrangement that is optimal under the circumstances.

Barter in a Domestic Setting

In recent years, the high volume of barter observed in Russia's domestic trade has rekindled analysts' interest. Several arguments have been made in attempt to explain the use of barter in international transactions. Ritter (Chapter 21) focuses on barter as a way of transacting when paper money has not been credibly established. By contrast, Williamson and Wright (Chapter 22) show that, in the presence of private information, barter can lead to an equilibrium in which only low quality goods are produced. The introduction of fiat money expands the range of trading strategies and options. Moving from barter to reliance on fiat money thus promotes production and exchange and enables agents to choose strategies that increase the probability of acquiring high-quality output. These analytical strands therefore contribute additional insights regarding the benefits of using money. Yet another focus of this literature is on the functions served by barter, which include evading taxes, exercising price discrimination/market power, and dealing with poor financial intermediation. While these latter ideas were already included in the literature reviewed earlier, they are now resurfacing in more elegant models, if still in working paper form (e.g. Guriev and Kvassov, 2000).

Barter and Countertrade: Conclusion and Prospects

The foregoing overview of the literature on barter and countertrade has shown an evolution in the description of the phenomenon from early explanations and critical analysis of same, to rigorous and formal hypotheses and their empirical verification. More than two and a half decades have elapsed since its initial study, and the fact that the range and formal complexity have increased significantly during this time makes it appropriate for us to summarize now what has been contributed and learned.

The first important lesson is that the relationship between countertrade and such alleged policy objectives as addressing currency shortages is somewhat tenuous. A more useful approach appears to be the study of the economic motivations for countertrade.

Mirus and Yeung (Chapter 23) attempt to take stock of the analytical results regarding the 'policy' and 'transactions costs' motives for countertrade. They do not favour the alleged policy motives emphasized by earlier commentators. Synthesizing the transactions cost motive deriving from difficulties in dealing with 'information asymmetry' and 'opportunistic behaviour', they reiterate that countertrade represents bundled transactions that are devised to mitigate these problems.

Restructuring, privatization, liberalization and development of markets in East and South may therefore reduce the frequency of countertrade. Reduced ownership restrictions are likely to shift organizational forms toward wholly owned production facilities and joint ventures. Improved knowledge, experience, and legal enforcement of contractual obligations will likely mean an increasing prevalence of longer-term and more sophisticated transaction contracts. Bundling should become less necessary in such a transformed environment.

However, bundled transactions as a way of dealing with information asymmetry, moral hazard problems, opportunistic behaviour, hedging needs, and other transaction difficulties are unlikely to disappear. While such problems are usually resolved by ownership integration and long-term contracts, there are situations where ownership is not desirable and where integration will cause diseconomies in management and other agency costs. When transactions are so complicated that monitoring and enforcement become costly, explicit contracting may be prohibitively difficult. Under such circumstances a bundled transaction might still be a viable solution.

Transaction cost economics (for example, Williamson, 1979) has shown that focusing on the transaction as the basic unit of analysis is a fruitful approach. In accordance with that approach and other advances in organizational economics, the contributions reviewed here have successfully identified and explicated differences that characterize alternative modes of governance.

By working out the microeconomic logic of its organizational form, the economics of barter and countertrade has arrived as an integral part of organization economics. Moreover, the literature illustrates that appropriately designed transactional governance is crucial for the efficiency of international economic interactions at the micro level.

References

Banks, Gary (1984), 'The economics and politics of countertrade', *World Economy*, **4**, 159–82.

Guriev, Sergei and Dmitry Kvassov (2000), 'Barter for price discrimination?', CEPR Discussion Paper No. 2449.

Tschoegl, Adrian E. (1985), 'Modern barter', *Lloyds Bank Review*, **158**, 32–40.

Williamson, Oliver E. (1979), 'Transaction cost economics: the governance of contractual relations', *Journal of Law and Economics*, **22** (2), 233–61.

Part I
Countertrade: Forms and Challenge of the Conventional Wisdom

[1]

BARTERS AND BUY-BACKS: LET WESTERN FIRMS BEWARE!

Non-monetary trade between Eastern-bloc firms and Western ones is not without certain drawbacks: repatriation of "profits" is often difficult; quality of goods, poor; and variety, limited.

ROBERT E. WEIGAND

International trade without money is flourishing today. Indeed, it is nearly the only way for some Western companies to do business with Eastern Europe, the developing countries, and, more recently, with the People's Republic of China. Recent deals include:

Armand Hammer negotiated an agreement to trade phosphate rock from Occidental Petroleum Corporation's mines in Florida for molten sulphur from Poland. The agreement would last twenty years and would involve about a million tons of phosphate rock a year and about 500,000 tons of sulphur. At the time the agreement was discussed, the market price for phosphate rock was about $33 a ton and molten sulphur was about $67 a ton. No money was expected to change hands unless market prices for the two products changed.

Control Data Corporation hoped to sell a new computer to the Soviet Union's Ministry of Culture, but the Ministry did not want to give up hard currency. So Control Data proposed that the Ministry lend some of Leningrad's Hermitage art collection to Western museums. Part of the proceeds would go to Control Data to pay for the computer. The Soviets would get their computer, Westerners would get to see a priceless art collection, and Control Data would get its money. In the Soviet-American confrontation following the invasion of Afghanistan, this deal was canceled.

Monarch Wine Company, a subsidiary of Manischewitz, is sending a team of American technicians to the People's Republic of China to teach the Chinese more about brewing, bottling, and packaging beer and vodka. Monarch will also furnish the Chinese with equipment to modernize the Chinese brewery and distillery. It will take back beer and vodka for its pay, acting as the exclusive distributor in the United States for the Tsingtao brand.

ROBERT E. WEIGAND is a professor of marketing at the University of Illinois at Chicago Circle.

These non-money arrangements are increasingly common and often involve huge amounts of capital.

BARTER DEALS

Barter—also known as counterpurchasing—is nothing more than trading some goods or services for other goods or services. ABBA is Europe's largest selling recording group, partly because it has agreed to take goods instead of hard currency from government trading organizations in eastern Europe. Sometimes it takes chemicals, sometimes fresh fruit, sometimes machine tools, all of which are sold for hard currency in the West by a trading company subsidiary of Beijerinvest (Sweden). Or, for another example, PepsiCo, a company that is intimately involved in international business, has been bottling Pepsi Cola in Hungary since 1974, but has been unable to repatriate its profits. So it used some of its accumulated revenue to produce the movie *The Ninth Configuration*. The movie was shot in Hungary (where most of the expenses were incurred), and PepsiCo used all those unconvertible forints it had accumulated over the years to pay for it. The movie is being distributed in the West where PepsiCo can collect its revenue in hard currency.

Triangular or quadrangular barter arrangements are more difficult to arrange, but certainly not unknown. One of the most celebrated barter deals is PepsiCo's swap with the Soviet Union. The arrangement involves Pepsi syrup being sent from its British plant to bottling plants in Novorossisk, Evpatoriya, and Tallinn. The Soviets exchange Stolichnaya vodka for the syrup and technical assistance. And Monsieur Henri, PepsiCo's own liquor distributor, markets the vodka. The barter arrangement is convenient to PepsiCo because the vodka acquired from the Soviet Union complements the other products sold by Monsieur Henri.

Each party in a barter arrangement negotiates and signs the contracts. Thus if an American company hopes to swap superphosphoric acid to the People's Republic of China for the right to Pohai Gulf oil leases off the China coast (presently being discussed by an American-based multinational firm) two contracts probably will be signed. One will oblige the Chinese to purchase a specific amount of chemicals at the world price during a specified time. The other contract will allow the American company to explore for oil and presumably extract and market their discoveries for a specified future period. Each party is expected to fulfill its part of each contract and to pay the other party in the event it should fail to perform. The non-performance penalties, of course, are written into the two contracts.

BUY-BACK DEALS

Buy-backs, also known as compensation trading, occur when one partner sells equipment, expertise, or technology to another party and takes its pay in the output of the facilities that the equipment, expertise, or technology has helped to build. For example Technip (France) is building a chemical plant in the People's Republic of China that will produce integrated olefins, aromatics, and fibres. The French have agreed to take back part of their pay in the plant's output, marketing them for hard currency in Western markets. More recently, Pierre Cardin has agreed to serve as a consultant to China, taking his pay in silks and cashmeres that will be marketed in the West under the Cardin label.

On the one hand, barter or compensation arrangements with other nations are attractive to Western businesses.[1] Such deals, many of which involve hundreds of millions of dollars, offer the opportunity to enter new markets not yet served by Western suppliers. Furthermore, the Western company that is prone to enter barter or compensation arrangements is

1. Robert E. Weigand, "International Trade Without Money," *Harvard Business Review*, November-December, 1977: 38.

"International trade without money is flourishing today. Indeed, it is nearly the only way for some Western companies to do business with Eastern Europe, the developing countries, and, more recently, with the People's Republic of China."

competitively ahead of those companies that refuse to enter such transactions: not to engage in such deals is nearly tantamount to excluding business with a large number of controlled economies.[2]

On the other hand, there are five major problems associated with non-monetary trade, most of which have not been adequately explored.

THE "SKINNY LIST"

Western traders who agree to non-money trade with controlled states cannot expect a rich assortment of products for their payment. Unhappily, the offered pay-back is likely to be goods that are in ample supply in Western markets. Just because Soviet nations produce a wide range of either consumer or industrial goods does not mean they are willing to trade all of those goods. It is far more likely that a trading organization will limit barter choices considerably. For example, Promsyrioimport, a trading organization in the Soviet Union, is interested in importing steel welding electrodes. But it insists that its supplier take cast iron tubes or steel pipes to complete the transaction. The Westerner would prefer to take back bicycles or farm machinery, but those products are the export responsibility of Raznoimport, a different trading organization.

The Soviet Union recently established the Main Administration For Compensation Arrangements With The West (MACAW), a government bureau that is supposed to reconcile the disparate interests of its trading organizations. If the effort is successful a Western partner may be able to market its produce to one trading organization but be free to receive products from a different trading organization. Nonetheless, this new bureau does not resolve the fact that the Socialist-bloc states usually offer only those products for which there is not a ready cash market in other countries.

PERSISTENTLY POOR QUALITY

The most common problem cited by those who receive products in payment from the Eastern-bloc countries is that often such goods are not suitable for sophisticated Western markets. Perhaps the best quick-and-dirty test of product quality is a visit to a department store in Prague, Warsaw, or Moscow. Western tourists are unlikely to find anything that they want to buy. Consumer goods are in short supply, and those that are available do not generally match the quality available in the West.

Such problems can be resolved but not easily. One common solution is to find buyers in markets that are not as discriminating as are Western customers. Specialized marketing institutions, mostly in Western Europe, have grown up in response to the need to switch products from one country to another. Barter houses usually charge substantial fees, but much of the commission (or margin, if you prefer) is passed along to the customer. The barter house, for example, agrees to take products from a Western customer that origi-

2. Pomiliu Verzariu, Scott Bozek, and JeNelle Matheson, *East-West Countertrade Practices* (Washington: U.S. Department of Commerce, 1978): 24-35.

57

nated in the Soviet bloc but pays the Western owner only 65 percent of the goods' nominal value. Then the barter house finds a customer in Thailand, Syria, Ghana, or Peru who is willing to pay 70 percent of nominal value. The barter house receives a 5 percent commission, the Western partner receives its cash, and the final customer gets something he or she can use.

Since products received in either barter or compensation trade must sometimes be heavily discounted (the 35 per cent in the example just cited is not unusual) the Western partner must generally build a comfortable premium into the price of the product he is sending to his trading partner. Astute international traders will effectively muddy the waters so that it is not evident that higher than usual prices are being charged. There is no advantage in affronting Socialist bloc trading organizations with the blunt assertion that much of their output must be dumped at distress prices. The Easterners may be asked for "special" prices because the Westerner wants to "open new markets" or because "unusually large quantities" are involved. Or the Easterner may be asked to pay "special charges" for technical assistance, charges that are free to cash customers.

The difficulty of selling Eastern-bloc products obliges Westerners to anticipate the likely price at which the products can be sold. Most traders follow this rule: Don't go into a deal unless you can see a way out of it.

A second solution to the quality problem, particularly applicable to buy-back arrangements, is to establish quality criteria that must be met by the compensation partner.

This approach is possible wherever objective measures of product quality are available and can be understood by both parties. For example, International Harvester furnished its compensation partner in Poland with exact specifications for tractor engine parts. It insists that the parts shipped to the West meet these standards, and it refuses to accept substandard parts. Such an approach requires that the Western partner have the confidence that its partner can attain a level of production that meets acceptable quality levels. In the absence of this certainty, the Western company may discover that none of the output is ever acceptable.

A third solution to the quality problem is to station technical personnel on site to assist the compensation partner in achieving and maintaining product quality. The success of this approach varies among countries. Some of the Socialist states are unwilling to allow temporary residency to foreigners, regardless of how desirable their technical role in the country may be. However, other countries welcome foreigners and are eager to bring low Eastern production standards up to acceptable Western levels.

GOODS DON'T FIT "IN HOUSE"

The goods that Western companies must take back—either through barter or compensation arrangements—rarely fit neatly into their factories, offices, or marketing channels. As I already suggested, barter houses prosper because they help solve this problem for their clients by finding customers for all kinds of unwanted products, at least if the price is right. However, many imaginative businesses have managed to find ways to use the products they receive either in their own production or to sell it through their own marketing channels. For example, Cadbury-Schweppes, Ltd. (U.K.) is licensed to bottle and market soft drinks in Bulgaria. Since profit repatriation is difficult, it takes back a substantial volume of fruits that it uses as raw materials for its English production operations. It also sells Bulgarian canned fruits and vegetables through its own marketing channels which reach British grocers. And the PepsiCo-Soviet barter arrangement that I described earlier is nearly an ideal example: the Stolichnaya vodka that Pepsi takes in barter fits neatly into the American company's marketing channel. Monsieur Henri, PepsiCo's distributor, did not sell vodka before the arrangement was completed, so no existing product in the line was displaced; furthermore, no additional fixed costs were involved except the initial promotional campaign.

However there is a risk that marketing people—those responsible for international sales—will go beyond the bounds of good judgment in deciding whether or not products they receive from non-money trade can be used in-house or fitted into existing marketing channels. There are ample international stories about companies that receive products that are less than ideal and then improvidently try to fit them into the firm's production plans. This is dangerous because goods received in non-money trade may rupture the routine purchasing patterns that the company's purchasing agents and buyers have worked long and hard to build up. This may not be serious if the new supplier can furnish the same products on a dependable time schedule in the future. But if the barter arrangement is a one-time event, the advantages of making the sale may be neutralized by the cost of a break in normal buying practices.

CLONING A NEW RIVAL

Another important disadvantage of engaging in non-money trade is that foreign goods may compete with the Western company's own products. Obviously, this does not occur when a Westerner ships machine tool counting units to an Eastern-bloc country and receives dried peaches in return. However, many industries—chemicals, for example—are con-

"Barter—also known as counterpurchasing—is nothing more than trading some goods or services for other goods or services. . . . Buy-backs, also known as compensation trading, occur when one partner sells equipment, expertise, or technology to another party and takes its pay in the output of the facilities that the equipment, expertise, or technology has helped to build."

cerned that they have traded away technology that their new Eastern trade partners can use to compete in Western markets. Suppose a Western firm agrees to furnish technology to help build plants and to take a substantial portion of their payment in chemicals as soon as the new plants begin to function. There is no assurance that the Eastern country will limit its shipments to the amount necessary to pay for the technology. Indeed, the opportunity to earn foreign exchange is one of the major reasons East European countries have selected chemicals suited to Western markets as an area for economic growth.

To compound the problem even further, some of the Soviet-bloc countries not only enjoy most-favored-nation status but they actually qualify for economic assistance as well—usually meaning low interest loans funded by various Western European governments! And the final irony, at least to those whose home markets are being invaded, is that the imported products may receive favored tariff treatment. In the early 1970s the developed countries abandoned non-discrimination when they elected to reduce or eliminate tariffs on products coming from the developing countries. Under United Nations auspices, the Generalized System of Preferences allowed each country (or grouping of countries) to list the countries and products which would be favored. For example, the initial American list, announced in late 1975, consisted of 2,724 products coming from 98 countries and 34 territories. Most of America's preference list consisted of raw materials and agricultural products. This was eminently sensible as long as the developing countries' products did not compete directly with those of the developed countries. But the developing countries today are shipping their products to the United States, Western Europe, and Japan and these products compete with and sometimes challenge the secure position of the high cost domestic ones. The developing countries' products are sometimes assembled in Western government-subsidized plants and pay zero tariffs. Many Western European businesses believe this is unfair. 59

There is little hope a barter house will keep home markets pure. In an era of instant communications and low cost shipping rates it doesn't take long for goods that are destined for Angola to show up in New Orleans. And ironically, the more the Western partner has insisted that only high quality products will be taken in trade, the greater is the likelihood that the goods will end up in Western markets.

Controlled economies use barter and compensation arrangements because such deals permit hitch-hiking on the Western partner's already developed marketing channels. Under different circumstances, a business complement would be highly desirable. For the Socialist states to provide the production facilities and the Western partner to provide the marketing capacity would be perfectly acceptable. But when Eastern-bloc products move through already established marketing channels in Western markets, they may do so at the expense of other products that are

"There are five major problems associated with non-monetary trade, most of which have not been adequately explored. . . . The most common problem cited by those who receive products in payment from the Eastern-bloc countries is that often such goods are not suitable for sophisticated Western markets."

already in the company line. For example, the Japan-Soviet Business Cooperation Committee has been slow to arrive at decisions concerning a copper mine, an asbestos mine, and a steel mill. The Soviets have long hoped to develop Siberia (where these projects would be located) and have expressed an interest in using Japanese capital and technical expertise. And the Japanese have long viewed Siberia as a source for much needed raw materials. However, the talks have stalled—particularly with respect to the steel mill—because Japan has enough steel from its 60 own mills and, unfortunately, the Soviets want to pay them with more steel.

There is no assurance, furthermore, that the Soviet states will not ultimately market their products through independently established marketing channels in the West. Although not the result of a barter or compensation arrangement, the Soviet-Fiat arrangement illustrates how new rivals can be unintentionally cloned. After protracted negotiations, Fiat agreed to help the Soviet Union build an automobile plant to serve the enormous local demand for cars. The size of the market and the pent-up demand for private transportation in the U.S.S.R. is well known. However, soon after the first cars rolled off the assembly line, Russian-built automobiles known in the West as "Ladas" began appearing, first in Belgium and shortly after in the rest of Western Europe, Africa, and more recently, the United States and Canada. It is unfortunate, at least from the Italian company's point of view, that the Lada looks and operates much like the Fiat.

HOW MUCH TO TAKE BACK?

Finally, the Eastern states and developing countries appear to be applying more pressure for barter and compensation arrangements today than just a few years ago. As little as five years ago, compensation arrangements in which the Western partner received about 80 percent of its pay in cash and the remaining 20 percent in goods were the rule. Receiving small amounts of Eastern products was little more than a token of the Western partner's good will. These small amounts of goods did not create the major problems that larger-scale barter and compensation arrangements have created.

Among the compensation contracts now being negotiated, the ratio of cash to goods is generally the inverse of what it was five years ago. Instead of receiving 80 percent cash and 20 percent goods, compensation arrangements increasingly call for the buy-back to hover around 80 percent or even higher. In many recent compensation arrangements, the compensation consists entirely of end products. And although still uncommon, there is trade talk that some Western partners are contracted to take back more goods than the value of a plant they build would warrant, sell those goods in Western markets, and return the hard currency balance to the East.

All this means that, as the phenomenon of doing business via barter and compensation arrangements expands, more markets will have to be found for poor products, new rivals will be unwittingly encouraged, labor unions will be antagonized as jobs are "exported," and business people at all levels will have to learn to accommodate an unusual assortment of goods taken in trade.

To some economists, the practices described in this article no doubt unleash quite different thoughts. On the one hand, non-money trading is simply one more manifestation of mercantilism. The methods may be different, but insistence on bilateral trading is no different in its intent from export subsidies, tax allowances for expatriate business people, or cheap transportation rates on the national shipping line. Its purpose is to assure that international trading accounts are balanced every year, not just country-by-country but even on a company-by-company basis. For example, the German "New Plan" of 1934 very carefully spelled out what goods could be imported, how much they would cost, and who Germany's trading partners would be. Under such restricted circumstances it is no surprise that Germany's international trade was so divorced from market preferences. The New Plan was intended, of course, to build an industrial base and ultimately a war machine.[3]

On the other hand, other economists may look on non-money trade as nothing more than a legitimate attempt by the less developed countries to gain access to markets in the developed countries. One theory, known as the "Vernon hypothesis," tells us that although industries originate in the wealthy industrialized countries, the locus of production may shift to developing countries later in the product's life cycle.[4] For example America was once a powerful leader in the production of textiles, shoes, steel, and automobiles. However, the technology of such industries is widely known, raw materials are almost universally available, and there are no serious patent or trade secret monopolies that prevent developing countries from being major producers of such goods. However, Vernon points out that industrialized countries may protect their markets through tariffs, quotas, stringent health and safety rules, "buy local" laws, and an assortment of other protectionist devices.

Economists can further argue that industrialized countries have not made enough trading concessions to accommodate the products of the Eastern bloc. Although the data vary, there are estimates that the Eastern bloc's debt to the West is about $56 billion. The Soviet Union is the leader, owing about $16.8 billion, and Poland runs a close second, owing about $13.5 billion. Perhaps the Eastern-bloc and developing countries have found a means of access to Western markets, a tying agreement that commands Western companies or countries to buy back products that they would prefer to produce at home or buy elsewhere. ☐

3. Howard S. Ellis, *Exchange Control in Central Europe* (Cambridge, Mass.: Harvard University Press, 1941).

4. Raymond Vernon, "The Trade Expansion Act In Perspective," *Emerging Concepts In Marketing* (Chicago: American Marketing Association, 1962), pp. 384-389. See also Raymond Vernon, "International Investment and International Trade In The Life Cycle," *Quarterly Journal of Economics*, May, 1966: 190-207.

5. Ministry for Inter-German Relations, Federal Republic of Germany, as reported in *The New York Times*, February 24, 1979: 35.

[2]

Bemerkungen–Notes

Countertrade and Foreign Exchange Shortages: A Preliminary Assessment

By

Rolf Mirus and **Bernard Yeung**

I. Introduction

It is often alleged that countertrade is a response to shortages of foreign exchange reserves. "Eastern European and some developing countries make demands for countertrade arrangements for a number of reasons: 1. They wish to minimize their outlay of scarce "hard" currency" [Minister of Supply and Services Canada, 1981, p. 1]. In the past few years, such statements have been made by practitioners, government officials and even academics[1]. It is surprising that this common allegation has not been subjected to much systematic analysis[2]. We are not aware of any rigorous analysis which reveals how countertrade alleviates foreign reserve shortages, nor can we find any critical test of the validity of the allegation. In this paper, we attempt to explore the relationship between countertrade and foreign exchange reserves in the hope of providing an answer to the question of whether countertrade is a means to deal with foreign reserve shortages.

Remark: The authors are grateful to Colin Hoskins for his helpful comments. All errors are ours. This paper was presented at the Academy of International Business Taipei Meeting.

[1] The following are just a few examples: Dennis [1982, p. 69] stated that, "The national Council (of China) has suggested four reasons for China's positive attitude towards countertrade. The first is its balance of payments problem. ... By obtaining a commitment from Western firms to make counterpurchases ... China hopes to improve its balance of payments". More recently, Cohen and Zysman [1986, p. 49] suggested that, "As hard currency has all but vanished from the major trading nations of Latin America, and uncommitted free money dried up in the OPEC nations, governments have turned to countertrade".

[2] Banks [1984] seems to be an exception. A number of recent papers concentrate on the relationship between countertrade and market imperfections. Examples are Murrell [1982], Parsons [1985], Kogut [1986], and Mirus and Yeung [1986a; 1986b]. The validity of the statements have been questioned. For instance, Miramon [1985, p. 27] stated that, "It is not sure that counertrade will allow developing countries to conserve their foreign exchange earnings. ... In the best of circumstances, (its) effect on the trade balance in convertible currencies is neutral".

It is desirable to explain our approach at the outset. Ideally, one would want to analyze the relationship between countertrade and the foreign exchange reserve position within the context of a full macroeconomic model which captures the important properties of the phenomenon, as well as other relevant economic variables. Such an approach, however, would be extremely difficult, if not impossible, because countertrade is a collective term for a variety of manifestations of economic behavior including contracting, agency relations, gaming aspects and the simple exercising of comparative advantage, as Murrell [1982], Kogut [1986], and Mirus and Yeung [1986a; 1986b] have shown. Since such a macroeconomic model is not likely to be available for some time, it is necessary to choose an alternative approach which allows us to make deductions of a general nature. Because our major concern is the validity of the statement that countertrade is a means to deal with foreign reserve shortages, we first clarify its analytical content. Two variants are obtained: *(i)* countries use countertrade to ameliorate their hard currency position, and *(ii)* countries experiencing debt service difficulties and being denied new credit resort to countertrade to obtain additional imports. Using widely accepted economic results, we then explore the required conditions for both cases and discuss their implications.

With respect to the first variant, our deduction is that countertrade in the form of simple barter or counterpurchase does not improve a country's foreign exchange position unless it improves economic efficiency in the sense that it leads to an increase in national income. Moreover, if counterpurchase does succeed in increasing otherwise unavailable import credits, the nation's foreign exchange position would actually deteriorate. The loss in reserves would be due to the fact that a lower (borrowing) interest rate results which, in turn, would stimulate absorption. The impact of countertrade in the form of buy-back has a time dimension since it almost always involves the construction of capital goods. It reduces a country's foreign exchange holdings in the short run but increases them in the longer run. These effects are more pronounced the more successful buy-back is in promoting the construction of investment goods. Our results suggest that if countertrade is indeed a response to foreign exchange shortages, it is because it improves economic efficiency. Therefore, the common assertions, that *(i)* countertrade is inefficient and *(ii)* it is a means of dealing with foreign exchange shortages, are not compatible.

With respect to the second variant, we shall argue that only under certain conditions is countertrade likely to facilitate additional imports: there must exist institutional imperfections that prevent countertrade earnings, unlike normal exports receipts, from being earmarked for debt repayments. Such an institutional imperfection seems to imply naivety on the part of the monitors of country credits. Its existence should be the exception rather than the rule.

In the following section, we first present our conceptual framework and then analyze the relationship between the foreign exchange position and barter/counterpurchase, as well as buy-back. In the third section, we explore the relation between countertrade and excess demand for imports.

II. Countertrade and Foreign Exchange Reserves

We begin by clarifying the term foreign exchange shortages. Foreign exchange shortages can refer to one of two situations which are *not* mutually exclusive. The first is that the domestic currency is artificially overpriced. In defending the exchange rate, the government's holdings of foreign exchange reserves are being depleted; exchange and credit control measures are often imposed to help defend the exchange rate. The second situation is that of a country with an inconvertible currency which does not have adequate amounts of hard currency to buy the imports it desires. We focus on the first situation here and analyze the second situation in the next section.

When the domestic currency is pegged at an unrealistically high price, exchange controls are often imposed. Countertrade can then be used to bypass exchange controls or to restore realistic export prices; it is used to facilitate trade. In this form, countertrade is a means to cope with, but not to reduce, shortages of foreign exchange which are policy-induced [Banks, 1984]. In essence, the problem is not an economic one, but one of policy. The question is whether countertrade can resolve the policy-induced disequilibrium. That is, can countertrade help improve a country's balance of payments or strengthen its currency? (This question, of course, is also relevant when there is no fundamental disequilibrium, but countertrade has the objective of improving the balance of payments or of strengthening the domestic currency.)

Most countertrading countries are characterized by an inconvertible currency; some are less developed countries which are heavily in debt and unable to attract much foreign capital. They have in common that the capital account of their balance of payments is relatively unimportant in comparison with the current account. (In fact, for some countries it is only the trade account that matters.) Moreover, in the various manifestations of countertrade, there is no substantial hard-currency inflow (and outflow). Our investigation, therefore, focuses on the impact of countertrade on the current account.

The usual definition of the current account is as follows:

(1) current account = exports – imports + net services[3].

It it easily shown that the current account is also equal to the following:

(2) current account = saving by the private sector – government budget deficit – investment.

Since the government budget deficit is just the negative of government saving,

[3] Net services = return of the country's holding for foreign assets – interest payments on domestic assets owned by foreigners + unilateral payments.

the current account can therefore be summarized as:

(2′) current account = aggregate domestic saving – investment.

In discussing the relationship between countertrade and foreign exchange reserves, the first definition is often made use of. It is argued that countertrade increases a country's exports and thus improves the country's foreign exchange earnings. This is not a fruitful way to analyze the issue inasmuch as an increase in countertrade exports is, by definition, always offset by an increase in countertrade imports of equal value. This approach would lead us to say that, all other things constant, the current account is not affected by countertrade.

The second identity proves to be more useful in analyzing the relationship between countertrade and the current account. Saving is a positive function of income and the interest rate. Investment is a positive function of the rate of return and is inversely related to the cost of capital. These important economic variables must be affected by countertrade if it is to significantly affect the current account[4]. It is along these lines that our argument will proceed.

1. Barter, Counterpurchase and Current Account

Countertrade involves simple barter, counterpurchase and buy-back [see, e.g. Mirus and Yeung, 1986b]. The first two types of countertrade usually do not involve investments. It is then reasonable to assume that these two types of countertrade do not significantly affect the investment item in (2′) so that the effects of simple barter and counterpurchase on the current account should be reflected by their impact on domestic saving.

Simple barter and counterpurchase affect saving through changes in aggregate income or the interest rate, or both. These types of countertrade affect aggregate income if they change the price of domestic goods in terms of foreign goods, and/or if they change economic efficiency. It is often suggested that countertrade is a form of monopolistic or monopsonistic behavior. In that event countertrade would improve the terms of trade of the country, thus its income, and consequently the current account via an induced increase in saving. This argument is, however, faulty because it confuses the concentration of buying and selling in the hands of a single state trader with the share of the world market held by the country's trade [Banks, 1984, p. 168]. Individual countertrading countries are, with rare exceptions, small economies and do

[4] It is quite obvious that the time perspective of the alleged causal relationship between countertrade and the balance of payments is the short run. Consequently, we concentrate on short-run economic relations. This allows us to treat the change of the important economic variables as exogenous to the balance of payments. Admittedly, payments imbalances lead to changes in the wealth position of a nation so that they have feedback effects on these economic variables. However, these long-run effects do not seem to critically affect the short-run relation between countertrade and the balance of payments and therefore can be put aside without serious implications.

not have any significant world market power; rather, they are usually price-takers. Indeed, it has been suggested that when pressed to accept countertrade deals, foreign trading partners increase the prices of their goods [Banks, 1984]. In that event, the countertrading country is indirectly imposing a tariff on its imports and hands over the tariff revenue to the foreign countertrading partner. As a consequence, the country's terms of trade and income are definitely decreased by countertrade. The effect is that the country's saving is reduced: rather than improving, the current account deteriorates.

There are, however, arguments that in some circumstances barter/ counterpurchase improves economic efficiency. For example, barter/counterpurchase can facilitate the exercise of trading nations' comparative advantage and can therefore lead to lower transaction costs [Mirus and Yeung, 1986b]. If economic efficiency is indeed enhanced, countertrade then helps to improve the current account because it leads to more income and hence more saving.

Our discussion reveals that the effect of countertrade on foreign exchange reserves via the income factor is quite clear-cut. If it increases income, it helps to improve the current account and thus increases a country's foreign reserve holdings. If it does not, it does not improve the foreign exchange reserves. These considerations have a clear implication: the assertions that countertrade is inefficient and that it is conducted to combat foreign exchange shortages are fundamentally incompatible.

It remains to pursue the effect of countertrade on the current account via the interest rate factor. Simple barter is a simultaneous exchange of goods within a relatively short period, hence unlikely to have a significant effect on the interest rate. In contrast, counterpurchase refers to the exchange of goods over time and may therefore have an effect on the interest rate. In a counterpurchase deal, the country insisting on counterpurchase obtains imports in exchange for trade credits. These trade credits are essentially claims on local goods if and when they are available in the future. In this form, counterpurchase represents an extension of credit by the foreign counterpurchaser to the local economy. Two cases are possible. In the case where the counterpurchasing country is facing a genuine credit shortage, counterpurchase constitutes a loan which is otherwise unavailable. It appears that in this case counterpurchase effectively lowers the country's borrowing interest rate (from, say, "infinity" to an affordable rate). Alternatively, if the country is not suffering from a credit crunch, counterpurchase can not represent an increase in the country's borrowing cost. So long as it has access to the world credit market, the country, by assumption, is able to borrow at the market interest cost should the credit cost of counterpurchase be deemed excessive. It is then clear that counterpurchase, in general, will not increase a country's borrowing cost. Hence, its effect on the current account, thus foreign exchange reserves, is non-positive as regards the interest rate factor.

From this perspective, counterpurchase will at best have a neutral effect on the foreign exchange shortage problem.

2. Buy-Back and Current Account

Buy-back involves the importation of capital goods in exchange for the future output of the facilities the capital goods helped to construct. Almost invariably, buy-back leads to the production of some investment goods in the local economy with the effect of raising national income. This increase in investment likely reflects a portion of the capitalised value of additional future and present incomes; additional saving would amount to only a fraction of the increase in present income induced by the new investment. It is, therefore, reasonable to argue that, while the investment goods are being constructed, the investment effect exceeds the saving effect so that the local economy experiences an adverse change in the current account. In later periods, when the capital goods are "on-stream", the current account should improve. From this perspective, it is obvious that buy-back does not offer any short-run help for a country's official reserve position.

It should be noted that buy-back can be conceived of as the borrowing of hard currency from the supplier of the capital goods who immediately collects back the hard currency as sales revenue. This in itself should not represent an increase in the borrowing country's foreign exchange reserves. Furthermore, if the country can borrow from the foreign company involved in the buy-back deal, it must have credit-worthiness to begin with. Therefore, buy-back does not generally lend itself to the argument that it resolves the credit shortage problem of the borrowing country.

It is instructive to pursue further the effect of buy-back on economic efficiency. If buy-back is inefficient, its imposition would reduce investment below what it would have been. In this situation, the short-run and long-run impacts on the current account will be smaller in magnitude. Moreover, the imposition of a buy-back requirement would lower the economy's rate of return (due to inefficiency). In turn, this would lower the savings rate as well as income, resulting in a negative side effect on the current account and, therefore, on the foreign exchange reserves. The overall short-run impact on the current account of an inefficient buy-back should still be negative, albeit mitigated. (But its short-run effect is positive when compared with the "what if" situation where the inefficient buy-back requirement is waived.)

Some writers have argued that countertrade can improve efficiency when market imperfections are present. For example, Murrell [1982] suggested that buy-back, as a signalling device, enhances the value of the underlying investment. Mirus and Yeung [1986a] theorized that buy-back facilitates the undertaking of some investment projects, including some which would otherwise be foregone. In these circumstances, buy-back leads to more construction of investment goods and accentuates the aforementioned negative short-run and positive long-run effects on the country's foreign exchange reserves. In addition, the improvement in economic efficiency means that the rate of return on the country's resources is increased so that both the interest rate and income are higher. Therefore, the savings rate of the country should increase representing a positive side effect on the country's foreign exchange reserves. It is, however, not conceivable that this side effect would negate the original adverse short-run effect of buy-back on foreign reserves (due to the increase in investment); the net short-run effect still ought to be negative. On the other hand, the positive long-run effect of buy-back will be reinforced by the side effect.

This discussion suggests that buy-back offers no immediate improvement in a country's official reserve position. Indeed, if buy-back induces investment, it will have an adverse short-run impact. It is then inappropriate to argue that buy-back is caused by foreign reserve shortages. Nor can it be said that it is an effective means of dealing with such shortages.

III. Countertrade and the Desire for Additional Imports

This section analyzes the suggestion that a country suffering from foreign exchange shortages and being denied new hard currency loans uses countertrade to raise its import consumption. Even though countertrade is a direct exchange of domestic for foreign goods, under normal circumstances there are no compelling reasons why countertrade imports can not be viewed as financed by trade credit against future exports. Countertrade then is equivalent to a foreign supplier extending credit to the countertrading country which in turn makes repayment in the form of future exports. Seen in this light, countertrading does not actually increase the country's purchases of imports beyond the present value of the future exports[5]. If countertrade has the effect of increasing imports, it must be due to some imperfections. In the following we discuss one such possibility.

Countries suffering from foreign exchange shortages are often those deeply in debt. As a consequence, they are subject to austerity programs and to close monitoring by their creditors. Part of their export earnings is likely earmarked for debt service and their expenditures on imports are closely scrutinized. One can say that their normal export earnings are "taxed", thusly constraining their import consumption. If countertrade exports are not subject to the same treatment and can avoid the "austerity tax", countertrade can indeed genuinely increase a country's access to imports. Simply put, countertrade is a form of "austerity tax" avoidance in that it takes advantage of a loophole in the security program of the country's creditors.

[5] This is not to deny the possibility that countertrade is an arrangement to elicit the maximum present value for the future exports.

An algebraic example will illustrate this idea. Let us suppose that for each unit of the debtor country's export earnings only the portion "a" can be used for imports while the remaining portion, "1–a", has to be paid to its creditors. Let us further assume that export proceeds from countertrade are not subject to the same treatment but can be used freely. Finally, we assume that a unit of resources exported in the form of countertrade can only purchase "b" units of imports to reflect the higher transaction cost of this trading practice; "b" would ordinarily be less than one.

Under these circumstances, for each unit devoted to normal exports, the country can only enjoy "a" units of imports ("a" is smaller than one) and "1–a" are used for debt service. If the country can divert a portion "c" of the same unit to countertrade, it can enjoy instead a+(b–a)c units of imports and only (1–a)(1–c) units of its resources go towards servicing its debt. This amounts to a "home-made" rescheduling of its debt. The gain in import consumption is (b–a)c and the reduction in debt repayment is (1–a)c. Provided "b" is larger than "a", the country succeeds in increasing its import consumption. As long as the country's marginal rate of substitution between import consumption and debt repayment is larger than (1–a)/(b–a), it will conduct countertrade (until the two terms are equalized).

This is a situation of asymmetric institutional treatment of normal and countertrade exports. The larger "b" is, the smaller "a" is, and the larger the marginal rate of substitution is between imports and debt repayments, the more likely countertrade becomes. These comparative static results are intuitively appealing. A small "a" represents a very severe "austerity tax" so that only a small portion of normal export earnings is allowed for import purchases. A large "b" means that countertrade is not very costly. The marginal rate of substitution between imports and debt repayments is large when import consumption is small relative to debt repayments. Under these conditions it is reasonable to expect that the country will be more inclined to resort to countertrade.

We thus have a case to support the notion that countertrade is conducted to fulfil a country's (excess) desire for imports. However, the case rests on asymmetric treatment of countertrade exports. The condition implies that countertrade escapes the creditors' audit, or that creditors are naive. While there may be some truth to this, we think such institutional imperfection to be the exception and short-lived, hence not applicable to too many situations.

IV. Conclusion

This paper has analyzed the relation between foreign exchange shortages and countertrade. Shortages in foreign exchange reserves can mean that a country is in need of increasing its reserve holdings or that it does not have the foreign exchange reserves to meet its desire for additional imports.

For the first variant, our analysis shows that barter and counter purchase increase foreign exchange reserves only if they improve economic efficiency. It follows that countertrade can not be both inefficient and a resolution to foreign exchange shortages. Buy-back adversely affects a country's foreign exchange reserves in the short run though it has a favourable long-run effect. (This pattern is more (less) pronounced if buy-back induces additional investment (inefficiency).) It follows that buy-back is not a suitable means for dealing with a deficiency of foreign exchange reserves in the short run, nor is it a natural consequence thereof.

For the second variant, our analysis suggests that countertrade can fulfil a country's excess desire for imports if there exists an institutional imperfection in the sense that normal export earnings can not be freely applied to the purchase of imports while the constraint does not apply to countertrade earnings. This institutional imperfection ought to be the exception rather than the rule.

We think the allegation that foreign exchange shortages lead countries to countertrade is very likely invalid. Our analysis points out that only efficiency-improving barter and counterpurchase can help to alleviate shortages in foreign reserves. These types of countertrade seem to account for only a small portion of countertrade. Other types of countertrade, including the prevalent buy-back, will adversely affect a country's balance of payments position. It is, therefore, unlikely that countries resort to countertrade because of shortages of foreign currencies. The economic incentives for countertrade suggested by Murrell [1982], Kogut [1986], and Mirus and Yeung [1986b] are more credible causes for countertrade than foreign reserve shortages. On the other hand, if countries indeed resort to countertrade in the hope of alleviating their shortages of foreign currencies, our analysis shows that their hope will likely not be fulfilled.

Our analysis suggests further that the economic consequences of countertrade are intimately related to its effect on economic efficiency. This means that more theoretical and empirical studies of the impact of countertrade on economic efficiency are warranted.

The approach taken in this paper is based on simplified but widely accepted economic relationships. As such, this effort represents a modest beginning of an analytical task that, in our view, is long overdue. Future work would entail exploring the relationship between countertrade, the foreign reserves position and imports within the framework of a full macroeconomic model that can properly take into account the size of the various impact and feedback effects.

References

Banks, Gary, "The Economics and Politics of Countertrade". *The World Economy,* Vol. 4, 1984, pp. 159–182.

Cohen, Stephen S., John Zysman, "Countertrade, Offsets, Barter, and Buybacks". *California Management Review,* Vol. 28, 1986, No. 2, pp. 41-56.

Dennis, Robert D., "The Countertrade Factor in China's Modernization Plan". *The Columbia Journal of World Business,* Vol. 17, 1982, Spring, pp. 67-75.

Kaikati, Jack G., "Marketing Without Exchange of Money". *Harvard Business Review,* Vol. 60, 1982, pp. 72-74.

Kogut, Bruce, "On Designing Contracts to Guarantee Enforceability: Theory and Evidence from East-West Trade". *Journal of International Business Studies,* Vol. 17, 1986, pp. 47-62.

Minister of Supply and Services Canada, "Countertrade, from a World Perspective". *Canadian Commercial Corporation Report,* February 1981, pp. 1-13.

de Miramon, Jacques, "Countertrade: An Illusory Solution". *The OECD Observer,* May 1985, No. 134, pp. 24-29.

Mirus, Rolf, Bernard Yeung [1986a], "Buy-Back in International Trade: A Rationale". *Weltwirtschaftliches Archiv,* Vol. 122, 1986, pp. 371-374.

-, - [1986b], "Economic Incentives for Countertrade". *Journal of International Business Studies,* Vol. 17, 1986, Fall, pp. 27-39.

Murell, Peter, "Product Quality, Market Signalling and the Development of East-West Trade". *Economic Inquiry,* Vol. 20, 1982, pp. 589-603.

Parsons, John E., *A Theory of Countertrade Financing of International Business.* Massachusetts Institute of Technology, Finance Department, Sloan School of Management Working Paper, 1632/85. Cambridge, Mass., March 1985.

[3]

SOME EMPIRICAL DIMENSIONS OF COUNTERTRADE

Jean-Francois Hennart*
The Wharton School

Abstract. This paper discusses some of the recent theories of why countries impose countertrade obligations and compares some of the implications of these theories with data obtained from a comprehensive database of countertrade transactions.

One of the major developments in international trade in the last decade has been the spread of a range of unconventional trade practices which have come to be defined by the generic term of countertrade. This development has attracted the attention of academics and practitioners, and there are now a number of excellent books and articles that analyze this phenomenon (for example, Alexandrides and Bower [1987]; Elderkin and Norquist [1987]; Fisher and Harte [1985]; Huszagh and Huszagh [1986]; Khoury [1984]; Korth [1987]; Verzariu [1980, 1985]; Yoffie [1984]. This literature has raised some very interesting questions. One of these is why countries impose countertrade obligations.

This article constitutes one of the first attempts at presenting data on countertrade so as to permit a preliminary assessment of the relevance of the major explanations given for countertrade. The data dispel some widely held views about countertrade; the oft-noted relationship between a country's credit rating and its propensity to countertrade is not as strong as commonly held; on the other hand, the data support the rival hypothesis that some forms of countertrade, buy-back and counterpurchase, are substitutes to foreign direct investment (FDI). The tables also show a surprisingly large volume of countertrade between developing countries themselves. But perhaps the most important finding is that each countertrade type seems to have its own separate motivations. The next section presents a typology of countertrade transactions. This is followed by a brief section summarizing the competing explanations given for countertrade. The relevance of these

---

*Jean-Francois Hennart is Anheuser-Busch Assistant Professor of Management at The Wharton School, University of Pennsylvania. The focus of his research is the application of transaction costs theory to international business.

I am indebted to Michael Morrison for his help, and to Erin Anderson for assistance and comments. Valuable comments were also received from Bernard Yeung and from two anonymous referees. Eduardo Francisco provided valuable help by setting up the database. Charmilla Chatterjee and Kathleen Saul helped with the programming. Grace Lao and Christine Tutay were outstanding research assistants. Thanks also to Donald Lecraw for help in procuring some source materials. Earlier versions of this paper were presented at the AIB meetings in San Diego in October 1988 and at the EIBA meetings in Berlin in December 1988. Financial assistance from the General Electric Foundation through the William Wurster Center for International Management Studies is gratefully acknowledged.

Received: January 1989; Revised: July & September 1989; Accepted: September 1989.

explanations is then examined in light of the data. The conclusion summarizes the main findings and suggests avenues for further research.

TYPES OF COUNTERTRADE

The term "countertrade" is used to describe six types of transactions: barter, clearing arrangements, switch trading, buy-back, counterpurchase, and offset. All these transactions have one characteristic in common: in each, a seller provides a buyer with goods or services and promises in return to purchase goods or services from the buyer [Banks 1983, p. 160]. Because countertrade usually results in a two-way flow of commodities, it is often considered to be only barter. In fact, there are important differences between barter, clearing arrangements, and switch trading, on the one hand, and the three other types of countertrade, buy-back, offset, and counterpurchase on the other. The first group of transactions is undertaken to avoid using money, while the main feature of the second group is the imposition of reciprocal commitments. Figure 1 provides a schematic classification of these six types of countertrade.

Barter (abbreviated as BT) is the direct exchange of goods and services between two parties without the use of money. Barter usually involves the swap of one product for another, but a large number of barter exchanges can be consolidated into a *clearing arrangement* (CA). In this form of barter, each party agrees, in a single contract, to purchase a specified (usually equal) value of goods and services. Each country sets up an account that is debited whenever one country imports from another. At the end of the period, imbalances are cleared through hard currency payments or transfer of goods. A clearing arrangement merely introduces the concept of credit to a barter arrangement, thereby allowing a barter transaction to be settled in a non-instantaneous fashion. The inflexibility inherent in a clearing arrangement can be alleviated by *switch trading*, which consists in buying a country's position in exchange for hard currency and selling it to another customer.

In contrast to barter, the other forms of countertrade, offset, buy-back, and counterpurchase involve the use of money or credit.[1] They consist of two parallel money-for-goods contracts. The crucial feature of these contracts is the imposition of reciprocal commitments. The commitment requested from the exporter may consist in reciprocal purchases, as in the case of buy-backs and counterpurchase, or in a complex menu of reciprocating concessions, as in the case of offsets.

In a typical *buy-back* (BB) transaction, the exporter transfers technology (embodied in plant and equipment, or disembodied), and agrees to purchase in return a certain percentage of the plant's output over a given number of years. Note that, contrary to popular impressions, buy-back agreements do not usually involve the barter of plant and equipment for resultant output. Instead, buyback contracts stipulate two parallel money transactions: when the project is completed, the plant seller is paid in full by the buyer from

FIGURE 1
Classification of Forms of Countertrade

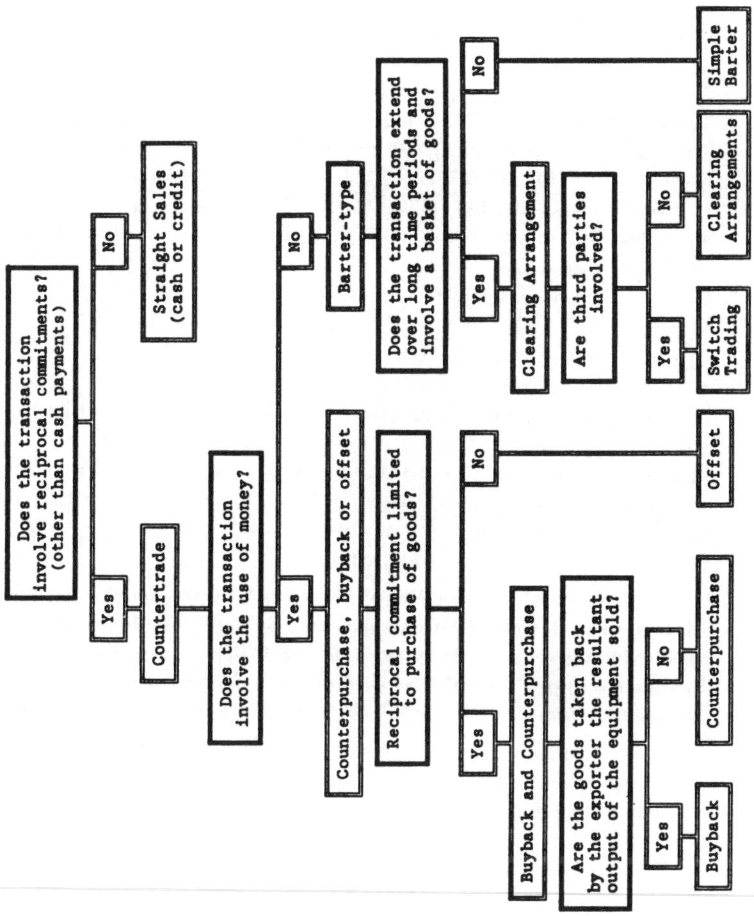

hard currency borrowed from eastern or western sources. The buyer then uses the proceeds of the sale of the output to the plant seller to repay the lender [Verzariu 1980, p. 93; 1985, p. 28; McVey 1980, p. 202; United Nations 1984, p. 10). For example, two British firms, ICI and Davy Powergas, sold in 1977 a methanol plant to the Soviets for 250 million dollars and agreed to take back 20% of the production of the plant over the 1981-1990 period for an estimated 350 million dollars.

Counterpurchase (CP) involves, like buy-back, two parallel hard currency contracts, but differs from buy-back insofar as the goods that are taken back by the western seller of goods or equipment are not produced with the equipment sold. The western exporter agrees to buy unrelated goods from a shopping list set up by the importer. The list may change from time to time, but the commitment is to buy from the list as it stands at a later date, at prices posted at a later date. The list often contains light manufactures and consumer items which do not have a ready market. For example, in 1977 Volkswagen sold 10,000 cars to East Germany, and agreed to purchase goods from a list set up by the East Germans over the next two years, up to the value of the cars sold to East Germany [Shuster 1980].[2]

The term *"offset"* (OF) is used to describe the imposition on exporters of a more complex basket of reciprocal concessions. When governments make large purchases from foreign companies, they increasingly insist that the purchase price be offset in some way by the seller. The latter has to agree to source some of the production locally, to increase its imports from the country, or to transfer technology. Offsets are particularly common in the purchase of weapons, but they are also imposed by government agencies on imports of non-military equipment.

The term countertrade thus covers contracts with two main purposes. The first type are barter contracts, and they are undertaken to avoid using money or to avoid having to set a money-price. The second type (offset, buy-backs, and counterpurchase) makes use of hard currency. The main feature of these contracts is the presence of reciprocal commitments.

METHODOLOGY

The only empirical evidence concerning countertrade comes from surveys of exporters, such as those directed by Bussard [1983, 1986]. Although extremely informative, these surveys only cover U.S. exporters. They tend also to lump together all types of countertrade. Yet we have seen that each type of countertrade has a somewhat different rationale (hence the present study that reports on countertrade transactions worldwide and that separates them by type).

The approach used was to rely on published sources. An informal telephone survey of countertrade observers and practitioners was made to identify possible sources. *Countertrade Outlook*, a weekly newsletter that reports on "countertrade and non-traditional trade" developments throughout the world, was consistently ranked as the most comprehensive and reliable of all publications dealing with countertrade. All issues of *Countertrade Outlook* between the first issue (June 1983) and the last issue of 1986 were surveyed. For each reported countertrade deal, we recorded the type of countertrade, the name and country of the seller, the goods sold, the name and country of the buyer, and the goods offered by the buyer as take-backs. The database includes all countertrade contracts that were mentioned as having been signed between June 1983 and December 31, 1986. The compilation yielded 1,277 transactions, of which 694 were classified as clearing arrangements, 171 as barters, 298 as counterpurchase, 71 as buy-backs, and

43 as offset.[8] The coding was done by an assistant, who was given a list of coding rules. Exchanging of goods for goods, without the use of money, was classified as barter if the exchange was not undertaken within existing clearing arrangements. Offsets are sometimes distinguished from counterpurchases by the fact that they involve military purchases; here transactions were classified as offsets if they involved more than a simple reciprocal sale, i.e., if the agreement obligated the seller to transfer technology, to subcontract to local firms, or to make direct investments in the buying country. All entries were reviewed by the author for correct classification.

The data source contains some biases. According to the editor of *Countertrade Outlook*, countertrade done by small countries tends to be underreported, while other countries where the magazine has correspondents tends to be over-represented in relation to their importance in global countertrade.[9] To minimize the impact of these potential biases, the analysis is conducted in terms of groups of relatively homogeneous countries.

In each trade, there is one or more buyer(s) and seller(s). Buyer, in this context, refers to the party that imposes a countertrade obligation, usually (but not always) a LDC or an Eastern European country. The seller, on the other hand, is the party that accedes to countertrade demands. It is usually a firm based in a developed country. The distinction between buyer and seller applies to buy-backs, counterpurchase, and offset, but is difficult to make for barters and clearing arrangements, since in this case it is impossible to determine in practice the trading partner that imposed a reciprocal obligation.

ANALYSIS OF THE DATA

Table 2 shows the total number (frequency) of deals that were coded. Clearing arrangements account for nearly half of the reported instances of countertrade, in part because they tend to be reported officially. The second most common form of countertrade in the database is counterpurchases. Offsets are the least common variety. These results are generally consistent with those found from surveys (for example, Bussard [1983]), except that barters seem here to be relatively more numerous.

Tables 3 and 4 tabulate the number of countertrade deals of each type with the countries that imposed them (the buyers) or responded to them (the sellers).[10] Countries were aggregated into five groups: the Developed Countries (Group 1), OPEC members (Group 2), Centrally Planned Economies (Group 3), Middle-Income Countries (Group 4), and Low-Income Countries (Group 5). The classification is that used by the World Bank (the distinction between low-income developing, middle-income developing, and developed country is based on per capita income). The composition of each group is given in the Appendix.

The main impression given by Table 3 is that each group of countries has a propensity to undertake a particular type of transaction. A chi-square test

TABLE 2
Total Number of Countertrade Deals, 1983-86

Type of Deals	Number of Deals	% of total
Involving no Currency		
Clearing Arrangements	694	54.3
Barters	171	13.4
Involving Currency and Reciprocity		
Buy-backs	71	5.5
Counterpurchases	298	23.2
Offsets	43	3.3
Total	1,277	100.0

TABLE 3
Number of Countertrade Deals by Type and Country Group of Buyers

	Country Group					
Countertrade Type	Developed Countries	Centrally Planned Economies	OPEC Members	Middle-Income Developing	Low-Income Developing	Total
Counterpurchase	12	72	104	88	20	296
Buy-back	1	55	6	11	0	73
Offset	15	1	7	15	1	39
Total	28	128	117	114	21	408

shows that the null hypothesis that all observations come from the same population is rejected at the 99% confidence level (chi-square=151.69). OPEC, middle-income developing, and low-income developing countries impose more counterpurchases, CPEs more buy-backs, and developed and middle-income developing countries more offsets than would be expected if there were no relationship between country group and countertrade type. CPEs had a particularly high frequency of buy-backs, accounting for fifty-five deals out of seventy-three, or three-fourths of the total. Note that there is only one instance of a buy-back imposed by a developed country in our sample. As we will see, this finding is consistent with the view that buy-backs are a second-best substitute to foreign direct investment. CPEs and low-income developing countries are not active in offsets for two separate reasons: CPEs are prohibited from purchasing weapons in the West, while low-income developing countries cannot afford the type of sophisticated weapons sold under offset. This differential frequency of types of countertrade across groups of countries suggests that it is unlikely that a single factor (such as lack of foreign exchange) could account for this complex phenomenon.

Table 4 is a tabulation by seller country. The table shows a definite pattern in the extent to which specific countries are subject to countertrade obligations

TABLE 4
Number of Countertrade Deals by Type and Country Group of Sellers

	Country Group					
Countertrade Type	Developed Countries	Centrally Planned Economies	OPEC Members	Middle-Income Developing	Low-Income Developing	Total
Counterpurchase	194	29	5	67	13	308
Buy-back	63	11	0	3	0	77
Offset	56	2	0	1	0	59
Total	313	42	5	71	13	444

(the chi-square value of 41.97 is significant at the 99% confidence level). OPEC and developing countries have higher observed than expected counterpurchase frequencies. This is also the case for developed countries and CPEs with buy-backs, and for developed countries with offsets. Thus although the bulk of counterpurchase requirements has been imposed on exporters from the developed countries, they have been relatively less subject to these obligations than OPEC and developing countries. Note also the significant number of cases involving middle-income developing countries and CPEs selling technology and equipment under buy-back.

Tables 5 through 8 show the structure of countertrade by type and country group. Table 5 provides this information for barter deals. No attempt is made in this case to differentiate between buyer and seller, so the table is symmetrical along the diagonal. As the table shows, the most common form of barter involves two middle-income developing countries; this is consistent with the view that barter is used to avoid repayment of external debt. There is here a coincidence of wants, as both countries are eager to shelter their export earnings from creditors. Barter is also common between developed countries and middle-income developing countries, and between middle-income developing countries and CPEs. The total absence of barter deals between OPEC members and between developed countries supports the view that barter is used to bypass cartels and commodity agreements: OPEC members do not sell oil to each other, so there are no opportunities to use barters in such trades. Also, most developed countries have similar types of price support programs, so agricultural surpluses cannot usually be bartered with other developed countries.

Table 6 presents the matrix of counterpurchase transactions. The columns represent sellers, and the rows buyers. Counterpurchase appears as imposed principally by OPEC, middle-income developing countries, and CPEs, on developed countries mostly, but also on middle-income developing countries. Note the relatively low incidence of counterpurchase imposed by developed and low-income developing countries.

The idiosyncratic characteristics of buy-backs appear clearly in Table 7. Buy-backs are clearly an East-West phenomenon, with more than two-thirds

TABLE 5
Matrix of Countertrade, Barter Only

	Country Group					
Country Group	Developed Countries	Centrally Planned Economies	OPEC Members	Middle-Income Developing	Low-Income Developing	Total
Developed countries	0					0
Centrally planned economies	15	3				18
OPEC members	16	3	0			19
Middle-income developing	30	26	18	31		105
Low-income developing	7	10	1	8	2	28
Total	68	42	19	39	2	170

TABLE 6
Matrix of Countertrade, Counterpurchase Only

	Country Group of Sellers					
Country Group of Buyers	Developed Countries	Centrally Planned Economies	OPEC Members	Middle-Income Developing	Low-Income Developing	Total
Developed countries	7	2	2	1	0	12
Centrally planned economies	47	2	1	22	3	75
OPEC members	75	4	1	21	3	104
Middle-income developing	55	19	1	15	4	94
Low-income developing	9	1	0	7	3	20
Total	193	28	5	66	13	305

TABLE 7
Matrix of Countertrade, Buy-backs Only

	Country Group of Sellers					
Country Group of Buyers	Developed Countries	Centrally Planned Economies	OPEC Members	Middle-Income Developing	Low-Income Developing	Total
Developed countries	0	1	0	0	0	1
Centrally planned economies	50	3	0	2	0	55
OPEC members	11	0	0	0	0	11
Middle-income developing	4	8	0	0	0	12
Low-income developing	0	0	0	0	0	0
Total	65	12	0	2	0	79

TABLE 8
Matrix of Countertrade, Offsets Only

Country Group of Buyers	Country Group of Sellers: Developed Countries	Centrally Planned Economies	OPEC Members	Middle-Income Developing	Low-Income Developing	Total
Developed countries	18	0	0	0	0	18
Centrally planned economies	1	0	0	0	0	1
OPEC members	16	0	0	0	0	16
Middle-income developing	14	2	0	1	0	17
Low-income developing	1	0	0	0	0	1
Total	50	2	0	1	0	53

of all buy-backs imposed by CPEs, almost all of them on developed countries. Note however that OPEC countries and middle-income developing countries have also imposed buy-backs on both developed countries and CPEs. The table shows only one case of buy-back involving developing countries as buyers: if buy-backs are a "second best" substitute to FDI and are imposed to reduce opportunism in the purchase of technology, then countries that put few limits on incoming investment (by and large the developed countries) will choose this institutional form in preference to buy-backs. The only case of buy-back imposed by a developed country is a 1985 agreement between Australia and Romania, in which Romania agreed to supply mining and handling equipment for an iron ore mine, and take payment in iron ore. Since Eastern European countries have generally been reluctant to make equity investments abroad, and since Australia had then stringent limits of foreign ownership of natural resources, this apparent exception is in fact consistent with the view that buy-backs are second-best substitutes to FDI.

The table also shows eight other cases where a CPE sold technology and equipment under buy-back to a non-CPE buyer, and was asked to take back the output. One of these cases is that of Greece, which has recently bought an alumina plant from the USSR under buy-back.[11] These eight observations, and the two cases where a middle-income developing country sold technology under buy-back to a socialist country, suggest that the use of buy-back to signal product quality is not limited to East-West trade, and/or that buy-back is a mechanism to reduce transaction costs in the sale of technology. Developing countries and CPEs do not generally have an established reputation as reliable sellers of plant and equipment. We would expect, therefore, that countries that buy technology from these vendors would require the latter to take back the resultant product so as to minimize the risk that they will be sold inferior or obsolete technology. Similarly, one interpretation of the data is that CPEs enter into buy-backs with developing countries to stimulate the development of resources for which they are the main buyer. This is clearly the case of Greece's alumina plant, for which the USSR and Romania will be the sole customers.

Offsets, on the other hand, are shown in Table 8 to involve almost exclusively developed countries selling to a variety of buyers. Of interest is the negligible role played by CPEs. This is explained by the fact that offsets usually involve weapons, and that trade in these products between East and West is severely constrained by considerations of national security.

Looking at Tables 3 to 8, one is struck by the large share of countertrade that is carried out among middle-income developing countries. Most theories of countertrade have focused on East-West and on North-South trade. This suggests that more attention needs to be paid to the motivations for South-South countertrade. Note that barter accounts for most of the transactions between middle-income developing countries (compare Table 5 with Tables 6, 7 and 8). As was argued above, this is consistent with the view that barter can be used by heavily indebted countries to avoid repayment of debt.

The database also provides information on the products that are traded through countertrade. Tables 9, 10, and 11 tabulate the goods sold by each group of countries under countertrade. In the case of barter, the product count reflects products sold by each group of countries. The product count for counterpurchase and buy-back is that of goods taken back by the technology seller or the initial exporter. The last column shows the product composition (in value) of exports of the relevant country group in 1985, as published in the *Handbook of International Trade and Development Statistics*. This column reflects the prior distribution of all feasible deals.

Table 9 shows that the proportion of CPE barter, counterpurchase, and buy-back sales that were manufactures (70%, 59.3% and 56.8%), was higher than the proportion of manufactures in their overall trade (47.7%). The difference was statistically significant at the 95% confidence level in the case of counterpurchase and barter, and at the 90% level in the case of buy-backs. This means that manufactures were more likely to be exported under countertrade than were other CPE exports. Note that we are comparing product count with value data, due to the lack of data on the value of countertrade transactions. A chi-square test shows that the hypothesis that the rows and columns are independent cannot be rejected: there seems to be no relationship between product category and countertrade type in the case of CPEs.[12] In other words, buy-back deals are no more likely to involve manufactures than barter and counterpurchase transactions. This seems to be at variance with Murrell's hypothesis that buy-backs are used to signal product quality in the West. Recall that because product quality is more variable in manufactures (and especially in industrial equipment-SITC 7) than in food, raw materials and fuels, Murrell had hypothesized that the proportion of goods from SITC 7 taken back under buy-back should be greater than that taken back under counterpurchase (H4). On the

TABLE 9
Distribution of Products Taken Back under Countertrade from Centrally Planned Economies

Product Categories	SITC Group	Countertrade Type: Barter Number	Barter %	CP Number	CP %	BB Number	BB %	% of all Trade
Food and raw materials	0,1,2,4	8	16	12	20.3	15	29.4	18.9
Fuels	3	7	14	12	20.3	7	13.7	33.4
Manufactures	5-9	35	70	35	59.3	29	56.8	47.7
Of which	7	(15)	(30)	(10)	(16.9)	(15)	(29.4)	
Total		50	100	59	100.0	51	100.0	100.0

Source: Trade by Commodity: UNCTAD, *Yearbook of International Trade and Development Statistics, 1987 Supplement.*

TABLE 10
Distribution of Products Taken Back under Countertrade from OPEC Member Countries

Product Categories	SITC Group	Countertrade Type: Barter Number	Barter %	CP Number	CP %	% of all Trade
Food and raw materials	0,1,2,4	5	13.1	40	39.0	4.1
Fuels	3	29	76.3	10	10.0	91.8
Manufactures	5-9	4	10.6	52	51.0	4.1
Of which	7	(0)	(0.0)	(3)	(3.0)	
Total		38	100.0	102	100.0	100.0

Source: Trade by Commodity: UNCTAD, *Yearbook of International Trade and Development Statistics, 1987 Supplement.*

other hand, the fact that the industrial distribution of buy-backs is no different than that of barters and counterpurchases is not inconsistent with the view that buy-backs and counterpurchases are second-best substitutes for FDI.

Table 10 provides the same data for OPEC countries. What is striking are the differences between the type of products sold under barter and those sold under counterpurchase.[13] Crude oil makes up the bulk (76%) of the products sold under barter, but only 10% of those sold under counterpurchase. Conversely, only 10% of the barters involve manufactures vs. 51% of the counterpurchases. This reinforces the point made earlier that barter and counterpurchase have very different motivations: barter is useful to shave on cartel prices, while counterpurchase is imposed to help penetrate foreign markets. Since successful distribution of manufactures generally requires the distributor to make greater transaction-specific investments than in the case of food, raw materials, or fuels, we would expect counterpurchase

TABLE 11
Distribution of Products Taken Back under Countertrade from High and Low-Income Developing Countries

Product Categories	SITC Group	Countertrade Type: Barter Number	Barter %	CP Number	CP %	BB Number	BB %	% of all Trade
Food and raw materials	0,1,2,4	49	69.0	29	35.8	6	54.5	32.9
Fuels	3	6	8.4	3	3.7	1	9.0	18.4
Manufactures	5-9	16	22.5	49	60.4	4	36.3	48.7
Of which	7	(3)	(4.2)	(12)	(14.8)	(1)	(9.0)	
Total		71	100.0	81	100.0	11	100.0	100.0

Source: Trade by Commodity: UNCTAD, *Yearbook of International Trade and Development Statistics, 1987 Supplement.*

to be more useful for the export of manufactures than for that of food and raw materials.

Tables 9, 10 and 11 also show that the proportions of counterpurchase sales by CPEs, OPEC and developing countries that are manufactures are greater than that of manufactures in their overall exports. The difference is statistically significant at the 95% confidence level (at the 99% level for less-developed countries). This provides some support for arguments (such as those made by Mirus and Yeung [1986] and Hennart [1989]) that counterpurchase is used as a second-best method to secure marketing assistance from the West.

Product data for all developing countries is presented in Table 11. Note again the differences between the product composition of barter and counterpurchase transactions: barters are heavily concentrated in raw materials (69% of all bartered products), while products sold under counterpurchase are mostly manufactures (60.4% of all counterpurchase take-backs). A chi-square test shows that there is a relationship between product category and countertrade type (chi square=22.54, $p<.001$), with barters used for raw materials and counterpurchases used for manufactures more frequently than if the probability distributions in both columns were the same. Since most products supported by cartels are agricultural and mineral commodities, this is consistent with the view that barters, because they disguise prices, are useful to shave prices on cartelized commodities. This goal cannot be attained through counterpurchase. As noted above, the high proportion of manufactures among counterpurchased products is also consistent with the hypothesis that counterpurchase is a marketing tool for differentiated products. Note also the high proportion of food and raw materials among the goods taken back under buy-back, a finding consistent with the hypothesis that buy-back is a substitute for FDI.

Tables 12, 13 and 14 relate a country's propensity to impose countertrade to their credit rating. If these forms of countertrade are undertaken in response to difficulties in obtaining hard currency credits, then the bulk of countertrade transactions ought to be imposed by countries with a low credit rating. Countries are classified in three groups: the first group contains countries that had a rating equal or below the median, the second group, countries with a rating above the median, and the third group, countries for which a credit rating was not available. Countries with the lowest credit rating accounted for 16% of all reported buy-back deals, 25% of all counterpurchase deals, and 38% of all barter deals (the total is the number of deals in countries for which credit rating was known).[14] Since countries with a low credit rating account for 9% of world trade, this suggests the existence of a strong relationship between a country's low creditworthiness and its propensity to barter, and a weaker one with its propensity to counterpurchase and buy-back. The fact that the relationship is stronger with barter than with buy-back or counterpurchase is consistent with H3.

Tables 15 and 16 compare a country's propensity to impose buy-backs and counterpurchase with the restrictions it puts on incoming foreign direct investment.[15] If buy-backs are a second-best solution to the problem of acquiring technology, the first-best being foreign direct investment, then countries that restrict incoming foreign direct investment should be the ones requesting buy-back commitments from the firms that sell them technology. Table 15 provides strong support for this hypothesis: 80% of all buy-backs were imposed by twenty-eight countries with very high or high barriers on incoming investment. This percentage is higher than the share of world trade by countries of these two groups (15%), and the difference is highly significant ($z=14.0$).

Table 16 also supports the view that counterpurchases are substitutes for vertical integration between manufacturing and distribution. Effective distribution of differentiated goods often requires a hierarchical link between production and distribution, i.e., vertically-integrated channels [Hennart 1989]. Producers in countries that ban or severely restrict incoming FDI cannot use vertically integrated marketing channels, and must instead rely on contracts. Counterpurchases are sophisticated export-marketing contracts with an enforceability that is greater than simple distribution contracts, but lower than FDI. They should therefore be used mostly by countries that have imposed severe restrictions on incoming FDI. Table 16 provides support for this hypothesis. Sixty-five percent of all counterpurchase contracts were imposed by countries with very high or high barriers to incoming FDI, a proportion significantly higher than their share of world trade (14%).

TABLE 12
Credit Rating and Buy-back Frequency

	1985 Credit Rating			
	Below and Equal to Median	Above Median	Unknown	Total
Number of Countries in Group	54	53	61	168
Number of BB deals	11	55	4	70
Percent of all deals	15.7	78.6	5.7	100
Share of World Trade of Countries in Group	9.0	89.5	1.5	100

Sources: Credit Rating: *Institutional Investor.*
Trade: International Monetary Fund, *Directions of Trade.*

TABLE 13
Credit Rating and Counterpurchase Frequency

	1985 Credit Rating			
	Below and Equal to Median	Above Median	Unknown	Total
Number of Countries in Group	54	53	61	168
Number of CP deals	61	170	14	245
Percent of all deals	24.9	69.4	5.7	100
Share of World Trade of Countries in Group	9.0	89.5	1.5	100

Sources: Credit Rating: *Institutional Investor.*
Trade: International Monetary Fund, *Directions of Trade.*

TABLE 14
Credit Rating and Barter Frequency

	1985 Credit Rating			
	Below and Equal to Median	Above Median	Unknown	Total
Number of Countries in Group	54	53	61	168
Number of BT deals	122	197	19	338
Percent of all deals	36.1	58.3	5.6	100
Share of World Trade of Countries in Group	9.0	89.5	1.5	100

Sources: Credit Rating: *Institutional Investor.*
Trade: International Monetary Fund, *Directions of Trade.*

TABLE 15
Barriers to Investment and Buy-back Frequency

	Host Country Barriers to New Investment					
	Very High	High	Medium	Low	No Data	Total
Number of Countries in Group	14	14	31	21	88	168
Number of BB deals	17	39	11	1	2	70
Percent of all deals	24.3	55.7	15.7	1.4	2.8	100
Share of World Trade of Countries in Group	4.5	9.9	28.4	52.9	4.2	100

Sources: Barriers to New Investment: Business International, Country Assessment Service.
Trade: International Monetary Fund, *Directions of Trade.*

TABLE 16
Barriers to Investment and Counterpurchase Frequency

	Host Country Barriers to New Investment					
	Very High	High	Medium	Low	No Data	Total
Number of Countries in Group	14	14	31	21	88	168
Number of CP deals	36	123	64	9	13	245
Percent of all deals	14.7	50.2	26.1	3.7	5.3	100
Share of World Trade of Countries in Group	4.5	9.9	28.4	52.9	4.2	100

Sources: Barriers to New Investment: Business International, Country Assessment Service.
Trade: International Monetary Fund, *Directions of Trade.*

CONCLUSION

This paper has presented some evidence on the patterns taken by countertrade. Although the information presented in this paper is derived from what is believed to be the largest database of countertrade transactions available, caution must be exercised in interpreting the tables, as the database undoubtedly only includes a fraction of all countertrade deals that were initiated over the period. As mentioned earlier, the proportion of countertrade deals reported depends also on whether *Countertrade Outlook* had correspondents in that particular country. Because of the lack of reliable data on value, the analysis has been conducted in terms of the number of countertrade agreements. This make it difficult to evaluate the relative importance of countertrade in the total trade of countries and of products.

In spite of the limitations of the data, the tables provide some interesting insights into the countertrade phenomenon. The most important finding is that each type of countertrade has its own patterns and is motivated by different factors. Even at the fairly broad level of aggregation used here, there are major differences among country groups in their use of countertrade. This suggests that future empirical research should be conducted at a disaggregated level and should focus on the differential use of particular types of countertrade by particular groups of countries.

NOTES

1. Although imbalances in clearing arrangements are sometimes settled through hard currency payments, the intended function of clearing arrangements is to swap goods for other goods, and thus to avoid the use of hard currency.

2. Counterpurchase differs from clearing arrangements insofar as it involves payment in foreign currency. In a clearing arrangement, importers pay and exporters get paid in local currency.

8. Switch trading was coded as clearing arrangement.

9. These countries are Columbia, the Dominican Republic, Guatemala, Thailand, and Zimbabwe.

10. The number of deals in these tables may vary from the totals of Table 2 for two reasons: (1) data may be missing for some observations and (2) some agreements may involve more than one seller or more than one buyer. In that case, the agreement is counted once for each buyer or seller country.

11. Greece is classified as a middle-income developing country.

12. The chi-square was 7.41, which is not significant at the 90% confidence level.

13. A chi-square of 64 allows us to reject the hypothesis that there is no relationship between countertrade type and product class at the 99% confidence level.

14. For barters, the number of transactions is the sum of those undertaken by both buyers and sellers. For example, in the case of a barter undertaken between Algeria and Canada, the table would contain one entry for Canada and one entry for Algeria.

15. The data for barriers to investment was obtained from the original worksheets for Business International's *Country Assessment Service* for January 1985. The data describes the level of limits on new investment, with a score of 0 meaning no foreign equity allowed, and 10 no limits on foreign investment. I formed the following categories: Very high limits = score of 0 to 2 (basically no foreign equity allowed); high limits = score of 3 to 5 (only minority foreign investment allowed); medium limits = score of 6 to 8 (local equity required or strongly recommended); low limits = 9-10 (no limits on FDI).

APPENDIX

Countries were aggregated into five groupings: the developed countries [Group 1], OPEC members [Group 2], centrally planned economies [group 3], Middle-income developing countries [Group 4], and Low-income developing countries [group 5]. The assignment of countries to each group (with the exception of groups 2 and 3) follows that used by the World Bank (1979). Low-income developing countries are countries with 1977 per capita income less or equal to US$300. Middle-income developing countries had a 1977 per capita income above US$300.

Developed Countries

W. Germany	Australia	U.S.	Italy
Finland	Austria	Ireland	Sweden
New Zealand	Belgium	Canada	France
Switzerland	U.K.	Norway	Japan
Netherlands	Denmark		

Centrally Planned Economies (CPEs)

USSR	Yugoslavia	Romania	Poland
Hungary	E. Germany	Czechoslovakia	Bulgaria
Cuba	Mongolia	Albania	N. Korea
Vietnam	China		

OPEC Countries

Nigeria	Algeria	Saudi Arabia	Libya
Iraq	Iran	Kuwait	Qatar
Venezuela	Ecuador	Gabon	Indonesia
U.A.E.			

Middle-Income Developing Countries

Egypt	Cameroon	Ghana	Honduras
Thailand	Senegal	Philippines	Zambia
Congo	Zimbabwe	El Salvador	Morocco
Bolivia	Ivory Coast	Jordan	Colombia
Guatemala	Korea	Nicaragua	Dominican Rep.
Peru	Tunisia	Syria	Malaysia
Guyana	Turkey	Mexico	Jamaica
Lebanon	Chile	Taiwan	Panama
Costa Rica	S. Africa	Brazil	Uruguay
Argentina	Portugal	Hong Kong	Greece
Israel	Singapore	Spain	Barbados
Belize	Malta	Surinam	Trinidad

Low-Income Developing Countries

Afghanistan	Burma	Cambodia	Bangladesh
Laos	Ethiopia	Mali	Nepal
Somalia	Burundi	Chad	Rwanda
Upper Volta	Zaire	Malawi	India
Mozambique	Niger	Pakistan	S. Leone
Tanzania	Benin	Sri Lanka	Malagasy
Kenya	Uganda	Mauritania	Sudan
Angola	Togo	Botswana	Guinea
Eq. Guinea	Cape Verde		

REFERENCES

Alexandrides, C. & B. Bowers. 1987. *Countertrade: Practices, strategies, and tactics*. New York: Wiley.

Banks, G. 1983. The economics and politics of countertrade. *The World Economy*, 6: 159–82.

Bussard, W. 1983. A view on countertrade. Paper presented at the Countertrade Conference, New York, December.

_____. 1986. New study reveals U.S. needs in countertrade. News release, U.S. Association of Countertrading Corporations.

Elderkin, K. & W. Norquist. 1987. *Creative countertrade*. Cambridge: Ballinger

Hennart, J.-F. 1986. The causes of countertrade. Working paper, Center for International Management Studies, The Wharton School.

_____. 1989. The transaction costs rationale for countertrade. *Journal of Law, Economics, and Organization*, 5, 1: 127-53.

Huszagh, S. & F. Huszagh. 1986. International barter and countertrade. *International Marketing Review*, 3: 7-19.

Khoury, S. 1984. Countertrade: Forms, motives, pitfalls, and negotiation requisites. *Journal of Business Research*, 12: 257-70.

Korth, C. 1981. Barter—An old practice yields new profits. *Business*, September/October: 2-8.

_____. 1987. *International countertrade*. New York: Quorum Books.

McVey, T. 1980. Countertyrade and barter: Alternative trade financing by Third World nations. *International Trade Law Journal*, 6: 197-220.

Mirus, R. & B. Yeung. 1984. Economic incentives for countertrade. Working paper, University of Alberta.

_____. 1986. Economic incentives for countertrade. *Journal of International Business Studies*, 17, 3: 27-40.

_____. 1987. Countertrade and foreign exchange shortages. *Welwirtschaftliches Archiv*, 123: 535-44.

Murrell, P. 1982. Product quality, market signalling, and the development of East-West trade. *Economic Inquiry*, 20, October: 589-603.

Shuster, F. 1980. Barter arrangements with money. *Columbia Journal of World Business*, Fall.

United Nations Commission for Europe. 1984. *The financing of large scale compensation projects in East-West trade since 1970*. Geneva: Economic Commission for Europe.

Verzariu, P. 1980. *Countertrade practices in East Europe*. Washington, D.C.: U.S. Department of Commerce.

_____. 1985. *Countertrade, barter and offsets: New strategies for profit in international trade*. New York: McGraw-Hill.

Yoffie, D. 1984. Profitting from countertrade. *Harvard Business Review*, May-June: 8-12.

Part II
Countertrade as Solution to Transactional Difficulties: Early Analytical Literature

[4]

PRODUCT QUALITY, MARKET SIGNALING AND THE DEVELOPMENT OF EAST-WEST TRADE

PETER MURRELL*

Countertrade, a contractual form in which there is a two-way flow of goods, occupies a position of significance in East-West trade. In this paper, it is shown that countertrade can solve problems which arise when the quality of Eastern European products is unknown. Using the market signaling literature, a theory is formulated in order to make predictions concerning the use of countertrade. Countertrade will be particularly useful when quality information is important but cannot be obtained directly and when a country has a poor quality reputation. These predictions are supported by empirical tests.

INTRODUCTION

During the last decade, there has been a major change in the trade relations between the developed capitalist countries and the nations of Eastern Europe.[1] Spurred by a variety of political and economic decisions, East-West trade has grown at a faster rate than world trade in general. Concurrently, a new contractual form, countertrade, has risen to a significant position. Under countertrade, there is a two-way flow of goods between a single Western company and an Eastern country (with perhaps an offsetting monetary transaction). Precise estimates of the significance of countertrade are difficult to obtain because international trade transactions are not classified by type of contract. However, one Hungarian source has estimated that countertrade agreements accounted for 25-35% of East-West trade in 1977 *(Business Eastern Europe (BEE)*, 1978, p. 280).[2] According to a recent OECD study (1981, p. 57), Eastern European governments view countertrade as a permanent and increasingly important part of their trade relations with the West.

*Associate Professor of Economics, University of Maryland, and Senior Research Fellow, International Institute of Management, Berlin. I would like to thank Charles Brown, Chris Clague, Dennis Mueller, Mancur Olson, and two anonymous referees for helpful advice.

1. In this paper, Eastern Europe is taken to include Czechoslovakia, the USSR, Hungary, Poland, Bulgaria, Romania, and the German Democratic Republic (GDR). These nations will be referred to collectively as the 'East' and the adjective 'Eastern' will apply to them. The developed capitalist nations are taken to be Canada, U.S.A., Japan, and all Western European nations. These nations will be referred to as the 'West' and the adjective 'Western' will apply to them.

2. *Business Eastern Europe* is a trade journal intended to give Western business people relevant information on developments in Eastern Europe. As such it is regarded in this paper as the most reliable source for qualitative information on recent developments in East-West trade; on the negotiating stances of Eastern countries; and on the attitudes of Western traders.

Economic Inquiry
Vol. XX, October 1982

There are two distinct forms of countertrade: counterpurchase and buy-back.[3] Under buy-back, the Western company sells capital equipment to an Eastern enterprise.[4] The enterprise then uses that equipment to produce output, some of which is bought by that same Western company. Thus, buy-back consists of two contracts, signed at the same time, but implemented over different periods. Under counterpurchase, the item sold by the Western company is not used in the manufacture of the goods bought by the Western company. For counterpurchase, implementation of the two contracts can have any temporal ordering.[5] Of the two types of countertrade, buy-back is the more important *(BEE* 1977, p. 10) and Eastern European countries are emphasizing buy-back (McMillan 1977, p. 1214).

The initiation of countertrade proposals by Eastern European nations can be viewed as a natural response to the pressure to increase exports to the West. Given an historical preference for bilateralism together with the constraint that some Eastern enterprises must earn their own foreign exchange, countertrade is a natural institutional response. Nevertheless, countertrade is often costly to Western companies *(BEE* 1977, p. 10, 1978, p. 289) and can be dropped by Eastern enterprises in return for other considerations *(BEE* 1977, p. 313). Thus, for countertrade to be successful it must offer other advantages apart from being a natural institutional response.

In this paper, market signaling theory is applied to explain the existence of countertrade, and especially buy-back. In section 2, salient points from the signaling literature are reviewed and their relevance to countertrade formulated. In section 3, a simple model is used to delineate the factors which influence the likelihood that countertrade will be used. In section 4, the model's predictions are tested. The paper concludes with some implications of the argument for the development of East-West trade.

I. THE RELEVANCE OF MARKET SIGNAL THEORY

When buyers do not know the quality of a specific product, they may attribute average market quality to each item. The average quality of items supplied will increase with price because sellers usually know quality. As Akerlof (1970) has shown, these assumptions will imply that less trade takes place when buyers do not know quality than when quality is easily ascertainable. Prospective Western buyers of Eastern products may be in the same position as buyers in Akerlof's model. Those buyers may have little prior information on the quality of goods made by a particular

3. Further details on countertrade arrangements in general can be found in Matheson, McCarthy and Flanders (1977), McMillan (1977), or St. Charles (1974).

4. Capital equipment includes such intangibles as the know-how to use a specific technology.

5. If credit is needed by the Eastern enterprise, it is negotiated through the usual finanacial channels (Matheson, McCarthy, and Flanders (1977), p. 1282). Of course, the existence of the countertrade deal may make credit easier to obtain.

Eastern enterprise and there may be no direct way to obtain quality information. Buyers may estimate quality at the average level for the enterprise's country.[6] Thus, following Akerlof's predictions, the market equilibrium may be such that Eastern enterprises do not find it worthwhile to export high quality goods to the West.

Consider an Eastern country which has a poor quality reputation but which wants to begin selling higher quality goods in Western markets. Enterprises in that country must discourage buyers from using country-of-origin to judge quality. Spence (1974) has shown that, if quality cannot be directly observed, sellers have an incentive to convey information by indirect methods: to signal quality. It is the central thesis of this paper that, under some circumstances, a countertrade contract will be such a signal.

A Western company which sells an item of capital equipment will sometimes know the quality of items made on its equipment. The company will usually have designed and manufactured the equipment and often will have had the most experience in using the equipment.[7] The company may know how much the quality of output varies with quality of labor input. Possibly, input quality will influence output quantity but not output quality. In such a case, the use of the capital equipment made by the Western company will be a signal of product quality by the enterprise. Therefore, in every buy-back deal there is a potential quality signal.

For many durable goods, a crucial element of quality is speed of after-sales service and reliability of supply of spare-parts. An Eastern enterprise without previous experience in the West will need to signal its intentions about these elements of product quality. One way to signal such intentions would be for the enterprise to place itself in a position of dependence on the Western company. The enterprise will be dependent on the company if that company is a supplier of capital equipment. Capital equipment requires technological updates and after-sales service which the Western company can threaten to withhold should the need arise. If the company is able to impose large costs on the enterprise, it can be more confident that the enterprise will be reliable in the future. By placing themselves in a position of mutual dependence, the two parties are signaling the reliability of their future conduct.

Mutual dependence is less likely to be an element of counterpurchase than buy-back. Often under counterpurchase, two different Eastern enterprises participate in the two trade flows and the Western company does not necessarily sell capital equipment. Then mutual dependence could be absent. In contrast, buy-back is always conducted between one enterprise and one company and always involves a Western sale of capital equipment. Thus, in examining the market signaling advantages of countertrade, one must focus on buy-back.

6. Later, I provide evidence that buyers make such assumptions.

7. 'Turnkey' factories are often supplies by the company which uses the equipment in the West.

The foregoing argument has used two unsubstantiated assumptions: (i) that Eastern European countries do have a poor quality reputation and (ii) that country-of-origin is used as a quality signal in the absence of other quality information. It is appropriate to provide some justification for these assumptions before proceeding further.[8]

The literature on East-West trade is replete with references to the poor quality of East European products (see, for example: Brown and Marer (1973, p. 191), Brown and Neuberger (1968, p. 15), Karcz (1973, p. 214), and Pryor (1963, p. 176)). Moreover, poor quality in non-priority sectors is a consequence of the economic management used in centrally-planned economies (Kornai 1959, p. 57). The cause of poor quality being systemic, prospective Western buyers would be thoroughly rational in assuming, in the absence of contrary information, that Eastern European goods are of poor quality. However, quality reputations are not the same for all Eastern European countries. The products of the GDR and Czechoslovakia are generally regarded as superior in quality to those of other Eastern countries (*BEE* 1971, pp. 57, 204, 301 and 1978, pp. 140, 201, 283). Montias (1976, p. 31) rates these two countries as the only Eastern European nations to penetrate Western markets for manufactured goods.

Given the foregoing, it is not surprising that country quality reputations affect market behavior. The following is typical of advice by *Business Eastern Europe* (1977, p. 187): "Romanian goods from the Romanian machine-building industry must be heavily discounted on Western markets because of poor after-sales service." The discounting on Western markets shows that country-of-origin is being used as a signal.[9] Statistical studies provide similar evidence. When comparing prices of Eastern goods sold on Western markets to the prices of exactly equivalent Western goods, Eastern goods have lower prices. The price differential is greatest on machinery, less on non-machinery manufactured goods, and least on raw materials. (Marer (1972) has summarized the results of a number of studies. Similar evidence can be found in Brada and Wipf (1976).) Not only can the lower prices be explained by the use of country-of-origin to judge quality, but also the discount is highest on those goods for which quality is most important. There is also evidence that the meaning of the country-of-origin signal varies within Eastern Europe. Czechoslovakian goods command higher prices in OECD markets than equivalent Polish, Hungarian, or Romanian goods (Brada and Wipf (1976, p. 130). Use of a superior country-of-origin quality signal for Czechoslovakian goods would account for such a result.

8. Note that these assumptions are sufficient, but not necessary, conditions justifying the importance of good-specific signals. Thus, the argument that buy-back is an important signal does not necessarily depend on these assumptions.

9. Country-of-origin is also used in Western markets. Reynolds and Gregory (1965, p. 190) observe that Puerto Rican manufacturers disguise the origin of their products when selling on the local market "because consumers will not buy the local product (if they can identify it as such) because of the poor reputation for quality."

II. A MODEL OF THE FACTORS INFLUENCING THE FORMATION OF BUY-BACK DEALS

In this section, I present a model of negotiations between an Eastern enterprise and a Western firm. The model is suggestive of, rather than a complete description of, the factors influencing contract choice. Construction of a complete model would be most cumbersome in view of the variety of institutional arrangements within Eastern Europe. As the model's conclusions are unsurprising and are later subjected to testing, little would be gained from a lengthier description of the behavior of Eastern enterprises.

An Eastern *enterprise* is negotiating to buy a *factory* from a Western *company* and concurrently trying to sell the product made in that factory to the Western company. (In the following, the underlined words will be used without the geographical adjectives.) The following assumptions are used:

(a) The factory is available only on Western markets, which are competitive.

(b) The enterprise will choose between 100% buy-back or no buy-back.[10] The company is an "arrangement-taker" in that it offers various contracts and allows the enterprise to choose between them.

(c) The objective of the enterprise is to maximize output sold subject to a profit constraint set by higher authorities. This is one of many enterprise goals which have been followed in Eastern Europe. Assuming maximization of output leads to a simple diagrammatic analysis. However, the same results are obtained if maximization of profits or revenues is the goal.

(d) The product is produced under non-increasing returns to scale.

(e) The product has quality μ^*. Exact knowledge of quality can be obtained by paying c per unit, the cost of tests (c may be infinite). The company selling the factory knows product quality.[11]

(f) In the absence of buy-back and quality testing, a buyer of the product assumes quality equals $\bar{\mu}\,(< \mu^*)$, average product quality in the enterprise's country.

(g) A company concluding a buy-back deal does not use the product and must resell it. The company can signal μ^* by using trademarks or guarantees. Costs incurred in this selling process are embodied in the factory's price.

(h) After the conclusion of a buy-back deal, the enterprise can convince potential buyers that product quality equals μ^* by informing buyers

10. This assumption simplifies the analysis by limiting possible outcomes to two alternatives instead of a whole spectrum of contracts.

11. This assumption is not intended to imply that the seller of any factory will always know quality but rather that we are restricting attention to the case where the seller has such knowledge.

FIGURE 1

Demand and Supply for the Eastern Product *(Y)*

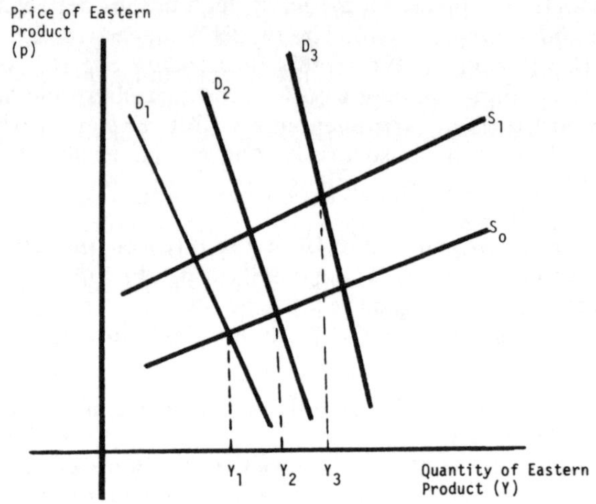

about the actions of the company involved in the deal. The original contract is thus a further signal.[12]

The decision facing an enterprise is represented in figure 1. There will be two supply curves for the Eastern product because costs are higher under buy-back than when the factory is bought for cash: S_1 following buy-back, and S_0 relevant after a cash purchase. Under the foregoing assumptions, both supply curves will be coincident with the relevant long-run average cost curves (counting minimum profits as costs). There are three demand curves for the product.[13] $D_1(p, \bar{\mu})$ is relevant if no buyer ascertains quality (p is product price). $D_2(p, \mu^*, c)$ is demand when buyers pay c to test quality. $D_3(p, \mu^*)$ is demand after a buy-back deal has been concluded. The demand curves have the following properties:

$$\frac{\partial D_i}{\partial p} < 0, \; i = 1, 2, 3; \quad \frac{\partial D_1}{\partial \bar{\mu}} > 0; \quad \frac{\partial D_i}{\partial \mu^*} > 0; \; i = 2,.3; \quad \frac{\partial D_2}{\partial c} < 0;$$

$D_1(p, \bar{\mu}) < D_3(p, \mu^*)$ for $\mu^* > \bar{\mu}$; and $D_3(p, \mu^*) > D_2(p, \mu^*, c)$ for all p, μ^*, and c.

12. Assumptions (g) and (h) can be changed without changing the conclusions. In particular, one could change (g) to include a situation in which the company uses the product as a production input. Or, (h) could be replaced with a much weaker assumption, in which buyers buying direct from the Eastern company assume product quality is between $\bar{\mu}$ and μ^*. Any changes in (h) and (g), however, would necessitate a different formulation of the model.

13. No explicit assumption is made about market structure. All one need assume is that competitors of the enterprise react in an unchanging manner to the enterprise's price changes.

On figure 1, the intersection of D_3 and S_1 gives the price-output combination for buy-back. The intersection of D_2 and S_0 gives the price-output combination when buyers test for quality. The intersection of D_1 and S_0 is relevant when buyers do not ascertain product quality. The outputs of the Eastern enterprise in each situation (Y_1, Y_2, and Y_3) can be ordered by magnitude in any pattern. (The situation depicted is one in which a buy-back deal is best.) An immediate conclusion from the model is that if nothing is learned from buy-back then $D_1 = D_3$ and $Y_1 > Y_3$, so that buy-back is inferior. A market signal is a necessary condition for the use of buy-back.

To obtain testable hypotheses, simple comparative statics results can be derived. When c decreases, D_2 moves to the right and the probability that Y_2 will be to the right of Y_3 increases. Hence, the likelihood of buy-back declines. Thus, buy-back is more likely the higher the cost of testing product quality. The second testable hypothesis focuses on the country quality signal, $\bar{\mu}$. If $\bar{\mu}$ increases, D_1 moves to the right. Thus, the probability that Y_1 is to the right of Y_3 is higher for enterprises in countries with a higher quality reputation. Hence, buy-back is more likely the lower is the Eastern country's quality reputation.

Before turning to the tests, two qualifications must be made. First, if institutional pressure for countertrade is strong, enterprises may sign countertrade contracts solely because of this pressure. One should not conclude that market signaling is the sole reason for countertrade. The appropriate conclusion from the above analysis is that the signaling property of buy-back will influence both the pattern of countertrade and the extent to which it is regarded as successful by Eastern European authorities.

Second, the Eastern enterprise need not be aware that the quality signal is a property of successful buy-back. A signal can have an appropriate effect even when the signaler is unaware of the information being conveyed. Thus, the model is consistent with a scenario in which countertrade began as an institutional response to changing trade conditions. Given some negotiating flexibility, countertrade proposals in which signaling was an element would succeed while others would fail. The pattern of successes and failures predicted by the foregoing hypotheses would occur even if Eastern negotiators did not understand the element of signaling in countertrade.

III. TESTS OF THE EFFECTS OF MARKET SIGNALING ON TRADE PATTERNS

For the tests, it is necessary to identify goods for which quality signals are important. Quality signals will be important determinants of market behavior if two conditions are satisfied. First, the buyer must think that quality is crucial to a good's performance and that quality could vary.

Second, quality must be difficult to ascertain before purchase. Thus, the following characteristics of goods are important:

(a) *Durability.*[14] The more durable a good, the less likely that it can be used in a normal manner and quality ascertained before purchase. Also, durable goods usually require after-sales service and supply of spare parts, the reliability of which cannot be tested before sale.
(b) *Indivisibility.* The greater the value of the smallest testable unit, the more expensive is randomized testing requiring destruction.
(c) *Proportion of raw material in total value.* The greater the manufacturing input relative to raw material input, the more quality depends on decisions made by the manufacturer. Therefore, quality variation will be more likely.

The exact identification of goods for which a signal is necessary would involve extended study. However, it is easy to identify one product group which is more likely to contain goods with the above characteristics than other groups. As this study examines trade flows, the Standard International Trade Classification (SITC) is a natural tool for classification purposes (see United Nations 1975). Of the one digit SITC groups, group 7, Machinery and Transport Equipment, has a large proportion of the goods that have the characteristics which make quality signaling important. In Appendix I, the use of group 7 goods as those which require signals is given further justification.[15]

The tests use data on countertrade contracts. As that data is from a nonstandard source *(Business Eastern Europe)*, a brief description of the data is required. A lengthier description is contained in Appendix II. Each week BEE describes contracts signed between Western companies and Eastern enterprises. The descriptions are detailed enough to obtain the following information: (a) whether the contracts are counterpurchase, buy-back, or for cash, and (b) the SITC group for any Eastern European export, or potential export, connected with the contract. For contracts listed during 1977-78, the following information was found:[16]

(i) The SITC group of the good to be produced on the capital equipment sold to an Eastern enterprise for cash ('the product group of a cash deal').

14. By durability I do not mean the opposite to perishable but rather the fact that the product is normally used over an extended period of time.

15. There is ample evidence that East European group 7 exports to the West are low compared to both Eastern European production of these goods and to the Eastern European level of development (see, for example, Kadar 1977). Thus, the use of group 7 and the interpretation of East-West trade given in the opening paragraphs of section 2 are consistent.

16. For countertrade contracts before 1977, information is available in Matheson, McCarthy and Flanders (1977). Therefore, as the numbers of buy-back and counterpurchase contracts signed during 1977-78 were small compared to the number of cash contracts, the sample has been augmented with pre-1977 countertrade contracts. This augmentation is for the tests of Hypotheses 1 and 2 but *not* for Hypotheses 3 and 4 for which it is important to have a measure of the relative importance of buy-back versus cash and counterpurchase contracts.

(ii) The SITC group of the Eastern product to be exported in a buy-back agreement ('the product group of a buy-back deal').
(iii) The SITC group of the Eastern product to be exported in a counterpurchase agreement ('the product group of a counterpurchase deal').

For each hypothesis tested, three overlapping sets of data were used in order to ensure that the results do not solely reflect one country's experience. Hungary and the Soviet Union account for a disproportionate share of the contracts. The policies of both these countries are not typical of Eastern Europe. As the Soviet Union has relied heavily on the export of raw materials, one would not expect its data to provide strong support for the signaling hypotheses. Hungary has liberalized its economy and allowed more flexibility in negotiations than other Eastern European countries. If the hypotheses are correct one would expect strong results for Hungary. Thus, to ensure that the results are not unduly affected by the specific policies of these two countries, three data sets are used. First, the results are presented for all 7 Eastern European countries. Then the Soviet Union is excluded from the data in order to focus on the countries which have not been able to rely on exports of natural resources. Then Hungary is also excluded in order to ensure that its data do not dominate the results.

The results to be tested were derived in the previous section. It was predicted that buy-back contracts will be more likely to be chosen when a quality signal is necessary and other contractual forms are more likely to be chosen when quality is more easily ascertainable. Since group 7 goods have been identified as those for which a quality signal is necessary, a natural hypothesis is:

> *Hypothesis 1.* The proportion of all buy back contracts which involve a product from group 7 will be greater than the proportion of all cash contracts which involve a product from group 7.

The test results for this hypothesis are presented in the first three lines of table 1. When all 7 countries are included in the data, 59% of all the buy-back contracts involve an Eastern product which is classified in SITC group 7. In contrast, 26% of cash contracts involve a group 7 product. The usual test statistic for a difference between proportions, which has a standard normal distribution, equals 6.3. The critical points (which apply to all the tests) are 2.33 for a 99% significance level and 1.64 for a 95% significance level. Thus, all three sets of data strongly support hypothesis 1.

There is a possible objection to hypothesis 1 as a test of the influence of signaling. The product in a buy-back contract is always exported. In contrast, there is no assumption that the product made on a piece of capital equipment bought in a cash deal is exported. Thus, if for any reason group 7 products are more readily exportable than other products, the data would support hypothesis 1 even if there were no signaling effects of buy-back. As the Eastern product in a counterpurchase contract is exported,

TABLE 1

Test Results

Hypothesis Tested	Test Statistics	COUNTRIES USED IN THE DATA SET 7 (all)	6 (excl. USSR)	5 (excl. USSR & Hungary)
1	Buy-back Proportion	0.59	0.62	0.56
	Cash Proportion	0.26	0.30	0.29
	Standardized difference	6.30**	5.11**	3.23**
2	Buy-back Proportion	0.59	0.62	0.56
	Counterpurchase Proportion	0.20	0.28	0.33
	Standardized difference	4.86**	3.76**	1.90*
3	High-signal Proportion	0.14	0.14	0.14
	Low-signal Proportion	0.20	0.31	0.13
	Standardized difference	0.92	2.29**	–0.15
4	High-signal Proportion	0.38	0.38	0.38
	Low-signal Proportion	0.64	0.73	0.58
	Standardized difference	1.75*	2.53**	1.14

** = significant at the 99% level; * = significant at the 95% level.

the objection can be countered by comparing the patterns of counterpurchase and buy-back contracts. Market signals are more likely to be important determinants of buy-back contracts than of counterpurchase contracts. Therefore, one would test:

> *Hypothesis* 2. The proportion of all buy-back contracts which involve a product from group 7 will be greater than the proportion of all counterpurchase contracts which involve a product from group 7.

Two of the test statistics (see table 1) are significant at the 99% level and the other at the 95% level. The results of Hypotheses 1 and 2 together give strong support to the signaling interpretation of countertrade. The fact that the least significant test statistic, for both hypotheses, is the one in which Hungary is excluded, provides additional support for that interpretation. As Hungarian enterprises have more negotiating flexibility than other East European enterprises, that country's data should show the strongest effects of signaling. Nevertheless, the results in the last column of table 1 ensure that signaling phenomena also affect the data of other countries.

The second prediction of the theory focuses on the notion of a national quality reputation. The model showed that the higher the country-of-origin quality signal the less likely that enterprises would use buy-back. The GDR and Czechoslovakia were identified as two countries with high quality reputations relative to the rest of Eastern Europe. Therefore, one can test the effects of country-of-origin signals by examining the following hypothesis:[17]

> *Hypothesis* 3. Let GDR and Czechoslovakia constitute the high signal group and Romania, Poland, Hungary, USSR, and Bulgaria the low signal group. Then the high signal group has a lower ratio of buy-back deals to all factory sales (*i.e.*, the sum of cash and buy-back deals) than the low signal group.

With Hungary included and the Soviet Union excluded, the test statistic for Hypothesis 3 is significant. For the two other sets of data, the test statistic is not significant. The results may be a reflection of the fact that enterprises in countries other than Hungary do not have much flexibility in avoiding institutional pressure for countertrade. Thus, one is led to seek a test which is not affected by this pressure: a comparison of counterpurchase and buy-back. As signaling is more likely to be a property of buy-back than of counterpurchase, buy-back will be more important relative to counterpurchase in low signal countries than high signal countries. Thus, one would test:

> *Hypothesis* 4. The proportion of all countertrade contracts which are buy-back contracts is higher for low signal than high signal countries.

Two of the statistics support the hypothesis significantly. However, when the Soviet Union and Hungary are excluded, the statistic is non-significant. (In the non-significant case, the difference of proportions has the expected sign. The standard errors are large due to the small number of contracts.) The test results for hypothesis 4 support the prediction that a country-of-origin quality signal affects trade patterns and that buy-back may be a means of overcoming a poor quality reputation.

17. See footnote 16 for the data included in this test. In formulating the test, it would have been appropriate to ensure that the test results are not due to the differing policies of companies which trade in different Eastern European countries. However, it is impossible to control for company behavior because each Western company accounts for only a small number (often one) of contracts. Nevertheless, there are a number of examples in the data of Western companies using different contractual forms in different countries. Thus, insofar as one can ascertain from the data, the results are not due to the preferences (geographical or contractual) of Western companies.

IV. CONCLUSION

The statistical results of section 3 support the theory that informational difficulties, and therefore market signals, affect the pattern of East-West trade. The results show that countertrade, and especially buy-back, can play an important role when quality information is unobtainable. In light of these results, the usual conclusion, that countertrade is a retreat towards bilateralism without any significant advantage (OECD 1981, p. 7), should be reevaluated.

Two further conclusions can be drawn. The first is based on the argument that knowledge of a production process can lead to an estimate of product quality. Presumably, this argument is relevant for trade relationships between any countries. Thus, in intra-Western trade there must be an institution which plays a role analogous to countertrade. The multinational corporation could be such an institution.[18] Thus, the presence of countertrade in East-West trade may be a result of the absence of multinational corporations in Eastern Europe.

One can also conclude that countertrade may lead to a gradual improvement in Eastern European trade performance. Every high quality good sold in the West will change Western perceptions of East European quality. As the country-of-origin signals change, it will become easier for Eastern enterprises to sell goods in the West. Thus, a buy-back contract is not only an investment in Western technology but also an investment in a country's quality reputation.

APPENDIX I:

The Use of Group 7

The strongest argument for using group 7 goods as those for which signaling is necessary is that all goods in group 7 are durable and most durable goods are in group 7. The test results are primarily due to a different pattern of behavior in group 7 (machinery and transport equipment) than in group 5 (chemicals) and 6 (manufactured goods classified chiefly by material). The names of these groups indicate that the use of group 7 is appropriate.

Evidence from other research can also be used. Nelson (1974) has distinguished between search goods and experience goods. Search goods are those whose quality can be ascertained before purchase. Experience goods are those goods whose quality can be ascertained only by experience. Nelson also distinguishes between experience durable and experience nondurable: the latter group consisting of goods which can be sampled at

18. The argument would be consistent with Williamson's (1975) organizational theories. The information problems solved by countertrade can, in a Western context, be solved by internalization of trade in a hierarchical organization.

small cost. Thus, "experience durable" goods are ones for which quality signals are important. Thus, if the use of group 7 is appropriate, Nelson's experience durable goods will be in group 7 while experience non-durable and search goods will not. Of 40 goods classified by Nelson (1974, p. 739), 35 classifications are consistent with this prediction, 3 are inconsistent and 2 are ambiguous. The use of group 7 is broadly consistent with Nelson's work.

APPENDIX II:

The Data

This appendix supplements the text's description of data collection by listing the rules employed in interpreting the *BEE* contract descriptions.

(a) The only *BEE* entries used were those in which it was explicitly stated that contracts had been signed.
(b) Where there was no mention of countertrade it was assumed that the sale was for cash (this assumption, if inappropriate, would only bias the tests toward acceptance of the null hypothesis).
(c) The SITC group was found by comparing the *BEE* description to the United Nations classification tables (see United Nations, 1975). In a small number of cases, it was not possible to find the SITC group number. In such cases, the contract was not included in the sample.
(d) For a few cases, the exports in a counterpurchase contract consisted of an assortment of goods. If the goods were either all in group 7 or all not in group 7 the counterpurchase was counted as one contract. If some goods were in 7 and others not, the contract was counted twice, once in 7 and once outside 7.
(e) Buy-back is only possible if the Eastern product is exportable. To include in cash sales only contracts in which buy-back would have been possible, cash sales were excluded if the product to be made in Eastern Europe as a result of the contract was not exportable.
(f) Buy-back is only possible when a complete salable item is made on the Western equipment. To include in cash sales only contracts in which buy-back would have been possible, cash sales were excluded if the item sold was only peripheral to the production process.
(g) Production process licenses were counted as sales of capital equipment for two reasons. First, knowledge of the production process provides the signal, and a license is evidence of this knowledge. Second, *BEE* estimates that 98% of license sales are eventually followed by sales of equipment.

The data collected using these rules is presented in table 2.

TABLE 2

The Structure of Countertrade

(1) Country	(2) Type of Contract	(3) Number of Contracts in SITC Group 7	(4) Number of Contracts in SITC Groups 0-6, 8, 9	(5) Total Contracts Signed in 1977-78
	Cash	19	20	39
Poland	Buy-back	15	14	8
	Counterpurchase	2	11	4
	Cash	18	38	56
Hungary	Buy-back	42	22	47
	Counterpurchase	2	11	13
	Cash	6	23	29
Romania	Buy-back	7	0	3
	Counterpurchase	2	0	2
	Cash	2	3	5
Bulgaria	Buy-back	0	0	0
	Counterpurchase	3	1	2
	Cash	2	14	16
Czechoslovakia	Buy-back	1	0	1
	Counterpurchase	1	2	2
	Cash	1	14	15
GDR	Buy-back	1	5	4
	Counterpurchase	2	6	6
	Cash	26	100	126
USSR	Buy-back	1	6	7
	Counterpurchase	0	16	16

SOURCES: 1977-78 issue of *Business Eastern Europe;* Matheson, McCarthy, and Flanders (1977), pp.1304-11.

NOTE: The data in column (5) only includes contracts listed in the first source. The data for buy-back and counterpurchase in columns (3) and (4) includes contracts listed in both sources.

REFERENCES

Akerlof, George A., "The Market for 'Lemons': Quality Uncertainty and the Market Mechanism," *Quarterly Journal of Economics*, August 1970, *84*, 488-500.

Brada, Josef and Wipf, Larry, "The Export Performance of East European Nations in Western Markets," *Weltwirtschaftliches Archiv*, 1975, *111*, 121-137.

__________, "Romanian Exports to Western Markets," in *Quantitative and Analytical Studies in East-West Economic Relations*, ed., J. Brada, International Development Research Center, Indiana University, Bloomington, 1976.

Brown, Alan A. and Marer, Paul, "Foreign Trade in the East European Reforms" in *Plan and Market*, ed., M. Bornstein, Yale University Press, New Haven, 1973.

Brown, Alan A. and Neuberger, Egon, "Foreign Trade of Centrally Planned Economies: An Introduction," in *International Trade and Central Planning*, University of California Press, Berkeley, 1968.

Kadar, B., "The Commodity Pattern of East-West Trade," *Acta Oeconomica* 1977, *18*, 153-165.

Karcz, Jerzy F., "Agricultural Reform in Eastern Europe," in *Plan and Market*, ed., M. Bornstein, Yale University Press, New Haven, 1973.

Kornai, Janos, *Overcentralization in Economic Administration*, Oxford University Press, Oxford, 1959.

McMillan, Carl H., "East-West Industrial Cooperation," in *East-European Economies Post-Helsinki*, U.S. Congress, Joint Economic Committee, 95th Con., 1st sess., Washington, 1977.

Marer, Paul, *Post-War Pricing and Price Patterns in Socialist Foreign Trade*. International Development Research Center, Indiana University, Bloomington, 1972.

Matheson, Jenelle, McCarthy, Paul and Flanders, Steven, "Countertrade Practices in Eastern Europe," in *Eastern European Economies Post-Helsinki*, U.S. Congress, Joint Economic Committee, 95th Cong., 1st sess., Washington, 1977.

Montias, John Michael, "Socialist Industrialization and Trade in Manufactures," in *Quantitative and Analytical Studies in East-West Economic Relations*, ed., J. C. Brada, International Development Research Center, Indiana University, Bloomington, 1976.

Nelson, Phillip, "Advertising as Information," *Journal of Political Economy*, July 1974, *82*, 729-54.

Pryor, Frederic L., *The Communist Foreign Trade System*, The M.I.T. Press, Cambridge, 1963.

Reynolds, Lloyd G. and Gregory, Peter, *Wages, Productivity, and Industrialization in Puerto Rico*, Irwin, Homewood, 1965.

St. Charles, David P., "East-West Business Arrangements: A Typology," in *Changing Perspectives in East-West Commerce*, ed., Carl H. McMillan, Heath-Lexington, Lexington, Mass., 1974.

Spence, A. Michael, *Market Signaling: Informational Transfer in Hiring and Related Screening Processes*, Harvard University Press, Cambridge, 1974.

Williamson, Oliver G., *Markets and Hierarchies: Analysis and Antitrust Implications*, The Free Press, New York, 1975.

Wolf, Thomas A., "East-West European Trade Relations," in *Eastern European Economies Post-Helsinki*, U.S. Congress, Joint Economic Committee, 95th Cong., 1st sess., Washington, 1977.

Business Eastern Europe, Business International S.A., Geneva, Weekly.

OECD, *East-West Trade: Recent Developments in Countertrade*, Paris, 1981.

United Nations, Department of Economic and Social Affairs, Statistical Office. *Standard International Trade Classification Revision 2*. United Nations: New York, 1975.

[5]

ON DESIGNING CONTRACTS TO GUARANTEE ENFORCEABILITY: THEORY AND EVIDENCE FROM EAST-WEST TRADE

Bruce Kogut*
The Wharton School

Abstract. This article suggests how the literature on East-West trade and the choice of contracts can be integrated into recent work on the theory of the multinational corporation and contract enforceability. By using the properties of foreign direct investment as a benchmark, it explains why one type of contract tends to prevail over another. The explanation rests on the premise that because of the prohibition on FDI, contracts are used which most closely replicate the benefits of intra-firm trade, while providing managerial and risk-shifting services to the eastern partner.

Current theories of the multinational corporation propose that the higher costs of transacting through the market rather than within the firm explain the existence of foreign direct investment. These costs stem from the failure to appropriate returns on knowledge and technology transfer, to guarantee quality of production and the maintenance of brand names, or to avoid costly arbitration in the case of non-performance.[1] Assuming that the foreign firm possesses a competitive advantage in the form of intangible assets, foreign direct investment occurs, therefore, when the costs of market or contractually-mediated transactions outweigh those of intra-firm trade. From this perspective, foreign direct investment theory weds a theory of imperfect competition stemming from intangible assets to a theory of the multinational corporation which explains imperfections in the sale of these assets.

In the context of East-West trade, foreign direct investment is largely prohibited. There exists, therefore, the following dilemma. On the one hand, the centrally-planned economy desires not only the importation of

* Bruce Kogut is an assistant professor at the Wharton School. In 1983, he taught at the Stockholm School of Economics. Dr. Kogut received his Ph.D. from the Sloan School of Management, Massachusetts Institute of Technology, in 1983.

I thank Jean Francois Hennart, Donald Lessard, Michael Piore, Richard Robinson, Jan Erik Vahlne, Louis Wells, and the anonymous referees for their criticism and advice, as well as to George Stathakis and Walter Glass of the World Trading Division of General Electric and Donald Green of Chase Manhattan Bank for useful discussions. Part of this research was financed by grants from the University of Pennsylvania and the Reginald H. Jones Center of the Wharton School.

Date Received: October 22, 1984; Revised: March 1, 1985/July 8, 1985; Accepted: July 8, 1985.

particular goods, but also contractual mechanisms by which it can acquire risk-shifting and managerial services. On the other hand, the western firm is concerned not only with the pricing of the contract, but also with the enforceability of its terms. The selection of a one type contract over another depends, therefore, upon the extent to which it provides these services within a framework which assures enforceability.

The relevance of contract selection is particularly important when placed in the wider context of the growing use of countertrade agreements that serve as conduits for world trade. For example, some recent estimates published in the popular press have indicated that countertrade may be responsible for 20 percent of world trade. The impetus behind the apparent growth in countertrade stems clearly from the financial constraints facing many countries. No matter what the impetus, however, the existence of these contracts rests on the use of contracts to shift risk onto one of the partners in order to finance and market the payment in kind.

Despite the relative novelty in the expansion of these activities, there exists tremendous information on the nature and risks of these contracts from East-West trade. Yet, whereas there has been substantial descriptive information on the motives for and problems of cooperative ventures (which include countertrade and other long-term agreements entailing coordination between two or more firms), there has been no attempt to analyze these activities in the context of a more general theory of the governance design of the economic activities of the firm. As a result, it is theoretically impossible to extend our understanding of East-West trade to explain the existence and structure of similar kinds of activities in other regions of the world.

This article moves in the direction of creating a more comprehensive explanation of contract design in East-West trade by developing a link between the literature on contract enforceability to recent theories of foreign direct investment and economic governance. In developing this link, this paper avoids much of the contractual complexity and concentrates upon three features which are of analytic interest. Two of these features are managerial and risk-shifting services. They characterize the *substance* of the contract. Managerial services involve the transfer of technology or the provision of superior market information and distribution access. Risk-shifting involves the transfer of price and/or sales volume variability from the eastern to the western partner. The demand for these services, it is shown in section one, is derived from structural weaknesses in centrally-planned economies to trade on world markets.

In addition to managerial and risk-shifting services, a third feature of contract choice is the question of enforceability. Enforceability characterizes the *design* of the contract. The terms of many contracts often leave the western partner in a hostage position which influences its willingness to supply these services. There exists, then, an enforcement problem, because by shifting the market risk, the incentives for quality production, for example, are reduced. If the sales contract is coupled with an agreement that delays payment, then there is also an elimination of incentives to perform on the implicit debt contract in certain cases.

A transaction cost analysis suggests that such a relationship is likely to be characterized by monitoring and arbitration costs. We would expect that these services would be provided within the firm rather than through the market place. In other words, foreign direct investment should be the governance structure for such types of transactions.

By using the properties of foreign direct investment as a benchmark, this paper explains why one type of contract is chosen over another. The explanation rests on the premise that because of the prohibition on FDI, contracts are used which most closely replicate the enforceability of proprietary claims inherent in intra-firm trade, yet provide the services of risk-shifting and management. The next section analyzes some chronic weaknesses in the foreign trade sector of the centrally-planned economy which generate the need for certain kinds of services. Section two presents a typology of some commonly used contracts in East-West trade in terms of their managerial, risk-shifting and enforcement capabilities. The third section presents some empirical data to test qualitatively the contention that self-enforcing contracts predominate over other alternatives. The conclusions suggest extensions of the findings to other areas of research and point also to implications for a revival of a macroeconomic story of foreign direct investment.

The methodology of this article is similar to that used by Williamson (1980). First, we establish *a priori* what kinds of discriminating criteria can be used to evaluate the merits of a contract. Next, contracts are compared in terms of whether they meet these criteria. Based upon this qualitative assessment, a prediction is made as to which contract is likely to be predominant. We do not expect that only one contractual form will exist. But to the extent that our criteria captures most of the underlying phenomena, we can expect one contract to be predominant for specified classes of traded goods and services. An examination of unexplained variance by a case-by-case method—which we do not attempt here—is needed to pinpoint the institutional facets which explain these deviations. We do not attempt such an investigation in this article, though it is hoped that the framework developed below may be used in future studies in order to increase the comparability across case studies to study questions of contract design.

WEAKNESSES IN FOREIGN TRADING

The motives for eastern European countries and the Soviet Union to import risk-shifting and managerial (especially marketing) services stems from systematic weaknesses in the organization of their foreign trade activities. The use of long-term contracts is by no means isolated to East-West trade or to trade between developing and developed countries. What makes East-West trade particularly interesting is that there are chronic weaknesses regarding the capacity of the centrally-planned economy (CPE) to respond to price variability and/or sales volume variability, weaknesses which promote the use of contracts, such as countertrade agreements. These contracts are, consequently, used relatively frequently. This section explains the weaknesses of the CPE in terms of three primary factors: 1) slow reactions to market changes, 2) insensitivity to buyers' needs, and 3) costly mechanisms of risk shifting. Though the details of our analysis are based on the German Democratic Republic (GDR), it applies generally to other East European countries.

Slow Reactions to Market Changes

A common complaint in the managerial literature published in the GDR concerns the slow reactions of firms to changes in foreign markets.[2] Import demand is, thus, fairly unresponsive to changes in foreign prices, as suggested by the price elasticities of the GDR's demand for western imports.[3] In a study by Vanous (1981), the price elasticity of the GDR's demand for western machinery and consumer goods were estimated to be nearly perfectly inelastic. Estimates for other commodities were found to be unstable. Similar results were found for the price elasticity of import demand of other centrally-planned economies.

Three factors explain the GDR's slow response to changes on world markets. First, profit and price rules lead to suboptimal decisions. In the GDR, the foreign trade enterprise (FTE) earns profits on two principal sets of transactions.[4] The first set is sales between the FTE and the domestic manufacturer, which are valued at internal prices fixed for one year or longer duration. The second set of transactions are sales between the FTE and the foreign firm. The FTE receives an annual target of sales valued at forecasted prices and exchange rates. From this target, the FTE is permitted to retain a planned profit. Exogenous changes in prices or exchange rates which result in windfall earnings (losses) are taxed away (subsidized). The FTE is under, therefore, no incentive to alter its sales plan when prices or exchange rates change. These changes do not affect the commission earned on its internal transactions or affect its profits on foreign sales. To the extent that central planners are always at an information disadvantage relative to the firm, the FTE has, in fact, the perverse incentive of arbitraging the fixed prices and exchange rates imposed by the plan.

Second, flexibility is constrained by the absence of surplus capacity. Most centrally-planned economies operate under what has been called taut planning.[5] Taut planning denotes the setting of targets such that capital and labor resources must be fully utilized in order to satisfy the plan goals. Of the many dysfunctional effects of taut planning, the most pertinent for the implications of foreign trade is the implied lack of surplus capacity to meet unexpected surges in foreign demand.

Last, planning mechanisms constrain sales and production flexibility. FTEs are not able to change contracts due to the nature of the plan. Production is earmarked for either internal manufacturers who must meet their plan or for foreign buyers with long-term contracts. Since the FTE incurs stiff penalties for delays in meeting contractual obligations, it cannot shift sales to the high price bidder. Moreover, long-term contracts are especially prevalent between firms of CMEA countries. Some 70% of the trade of the GDR is with CMEA countries and this trade cannot be redirected. When foreign demand increases, the firm is not in the position to meet new orders. The upper tail of the returns distribution is truncated, since the firm cannot increase production to take advantage of higher output prices.

Insensitivity to Buyers' Needs

Production of high quality and technologically-sophisticated products has been a chronic difficulty for the CPE. In addition to anecdotal evidence, some indications of quality problems of traded goods can be inferred, as Holzman (1979) points out, from data on the composition of trade. Sales of machinery are less price sensitive, more quality sensitive relative to sales in commodities. In East-East commerce, notes Holzman, trade in machinery plays a significant role. In East-West commerce, eastern machinery exports is markedly less important relative to raw materials, suggesting the difficulty of East European countries and the Soviet Union to compete on quality. Even for the GDR, which is purported to be more developed of the CMEA countries, a similar reversal in trade composition can be seen.

In part, this failure is an outcome of the sellers' domination of commercial transactions in domestic trade. Sellers' domination stems from principally two causes. Above all, there is a lack of competition between domestic firms in the home and foreign market. Because firms are given administratively-determined incentives to minimize costs, there is no recognized need to encourage competition.

A second cause is that the CPE tends to be "resource-constrained." The binding constraint on the firm is not demand for its goods, but the supply of its inputs.[6] Industrial consumers have a soft budget constraint insofar that increases in the costs of their inputs can be passed onto the consumer or subsidized by the state. As a result, firms are not compelled to improve the quality of their products, since demand is price and quality insensitive.

In addition to the condition of a sellers' market, production is not responsive to demands for quality and technology changes given the nature of the technology plan. Not only are inputs and final goods balanced and planned in the centrally-planned economy, but technology is also planned over a five-year horizon. A serious drawback to the planning of technology is the inflexibility of the plan to unexpected developments.[7]

Intolerance towards Risk

The riskiness of trading on world markets poses complex problems to the operation and success of a planned economy. The intolerance towards risk stems from at least three factors. First, the factors of production are not flexible in the long-term plans. Second, because bonuses are tied to profitability, changes in foreign prices and demand have direct consequences for income distribution. Lastly, because of the linking of the bonus system to the plan, the riskiness of foreign sales distorts the incentive system by rendering it more arbitrary. From the point of view of the CPE, therefore, the riskiness of foreign prices and sales interrupts planning mechanisms and distorts internal incentives.

Risk from foreign sales can be reduced either through diversification or shifting. Diversification is achieved by the pooling of different capital assets with less than perfectly correlated returns. In a capitalistic economy, the concept is easily illustrated by a portfolio of securities which can be generally shown to have a total variance lower than the sum of the variances of the individual securities. Risk shifting is the transfer of risk to individuals or firms which are willing to bear it. An illustration of risk shifting is a forward contract which guarantees an individual the right to buy or sell foreign exchange at a fixed price at a certain point in time from a bank. The bank bears, therefore, the risk that the spot rate may deviate from the contracted forward rate. Thus, there are two relevant questions: who bears the risk? and how is risk reduced?

The GDR has created two mechanisms to reduce the variability in bonuses due to price changes on the foreign market. First, any exogenous change in prices (that is, changes which do not stem from changes in product quality or marketing) results in either subsidies if losses ensue or taxes if gains are incurred. The effectiveness of this policy rests on the abilities of central authorities to infer managerial performance from exogenous price disturbances and the bargaining capabilities of firms. The second mechanism is the creation of risk and reserve funds to encourage the use of new technologies and to buffer wages against losses to the bonus fund.

The state subsidies and risk funds shift the incidence of risk from the firm onto the central authority. The risk profile at the central level differs, however, from that of the individual firms, since by the pooling of investments across different industries, the variance of the individual activities is reduced through diversification. The CPE may, therefore, seek to replicate the diversification effects of a portfolio of securities by investing across industries. Clearly, risk reduction through the diversification of real economic activity is costly and inefficient, for the benefits of economies of scale and comparative advantages are lost. (Within the Council on Mutual Economic Assistance, long-term specialization agreements partially permit a division of labor while eliminating risk through essentially barter arrangements.)

Alternatively, risk can be reduced through inward and outward portfolio or foreign direct investment. For example, by investing in foreign extraction industries, increases in the price of raw materials can be hedged. Or by permitting inward direct investment, some of the risk of production can be shifted to foreign investors. As noted before, however, inward flows of proprietary capital is prohibited, and outward flows are negligible. Though portfolio flows are an insignificant proportion of total international investment, the prohibition on foreign direct investment greatly restricts the CPEs relative to other regions in the world. (Data is provided in the third section.)

A more relevant mechanism than diversification for the CPE is the shifting of risk. A major obstacle is that forward contracts are traded only for a limited number of goods, primarily homogenous commodities. Even if contracts existed for all goods, two types of costs would be associated with their use. First, such contracts entail transaction costs. Second, long-term contracts prevent the CPE from altering its production mix as relative prices change. Thus, there are real opportunity costs.[8] Parenthetically, it should be noted that unlike participation in world equity markets, the use of forward or future contracts does not provide any diversification benefits. Consequently, the CPE faces limited opportunities to reduce risk through diversification.

CONTRACTUAL SERVICES

Given the organizational properties discussed in section one, the centrally-planned economy can seek to remedy its institutional weaknesses through various forms of contracts. The implications of these weaknesses can be usefully grouped under deficient managerial expertise and risk-shifting mechanisms. Slow response time implies that the changes in foreign markets are weakly transmitted or that market signals are not salient in respect to managerial incentives. Similiarly, poor product quality represents a lack of technical and managerial expertise or the incentives to produce competitive goods. The prohibition on foreign direct investment deprives the CPE of efficient ways to diversify and shift risk.

Contracts with western firms can be designed to provide these functions. A western firm contributes managerial services and information regarding the opportunity or scarcity values of economic resources, the demand characteristics of foreign markets, and technology. In addition to providing information on present and forecasted trends, western firms provide distribution, marketing and advertising services, areas in which socialist countries have been historically weak.

Contracts can also be designed to provide risk-shifting services. A western firm may be more willing than its eastern counterpart to bear the risk for principally three reasons. First, by participating in diversified world or national financial markets, its shareholders can more easily reduce the total risk. Second, it is able to bear the risk more easily, because its factors of production, namely labor, are not fixed. To the extent to which factor markets are competitive and supply elastic, firms can respond to demand surges and, by laying off workers, to shortfalls. Lastly, given long-standing relationships with banks and other financial institutions, risk can be laid off through hedging and other financial means at lower transaction costs.

Despite the incentives for the transfer of managerial skills and risk-shifting functions, obstacles to their provision exist due to the costs of contract enforceability. The willingness of the western firm to supply managerial and risk-shifting services is partly a function of the extent to which a contract is enforceable. The problem is, of course, the same for the eastern firm, but the key difference is that it is invariably the western firm which has incurred the up-front investment and exposure.

Contract enforceability can be assured either by effective recourse to third-party arbitration or by the creation of self-enforcing instruments. Recourse to third-party arbitration is often undesirable, for the costs of arbitration and redress are not insignificant and involve prolonged settlement. Under the law of most socialist countries, penalties can only be levied against the assets of the FTE rather than against those of the manufacturer. The assets of the former usually consist only of office property and furnishings. On the other hand, the track record for arbitration in socialist countries is not notoriously poor.[9] But arbitration in any environment is costly and deters contractual agreement if the probability of conflict is significant.

An alternative is the creation of a self-enforcing contract.[10] A self-enforcing contract is created when any willful breach in its provisions leads automatically to penalties for the violator in an amount greater than the potential gain. An example of a self-enforcing contract relevant to East-West trade is the case of co-production in which two firms make bilateral asset-specific investment; the production of one firm is valueless without the component of the second firm. Another example is investment levered through the issue of foreign debt in export industries which produces uniquely for export to the West. Thus, default on the loans is restrained by the hostage nature of the export product.[11] In both of the above examples, the stakes of the two parties are secured through the creation of bilateral hostage exposure.

Trade based on long-term agreements can be channeled through numerous types of contracts. These contracts vary in their provision of managerial, risk-shifting, and self-enforcing services. The principal contracts in East-West trade are briefly considered below and summarized in Table 1.

1. *Spot trading:* Since goods are exchanged for their monetary or barter value, there is no provision of managerial skills and risk-shifting services. Contracts are self-enforcing since payment is immediate.
2. *Industrial cooperation:*

   a. *Compensation:* Compensation agreements vary in type, but most commonly consist of two contracts. The first contract states the value and quantity of the good or equipment sold by the western firm to the CPE partner. The second contract is an agreement by the western party to purchase in the future either the production derived from the sold equipment or other goods. The value of the second contract can be less

TABLE 1

Type of Contract	Managerial Skills	Risk Shifting	Self-Enforceability
Spot trading	No	No	Yes
Trading on long-term contracts	No	Yes	No
Industrial Cooperation:			
a. Compensation	No	Yes	No
b. Co-production	Yes	Yes	Yes
c. Joint Ventures	Yes	Yes	Yes
Foreign Direct Investment	Yes	Yes	Yes

than, equal, or sometimes greater than the value of the first contract. These contracts can be discounted and sold to third parties. Such agreements provide no explicit managerial services in terms of product development and production management, though the western partner can behave as a sales agent. Risk-shifting benefits are acquired by the eastern partner since payment is made essentially through the issuance of a financial instrument with a payout fixed to the stochastic value of the production. (When the western firm has the choice among several products, the financial instrument is analogous to an issuance of a bond indexed to different commodities, among which the bondholder may choose.) The western or third-party purchaser of this contract bears the risk of fluctuations in the value of the tied product. A compensation contract is not self-enforcing, since the western firm provides an up-front product and payment is made in the future.

b. *Co-production:* Co-production agreements provide all three types of services. Co-production contracts assign the western and eastern partner the responsibility to manufacture particular components of a final good. Usually, the western partner provides the components with embodied technology of a proprietary nature. (The western partner also frequently manufactures the complete component in plants outside the partner's country.) By providing production information and marketing skills, a co-production agreement transfers managerial services. Since payment is made in real goods, the eastern partner is not exposed to fluctuations in the unit demand. Net profitability is, however, risky, since the cost of inputs is uncertain. Finally, such contracts are self-enforcing, for as long as the CPE firm must dedicate non-fungible capital assets to the production of these components, any cessation of transactions would render valueless the capital investment.

c. *Joint venture:* Joint ventures are clearly the most direct channel of providing managerial and risk-shifting services. The western partner participates directly in management decisions, and part of the capital investment risk is borne through equity interests. Whether such contracts are enforceable depend upon the nature of the investment. When the value of the investment is dependent upon a continuing stream of western technology, the agreement is self-enforcing. When the investment is a one-time sunk cost, the western partner's interests are exposed to *ex post* renegotiation or expropriation. We would not expect joint venture under such circumstances given *ex ante* recognition of the unilateral hostage position. Historically, there are a number of examples of joint and fully-owned ventures where the investment was essentially hostage and suffered the costs of renegotiation. (These cases are generically described as "obsolescent bargains" and are particularly common in the mineral extraction industries.)[12]

3. *Foreign Direct Investment:* The joint venture discussed above is, of course, a special case of this type of contract. The above description of the joint venture applies to a hundred percent equity investment with the exception that it is only the government, and not the contractual partner as well, which poses the threat.

In light of the above analysis, contracts can be seen to vary in their provisions of managerial, risk-shifting, and self-enforceability services. The use of these contracts is a function not only of the characteristics of the market and the traded goods, but also the institutional stability of the environment. In the next section, the selection of contracts is analyzed in terms of choosing the correct governance structure for the sale of managerial expertise and risk shifting.

EMPIRICAL EVIDENCE

The importance of the above contracts in East-West trade can be understood by looking at data for trade in other regions. Though no estimates have been made of the amount of trade funneled through contracts, some data exists for the amount of intra-firm, relative to total trade, flows. This ratio is particularly interesting, for it provides information on the significance of foreign direct investment in channeling goods within the firm rather than through markets. A study by the United Nations indicates that 29% of United Kingdom exports and 30% of Swedish exports are conducted on an intra-firm basis.[13] Helleiner (1979) provides data on intra-firm imports into the United States for 1977. His calculations are given in Table 2. The disparity between the regional ratios given in the table below underlines the minimal importance of foreign direct investment as a conduit for goods in the case of the United States and East European and Soviet trade. Though the above data cannot be extrapolated to other countries without care, it is likely that similar trends towards low intra-firm trade between the East and West would be found overall.

If intra-firm trade is relatively insignificant, how important are long-term trade contracts in East-West trade? Unfortunately, neither western firms, nor East European governments provide exhaustive information on the volume of trade flows and the details of the contracts. Rough estimates for some have been provided by two surveys. One study by a group in

TABLE 2

United States Intra-Firm Imports by Region

Product Type	Developed countries	CPEs*	Developing countries	Total
Primary	41.3%	2.8%	49.1%	47.0%
Semi-manufactured	43.4%	8.9%	17.0%	37.6%
Manufactured	61.6%	8.1%	37.0%	53.6%
Total	53.7%	7.7%	43.4%	48.4%

* Yugoslavia and Cuba included.

the Federal Republic of Germany found that approximately 15% of all FRG trade with the East is channeled through counter trade agreements (e.g. compensation or buy-back).[14] A recent OECD study (1981) estimates buy-back contracts between 1969-80 to have been worth between $30 to $48 billion of western exports, $35 to $42 billion of imports from the East.

If indeed some contracts are substitutes for intra-firm trade through foreign direct investment, we predict that these contracts will be relatively abundant. Based on the analysis summarized in Table 1, co-production agreements were argued to provide functions of managerial services, risk-shifting, and enforceability. Thus, co-production agreements resemble most approximately foreign direct investment.

Unfortunately, there is no data which break down trade according to contractual channels. Some rough evidence is provided by a survey conducted by the Economic Commission for Europe.[15] The survey sampled 314 contracts which were in operation as of September 1978. These contracts are categorized under licensing, buy-back, co-production and specialization, sub-contracting, joint venture, joint tender, and tripartite agreements. Joint ventures include equity investments both in eastern Europe and in third countries. Specialization, for our purposes, has identical characteristics as co-production. The findings of the survey are given in Table 3.

The striking aspect of their results is the predominance of the use of co-production agreements. Interestingly, in the cases of Czechoslovakia and Romania, co-production agreements were displaced by joint ventures as the dominant form of contracting, an unsurprising result as joint ventures are a form of internalizing transactions. An outlier is the case of the GDR, for which buy-backs were the most frequent type of contract. (Buy-back agreements obligate the western firm to purchase a specified amount of goods produced by the plant equipment it initially sold.) Some care is needed in interpreting the data by country, however, due to small sample problems. The GDR comprised only 2.2% of the sampled contracts; Czechoslovakia, 2.9%; and Romania, 8.9% Some indication of the trade-off between joint ventures and co-production at the country level can be inferred for the case of Yugoslavia. (These results are not reported in the table.)

TABLE 3

Share of the Various Types of Contract in the Total Number of Industrial Co-operation Contracts, with Breakdown by Country

(in %)

	Licensing	Buy-Back	Co-Production	Sub-Contract	Joint Venture	Joint Tender	Tripartite Agreement
Bulgaria	––	––	63.7	9.1	27.3	––	––
Hungary	2.6	1.3	44.7	9.2	17.1	5.2	19.7
Poland	22.2	24.1	37.0	3.8	1.9	7.4	3.7
GDR	––	71.4	28.6	––	––	––	––
Romania	––	3.6	14.3	7.2	67.9	––	7.1
Czechoslovakia	22.2	––	11.1	––	66.7	––	––
USSR	2.4	27.2	57.4	––	8.6	3.9	0.8
TOTAL	6.1	17.4	45.2	3.8	16.9	4.2	6.4

Source: Economic Commission for Europe, *East-West Industrial Cooperation*, United Nations, New York, 1979.

Joint Ventures included both sales and production agreements. Joint Tenders refer to the execution of an investment project by a western and eastern firm.

Tripartite agreement is the same as a joint tender, except that a third partner from a developing country is added.

(Figures derived from a sample of 314 contracts at end of September 1978.)

Based on a sample of 100 Yugoslavian contracts, the ECE surveys co-production and specialization agreements to comprise only 19.2% of all contracts, whereas joint ventures comprised 66.2%. Despite the crude nature of the data, the evidence supports the *a priori* claim that co-production agreements are imperfect substitutes for foreign direct investment.

Similar results were found in other surveys.[16] One study found co-production and specialization agreement comprised 35.4% of Swedish contracts with eastern partners, though 41.7% were in the form of buy-back or compensation. Another survey found that in 1977, 58.2% of sampled Hungarian contracts consisted of co-production agreements; another 8.7 were specialization agreements.

Unquestionably, the above data is not conclusive. First, Table 3 presents data according to the number of contract types used, whereas the volume of trade channeled through each contract is also of interest. Such information is not available, probably because of its proprietary value. Parenthetically, it should be noted that the relative importance of market transactions does not vitiate the findings. Some trade will be eliminated in the absence of foreign direct investment or may shift to the market, thus raising the proportion of spot trading.

Secondly, as suggested by the above comment, the structure of trade between the East and West is likely to differ from that of other regions. Thus, the use of western data for purposes of comparison is not a perfect control. One way to strengthen this comparison is to compare the use of contracts and foreign direct investment at a sectoral level. Though there is no data broken out by sectors, the available evidence suggests that co-production agreements are more common in industries with advanced technology, whereas compensation is used for standard goods.[17] Such a trend is consistent with the claim that technology transfer tends to be internalized through foreign direct investment or through similar contractual alternatives.

Certain factors suggest, moreover, that these numbers have a conservative bias in estimating the substitutability of contracts for internalization. One bias is that the externalities between contracts are not included in these numbers. Some contracts which are not self-enforcing can be *bundled* with other agreements through cross-default provisions. For example, debt contracts include cross-default provisions which often stipulate that default on one obligation results in default on all outstanding debt. Or a western firm involved in a compensation agreement may also enter into a co-production contract. The western partner can protect against losses by maintaining other plants which produce the part manufactured by the eastern firm. Default on providing quality goods as required by the compensation contract leads to cancellation of the other agreement. Another downward bias stems from the possibility that the risk of default can be priced and embedded in the cost of contracts which are not self-enforcing. (While this is possible, such added costs repress the use of these types of contracts and can even increase the probability of breach of contract if payment is not up front.) The failure to account for externalities or for monetary compensation tends, therefore, to understate the extent to which some contracts substitute for internalization.

CONCLUSIONS

This article has sought to relate two disparate phenomena to explain the selection of contracts in East-West trade, namely, the structural weaknesses of planned economies which generate the need to import managerial and risk-shifting services and the design of contracts which minimize hazards attached to the provision of these services. The explanation is significant for two bodies of literature. First, it suggests how research on countertrade and contractual choice can be integrated with recent theories of foreign direct investment.

A second body of literature for which these findings have particular relevance concerns the creation of contracts and other institutional mechanisms by which trade, finance, and services are channelled in order to redress structural weaknesses of developing and developed countries. Data does not presently allow speculation on the impact of the design of governance structures at both a micro- and macro-level on the varied economic performance of the different East European countries. The above analysis suggests, nevertheless, that a key question in international business is how the institutional structure of trade and the enforceability of proprietary claims affect the composition and volume of trade between countries as well as their creditworthiness in international financial markets.

NOTES

1. Transaction-cost economics has been most influentially developed by Williamson. (See Williamson, 1975 and 1979.) For independent developments in the literature on foreign direct investment, Buckley and Casson, 1976; Magee, 1976; Rugman, 1980; Calvet, 1981; and Hennart, 1982. (For a review, see Kogut, 1983.) It seems obvious, however, that internalization theory is a subset of the general theory of transaction-cost economics, with the difference that macro-economic variables must be considered in the former to explain the location of foreign direct investment.

2. See, for example, Bayer and Kosser, 1981.

3. While export supply price elasticities are also of interest, their estimation is hindered by severe problems regarding relative prices and capital constraints.

4. A discussion of a third source of profits, that of meeting the currency plan, is suppressed, for lack of information on its importance.

5. The concept of taut planning was first developed by Hunter, 1961.

6. The following draws from Kornai, 1981.

7. Technology must be planned for an annual and five-year duration. Since the technology plan has a constrained claim on economic resources, a stochastic increase in the demand for a certain kind of technology cannot be any more easily accommodated than the change in the demand for any input.

8. This can be demonstrated analytically. Assuming that the profit function is convex, Varian shows that profits are higher with flexible than with fixed prices. Define the profit function as F(P, W), where P is the price of the output and W is the cost vector for the inputs. A fixed price is calculated as a weighted average of two prices (P1 and P2), with weights q and 1 – q, respectively. By the convexity of the profit function, it follows:

$$qF(P1, W) + (1 - q)F(P2, W) > F(qP1 + (1 - q)P2, W)$$

The intuition behind this result is that production is not constant. When prices go up, the firm produces more, and thus profits are higher. See Varian, 1978.

9. For a short description on arbitration, see Grzybowski, 1972.

10. For an excellent statement on self-enforcing contracts, see Klein, Crawford, and Alchian, 1978, who derive equilibrium conditions for investments in enforceability, and Telser, 1980, who works out the intertemporal setting. A recent treatment comparing contingent contracting, arbitration, and monitoring costs can be found in Shavell, 1984.

11. Loan conditionality on the Siberian pipeline is an illustrative case. Western banks and firm stipulated as a condition for granting credit that no eastern European country be allowed to participate in the building of the pipeline. In the case of default, therefore, the gas cannot be costly redirected to other CMEA countries.

12. A classic statement of this problem is given in Vernon, 1971.

13. Figures are drawn from Helleiner, 1979.

14. See F. L. Altmann and H. Clement, 1979, *Die Kompensation als Instrument in Ost-West Handel;* cited in OECD, 1981.

15. Reported in Economic Commission for Europe, 1979, *East-West Industrial Cooperation.*

16. Reported in "Reciprocal Trading Agreements in East-West Trade," *Economic Bulletin for Europe,* 1982.

17. See "Trends in East-West Industrial Cooperation," *Economic Bulletin for Europe,* 1981.

REFERENCES

Bayer, L. and Kosser, K. H., 1980, *Effektiver Exportieren: Erfahrungen und Aufgaben der Leitung in Kombinaten und Betriebe,* Berlin: Verlag Die Wirtschaft.

Buckley, R. and Casson, M., 1976, *The Future of Multinational Enterprise,* London: MacMillan.

Calvet, A. L., 1981, "Foreign Direct Investment Theories and Theories of the Multinational Corporation," *Journal of International Business Studies,* 12, Spring/Summer: 43-60.

Grzybowski, K., 1972, "Arbitral Tribunals for Foreign Trade in Socialist Countries," in Kazimierz Grzybowski, ed., *East-West Trade,* Dobbs Ferry, NY: Oceana Publications.

Helleiner, G. K., 1979, "Transnational Corporation and Trade Structure: The Role of Intra-Firm Trade," in *On the Economics of Intra-Industry Trade*, Herbert Giersch, ed., Tuebingen: J. C. B. Mohr.

Hennart, J. F., 1982, *The Theory of the Multinational Firm*, Ann Arbor: University of Michigan Press.

Hunter, H., 1961, "Optimum Tautness in Developmental Planning," *Economic Development and Cultural Change*, 9:561-572.

Klein, B., Crawford, R. G., and Alchian, A. A., 1978, "Appropriable Rents, and the Competitive Contracting Process," *Journal of Law and Economics*, 21, October: 561-572.

Kogut, B., 1983, "Foreign Direct Investment as a Sequential Process," *The Multinational Corporation in the 1980s*, ed., C. P. Kindleberger and D. Audretsch, Cambridge, MA: MIT Press.

Kornai, J., 1981, *The Economics of Shortage*, Amsterdam: North Holland Press.

OECD (Organization for Economic Cooperation and Development), 1981, *East-West Trade: Recent Developments in Countertrade*, Paris.

Pisar, S., 1970, *Coexistence and Commerce: Guidelines for Transactions between East and West.* New York: McGraw Hill.

Rugman, A., 1980, "Internalization as a General Theory of Foreign Direct Investment: A Re-appraisal of the Literature," *Weltwirtschaftliches Archiv*, 116: 365-79.

Shavell, S., 1984, "The Design of Contracts and Remedies for Breach," *Quarterly Journal of Economics*, February: 121-147.

Telser, L. G., 1980, "A Theory of Self-Enforcing Agreements," *Journal of Business*, 22, January: 27-44.

Vanous, J., 1981, "The Determinants of Imports of the CMEA Countries from the West," *Jahrbuch der Wirtschaft Osteuropas–Yearbook of East-European Economics*, Munich: Olzog Verlag.

Varian, H., 1978, *Microeconomic Theory*, New York: Basic Books.

Vernon, R., 1971, *Sovereignty at Bay: The Multinational Spread of U.S. Enterprises*, New York: Basic Books.

Williamson, O. E., 1975, *Markets and Hierarchies: Analysis and Anti-trust Implications*, New York: Free Press.

Williamson, O. E., 1979, "Transaction-Cost Economics: The Governance of Contractual Relations," *Journal of Law and Economics*, 22, October: 233-61.

Williamson, O. E., 1980, "The Organization of Work: A Comparative Institutional Assessment," *Journal of Economic Behavior and Organization*, 1, January: 5-38.

[6]

ECONOMIC INCENTIVES FOR COUNTERTRADE

Rolf Mirus* and Bernard Yeung**
University of Alberta

Abstract

This paper examines countertrade using standard economic theory. We show that in many circumstances countertrade is a rational response to transaction costs, information asymmetry, moral hazard-agency problems, and other market imperfections. This paper also integrates countertrade into international business theories. Some preliminary hypotheses, that may be empirically testable after refinement, are developed.

As reports of countertrade arrangements have become frequent, academic interest has increased. Many popular explanations have been advanced, among them shortage of foreign exchange, balance of payments difficulties, exercise of monopsony power, and imposition of trade barriers. It has also been alleged that countertrade is an inefficient form of international trade and that it represents a retrograde development. Most of these arguments have not been established theoretically, nor have they been tested empirically.

Countertrade does not usually take the ancient form of barter and its existence does not imply the decline of international business into

---

*Rolf Mirus is Professor of International Business and Finance at the University of Alberta. He holds a doctorate in economics from the University of Minnesota and his research interests are in the area of international financial markets and managements.

**Bernard Yeung is Assistant Professor of International Business and Finance at the University of Alberta. He holds a Ph.D. in International Business from the University of Chicago, and his major research interest is in applying economic theory to international business phenomena.

Both authors are currently involved in a project to transfer management education to China under the auspices of the Canadian International Development Agency.

This paper was presented at the Administative Sciences Association of Canada Montreal Conference (May 1985). We would like to thank the conference reviewers for their comments.

We are grateful to our colleagues, Giovanni Barone-Adesi, Randy Chapman, Ted Chambers and Colin Hoskins, for their helpful comments. We also acknowledge the valuable suggestions of three anonymous referees.

Received: June 1985; Revised: November 1985 & February 1986; Accepted: February 1986.

bartering, but rather a complicated contractual exchange of economic resources, either contemporaneously or intertemporally. At the same time, countertrading parties normally have the option of diverting their resources into money-mediated trade elsewhere. It is therefore evident that a more thorough understanding of countertrade requires an examination of the trading parties' incentives for bypassing money-mediation. This paper undertakes such an examination through the application of economic theory.

The results suggest that countertrade is a rational economic response to differential transaction costs, information asymmetry, incomplete markets (in particular, the lack of forward and future markets), and political and ownership constraints that lead to principal-agency problems. In other words, countertrade occurs in situations where the superiority of market-mediated transactions is not well established; it may even lead to transactions that would otherwise not occur. In consequence, countertrade is not generally inefficient; indeed it often promotes rather than inhibits the growth of international business.

Our analysis also points out that countertrade involves a class of international transactions that can be viewed as vertical or horizontal integration of economic activities while ownership remains separate. Therefore, countertrade can be seen as a hybrid of joint venture, franchising, vertical integration, and foreign direct investment, under political and ownership constraints. The contribution of this paper is that it shows countertrade as an integral part of the theory of international business.

In section two, we provide an elementary conceptualization of countertrade contracts. Section three explains "intertemporal" countertrade, often referred to as "buy-backs" in the literature and section four discusses simple barter ("contemporaneous" countertrade). These two sections give rise to five simple hypotheses which may become suitable for empirical verification after some further refinement. Finally, in the fifth section we briefly extend our analytical result to the case of counter-purchase.

CONCEPTUALIZATION OF THE COUNTERTRADE PROBLEM

Countertrade involves "simple barter", "buy-back", and "counter-purchase". This paper suggests economic incentives for the first two types of countertrade and argues that some of the results may also be applicable to counter-purchase.[1] In the following, we present the motivation for our analysis.

Diverse and complex as the actual forms are, countertrade is characterized by a significant substitution of payment in kind for payment in an international money. To explain countertrade satisfactorily, the economic motivation for this preference needs to be uncovered. Two observations may help in this context. First, countertrade involves the exporter's and the importer's resources which usually have alternative uses. The opportunity costs of these resources are not less than their prices in money-mediated market transactions, and presumably countertraders would cover at least these opportunity costs. For both parties to a countertrade there must then exist compatible economic incentives in order to forego ordinary market alternatives. Second, countertrade is often conducted in tightly controlled and/or less developed economies. In these economies, a competitive price system, pure profit motive, and private ownership of the means of production (especially foreign) are often absent. Also, market imperfections are the norm and business skills are often scarce, while foreign investors face many restrictions and a lack of information about the business environment. Were it not for these factors, countertrade would perhaps be displaced by money-mediated transactions in the form of commodity trade, factoring, forward sales, foreign direct investment and other forms of internalization. Based on these two lines of thought, we develop our analysis.

INTERTEMPORAL BUY-BACK[2]

Intertemporal buy-back is the most prevalent form of countertrade (Walsh 1984). It usually involves the export of a technology package, frequently amounting to the provision or construction of an entire plant combined with start-up operating assistance. The buyer pays the technology supplier by delivering a share of the output in the future. There are some unique aspects to technology and capital packages that are significant in this context. First, they are ambiguously defined bundles of goods and their quality is difficult to judge ex ante for anyone except the supplier. Second, physical capital usually requires continuous maintenance; the effort devoted to this is also difficult to observe for outsiders. Third, most physical capital and technology is in the form of highly specialized assets and can only be altered slowly and/or at high costs. Investment in capital and technology is mostly provided by the final user due to these market imperfections.

A firm motivated by a desire to integrate horizontally or vertically, or to benefit from firm-specific advantages, would want to apply its capital and technology in production abroad. However, due to high ownership costs and political constraints, it may be prevented from assuming ownership. In this situation, the imperfections intrinsic in markets for capital and technology are not overcome by internalization, resulting in the divergence of the economic interests of the user and supplier of capital and technology. This problem is aggravated by the information asymmetry between the user and the supplier. We argue that buy-back is a rational contractual resolution to market imperfections and is, in fact, a substitute for internalization in three kinds of situations.

Buy-back as a Double Coincidence of Wants

In the simplest case, where the quality of the capital/technology package is unimportant, buy-back is simply the result of a double coincidence of wants. This notion is best illustrated by the following scenario. A firm is searching for access to a needed raw material and has a firm-specific advantage in its mining and processing. This firm may be bothered by the absence of long-term futures and forward markets for the raw material in question. It would normally respond by backward integration to assure itself of a reliable source of supply. Of course, there may exist other benefits in this integration. When the resource exists in an environment where ownership is impossible (e.g., in the People's Republic of China) or perceived as prohibitively expensive (e.g., in South Africa), the usual response of vertical integration is precluded.

For the owner of the resources the alternatives to countertrade are to allow foreign ownership and receive tax income, or to buy the technology package and develop the market for output. The first alternative may not be better than countertrade if there is a preference for ownership or control. The second alternative can also be inferior to countertrade, as there are costs of market penetration and uncertainty concerning future sales. In addition, it may be difficult to determine a money price acceptable to both the buyer and the seller. Offering output in return would lower market penetration costs, especially for the inexperienced producer, although less learning benefits would be gained. In addition, this tactic establishes a much needed long-term continuous forward sale with obvious economic advantages. There may thus be powerful economic incentives for countertrade. The market development need of the resource-owner and the backward integration motive of a foreign firm constitute a double coincidence of wants that obviates the need for money. Generalizing from these considerations, we hypothesize the following:

> H1: Intertemporal buy-back of natural resources is more likely the more expensive forward purchase of input supply by the user, the more expensive (or prohibitive) foreign ownership, the more advantageous vertical integration to the capital owner, and the more costly market penetration/development for the owner of the natural resources.

It is desirable to examine the nature of the capital and technology involved in the development of the original resources and the production of the commodity. If this capital/technology package is homogeneous and has a competitive market, the pure motives for countertrading are forward sales, savings in market development cost (by the owner of the resource) and backward integration (by the capital/technology supplier). Countertrade is merely the result of a double coincidence of wants. If the package is heterogeneous so that potential suppliers have differential provision costs (these may include management and maintenance costs), countertrade gives further advantages to the resource owner. The heterogeneity property means that a standard price for the package may not be readily available (to the owner of the resource), nor are the differential costs usually observable at reasonable expense, especially for less developed countries. Through countertrade the resource-owner avoids a cost accounting problem: no explicit mutual agreement on the price of capital is needed. The resource-owner is then protected against overstatement of capital costs. Moreover, the moral hazard problem of shirking behavior by the capital/technology supplier is avoided because the capital supplier is compensated by what his technology produces. Lastly, the countertrade scheme ensures that the most efficient capital supplier, the one who is able to extract the highest expected net economic benefits from the final output, is the most competitive bidder. Thus, most economic rent can be extracted. Since all these advantages are also available in a revenue-sharing contract, the prime motive for countertrade must still be convenient forward sale, i.e., savings in marketing cost.

This explanation of countertrade hinges on the double coincidence of wants: the internalization need of the foreign firm encountering high ownership costs and the desire by the owner of the local resources for production and market development. It appears that this is the only way to explain the simplest case, where heterogeneity of capital and technology is not important to the buyer, as there is no fundamental economic conflict between the buyer and seller and countertrade is used for no other purposes. This explanation, however, may also be extended to the more complicated cases analyzed below.

Buy-back as an Incentive Contract - Output with a Quality Dimension

In the presence of ownership constraints, where the final user of the capital and technology is not the supplier of the package, there is no guarantee that the recipient and the supplier of the package have compatible economic interests. Generally, it is not in the supplier's interest to provide quite the technology the recipient desires, and the behavior of the former is not observable (ex ante, at least). This gives rise to a subtle principal-agency problem.[3] In this subsection we show that when the output has a distinct quality aspect, which is determined by the quality of the production technology, countertrade is an incentive compatible contract that allows both parties to achieve their objectives: integration for the technology-supplier and the transfer of quality technology for the recipient.

The quality attribute of a capital and technology package is often unidentifiable to anyone but the supplier. When a capital/technology transfer takes place, a problem is caused by the fact that the capital/technology recipient has inferior information about its quality. The supplier will have an incentive to overstate (undersupply) the quality of the capital/technology he provides, as long as the supply cost increases with quality and/or his revenue increases with the claimed quality; this represents a typical principal-agency problem. Conceivably, when profits are the only objectives for the supplier and the recipient, a revenue-sharing contract that resolves the problem can be constructed.[4,5]

If the technology recipient's desire is not just profits from the final output but also the quality of the technology transferred, another dimension is added to the principal-agency problem. The quality decision made by the supplier is fundamentally unobservable (at least, ex ante) to the recipient and cannot be controlled directly. In particular, under an ordinary revenue-sharing contract, the supplier has the freedom to choose both the quality and quantity of output; the resultant quality in technology transfer may not satisfy the recipient's demand.

By writing a contract that gives the supplier, in return for the technology, a fixed quantity of output for a specified number of years, the recipient has a means to influence the supplier's provision of quality.[6] The assumption is that the distinct quality attribute of the output is determined, in a monotonic manner, by the quality of the capital/technology input. Usually, the price of the output varies with its perceived quality. In this situation the supplier's decision on quality is dependent on its stipulated quantity return. If quantity and quality are substitutes (complements) from the supplier's point of view, a decrease (an increase) in its quantity return will induce more supply in quality. Therefore, the quantity-sharing contract is a desirable incentive contract for the recipient to offer whenever the supplier's decisions on quantity and quality are not independent.[7]

A caveat is that with this type of contract the supplier has no incentive to conceal its quality decision, either ex ante or ex post. First, a statement of the quality provision is not required in the contract. Second, the supplier's actual payoff depends only on the actual input in quality. On the other hand, the supplier does have an incentive to misrepresent the functional relationship between its quality decision and its quantity return. We conjecture that this problem is not material if a hedonic market price function for the output is observable ex ante. The quantity buy-back contract may also have the favourable signalling effect mentioned in Murrell (1982). Of course, the countertrade arrangement does not displace further monitoring requirements in technology transfer. Still, it is reasonable to propose the following hypothesis:[8]

> H2: When technology transfer with a quality dimension is involved, countertrade (in buy-back form) is more likely the more unobservable the quality dimension, the less available services for monitoring supply performance, the stronger the recipient's desire for quality, and the more explicit and stronger the relationship between the quality decision of the supplier and its quantity return.

The significant implication, of course, is that foreign exchange shortage has nothing to do with this type of arrangement. It is the very nature of markets for technology, information asymmetry coupled with ownership constraints, that explain the phenomenon: countertrade is an incentive contract that ensures the transfer of desirable quality technology and post-installation service performance. In this type of contract, the recipient influences the supplier's decision on the quality of the technology and capital transferred by stipulating a quantity of final output in return. The crucial assumption that leads to the incentive compatibility is the relationship between the quality of the technology and capital input on the one hand, and per unit value of the final output on the other. Without this relationship, our result does not obtain.

Buy-back as an Incentive Contract - A Differentiated Product Used as an Input by the Technology-Supplier.

Buy-back is an incentive contract in the more complicated case whereby a firm contracts to provide a production facility to another accepting in return some of the output for use in further production. We assume that the output is production process-specific, so that other firms would find it costly and time-consuming to adjust their production process to make use of the good. It would be equally difficult for the original firm to find a replacement for the input. An example would be the recent construction of an engine production plant in the German Democratic Republic by VW. As compensation the company receives every year during a specified period a fixed quantity of the engines produced. In comparison with the previous case, the complexity of the situation increases due to a time inconsistency problem and a double information asymmetry problem.

A time inconsistency problem exists because of the putty-clay nature[9] of the project and prohibition of ownership. Assuming the motives of the technology-supplier include the diversification of sourcing, cost reduction, and collection of economic rents on its firm-specific advantage, the normal solution would be to internalize the market by means of foreign direct investment. This choice is not feasible if there are restrictions on, or high cost associated with ownership. In such a situation, a contractual arrangement between the technology-buyer and supplier becomes necessary. The technology-buyer would face significant risks if a plant were purchased and some of its output in subsequent periods were sold back to the technology-supplier. As market transactions these would be separated and sequential in nature. By the putty-clay feature of the project, the current seller of the technology would be the sole future customer for the product. In later periods, he has the incentive and ability to monopsonistically depress the price of the output, or to increase the price of the management and production services provided. In anticipation of being "locked-in and ripped-off," the technology-buyer might want to cut short the local commitment. A similar fear may also exist on the technology-supplier's side. He may worry that, in the later periods, the plant owner (the technology recipient) may suddenly monopolistically inflate the price of the output. Given that a steady supply of this output at a predetermined price is vitally important to him, he may then want to cut short his technology and capital commitment in the construction of the plant. These circumstances, in a non-cooperative Nash game setting, would result in an equilibrium of less/lower technology being coupled with lower amounts of (local) labor as compared to the internalization outcome. In the extreme, it is possible that no plant would be built. In short, in this particular case the time inconsistency of the decisions necessitates a credible contract that ties the value of technology to the value of future output. For both parties such a contract should be an improvement over the non-cooperative Nash outcome.

When a contract is specified in terms of prices, however, there is still the double information asymmetry problem. The problem arises from the fact that the valuation of the output, which is tied to the value of its marginal physical productivity in further production, is much better known to the technology-supplier. From the perspective of the technology recipient this creates the possibility that the supplier will understate the value of the output in contract negotiations that try to specify a mutually agreed money-price. The net cost of the output to the technology-supplier is the price he pays for the local participation. This price will be positively related to the agreed money-price of the output. Therefore, the technology-supplier will have an incentive to understate his valuation of the output. The supplier can also inflate the value of other management and production services and, at the same time, undersupply the promised provisions. The technology recipient may be hard pressed to assess the quality, reliability and, thus, the value of the technology. On the other hand, because of the lack of a competitive local factor market,[10] the technology-supplier may have an information disadvantage as regards the shadow price and the productivity of local participation. The supplier may be suspicious that the local partners inflate their factor cost schedules (practicing monopsonistic pricing). Hence, a severe double "informational-asymmetry-moral-hazard" problem exists.

A contract that specifies physical quantities can first of all overcome the problem of quantity-quality substitution referred to in the previous case. It thus satisfies the recipient's desire for state-of-the-art technology. But even when quality is not an issue, a quantity contract will conceivably induce the supplier to reveal his valuation of the product by furnishing technology to the extent that the marginal revenue from extra technology is equated to its marginal cost. Similarly, the recipient has no incentive to waste labour resources or to put less than the best effort forward. In this fashion, the countertrade contract is an institutional choice that overcomes difficulties that, in all likelihood, prevent a market solution. At the same time, there is good reason for the two parties to contract to exchange technology for output because this is the original motive for the transaction. Viewed in this light, the observed practices are a substitute for foreign direct investment and are the direct result of the high costs of ownership.[11]

Finally, it appears that countertrade, in the present case, is efficiency-improving. There are four possible relationships between the technology supplier, who wants to internalize a firm-specific advantage, and the technology recipient, who wants a local industry: (i) no deal, (ii) the non-cooperative Nash equilibrium, (iii) a monetary contract equilibrium, and (iv) a countertrade equilibrium. Our analysis suggests that countertrade is the most Pareto-efficient among the last three equilibria. Countertrade then materializes if it is more Pareto-efficient than the no deal situation. If this is indeed the case, countertrade is efficiency-improving and creates trade. This argument also applies to the previous case (case (b)).As a tentative hypothesis we would argue that:

> H3: Given informational asymmetry, the more costly is ownership, the more likely is this type of countertrade. Also, it follows that the more "putty-clay" the nature of a plant (i.e., the more "lock-in" and "rip-off" is

possible), the more likely is this type of countertrade contract.

Our analysis of buy-back has thus progressed from a simple situation of double coincidence of wants to the present complicated case. Buy-back arises as a rational economic resolution to market imperfections caused by high ownership costs[12] (or politically motivated ownership constraints) and information asymmetry. It is not necessarily an inefficient form of international trade, nor is it inevitably a reflection of a shortage of foreign exchange. Countertrade is simply a substitute for other more standard forms of internalization under the conditions outlined. In this sense, our analysis links countertrade to the existing theory of international business.

CONTEMPORANEOUS COMMODITY EXCHANGE

Simple barter is of a one-time, simultaneous exchange of often unrelated commodities. Again, it is troubling to accept foreign exchange shortage as a general explanation for the occurrence of this type of international transaction when countries such as the Soviet Union or the German Democratic Republic are involved. These are nations with relatively good international credit standing that should have little trouble raising the necessary import/export financing for such one-time deals, even on a more or less ongoing basis. Indeed, a nation that has successfully arranged a barter trade could have instead used the good "exported" in the barter deal as collateral for a foreign exchange loan so as to finance the very same imports. Moreover, countries that experience the most severe credit problems do not seem to be the most active in seeking countertrade deals.[13] It would appear that there must have been a political decision that is at the root of some of the observed countertrade: the decision not to access financial markets. It is idle to speculate why one would forego borrowing but perceived loss of independence or loss of face might be possible motives. In the following, we suggest two different reasons for countertrades.

It appears that foreign exchange shortage or rationing and other forms of capital control can explain some countertrade when we focus on the Western suppliers. When an exporter has identified a customer and an order is likely, the fact that foreign exchange is rationed in the importer's country implies a time-consuming foreign exchange allocation process, so much so that uncertainty surrounds not only the conclusion of a contract but also its value. In this setting, the supplier may accept payment in terms of a marketable commodity to move the deal forward in time. This will be more likely the longer the expected waiting time and the higher the uncertainty of being able to conclude a money-based contract.[14] In a very real sense, countertrade here is akin to selling an account receivable (i.e., factoring). Moreover, in this context, countertrade may actually be seen as an officially sanctioned way of bypassing a black market for foreign exchange.[15] We, therefore, tentatively hypothesize the following:

H4: Given regulatory difficulties in currency exchanges, simple barter is more likely to occur the greater the uncertainty, the longer the expected waiting time for the foreign exchange allocation and the lower the implicit marketing cost of the countertrade goods.[16]

The nature of some observed countertrade transactions suggests further possible rationales. When, for example, VW sells compact cars to the German Democratic Republic in return for canned hams, the impression gained is that the GDR wants to sell a temporary excess supply. Such situations tend to have a low probability of recurrence. In the normal course of events, (additional) exports of this product would saddle the seller with extra search and transactions costs (in either direct sale or indirect sale through a marketing agent). By availing itself of VW's familiarity with Western markets, cars-plus-marketing services are obtained for ham, while the benefit of learning from the experience of direct sale is foregone. From the countertrader's point of view, two necessary imports, in this example cars and marketing services, can apparently be more cheaply obtained bundled together[17] and the shared savings may exceed the loss due to the foregone learning benefit from direct sales experience. The other side of the deal is that the Western firm gets a bundle: a product and reduced uncertainty regarding future market access. Payment consists of its own goods and marketing services. The Western exporter stands to gain whenever the sum of the net (of marketing cost) gain of the goods accepted and the long-run benefit of more certainty in future market access is not less than the cost of its exports. From that perspective, countertrade is economically more efficient than the same trade conducted in terms of money, and it is conducted to save search and transaction costs. The scenario reveals that countertrade is an exchange of bundled goods and services according to comparative advantage. This cost-benefit analysis leads to the following tentative hypothesis.

H5: Simple barter is more likely the lower the benefit of learning from direct sales experience, the higher the cost of direct sale of a stochastic commodity surplus with low probability of recurrence, and the lower the implicit cost of marketing services for the Western supplier.

Our assessment of simple barter would lead to the conclusion that the often stated reason giving rise to the practice, that is foreign exchange shortage, is at best a partial and somewhat, superficial explanation. The deeper causes must be sought in government policy choices regarding access to financial markets and bureaucratic delays inherent in maintaining overvalued exchange rates. In this light, countertrade appears to be a form of uncertainty resolution from the Western supplier's point of view.

In addition, given the specialized nature of marketing skills and the comparative advantage of Western firms in market knowledge, countertrade may be a reflection of high transactions and search costs faced by a trader in Eastern Europe (or elsewhere) when trying to dispose of occasional surplus production. These observations amount to bringing observed countertrades into the fold of the theory of the firm. It shows that the firm rationally responds to market conditions: countertrade may be more Pareto-efficient than ordinary trading modes; it helps markets function.

COUNTER-PURCHASE

There is now need to discuss counter-purchase and to assess the extent to which our explanations also apply to this case. In a typical counter-purchase arrangement, a seller, usually from the Western world, is partially paid in terms of trade credits that must, subject to a time and an availability constraint, be used for purchase from a prespecified list of goods. (Part of the payment may be made in convertible currencies.) While these trade credits are sometimes negotiable, nonfulfillment of a counter-purchase commitment usually invokes a penalty clause, such as a reduction in the trade credits. The essential feature of counter-purchase is the exchange of goods delivered now for goods delivered in the future. From this perspective, counter-purchase is similar to simple barter (contemporaneous exchange of goods), albeit more complicated. Some of our results in the previous section should apply to counter-purchase.

First, making payments in terms of credits that can only be used for future purchases from a prespecified list of local products is essentially a form of exchange control. Hence, the relationship between exchange control and simple barter applies to counter-purchase and a firm will accept counter-purchase requirements if the price is sufficiently attractive. Second, given that Western firms not infrequently have specialized marketing skills or easier access to them, a counter-purchase requirement can be viewed as a form of forward purchase of the Western firm's marketing skills by the local countertrader. The conceptualization of barter as an exchange of bundled goods and services based on comparative advantage is then also applicable to counter-purchase.

Counter-purchase, however, is not identical to simple contemporaneous exchange of goods. Even though the economic incentives may be similar, there are usually other complications. Counter-purchase is, by definition, intertemporal and hence has a forward selling aspect. There is also more uncertainty in counter-purchase because some of the goods on the shopping list may not be available. Moreover, the timing of the purchases is uncertain. The nature of counter-purchase arrangements may facilitate gaming behavior or, possibly, be a result thereof. On the surface our analysis thus appears generally applicable to counter-purchase but, given the unique features noted, explanations for this trading practice warrant further research.

CONCLUSION

We have attempted to explain observed countertrade transactions using the standard tools of economic analysis. While this may be a narrow view, some headway had been made toward moving the discussion from the descriptive to the analytical. For example, we found that contemporaneous countertrade can be the result of attempts to save search costs and transaction costs. Alternatively, it can be viewed as a form of factoring a future receivable.

In the case of intertemporal countertrade, which almost inevitably involves the transfer of complex technology, the root of countertrade is to be found in the high cost of foreign ownership which makes more severe the problems of information asymmetry, of moral hazard, and of decisional time inconsistency. Countertrade is revealed as a contractual resolution to these problems, and it is also a rational substitute for foreign direct investment. As a cost-saving arrangement and, sometimes, as an efficiency-improving, incentive-compatible form of contracting, countertrade is neither an inefficient form of trade nor, as is commonly alleged, is it detrimental to the growth of international business. We conclude that countertrade arrangements may be a rational response of economic agents to environmental constraints and market imperfections; that they do not necessarily represent inefficient economic exchange. Obviously, we do not claim that our analysis has comprehensively explained all manifestations of countertrade, nor do we assert that countertrade can only be explained by the tools of positive economics. Nevertheless, our approach should be seen as a first step towards a more rigorous and general analysis of countertrade. Suggestions for further work include refinement of our hypotheses for empirical testing and formalization of the arguments.

NOTES

1. Counter-purchase is not a major focus of this paper because we do not have a satisfactory general explanation for it. Interested readers may consult a recent paper by John Parsons (1985) that discusses counter-purchase extensively. In general, his analysis is very close to ours.

2. We originally differentiated buy-back according to the degree of standardization of output and analyzed it accordingly. A referee pointed out that the heterogeneity of production technology is the really crucial factor in our analyses. We subsequently revised our discussion of buy-back and gratefully acknowledge the reviewer's insightful comment. See also footnote 7.

3. A review of this problem is provided in MacDonald (1984).

4. Solutions to the problem are discussed in Ross (1973), MacDonald (1984) and articles cited therein.

5. Up to now, the relationship between the quality of the output and that of the technology does not play a crucial role. The argument is applicable to standard output with negligible quality attributes.

6. Analytically, a regressive quantity-sharing contract has the same effect on the firm's quality/quantity choice behavior as a fixed quantity contract.

7. If the output is standard but input productivity is affected by the quality of the technology, the technology supply is a function of the price of output. Either a revenue-sharing rule or an output-sharing rule can influence the technology supply and there is no presumption as to which of these will be the outcome. Conceivably, the output-sharing rule (buy-back) is sometimes, and only sometimes, the outcome. This points out that the relationship between the quality of the output and that of the technology is only one of the sufficient conditions for buy-back, not a necessary one. On the other hand, the unidentifiable quality attribute of the technology is neither a sufficient nor a necessary condition for buy-back.

8. The analysis in this subsection can be illustrated by a formal mathematical model. To preserve the non-mathematical nature of this paper, this is not provided.

9. By assumption the output is not readily useful to other producers.

10. This is an assumption that is realistic for many socialist countries and for some developing countries.

11. As we do not yet have a formal proof of its general validity, this point is conjectural. We also speculate that the buy-back provision contributes to the overall credibility of the countertrade contract.

12. Note that this cost can be the intrinsic internalization cost and/or the cost of political risk exposure. Psychological and economic costs of rendering ownership control arise for the original resource-owner.

13. Recently, there is evidence that some Latin American countries are also actively seeking countertrade.

14. Just as the currency of invoice is negotiable and acceptance of local currency can garner a contract, "invoicing" in goods may hasten a sale.

15. When the currency value deviates from the true market value, the money prices of trading commodities do not necessarily reflect the true market prices. From this perspective, countertrade is a way to adjust the relative prices at which goods are traded when their nominal prices do not reflect their real values. See Adrian E. Tschoegl (1985), p. 2.

16. This point includes Weigand's (1980) argument as a subcase.

17. This bundling suggests some market imperfections. Increased competition and specialization tends to unbundling in competitive markets unencumbered by regulation. The offshore financial markets are a case in point.

REFERENCES

Akerlof, George A., The Market for Lemons: Quality Uncertainty and the Market Mechanism, *Quarterly Journal of Economics*, 84, 1970, pp. 488-500.

Calvet, A.L., Foreign Direct Investment Theories and Theories of the Multinational Firm: A Canadian Perspective. In K.C. Dawan, Hamid Etemad and Richard W. Wright, eds., *International Business: A Canadian Perspective*, p. 281. Don Mills, Ontario: Addison-Wesley, 1981.

Culpan, Refik, Emerging Countertrade Practices, The Case of Brazil, Academy of International Business, Annual Meetings, Cleveland, October 1984.

Dennis, Robert D., The Countertrade Factor in China's Modernization Plan, *Columbia Journal of World Business*, 17, 1, Spring 1982, pp. 67-75.

Kaikati, Jack G., Marketing Without Exchange of Money, *Harvard Business Review*, November-December 1982, pp. 72-74.

Librowicz, Michel and Serruya, Michel, Countertrade, A Partial Solution to the Liquidity Crisis, Academy of International Business, Annual Meetings, Cleveland, October 1984.

MacDonald, Glenn M., New Directions in the Economic Theory of Agency, *Canadian Journal of Economics*, Vol. 1, No. 3, August 1984, pp.415-440.

Murrell, Peter, Product Quality, Market Signalling and the Development of East-West Trade, *Economic Inquiry*, Vol. 20, No. 4, October 1982, pp. 589-603.

Parsons, John E., A Theory of Countertrade Financing of International Business, Finance Department, Sloan School of Management, Massachusetts Institute of Technology, Working Paper 1632-85, March 1985.

Rosen, Sherwin, Hedonic Prices and Implicit Markets: Product Differentiation in Pure Competition, *Journal of Political Economy*, Vol. 82, No. 1, February 1974, pp. 34-55.

Ross, Stephen A., The Economic Theory of Agency: The Principal's Problem, *American Economic Review*, 63, 1973, pp. 134-139.

Tschoegl, Adrian E., Barter, *Lloyd's Bank Review*, 1985.

Walsh, James I., Countertrade Megatrends: Where Are We Now? How Did We Get Here? And What Next?, Academy of International Business, Annual Meetings, Cleveland, October 1984.

Weigand, Robert E., Barters and Buy-Backs: Let Western Firms Beware!, *Business Horizons*, Vol. 23, No. 3, June 1980, pp. 54-61.

____________, International Trade Without Money, *Harvard Business Review*, November-December 1977, pp. 28-42.

[7]

The Transaction-Cost Rationale for Countertrade

JEAN-FRANÇOIS HENNART
University of Pennsylvania

1. INTRODUCTION

One of the salient developments in international trade in the last ten years has been the increasing importance of countertrade. This generic term is used to describe unconventional trade practices that impose some sort of reciprocity. Although there is disagreement on how much of world trade is subject to countertrade requirements, most experts agree that countertrade accounts for at least 15 percent of world trade and that the percentage is growing rapidly (UNCTAD, 1986a:79).

This development has puzzled economists because they have equated countertrade with barter, and trade for goods is much inferior to trade for money. Money, surely one of man's greatest inventions, allows trades to be multilateral and spread over time. Barter, on the other hand, requires them to be bilateral and instantaneous (Jevons). It has also worried officials of the U.S. government and of various multilateral bodies, such as the Organization

I would like to thank Oliver Williamson, Roberta Romano, two anonymous referees, Adrian Tschoegl, Bruce Kogut, Franklin Root, and especially Erin Anderson for helpful comments on earlier drafts. I have also benefited from conversations with Willis Bussard, Mark Casson, Frank Horwitz, Tro Kortian, and Michael Morrison. Laurent Jacque, Andrew Kimball, Peter Lorange, Howard Perlmutter, and Weijian Shan brought some of the literature to my attention. I am indebted to Edith Ward and J. R. Mikton for providing me with UN documents. Michael Morrison, Donald Lecraw, Eduardo Francisco, Michael Castleman, Christine Tutay, and Dan Riemer provided valuable help in building the data base. This research was supported by a grant from the General Electric Foundation through the William H. Wurster Center for International Management Studies.

Journal of Law, Economics, and Organization vol. 5, no. 1 Spring 1989
 ISSN 8756–6222

for Economic Cooperation and Development, the General Agreement for Tariff and Trade, and the International Monetary Fund, because the spread of countertrade weakens the multilateral system of trade and payments that has worked so well since 1945 (de Miramon).

Much of the literature has ascribed the growth of countertrade to the heavy indebtedness of an increasingly large number of developing countries. Countertrade is seen as a way for these countries to solve their foreign exchange shortages. This article argues that saving on foreign exchange is not the only reason nor even perhaps the main reason for countertrade. The two most commonly used forms of countertrade can be explained instead as attempts to build reciprocity in order to reduce transaction costs in the international market for intermediate products, technology, and distribution services.

Section 2 shows that the term *countertrade* includes contracts with very different characteristics. In section 3, the usual view that countertrade is an answer to foreign exchange shortages is shown to be only partially valid. Section 4 argues that countertrade can be seen as a device to reduce transaction costs in the international market for intermediate products, distribution services, and technology.

2. WHAT IS COUNTERTRADE?

The term *countertrade* is used to describe a variety of trade practices that can be categorized into four main types: classical barter (one contract, short-term orientation, no money used), commercial compensation (multiple contracts, short-term orientation, money used), industrial compensation (multiple contracts, long-term orientation, money used), and offset (multiple contracts, long-term orientation, money used, involves sometimes investment). All these transactions have one characteristic in common: in each a seller provides a buyer with goods and services and promises in return to purchase goods and services from the buyer (Banks, 1983:160).[1] Because countertrade usually results in a two-way flow of commodities, it is often likened to barter. In fact, there are important differences between barter and the three other categories of countertrade.

The *classical barter* category includes transactions that are short term, are effected by a single contract, and consist of the direct exchange of goods and services between two parties without the use of money. *Barter* is a one-shot transaction that involves the swap of one product for another. A large number of barter exchanges can be consolidated into a *clearing arrangement*. In this form of barter, each party agrees, in a single contract, to purchase a specified, and usually equal, value of goods and services. The contract value is expressed in nonconvertible, clearing account units (usually

1. In the case of offset, the buyer may also promise to make investments in the country.

called clearing dollars). Each country sets up an account which is debited whenever one country imports from the other. At the end of the trading period, imbalances are cleared through hard currency payments, transfer of goods, or payment of a penalty. The inflexibility inherent in clearing arrangements can be alleviated by *switch trading*, which consists in buying a country's position in exchange for hard currency and selling it to another customer.

In contrast to barter, the other forms of countertrade—commercial compensation, industrial compensation, and offset—involve the use of money or credit. When governments make large purchases from foreign companies, they increasingly insist that the purchase price be offset in some way by the seller. The seller has to agree to subcontract some of the production to local producers, to increase its imports from the purchasing country or to transfer technology. Such a quid pro quo is called *offset*. Political factors are important in explaining this type of countertrade and are sufficiently complex that a discussion of offsets is better left to another time.

Industrial compensation includes trade arrangements that are long term in nature and consist of separate but linked money-for-goods contracts. The most common type of countertrade is *buy-back*, or *compensation*. In a typical buy-back transaction, the exporter transfers technology (either embodied in plant and equipment or disembodied), and agrees to purchase in return a certain percentage of the plant's output over a given number of years. For example, two British firms, ICI and Davy Powergas, sold a methanol plant in 1977 to the Soviets for $250 million and agreed to take back 20 percent of the production of the plant over the 1981–90 period for an estimated $350 million. A variant of buy-back is called *loan-and-import*. Under this scheme, a user of an input provides financing, and sometimes equipment, to develop a new source of supply. The borrower then signs a long-term supply contract with the lender, the loan being repaid from the proceeds of these deliveries (Walsh).

Commercial compensation includes a variety of trade practices that involve, like buy-back, two parallel hard currency contracts, but they differ from buy-back insofar as the goods that are taken back by the seller of goods or equipment are not those produced with the equipment sold. Another difference is that the reciprocal obligations are fulfilled within a much shorter period of time, usually three to five years. In *counterpurchase* transactions, an exporter agrees to buy, within a few months to a few years, unrelated goods from a shopping list set up by the importer. The list may change from time to time, but the commitment is to buy from the list as it stands at a later date and at prices posted at that time. The list often contains light manufactures and consumer items that do not have a ready market. For example, in 1977 Volkswagen sold ten thousand cars to East Germany and agreed to purchase goods from a list set up by the East Germans over the next two years, up to the value of the cars sold to East Germany (Shuster).

A variant of this is *advance purchase*, in which the order of the transactions is reversed.

The term *countertrade* thus covers contracts with two main purposes. On one hand, barter contracts are undertaken to avoid using money or setting a price. The other three types make use of money, and their main feature is reciprocity.

Likening countertrade to barter is unfortunate, for barter makes up a relatively small proportion of the countertrade of Western firms. A survey of 122 U.S. firms by the National Foreign Trade Council shows counterpurchase, with 55 percent of all transactions, to be the most common form of countertrade, followed by offset, 24 percent; barter and switch trading, 12 percent; and buy-back, 9 percent (Bussard, 1983). My survey of all countertrade transactions reported in *Countertrade Outlook* over the mid-1983 through 1986 period shows counterpurchases to be the most common practice, with 51 percent of all transactions, followed by barter (29 percent), buybacks (13 percent), and offset (7 percent). (See Appendix 1 for details.)

3. COUNTERTRADE AS A WAY TO SAVE ON FOREIGN EXCHANGE

Why would a country engage in such complicated forms of transactions when much more efficient alternatives would seem to be available? A view commonly held by both academics and practitioners is that a shortage of hard currency is the main cause of these heterodox trade practices (Elderkin and Norquist, 1987:11; Haendel, 1984:1; McVey, 1980:197).[2] The recent development of countertrade would be directly linked to the heavy indebtedness of Soviet bloc and developing countries.

If countertrade results from foreign exchange shortages or from the difficulties that indebted countries experience in obtaining trade credits, then it must be because countertrade can save on foreign exchange. But a careful analysis shows that this is not generally true. Of all four types of countertrade, only barter can be shown to have this property, and only under very specific conditions (Banks, 1983). It is difficult to see, on the other hand, how counterpurchase and buy-back could help solve a country's shortage of hard currency.

Buy-backs, like counterpurchases, consist of separate but linked money-for-goods contracts. The ICI-Davy buy-back mentioned earlier involved three separate contracts. The first was for the sale of the methanol plants for hard currency. A second contract extended credit to the Russians for the purchase of the equipment and set the terms of repayment. A third contract specified the terms and conditions of the purchase by ICI and Davy of the methanol to be produced in the plant. Note that, contrary to popular impres-

2. See, however, Banks (1983), Mirus and Yeung (1987), and Kostecki for criticisms of this view.

sions, buy-back arrangements do not usually involve the barter of plant for resultant output but consist of two parallel money transactions. At the completion of the project the plant seller is paid in full by the buyer from credits obtained from Eastern or Western sources. The plant buyer then repays the lender with the proceeds of the sale of the output to the plant seller (Verzariu, 1980:93; Loeber and Friedland; McVey, 1980:202; United Nations Economic Commission . . . , 1984:10).

As in this example, buy-backs usually require hard currency outlays or credit, since exporters of plant and equipment usually do not agree to wait the number of years it would take for the plant to come on-line before being paid in the resulting product. One could argue that the assurance of a ready market for the goods produced with the project would improve its credit rating in the eyes of a Western bank. In practice, lenders do not take the buy-back contract as security. They require that no mention of the Western firm's commitment to purchase the plant's output appear in the export contract and consider the borrower solely liable for repayment of the loan (Verzariu, 1980:27). Buy-backs cannot therefore reduce either outlays of foreign exchange or the need for credit, and they do not improve the borrower's creditworthiness.[3]

Counterpurchase also involves two separate contracts, each paid in hard currency. A counterpurchasing country must pay (or borrow) hard currency for its imports and gets hard currency back when the return transaction is completed. Because imports are usually delivered first, and because counterpurchase obligations often cover only a part of import value, the exports from the counterpurchasing country cannot be used to finance the import (Jones, 1984:15; Welt, 1984:59).

While a superficial view of countertrade arrangements has led most observers to equate them with barter, an examination of their stipulations reveals that two major types of countertrade—counterpurchase and buy-backs (and their variants)—are not barter transactions and cannot help countries reduce their outlay of hard currency or improve their ability to borrow foreign exchange. Since we have seen above that these two types make up more than half of all countertrade transactions, explanations in terms of foreign currency shortages are bound to have only limited explanatory power.

Table 1 tabulates the extent to which countries used countertrade and their debt-service ratio in 1983. The table does not show a clear relationship between the variables, and a chi-square test confirms the absence of a relationship between indebtedness and countertrade.[4] This suggests that the

3. One reason for the banks' reluctance to take buy-back commitment as security is because buy-backs are usually entered into by governments, and there is no guarantee that the cash flow generated by the project will be used to repay the debt. Therefore the lending bank will consider the country's overall creditworthiness. Buy-back will not allow such countries to exceed their credit limits (Banks, 1983:166).

4. Columns 2 and 3 and rows 2 and 3 were aggregated because of small sample size.

Table 1. Countertrade and Debt, 1983

	Number of LDCs and Eastern European Countries with a Debt Service Ratio	
Countertrade Frequency	over 25%	25% or less
Above average	7	8
Average	7	9
Below average	4	5

Average countertrade frequency is 2 to 4%.

Source: Kostecki, 1987.
Rows 2 and 3 were added to calculate chi-square, which is close to zero (chi-square critical, 1, .05 = 3.84). The null hypothesis that countries with high debt service ratio are no more likely to countertrade than countries with low debt service ratios is supported.

reasons for the development of buy-back and counterpurchase must be sought elsewhere.

4. COUNTERTRADE AS A DEVICE TO REDUCE TRANSACTION COSTS

Whereas the main characteristic of barter is the fact that it effects trade without the use of currency, the distinguishing mark of all other types of countertrade is their reciprocal nature. Of the three, offset is the most complex, arising from the interaction of political and economic factors. In this section we concentrate on industrial (buy-back and loan-and-import) and commercial compensation (counterpurchase) and argue that they constitute attempts at reducing transaction costs.

As Williamson has shown, market exchange suffers from high transaction costs whenever small-number conditions prevail, uncertainty is high, and there is high information asymmetry between the parties. In that case, one party can be "held up" by the other. Hierarchical coordination is an efficient solution in such cases because it reduces the incentives that the parties have to exploit each other by replacing price with behavior constraints.

Assume, however, that international hierarchical coordination is not possible, because host governments will not allow incoming foreign direct investment and home firms are unable or unwilling to expand overseas. One way to reduce transaction costs, and thus to motivate parties to make transaction-specific investments, is to transform a unilateral supply relation into a bilateral one, in which A's sale to B will be contingent on B's selling to A. Reciprocity can be used to equalize the exposure of the parties (Williamson, 1985:191). This line of argument suggests that buy-back, loan-and-import, and counterpurchase contracts will be used in situations where high transaction costs would otherwise prevent international trade from taking place.[5]

There are two main circumstances in which transaction costs are likely to be high: (1) when there is significant information asymmetry between the parties, or (2) when the market is narrow because of scale economies, transportation costs, or a need to make transaction-specific investments. Let us examine these two cases in greater detail.

4.1. Technology

Knowledge has one main attribute that makes its market exchange costly: its characteristics are, by definition, unknown to the buyer. The seller, on the other hand, is reluctant to provide this information because, if he did so, he would be transferring his knowledge free of charge. There are two basic solutions to this problem of "buyer's uncertainty": they consist in embedding knowledge in (1) physical goods and (2) patents. Embedding knowledge in physical goods facilitates its sale, since physical goods are tangible. Embedding knowledge in a patent allows the innovator to divulge the characteristics of the knowledge he has for sale by granting him a monopoly on its use. The efficiency of the patent system thus depends crucially on the degree to which the know-how can be put on paper (on its nontacitness), as well as on the strength of the legal protection given to patents. The higher the tacit component in the technology package, and the weaker the legal protection afforded patentors, the less efficient markets will be in transferring knowledge.

Except for the case of older, patented knowledge, where the patent provides full information on the technology for sale, the seller of technology (embodied in a plant or disembodied, as in a license or a technical assistance agreement) usually knows better than his customer the value of the technology that is for sale. He knows the characteristics of the equipment he is selling, the quantity, quality, and cost of the prospective output, and new technological developments that could make the plant or license obsolete.

Given this information asymmetry, a simple sale contract would encourage the seller to behave opportunistically. The reason is that the seller of the plant (or the licensor) is paid a lump sum at the conclusion of the transfer. He has consequently strong incentives to minimize the cost of providing the knowledge and no continuing interest in the operation. The problem does not arise in the case of a traditional foreign direct investment (FDI) because the return to the investor then comes from the difference between the plant's revenues and its costs. The investor is therefore motivated to make the most efficient technology transfer.

A country that bans incoming FDI cannot use this device and must protect

5. The point that East-West contracts serve to increase enforceability was first made by Bruce Kogut (1986). See also Mirus and Yeung (1986) and Parsons.

itself by drawing detailed specifications and performance guarantees. There are, however, problems with this approach. First, the quantity and quality of the plant's output depends on the joint performance of both the equipment seller and the plant's operator. Failure to produce output of a given quality at the predicted cost and up to the plant's designed capacity can be caused by inadequate performance by either the plant seller or the buyer, or both. Often it is difficult to apportion responsibility, making it possible for equipment sellers to avoid damage to their reputation when their performance is defective. The buyer could alleviate this problem by specifying in detail the seller's obligations. The buyer could, for example, carefully describe the specifications of the equipment he wants to buy. But since in most cases the seller has better knowledge than the buyer of the technical choices to be made, the equipment specifications drawn by the buyer may not result in the cheapest solution. Consultants can be employed, but their advice is not always unbiased.

A second potential problem is that the economic value of the plant often depends on continued after-sale service. In a straight sale of equipment, the seller, once paid, has few incentives to provide this service free of charge. Indeed, the seller is often in a position to ask excessive compensation for such service because, though there may be a number of competitors ex ante, the successful bidder is often, ex post, the only one with detailed knowledge of the technology in place.

In theory, a contract could be written that (1) would stipulate that no payment be made until the facility (or the license) works as intended, (2) would provide for completion guarantees to be forfeited should the plant not perform as expected, and (3) would obligate the technology seller to provide continuous after-sales assistance.

In practice, contracts provide only limited protection. Consider, for example, the usual stipulations found in turnkey contracts, which were developed in the 1960s to sell complete plants to Eastern Europe. Turnkey contracts have been extensively used since by other countries, such as Algeria, that have discouraged incoming foreign direct investment. Under such contracts the contractor is paid to set up a complete production unit. He is responsible for feasibility studies, technology and know-how, design and engineering, equipment, and the construction of the plant. His obligations are normally fulfilled when the plant is fully operational (Oman).

An examination of turnkey contracts, however, shows that they provide only limited protection. Although they specify that the contractor will be paid the remaining sums due upon the satisfactory completion of trial runs, those runs are usually made by the contractor's personnel and last only twenty-four hours. This provides little guarantee that the plant will operate as planned in normal circumstances—when run by the buyer on a day-to-day basis. Completion guarantees are also typically low, on average 5 to 10 percent of the contract value (Salem and Sanson-Hermitte).

As a result, turnkey contracts do not seem to have effectively protected technology buyers against opportunism by the seller. This is evident in a piece by Kemal Abdallah-Kodja, who was Algeria's minister of planning and one of the main forces behind Algeria's reliance on turnkey contracts. According to Abdallah-Kodja, the purchase of plants through these contracts had a number of drawbacks. First, they proved to be very expensive because contractors covered themselves against all possible contingencies. Because they lacked technological information, Algerians were unable to check on the reasonableness of the quoted price. The bidding process failed to disclose the required information because the number of potential suppliers was usually small. Second, the local operator often found himself unable to run the plant after delivery had taken place because he lacked the necessary managerial and technical skills. Third, the buyers were ill equipped to verify that they were getting what they wanted. Trials showed that the plant worked, not that the fundamental design and technical choices were correct. The validity of these choices became apparent only after many years (Abdallah-Khodja, 1984:33–34).

Algeria's answer to these problems was to extend the scope of the contract to include responsibility for the effective transfer of tacit production and management skills. A new contract, called "product-in-hand," made the plant seller also responsible for running the project with the buyer's personnel during the first two to three years of operation, thus requiring him to train successfully local management and workers. These contracts stipulated that the contractor would be paid in full (except for a bank guarantee) sixty days after completion of successful tests by the buyer's staff under the contractor's supervision. Two years later, a joint commission would evaluate how well the plant was running under local control. If performance was satisfactory, the contractor would be refunded the bank guarantee he had posted (United Nations Centre . . . , 1983:38, 48). These clauses protected the buyer against the risk of not being able to run the plant after taking delivery and against any hidden flaws that could not be detected at the trials stage.

The difficulties experienced with product-in-hand contracts show the limits of a straight contractual solution to technology transfer. Because they shift considerable risk to the plant seller, these contracts are considerably more expensive (30 to 50 percent more costly than turnkey contracts in Algeria's case). There are fewer bidders, often only one or two, which makes price comparisons difficult. And last, the contracts are difficult to enforce because sellers have consistently refused to post guarantees of more than 5 to 10 percent of the value of the contract. This sum is much smaller than the cost to the buyer of inadequate performance or delay. Furthermore, when such incidents arise, the contractor is the only one able to set the plant right. He is in a strong bargaining position and can shift to the buyer much of the cost of completing the project (Abdallah-Khodja, 1984:34–35).

There seems, therefore, to be clear limits on the ability of a technology buyer to protect himself from opportunism by writing contracts that specify in detail all the seller's obligations. This conclusion was also reached in a United Nations technical paper on turnkey and product-in-hand contracts (United Nations Centre . . . , 1983:48).

How then can the buyer obtain effective assurances that the equipment seller will provide a well-functioning plant, effective training of the buyer's work force, and after-sales service? One way is to write a buy-back contract—that is, make the purchase of the plant contingent on the seller buying the plant's output. Forcing the seller of equipment to purchase its output provides a number of effective guarantees.

First, it ensures that the technology for sale is capable of producing a competitive product. If a plant supplier intends to sell obsolete equipment, or if he plans to cut corners and thus knows the plant will yield substandard output, he will be unwilling to contract for the product except for a very low price; this will send a signal to the buyer (Mirus and Yeung, 1986; Parsons, 1985:32).[6]

This was confirmed in John Holt's survey of U.S. agricultural and construction equipment companies involved in selling technology to Eastern Europe. He found that four of the eight firms he interviewed protected themselves from competition from their Eastern European customers by withholding their latest technology. Three of the four companies that were subject to buy-back obligations, however, pointed out that such a strategy is self-defeating: "If the U.S. company has become dependent upon the Western country's production for itself or its subsidiaries or is responsible for marketing the Eastern product outside the CMEA area, the latest technology must be incorporated in the product to make it as competitive as possible" (Holt, 1977:86).

Second, forcing the seller to buy back part of the plant's output at contracted prices also ensures that the plant seller will make realistic estimates of the level of future demand for the product. If he misleads the equipment buyer about the sales prospects for the output and makes overly optimistic predictions, the world market price will fall, and he will be stuck with overpriced goods. By agreeing to take some of the plant's output at a price fixed ex ante, the supplier of the plant and equipment demonstrates his confidence in his forecasts of future demand (Parsons, 1985:33).

Last, buy-back contracts may ensure that the plant seller will provide continuous assistance until the plant functions as planned under local control. This is the case if the plant seller is repaid in the resulting product, but we

6. One additional feature of buy-back contracts seems to support my hypothesis that they serve to decrease the costs of transferring technology: when a plant involves subcontractors, each is made responsible for taking a share of the resultant product corresponding to his share of the total project (United Nations Economic Commission . . . , 1985:6). This suggests that buy-backs are used to enforce good performance.

have seen that this is not the norm, as the sale of the equipment is usually financed by a bank from either the seller's or the buyer's home country.

Why then does a plant seller feel obliged to provide assistance if he has been paid in full? The first reason is that the plant seller may have made transaction-specific investments to dispose of the buy-back goods—for example, in arrangements called "co-production" whereby the Eastern deliveries consist of components of a particular Western product (Kogut, 1986). Mirus and Yeung (1986:33) cite an agreement between Volkswagen and East Germany, by which Volkswagen agreed to deliver a complete production line capable of producing 286,000 engines per year. The line, in operation in West Germany, was dismantled and moved to East Germany. In return for the production line and a licensing agreement, East Germany delivers to Volkswagen 100,000 motors per year. The tie created a commitment on the part of VW to maintain a supply of spare parts and machine standards and to communicate to East Germany any improvements it might make in engine production (Parsons, 1986:36). In our previous example, the methanol obtained from the plant sold by ICI to the USSR was to be used in a new $65 million ICI plant to produce animal feedstuffs (United Nations Economic Commission . . . , 1984:28). Failure to obtain the resulting product in requisite quantity and quality would have imposed substantial costs on ICI, as world demand for methanol was increasing rapidly and shortages were forecast (Business Eastern Europe, May 27, 1977, p. 163; Chemical Market Review, May 14, 1979:7).

The enforceability of buy-back contracts is weaker if the plant seller disposes of alternate sources of supply, but it is nevertheless stronger than in the case of a turnkey contract. First, the plant seller usually purchases the takebacks at a discount (United Nations Economic Commission . . . , 1982:288). This provides him with an interest in purchasing the plant's output and hence in transferring state-of-the-art technology and providing after-sale assistance.

We have seen that under a turnkey contract it is difficult for a plant buyer to prove that the seller has not fulfilled his obligations and that he is fully responsible for the plant's substandard performance. In contrast, a plant seller's failure to take back agreed quantities at an agreed-upon price represents a clear breach of contract, so that the burden of proof is reversed. The plant seller must now prove that his failure to take back the output is the fault of the plant buyer.

Because buy-backs do not give the plant seller a direct stake in the profits resulting from the investment, they provide technology sellers with weaker incentives to transfer technology efficiently than under FDI. For example, they do not protect the plant buyer against false promises concerning the plant's operating cost (Parsons, 1985:30). Because equity links (wholly owned subsidiaries or joint ventures) provide better guarantees of efficient technology transfer, they are likely in many cases to be the preferred institutional form. Thus the use of buy-backs should be concentrated in countries that severely restrict FDI.

To test this proposition, I established a list of buy-back contracts signed between mid-1983 and the end of 1986, as reported in *Countertrade Outlook* (see Appendix 1 for details). Sixty-one of the seventy-five buy-back agreements on the list, or 81 percent, were initiated by fifteen countries that impose very high barriers on incoming FDI (for definitions and the list of countries in this category, see Appendix 2). By comparison, these countries accounted for only 25 percent of the world's GNP. Similarly, there is some rough evidence that buy-backs make up a larger proportion of contracts for the transfer of technology to countries that ban equity investments than to those that allow them. A survey of East-West contracts in operation as of September 1978 found that buy-backs made up 90 percent of the contracts in the seven Soviet bloc countries which had at that time strong restrictions on FDI; this was in contrast to 9 percent for joint venture arrangements. In Yugoslavia, which allows joint ventures, the proportions were 30 percent buy-backs and 70 percent joint ventures (United Nations Economic Commission . . . , 1979).[7]

4.2. Loan and Import

The second situation in which contracts may not provide effective protection is when the market for an intermediate product is narrow, whether because of high transportation costs, scale economies, or the need to make transaction-specific investments.

Consider the position of an owner of a resource—for example, a particular type of mineral deposit—who has only a single potential customer. This can happen if the ore is of a specific grade and composition, for processing plants incur lower costs if they are tailored to the characteristics of the ore (as in the case of bauxite; Stuckey, 1983:47). Alternatively, transportation costs and the need for dedicated infrastructure may make a mine dependent on a single buyer, as is often the case for oil or low-grade minerals. The owner of the resource could invest in a mine and then sell the output to the sole customer. But since the seller's investment is sunk, the buyer would then be able to negotiate a very low price, expropriating the seller's quasi-rent. The most efficient solution is for the mine and the downstream facilities to be vertically integrated. If the host government outlaws incoming FDI, and the mining firm is unable to integrate downstream into foreign processing of its ores,

7. Based on a survey by the United Nations Economic Commission for Europe (1979) of 444 contracts in operation in Bulgaria, Hungary, Poland, the GDR, Romania, Czechoslovakia, the USSR, and Yugoslavia. The figures differ from those quoted by Kogut (1986) because 77 contracts involving undertakings outside these countries were excluded and because all contracts for which payment was in resultant product were categorized as buy-backs.

the next best strategy would be for the seller to enter into a long-term contract with the buyer.

As the historical evidence shows, long-term contracts cannot provide full protection, because the environment often changes in ways that cannot be anticipated when the contract is written. The long-term bauxite supply contracts signed in the late 1960s between Japan and Australian, Malaysian, and Indonesian bauxite producers are a good example. Their length was ten to twenty years, and the price was denominated in dollars. The collapse of the Bretton Woods system of fixed exchange rates and the doubling a few years later of the price of energy resulted in the sellers having to accept both lower prices and lesser quantities (Stuckey, 1983:121–23). This is not an isolated case. Most steel companies, for example, have reneged on earlier long-term supply contracts for iron ore, and today these contracts provide "little, if any, assurance that the annual tonnages will be lifted" (Franz et al., 1986:30). D'Cruz (1979:139) also documents that when the price of coal shot up in 1974 U.S. producers diverted shipments they had contracted to sell to Japan to the more remunerative spot market. This led one observer to conclude that "long-term contracts have been observed only in their breach" (Rogers, 1986:28).

Transaction costs can be reduced, however, by having the buyer post a bond to be forfeited in case of breach. This is the solution adopted in the case of loan-and-import contracts. Under this scheme, firms based in Western countries, but also Japan, have extended loans at concessionary terms to foreign entrepreneurs to finance the development of mines and smelters in exchange for long-term supply contracts (Walsh). Repayment of the loan is typically made by deducting an agreed-upon amount from the price of the mine output sold to the lender (D'Cruz, 1979:185). Because resource owners will be reluctant to make investments geared to a single customer, and because they believe that long-term sales contracts may be opportunistically renegotiated once the investment is made, the buyer must post a bond to signify his willingness to abide by the contract. By offering financing, the buyer binds himself to take the contracted quantities, for if he fails to do so he can expect the mine owner not to repay the loan. This type of countertrade can be seen as a device to induce independent entrepreneurs to make transaction-specific investments when foreign direct investment is not possible.

Although contracts under which the buyer provides financing to induce the seller to make transaction-specific investments have been described as loan-and-import contracts in the mining literature, this rationale also accounts for some contracts in manufacturing that are sometimes called buybacks. For example, IKEA, a Swedish furniture company, recently granted a loan to a Polish company to finance the purchase of equipment for the firm's furniture factory. In return, the firm will supply furniture components to IKEA, some of which will repay the loan. Since the components are designed to IKEA's specifications and are bundled with other IKEA components, the Polish firm is dependent on IKEA for marketing its output (*Countertrade Outlook*, 8/10/1987, p. 3).

We would expect loan-and-import schemes to be used when the FDI alternative is relatively expensive. Such is the case when vertical integration abroad is prevented by host-country regulations or when it is subject to high risk of confiscation. Firms based in some countries, principally communist countries and LDCs, also find it difficult to expand abroad because of lack of managerial skills, foreign exchange regulations, or ideological preference for nonequity relationships.

What we know of loan-and-import contracts supports these predictions. Most such contracts have been used to procure inputs (1) from countries that severely restrict FDI, (2) in sectors where FDI is particularly discouraged and subject to strict restrictions, (3) for firms unable or unwilling to invest abroad, and (4) from new projects with no alternative customers.

1. Many contracts in which the lender's primary motivation is the procurement of reliable sources of inputs and the borrower's is protection against ex post renegotiation have been signed by Western firms with Eastern European countries. Probably the most famous involved the sale of Russian gas to Western Europe (Loeber and Friedland), and similar contracts have been signed for delivery of Polish copper and coal to Western markets (United Nations Economic Commission . . . , 1984).

2. Most loan-and-import contracts involve mineral industries, a sector in which FDI has been particularly discouraged by host countries and in which the danger of expropriation is highest (Walsh). Data on the relative use of loan-and-import schemes by Japanese firms in their international operations show that this technique was disproportionately used for the extraction of oil and minerals (Ozawa, 1984, table 3-a).[8]

3. Loan-and-import schemes often are used by firms for which the FDI alternative is relatively expensive. Firms based in East European countries, which have an ideological preference for nonequity modes, have extensively used loan-and-import schemes to procure national resources. For example, the Soviet Union extended loans to Iran to build a gas pipeline serving the USSR, with repayment to be made in gas deliveries. Such contracts have been signed, too, by Eastern European nations with Turkey, Greece, and other developing countries (Dobozi, 1983:27–29). LDCs do not usually possess the capital and managerial resources to integrate vertically abroad, and they have also used this device.[9] In addition, Japanese companies have experienced greater difficulties in expanding abroad than have their Western counterparts. The problems arise from Japan's long isolation from the rest of

8. Ozawa shows that interest on loans made up 93.5 percent and dividends 0.5 percent of the overseas revenues of large Japanese companies involved in mineral and oil extraction; the comparable figures for Japanese manufacturing firms were 18.7 and 37.2 percent.

9. For example, Iran had agreed to provide credits to India for the development of the Krudemuth iron ore deposits, to be repaid in iron ore.

the world, its poor reputation because of its actions before and during World War II in potential host countries in Southeast Asia, and, until the 1980s, domestic restrictions on capital exports and a shortage of capital at home. McKern (1976:76) has shown that, in contrast to American and European firms which undertook FDI in Australia in the 1960s and early 1970s to secure sources of raw materials, the Japanese used loan-and-import for that purpose. As capital controls were relaxed and Japanese ore buyers gained experience in foreign operations, they shifted toward greater use of equity investments.

4. Last, the view of loan-and-import contracts as bonds posted by the buyer suggests that buyers will use them to stimulate investments in new plants which, for technical or geographical reasons, are dedicated to them. D'Cruz's study of the Japanese procurement of cooking coal confirms this prediction. The Japanese relied on loan-and-import contracts to develop coal mines (and the necessary transport infrastructure) in new production areas (Australia and Western Canada). Because of transportation costs, these mines could serve only Japan, and loans had to be extended to convince producers to undertake production for which there was no other realistic market (D'Cruz, 1979:190–93, 281–82).

4.3. Distribution

Countertrade can also be seen as a device to reduce the costs of arranging for the international marketing of products. There is clear evidence that countries that impose counterpurchase requirements do so in order to increase and diversify their exports. Eastern bloc countries, which have experienced difficulties in selling manufactured goods to the West, have used counterpurchase to push these exports: their counterpurchase lists usually feature manufactures, whereas readily marketable products, such as raw materials, are sold through normal channels. Many counterpurchase contracts also require the Western firm to provide the name of the final customers of goods taken back. Goods for which Western traders find a reliable market are subsequently taken off counterpurchase lists and sold directly to the ultimate buyer ("Locating . . . Goods," 1979; Business International, 1977:81).

LDCs have also used counterpurchase to push nontraditional exports. In Ecuador, India, and Indonesia, firms that sell to government authorities must take back nontraditional exports or, if they counterpurchase traditional exports, must sell them in new markets (Goldstein, 1984:10). In India, one of the main countertraders, the Minerals and Metals Trading Corporation (MMTC), provides selective incentives to take back nontraditional exports. According to MMTC's director, "the endeavour is to create markets for new goods or services, and to provide traditional exports with new markets" ("India . . . ," 1988:50).[10] Furthermore, many countries stipulate that counterpurchased goods must not be resold in third markets and that the end user must be made known (Banks, 1983:161; Graubart and Sachs, 1984:32). Additionality—adding exports that do not replace existing exports—is also typically required.

Many observers have argued that counterpurchase is not a particularly efficient method of expanding exports (de Miramon). Western firms that take back counterpurchase goods do not always market them themselves, but sometimes sell them at a discount to trading companies. These companies may dispose of the goods by selling to traditional customers at cut-rate prices, thus displacing existing markets. Additionality is difficult to enforce, as "new markets" may be nothing more than transshipment points (Graubart and Sachs, 1984:30).

Commentators have noted that the use of counterpurchase as a marketing tool has other drawbacks. The seller (especially if it is a trading company) has no commitment to the product, and the goods will typically be sold on an as-is basis, with no promise of after-sales service or any quality guarantee. Shifting the marketing function to a Western exporter does not give the countertrading country the opportunity to develop its marketing skills and does not provide the feedback needed to adapt its exports to its customers' requirements (Banks, 1983:168).

Why then use counterpurchase? If most such products are eventually marketed by trading companies, could not countries contract directly with these intermediaries for the international marketing of their exports? Why should countries enter complex countertrade transactions when, as Roger (1986:14) says, "the services of clever international traders are directly available to developing countries' exporters"?

The answer is that there are many cases where the purchase of distribution services is subject to high transaction costs. Effective distribution often requires the distributor to make transaction-specific investments. The successful introduction of a new differentiated product or that of an existing differentiated product to a new market requires substantial, up-front investments to find customers and to learn how to price, demonstrate, and service the product. Often these investments are specific to a particular producer. The trader may find, after making significant up-front investments in the expectation of a long-lived relationship, that he is bypassed by the exporter once sales start to pick up. As a result, traders are usually reluctant to make

10. MMTC has classified products into four categories. Traditional exports (for example, ready-made garments within quota restrictions) are not offered for export under countertrade. A second list includes products (e.g., raw cotton) that earn countertrade credits for 50 percent only of their export value. Products more difficult to sell (such as handicrafts) earn credits for 100 percent of their export value. Last, some items (including tourism packages, electronic components, and computer software) earn credits at 150 percent of their export value ("India . . . ," 1988:51).

supplier-specific investments to market products from sources they do not control through equity stakes. Consequently, exporters to new markets and manufacturers of new products requiring substantial demonstration and service or specialized distribution facilities (for example, refrigeration) have found it difficult to motivate traders to provide the requisite level of investment (Anderson and Coughlan; see also Keegan, 1984:391).

Some support for this view comes from a study done for General Electric Trading Company on the cost and availability of traders to handle the firm's countertrade obligations. The study found that subcontractors were available "at reasonable cost for countries offering commodity products with an established product history" but that help was "virtually nonexistent or highly expensive in differentiated products and in countries offering products not traditionally exported" (General Electric Trading Co., n.d.:39).

Historically, the solution to this problem has been vertical integration between manufacturing and trading (Hennart, 1982). By the turn of this century, British and American manufacturers of new machines and durable consumer goods, dissatisfied by the performance of their agents, had integrated vertically into foreign sales subsidiaries (Nicholas; Porter and Livesay). Similarly, Japanese manufacturers are now edging out the trading companies that initially marketed their exports and are replacing them with company sales subsidiaries (Yoshino). Eastern European countries have also found that traders were often less than diligent in pushing difficult-to-market goods and have started to establish marketing subsidiaries in the West (MacMillan).

There are two ways by which manufacturing and overseas distribution can be integrated. Manufacturers in the home market can establish sales subsidiaries overseas—the pattern described in Nicholas and Porter and Livesay. Alternatively, firms with developed distribution systems in the home market can establish production facilities in foreign countries. This was the motive behind the international expansion of banana firms such as United Fruit.

Assume, however, that the home country restricts incoming FDI and is either unable or unwilling to set up marketing networks abroad. Counterpurchase can then serve as the next best way to market effectively in the West. By telling suppliers that they will import only if the supplier takes back and markets their products, countertrading countries can force them to make marketing investments they otherwise would not undertake. The Western exporter forced to take back the countertrading country's products can be expected to make a greater commitment to market the goods because failure to do so would jeopardize future sales.

Traders are well aware of this fact. For example, David Swanson, senior vice president of Continental Grain, argues that the foreign country exporter may often obtain greater benefits by contracting with the captive countertrade unit of a major corporation than with a trader: "The point is that there often are longer-term commitments underpinning countertrade transactions. These longer-term commitments are more likely to be undertaken by the captive countertrade organization . . . than by a more purely trade-oriented company which, almost by definition, is not interested in long-term investment" (Swanson, 1985:46).

Note that the case of counterpurchase differs from those analyzed previously. Buy-back and loan-and-import arrangements involve symmetrical exposure: in buy-back, for example, the technology buyer, exposed to contractual hazards, balances his exposure by making his purchase of technology conditional on another trade where the technology seller is similarly exposed. Counterpurchase contracts, on the other hand, do not result in mutual exposure. A distributor who has invested in transaction-specific assets is exposed to renegotiation by the counterpurchasing country, but the country that has imposed counterpurchase is not. Instead, counterpurchase can be seen as the use by importers of their monopsonistic power to persuade exporters to make transaction-specific investments.[11]

Admittedly a country could use its monopsonistic power to obtain from exporters lower prices on imports. But if, as is often the case for Eastern European countries or LDCs, Western exporters enjoy a substantial cost advantage over indigenous firms in making marketing investments, then imposing counterpurchase obligations may constitute an efficient use of monopsonistic power, especially if countries believe that the development of exports entails significant positive externalities.

If counterpurchase is motivated by these factors, we would expect importing countries to insist that only goods that require extensive, supplier-specific marketing support be taken back in counterpurchase. Conversely, exporters can be expected to attempt to minimize their obligations by taking back commodities that require only general-purpose assets in their marketing. We have seen that to prevent this, counterpurchasing countries have required sellers to take back nontraditional exports and goods destined for new markets. Counterpurchase contracts often contain clauses prohibiting reexport to third countries (UNCTAD, 1986b:9). Most Eastern European countries prohibit the transfer of counterpurchased goods to traders or will reduce the counterpurchase ratio if the Western exporter takes the goods in-house or distributes them through its own sales network (Business International, 1984:90; *Countertrade Outlook*, 9/21/1986:2).[12]

Through stipulations like these, counterpurchase is often successful in forcing firms either to use the take-backs in-house or to induce their clients to buy them. The National Foreign Trade Council survey mentioned above found that 45 percent of all countertrade goods were used in-house and an additional 8 percent were sold to suppliers. In many cases take-backs are used as inputs in the firm's production process, creating a new market for

11. I thank the editors for bringing this point to my attention.

12. Albania, Bulgaria, Czechoslovakia, Hungary, and the USSR generally bar third-party involvement (see ACECO, 1985:85–92).

the country imposing counterpurchase, as Western firms switch suppliers to accommodate the take-backs. For example, when Pfizer found its sales of poultry vaccines to Brazil subject to counterpurchase requirements, it searched that country for take-backs, and "found that the country was producing glass vials that were competitive in quality and price. The company switched from sourcing these from its traditional supplier in France to the Brazilian manufacturer. It now not only takes the product to meet its own in-house needs, but also supplies Brazilian glass vials to other countries in Central America" (Business International, 1984:83).

Countries that do not succeed in having their products taken as inputs may still be able to tap the extensive marketing network of Western multinational firms and to benefit from their marketing experience. Witness Coca-Cola's efforts to market the wine of Slovin, its Yugoslav bottler. Slovin made its syrup purchases contingent on Coke's exporting its wine, but the wine was poorly made and unattractively presented. Coca-Cola called in experts who completely changed Slovin's wine production methods, chose a new name, and had a new label designed and printed in Italy. It then was able to successfully sell the wine in the United States (Martin and Ricks). Coca-Cola was motivated to make such a long-term investment because it knew its continued syrup sales depended on it.

Similarly, counterpurchase has helped Eastern European countries sell car accessories in the West. The accessories are made to Daimler Benz's specifications and sold under the company brand name through its dealer network (Business International, 1977:159). Some companies will even go so far as to create new industries in counterpurchasing countries. Unable to find goods to take against the vehicles it wanted to sell to Jamaica, General Motors established the first data processing plant in that country to handle data for U.S. firms (Elderkin and Norquist, 1987:120–21). A similar commitment would not have been obtained without countertrade.[13]

If counterpurchase is used to approximate the benefits of an equity tie between manufacturers and distributors in the absence of FDI, then we should observe the following: (1) countries that practice counterpurchase should be those that hinder incoming FDI and that have no home-based multinational firms, and (2) the products offered for counterpurchase should be those that require a strong marketing input.

The survey of countertrade transactions described in Appendix 1 provides

13. Another possible reason counterpurchase might be preferable to the outright purchase of marketing services is its ability to shift some of the marketing cost to the Western exporter (Graubart and Sachs, 1984:25). There is some evidence that this has been the case. the NFTC survey of U.S. countertraders found that 18 percent of the respondents had to absorb all disposition costs, and another 34 percent shouldered a part of such costs. As a result, 18 percent experienced a loss on the overall transaction (Bussard, 1983). There are reasons to believe that this is likely to be a temporary phenomenon, as Western firms learn from their mistakes. Indeed, a 1986 survey of major U.S. exporters found that only 7 percent reported a loss on their countertrade transaction (Bussard, 1986).

some support: Forty-seven percent of the total number of recorded counterpurchase transactions were imposed by countries that had very high barriers to incoming investment.[14] The list includes East European countries and LDCs. Moreover, manufacturers in these countries have embryonic international marketing networks (MacMillan). Their marketing effort is handicapped by the fact that international marketing is performed not by the exporter itself but by foreign trade organizations. The LDCs on the list, such as Indonesia, China, India, and Colombia, do not possess the management skills necessary to expand internationally and to scale the "formidable barriers to entry into exports markets abroad" (de la Torre). Restricting incoming FDI cuts them off from the international marketing networks of Western multinationals, and we would therefore expect them to turn to counterpurchase as the next best solution.

Our analysis suggests also that goods that are offered in counterpurchase should be primarily manufactures, which require more marketing support than commodities. We saw in the beginning of this section that manufactures are featured prominently in counterpurchase lists. Have counterpurchasing countries been successful in persuading Western firms to take back these manufactured goods? There is some evidence that the answer is yes. A study of the products taken back in countertrade shows that the relative importance of manufactured goods increased between 1980 and 1987 (Montagnon). The data base of countertrade transactions described in Appendix 1 shows that 43 percent of the products imported from centrally planned economies (CPEs) and LDCs in fulfillment of counterpurchase obligations were manufactures. This percentage was higher than the share of manufactures in their overall exports (34 percent). This is an admittedly crude comparison because we are comparing value data to a product count, but value data on counterpurchases by product type are not available.[15]

In conclusion, there is evidence that CPEs and LDCs have attempted to leverage their bargaining power as buyers to obtain marketing support from their suppliers and that they have been partially successful. By linking imports to exports, countries that do not have their own international marketing networks and object to foreign control of their manufacturing sector have found it possible to persuade multinational manufacturing firms to develop markets for their goods. The latter used the products as inputs or sold them to their industrial suppliers, customers, or final consumers through their marketing network. Although negotiation costs of counterpurchase are often high, such contracts may provide, in the absence of equity links, a second-

14. By comparison, the countertrading countries that had high barriers to incoming investment accounted for 31 percent of the world's GNP. They had therefore a higher propensity to counterpurchase than we would expect from their size.

15. For details, see Appendix 1. The percentage of manufactures in the total value of exports of LDCs and CPEs was calculated from country figures in UNCTAD, 1988, table 4.1. The weights used were 1985 exports.

best answer to the problem faced by LDCs and CPEs in penetrating Western markets.

5. CONCLUSION

This article has argued that the most common reason advanced to explain countertrade—the need to solve hard currency shortages—has only limited explanatory power. Some forms of countertrade, such as buy-back and counterpurchase, can be seen instead as devices to reduce the high transaction costs that affect three types of international transactions: the purchase of poorly protected technology, the sale of intermediate products in small-number conditions, and the purchase of marketing services when the distributor needs to make up-front, transaction-specific investments. In these circumstances buy-back and counterpurchase can be seen as attempts to reduce transaction costs by providing what amounts to a bond or hostage. They substitute for hierarchical coordination when the political desire for national sovereignty pushes a country to ban both inflows and outflows of foreign direct investment.[16]

The empirical evidence generally confirms these observations. Since buy-back and counterpurchase probably make up more than half of all countertrade transactions, a country's countertrade intensity should be correlated with the degree to which it restricts incoming FDI. Table 2 relates estimates of a country's total countertrade intensity to the level of its restrictions on incoming FDI. The table shows that countries that practice countertrade heavily are also those that severely restrict incoming FDI. Of the fifteen countries that were heavily involved in countertrade in 1983, nine had a full or partial ban on incoming FDI, and six had strong restrictions on the per-

Table 2. Countertrade and Restrictions on Incoming FDI, 1983

	Number of LDCs and Eastern European Countries in which restrictions to incoming FDI are		
Countertrade Frequency	very high	high	moderate
Above average	9	6	0
Average	5	10	1
Below average	2	4	2

Average countertrade frequency is 2 to 4%.

Sources: Countertrade frequency: Kostecki, 1987; barriers to incoming FDI: see Appendix 1.

Columns 2 and 3 and rows 2 and 3 were added to calculate chi-square, equal to 3.93. Since chi-square critical (1, .05) = 3.84, the null hypothesis that countries that restrict incoming FDI have the same propensity to countertrade as countries that do not is rejected at the 5% level.

16. Because of its complexity, countertrade imposes heavy negotiation costs on the parties. As such it is clearly a second-best solution to the problems described above.

centage of equity allowed foreign investors. Conversely, of the sixteen countries with strong restrictions, nine had above average countertrade activity.[17] A chi-square test shows that the hypothesis that countertrade intensity is independent of restrictions on incoming FDI is rejected at the 5 percent confidence level.[18]

My analysis has two important implications. First, as a significant percentage of countertrade transactions has little to do with foreign exchange shortages, changes in the debt situation of LDCs should have only a moderate impact on the development of countertrade. Second, the future of buy-back and counterpurchase depends on restrictions by host countries on foreign direct investments. Should the trend in LDCs toward a generally more favorable attitude toward incoming FDI continue, these forms of countertrade may experience a relative decline. This last point seems supported by recent developments in China, where the relative importance of buy-back agreements has been declining with the enactment of joint venture legislation (Chen, 1986:27).

This article does not claim to present a general theory of countertrade; it deals only with two of its forms, albeit the most common. As shown by Banks (1983, 1985), barter arises for quite different reasons. Furthermore, the factors that have led to the development of buy-backs and counterpurchase are complex. The institutional context of centrally planned economies, such as administrative trade and exchange controls and incentives systems that privilege exports, is clearly relevant (Parsons; Kostecki, 1987:10–11). No unicausal theory can satisfactorily account for all the features of buy-backs and counterpurchase. Nevertheless, I hope I have shown that transaction-cost economizing can throw light on a number of features of this ill-understood phenomenon.

APPENDIX 1. DATA BASE ON COUNTERTRADE TRANSACTIONS

Information on countertrade transactions was obtained from weekly issues of *Countertrade Outlook*. This publication, which reports on countertrade and nontraditional trade throughout the world, is generally considered to be the most complete and reliable of all publications in the field. All issues from the first, April 1983, to December 31, 1986, were consulted. Only transactions that were reported as signed were entered in the data base. For each trans-

17. Note that these countertrade estimates include barters and offsets as well as counterpurchases and buy-backs.

18. To verify the robustness of the present results, a separate test was run using data on barriers to incoming FDI obtained from Business International. The resulting chi-square (3.95) confirmed our previous findings.

action, the date, the type of countertrade, the name and country of both seller and buyer, the goods sold, and those taken by the seller as take-backs were recorded. The compilation yielded 304 counterpurchases, 171 barters, 75 buy-backs, and 42 offsets.

APPENDIX 2. BARRIERS TO INCOMING INVESTMENT

The data on country barriers to incoming FDI describe the situation as of the end of 1983 and were obtained from a compilation of the following sources:

Annual Report on Exchange Arrangements and Exchange Restrictions. Washington, D.C.: International Monetary Fund, various years.

National Legislation and Regulations Relating to Transnational Corporations. New York: United Nations Center for Transnational Corporations, vol. 4 (1985) and vol. 5 (1986).

R. Hammer, G. Simonetti, and C. Crawford. *Investment Regulations around the World.* New York: John Wiley, 1983, and *Supplement*, 1984.

Investment Laws of the World. Dobbs Ferry, N.Y.: Oceana Publications.

Countries for which information was available were classified in three categories. Those in category 1, "very high barriers," are countries that ban outright FDI in all or a majority of activities and, if they allow any investment in some sectors, do not allow majority-owned foreign investments.

Category 2, "high barriers," include countries that forbid FDI in a significant number of sectors and require joint ventures in a significant number of sectors left open to foreign investors.

Category 3, "moderate barriers," include countries that do not ban investment in any sectors which most Western countries leave open to foreign investment (see note below) and that do not put any restrictions on foreign equity share.

The following is the list of countries for which data on both countertrade frequency and barriers to foreign direct investment were available. Countries starred are those for which Kostecki did not provide countertrade frequency.

Very high barriers:

Albania	India
Algeria	Indonesia
Bulgaria	Iraq
China	Poland
Colombia	Romania
Czechoslovakia	USSR
East Germany	Venezuela
Hungary	Yugoslavia
*Cuba	*Libya
*Mozambique	*Vietnam
*Iran	*North Korea

High barriers to investment:

Bangladesh	Nigeria
Brazil	Pakistan
Costa Rica	Peru
Ecuador	Philippines
Egypt	Saudi Arabia
Honduras	Thailand
South Korea	Tunisia
Malaysia	Turkey
Mexico	Uruguay
Morocco	Zambia

Moderate barriers:

Argentina
Chile
Dominican Republic

Since the majority of even the most liberal countries ban foreign investments in selected sectors considered sensitive, such as the press, radio and television, utilities, and armaments, a ban on investment in those sectors was not considered a ban on investment for the purpose of this study. Thus no country, even those in category 3, can be said to be fully open to incoming FDI.

REFERENCES

Abdallah-Khodja, Kemal. 1984. "Algeria's Experience with New International Investment Relations." In C. Oman, ed., *New Forms of International Investment in Developing Countries: The National Perspective.* Paris: OECD.

ACECO, 1985. *Practical Guide to Countertrade.* New York: Metal Bulletin.

Alexandrides, Costas, and Barbara Bower, 1987. *Countertrade: Practices, Strategies, and Tactics.* New York: Wiley.

Anderson, Erin, and Anne Coughlan. 1987. "International Market Entry and Expansion via Independent or Integrated Channels of Distribution." 51 *Journal of Marketing* 71–82.

Banks, Gary. 1983. "The Economics and Politics of Countertrade." 6 *World Economy* 159–82.

———. 1985. "Constrained Markets, 'Surplus' Commodities and International Barter." 38 *Kyklos* 249–67.

Business International. 1977. *Solving East European Business Problems.* Geneva: Business International.

———. 1984. *Threats and Opportunities in Global Countertrade.* New York: Business International.

Bussard, Willis. 1983. "A View on Countertrade." Paper presented at the Countertrade Conference, New York, December.

———. 1986. "New Study Reveals U.S. Needs in Countertrade." News release, U.S. Association of Countertrading Corporations.

Chen, Nai-Ruenn. 1986. *Foreign Investment in China: Current Trends*. Washington, D.C.: International Trade Administration, U.S. Department of Commerce.

D'Cruz, Joseph. 1979. "Quasi-Integration in Raw Materials Markets." D.B.A. diss., Harvard Business School.

Dobozi, Istvan. 1983. "Economic Interaction between East and South—the Mineral Resource Dimension." 2 *Raw Materials Report* 25.

Elderkin, Kenton, and Warren Norquist. 1987. *Creative Countertrade*. Cambridge: Ballinger.

"Financing and Buyback Clinch Largest UK-USSR Deal." 1977. *Business Eastern Europe*, May, 162–64.

Franz, Juergen, Bo Stenberg, and John Strongman. 1986. *Iron Ore: Global Prospects for the Industry, 1985–95*. Washington, D.C.: World Bank.

General Electric Trading Company. N.d. "A Field Study in Countertrade at General Electric Trading Company." An unpublished report written under the direction of David Yoffie.

Goldstein, E. "Countertrade: A Stop-Gap Solution to Foreign Exchange Shortages," research paper no. 8424, Federal Reserve Bank of New York.

Graubart, Steven, and Donald Sachs. 1984. *Countertrade between the Industrialized West and the Developing Nations*. Washington, D.C.: International Planning and Analysis Center.

Haendel, Dan. 1984. "International Barter and Countertrade." Staff Paper no. 14, National Center for Export-Import Studies.

Hennart, Jean-François. 1982. *A Theory of Multinational Enterprise*. Ann Arbor: University of Michigan Press.

———. 1986. "What Is Internalization?" 122 *Weltwirtschaftliches Archiv* 791.

Holt, John. 1977. "Industrial Cooperation in Eastern Europe: Strategies of U.S. Agricultural and Construction Equipment Companies." 12 *Columbia Journal of World Business* 80.

"India: Can Countertrade Achieve Its Promise?" 1988. *Trade Finance*, March, 49–51.

Jevons, Stanley. 1883. *Money and the Mechanism of Exchange*. London: Keagan Paul, Trench and Co.

Jones, Stephen. 1984. *North-South Countertrade*. Special Report no. 174. London: Economist Intelligence Unit.

Keegan, Warren. 1984. *Multinational Marketing Management*. 3d ed. Englewood Cliffs, N.J.: Prentice-Hall.

Kogut, Bruce. 1986. "On Designing Contracts to Guarantee Enforceability: Theory and Evidence from East-West Trade." 17 *Journal of International Business Studies* 47.

Kojima, K., and T. Ozawa. 1984. *Japan's General Trading Companies*. Paris: OECD.

Kostecki, Michel. 1987. "Should One Countertrade?" 21 *Journal of World Trade Law* 7.

Kronman, Anthony. 1985. "Contract Law and the State of Nature." 1 *Journal of Law, Economics, and Organization* 5.

Lecraw, Donald. 1988. "Countertrade: A Form of Cooperative International Business Arrangement," in Farok Contractor and Peter Lorange, *Cooperative Strategies in International Business*. Lexington, Mass.: Lexington Books.

"Locating Unavailable Countertrade Goods." 1979. *Business Eastern Europe*, August 31.

Loeber, Dietrich, and Ann Friedland. 1983. "Soviet Imports of Industrial Installations under Compensation Agreements: West Europe Siberian Pipeline Revisited." 18 *Columbia Journal of World Business* 51.

McKern, Bruce. 1976. *Multinational Enterprise and Natural Resources*. Sydney: McGraw-Hill.

MacMillan, Charles. 1982. "The Foreign Investment Activity of the Comecon Countries: Actors and Strategies." University of Reading, Discussion Paper in International Investment and Business Studies.

McVey, Thomas. 1980. "Countertrade and Barter: Alternative Trade Financing by Third World Nations." 6 *International Trade Law Journal* 197.

———. 1984. "Countertrade: Commercial Practices, Legal Issues, and Policy Dilemmas." 16 *Law and Policy in International Business* 1.

Martin, E., and T. Ricks. 1985. "Selling Tool: Countertrade Grows as Cash-Short Nations Seek Marketing Help." *Wall Street Journal*, March 13, 1.

Matheson, Jenelle, Paul McCarthy, and Steven Flanders. 1977. "Countertrade Practices in Eastern Europe." In Joint Economic Committee, 95th Cong., 1st Sess., *East European Economies Post-Helsinki*. Washington, D.C.: U.S. Government Printing Office.

"Methanol Demand to Grow 7 percent / year through 1984; Shortages foreseen despite New Capacity," 1979. *Chemical Market Review*, May 14, 7.

de Miramon, Jacques. 1985. "Countertrade: An Illusory Solution." *OECD Observer*, no. 134, 24.

Mirus, Rolf, and Bernard Yeung. 1986. "Economic Incentives for Countertrade." 17 *Journal of International Business Studies* 27.

———. 1987. "Countertrade and Foreign Exchange Shortages." 123 *Weltwirtschaftliches Archiv* 535.

Montagnon, Peter. 1988. "Countertrade Is No Longer the Business It Was." *Financial Times*, May 25.

Murrell, P. 1982. "Product Quality, Market Signaling and the Development of East-West Trade." 20 *Economic Inquiry* 589.

Nicholas, Steve. 1983. "Agency Contracts, Institutional Modes, and the Transition to Foreign Direct Investment by British Manufacturing Multinationals before 1935." 48 *Journal of Economic History* 675.

Oman, Charles. 1984. *New Forms of International Investment in Developing Countries*. Paris: OECD.

Organisation for Economic Cooperation and Development. 1980. *East-West Trade: East-West Trade in Chemicals*. Paris: OECD.

———. 1981. *East-West Trade: Recent Developments in Countertrade*. Paris: OECD.

———. 1985. *Countertrade: Developing Country Practices*. Paris: OECD.

Ozawa, Terutomo. 1984. "Japan's 'Revealed Preference' for the 'New Forms' of Investment: A Stock Taking Investment." In C. Oman, ed., *New Forms of International Investment in Developing Countries: The National Perspective*. Paris: OECD.

Parsons, John. 1985. "A Theory of Countertrade Financing in International Business." Working Paper no. 1632—85, Sloan School of Management, MIT.

Porter, Glen, and Harold Livesay. 1971. *Merchants and Manufacturers: Studies in the Changing Structure of Nineteenth Century Marketing*. Baltimore: Johns Hopkins Press.

Roehl, Thomas. 1982. "The General Trading Companies: A Transaction Cost Analysis of Their Function in the Japanese Economy." In M. G. Harvey and R. F. Lusch, eds., *Marketing Channels: Domestic and International Perspectives*. Norman: Center for Economic Research, University of Oklahoma, 86.

Roger, N. 1986. "Countertrade: A Developing Country Policy Perspective." Unpublished manuscript, the World Bank.

Rogers, Christopher. 1986. "Long Term Contracts and East-West Trade in Non-Fuels Minerals." International Institute for Applied Systems Analysis, East-West Mineral Trade Project.

Salem, M., and M. A. Sanson-Hermitte. 1979. *Les Contrats "Clé en Main" et les Contrats "Produit en Main."* Paris: Librairies Techniques.

Shuster, F. 1980. "Barter Arrangements with Money." 15 *Columbia Journal of World Business.*

Stuckey, J. 1983. *Vertical Integration and Joint Ventures in the Aluminum Industry.* Cambridge, Mass.: Harvard University Press.

Swanson, D. 1985. "Trading Companies: The Reluctant Countertraders." In *Countertrade in the World Economy.* New York: Group of Thirty, 45–52.

de la Torre, Jose. 1971. "Exports of Manufactured Goods from the Developing Countries: Marketing Factors and the Role of Foreign Enterprise." D.B.A. diss., Harvard Business School.

Tschoegl, Adrian. 1978. International Barter. Working Paper no. 996-78, Sloan School of Management.

United Nations Centre on Transnational Corporations. 1983. *Features and Issues in Turnkey Contracts in Developing Countries: A Technical Paper.* New York: United Nations.

United Nations Conference on Trade and Development (UNCTAD). 1986a. *Trade and Development Report.* New York: United Nations.

———. 1986b. "Countertrade: Background Note by the UNCTAD Secretariat." Mimeo.

———. 1988. *Handbook of International Trade and Development Statistics: 1987 Supplement.* New York: United Nations.

United Nations Economic Commission for Europe. 1979. *East-West Industrial Cooperation.* New York: United Nations.

———. 1982. "Reciprocal Trading Arrangements in the Chemicals Industry: The Experience of Selected Western Chemicals Producers and Plant Contractors in East-West Trade." 34 *Economic Bulletin for Europe* 283.

———. 1984. *The Financing of Large Scale Compensation Projects in East-West Trade since 1970: Mechanisms, Patterns, and Trends.* Geneva: UN Economic Commission for Europe.

———. 1985. *Contractual Features of Countertrade Transactions in East-West Trade.* Geneva: UN Economic Commission for Europe.

Verzariu, Pompiliu. 1980. *Countertrade Practices in East Europe.* Washington, D.C.: U.S. Department of Commerce.

———. 1985. *Countertrade, Barter and Offsets: New Strategies for Profit in International Trade.* New York: McGraw-Hill.

Walsh, James. 1982. "The Growth of Development for Import Projects." 8 *Resources Policy* 277.

Welt, Leo. 1984. *Trade without Money: Barter and Countertrade.* New York: Law and Business.

Williamson, Oliver. 1985. *The Economic Institutions of Capitalism.* New York: Free Press.

Yoshino, Michael. 1976. *Japan's Multinational Enterprises.* Cambridge: Harvard University Press.

Part III
The Literature in the Nineties: Double Moral Hazard, Hostage Exchange, and Quantity Stipulation

[8]

Tying Trade Flows: A Theory of Countertrade with Evidence

By DALIA MARIN AND MONIKA SCHNITZER*

A countertrade contract ties an export to an import. Usually, countertrade is criticized as a form of bilateralism and reciprocity and thus as an inefficient form of international exchange. In this paper we argue that there are circumstances in which the tying of two technologically unrelated trade flows may be efficiency-enhancing. We show that countertrade can be an efficient institution in international trade that solves moral-hazard problems and restores creditworthiness of highly indebted countries. We test the implications of our model using a sample of 230 countertrade contracts. (*JEL* D23, F13, F34, L14)

In a countertrade agreement an export is tied to an import. Typically, a firm in a developed country (DC-firm) exports to an Eastern European (EE) or a developing country (LDC) and commits itself (in a second contract) to import goods from this country in return. A Western bank is often involved to finance both transactions. Traditionally, countertrade is seen as a form of bilateralism and reciprocity and, thus, as an inefficient form of international exchange.[1] In this paper we argue that there are circumstances in which tying an export to an import may reduce transaction costs and yield efficiency gains. In particular, we show that countertrade can solve contractual problems that arise in technology trade and imperfect capital markets which otherwise would prevent the realization of gains from trade.

Even though most experts agree that countertrade accounts for a large and rapidly growing proportion of international trade (according to most estimates between 10 and 20 percent of world trade), it is quite difficult to get reliable data on the exact volume and features of these transactions.[2] In order to obtain data on the specific features of countertrade arrangements we carried out a survey among countertrading companies located in Austria (the majority of which are trading companies or subsidiaries of multinationals). Our sample contains detailed information on 230 countertrade contracts signed by firms from OECD countries and trade organizations in EE or LDC's in 1984–1988.[3]

* Marin: Department of Economics, Humboldt University Berlin, Spandauer Str. 1, D-10178 Berlin, Germany, and Center for Economic Policy Research; Schnitzer: Wirtschaftspolitische Abteilung, University of Bonn, Adenauerallee 24, D-53113 Bonn, Germany. This project was started while the first author visited Harvard University and the second author visited the Massachusetts Institute of Technology and Boston University. We thank Jonathan Eaton, Elhanan Helpman, Paul Krugman, Albert Ma, Mike Riordan, Klaus Schmidt, and two anonymous referees for helpful comments and suggestions. The paper also benefited from presentations at Harvard University, MIT, Boston University, University of Bonn, and at the European Summer Symposium in Economic Theory in Gerzensee. Financial support by the Austrian Science Foundation and by the Deutsche Forschungsgemeinschaft through SFB 303 and through a research grant is gratefully acknowledged.

[1] Countertrade is discussed under the heading "Trade Related Investment Measures (TRIMS)" in the GATT negotiations (Stephen Guisinger, 1987). For the different political views on countertrade see OECD (1985).

[2] Countertrade does not show up in the official trade statistics. It is hard to measure because (in the case of barter) there are often no prices attached to the trade flows and (in the case of buyback and counterpurchase) the trade flows occur in different periods. Furthermore, governments have an incentive to play down the role of countertrade because it is regarded as a potential trade barrier by the GATT. For estimates, see Grant T. Hammond (1990) and OECD (1981, 1985).

[3] For more details on this data set see Marin (1990) and Section III-A.

In our data set, the three main forms of countertrade are represented: barter, counterpurchase, and buyback. Barter is a spot transaction in which the two trade flows occur simultaneously and no foreign exchange is used. The export is paid for with the import. In counterpurchase and buyback arrangements, in contrast, the two transactions are carried out sequentially, and each flow is paid for in foreign exchange. With buyback there is also a technological relationship between the original export and the subsequent import, one flow consisting of plants and/or machinery and the other of output produced with this equipment.

Most explanations of countertrade suggested in the descriptive literature ascribe the increasing importance of reciprocal trade to the high indebtedness of developing and Eastern European countries. Often, these countries face a shortage of foreign exchange, and their low creditworthiness makes it impossible to finance imports with a simple loan from an international bank. Countertrade is seen as an arrangement that allows an importing firm to save on foreign exchange (OECD, 1981, 1985). However, the only form of countertrade that actually avoids the use of hard currency is barter, and barter accounts for only a small proportion of total countertrade. Surprisingly, by far the dominant form is counterpurchase. This has been reported by many studies and is confirmed by our own sample in which counterpurchase makes up for more than three-quarters of total countertrade (see e.g., Stephen F. Jones and Ashley Jagoe, 1988; OECD, 1981, 1985).[4] Moreover, there are some features of countertrade that cannot be attributed to credit constraints caused by high indebtedness. In particular, one important feature that needs to be explained is why the trade pattern of exports in countertrade differs significantly from that in untied trade. In our sample, 70 percent of all countertrade exports from DC firms were technology-related and investment goods, as opposed to only 30–40 percent of total trade.[5]

Why are countertrade exports predominantly technology goods? John E. Parsons (1985, 1987) reports that the sale of technology is particularly prone to incentive problems. For example, the value of a plant or some equipment to the buyer is directly affected by actions of the seller which are difficult to specify in a contract, such as the level of care with which a plant is set up and workers are trained, or the supply of after-sale services and technological advances.[6] Parsons proposes buyback contracts as a solution to this moral-hazard problem. A buyback contract gives the DC-firm an incentive to spend more effort in setting up the plant properly in order to improve the quality of the output it is paid with. This argument has been modeled formally by Raissa Chan and Michael Hoy (1991) and Chong J. Choi and Daniel Maldoom (1992). Note that the technological relation between the two goods is essential for this contract to work. However, like barter, buyback accounts for a surprisingly small fraction of all countertrade transactions (see footnote 4).

In this paper we want to show that *counterpurchase*, the dominant form of countertrade, can solve both the creditworthiness problem and the technology-transfer problem even

[4] In our sample, the respective percentages of all countertrade transactions are 76.6 percent for counterpurchase, 11.3 percent for barter, and 12.2 percent for buyback.

[5] Similar evidence is found by Willis A. Bussard (1987). Note that this discrepancy between export patterns of countertrade and total trade can also be found in country-specific comparisons. As an example, consider former Czechoslovakia (57 of 230 cases in our sample), where 66.7 percent of all exports in countertrade were technology goods, as opposed to 42.72 percent in total trade of this country. Similarly, for Hungary (33 of 230 cases) the respective percentages are 51.5 for countertrade versus 33.68 for total trade, and for Poland (16 of 230 cases) the percentages are 87.5 as compared to 31.75. The numbers for total trade are taken from OECD's (1990) *Foreign Trade by Commodities*, Vol. 5, Series C.

[6] Similarly, the seller of a production plant may have superior information regarding the quality or future value of the commodity to be produced with the plant, which leads to a problem of adverse selection. The negative implications of both of these incentive problems on international technology transfer have been emphasized by several authors (see Kemal Abdallah-Khodja, 1984; Bruce Kogut, 1986; Rolf Mirus and Bernard Yeung, 1986; Jean François Hennart, 1989).

though foreign exchange is used and the two goods are not technologically related. For this purpose we set up the following stylized model. On the one hand there is a DC-firm which wants to export a plant, machinery, know-how, or other investment goods to a developing or Eastern European country. These are complex and sophisticated products, and it is difficult to specify all aspects of these goods in a complete contingent contract. The DC firm may be tempted to undersupply "quality" (including spare parts, technology advances, etc.) and blame adverse circumstances in the LDC or EE country for unsatisfactory performance. On the other hand, the LDC or EE country lacks creditworthiness due to large debts, and the DC firm cannot be sure that the export is actually going to be paid for.

How can tying two transactions mitigate these moral-hazard problems? In our model the second deal (the import from the LDC/EE) creates a "hostage" (in the language of Oliver E. Williamson [1983]) that deters cheating on quality *and* defaulting on the payment in the original export. First of all, the import goods serve as deal-specific collateral which gives the LDC/EE country an incentive to fulfill its financial obligations.[7] Secondly, the contract is designed such that the value of this collateral depends on the quality decision of the DC firm in the first transaction, even though there is no technological relationship between export and import goods. This contractual arrangement makes the DC firm internalize the externality its quality decision has on the LDC/EE country.

Note that without the subsequent import the gains from trade of the technology export could not be realized. Thus, even if the second deal could be carried out more efficiently with a third party (e.g., a trading company specialized in marketing imports from developing or Eastern European countries), it may still be optimal to link the two transactions in a countertrade arrangement. We show, however, that it is possible to renegotiate the subsequent import such that the technology-exporting DC firm markets the import through a specialized trading company without affecting the incentives in the first transaction.

Based on our sample of 230 countertrade contracts we test several implications of our theory. The data support our hypothesis that countertrade is chosen to secure efficient technology transfer to developing countries and Eastern Europe and to restore creditworthiness of countries with large debts. An advantage of our data set is that it contains a (comparatively) large number of observations and detailed information on each individual contract. In contrast, most of the few other empirical studies on countertrade rely on more aggregate information such as estimates of the volume of countertrade per country or per industry.[8]

Until recently, the analysis of contracts and institutions that govern trade has been neglected in trade theory, which focuses on endowments, technologies, preferences, and the nature of competition in international markets as determinants of trade. A notable exception is the paper of Avner Greif et al. (1994), who analyze merchant guilds in the middle ages as an efficiency-enhancing institution to deal with moral-hazard problems in "international" trade. There is also a small theoretical literature on countertrade that deals with other possible explanations for this phenomenon. Richard E. Caves and Marin (1992) suggest that countertrade may be used by DC companies as an instrument of price discrimination. Tore Ellingsen (1991) considers a strategic setting in which countertrade facilitates profit-shifting from competitors to the countertrading firm. Ellingsen and Lars A. Stole (1992) see

[7] In the sovereign-debt literature the "reputation theory" suggests that a country will not repudiate its debt if otherwise it risks not participating in international financial markets in the future. In our model, the introduction of a second profitable deal which serves as a collateral guarantees that the debtor will fulfill his financial obligations. Thus, long-term interaction and reputation effects are not necessary to enforce repayment by the debtor.

[8] The studies of Hennart (1989) and Hennart and Erin Anderson (1993), which also focus on transaction costs as a rationale for countertrade, test the hypothesis that countertrade is a second-best alternative to direct foreign investment by looking at country data. They find supporting evidence that countertrade is more frequently used by countries that restrict direct foreign investment. However, their tests are based on only 39 and 84 observations, respectively.

government-mandated countertrade as a strategic commitment for buyers not to purchase unless there are reciprocal sales. Erwin Amann and Marin (1994) suggest that countertrade provides a mechanism for risk-sharing between parties when no futures markets for the good of the LDC/EE country exists.

The rest of the paper is organized as follows. Section I introduces the model and outlines our basic argument. In Section II we show conditions under which countertrade can solve the moral-hazard problems described in Section I. Section III derives testable predictions from the model which are then put to an econometric test. Finally, Section IV concludes and discusses the relevance of the model for Eastern European economies in transition. Some of the mathematical proofs are gathered in the Appendix.

I. The Model

A. *The Double Moral-Hazard Problem*

Consider two parties, A and B, where A is a company in a developed country (DC) and B is a trade organization in Eastern Europe or a developing country. A wants to export a technology, like a turnkey factory, machinery, or some other investment good, to B. This technology, in the following called "good 1" or the "export," is used by B to produce goods which are then sold on the world market. B's valuation of good 1 can be thought of as his profits generated with good 1 (including spillover effects this technology may have on other industries in the LDC or EE country). This valuation is higher the more effort A spends in order to produce a high-quality product (including after-sale service, delivering spare parts, technological upgrades, etc). The problem is that quality is not observed by B when good 1 is delivered, nor is it verifiable to an outsider like the courts, and thus cannot be specified unambiguously in a contract. For simplicity we assume that there are only two different quality levels, "high" and "low" quality.[9] Since our focus is on incentive problems, we are interested mainly in how much costs and valuations increase if high quality is delivered instead of low quality. Thus, to save on notation we normalize A's production costs for low quality and B's valuation for low quality to 0. Producing high quality increases A's costs by k and B's valuation by v_1.[10] To make the problem interesting, we impose the following.

ASSUMPTION 1:

$$v_1 - k > 0.$$

Thus, producing high quality is efficient. However, there is a genuine moral-hazard problem in that firm A has an incentive to cheat on quality.

To make matters worse, there is a second moral-hazard problem related to B's payment for good 1. B does not have enough liquidity to pay for good 1 in cash at the date of delivery. In principle, the transaction could be financed with a credit, either from a commercial bank or from firm A directly, which has to be paid back out of B's profits generated with good 1. Note that if this credit could be guaranteed by the government of B's country, there would be no problem. If, however, B's country is highly indebted it is likely to be credit-constrained due to the sovereign-debt problem. The problem is that B's government cannot be forced by the courts in A's country to repay its debt. It has to meet this obligation voluntarily, either for reputational reasons in order to maintain future access to international financial markets or because it wants to avoid the international trade sanctions which may be triggered by default on a loan. If an LDC or EE country is highly indebted already, the gains from default on existing debt may outweigh the expected future losses, and Western banks will be reluctant to offer additional credit (see Jonathan Eaton, 1993).

[9] All our results can be generalized to the case of a continuous quality variable. See footnote 16.

[10] We rule out the possibility that the level of quality can be deduced from A's production cost or B's profits. Both parties can shift accounting costs and profits between different divisions and activities, such that it is impossible for the courts to infer the quality from accounting data.

In our model there is no difference whether B gets a credit from A or from a commercial bank. For simplicity, we assume that any credit is provided by A directly. We want to allow for the possibility that A can enforce at least some repayment up to an amount $r \geq 0$, which represents assets that B's country holds abroad and that A can seize in case of default. However, the more severely indebted B's country, the more creditors have to share any assets that can be seized in case of repudiation, and thus the smaller will be r, the repayment that can be enforced by A.

ASSUMPTION 2: *B is credit-constrained on international capital markets, and A can enforce payments only up to an amount $r < k$.*

That is, payment of r is insufficient to cover A's cost to produce high quality. Hence, there is a second moral-hazard problem in that B has to be induced to pay for the transaction.

Considered in isolation, the outcome of this double moral-hazard problem must be inefficient. It is neither possible to induce A to deliver high quality, nor to get B to pay more than $r < k$. Thus, if at all, only the inferior-quality good can be traded.

B. *Creating a Hostage*

How can a countertrade arrangement help to overcome the double moral-hazard problem? Suppose the parties find a second transaction to be carried out after B has realized his payoff from good 1 and has paid p_1. This time B is supposed to deliver one unit of another good, in the following called "good 2" or "import," to firm A. Good 2 will typically be a standardized consumption good, the quality of which can more easily be verified and controlled through a contract. Furthermore, let us assume that A (a large company in a Western country) is neither liquidity- nor credit-constrained, and that the courts in A's country will enforce the payment for good 2. Thus, while B cannot be forced to carry out the second deal, there are no other contractual hazards.

Let v_2 denote A's valuation for good 2 and let p_2 denote the price A agreed to pay. In order to produce good 2, B has to incur investment and production cost $c > 0$ (in hard currency), for example, to buy machinery or inputs on the world market. In addition to the payoff $p_2 - c$, B may receive a nonverifiable benefit $b \geq 0$ if the second trade takes place. The idea is that B learns how to market the good on the world market, that he acquires information about consumers' tastes or about the production technology, or that there is a goodwill effect: consumers learn about the quality of B's good which makes it more profitable to sell other goods later on.[11] The second transaction is interesting only if there are gains from trade.

ASSUMPTION 3:

$$v_2 + b - c > 0.$$

How does the design of the second transaction affect the incentives in the preceding technology trade? First, it generates an additional collateral for firm A. If by the time A has to pay p_2 B has not fully paid p_1, A can withhold the difference from its own payment. Of course, this requires that B has an interest to deliver good 2 to A. The contract has to be designed such that B wants to deliver good 2 even if this means that its payment p_1 becomes enforceable. Note that B cannot breach the contract and sell good 2 to a third party C in some other developed country. If this were to happen, A could refer to its countertrade contract which promises good 2 and use courts in C's country to seize good 2 as soon as it is delivered.[12] We assume that the probability of success of this legal action is sufficiently high to make a separate deal between B and C unprofitable.

Second, the contract can be designed such that B's ability to finance the production cost

[11] These are important considerations for firms in EE or LDC countries (see e.g., Hennart, 1989).

[12] Goods and cash flows from countertrade transactions are frequently used as collateral (see e.g., Leo G. B. Welt, 1984 p. 61; Pompiliu Verzariu, 1985 p. 111; James M. Barkas, 1987 p. 80). A similar theoretical effect can be found in Patrick Bolton and David Scharfstein (1990). They show that a firm will not default on its debt if the availability of a second loan is made contingent on the repayment of the first one.

c depends on the quality level of good 1. Suppose A cheats on quality. Then B's profit is reduced by v_1. If p_1 and p_2 are chosen appropriately, this reduction in B's profits will make it impossible for B to pay for c, and the second trade is lost.[13] Party A might be willing to renegotiate and offer additional money to B in order to rescue the gains from the second transaction. However, cheating on quality is inefficient. Therefore, A will have to put in more money now than was gained from cheating on quality in the first transaction. This way, A can in fact be made residual claimant for its own quality decision.

The sequence of events is summarized in Figure 1. A and B negotiate prices p_1 and p_2 at date 0. At date 1, A chooses the quality level which determines B's profit from good 1. This decision is denoted by $q \in \{0, 1\}$, where $q = 1$ denotes high quality and $q = 0$ denotes low quality. At date 2, B chooses whether or not to pay p_1. If he does not pay p_1, A receives r. Furthermore, B can invest c and produce good 2. This decision is denoted by $d \in \{0, 1\}$. If $d = 1$, then at date 3, good 2 is delivered and A has to pay p_2; otherwise there is no trade and no payment. All payments are measured in date-3 money. The utility functions of A and B are given by

$$(1) \quad U_A = p_1 - qk + d[v_2 - p_2]$$

$$(2) \quad U_B = qv_1 - p_1 + d[p_2 - c + b].$$

II. Countertrade as an Efficient Institution

Given Assumptions 1 and 3, the first best requires that A chooses $q = 1$ at date 1 and B chooses $d = 1$ at date 2. We say that a countertrade contract (p_1, p_2) implements the first best, if (given p_1 and p_2) there is a unique subgame-perfect equilibrium outcome in which A chooses high quality, B pays p_1, and the second transaction takes place. Furthermore, both parties have to agree to countertrade voluntarily. To show the conditions under which such a contract exists we proceed in two steps. In the following subsection we consider the case in which no renegotiation is possible. That is, A cannot increase its payment p_2 in case it delivered low quality in order to rescue the second deal. This case applies when A is engaged in countertrade transactions repeatedly and has built up a reputation not to renegotiate. In Subsection II-B we allow for renegotiation, and we consider the possibility of including third parties in the transaction (e.g., some company C which has a higher valuation for good 2 than A).

A. *No Renegotiation*

We solve the game induced by a contract (p_1, p_2) by backwards induction, looking for conditions on prices and exogenously given parameters such that there is a unique subgame-perfect equilibrium implementing the first best. Note first that without loss of generality we can restrict attention to prices satisfying

$$(3) \quad p_1 < p_2 + r.$$

In order to enforce p_1, A can seize r, and, if the second deal takes place, A can retain the payment p_2. Thus the highest payment that can be enforced is $r + p_2$, and it is a strictly dominated strategy for player B to pay more.[14]

Now consider B's decision at date 2 whether or not to carry out the second deal. If B chooses $d = 0$, then it is clearly optimal to pay p_1 if and only if $p_1 \leq r$. On the other hand, if B chooses $d = 1$, then he cannot avoid paying

[13] In the corporate-debt literature there is an interesting parallel to our use of a financial constraint as an incentive device. Oliver Hart (1991) considers a manager whose action has an externality on outside investors. The manager might not want to liquidate the firm when it would be profitable to do so. The optimal debt-repayment schedule is designed such that the manager faces a financial constraint and is forced to come to the capital market for additional funds. This way, he can be induced to liquidate the firm when it is in the interest of outside investors to do so.

[14] Rewriting condition (3) as $p_2 > p_1 - r$ highlights the similarity with the condition for debt repayment in the sovereign-debt literature. The debtor will meet his debt-service obligations only if he expects to receive a subsequent net resource transfer from creditors if he repays (see Eaton, 1993).

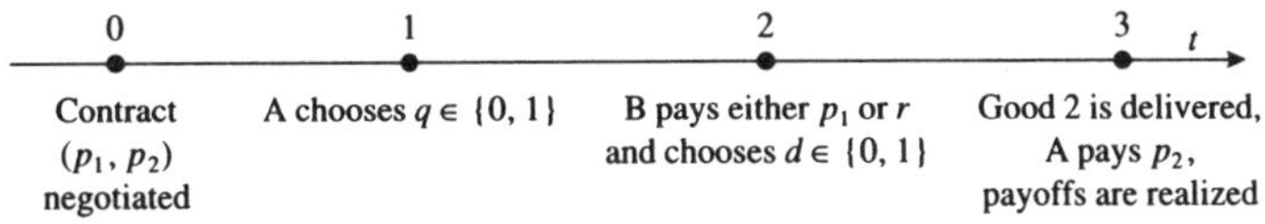

FIGURE 1. TIME STRUCTURE

p_1 [given that (3) holds] because A can use $p_2 + r$ as collateral. Thus, B strictly prefers to carry out the second deal if and only if

$$(4) \quad v_1 - p_1 + p_2 + b - c > v_1 - \min\{p_1, r\}.$$

Note that B's incentive to carry out the second deal is independent of whether or not A delivered high quality in period 1. This is due to the fact that there is no technological relationship between goods 1 and 2. However, A's quality decision has an impact on B's financial constraint. In order to finance the investment and production cost c, B can use his profits from the first transaction, $qv_1 - p_1$, and he can take a credit up to the amount $p_2 + r$, which is secured by the payment he is going to receive (p_2) and his assets (r).[15] Thus, if we want B to be able to finance the second transaction if and only if A delivered high quality ($q = 1$), then p_1 and p_2 must be chosen such that:[16]

$$(5) \qquad v_1 - p_1 + p_2 + r \geq c$$

$$(6) \qquad -p_1 + p_2 + r < c.$$

Next, consider A's decision at date 1, whether or not to produce high quality. If (4), (5), and (6) hold, then the second transaction will take place if and only if $q = 1$. Thus, A strictly prefers to deliver high quality if and only if

$$(7) \quad p_1 - k + v_2 - p_2 > \min\{p_1, r\}.$$

[15] Note that b cannot be used as collateral, because it is an unverifiable spillover benefit that cannot be seized by potential creditors.

[16] If quality is a continuous variable then (5) and (6) have to be replaced by a condition which requires that B can finance c if and only if efficient quality is delivered.

Finally, at date 0 both parties have to participate voluntarily in the countertrade transaction. The participation constraints of A and B are given by

$$(8) \qquad p_1 - k + v_2 - p_2 \geq 0$$

and

$$(9) \qquad v_1 - p_1 + p_2 + b - c \geq 0$$

respectively.

In summary, if for a given pair of prices (p_1, p_2) conditions (3)–(7) are satisfied, then there is a unique subgame-perfect equilibrium in which A chooses high quality, B pays p_1, and the second trade takes place. Furthermore, if (8) and (9) hold, then both parties benefit from the countertrade transaction. This proves the following.

PROPOSITION 1: *If there exist prices (p_1, p_2) satisfying (3)–(9), then a countertrade contract (p_1, p_2) implements the first best.*

Theorem 1 gives necessary and sufficient conditions for the existence of an efficient countertrade contract.

THEOREM 1: *There exists a countertrade contract (p_1, p_2) which implements the first best if and only if the following conditions hold:*

(i) $v_2 + b - c > k$
(ii) $v_2 - k + v_1 + r \geq c$
(iii) $v_2 > k - r$
(iv) $b > 0$.

PROOF:

Note first that, given Assumptions 1 and 2, condition (9) is implied by (4) and can be ignored. The first part of the proof is to show that (3)–(8) imply (i)–(iv). First, (4) and (7) imply that

$$(10)\quad c - b - \min\{p_1, r\} < p_2 - p_1 < v_2 - k - \min\{p_1, r\}$$

which in turn implies condition (i),

$$v_2 + b - c > k.$$

That is, the gains from trade from the second transaction have to be larger than A's gain from cheating on quality in the technology trade.

Condition (5) requires that $v_1 - p_1 + p_2 + r \geq c$ (i.e., B has to be able to finance the second deal if A delivered high quality). Together with A's participation constraint (8), which puts an upper bound on the net payment from A to B by imposing that $p_2 - p_1 \leq v_2 - k$, this implies condition (ii),

$$v_2 - k + v_1 + r \geq c$$

saying that A's maximum transfer to B ($v_2 - k$) plus B's own funds ($v_1 + r$) must be sufficient to finance c.

Next, condition (3) requires that $p_1 - p_2 < r$; otherwise p_1 cannot be enforced. On the other hand, (8) requires that $p_1 - p_2 \geq k - v_2$ to make it worthwhile for A to participate. This implies condition (iii),

$$v_2 > k - r$$

(i.e., A's valuation of good 2 must be big enough to compensate it for the costs of producing high quality that are not covered by B's minimal repayment r).

Finally, (4) (the incentive constraint for B) requires $p_2 - p_1 > c - b - \min\{p_1, r\}$, while (6), the condition ensuring that B cannot finance the second deal if A delivered low quality, imposes $p_2 - p_1 < c - r$. Together, these conditions imply condition (iv),

$$b > r - \min\{p_1, r\} \geq 0.$$

The second part of the proof, showing that (i)–(iv) imply (3)–(8), is relegated to the Appendix.

Note first that the set of parameters satisfying (i)–(iii) is not empty. As an example, choose v_2 large enough and c sufficiently small such that $v_2 - c > k$; then (i)–(iii) hold. The theorem also requires that b, the nonverifiable benefit of B from the second transaction, is strictly positive. If $b = 0$ and (i)–(iii) hold, then there is still a countertrade contract (p_1, p_2) and a subgame-perfect equilibrium given (p_1, p_2) in which the first best is achieved. However, this equilibrium is no longer unique. In this case (4) and (6) hold with equality, so B is indifferent whether or not to carry out the second deal, and he could do so even if A delivered low quality. Thus, requiring $b > 0$ is essentially a tie-breaking rule guaranteeing a unique subgame-perfect equilibrium.[17]

Of course, countertrade is not always an efficient remedy to solve the underlying incentive problems. Considering (i)–(iv) again, it is easy to see that these conditions are less likely to be satisfied if the incentive for A to cheat on quality, measured by k, is very big, and the minimum payment that can be enforced from B, r, is very small. Thus, the incentive problems may not be too severe. On the other hand, countertrade is more likely to be an efficient institution the higher the gains from the second trade (i.e., the bigger $v_2 + b$ and the smaller c). All this is quite intuitive. Countertrade is supposed to solve the double moral-hazard problem by introducing a "hostage," which is lost if either party cheats in the first transaction. For this construction to work it has to be the case that the hostage is sufficiently valuable as compared to the gains from cheating.

[17] A strictly positive b is consistent with the import pattern that we observe for countertrade. In our sample, 67 percent of all countertrade imports from LDC's and EE are manufactured investment and consumption goods as opposed to only 35–40 percent in total trade. (For similar numbers see also Hennart [1989]). As argued above, marketing these goods through a Western firm opens new markets for B and generates positive spillovers on its future transactions with Western markets.

What can we say about the prices p_1 and p_2 that implement the first best? If conditions (i)–(iv) are met, there exists a continuum of price pairs (p_1, p_2) satisfying (3)–(9). Note that, for any such price pair with $p_1 \geq r$, there exists another price pair (p_1', p_2') which also implements the first best, where $p_1' \leq r$, $p_2' = p_2 - (p_1 - p_1')$, and

$$c - b \leq p_2' \leq v_2 - k. \tag{11}$$

This price pair has a natural interpretation: B is asked to pay for the first loan an amount that can be enforced anyway, and A is compensated for its costs in transaction 1 (mainly) through the second transaction. As condition (11) shows p_2' has to be chosen such that the second deal is sufficiently attractive to both A and B; that is, their incentive constraints (4) and (7) have to be satisfied.

B. *Renegotiation and Third Parties*

An important question is whether a countertrade contract still achieves the first best when A and B cannot commit not to renegotiate the initial contract. An opportunity for an *ex post* Pareto improvement arises off the equilibrium path. Suppose A delivered low quality in the first transaction. We have chosen p_1 and p_2 such that B is not able to finance the second deal in this case. However, A could offer to raise p_2 (i.e., put in additional money), in order to rescue the gains from trade from the second transaction. In the Appendix we prove the following lemma.

LEMMA 1: *Suppose A defaults on quality but offers to increase p_2 by at least*

$$\underline{\Delta} = c + p_1 - p_2 - r. \tag{12}$$

Then B will deliver good 2.

If we want to make sure that A strictly prefers to deliver high quality and stick to the old contract, rather than cheating on quality in the first transaction and putting in the minimum amount $\underline{\Delta}$, the following renegotiation constraint has to be satisfied:

$$\begin{aligned} p_1 - k + v_2 - p_2 &> p_1 + v_2 - p_2 - \underline{\Delta} \\ &= p_1 + v_2 - p_2 - (p_1 - p_2 + c - r) \\ &= v_2 + r - c \end{aligned} \tag{13}$$

or, equivalently,

$$p_2 - p_1 < c - k - r. \tag{14}$$

Note that this condition implies (6). The contract (p_1, p_2) is "renegotiation-proof" if the possibility of mutually beneficial renegotiation does not upset the equilibrium, that is, if it satisfies condition (14).

THEOREM 2: *Suppose A and B can renegotiate after A has chosen q but before B decides on d. A countertrade contract (p_1, p_2) that implements the first best and that is renegotiation-proof exists, if and only if in addition to (i)–(iv) the following conditions are met:*

(v) $c > k$
(vi) $b > k$.

PROOF:
Let us first show that (v) and (vi) are implied by (3)–(8) and (14). The renegotiation constraint puts a lower bound on the net payment from A to B: $p_2 - p_1 < c - k - r$. Along with (3), we have

$$-r < p_2 - p_1 < c - k - r \tag{15}$$

which implies condition (v),

$$c > k$$

(i.e., A's gains from cheating in the first transaction have to be smaller than the total cost to produce good 2).

Condition (4), the incentive constraint of B, imposes an upper bound on A's net payment to B: $p_2 - p_1 > c - b - \min\{p_1, r\}$. Along with the renegotiation constraint (14), this implies that

$$(16) \qquad c - b - \min\{p_1, r\} < p_2 - p_1 < c - k - r$$

which in turn implies condition (vi),

$$b > k.$$

Again, A's incentive to cheat on quality may not be too big. The second part of the proof, showing that (i)–(vi) imply (3)–(8) and (14) is relegated to the Appendix.

Thus, Theorem 2 shows that the first best can be implemented with a renegotiation-proof countertrade contract if A's incentive to cheat on quality is not too big. Note that condition (iv) of Theorem 1 is implied by condition (vi).

There may also be a possibility to renegotiate by including a third party in the contract. Suppose that there is another firm C in a developed country that is specialized in marketing good 2. Suppose C is more efficient than A in carrying out the second transaction (i.e., C's valuation for good 2 is $v_2 + \varepsilon$, $\varepsilon > 0$). Then there is scope for a Pareto improvement by including C in the countertrade contract. Note that A owns good 2. Thus it can sell it to C for a price p_2', such that $v_2 \leq p_2' \leq v_2 + \varepsilon$. B's utility is unaffected by this transaction, and its permission is not required. The following theorem shows that this form of renegotiation does not upset the efficient equilibrium and actually increases the scope for countertrade.

THEOREM 3: *Suppose there exists an efficient countertrade contract* (p_1, p_2). *Renegotiation with a third party C, whose valuation for good 2 is* $v_2 + \varepsilon$, $\varepsilon > 0$, *does not upset the efficient equilibrium induced by* (p_1, p_2). *Furthermore, the existence of such a third party relaxes conditions (i)–(vi) and thus increases the set of parameters under which countertrade implements the first best.*

PROOF:

Suppose A sells good 2 to C at a price $p_2' = v_2 + \varepsilon'$, $0 \leq \varepsilon' \leq \varepsilon$. Replacing v_2 by $v_2 + \varepsilon'$ in conditions (3)–(8) and (14) relaxes these conditions. Thus, choosing high quality, paying p_1, and delivering good 2 is still an equilibrium.

Considering (i)–(vi), v_2 appears on the left-hand side of (i)–(iii) and is irrelevant for (iv)–(vi). Thus, increasing v_2 by ε' relaxes these conditions.

Theorem 3 shows that the main disadvantage usually associated with countertrade, namely, that there has to be a double coincidence of needs, is not really a problem, since the parties can include a third party into the contract. In fact, this is frequently done in reality. In our empirical investigation we found that most firms in developed countries that countertrade with LDC or EE countries have a division specialized in finding an appropriate buyer for the goods imported from these countries.

III. Theoretical Predictions and Empirical Evidence

In this section we discuss some testable predictions from our theoretical model, look for proxies for the variables we would like to measure, and estimate whether or not the derived predictions are consistent with the data on actual countertrade contracts in our sample.

A. *The Data*

The companies included in our sample of 230 contracts are either firms producing in Austria or subsidiaries of multinational enterprises with their own in-house countertrade division located in Austria, or else other firms in OECD countries using an international trading firm in Vienna to carry out the countertrade transaction. Thirty percent of the Western firms in the sample are based in the European Community and 62.7 percent are based in other industrialized countries, including Austria, Sweden, Japan, and the United States. Each firm was asked for information on about 40 aspects of each countertrade transaction.

TABLE 1—DEFINITION OF VARIABLES AND SAMPLE STATISTICS

Variable	Number of observations	Description	Mean	Minimum	Maximum	Standard deviation
DEBT[a]	226	total debt of EE/LDC country as percentage of GNP	38.94	4.50	326.60	37.54
COMP	230	compensation ratio: import value as percentage of export value	71.38	2.00	400.00	51.44
XCLASS	229	type of product exported: manufacturing plants and machinery	(dummy = 1, 173 observations)			
MDIF	224	type of product imported: horizontally and/or vertically differentiated good	(dummy = 1, 116 observations)			
MPOS	221	market position of EE/LDC firm: leading producer	(dummy = 1, 32 observations)			
Contract type:	230					
Barter			(26 observations)			
Buyback			(28 observations)			
Counterpurchase (CPURCH)			(176 observations)			

[a] From the World Bank's *World Debt Tables*, various years.

The countertrade partner in the Eastern European or developing country was a state agency (85.2 percent of the cases), a state-owned enterprise (9.1 percent), or a private firm (5.7 percent). Due to Austria's geographic proximity to Eastern Europe, East–West countertrade accounts for more than four-fifths of all deals in our sample. More specifically, 14.8 percent of the transactions are with the former Soviet Union, 24.8 percent with the former Czechoslovakia, 14.3 percent with Hungary, 7 percent with Poland, 4.3 percent with Romania, 6.5 percent with former East Germany, 6.5 percent with Bulgaria, 6.1 percent with the former Yugoslavia, and 0.9 percent with Albania. In contrast, North–South countertrade is underrepresented in the sample. Only 5.7 percent of the transactions took place with Africa, 3 percent with Asia, 2.6 percent with South America, and 2.2 percent with China. The deals in our sample are mostly very large in size, ranging from U.S. $8,400 to U.S. $635 million, with a mean of U.S. $11.1 million. All statistics presented in this paper are based on the number of contracts, rather than trade volume, as the unit of analysis.

Table 1 describes the variables included in the following empirical analysis and reports on some sample statistics.

B. *Counterpurchase versus Barter*

In barter agreements, where no payments in cash are made, the value of the import is chosen in order to provide sufficient payment for the value of the DC firm's export. This is reflected by the compensation ratio, which measures the value of the import as a percentage of the export value. For barter contracts this ratio is typically around 100 percent. If counterpurchase were just another form of barter and motivated only by financial constraints we would expect counterpurchase contracts to show a similar pattern of compensation ratios. However, the two patterns differ significantly, indicating that counterpurchase is driven also by other motivations, as our theory suggests.[18]

If counterpurchase serves different functions than barter, then this should be re-

[18] The mean compensation ratio of counterpurchase contracts in our sample is 61.2 (with a variance of 45.31), as opposed to 107.4 for barter (with a variance of 28.77). An analysis of variance (ANOVA) and a Kolmogorov-Smirnov test both confirm that the distributions of compensation ratios for barter and counterpurchase differ significantly.

flected by the variables that explain the choice between barter and counterpurchase. We would expect that counterpurchase rather than barter will be chosen if the LDC or EE firm wants to make sure that the DC firm provides efficient quality.[19] This leads to our first hypothesis.

Hypothesis 1: The contract will be counterpurchase rather than barter when there is a problem to induce the DC firm to deliver high-quality technology goods.

To estimate the effect of contract characteristics on the choice of contractual form, we use both ordinary least-squares (OLS) and logit regressions. Table 2 presents the results of testing Hypothesis 1 using the choice between counterpurchase and barter as the independent variable. A's incentive to cheat on quality is proxied by the variable XCLASS. XCLASS is a dummy variable that takes the value of 1 if the good exported by the DC firm is a manufacturing plant or machinery and 0 in all other deals. The underlying presumption is that in the case of technology exports the incentive problems are more severe. The coefficients for XCLASS prove to be consistently positive and significant. This suggests that the presence of technology increases the probability that the contract form will be counterpurchase rather than barter. We also include DEBT as a measure for B's creditworthiness in our regressions. DEBT stands for the ratio of debt over GNP of the country in which B is located. The coefficients for DEBT have a negative sign [though the coefficients are statistically insignificant in specifications (i) and (iii)], indicating that the parties will sign a barter agreement rather than counterpurchase when the EE/LDC's debt problems are severe. In this case, B's lack of creditworthiness cannot be overcome, and only barter contracts are feasible (where in fact no credit is given).

In specifications (ii) and (iv) XCLASS is replaced by XCLASS $\times$ ln(DEBT) to focus on those cases of technology exports that were accompanied by high indebtedness, since it is for those cases that our theory predicts counterpurchase to provide optimal incentives. The coefficients have the expected positive sign and are statistically significant. A comparison of specifications (i) and (ii) with (iii) and (iv) shows that both OLS and logit regressions generate very similar results, which confirms that OLS is a good linear approximation in this problem.

C. *Counterpurchase and Compensation Ratios*

Our model predicts that the prices p_1 and p_2 are chosen to provide optimal incentives to both parties involved in the countertrade deal. Thus, an important test of our theory is to check how actual contracts in our data sample react to different incentive problems identified by our model. Note that the model does not allow for point predictions of p_1 and p_2. However, counterpurchase implements an efficient allocation only if $p_2 - p_1$ can be chosen in an interval whose bounds are given by constraints (3)–(8) [and (14)] (conveniently expressed in terms of $p_2 - p_1$ in the Appendix). Suppose that the upper bound of this interval is reduced because of a change in the exogenous variables of the model. If $p_2 - p_1$ is close enough to the upper bound, it will have to go down as well. Similarly, if a change in the exogenous variables leads to an increase of the lower bound, $p_2 - p_1$ has to go up. This observation allows us to derive several testable predictions for $p_2 - p_1$.

Before doing so, note that in our model we have normalized quantities to 1, whereas in our sample, multiple items may have been traded. Thus, the relevant variables to look at in our data set are import and export values.

[19] Recall that our theory requires that B faces a financial constraint when A delivers low quality. This is the case only when the deal is sufficiently large. A back-of-the-envelope calculation suggests that the deals have been large enough to make the foreign-trade organisations (FTO's) in Eastern Europe face this constraint. In 1985 the average countertrade technology export to former Czechoslovakia in our sample made up 26 percent of the trade value of a typical FTO. Similar calculations for Hungary and Poland make the typical countertrade technology export 18 percent and 9 percent, respectively, of the average trade value of the typical FTO.

TABLE 2—CHOOSING COUNTERPURCHASE VERSUS BARTER, DEPENDENT VARIABLE = CPURCH

	OLS		Logit	
Independent variable	(i)	(ii)	(iii)	(iv)
XCLASS	0.14 (0.005)		1.23 (0.007)	
ln(DEBT)	−0.03 (0.20)	−0.07 (0.013)	−0.34 (0.195)	−0.53 (0.043)
XCLASS × ln(DEBT)		0.05 (0.002)		0.36 (0.006)
Intercept	0.89 (0.000)	0.99 (0.000)	2.39 (0.000)	3.06 (0.000)
Adjusted R^2:	0.04	0.05		
F:	5.3 (0.006)	6.3 (0.002)		
−2(log likelihood):			132.9	132.2
Percentage correct:			88.4	88.4

Notes: The table reports ordinary least-squares and logit regressions of 202 observations. Numbers in parentheses are p values. Definitions of variables are as follows:

CPURCH Dummy variable equal to 1 when contract is counterpurchase and equal to 0 when contract is barter

XCLASS Dummy variable equal to 1 when export to EE/LDC is manufacturing plant or machinery and equal to 0 for all other exports

ln(DEBT) Natural log of debt as percentage of GNP of LDC or EE country.

Since some of the deals in our sample are extremely large and others are rather small in value, the differences of import value and export value vary a lot over different contracts. To control for possible size effects we normalize these differences by dividing each difference by its export value which yields as a proxy the compensation ratio (import value)/(export value).

Hypothesis 2: The greater A's incentive to cheat on quality, the lower will be the compensation ratio.

An increase in k reduces the right-hand side of (7) and leaves all other constraints unaffected. [If (6) is replaced by (14) in order to guarantee renegotiation-proofness, the right-hand side of (14) is also reduced.] Thus, $p_2 - p_1$ is restricted to be smaller. Intuitively, when A's incentive to cheat on quality increases, the contract needs to give A a larger profit in transaction 2 in order to make sure that A is interested in the second deal. This calls for a lower net transfer to B. As above, A's incentive to cheat on quality is captured by XCLASS, a dummy variable equal to 1 if the export good is a technology-related product.

Hypothesis 3: The lower B's creditworthiness, the larger will be the compensation ratio.

A decrease in r increases the left-hand side of (3) and (5) as well as the right-hand side of (6) and thus is associated with a higher $p_2 - p_1$. The variable r stands for the assets A can seize in case of B's default. Intuitively, the smaller the contractible collateral, the lower B's creditworthiness, and thus the larger the collateral generated by the second deal needs to be. As a proxy for B's creditworthiness we again use DEBT, the ratio of debt to GNP, assuming that B's creditworthiness decreases as DEBT increases.

Hypothesis 4: The smaller B's unverifiable benefit from carrying out the second transaction (his gain in goodwill b) the higher will be the compensation ratio.

A decrease in b increases the left-hand side of (4) and does not affect any other constraint. Thus, $p_2 - p_1$ has to be bigger. The reason is that, the smaller the spillover benefit on B's future transactions, the higher must be A's net transfer to B in order not to violate B's incentive to carry out the second deal. We use MDIF as a measure for the gain in goodwill, b, that B has from carrying out the second deal. MDIF is a dummy variable that is equal to 1 if the good imported from the EE country or LDC is horizontally or vertically differentiated and 0 otherwise. The idea is that when B as a new entrant on A's market sells differentiated goods he has to convince consumers about the quality of his products. Consumers learn the quality of these goods by using them. Therefore, when good 2 is differentiated, sales on A's market generate an informational externality about the quality of good 2, thereby contributing to B's future profits.

Hypothesis 5: The smaller A's profit from marketing good 2, the smaller will be the compensation ratio.

A reduction of v_2 decreases the right-hand sides of (7) and (8) and forces $p_2 - p_1$ to become smaller. A lower valuation of the second good makes it more difficult to satisfy A's incentive and participation constraints, requiring a lower net transfer from A to B. We proxy the profitability with which firm A can sell good 2 with the dummy variable MPOS. MPOS is a dummy variable set equal to 1 if the EE/LDC firm is a leading producer of the good exported to the developed country, and 0 in all other cases. It is assumed here that if the market for good 2 is highly concentrated, then A's profit from marketing good 2 will be bigger.

Table 3 presents the results of testing Hypotheses 2–5 for counterpurchase contracts (excluding barter and buyback). The coefficients of XCLASS are negative and significant for all specifications, confirming Hypothesis 2. When the developed-country firm delivered technology, the contracts were designed with lower compensation ratios to increase the technology seller's stake in the second deal.[20] The coefficients on DEBT have the expected positive sign, as posed by Hypothesis 3, and are significant for all specifications.

In specification (ii) we include MDIF in our regression to test Hypothesis 4. The negative sign of the coefficient confirms Hypothesis 4, and the inclusion of MDIF improves the overall statistical properties of the regression. Hypothesis 5 is tested in specification (iii). The estimated coefficient of MPOS is consistent with the hypothesis that a higher profitability of marketing good 2 tends to increase the compensation ratio. Finally, in specification (iv), XCLASS is again replaced by XCLASS × ln(DEBT) to focus on those cases of technology exports that were accompanied by high indebtedness. This leads to a loss in R^2 but at the same time improves the statistical properties of all other variables included in the regression.

IV. Summary and Conclusions

In this paper we have shown that countertrade can be an efficient institution that mitigates incentive problems prevalent in East–West and North–South trade. In this arrangement, the import from Eastern Europe or the developing country serves as a "hostage" which induces both trading partners to fulfill their contractual obligations in the original export. In particular, if the DC firm delivers poor quality or if the EE or LDC company defaults on its payment, the second transaction is jeop-

[20] The reader might ask whether this negative impact of technology exports on compensation ratios is simply due to the fact that technology exports like manufacturing plants are typically very large and that there may not be enough valuable imports to offset these exports. To check this possibility we calculated the correlation coefficient between the export values and the compensation ratios, which is −0.03, indicating that the two variables are not correlated. This confirms that the negative coefficient in our regression is not just driven by size effects.

TABLE 3—DETERMINING THE DEGREE OF TYING, DEPENDENT VARIABLE = ln(COMP)

Independent variable	(i)	(ii)	(iii)	(iv)
ln(DEBT)	0.38**	0.39**	0.34**	0.59**
	(4.88)	(4.96)	(4.18)	(5.02)
XCLASS	−1.10**	−1.02**	−1.00**	
	(6.70)	(6.31)	(6.19)	
MDIF		−0.27*	−0.29*	−0.45**
		(1.93)	(2.08)	(3.05)
MPOS			0.38	0.49*
			(1.81)	(2.18)
XCLASS × ln(DEBT)				−0.01**
				(3.17)
Intercept	3.31**	3.37**	3.47**	2.22**
	(11.38)	(11.28)	(11.57)	(6.34)
F:	37.9**	26.6**	21.1**	12.4**
Adjusted R^2:	0.30	0.31	0.33	0.22

Notes: The table reports ordinary least-squares regressions of 176 observations. Numbers in brackets are t values. Definitions of variables are as follows:

ln(COMP) Natural log of import value as percentage of export value

ln(DEBT) Natural log of debt as percentage of GNP of LDC or EE country

XCLASS Dummy variable equal to 1 when export to EE/LDC is manufacturing plant or machinery and equal to 0 for all other exports

MDIF Dummy variable equal to 1 when import from EE/LDC is horizontally or vertically differentiated product and equal to 0 when import is homogenous product

MPOS Dummy variable equal to 1 when EE/LDC producer has leading market position and equal to 0 for all other import goods.

* Statistically significant at the 5-percent level.

** Statistically significant at the 1-percent level.

ardized. Tying two trade flows can thus promote efficient technology transfers from developed countries to Eastern Europe and developing countries and at the same time increase their creditworthiness. Our data on actual countertrade transactions seem to be consistent with the implications of our model.

Our analysis suggests that countertrade might play an important role in transition economies in Eastern Europe. These countries face two problems. First, their creditworthiness is poor and in some cases deteriorating further.[21] Second, there is only modest direct foreign investment due to the high political uncertainty in the transition period. Thus, the amount of foreign resources available for investment in these countries is limited. Under these circumstances, countertrade may continue to be an important institution to facilitate trade and to finance imports of technology from developed countries.

APPENDIX

PROOF OF THEOREM 1 (second part):

We have to show that if (i) – (iv) hold, then there exist (p_1, p_2) satisfying (3) – (8). Note

[21] In recent years Russia experienced a sharp increase in countertrade in its trade with the West. This fits well the story of our model since the increasing importance of countertrade went hand in hand with a significant deterioration of Russia's creditworthiness.

that, if $p_1 \geq r$, then only the difference $p_2 - p_1$ matters in conditions (3)–(8), and we are free to fix the absolute value of p_1 as we like. For example, we can set $p_1 = r$. Thus, without loss of generality, we can restrict attention to prices $p_1 \leq r$. Rewriting conditions (3)–(8) and substituting $p_1 = \min\{p_1, r\}$ we get:

$$(3') \qquad A \equiv -r < p_2 - p_1$$

$$(4') \qquad B \equiv c - b - p_1 < p_2 - p_1$$

$$(5') \qquad C \equiv c - v_1 - r \leq p_2 - p_1$$

$$(6') \qquad p_2 - p_1 < c - r \equiv D$$

$$(7') \qquad p_2 - p_1 < v_2 - k - p_1 \equiv E$$

$$(8') \qquad p_2 - p_1 \leq v_2 - k \equiv F.$$

These conditions impose some restrictions on the choice of p_1. Lower bounds on p_1 are imposed by (4′) and (6′) and by (4′) and (8′):

$$(A1) \qquad p_1 > r - b \equiv G$$

$$(A2) \qquad p_1 > c - b - v_2 + k \equiv H.$$

Upper bounds on p_1 are imposed by (3′) and (7′) and by (5′) and (7′):

$$(A3) \qquad p_1 < v_2 - k + r \equiv I$$

$$(A4) \qquad p_1 < v_2 - k - c + r \equiv J.$$

Also, we restrict attention to prices p_1 such that

$$(A5) \qquad p_1 \leq r \equiv K.$$

We can find a p_1 within these bounds if and only if $G < I, G < J, G < K, H < I, H < J$, and $H < K$. $G < I$ is implied by (i), $G < J$ is implied by Assumptions 1 and 3, $G < K$ is implied by (iv), $H < I$ is implied by (i) and (iii), $H < J$ follows from (i) and (ii), and $H < K$ follows from (i) and the fact that $r \geq 0$.

Pick any $p_1 \leq r$ satisfying (A1)–(A4). There exists a p_2 such that (p_1, p_2) satisfy (3′)–(8′) if $A < D, A < E, A < F, B < D, B < E, B < F, C < D, C < E$, and $C < F$. By the choice of p_1, we know already that $A < E, B < D, B < F$, and $C < E$. $A < D$ is trivially satisfied. $A < F$ is equivalent to (iii), and $B < E$ is equivalent to (i). $C < D$ follows from $v_1 > 0$. Finally, $C < F$ is implied by (ii).

PROOF OF LEMMA 1:

Note first that B can finance the production cost c for the second good if p_2 is increased by Δ such that

$$(A6) \qquad -p_1 + p_2 + r + \Delta \geq c.$$

Furthermore, B has to accept this offer voluntarily. If he does so, his final payoff is given by

$$(A7) \qquad -p_1 + p_2 + \Delta - c + b.$$

If he rejects he will only pay $\min\{p_1, r\}$ for good 1. Thus, B's participation constraint requires that

$$(A8) \qquad -p_1 + p_2 + \Delta - c + b \geq -\min\{p_1, r\}.$$

A successful renegotiation offer has to satisfy both (A6) and (A8):

$$\begin{aligned}(A9) \qquad \Delta &\geq p_1 - p_2 + c \\ &\quad + \max\{-b - \min\{p_1, r\}, -r\} \\ &= p_1 - p_2 + c \\ &\quad - \min\{\min\{p_1 + b, r + b\}, r\} \\ &= p_1 - p_2 + c - \min\{p_1 + b, r\} = \underline{\Delta}.\end{aligned}$$

Recall that (4′) and (6′) imply that $p_1 > r - b$. Therefore,

$$(A10) \qquad \underline{\Delta} = p_1 - p_2 + c - r.$$

PROOF OF THEOREM 2 (second part):

We have to show that, if (i)–(vi) hold, then there exist (p_1, p_2) satisfying (3′)–(8′) and (14). Recall that (14) implies (6). The proof follows the lines of the proof of Theorem 1, where (6′) is replaced by (14′):

$$(14') \qquad p_2 - p_1 < c - k - r \equiv D'.$$

This tightens the lower bound imposed on p_1. Conditions (4′) and (14′) impose

$$\text{(A11)} \qquad p_1 > k + r - b \equiv G'.$$

Note that $G' < I$ is implied by (i), (v), and (vi); $G' < J$ is implied by (i) and Assumption 1; and $G' < K$ follows from (vi). Thus, we can find a $p_1 \leq r$ satisfying (A2)–(A4) and (A11).

Pick any such p_1. There exists a p_2 such that (p_1, p_2) satisfy $A < D'$, $A < E$, $A < F$, $B < D'$, $B < E$, $B < F$, $C < D'$, $C < E$, and $C < F$. By choice of p_1, $B < D'$. $A < D'$ is equivalent to (v), while $C < D'$ is implied by Assumption 1. The other inequalities have been checked in the proof of Theorem 1 already.

REFERENCES

Abdallah-Khodja, Kemal. "Algeria's Experience with New International Investment Relations," in Charles Oman, ed., *New forms of international investment in developing countries: The national perspective.* Paris: Organization for Economic Cooperation and Development, 1984.

Amann, Erwin and Marin, Dalia. "Risk-Sharing in International Trade: An Analysis of Countertrade." *Journal of Industrial Economics*, March 1994, *42*(1), pp. 63–77.

Barkas, James M. "A Bank's Role in Facilitating and Financing Countertrade," in Christopher M. Korth, ed., *International countertrade.* New York: Quorum, 1987, pp. 77–83.

Bolton, Patrick and Scharfstein, David. "A Theory of Predation Based on Agency Problems in Financial Contracting." *American Economic Review*, March 1990, *80*(1), pp. 94–106.

Bussard, Willis A. "An Overview of Countertrade Practices of Corporations and Individual Nations," in Christopher M. Korth, ed., *International countertrade.* New York: Quorum, 1987, pp. 13–25.

Caves, Richard E. and Marin, Dalia. "Countertrade Transactions: Theory and Evidence." *Economic Journal*, September 1992, *102* (414), pp. 1171–83.

Chan, Raissa and Hoy, Michael. "East–West Joint Ventures and Buyback Contracts." *Journal of International Economics*, May 1991, *30*(3-4), pp. 331–43.

Choi, Chong J. and Maldoom, Daniel. "A Simple Model of Buybacks." *Economic Letters*, September 1992, *40*(1), pp. 77–82.

Eaton, Jonathan. "Sovereign Debt: A Primer." *World Bank Economic Review*, May 1993, *7*(2), pp. 137–72.

Ellingsen, Tore. "A Model of Countertrade." London School of Economics Discussion Paper EI/3, March 1991.

Ellingsen, Tore and Stole, Lars A. "Mandated Countertrade as a Strategic Commitment." Mimeo, Stockholm School of Economics, September 1992; *Journal of International Economics* (forthcoming).

Greif, Avner; Milgrom, Paul and Weingast, Barry R. "Coordination, Commitment, and Enforcement: The Case of the Merchant Guild." *Journal of Political Economy*, August 1994, *102*(4), pp. 745–76.

Guisinger, Stephen. "Investment Related to Trade," in Michael J. Finger and Adrzej Olechowski, eds., *The Uruguay Round: A handbook for the multilateral trade negotiations.* Washington, DC: World Bank, 1987, pp. 217–25.

Hammond, Grant T. *Countertrade, offsets, and barter in international political economy.* London: Pinter, 1990.

Hart, Oliver. "Theories of Optimal Capital Structure: A Principal–Agent Perspective." Mimeo, Massachusetts Institute of Technology, March 1991.

Hennart, Jean-François. "The Transaction-Cost Rationale for Countertrade." *Journal of Law, Economics, and Organization*, Spring 1989, *5*(1), pp. 127–53.

Hennart, Jean-François and Anderson, Erin. "Countertrade and the Minimization of Transaction Costs: An Empirical Examination." *Journal of Law, Economics, and Organization*, October 1993, *9*(2), pp. 290–313.

Jones, Stephen F. and Jagoe, Ashley. *Third World countertrade: Analysis of 1,350 deals involving developing countries, 1980–87.* Newbury, U.K.: Produce Studies, 1988.

Kogut, Bruce. "On Designing Contracts to Guarantee Enforceability: Theory and Evidence from East–West Trade." *Journal of International Business Studies*, Spring 1986, *17*(1), pp. 47–61.

Marin, Dalia. "Tying in International Trade." *World Economy*, September 1990, *13*(3), pp. 445–62.

Mirus, Rolf and Yeung, Bernard. "Economic Incentives for Countertrade." *Journal of International Business Studies*, Fall 1986, *17*(2), pp. 27–39.

OECD. *East–West trade: Recent developments in countertrade.* Paris: Organization for Economic Cooperation and Development, 1981.

______. *Countertrade: Developing country practices.* Paris: Organization for Economic Cooperation and Development, 1985.

Parsons, John E. "A Theory of Countertrade Financing of International Business." Mimeo, Massachusetts Institute of Technology, March 1985.

______. "Forms of GDR Economic Cooperation with the Nonsocialist World." *Comparative Economic Studies*, Summer 1987, *29*(2), pp. 7–18.

Verzariu, Pompiliu. *Countertrade, barter, and offsets: New strategies for profit in international trade.* New York: McGraw-Hill, 1985.

Welt, Leo G. B. *Trade without money: Barter and countertrade.* New York: Law and Business, 1984.

Williamson, Oliver E. "Credible Commitments: Using Hostages to Support Exchange." *American Economic Review*, September 1983, *73*(4), pp. 519–40.

[9]

ELSEVIER European Economic Review 42 (1998) 705–716

EUROPEAN ECONOMIC REVIEW

Economic incentives and international trade

Dalia Marin[a,c,*], Monika Schnitzer[b,c]

[a] *Humboldt University Berlin, Department of Economics, Spandauer Str. 1, D-10178 Berlin, Germany*
[b] *University of Munich, Department of Economics, Akademiestr. 1/III, D-80799 Munich, Germany*
[c] *CEPR, London, UK*

Abstract

This paper studies the importance of incentives as a determinant of international trade flows. We argue that barter, countertrade and foreign direct investment can be seen as efficient institutions that mitigate contractual hazards which arise in technology trade, marketing and imperfect capital markets. Paying an import with export goods rather than cash (barter) helps to overcome incentive problems that arise in debt repayment of highly indebted countries. Payment in export goods removes the anonymity of the medium of exchange and thus allows to create a collateral for the creditor. Furthermore, tying an import with an export (countertrade) helps to solve the incentive problems related to the technology transfer to developing countries. The export flow serves as a 'hostage' that deters cheating on the quality of the imported technology good. The predictions of the two models are consistent with the pattern of trade of actual barter and countertrade contracts. © 1998 Elsevier Science B.V. All rights reserved.

JEL classification: F13; F34; L14

Keywords: Institutions and trade; Sovereign debt; Commodity money; Technology transfer; Foreign direct investment

* Correspondence address: Humboldt University Berlin, Department of Economics, Spandauer Str. 1, D-10178 Berlin, Germany. E-mail: marin@wiwi.hu-berlin.de.

PII S0014-2921(97)00133-5

1. Introduction

Economic incentives and institutions as a determinant of trade have received relatively little attention from traditional trade theory. The main reason for this neglect seems to be that contract theory and the theory of international trade belong to two strands of the literature with separate traditions. In this paper we argue that there is much to be gained by merging these two fields. Incentives and economic institutions can play an important role in explaining international trade beyond the known determinants of trade like factor endowment, productivity, preferences, and market structure. They are particularly relevant for the explanation of international business activities such as foreign direct investment, joint ventures, alliances, barter, countertrade and other forms of international partnership, the so-called 'new forms of international business'.[1]

Table 1 illustrates with the example of East–West trade that trade takes a variety of different institutional forms. At one end of the spectrum there are spot transactions like conventional exports and imports, at the other end common ownership like joint ventures and foreign direct investment. Tying contracts like international barter and countertrade take a middle position. In a typical barter and countertrade transaction a firm or a trade organization in Eastern Europe (or a developing country) imports from a developed country and commits itself to export goods to this country in return. Thus, barter and countertrade are market transactions which bind the parties together.

Why do we observe these different contract forms in international trade? Some experts have argued that in particular barter and countertrade are an outcome of central planning. Due to a political ownership constraint, joint ventures and foreign direct investment were rare before 1989 and started to grow only since then.[2] But as Table 1 shows, although barter and countertrade declined in some countries (like the Czech Republic, Poland and Hungary) their importance increased in others (like the former Soviet Union, Bulgaria and Romania). Barter also regained importance in domestic trade in most of the former Soviet Union.[3] Furthermore, the same institutional arrangements can be found in trade with developing countries.[4] An alternative explanation is therefore warranted. We instead see these forms as institutional arrangements which promote efficient international exchange when parties have short run temptations to cheat and when alternative mechanisms, e.g. based on repeated interaction, fail

[1] Oman (1984).

[2] See also Lankes and Venables (1996).

[3] Estimates suggest that in the Ukraine 43% of exports and 50–70% of domestic trade took the form of barter in 1994. In Russia barter as percent of industrial sales increased from 6% in 1992 to 40% in the first quarter of 1997; see Transition Report 1997, European Bank for Reconstruction and Development, London.

[4] See OECD (1981, 1985).

Table 1
The institutional structure of East–West trade

		Exports Imports (%)	Barter Countertrade[a] (%)		Joint ventures Foreign direct investment[b] (%)	
Before 1989		~ 60	~ 40		0	
After 1989			1990	1995	1990	1995
	Hungary				3.6	22.7
	Poland				0.4	8.6
	Czech Republic				1.2	12.0
	Slovakia				0.6	2.9
	Russia		~ 50		1.6	4.3
	Romania		~ 10	~ 6	1.2	4.0
	Bulgaria				0.9	2.7
	Ukraine		~ 50	~ 20[c]		

Source: World Investment Report 1994 and 1996; Countries in Transition 1996. The Vienna Institute for Comparative Economic Studies; OECD: East–West Trade: Recent Developments in Countertrade, 1981.
[a] Percentage of total trade.
[b] Incoming foreign direct investments as a ratio of total imports of the respective country.
[c] 1996.

to be effective. Formal institutions are therefore required to substitute for informal arrangements such as reputation.[5]

In this paper we focus on barter and countertrade to analyse the role of formal institutions which govern international trade. Two stylized facts on countertrade and barter stand out that need to be explained. First, they tend to take place in countries which are highly indebted. The debt to GDP ratio of countertrading countries varies between 4.5% and 327%. Second, the trade pattern within barter and countertrade differs significantly form that in conventional trade. Table 2 illustrates this on the example of East–West trade. Within countertrade and barter more than 70% of Eastern European imports from the OECD are machinery and equipment compared to 36% in conventional imports. On the export side, Eastern Europe's exports to the OECD consist of 36%

[5] Bulow and Rogoff (1989) show that reputation as an enforcement mechanism fails to be effective in international capital markets when the debtor can costlessly switch to cash in advance contracts. In a notable paper, Greif et al. (1994) analyse merchant gilds in the Middle Ages as an efficiency enhancing institution to deal with moral hazard problems in international trade when a reputation mechanism cannot solve these incentive problems. For an overview of other institutions governing international trade in the Commercial Revolution see Greif (1992). For an institutional approach to the form of trade liberalisation see Yarbrough and Yarbrough (1992).

Table 2
Pattern of trade with Eastern europe in 1987

	Imports from OECD countries[a] (%)		Exports to OECD countries[a] (%)	
	Countertrade (1)	Total trade[b] (2)	Countertrade (3)	Total trade[b] (4)
Machinery and equipment	70.9	35.7	35.5	17.7
Consumer goods	8.8	8.2	31.9	16.4
Basic goods	3.6[d]	43.7[c]	18.4[d]	47.9[c]
Chemicals	8.8		8.2	
Services	4.0	n.a.	6.0	n.a.
Foods and agricultural products		10.4		10.9

Source: Sample of 230 countertrade comtracts; Comecon Data 1989. The Vienna Institute for Comparative Economic Studies, Vienna.
[a] The percentages of columns 1 and 3 refer to the total of 230 countertrade contracts of the sample. The percentages of columns 2 and 4 refer to imports and exports of Eastern Europe. Eastern Europe is here defined as to consist of Poland, Hungary, Czechoslovakia, and the Soviet Union. These four countries cover more than 60 percent of the 230 countertrade contracts of the sample. The four countries enter with the following respective weights: 0.115, 0.235, 0.407 and 0.243. These weights correspond to the importance of the respective country in the countertrade sample.
[b] This column gives the CMEA classification of commodity groups called CMEA Trade Nomenclature (CTN): CTN1 machinry and equipment, CTN9 consumer goods, CTN2-5 basic goods and CTN6-8 food and agricultural products.
[c] Includes chemical products also.
[d] Includes food and agricultural products also.

machinery and equipment and 32% consumer goods within countertrade, while the same categories account for only 18% and 16%, respectively, in conventional exports.

Barter and countertrade are typically criticized for their inefficiency because of their reciprocity features and the need of a double coincidence of wants. We therefore ask two questions. First, why would parties want to tie an import with an export (countertrade)? Second, in a fully developed monetary world economy why would parties agree to pay in goods rather than money (barter)? The answer that we give in this paper is that by doing so the trade partners can solve incentive problems which otherwise would prevent trade from taking place at all. In Section 2 we show that paying with goods rather than money helps to overcome the creditworthiness problem of highly indebted countries. In Section 3 we focus on the import pattern of countertrade and show that countertrade promotes efficient technology transfer and thus is a first best substitute for common ownership like foreign direct investment. In Section 4 we derive the export pattern of barter by identifying which goods will qualify as means of payment.

2. The institutional organization of trade

Consider two potential trade partners, A, a firm in a Western country, and B, a firm in an Eastern European or developing country. B would like to buy one unit of good 1 from A but since he is short of foreign exchange he cannot pay when good 1 is delivered. One period later, B can produce and sell one unit of good 2 on the world market to generate sufficient revenues to pay for good 1. The problem is, however, that A cannot enforce this payment unless B provides a collateral that A can seize in case of repudiation. Assets in B's country cannot serve as collaterals since in case of conflict A depends on the cooperation of B's country to enforce her claim on these assets. Thus, B's creditworthiness depends on his ability to provide collaterals that are in A's reach if he should refuse payment. In the remainder of this paper we will focus on the case where B is highly indebted already, so that almost no collaterals are left for additional transactions like buying good 1 on a credit basis.

To make ideas precise let v_1 denote B's valuation of good 1 and c_1 denote A's production cost. B's revenues from selling good 2 on the world market are given by v_2 and his production cost are c_2. Finally, a represents the amount of collateral that B has left to guarantee future payments. We assume that $v_1 > c_1$, $v_2 > c_2$ and $v_2 > c_1$, i.e. both transactions are potentially profitable and B's revenues from selling good 2 are sufficient to cover A's productions cost for good 1 (we assume that there is no discounting). However, $a < c_1$, i.e. if A sells good 1 on a credit basis she cannot insure a repayment sufficiently high to recover her production cost. Thus, a conventional trade cannot take place because B cannot guarantee that he will pay for good 1 once he has sufficient funds available.

Suppose now that instead of selling good 2 himself B promises to deliver good 2 to A as payment of good 1. Why should this make any difference to A? The point is that in case of such a barter contract A acquires property rights on good 2 which can now serve as an additional deal-specific collateral. If B should try to cheat on A and sell good 2 on the world market instead of delivering it to A as specified in the barter contract A can ask courts to intervene. In this case B's expected payoff from going to the world market is reduced to $\pi_2 \leq (v_2 - c_2)$. Thus, B voluntarily delivers good 2 to A if and only if

$$v_1 - c_2 \geq v_1 - a + \pi_2. \tag{1}$$

On the other hand, A is willing to deliver good 1 to B if and only if condition (1) is satisfied and in addition

$$v_2 - c_1 \geq 0. \tag{2}$$

Proposition 1. *Barter trade can overcome B's lack of creditworthiness if and only if*

$$v_2 \geq c_1 - a + c_2 + \pi_2. \tag{3}$$

Proof. See the appendix.

Proposition 1 shows that the moral hazard problem of debt repayment can be solved only if the problem of creditworthiness is not too severe; i.e. a is not too small, if the deal-specific collateral v_2 is sufficiently large, and if π_2 is sufficiently small; i.e. if A can successfully label good 2 as her property.[6] The advantage of paying with goods rather than money is that goods are less anonymous than money and thus they can be earmarked as property of the creditor. If A could not label and identify good 2 as her own collateral in case of conflict, nothing could keep B from selling it to someone else. But since goods act like special purpose money they are better collaterals than cash.[7]

So far we have implicitly assumed that good 2 is homogeneous like basic goods and commodities. This means in particular that it involves no quality problem. If good 2 is instead differentiated like consumer and investment goods an additional incentive problem arises, because B may deliver low quality. This tends to make differentiated goods less liquid than homogeneous products.

To capture this idea suppose that there are just two quality levels, high and low, and that product quality is not verifiable. With high quality, the production cost of good 2 are c_2 and the valuation is v_2, with low quality, both production cost and valuation are normalized to 0. Since A cannot verify the product quality B is tempted to fulfill his payment obligations at no cost by delivering a low quality good 2. If this happens, A cannot even claim collateral a even though good 2 is worthless to her.

This problem is particularly acute if B has not sold this good before and thus potential customers have no experience with it. One possible solution is that A invests in the marketing of good 2 on the world market to make new consumers learn about B's product and product quality. As a result, B experiences a positive spillover on his future export revenues if he delivers good quality now. Let b denote B's future gain if A makes a marketing investment i and B delivers high quality. Then B prefers to deliver high quality to low quality if and only if

$$v_1 + b - c_2 \geq v_1, \tag{4}$$

[6] See Marin and Schnitzer (1997) for a discussion how this relates to the literature on sovereign debt.

[7] For the use of countertrade goods as collaterals see Marin and Schnitzer (1995, 1997) and the references cited there.

and he prefers to deliver high quality rather than not to deliver at all if and only if

$$v_1 + b - c_2 \geq v_1 - a + \pi_2. \tag{5}$$

Note that Eq. (5) implies Eq. (6) if $a \geq \pi_2$. A will deliver good 1 and carry out the necessary marketing investment i for good 2 if and only if

$$v_2 - c_1 - i \geq 0. \tag{6}$$

Proposition 2. *If differentiated goods are chosen to collateralize B's future payment barter trade can restore B's creditworthiness if and only if*

$$v_2 - c_1 - i \geq 0 \geq c_2 - b - \min(0; a - \pi_2). \tag{7}$$

Homogeneous and differentiated goods differ in two dimensions, in their liquidity and (potentially) in their anonymity. Differentiated goods are less liquid than homogeneous products because of the uncertainty about product quality. But they also have the advantage that B can be given an additional incentive to fulfill his contractual obligation by helping him to market goods that otherwise are difficult to export. In addition, differentiated goods can be made even less anonymous with A's marketing investment which again improves their property as a collateral.[8]

3. The import pattern

In this section we focus on the question why it might be desirable to tie an import with an export. So far we have assumed that good 1 is homogeneous and no incentive problem on A's side arises in this transaction. But as Table 1 shows most imports to EE or LDCs within countertrade consist of technology and machinery where similar quality problems are present. Since it is often difficult for B to verify the quality of technology goods he cannot legally condition his payment on A's quality choice. This means that A has low-powered incentives to deliver high-quality technology in the first place. This phenomenon has become known as the problem of technology transfer to developing countries.

To illustrate this suppose that A can deliver two different quality levels but B cannot verify this quality on delivery. We normalize values such that if high quality is delivered, B's valuation is v_1 and A's production cost are c_1, with $v_1 > c_1$. If low quality is delivered both production cost and B's valuation are

[8] An empirical analysis how different types of goods can be ranked with respect to their liquidity and anonymity can be found in Marin and Schnitzer (1997).

zero. Suppose furthermore that B agrees to pay good 1 by delivering a differentiated good as described in the previous section.

The following argument shows how a countertrade contract can induce A to deliver high quality. The idea is to make B's payment contingent on A's quality choice in the sense that if A delivers low-quality technology, B will not be able to produce good 2 because he cannot generate enough revenues from the technology and thus has not enough funds to purchase the inputs required for the production of good 2. Thus, if A cheats on quality she loses her collateral. Although good 1 and 2 are not technologically related the countertrade contract establishes a financial link. In order for B to hit a financial constraint in case of bad quality we need the following two conditions.

$$a + v_1 - c_2 \geq 0, \tag{8}$$

$$a - c_2 \leq 0. \tag{9}$$

Condition (8), on the one hand ensures that B can finance good 2 out of his revenues from using good 1 and potentially collateral a. Condition (9), on the other hand, implies that B cannot finance good 2 out of this collateral a alone and thus cannot produce and deliver good 2 if low quality technology is delivered.[9] Recall that conditions (4) and (5) above make sure that B delivers a high-quality product as payment for good 1 if he is able to do so. A in turn is willing to deliver high quality (and make the relevant marketing investment) if and only if condition (6) is satisfied.

Proposition 3. *Countertrade can induce an efficient technology transfer and restore B's creditworthiness if only if*

(i) $v_1 - c_1 + v_2 - c_2 + a \geq i$,
(ii) $b \geq c_2 \geq a$,
(iii) $b \geq \pi_2$,
(iv) $v_2 + b - c_2 - i \geq \max\{0, \pi_2 - a\} + c_1$.

Proof. See the appendix.

Proposition 3 proves that a market transaction, if embedded in a countertrade arrangement, can achieve an efficient technology transfer and is thus a first best substitute for a hierarchical solution like foreign direct investment. The point is that the export flow serves as a hostage in the sense of Williamson (1983) which deters cheating on the import of the technology good because if A cheats

[9] Note that b cannot be used as collateral because it is an unverifiable spillover benefit that cannot be seized by potential creditors.

she loses her collateral.[10] Conditions (i) to (iv) imply that for this construction to work the hostage has to be sufficiently valuable, measured by $(v_2 + b - c_2)$, compared to the gains from cheating as measured by c_1 and π_2. Our contractual solution to *A*'s moral hazard problem uses the fact that *B* faces a financial constraint. If *B* were able to produce good 2 all by himself, independent of what *A* delivers, then condition (9) could not be satisfied and *A* could not internalize her own quality decision. Thus, the fact that barter is used by countries with a severe financial constraint makes it particularly effective to solve the problem of technology transfer.[11]

4. The export pattern

In this section we ask which goods are chosen as collateral, i.e. what determines the pattern of exports in barter trade. Trade theory predicts that the trade pattern of a particular country is determined by its comparative advantage. This implies that *B* should use the goods as payment which yield the highest possible surplus, i.e. in which *B*'s country has a comparative advantage. Even if there is a bilateral monopoly situation as in our case, the Coase Theorem still predicts that in the absence of transaction costs *A* and *B* choose the most efficient product as collateral. However, the incentive problems considered in this paper may make this impossible.

We have seen that in order to solve *B*'s creditworthiness problem it is important to make sure that *B* voluntarily delivers good 2 and, if it is differentiated, that it is of high quality. This suggests (and is proved formally in the appendix) that homogeneous goods are preferable as means of payment in barter since they involve no additional quality problem. But our analysis in the previous section also suggests that differentiated products are to be preferred as 'hostage' for *A*'s technology since a positive marketing benefit *b* is required to achieve an efficient technology transfer (see condition (ii) of Proposition 3) because it makes it easier to provide incentives for *B* to deliver good 2 without violating his financial constraint. We expect these incentive problems to be reflected in the pattern of exports in barter. Our theory predicts that countries which differ in their creditworthiness will show a different pattern of barter trade. More specifically, countries with low creditworthiness will use more liquid goods, i.e. homogeneous goods as means of payment for their imports,

[10] Parsons (1985, 1987) and Chan and Hoy (1991) have argued that countertrade can mitigate the technology transfer problem if the export good is produced directly with the technology imported. Our solution, however, does not require such a technological link between the two trade flows.

[11] A more extensive analysis including also renegotiation can be found in Marin and Schnitzer (1995).

714 D. Marin, M. Schnitzer / European Economic Review 42 (1998) 705–716

Table 3
Creditworthiness and trade pattern

	Barter exports in percent	Debt/GDP Mean	Std. dev.	No. of cases
Eastern Europe[a]	86.2	33.8	26.4	194
Export pattern[b]				
Investment goods	38.7	28.8	24.1	75
Consumer goods	35.6	38.3	28.6	69
Basic goods	13.4	34.4	26.3	26
Chemicals	7.2	33.4	22.9	14
Services	5.2	42.8	30.4	10
Developing countries[c]	13.8	76.6	72.1	27
Export pattern[d]				
Consumer goods	22.2	51.4	33.4	6
Basic goods	51.9	97.1	81.2	14
Chemicals	25.9	57.4	72.6	7
Total		39.1	37.7	221
ANOVA	$F = 35.2$, Marginal significance 0.000			

[a] Former Soviet Union, former GDR, former Czechoslovakia, Hungary, Poland, former Yugoslavia, Rumania, Bulgaria, Albania.
[b] Brazil, Ecuador, Argentina, Nicaragua, Philippines, Indonesia, Malaysia, China, Israel, Iran, Egypt, Algeria, Syria, Cyprus, Togo, Zambia, Zimbabwe.
[c] The percentages in the first column refer to total barter exports from Eastern Europe.
[d] The percentages in the first column refer to total barter exports from LDCs.

while countries more concerned about technology transfer will use differentiated goods to collateralize their future payment.

We confront this prediction with data on 230 countertrade and barter contracts in Table 3 where we examine (with an analysis of variance ANOVA) whether developing countries and Eastern European countries show a different pattern of specialization.[12] This is indeed supported by the data. Developing countries with an average debt to GDP ratio of 76.6 are substantially less creditworthy than Eastern Europe with an average debt to GDP ratio of 33.8 in 1987. Moreover, under central planning, when the system prohibited foreign ownership of assets, Eastern Europe was much more concerned about achieving an efficient technology transfer than the developing countries with no such political ownership constraint on foreign assets. Table 3 confirms that developing countries use predominatly the most liquid goods, basic goods, as means of

[12] For details on this data set see Marin (1990).

payment in barter. In contrast, Eastern Europe with its better creditworthiness and concern about technology transfer uses differentiated goods like consumer and investment goods as means of payment in barter. Payments in consumer goods provided a sufficiently valuable hostage to deter cheating on the technology imports.

Appendix A.

Proof of Proposition 1. The necessity of Eq. (3) is straightforward to see. To prove its sufficiency note that Eq. (2) is satisfied by assumption. The only possible problem thus is that condition (1) is violated, i.e.

$$c_2 + \pi_2 - a > 0. \tag{A.1}$$

If this were the case A could induce B to deliver good 2 by making a voluntary monetary side payment s conditional on B's delivery. As long as (3) holds it is possible to find a side payment such that

$$v_2 - c_1 - s \geq 0 \geq c_2 + \pi_2 - a - s. \qquad \text{Q.E.D.} \tag{A.2}$$

Proof of Proposition 3. To prove necessity, note that condition (i) is implied by Eq. (8) together with Eq. (6), condition (ii) by Eq. (9) together with Eq. (4), condition (iii) by Eq. (9) together with Eq. (5), and condition (iv) by Eq. (6) together with Eqs. (4) and (5), respectively. To prove sufficiency, note further that (i) ensures that Eqs. (8) and (6) can be fulfilled, possibly by making a side payment s such that $a + v_1 - c_2 + s \geq 0 \geq c_1 + i - v_2 + s$. Furthermore, (ii) guarantees that Eqs. (9) and (4) are satisfied. Finally, (iii) ensures that Eq. (5) can be satisfied, possibly by making a side payment s from A to B in case of delivery such that $b - c_2 + a - \pi_2 + s \geq 0 \geq a - c_2 + s$. Q.E.D.

Proposition 4. *The creditworthiness problem creates a bias towards choosing homogeneous goods as collateral in the following sense:*

(a) *If a homogeneous good is more efficient than a differentiated good and the differentiated good fulfills all incentive constraints, then the homogeneous good does so too.*

(b) *If a differentiated good is more efficient than a homogeneous good and the homogeneous good fulfills all incentive constraints, it is possible that the differentiated goods does not and thus cannot serve as a collateral.*

Proof. To prove part (b) consider the following example. Suppose first that the differentiated good is more efficient than the homogeneous one in the sense that $v_2^{\mathrm{d}} - c_2^{\mathrm{d}} + b - i > v_2^{\mathrm{h}} - c_2^{\mathrm{h}}$. Suppose further that $a - \pi_2 > c_2^{\mathrm{h}}$ but that $b < c_2^{\mathrm{d}}$. Then the incentive constraint for homogeneous goods, (1), is satisfied but not for differentiated goods, (4). Since quality is nonverifiable A cannot induce B to deliver high quality by promising an additional side payment in case of high quality. Thus, it is not possible to use the differentiated good as a collateral even though it is more efficient.

To prove part (a) suppose that the homogeneous good is more efficient and that the incentive constraint for differentiated goods (5) and (6) are fulfilled. Since condition (8) for differentiated goods is more restrictive than condition (3) for homogenous goods this implies that the incentive constraint for homogeneous goods, Eq. (1), can be satisfied too, if necessary by offering an additional side payment to B in case of the (verifiable) delivery of good 2. Q.E.D.

References

Bulow, L., Rogoff, K., 1989. A constant recontracting model of sovereign debt. Journal of Political Economy 97, 155–178.

Chan, R., Hoy, M., 1991. East–West joint ventures and buyback contracts. Journal of International Economics 30, 331–343.

Greif, A., 1992. Institutions and International Trade: Lessons from the commercial revolution. American Economic Review 82, Papers and Proceedings, 128–133.

Greif, A., Milgrom, P., Weingast, B.R., 1994. Coordination, commitment, and enforcement: The case of the merchant guild. Journal of Political Economy 102, 745–776.

Lankes, D., Venables, A., 1996. Foreign direct investment in economic transition : The changing pattern of investments. Economics of Transition 4, 331–347.

Marin, D., 1990. Tying in international trade. The World Economy 3, 445–462.

Marin, D., Schnitzer, M., 1995. Tying trade flows : A theory of countertrade with evidence. American Economic Review 85, 1047–1064.

Marin, D., Schnitzer, M., 1997. The economic institution of international barter. CEPR Discussion Paper No 1658, London.

OECD, 1981. East–West trade: Recent Developments in Countertrade, Paris.

OECD, 1985. Countertrade: Developing Country Practices, Paris.

Oman, C. (Ed.), 1984. New Forms of International Investment in Developing Countries. OECD, Paris.

Parsons, J.E., 1985. A theory of countertrade financing of international business. Mimeo., Cambridge, MA. Massachusetts Institute of Technology.

Parsons, J.E., 1987. Forms of GDR economic cooperation with the nonsocialist world. Comparative Economic Studies 29, 7–18.

Yarbrough, B.V., Yarbrough, R.M., 1992. Cooperation and Governance in International Trade. Princeton University Press, Princeton.

Williamson, O., 1983. Credible commitments: Using hostages to support exchange. American Economic Review 73, 519–540.

[10]

Journal of International Economics 30 (1991) 331–343. North-Holland

East–West joint ventures and buyback contracts

Raissa Chan

Hongkong and Shanghai Banking Corporation Ltd

Michael Hoy*

University of Guelph, Guelph, Ontario N1G 2W1, Canada, and *University of Southampton, Southampton SO9 5NH, UK*

Received August 1989, revised version received August 1990

Contractual joint ventures (CJVs) and the buyback form of countertrade are popular methods that Socialist countries use to attract foreign investment. In this paper we explore some reasons why this is so and also explain two predominant characteristics of these contracts: the existence of sharing rules and minimum standard requirements on inputs. The model stresses the incentive problems involved when a (Socialist) host country, which does not allow foreign direct investment, uses a CJV to obtain the fruits of some knowledge-based production process from a multinational enterprise.

1. Introduction

Contractual joint ventures and the buyback form of countertrade are popular methods that Socialist countries use to attract foreign investment.[1] In this paper we explore some reasons why this is so and also explain two predominant characteristics of these contracts: the existence of sharing rules and minimum standard requirements on inputs.

*The second author's work on this paper was mostly done while visiting the Economics Department at the University of Southampton, whose support and hospitality were greatly appreciated. We wish to thank seminar participants at the universities at Guelph, British Columbia (the faculty of Commerce and Business Administration), Southampton, Munich, Exeter and York for useful comments, and in particular to Jim Brander, Ron Giammarino, Ray Rees, Clive Southey, and Barbara Spencer. Wai Fan Chan and Margaret Wheatstone both provided valuable research assistance. Also, the perceptive comments from two referees have led to substantial improvements in an earlier version. Any remaining shortcomings are, naturally, our own responsibility.

[1]Campbell (1988) reports that for the period 1979–85, following China's open door policy, contractual joint ventures make up 49% of all money committed for foreign investment while, for example, wholly owned foreign enterprises account for only 3%. Buyback is a specific form of joint venture that involves sharing of output rather than revenue. For a discussion of the importance of such practices in Eastern European countries, see OECD (1985, pp. 11–12) and Welt (1984).

Consider the following economic environment. A multinational corporation (MNC) possesses a 'knowledge-based production process'[2] that requires skilled labour or information which the host (Socialist) country does not possess. Moreover, the host country enterprise (HCE) resides in a socialist country that does not allow direct foreign investment (FDI).[3] Unable to write legally enforceable contracts for the 'purchase' of a specified quality level of the MNC's production process, a joint venture contract may be a suitable way to obtain the fruits of the said process. However, there is a natural tendency for either party to shirk if it is not the full residual claimant to the stream of profits from the production process. The problem of an insufficient supply of productive inputs that arises from free-riding in closed organizational forms, such as partnerships, is nicely illustrated by Holmstrom (1982), who shows that it is a consequence of imposing a balanced budget, when sharing output, that causes this phenomenon. The scope for contract forms which may limit such a 'double moral hazard' possibility is severely limited by the lack of a single comprehensive legal institution.

In this paper we consider the use of joint venture contracts as a means to ameliorate this problem. In particular, we present a simple model that shows that a sharing rule for output or revenues in conjunction with a set of minimum standards requirements on some inputs behave as complementary instruments to reduce the efficiency loss inherent in this environment. The model is presented in section 2 along with the essential results. In section 3 some simple extensions to the basic model are carried out and various related issues involving possible future research are considered, such as the possible role of technology transfer. A concluding section follows.

2. The model and results

To begin, consider a very simple model describing a joint venture between a multinational corporation (MNC) from an industrialized (Western) country and a host country enterprise (HCE) from a Socialist (Eastern) country. Together the enterprises represent the sole producer of the good in the host country, but with each providing a single input, x_w and x_e, respectively, used to produce an output $Q=Q(x_e,x_w)$. Both x_e and x_w (and possibly Q) represent quality adjusted levels. The following set of assumptions is made about the production process (subscripts e and w are used in place of x_e and x_w):

[2]For a discussion of this issue, but excluding the East–West aspect of the phenomenon, see Horstmann and Markusen (1987).

[3]This may be due to the divergence between market prices and true values of inputs in the host country, or simply political reasons.

$$Q_i > 0, \quad Q_{ii} < 0, \quad i = \mathrm{e}, \mathrm{w},$$
$$Q_{\mathrm{ew}} > 0, \quad \text{and} \quad Q(0, \cdot) = Q(\cdot, 0) = 0. \tag{1}$$

We also assume decreasing returns to scale and that $Q(\cdot,\cdot)$ is both strictly concave and twice continuously differentiable. The effects of relaxing some of these assumptions, in particular allowing for $Q_{\mathrm{ew}} < 0$, are considered later.[4]

Input prices for x_{e} and x_{w} are r_{e} and r_{w}, respectively, while P is the price of the output. For convenience we assume zero fixed costs and treat all prices as exogenously fixed.[5] Therefore, aggregate profit from production is as follows:

$$\Pi = PQ(x_{\mathrm{e}}, x_{\mathrm{w}}) - r_{\mathrm{e}}x_{\mathrm{e}} - r_{\mathrm{w}}x_{\mathrm{w}}. \tag{2}$$

We define the first-best equilibrium (FBE) as the pair of input levels $(\bar{x}_{\mathrm{e}}^{\mathrm{F}}, \bar{x}_{\mathrm{w}}^{\mathrm{F}})$ that maximize aggregate profits. It is useful, for purposes developed later, to generate what we call conditional first-best input choice functions, $x_{\mathrm{e}}^{\mathrm{F}} = \mathbb{F}_{\mathrm{e}}(x_{\mathrm{w}})$ and $x_{\mathrm{w}}^{\mathrm{F}} = \mathbb{F}_{\mathrm{w}}(x_{\mathrm{e}})$, as defined according to eqs. (3) and (4) below. For example, $x_{\mathrm{e}}^{\mathrm{F}} = \mathbb{F}_{\mathrm{e}}(x_{\mathrm{w}})$ depicts the profit-maximizing input level that the HCE would choose if it could costlessly determine and enforceably contract for some specified level of x_{w} to be provided by the MNC, thus allowing the HCE to be a full residual claimant to profits and eliminating any moral hazard problem. T_{ij}, $i, j = \mathrm{e}, \mathrm{w}$, $i \neq j$, represents a payment from enterprise i to j for the latter's input.

$$x_{\mathrm{e}}^{\mathrm{F}} = \mathbb{F}_{\mathrm{e}}(x_{\mathrm{w}}) : x_{\mathrm{e}}^{\mathrm{F}} = \operatorname{argmax} \Pi_{\mathrm{e}}^{\mathrm{F}} = PQ(x_{\mathrm{e}}, x_{\mathrm{w}}) - r_{\mathrm{e}}x_{\mathrm{e}} - T_{\mathrm{ew}}, \tag{3}$$

$$x_{\mathrm{w}}^{\mathrm{F}} = \mathbb{F}_{\mathrm{w}}(x_{\mathrm{e}}) : x_{\mathrm{w}}^{\mathrm{F}} = \operatorname{argmax} \Pi_{\mathrm{w}}^{\mathrm{F}} = PQ(x_{\mathrm{e}}, x_{\mathrm{w}}) - r_{\mathrm{w}}x_{\mathrm{w}} - T_{\mathrm{we}}. \tag{4}$$

The intersection of these curves gives the FBE. For later use, it is convenient to note that *aggregate* iso-profit lines satisfy the following properties relative to these $\mathbb{F}$-curves: (i) they have zero slope where they intersect the $\mathbb{F}$-curves, i.e. $\mathrm{d}x_{\mathrm{w}}/\mathrm{d}x_{\mathrm{e}}|_{\mathrm{d}\Pi=0} = 0$ along $\mathbb{F}_{\mathrm{e}}(x_{\mathrm{w}})$ and $\mathrm{d}x_{\mathrm{e}}/\mathrm{d}x_{\mathrm{w}}|_{\mathrm{d}\Pi=0} = 0$ along $\mathbb{F}_{\mathrm{w}}(x_{\mathrm{e}})$; and, within the region enclosed by the $\mathbb{F}$-curves they are (ii) negatively sloped and (iii) convex to the origin. These are all a result of concavity of the production function (see fig. 1).

With the first-best equilibrium (FBE) as a benchmark, we now analyse the properties of three types of equilibria that result from different forms of

[4]It is standard to assume that increasing one input leads to an increase in the marginal product of the other input(s). However, considering $Q_{\mathrm{ew}} < 0$ will allow for the possibility that these inputs are strategic substitutes (see section 3).

[5]As sole producer of the good in the host country, holding output price fixed is overly restrictive. However, it is shown in section 3 that one can use a more general formulation to relax these assumptions.

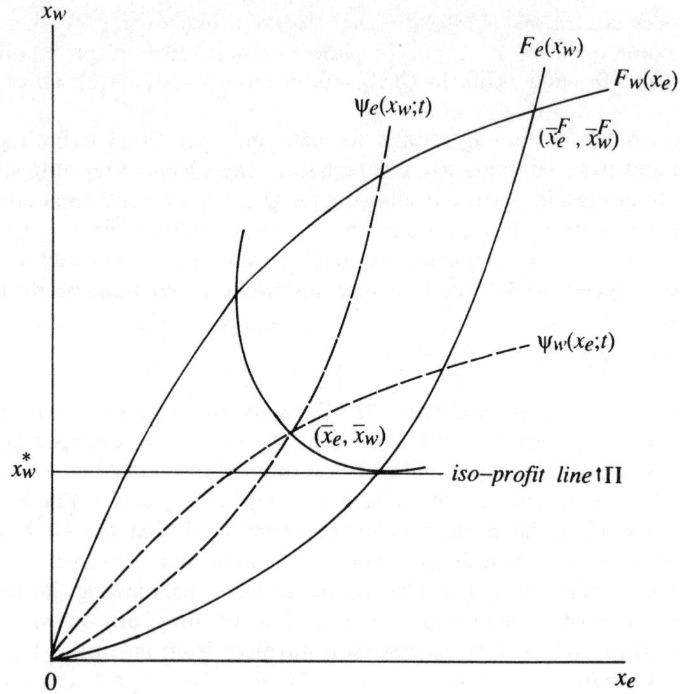

Fig. 1

contracts. First, let (t, T) define a sharing rule with $t \in (0, 1)$ being the share (fraction) of revenue or output received by the HCE and $(1-t)$ by the MNC. T is a lump-sum transfer from the HCE to the MNC, but may be negative. Profits for each enterprise are

$$\Pi_e = tPQ(x_e, x_w) - r_e x_e - T, \tag{5}$$

$$\Pi_w = (1-t)PQ(x_e, x_w) - r_w x_w + T. \tag{6}$$

Definition 1. A sharing rule equilibrium (SRE) is the outcome of each organization maximizing its profit [respectively eqs. (5) and (6)] for a given pair (t, T) on the basis of its conjecture about the other organization's choice, made in the standard Cournot–Nash fashion. The value of t is chosen to maximize aggregate profit.

A SRE is, therefore, a two-stage process similar to the model of warranties in Cooper and Ross (1985). In the second (noncooperative) stage, each organization chooses its input in order to maximize its profit given its (Cournot) conjecture about the other organization's input level. This leads to the following reaction functions:

$$x_e = \psi_e(x_w; t): x_e = \text{argmax}\, \Pi_e(x_e \mid x_w) = tPQ(x_e, x_w) - r_e x_e - T, \tag{7}$$

$$x_w = \psi_w(x_e; t): x_w = \text{argmax}\, \Pi_w(x_w \mid x_e) = (1-t)PQ(x_e, x_w) - r_w x_w + T. \tag{8}$$

It is clear from the first-order conditions to these maximization problems, which are given below as eqs, (9) and (10), that the value of T has no effect on the input choices:

$$tPQ_e(x_e, x_w) - r_e = 0, \tag{9}$$

$$(1-t)PQ_w(x_e, x_w) - r_w = 0. \tag{10}$$

The Cournot–Nash solution is indicated by $(\bar{x}_e, \bar{x}_w)$ in fig. 1. Upon total differentiation of the first-order conditions [eqs. (9) and (10)], it is easy to see that: (i) provided $Q_{ew} > 0$, the reaction functions are upward sloping with respect to the other organization's input, and (ii) an increase in t will shift the HCE's (MNC's) reaction function towards (away from) the $\mathbb{F}_e/(\mathbb{F}_w)$ curve. It is also easy to see that the HCE's reaction function will lead to (conditional) first-best input choices only if $t=1$ [i.e. $\psi_e(x_w; t) \equiv \mathbb{F}_e(x_w)$ iff $t=1$] while this is the case for the MNC only if $t=0$ [i.e. $\psi_w(x_e; t) \equiv \mathbb{F}_w(x_e)$ iff $t=0$]. Therefore the SRE cannot reproduce the FBE. The following comparison between these two equilibria is precisely analogous to Propositions 1 and 2 in Cooper and Ross (1985). It is therefore not proved here but is illustrated by fig. 1.[6]

Proposition 1. Suppose a unique SRE (sharing rule equilibrium) exists. It will have the following properties: (i) *the sharing rule will involve a t such that* $0 < t < 1$; (ii) *less of each input and hence less output will result in comparison with the first-best equilibrium (FBE); and* (iii) *a lower aggregate profit results than for the FBE.*

A sharing rule is one method of dealing with the two-sided moral hazard problem inherent in this economic relationship. A second we consider is the use of minimum standards requirements, which are generally also present in joint venture contracts. Other, more sophisticated, remedies such as imperfect monitoring may in practice be difficult to enforce given the absence of a

[6]Also, see Cooper and Ross (1985) for a discussion about uniqueness.

single, comprehensive legal system for enforcing contracts between the two parties.[7]

Thus, suppose the HCE is able to determine, before the production process begins, whether the input from the MNC achieves some minimal quality level, $\hat{x}_w$, which may well be less than the first-best one, $\bar{x}_w^F$. For example, certain credentials may signal a minimum quality level for some type of labour to be used. As an alternative to the SRE we have the following possibility.

Definition 2. Suppose the HCE contracts with the MNC to provide input level $\hat{x}_w$ in exchange for monetary compensation T_{ew}, with the HCE being a full residual claimant to the profits. Maximization of profits implies the HCE chooses its input level in a (conditional) first-best fashion; that is, $\tilde{x}_e = \mathbb{F}_e(\hat{x}_w)$ [see eq. (3)]. Such an outcome is referred to here as a minimum standards equilibrium (MSE).

Clearly, if $\hat{x}_w$ is 'close to' its first-best level, one can generate 'close to' first-best aggregate profits from this arrangement and the MSE will be preferred to the SRE. Alternatively, if $\hat{x}_w$ is 'close to' zero, then the profit from the SRE will dominate.

Proposition 2. (i) *A MSE with $\hat{x}_w = \bar{x}_w$, the level of input provided by the MNC in the SRE, generates higher aggregate profit than does the SRE.* (ii) *Aggregate profit for the MSE is monotonically increasing in $\hat{x}_w \in [0, \bar{x}_w^F)$.* (iii) *There exists a critical minimum quality level for $\hat{x}_w$, call it $x_w^*(<\bar{x}_w)$, such that the MSE will generate the same level of aggregate profit as does the SRE.*

Proof. (i) A MSE is characterized by $x_w = \hat{x}_w$ and $\tilde{x}_e = \mathbb{F}_e(\hat{x}_w)$, which maximizes $\tilde{\Pi}_e = PQ(x_e, \hat{x}_w) - r_e x_e - T_{ew}$. A SRE is characterized by the pair $(\bar{x}_e, \bar{x}_w)$, which satisfy eqs. (9) and (10). If $\hat{x}_w = \bar{x}_w$, it follows from eqs. (3), (7) and (9) that $d\tilde{\Pi}_e/dx_e = PQ_e - r_e > 0$ at $x_e = \bar{x}_e$. Therefore, $\tilde{x}_e > \bar{x}_e$, and $\Pi(\tilde{x}_e, \hat{x}_w) > \Pi(\bar{x}_e, \bar{x}_w)$ when $\hat{x}_w = \bar{x}_w$.

For (ii) and (iii) note that $\tilde{x}_e = \mathbb{F}_e(\hat{x}_w)$, i.e. $\tilde{x}_e$ is chosen so that $PQ_e(\tilde{x}_e, \hat{x}_w) - r_e = 0$. Upon total differentiation of this first-order condition we get $d\tilde{x}_e/d\hat{x}_w = -Q_{ew}/Q_{ee} > 0$. Since Q_{ew} and Q_{ee} are continuous functions, then so is $\mathbb{F}_e(\hat{x}_w)$. Moreover, aggregate profit for the MSE can also be written as a continuous function of $\hat{x}_w: \Pi_{MSE}(\hat{x}_w) = \Pi(\mathbb{F}_e(\hat{x}_w), \hat{x}_w) = PQ(\mathbb{F}(\hat{x}_w), \hat{x}_w) - r_e \mathbb{F}_e(\hat{x}_w) - r_w \hat{x}_w$. Since $\tilde{x}_e = \mathbb{F}_e(\hat{x}_w)$ is chosen to maximize $\tilde{\Pi}_e$, which differs

[7]An example of an imperfect monitor is given in Baron and Besanko (1987). However, such a monitor must be both observable and verifiable, requiring an impartial third party to enforce it. This is problematic given the institutional setup of this model. Also, see Eswaran and Kotwal (1985) for an alternative to monitoring in the similar setting of a principal–agent model where both engage in morally hazardous behaviour.

from Π only by the constant term T_{ew}, it follows that the envelope theorem can be applied to obtain $d\Pi_{MSE}/d\hat{x}_w = PQ_w - r_w > 0$ for $\hat{x}_w \in [0, \bar{x}_w^F)$. Thus, part (iii) is proved. Finally, since $\Pi_{MSE}(0) = 0$ and $\Pi_{MSE}(\hat{x}_w) > \Pi_{SRE}$, where Π_{SRE} is the level of aggregate profits under the SRE, result (ii) follows. □

The result that profit in the MSE is strictly greater than that for the SRE when the input level for x_w is the same for both is somewhat surprising. The reason is that in the MSE the HCE becomes a full residual claimant to profits. Therefore, one side of the moral hazard problem is eliminated and so aggregate profit is enhanced. A similar intuition underlies result (iii).

It can easily be shown for the case in which the MNC provides only one input that there is no advantage in combining a sharing rule with a minimum standards requirement.[8] Maximal aggregate profit is obtained either when the constraint $x_w \geqq \hat{x}_w$ is binding, in which case the optimal $t = 1$, a pure MSE, or, if the constraint is not binding, the pure SRE obtains. Moreover, by assuming that the HCE can always discern some positive, although possibly very low, level of quality for x_w, one can use this result to say something about equilibrium selection. For example, the equilibrium $\bar{x}_e = \bar{x}_w = 0$ could be excluded as long as one of the MSE or SRE generates positive profits, even if the level of $\hat{x}_w$ is not large enough for the MSE to dominate the SRE. We return to this point in section 3.

Despite these results, joint venture contracts generally include *both* a sharing rule for dividing output *and* minimum standard requirements for at least some of the inputs. Upon expanding the model to allow for more than one input from the MNC, we are able to see how these two instruments may be complements, rather than substitutes, for dealing with the presence of two-sided moral hazard. Therefore, we extend consideration to a production function with two inputs provided by the MNC, (x_{w1}, x_{w2}). We make analogous assumptions about the production function with obvious extensions (e.g. $Q_{ij} > 0$, $i, j = e, w1, w2$, $i \neq j$) plus the requirement that for any given fixed input, $Q(\cdot,\cdot,\cdot)$ is concave with respect to the other two inputs.

Definition 3. Suppose a MNC provides two inputs into the production process. A combined sharing rule–minimum standards equilibrium (CSRMSE) is the outcome of a minimum standards requirement being placed on one of the two inputs, say $x_{w1} \geqq \hat{x}_{w1}$, as in a MSE, and a sharing rule, (t, T), as in a SRE. Each organization maximizes profits accordingly and the value of t is the one that leads to maximum aggregate profit.

A scenario in which the HCE is able to assess to a substantive degree the

[8]The intuition is that if $x_w \geqq \hat{x}_w$ is binding, choosing a $t \in (0,1)$ will reduce the HCE's incentive to supply x_e, while if such a t encourages the MNC to provide $x_w > \hat{x}_w$, the constraint becomes redundant and the optimal t must be the same as for the SRE.

quality level of some of the MNC's inputs, but not others, is a plausible one. However, in a pure MSE the MNC has an incentive to shirk as much as possible with respect to inputs not amenable to minimum standards requirements. Therefore, a CSRMSE may lead to higher aggregate profit in such an environment than either a pure MSE or a SRE. Moreover, with complementarity among inputs ($Q_{ij}>0, i \neq j$), a quality requirement placed on one input provides an incentive to improve the quality level of other inputs by both organizations. The result of this is that, if possible, the stipulated quality level of the input in question might ideally be set at a level that is even greater than for the first-best case. With this exception, the impact of standards requirements in a CSRMSE is similar to that for the pure MSE case.

Proposition 3. The CSRMSE has the following properties: (i) *The optimal value for* $t \in (0,1)$ *as for a SRE.* (ii) *If the required quality level for the constrained input is equal to the level that would be chosen in the pure SRE (i.e. if* $\hat{x}_{w1} = \bar{x}_{w1}$*), then the CSRMSE will generate higher aggregate profit than will the SRE.* (iii) *Letting* $\Pi_C(\hat{x}_{w1})$ *represent aggregate profit in a CSRMSE as a function of* $\hat{x}_{w1}$*, it follows that* Π_C *is monotonically increasing in* $\hat{x}_{w1}$ *from zero to a level beyond where its marginal revenue product equals its cost (i.e.* $PQ_{w1} = r_{w1}$*).*

Proof. Since the MNC chooses x_{w2} in the same way as it chooses x_w in the SRE, result (1) follows trivially from Proposition 1.

To prove result (ii), compare the following problems:

$$\max_{\{t\}} \Pi = PQ(x_e, x_{w1}, x_{w2}) - r_e x_e - r_{w1} x_{w1} - r_{w2} x_{w2}$$

Problem 1 (*Pure SRE*):
(subject to)

$$tPQ_e - r_e = 0, \qquad \text{(P1-ci)}$$

$$(1-t)PQ_{w1} - r_{w1} = 0, \qquad \text{(P1-cii)}$$

$$(1-t)PQ_{w2} - r_{w2} = 0. \qquad \text{(P1-ciii)}$$

Problem 2 (*CSRMSE*):
(subject to)

$$tPQ_e - r_e = 0, \qquad \text{(P2-ci)}$$

$$x_{w1} = \hat{x}_{w1}, \tag{P2-cii}$$

$$(1-t)PQ_{w2} - r_{w2} = 0. \tag{P2-ciii}$$

Write the profit functions for Problems 1 and 2, respectively, as

$$\bar{\Pi}(t) = PQ(\bar{x}_e(t), \bar{x}_{w1}(t), \bar{x}_{w2}(t)) - r_e\bar{x}_e(t) - r_{w1}\bar{x}_{w1}(t) - r_{w2}\bar{x}_{w2}(t), \tag{11}$$

$$\tilde{\Pi} = PQ(\tilde{x}_e(t; \hat{x}_{w1}), \hat{x}_{w1}, \tilde{x}_{w2}(t; \hat{x}_{w1})) - r_e\tilde{x}_e(t; \hat{x}_{w1}) - r_{w1}\hat{x}_{w1} - r_{w2}\tilde{x}_{w2}(t; \hat{x}_{w1}). \tag{12}$$

Optimal t, call it t^*, for Problem 1 satisfies the following:

$$(PQ_e - r_e)\cdot\frac{d\bar{x}_e}{dt} + (PQ_{w1} - r_{w1})\cdot\frac{d\bar{x}_{w1}}{dt} + (PQ_{w2} - r_{w2})\cdot\frac{d\bar{x}_{w2}}{dt} = 0. \tag{13}$$

The same level of profit can be generated for Problem 2 with $\hat{x}_{w1} = \bar{x}_{w1}$ and the same $t = t^*$. Note that each term of eq. (13) in parentheses is positive and, w.l.o.g., assume the following configuration of signs: $d\bar{x}_e/dt > 0$, $d\bar{x}_{w1}/dt$, and $d\bar{x}_{w2}/dt < 0$. Upon totally differentiating the profit function for Problem 2 it follows that, at $t = t^*$, $d\tilde{\Pi}/dt > 0$. Thus, there is an optimal t for Problem 2 that generates higher profit.

To prove result (iii), totally differentiate $\tilde{\Pi}$, holding t fixed:

$$\frac{d\tilde{\Pi}}{d\hat{x}_{w1}} = (PQ_e - r_e)\frac{d\tilde{x}_e}{d\hat{x}_{w1}} + (PQ_{w1} - r_{w1}) + (PQ_{w2} - r_{w2})\frac{d\tilde{x}_{w2}}{d\hat{x}_{w1}}. \tag{14}$$

$(PQ_e - r_e)$ and $(PQ_{w2} - r_{w2})$ are positive from (P2-ci and P2-ciii). Moreover, provided Cournot–Nash stability holds, the comparative statics of Problem 2 lead to $d\tilde{x}_e/d\hat{x}_{w1}$ and $d\tilde{x}_{w2}/d\hat{x}_{w1} > 0$. Thus, result (iii) follows. □

3. Extensions and further considerations

For each type of equilibrium considered in this paper the share value t, where relevant, is assumed to be chosen to maximize aggregate profit, while the value of any lump-sum transfer (T or T_{ij}) is left undetermined [as in Cooper and Ross (1985)]. Since the lump-sum component does not affect marginal incentives, although it may affect participation decisions, any efficient bargaining process would be consistent with the modelling strategy used in this paper. Consider, for example, the outcome of the Nash bargaining solution for the SRE. Since each organization chooses its input to maximize its own profit conditional on the share t, we write $x_e = \bar{x}_e(t)$, $x_w = \bar{x}_w(t)$ and total revenue as $R(t) = PQ(\bar{x}_e(t), \bar{x}_w(t))$. The Nash bargaining problem can then be written

$$\max_{\{t,T\}} \Pi_e \cdot \Pi_w = [tR(t) - r_e\bar{x}_e(t) - T] \cdot [(1-t)R(t) - r_w\bar{x}_w(t) + T]. \qquad (15)$$

The solution is that t is chosen so as to provide maximal aggregate profit [i.e. $R'(t) - r_e\bar{x}_e'(t) - r_w\bar{x}_w'(t) = 0$], while T leads to an equal division of this profit (i.e. $\Pi_e = \Pi_w = \Pi/2$). In addition to showing that the first stage of the model can in fact be explicitly modelled within a bargaining framework, there are further advantages to this exercise. One is that it offers a possible resolution to the ambiguity about the level of the lump sum-component (T). It also shows how both parties may prefer any contract form that improves overall efficiency. This being the case, a MNC would benefit either by its own country's government enforcing the contractual obligations of its member firms, even when made with enterprises from countries that do not reciprocate, or by generating a reputation for always honouring its contractual obligations, even if they are not legally binding.

In section 2 we assumed $Q_{ew} > 0$, thus ruling out the possibility that inputs x_e and x_w are substitutes. Although allowing for $Q_{ew} < 0$ leads to some alterations, the main results are left intact.[9] Thus, the model allows for the possible case in which the HCE supplies labour, which is a substitute for the MNC's skilled labour. This would be particularly relevant when considering the possibility of technology transfer via learning in a dynamic framework.[10]

Another simple extension to this model would be to introduce uncertainty. For example, let $\mathcal{Q} = Q \times \varepsilon$, where ε is a random variable with a mean of 1 and support $[0, \infty)$. If we replace profit with expected profit as the objective function(s) and let the pair (t, T) represent a linear sharing rule, then all of the results in this paper will follow through with obvious changes.[11]

A very useful but straightforward generalization is to use net value functions, $V^e(x_e \mid x_w)$ and $V^w(x_w \mid x_e)$, as objective functions for the HCE and MNC without restricting them to contain complementary fractions of total revenue. By defining total value of the joint venture as $V = V^e + V^w$ and requiring only that these functions be concave, we can generate the same

[9]Result (ii) of Proposition 1 *may* be affected [see Cooper and Ross (1985)]. The results of Propositions 2 and 3 are also maintained with only slight variations regarding the shape of the profit functions defined in terms of $\hat{x}_w$ or $\hat{x}_{w1}$, as relevant. [*Note*: To allow $Q_{ew} < 0$ requires relaxing the assumption $Q(0, \cdot) = Q(\cdot, 0) = 0$.]

[10]Moreover, it would also allow for a richer description of industry structure with respect to other activities of the MNC. As noted in Bulow et al. (1985), the effect of using an input in one market may affect a firm's profits in a strategic manner in other markets.

[11]Assuming (t, T) to be independent of Q, however, implies linearity of the sharing rule, a restriction that may not be warranted under uncertainty [see Williams and Radner (1988)].

qualitative results but allow for a much broader interpretation. For example, doing so would allow for the introduction of prices, which depend on quantities, or the inclusion of external effects, which may accrue to the HCE's labour force through learning by doing.[12]

4. Conclusion

One predominant feature of contractual joint ventures between MNCs and enterprises in Socialist countries (e.g. China) is that revenues (or output, in which case the phenomenon is called buyback) are split on a percentage basis between the two parties involved. It is suggested by the results of this paper that this rule, in conjunction with minimum standards requirements which can be verified at the beginning of the production period, reflects the need to produce an arrangement that diminishes the incentives on both parties to shirk by providing less than first-best quality levels for inputs.[13] The model in this paper suggests that the outcome of a joint venture is likely to be less than fully efficient relative to FDI, where the MNC is a full residual claimant to profits, or arrangements whereby the HCE plays this role. However, because of the HCE's lack of information about the production process and the particular political and legal institutions in place, a contractual joint venture may reflect a sort of second-best outcome. Moreover, owing to the direct involvement of the HCE in a joint venture, it may be a more effective way to generate the externalities often associated with technology transfer [see, for example, Leung et al. (1989, p. 21)]. Therefore, the Chinese experience suggests that joint ventures may be more prevalent when technology transfer is an important component and that such relationships are likely to be more common between countries exhibiting a technology gap, although not one so large as to preclude the possibility of learning on behalf of the host country.

There may also be reasons for a MNC to prefer joint ventures to FDI when dealing with socialist (or 'politically sensitive') countries, with China being a good example. With a joint venture arrangement it is usually the case that neither party can continue proudction independently. Therefore,

[12]For example, China looks to joint ventures as a way to acquire not only production technologies, but also management techniques, design philosophy, etc. [e.g. see the statement by Zhao Ziyang in the *Beijing Review* (1988, p. 18) and Chan (1989) for further examples]. Also, see Findlay (1978) and Blomstrom and Wang (1989) for models that use an externality type relation to model the transfer of technology.

[13]In the case where the output quality is unobservable or not easily verified, the use of output splitting rather than revenue splitting helps to avoid any agency problems that might arise concerning the settling on a price to use in computing shares. From the point of view of the model in this paper, the distinction is unimportant.

there is no incentive for the host country to expropriate the nonhuman assets of the MNC. Thus, a joint venture will be particularly resilient in avoiding the threat of expropriation when the MNC's input is knowledge based. Other potential problems, such as the upholding of possible export restrictions on the HCE or input adjustments by the MNC (e.g. improvements to technology), would be easier to deal with in a continuing relationship. Such issues, however, can receive proper treatment only in an intertemporal model and so remain a future project.

One further advantage of joint ventures from the host country's perspective is the low foreign exchange requirement, especially in the case of the buyback form. In fact, this argument has been put forward as the sole rationale for such phenomena. If HCEs are faced with an imperfect (foreign) capital market, then this factor may indeed be important. However, host countries could instead allow FDI by MNCs in order to gain the fruits of the technology, while at the same time exporting some of the product and perhaps even charging a licence fee for access to their market, hence generating a net inflow of foreign exchange. Therefore, there are considerations beyond the foreign exchange restriction that explain the popularity of this phenomenon. Moreover, the 'foreign exchange rationale' explains neither the substantial differences in types of countertrade across countries (in particular, socialist vs. nonsocialist) nor the particular form of joint venture and buyback contracts observed.[14]

[14]For elaboration on this point as well as economic reasons that have been proposed for other types of countertrade, see Murrell (1982), Parsons (1985), Mirus and Yeung (1986), and Amann and Marin (1989).

References

Amann, E. and D. Marin, 1989, Barter in international trade: A rationale, Working Paper 257, Institute for Advanced Studies, Vienna.

Baron, D.P. and D. Besanko, 1987, Monitoring, moral hazard, asymmetric information, and risk sharing in procurement contracting, Rand Journal of Economics 18, 509–532.

Beijing Review, 1988, Zhao on coastal areas' development strategy, 36 (6), 18.

Blomstrom, M. and J.-Y. Wang, 1989, Foreign investment and technology transfer: A simple model, NBER Working Paper 2958.

Bulow, J.I., J.D. Geanakoplos and P.D. Klemperer, 1985, Multimarket oligopoly: Strategic substitutes and complements, Journal of Political Economics 93, 488–511.

Campbell, N., 1988, The patterns of equity joint ventures in China, Manchester Business School Working Paper 156.

Chan, W. F., 1989, The role of countertrade in China's economic development, University of Guelph, Mimeo.

Cooper, R. and T. W. Ross, 1985, Product warranties and double moral hazard, Rand Journal of Economics, Spring, 103–113.

Eswaran, M. and A. Kotwal, 1985, A theory of two tier labor markets in agrarian economics, American Economic Review 75, 162–177.

Findlay, R., 1978, Some aspects of technology and direct foreign investment, American Economic Review 68, 275–279.

Holmstrom, B., 1982, Moral hazard in teams, The Bell Journal of Econoomics 13, 324–340.

Horstmann, I. and J. R. Markusen, 1987, Licensing versus direct investment: A model of internalization by the multinational enterprise, Canadian Journal of Economics 20, 464–481.

Leung, H. M., J. T. Thoburn, E. Chau and S. H. Tang, 1989, Contractual relations, foreign direct investment, and technology transfer: The case of China, University of East Anglia Working Paper 43.

Mirus, R. and B. Yeung, 1986, Economic incentives for countertrade, Journal of International Business Studies 17, 27–39.

Murrell, P., 1982, Product quality, market signaling and the development of East–West trade, Economic Inquiry 20, 589–603.

OECD, 1985, Countertrade: Developing country practices (OECD, Paris).

Parsons, J.E., 1985, A theory of countertrade financing of international business, MIT Working Paper 1632–85.

Welt, L., 1984, Trade without money: Barter and countertrade (Harcourt Brace Jovanovich, New York).

Williams, S.R. and R. Radner, 1988, Efficiency in partnership when the joint output is uncertain, Northwestern Discussion Paper 760.

[11]

Economics Letters 40 (1992) 77–82
North-Holland

A simple model of buybacks

Chong J. Choi and Daniel Maldoom
University of Oxford, Oxford, UK

Received 27 March 1992
Accepted 24 June 1992

Buybacks are a type of contractual joint venture used in countertrade, where the good produced is allocated in fixed proportions to the parties involved. We show that buybacks can act as commitment devices when the quality of inputs cannot be contracted over.

1. Introduction

Countertrade arrangements comprise over 20% of international trade but have received little theoretical attention from international economists. It has been particularly important in the West's trade with Eastern Europe and shows little sign of diminishing. Caves and Marin (1992) have convincingly shown the importance of countertrade in a detailed empirical study. They have shown that the traditional argument for the existence of countertrade based on foreign exchange restrictions is not substantiated by their data.

A major category of countertrade is buyback arrangements. A buyback is a type of contractual joint venture where the good produced is allocated in fixed proportions to the parties involved. The purpose of this short note is to present a simple explanation of why buybacks are used. We consider that the correct explanation of these phenomena requires an investigation of the contracting and commitment problems which arise in international trade. These issues are important for two reasons. Firstly, there may be imperfect information at work, for example because of the inability of agents in international transactions to observe the quality of each others' goods. Difficulties in monitoring agents in other countries can be expected to create greater imperfect information problems for international transactions than for domestic ones. Secondly, due to geographical limits on legal jurisdiction, it is much more difficult to draw up an enforceable contract for an international transaction than it is for a domestic one. This makes it difficult for the parties engaged in an international transaction to use contracts as commitment devices.

In their recent work, Chan and Hoy (1991) tried to study buybacks by applying a simplified version of the double moral hazard model of Cooper and Ross (1985). Their paper is correct in identifying the importance of cross-frontier contracting problems and the design of incentive schemes, but fails to draw any substantial conclusions from this observation. In particular, they fail to ask the key economic question – why do buybacks occur?

The innovation in this note is that we show how buyback arrangements can act as a commitment

Correspondence to: Chong J. Choi, University of Oxford, The Queen's College, Oxford, OX1 4AW, United Kingdom.

0165-1765/92/$05.00

device that reduces the incentives for opportunism. A buyback arrangement can produce higher profits for those parties involved than one in which the good produced is sold in various markets to maximise revenue. This provides a simple explanation of the use of buyback arrangements in preference to other contractual arrangements and fits the stylised facts.

2. A stylised example of a buyback contract

We now consider a stylised example of a buyback contract. A high technology western firm wants to set up and produce output with an Eastern European firm. The western firm provides technology inputs in the form of capital; the eastern firm provides skilled labour for the plant. We assume that 1 unit of technology and 1 unit of labour combine to produce 1 unit of output. The quality of the output depends on the quality of the labour force and the quality of the technology supplied.

There is no legally enforceable mechanism for writing a contract conditional on the quality of either input or on the quality of the output. A balanced budget constraint on the enterprise means that incentives of the suppliers of inputs cannot wholly reflect their marginal effects on revenues, as noted in Holmstrom (1982). Thus the first will reduce the quality of their inputs below the joint profit maximising levels.

The purpose of our analysis is to see what would be the optimal contract under such conditions. The contracts we consider specify in what proportion profits will be shared between the two suppliers of inputs, a transfer payment between them and the method by which the output is allocated between the East and West. We compare two types of contracts: a buyback contract, and a 'market allocated' contract. Under a buyback contract, there is fixed division of output to the eastern and western markets. Under a market allocated contract, a middleman can observe the quality of the output and then allocate output optimally between the two markets. We show that the buyback contract is preferable to a market allocated contract, justifying the economic use of buyback arrangements.

3. The model

We assume that the eastern firm provides an input of quality x at cost $c_e(x)$ and that the western firm provides an input of quality y at cost $c_w(y)$. One unit of output is produced of quality $q(x, y)$. A proportion s of this output is sold in the East and $1-s$ in the West. This yields revenue $R_e(q, s)$ from the eastern market and $R_w(q, 1-s)$ from the western market. The total revenues from both markets are divided with a proportion t going to the eastern firm and $1-t$ to the western firm. We may define the profit functions for the two firms as follows:

$$\pi_e(x, y; s, t) = t\{R_e[q(x, y), s] + R_w[q(x, y), 1-s]\} - c_e(x);$$

$$\pi_w(x, y; s, t) = (1-t)\{R_e[q(x, y), s] + R_w[q(x, y), 1-s]\} - c_w(y).$$

A buyback contract between the eastern and western firms specifies t, the sharing of profits, and s, the sharing of output. It may also specify a transfer payment between the firms. We shall consider optimal contracts which maximise the joint profits of the two firms. Since transfer payments can be made costlessly between the firms any contract which did not maximise joint profit could not be Pareto efficient.

Given a particular contract, the two firms simultaneously choose the qualities of their inputs. The quality levels they choose are a Nash equilibrium of the game with payoff functions π_e, π_w. We assume that this game always has a pure strategy Nash equilibrium.

Let us now find the optimal buyback contract. As is standard in contract theory, we may think about maximising over the contracting variables t, s and over the quality levels x, y chosen by the firms, subject to the incentive compatibility constraints that these quality levels constitute a Nash equilibrium. The maximisation problem is

$$\text{(BB)} \qquad \max_{(x,y,s,t)} \pi_e(x, y; s, t) + \pi_w(x, y; s, t),$$

$$\text{such that} \quad \text{ICC}_e \quad \pi_e(x, y; s, t) \geq \pi_e(x', y; s, t) \quad \forall x',$$

$$\text{ICC}_w \quad \pi_w(x, y; s, t) \geq \pi_w(x, y'; s, t) \quad \forall y',$$

$$s \in [0, 1] \quad \text{and} \quad t \in [0, 1].$$

A market allocated contract specifies t, the sharing of profits and also any transfer payments. Unlike the buyback contract, it does not specify the allocation of output to eastern and western markets. We imagine that, once produced, the output is passed to a middleman who can observe its quality. The middleman, who could be interpreted as the manager of the plant, then decides how to share the output between the two markets in order to maximise total revenue. This mechanism is intended to capture the idea that there is an efficient international market for the output, and for this reason we call this a 'market allocated contract'. It should be noted that we have assumed that the quality of the output is *observable* (consumers and the middleman can observe it) but is not *contractable* (binding contracts cannot be conditioned on it).

We may construct the market allocated profit functions faced by the two firms by maximising over s, the sharing of output:

$$\pi_e^m(x, y; t) = \max_s \pi_e(x, y; s, t);$$

$$\pi_w^m(x, y; t) = \max_s \pi_w(x, y; s, t).$$

The same s maximizes both π_e and π_w, since it is the s which maximises total revenue. The optimal market allocated contract can be found from the maximisation problem:

$$\text{(MA)} \qquad \max_{x,y,t} \pi_e^m(x, y; t) + \pi_w^m(x, y; t),$$

$$\text{such that} \quad \text{ICC}_e' \quad \pi_e^m(x, y; t) \geq \pi_e^m(x', y; t) \quad \forall x',$$

$$\text{ICC}_w' \quad \pi_w^m(x, y; t) \geq \pi_w^m(x, y'; t) \quad \forall y',$$

$$t \in [0, 1]$$

The optimal market allocated problem is equivalent to one in which we choose s and face extra incentive compatibility constraints from the requirement that the allocation of output to the two markets be efficient if there is any deviation from the Nash equilibrium. Thus the optimal market allocation must solve:

$$\text{(MA}') \qquad \max_{x,y,s,t} \pi_e(x, y, s, t) + \pi_w(x, y, s, t),$$

$$\text{such that} \quad \text{ICC}''_e \quad \pi_e(x, y, s, t) \geq \pi_e(x', y, s', t) \quad \forall x', s'$$

$$\text{ICC}''_w \quad \pi_w(x, y, s, t) \geq \pi_w(x, y', s', t) \quad \forall y', s'$$

$$s \in [0, 1] \quad \text{and} \quad t \in [0, 1].$$

A proof of the equivalence of the maximisation problems MA and MA′ is given as an appendix. The set of constraints for the MA′ problem contains the set of constraints for the BB problem. Thus the buyback contract must give a total profit no smaller than the market allocated contract. Where one of the additional constraints on the MA′ problem binds, the buyback contract gives a strictly higher payoff than the market allocated contract. Providing changes in quality cause changes in the revenue maximising allocation of output to the two markets, it will be the case that some of these additional constraints bind and that the buyback contract is strictly better than the market allocated contract.

There is a simple economic interpretation of this result. In an optimal buyback contract, revenue is more responsive to changes in quality than under a market allocated contract. This is a straightforward application of le Chatelier's principle. If one of the firms deviates from the Nash equilibrium under a market allocated contract, the allocation of output to the two markets may be adjusted. Under the buyback contract, the allocation is fixed and so profits must decrease more than in the market allocated case. Thus there are stronger incentives to maintain the quality of inputs under the buyback contract since the firms can commit themselves to a greater potential loss of profit should they cut quality.

4. Discussion

This model provides a simple explanation of why buybacks should occur. It allows us to make a number of predictions. Firstly, the establishment of stable convertible currencies in Eastern Europe cannot be expected to reduce the proportion of trade occurring through buyback arrangements. This conclusion is in sharp contrast to the view held by some practitioners that countertrade is due to failures of the international monetary system.

Secondly, buybacks are of greatest benefit in trade between dissimilar economies. The model predicts that the greater the revenue loss from not being able to adjust the allocation of output once the quality of output is known, then the greater is the commitment power of a buyback contract. If the revenue functions in the two markets were very similar, there would be little revenue lost from committing to a particular allocation of output. In our stylised example of Western and Eastern European markets it might be reasonable to assume that the revenue from the western market is highly sensitive to quality, whereas the revenue from the eastern market is rather insensitive. Thus in order to maximise revenue, more of the output might be allocated to the West if it is of higher quality. Under such circumstances, the commitment value of the buyback contract is high. Thus we should expect to see more buyback arrangements across economic blocs rather than within them.

From a policy perspective, buyback arrangements should not be discouraged in favour of 'free market' policies of selling the output of joint ventures where it is most profitable. They provide a useful welfare improving commitment device.

There are strong similarities between our approach and the double moral hazard issue analyzed in the product warranty literature of Mann and Wissink (1988) and Demiski and Sappington (1991). As regards further research, this paper is incomplete is an important respect. We intend to include uncertainty into the model and produce a true double moral hazard formulation in which it is possible to contract over the quality of the output, but in which random and unobservable shocks affect the relationship between the quality of inputs and the quality of outputs. However, we have felt it appropriate to report these preliminary results because of the paucity of coherent economic explanations of countertrade and the success of this simple model in fitting the stylised facts.

Appendix: Equivalence of the MA and MA′ maximisation problems

MA → MA′: Let x, y, t be a solution to MA, and let

$$s = \operatorname*{argmax}_{s'} \pi_e(x, y; s', t) = \operatorname*{argmax}_{s'} \pi_w(x, y; s', t).$$

Then,

$$\pi_e(x, y; s, t) + \pi_w(x, y; s, t) = \pi_e^m(x, y; t) + \pi_w^m(x, y; t).$$

Also by ICC_e',

$$\pi_e(x, y; s, t) = \pi_e^m(x, y; t) \geq \pi_e^m(x', y; t) \quad \forall x'.$$

But

$$\pi_e(x', y', t) = \max_{s} \pi_e(x', y; s, t) \geq \pi_e(x', y; s', t),$$

and so

$$\pi_e(x, y; s, t) \geq \pi_e(x', y; s', t) \quad \forall x', s'.$$

Thus x, y, s, t, satisfies ICC_e''. Similarly, it satisfies ICC_w''. Thus, total profits in MA ≤ total profit in MA′.
MA′ → MA: Let x, y, s, t, be a solution to MA′. From ICC_e'',

$$\pi_e(x, y; s, t) \geq \pi_e(x, y; s, t) \quad \forall s.$$

Thus,

$$\pi_e(x, y; s, t) = \max_{s'} \pi_e(x, y; s', t) = \pi_e^m(x, y; t).$$

So

$$\pi_e(x, y; s, t) + \pi_w(x, y; s, t) = \pi_e^m(x, y; t) + \pi_w^m(x, y; t).$$

From ICC''_e

$$\pi_e^m(x, y; t) = \pi_e(x, y; s, t) \geq \pi_e^m(x', y; t) \quad \forall x',$$

and similarly for w. Thus, x, y, t satisfies ICC'_e, ICC'_w. Thus total profits in MA′ ≤ total profits in MA. We conclude that total profits in MA equal total profits in MA′.

References

Caves, R. and D. Marin, 1992, Countertrade transactions: Theory and evidence, Economics Journal, forthcoming.

Chan, R. and M. Hoy, 1991, East–West joint ventures and buyback contracts, Journal of International Economics 30, 331–343.

Cooper, R. and T. Ross, 1985, Product warranties and double moral hazard, Rand Journal of Economics 16, no. 1, Spring, 103–113.

Demiski, J. and D. Sappington, 1991, Resolving double moral hazard problems with buyout agreements, Rand Journal of Economics 22, no. 2, Summer, 232–240.

Holmstrom, B., 1982, Moral hazard in teams, Bell Journal of Economics 13, 324–340.

Mann, D. and J. Wissink, 1988, Money–back contracts with double moral hazard, Rand Journal of Economics 19, 285–292.

Part IV
Risk Sharing

[12]

THE JOURNAL OF INDUSTRIAL ECONOMICS 0022-1821 $2.00
Volume XLII March 1994 No. 1

RISK-SHARING IN INTERNATIONAL TRADE: AN ANALYSIS OF COUNTERTRADE

ERWIN AMANN AND DALIA MARIN

Countertrade agreements in international trade refer to a trade practice in which an exporter agrees to purchase back commodities proportional to his original export sale in the future. The paper provides a rationale for why such an agreement might be efficient. More specifically, the paper argues that countertrade represents a rational response to market incompleteness by allowing the forward selling of commodities where no organized future market exists. This way countertrade helps to reduce risk by providing information on future market conditions and by offering insurance against random fluctuations in market conditions.

I. INTRODUCTION

COUNTERTRADE IS a tying contractual arrangement in international trade. In a typical countertrade transaction one party imports a product and the exporting party commits herself to purchase from the first party commodities equal to a portion of the original export value at a future point of time. The products that the exporting party purchases in the future to fulfil the countertrade obligation are specified in a shopping-list and each commodity flow is paid in foreign exchange, that is the two sides of the transaction are linked but financially separate. Since the exporting party—typically a firm in a western industrial country—commits herself to the purchase of commodities in the future, countertrade agreements are long term in nature with a time horizon of up to 10 years.[1]

Since the mid seventies countertrade has started to grow rapidly. Reasonable estimates range the phenomenon between 10 and 20 per cent of world trade (see OECD [1985], deMiramon [1985]). Besides the formerly centrally planned economies (CPEs), many of the developing countries (LDCs) have turned to countertrade in the belief that it facilitates economic development in face of an increased foreign indebtedness. The very fact that mostly countries with serious foreign-exchange shortages are engaged in

[1] The typical countertrade transaction is the counterpurchase form of countertrade. Counterpurchase accounts for 77 per cent of countertrade, while the other two forms of countertrade—barter and buy back—occur less frequently. They have a share in countertrade of 11 and 12 per cent, respectively, see Marin [1990]. Barter is—in contrast to counterpurchase—a spot transaction in which both commodity flows are exchanged at more or less the same time without the involvement of foreign exchange, while buy back is similar to counterpurchase with the commodity flows standing in a technical relation to each other; typically one flow consists of machinery and the other one of products produced with the machinery.

countertrade led to the most popular explanation of the phenomenon that countertrade helps to finance imports without the use of hard currency thereby allowing these countries to overcome the foreign-exchange constraint.[2] This paper argues that countertrade can be understood as a second-best outcome in the absence of complete risk and future markets. Faced with a tight foreign-exchange constraint the countries imposing countertrade have become more risk averse when deciding on future export areas. Given the constraint, these countries have felt the pressing need for a guarantee that future exports will generate the foreign-exchange earnings that they are now lacking. In the absence of adequate insurance markets these countries have looked for alternative ways to insure against the risk that they face and the paper views countertrade to be such a substitute for an absent futures market.[3] This explains also why countertrade has increased since the mid seventies when foreign debt and hard currency shortages have started to become particularly binding in these countries. Viewed in this way, it is not the need to finance imports when there is a hard currency shortage that accounts for the occurrence of countertrade but the increased risk aversion due to a tight foreign-exchange constraint that has created the incentive for countertrade as an insurance contract.

In previous papers (Marin [1991], and Caves and Marin [1992]) we have shown that barter can be explained by the presence of market distortions in the form of monopoly power of the western firm or in the form of price cartels and other collusive arrangements on the part of LDCs. In this paper we focus on market incompleteness in the form of the absence of perfect risk and insurance markets as a rationale for countertrade. Since risk allocation is our major concern in this paper we exclude other potential reasons for the choice of a tied contractual arrangement. More specifically, the paper ignores "relationship-specific investment" as factors giving rise to a tying relationship.[4] Moreover, the analysis does not take into account that most risk-sharing arrangements have significant effects on moral hazard incentives and involve adverse selection problems.[5]

The paper comes in four sections. Section II gives the model and section III looks at the optimal risk sharing properties determining the extent of price adjustment over time, and the share of production insured. Section IV undertakes some comparative statics with respect to changes in the amount of risk and risk aversion which shows how the model can explain the increase of

[2] The argument seems not convincing because among countertrade only barter avoids the usage of hard currency while counterpurchase and buy back involve foreign exchange in the transaction so that they cannot be effective in easing the foreign exchange constraint (see Banks [1983]).

[3] For an argument along similar lines see Parsons [1985].

[4] See Williamson [1985] and Klein, Crawford and Alchian [1978].

[5] We concentrate on moral hazard issues and *ex-post* hold up problems as an explanation for why countertrade as a tying arrangement might outperform non-tied trading arrangements in Marin and Schnitzer [1993].

countertrade in world trade observed since the mid seventies. Section V concludes. An appendix provides the proofs of the propositions made throughout the paper.

II. THE MODEL

Consider two agents: a firm DC in a western industrial country producing the good X which the firm wants to export to a CPE or a LDC, and a party called CPE being a firm or a Foreign Trade Organization (FTO) in a CPE or a LDC. The DC-firm faces an entry barrier in CPE's market and is willing to offer something in exchange to the CPE for helping her overcome this barrier. The CPE, in turn, deals with the following decision problem. Faced with a tight foreign exchange budget constraint CPE is highly risk averse when deciding on which products to produce for future exports. It will scrutinize carefully competing choices for the use of productive resources with respect to their prospects of generating future foreign exchange earnings. In this situation futures markets would be especially valuable to CPE since they would provide it with information on future market conditions for the product it considers producing and additionally would offer insurance against random fluctuations in price. Thus by selling the product forward, the CPE could eliminate all the risk from its foreign exchange earnings (in the absence of any supply risk) by having a guaranteed price over the period for which the futures market is open. This way futures markets guarantee that an investment today is generating foreign exchange earnings in the future thus making the present foreign exchange constraint less binding. In the absence of such perfect risk markets CPE will look for alternative ways to insure itself against the market risk it faces.[6] It will make DC's market entry contingent on DC's provision of a private futures market. It will negotiate with DC for a forward contract in which the DC-firm commits herself to purchase at a future date the product M that CPE considers to produce. If the DC-firm agrees to such a contract counterpurchase serves as an insurance against future price fluctuations and the fact that an agreement is reached will give CPE a signal on the future demand for the product.

CPE's utility function is given by

$$U_M = E[R_M] - C_M - \frac{A_M}{2}\sigma^2_{R_M} \tag{1}$$

with $E(R_M)$ as the expected total revenue and C_M total cost. CPE is assumed to be risk averse with A_M being the coefficient of absolute risk aversion and

[6] Future contracts exist only for a narrow range of commodities and most of them expire in six months or less. The reason why they are confined to a narrow range of commodities is that they require product quality to be exactly identified which is obviously only possible for standardized products. That more distant contracts do not exist might be associated with the increased costs of operating such markets which suggest that alternative risk-sharing arrangements, like long-term contracts or vertical integration, are less costly. For the reason why better futures markets do not exist see Newbery and Stiglitz [1985].

with $\sigma^2_{R_M}$ as the variance of R_M. When CPE signs a countertrade agreement its total revenue and costs become

$$R_M = \sum_{t=1}^{d} p_t^M \frac{M}{d} + \sum_{t=1}^{d} p_t \left[\frac{M^0}{T} - \frac{M}{d}\right] + \sum_{t=d+1}^{T} p_t \frac{M^0}{T}$$

$$C_M = p_x X + C_0 + C_T$$

with p_x the price for DC's product X in the countertrade agreement, p_t^M the countertrade price that DC agrees to pay for CPE's product M over the duration of contract d. p_t is the future spot world market price for M that CPE receives when it sells M in a traditional spot transaction. CPE incurs costs C_0 when it decides to produce M with M^0 being the total volume that can be produced over the production period T.

When CPE does a spot transaction its outside option revenue and costs are

$$R_M^0 = \sum_{t=1}^{T} p_t \frac{M^0}{T}$$

and

$$C_M^0 = p_x^c X + C_0$$

with p_x^c the price for DC's product X that the CPE pays in the spot transaction. Comparing revenues and costs under the two alternative arrangements, the CPE's benefit of signing a countertrade agreement relative to a spot transaction will depend on the difference between the countertrade price p_x^c and the spot price p_x for X, on the transaction costs of agreeing to the contract C_T, and on the extent to which the countertrade contract reduces the price risk that it faces. The risk reducing role of countertrade, in turn, will depend on the contract duration d relative to the gestation period T, on the reduction in price variability (the difference between $\sigma^2_{p_t^M}$ and $\sigma^2_{p_t}$), and on the share of production M/M^0 for which the contract provides insurance. In the absence of any supply risk, the CPE can eliminate all the risk from its foreign exchange earnings by signing a countertrade agreement with the features $d = T, \sigma^2_{p_t^M} = 0$, and $M = M^0$. In other words, the CPE will have shifted all the risk to the DC-firm when the contract extends over the total production period T and over the total volume of production M^0, and the DC-firm buys CPE's production at a fixed price. The CPE will pay for the risk reduction (elimination) in the form of a higher price p_x for X (whether DC will find such a contract acceptable will be dealt with below). Note that the specification of the utility function (1) leaves CPE the outside option of buying an identical good X from somebody else than DC without imposing a countertrade agreement and of producing M without any risk sharing arrangement when the expected revenues of the investment exceed the risk involved.[7]

[7] Since the analysis abstracts from moral hazard incentives and adverse selection problems it is assumed that CPE offers only one good M which has no quality dimensions and which is known to the DC-firm at the date of signing the contract.

The DC-firm's utility, in turn, is given by

(2) $$U_X = E(R_X) - C_X - \frac{Ax}{2}\sigma^2_{R_X}$$

with $E(R_X)$ now DC's expected revenue, C_X her costs, and A_X the DC-firm's coefficient of absolute risk aversion. Under the countertrade contract the DC-firm's revenue and costs become

$$R_X = \sum_{t=1}^{d} (p_t - p_t^M)\frac{M}{d} + p_x X$$

and

$$C_X = c_x X + C_T$$

where c_x is DC's marginal costs. Under the spot transaction the DC-firm's revenue and costs are

$$R_X^0 = 0 \quad \text{and} \quad C_X^0 = 0$$

which reflects DC's entry barrier in CPE's market leaving her without an outside option to countertrade. DC's utility of signing a countertrade contract increases with the price-cost margin $p_x - c_x$ on X and with the possible profit that she makes when selling CPE's product—which depends on the expected value of the difference between the countertrade price p_t^M that DC pays to CPE for M and the price p_t that she gets when selling M on the world market. DC's profit of signing a countertrade agreement, however, decreases with the amount of risk that she agrees to bear—which depends on $\sigma^2_{(p_t - p_t^M)}$, the contract duration d, and the amount of M that she buys from CPE. Since the DC-firm faces an entry barrier in CPE's market the countertrade agreement can be viewed as an exchange of entry for a private futures market. It is assumed that DC is less risk averse than CPE, $A_X \leqslant A_M$ which is supposed to reflect the fact that DC being a firm in a market economy has more opportunities of risk spreading by, for example, reducing employment in a recession or going on the stock market than CPE who typically operates in a planned economy without any risk absorbing institutions.[8]

Furthermore, it is assumed that the spot world market price for M is generated by a random walk

(3) $$p_t = p_{t-1} + u_t \quad \text{with} \quad u_t \,\text{iid}(0, \sigma_p)$$

The countertrade price p_t^M that DC pays for M is supposed to be determined by the following price rule

(4) $$p_t^M = (1-\mu)p_t + \mu p_0 \qquad 0 \leqslant \mu \leqslant 1$$

[8] For the attitudes towards risk in CPEs and its difference to western market economies see Kogut [1986].

with p_0 as the present and p_t the future spot world market price for M and μ as the risk shifting parameter. If $\mu = 1$ the countertrade agreement is a "fixed price contract" in which DC agrees to buy M at the world market price p_0 prevailing at the date of contract agreement and remaining unchanged over contract duration while with $\mu = 0$, DC pays the price prevailing on the spot market for the countertrade good at the date of delivery which is referred to as a "spot price contract." For given d and M, the "fixed price contract" allocates all the risk to DC while in the "spot price contract" all the risk of future price variability remains with M. Any value of μ between 0 and 1 therefore describes a situation of risk sharing between DC and CPE.

III. OPTIMAL RISK SHARING PROPERTIES

In this section we determine the amount of price and output insurance that CPE will obtain from the DC-firm. DC and CPE will extend the contract over the whole gestation period of the investment, since the gains from risk sharing are maximized at this contract length.[9]

We assume a symmetric situation between DC and CPE and use the Nash Bargaining as a benchmark case in modeling the bargaining. The bargaining is a one shot game under complete information in which both DC and CPE simultaneously make an offer and an agreement is reached if both offers are compatible with each other.[10] We assume that $\sigma_p = 1$, $A_X = 1$, $A_M = \alpha > 1$, $\theta = p_0 M^0$ and $s = p_X X = p_0 M$. Furthermore, the two restrictions $d \leqslant T$, $\frac{M}{d} \leqslant \frac{M^0}{T}$ are assumed to hold; that is contract duration cannot exceed the gestation period of the investment T and CPE cannot deliver more than it produces. Since both DC and CPE have a common interest to extend the contract over the whole gestation period $d^* = T$, the bargaining over risk sharing takes place only with respect to μ and s. Normalizing U_M to 0, substituting (4) into (1) and (2) and taking expected values, the two utility functions rewrite then to

$$(1'') \qquad U_M = c_1 - s - \alpha_M(\Theta - \mu s)^2$$

$$(2'') \qquad U_X = -c_2 + s - \alpha_X(\mu s)^2$$

[9] For a proof that $d^* = T$ see Amann and Marin [1990].

[10] In a typical countertrade deal DC has the option of leaving the contract commitment by paying a penalty to CPE. In our model, however, DC is not free to leave the commitment once she has agreed to the contract. Thus we have made the assumption that the penalty costs of breaking the contract are infinite. This assumption can be justified by the fact that in reality the parties play repeated games in the form of having a continuous business relationship which prevents them from breaching. Breaking the contract for short run profit opportunities would upset future business terms thereby making the effective penalty costs very high. For empirical evidence supporting this see Marin [1990]. For a descriptive representation of countertrade deals see OECD [1981, 1985], Group of Thirty [1985] and Korth [1987].

with

$$c_1 = \min\{\Theta - C_0, \textstyle\sum_M\} + p_X^c X$$

$$c_2 = \qquad c_X X$$

$$\alpha_M = \frac{A_M}{2p_0^2}\frac{(2T+1)(T+1)}{6T}$$

$$\alpha_X = \frac{1}{2p_0^2}\frac{(2T+1)(T+1)}{6T}$$

where $\alpha_M \Theta^2 = \sum_M$

In the Nash Bargaining solution $W = (U_X - U_X^0)(U_M - U_M^0)$ is maximized which reflects the symmetry between DC and CPE. In order to find the optimal amount of insurance that DC provides to CPE the problem max W over μ and s is solved.[11]

Proposition 1. The optimal risk sharing properties with respect to μ and s are given by

$$\mu s = \left[\frac{\alpha_M}{(\alpha_X + \alpha_M)}\right]\Theta \tag{5}$$

which implies

$$\frac{\delta U_M}{\delta s} = \frac{-\delta U_X}{\delta s} \quad \text{and} \quad \frac{\delta U_M}{\delta \mu} = \frac{-\delta U_X}{\delta \mu}$$

Proof. in the Appendix

Proposition 1 states that the optimum amount of insurance that DC provides to CPE will depend on relative risk aversion only. If $\alpha_X = \alpha_M$, that is DC and CPE do not differ in their attitude towards risk, then the insurance covers a half of CPE's total production, while if DC is risk neutral, $\alpha_X = 0$, equation (5) (subsequently denoted by C_p) implies that DC insures CPE's total production and thus bears all the risk. C_p describes the loci of Pareto optimal risk sharing outcomes. At all points on the C_p curve DC's and CPE's indifference curves are tangential to each other reflecting that neither DC nor CPE can improve his/her utility through a change in s and/or μ without making the other worse off. A further implication of optimal risk sharing is that DC's and CPE's marginal rates of substitution of μ and s are equal. In other words, any increase in DC's utility through a marginal change in s and μ will be just offset by a decline in CPE's utility.

[11] For the concept of Nash Bargaining see van Damme [1987].

Proposition 2. If a Nash Bargaining solution exists in the interior of the strategy space $S = [0, 1] \times [0, \Theta]$ it will have the property of $(s, \mu) \in C_P$ and $U_X = U_M$.

Proof. in the Appendix

A geometrical illustration of Proposition 2 is given in Figure 1. In the (μ, s)-space the curve C_P is drawn which reflects the loci of Pareto optimal risk sharing outcomes. Furthermore, the figure shows three distinct indifference curves. The $U_X = 0$ and the $U_M = 0$ curves showing the (μ, s)-combinations at which DC's and CPE's utility, respectively, are zero and the $U_X = U_M$ curve giving the loci of equal splitting of the pie between DC and CPE. Any right downwards shift of the U_X = constant curve represents a higher utility level to DC since her benefit of signing the contract increases with lower μ and higher s, while any left upwards shift of CPE's indifference curve indicates an increase in CPE's payoff. The point E_M (the intersection between the $U_X = 0$ and the C_P curve) reflects an equilibrium outcome when CPE is a powerful FTO that moves first and gets the maximum risk reduction at which DC will still agree to the contract. The Nash Bargaining solution is illustrated by point E which is given by the intersection of the $U_X = U_M$ and the C_P curve.

The optimum amount of output insurance that CPE obtains in the Nash Bargaining is given by[12]

$$(6) \qquad (s^* - c_2) = \frac{(c_1 - c_2)}{2} + \frac{(\alpha_M - \alpha_X)}{2}\left[\frac{(\alpha_M \alpha_X)}{(\alpha_M + \alpha_X)^2}\right]\sum_M$$

$$= \frac{(c_1 - c_2)}{2} + \frac{(\alpha_M - \alpha_X)}{2}\sum_X$$

that is the optimal price s^* that CPE will pay for X will be such as to cover the risk costs $\sum_X$ that accrue to DC when she agrees to the contract $d^* = T$ and μ^* and, furthermore, the price will be such as to allocate half of the profits and half of the gains from risk sharing to X. Consider each of the right hand side expression of equation (6) separately. DC's risk cost $\sum_X$ will depend on the size of the original risk $\sum_M$ and on the difference in risk aversion between DC and CPE. If DC and CPE do not differ in their attitude towards risk, $\alpha_X = \alpha_M$, then DC's risk cost will be $1/4\sum_M$, that is DC will need to be compensated for a quarter of the original risk. The reason why DC's risk costs are only a quarter of CPE's original risk is that the insurance generates an externality in the form of gains from risk spreading as the risk is now shared between DC and CPE instead of borne by CPE alone. If $\alpha_X < \alpha_M$, that is DC is less risk averse than CPE, DC requires a smaller compensation for providing the risk market because of the following two reasons. One reason is that DC does not

[12] s determines M and thus the share of CPE's production insured because of the assumption of $s = p_X X = p_0 M$ making $M = s/p_0$ when setting $X = 1$.

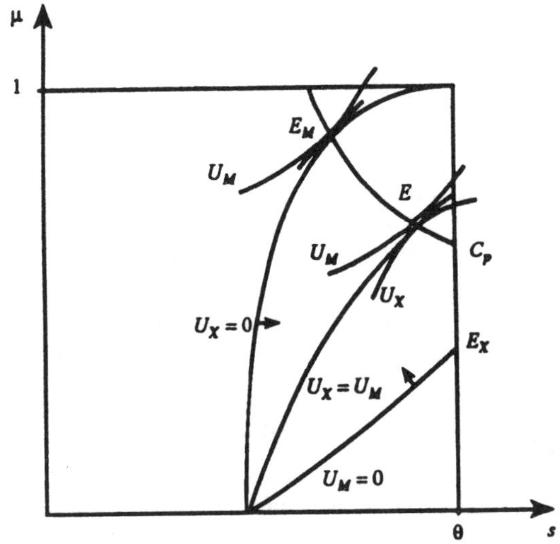

Figure 1
Optimal Risk Sharing

mind the risk as much as CPE which reduces the price that she asks for providing the insurance which is reflected in $\alpha_M\alpha_X/(\alpha_M+\alpha_X)^2 < 1/4$ when $\alpha_X < \alpha_M$. The second reason is that there are additional gains from risk sharing when $\alpha_X < \alpha_M$ since the contract allocates some of the risk to DC who cares less about it. These additional gains from risk sharing are divided equally between DC and CPE in the Nash Bargaining which is expressed by the term $1/2(\alpha_M-\alpha_X)$ in equation (6). Finally, the optimal price for X will depend on the level of profits c_1-c_2 that both agents earn in the transaction since in the Nash Bargaining these profits are split equally between them. This implies that the more (less) profitable the production of M the higher (lower) will s^* be while the reverse is the case for different sizes of DC's profit margin. s^* will be the lower the more monopoly power DC usually has in traditional transactions. Note that when the bargaining power of the agents is not as symmetric as the Nash Bargaining assumes but CPE is a powerful FTO making the offer of μ and s, then (6) reduces to $s^*-c_2=\sum_X$ implying that the price will just cover the risk that DC takes when supplying the futures market to CPE (this corresponds to the equilibrium point E_M shown in Figure 1).[13] The optimum amount of price insurance μ^* that corresponds to s^* is

[13] When $\alpha_X=\alpha_M$ equation (6) becomes $s^*-c_2=(c_1-c_2)/2$ with $(c_1-c_2)/2>\alpha\Theta^2/4$ reflecting that in this case the profits that are earned by both agents cover DC's risk cost $\sum_X=\alpha\Theta^2/4$ and the remaining profits are equally divided between them.

determined by

$$(7) \qquad \mu^* = \left[\frac{\alpha_M}{(\alpha_M + \alpha_X)}\right]\frac{\Theta}{s^*}$$

The higher the share of production for which the contract provides insurance s^*/Θ, and the smaller the difference in risk aversion between DC and CPE, the more will the contract need to look like a spot price contract (the smaller will μ need to be) in order to make DC accept the agreement. Note that the greater (lower) CPE's bargaining power the more (less) will the contract look like a fixed price contract as CPE will be able to achieve more price insurance at lower costs (compare equation (6) and (7) and the outcomes E_M and E in Figure 1).

IV. COMPARATIVE STATICS

In this section we undertake some comparative statics in order to see how changes in risk or risk aversion will affect the insurance features of the contract. Furthermore, we explore whether the gains from counterpurchase increase with larger risk aversion and thus look at whether the prediction of the model is consistent with our hypothesis that countertrade has increased since the mid seventies because the risk aversion of the CPEs and LDCs have increased in face of a tight foreign exchange constraint.

Consider Figure 2a for the effect of a change in the amount of risk on the

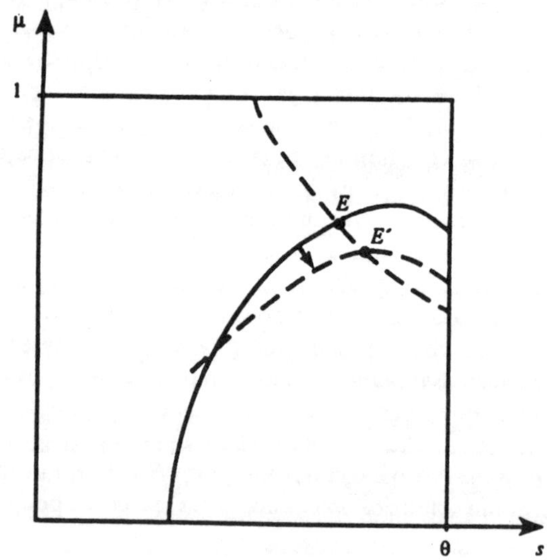

Figure 2a
Comparative Statics: $\Delta\sigma_p^2$

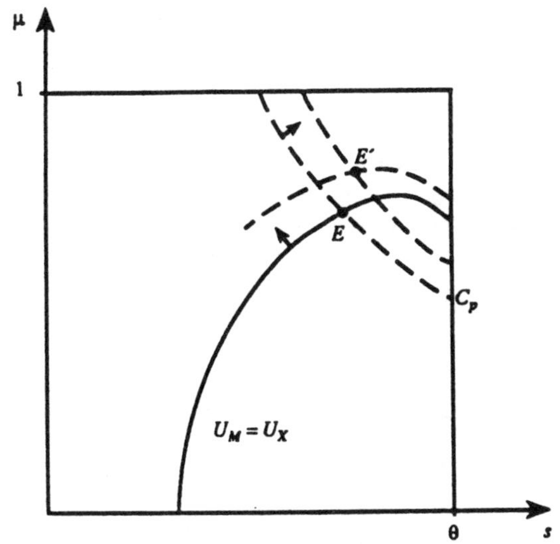

Figure 2b
Comparative Statics: ΔA_M

insurance features of the countertrade contract. Suppose that the amount of risk σ_p^2 increases and suppose further that DC's and CPE's attitude towards risk is not affected by this change in risk leaving A_M/A_X constant. A change in σ_p^2 leaves the C_p curve that describes the loci of Pareto optimal risk sharing unchanged since the Pareto outcomes depend on relative risk aversion only. An increase in σ_p^2 will shift the $U_X = U_M$ curve downwards as DC takes disproportionally more of the risk when she is less risk averse than CPE. In order for the utilities of both agents to remain the same CPE will need to pay a higher price for the insurance while getting a smaller amount of price insurance. Thus, an increase in risk will make the contract look more like a spot price contract and will require CPE to pay more for an insurance with less risk absorption. Figure 2b illustrates how the picture looks when CPE's risk aversion increases. An increase in A_M will shift the C_p curve upwards since the increase in relative risk aversion will now require DC to take a greater amount of risk from CPE in order for the gains from risk sharing to be maximized. The $U_X = U_M$ curve, in turn, will also shift upwards since CPE's greater risk aversion now means a lower benefit to him from the agreement requiring DC to compensate CPE for this loss in utility by offering more price insurance. s will also increase in response to the change in A_M because CPE is willing to pay more for a greater amount of price insurance or because CPE will want more output insurance when the amount of price insurance has increased. Thus, an increase in A_M will increase the amount of price and output insurance that CPE will receive in the contract.

In order to assess how the gains from countertrade are affected by an increase in CPE's risk aversion we distinguish two cases since the result depends critically on whether or not producing M is profitable without a risk sharing contract.

Case 1. $\Theta - C_0 > \sum_M$ that is the production of M is profitable without the countertrade insurance. In this case countertrade (CT) will increase in response to CPE's higher risk aversion. The first derivative of the gains from countertrade with respect to A_M is[14]

$$\frac{\delta CT}{\delta A_M} = \left[\frac{A_M^2}{(A_M+A_X)}\right]^2 \frac{\sum_M}{A_M} > 0$$

Case 2. $\Theta - C_0 < \sum_M$ that is the production of M is not profitable without the countertrade contract. In this case countertrade will decrease in response to an increase in A_M since

$$\frac{\delta CT}{\delta A_M} = \left[\frac{-A_X^2}{(A_M+A_X)^2}\right] \frac{\sum_M}{A_M} < 0$$

The reason for this result is as follows. When producing M is profitable without the insurance an increase in A_M makes the difference in risk aversion between DC and CPE larger which increases the gains from risk sharing stemming from the efficiency that arises when some of the risk is transferred to someone who cares less about it. However, when the production of M is not profitable without the insurance then an increase in A_M will lead merely to an increase in the costs of risk making CPE more reluctant to produce M in the countertrade contract. In other words, an increase in CPE's risk aversion makes the size of the pie larger when the production of M is profitable without any risk sharing arrangement, while it makes the size of the pie smaller when producing M is not profitable without an insurance. Thus, as long as the CPEs/LDCs produce goods with sufficiently high profits, an increase in their risk aversion will increase their demand for countertrade as additional gains from risk sharing can be exploited. This increase in risk aversion is our main explanation for why countertrade has increased since the mid seventies.[15]

V. CONCLUSIONS

In this paper we have developed a model explaining risk sharing arrange-

[14] The gains from countertrade are $(p_X^c - c_X)X + \min\{\Theta - C_0, \sum_M\} \geqslant \frac{A_X}{(A_X+A_M)}\sum_M + C_T$.

[15] From this follows that we expect these countries' demand for countertrade to decline with the reduction of their foreign debt. This result contradicts the view of international organizations who see countertrade to have increased because the CPEs/LDCs have increasingly become unable to earn sufficient foreign exchange in order to finance their imports and therefore are seen to use countertrade to export goods which they cannot export otherwise. See OECD [1981].

ments in international trade which play an especially important role in East–West trade and in trade with Developing Countries. The paper shows that countertrade contracts can be seen as a substitute for an absent futures market and, thus, as a second-best outcome when markets are incomplete. The model predicts that the agreement will tend to be a fixed price contract the smaller the risk is, the more the two parties differ in their attitude towards risk, and the more monopoly power the DC firm has in traditional transactions making the western firm which provides the insurance more willing to absorb a greater amount of risk at a price that the CPEs/LDCs are willing to accept. Finally, the model shows that the increase of countertrade in world trade observed since the mid seventies can be attributed to an increase in risk aversion of the CPEs/LDCs in face of a tight foreign exchange constraint.

By leading to more export stability countertrade might have promoted growth in the CPEs/LDCs.

A sufficient condition for countertrade to have a positive impact on the rate of investment and thus on the rate of growth is

$$\frac{A_X}{(A_X+A_M)}\textstyle\sum_M + C_T < \Theta - C_0 < \sum_M.$$

Countertrade will benefit the CPEs/LDCs in the form of higher investment when the investment becomes profitable under the risk sharing contract only. The reason why the investment might become profitable under countertrade when not being profitable without it is that the contract ties together two functions—the exporting of the good on the one hand and the provision of the insurance on the other. This way countertrade might accelerate investment and, thus, growth through export-led stability.[16]

ACCEPTED MAY 1993

ERWIN AMANN,
Department of Economics,
University of Dortmund,
Postfach 500,
D-4600 Dortmund 50,
Germany

and

DALIA MARIN,
Department of Economics,
Harvard University,
Cambridge, MA 02138,
USA.

[16] Whether more or less export stability will stimulate investment and growth is an open question, see Knudsen and Parnes [1975], Newbery and Stiglitz [1985].

APPENDIX

Proposition 1. The optimal risk sharing properties are given by

$$(1) \qquad s\mu = \frac{A_M}{A_M + A_X}\theta$$

Proof. CPE's and DC's indifference curves are determined by:

$$I_M: -1 + 2\alpha_M(\theta - s\mu)(\mu + s\mu'_M) = 0$$

$$I_X: 1 - 2\alpha_X s\mu(\mu + s\mu'_X) = 0$$

implying that $\mu + s\mu' > 0$. They are tangential to each other if and only if

$$2\alpha_M(\theta - s\mu) = 2\alpha_X s\mu$$

$$s\mu \lesseqgtr \frac{A_M}{A_M + A_X}\theta \Rightarrow \mu_M \lesseqgtr \mu_X \Rightarrow$$

there are Pareto improvements towards an increase (decrease) of μs. By the fact that $\alpha_M/(\alpha_M + \alpha_X) = A_M/(A_M + A_X)$ we get the desired result. □

Corollary 1. The utility of player CPE (DC) on the Pareto curve is monotonically increasing (decreasing) in μ. It is moreover linear in the interior of the strategy space $S = [0, 1] \times [0, \theta]$.

$$U_M = c_1 - s - \alpha_M \left(\frac{A_X}{A_X + A_M}\theta \right)^2$$

$$U_X = s - c_2 - \alpha_X \left(\frac{A_M}{A_X + A_M}\theta \right)^2$$

Remark: On the loci of the Pareto optima the division of the risk and thus $U_M + U_X$ remain constant.

Proposition 2. If there exists a Nash bargaining solution in interior S then it is determined by

$$(s, \mu) \in C_P$$

where C_P stands for Pareto Curve and

$$U_M = U_X$$

Proof. The first condition follows immediately. By Corollary 1 the Nash bargaining solution which is defined by arg max $U_M \cdot U_X$, maximizes

$$(\text{const.}_M - s)(s - \text{const.}_X)$$

The first order condition gives

$$s = \frac{\text{const.}_M - \text{const.}_X}{2}$$ □

REFERENCES

AMANN, E. and MARIN, D., 1990, 'Long-Term Contracts in International Trade', Centre for Economic Policy Research, Discussion Paper No. 413, London.

BANKS, G., 1983, 'The Economics and Politics of Countertrade', *The World Economy 2*, pp. 159–182.

CAVES, R. E. and MARIN, D., 1992, 'Countertrade Transactions: Theory and Evidence', *The Economic Journal*, 102, pp. 1171–1183.

GROUP OF THIRTY, 1985, *Countertrade in the World Economy*, New York.

KLEIN, B., CRAWFORD, R. C. and ALCHIAN, A. A., 1978, 'Vertical Integration, Appropriable Rents, and the Competitive Contracting Process', *Journal of Law and Economics*, 21(2), pp. 297–326.

KOGUT, B., 1986, 'On Designing Contracts to Guarantee Enforceability: Theory and Evidence from East–West Trade', *Journal of International Business Studies*, Spring, pp. 47–61.

KORTH, C. M. (ed.), 1987, *International Countertrade*, Westport, Quorum Books.

KNUDSEN, O. and PARNES, A., 1975, *Trade Instability and Economic Development*, Lexington.

MARIN, D., 1990, 'Tying in International Trade', *The World Economy 3*, pp. 445–462, Proceedings of the CEPR-NBER International Seminar on International·Trade, Cambridge, MA.

MARIN, D., 1991, 'Monopoly, Tying and Reciprocity: An Application to International Trade', Centre for Economic Policy Research, Discussion Paper No. 609, London.

MARIN, D. and SCHNITZER, M., 1993, *Tying Trade Flows: A Theory of Countertrade*, SFB 303, University of Bonn, Discussion Paper No. A-396.

DEMIRAMON, J., 1985, *Countertrade: An Illusionary Solution*, OECD Observer, Paris, OECD.

NEWBERY, D. M. G. and STIGLITZ, J. E., 1985, *The Theory of Commodity Price Stabilization*, Oxford, Clarendon Press.

ORGANIZATION FOR ECONOMIC COOPERATION AND DEVELOPMENT, 1981, *East–West Trade: Recent Developments in Countertrade*, Paris, OECD.

ORGANIZATION FOR ECONOMIC COOPERATION AND DEVELOPMENT, 1985, *Countertrade: Developing Country Practices*, Paris, OECD.

PARSONS, J. E., 1985, 'A Theory of Countertrade Financing of International Business, Sloan School of Management', MIT, Working Paper No. 1632–85.

VAN DAMME, E., 1987, *Stability and Perfection of Nash Equilibria*, Berlin–Heidelberg–New York, Springer.

WILLIAMSON, O., 1985, *The Economic Institution of Capitalism*, New York, Free Press.

Part V
Price Discrimination

[13]

1 The Economics of Reciprocity: Theory and Evidence on Bilateral Trading Arrangements

BY RICHARD E. CAVES*

MOST modern research on the theory of price discrimination in general equilibrium has sprung from the interest of countries in forming customs unions or free-trade areas. Yet these two forms of integration far from exhaust the kinds of preferential agreements that are observed in real life. The theorists have been conscious that their analyses potentially apply to a much wider set of arrangements – witness the titles of the two leading contemporary treatises [18], [38]. But they have not used their apparatus to explore all the positive and normative questions raised by some of these other types of discriminatory arrangements. Nor, perforce, has the general-equilibrium theory of discrimination been applied to these questions in practice.

The first section of this paper seeks to restate and extend parts of the theory of preferential trading, emphasising its relation to the simple theory of monopolistic discrimination. The second and third apply it respectively to two superficially disparate types of trading arrangements: bilateral trading agreements of the types used by less-developed economies; and 'reciprocity' deals between manufacturing firms, each of which produces an output that serves as an input to the other's production process. The similarity of these arrangements to each other has gone largely unnoticed,[1] and the application to them of the general-equilibrium theory of discrimination has been at best incomplete. I shall not contend that this theory provides a unique and sufficient explanation of either set of

* Harvard University.

[1] Compare [16, pp. 73–74].

arrangements – others will be noted – but that it is consistent with substantial amounts of evidence that we possess concerning their occurrence and effects.

1. The Theory of Reciprocal Trading Arrangements

Suppose that *m* entities barter *n* commodities among themselves, and that some subsets of entities form clubs and agree to trade some set of commodities among themselves at price ratios which differ from those prevailing between club members and the remaining traders. The general-equilibrium theory of preferential trading deals with arrangements taking this form. A club that we call a customs union covers all *n* commodities and normally commits its members to internal free trade (common internal opportunity-cost ratios for each member trading entity and among club members). The members adopt a common set of distortions between internal opportunity cost ratios and the external relative prices prevailing among the remaining traders; a free-trade area differs only in the absence of this latter step. A preferential trading area could clearly involve less than the full *n* traded commodities, or less than complete unification of internal opportunity-cost ratios among club members, or both. Indeed, the actual trading arrangements to be considered below share just these characteristics, usually covering two traders, two commodities (or at most a limited number), and leaving some divergence of the club's price ratio from the internal opportunity costs of its members.

Superficially, the theory of preferential trading as developed by Vanek [38] and Kemp [18] nicely matches this pattern of limited preferential arrangements. In order to achieve simplicity within a context of general equilibrium, it employs the minimum of three countries – two club members and the outside world – trading two commodities. It encompasses both small preferences – what Kemp calls a trading club – and complete free trade within the club. Numerous useful results have been derived concerning the conditions for gain to the club members, the distribution of gains (net of any compensation) among them, the resulting change in the welfare of excluded traders, the effect of unification of the club members' external tariff, and the like.

This theoretical model nicely matches the empirical cases to be investigated below, and it provides a seemingly apt analytical framework of discrimination in general equilibrium. Nonetheless, the theory of preferential trading has placed strikingly little emphasis on purposive welfare-maximising behaviour by a trader forming a preferential arrangement. The following would seem to be central questions:

(*a*) When trading entity A selects a potential partner B for forming a trading club, what traits does he seek in B that will maximise his gains from preferential trading?

(*b*) What distortion of the club's price ratio from that prevailing in the outside world maximises gains for the club (or its dominant member)?

Yet the first has received attention only in special contexts;[2] the second has been given a clear answer, but the answer has not been put to use ordering the taxonomy of cases governing the distribution of gains and losses from preferential trading. I shall first develop the simplest possible model of the discriminating monopolist in general equilibrium and then proceed with several theoretical cases chosen to supply findings useful in my subsequent review of bilateral trading arrangements and business reciprocity arrangements.

1.1 *Theory of discriminating monopoly in general equilibrium*

Reciprocal arrangements by definition involve the consent of two parties, whereas the simple theory of price discrimination[3] deals with unilateral action by a single seller able to divide his market. Yet no strong distinction should be made between them, since the willingness of customers to continue after a simple monopoly price is converted into a discriminatory price structure constitutes (in partial equilibrium) an acceptance of a bilateral trading arrangement as superior to the available alternatives. Furthermore, a discriminating monopolist could conceivably enter into an agreement with a favoured buyer to divide the increment of profits as a bribe, say, for declining to

[2] Primarily in papers investigating the consequences of social preferences regarding the mix of activities in which the nation's factor stock is employed, e.g. a desire for 'industry' *per se*. See [7] and [17, especially pp. 279–281]. But its applicability is clearly wider than this.

[3] The classic source is Robinson [25, chap. 15].

resell to the disfavoured customer. Thus it is clear that the considerations underlying simple price discrimination can support an attempt to explain barter-type trading arrangements in a setting where each trader in general is large enough to possess some monopoly/monopsony power in the markets for some commodities.[4]

As Henderson [16a] has shown, partial-equilibrium price discrimination is easily translated into general ebuilibrium with two commodities by the use of reciprocal demand curves, which I assume to be derived from the trade-indifference curves developed by Meade [22]. They thus reflect each entity's willingness to trade at any given price ratio after optimal internal adjustment of production and consumption is made.[5] In Figure 1.1, potential monopolist A exports commodity 2 and imports commodity 1 in its trade with both B and C, whose individual reciprocal-demand curves are illustrated (*OB* and *OC*). If B and C can be confronted with different terms of trade, implying that they cannot exchange commodities 1 and 2 costlessly between themselves,[6] A can select an offer which optimises his trading position with each of them separately. A is required to set prices which equate his internal marginal rates of substitution in production and consumption to his marginal rate of substitution through trade with each party. In terms of offer-curve geometry, this means equating the slopes of an appropriately chosen point on A's highest attainable trade-indifference curve and points on B's and C's offer curves.

The solution can be shown by constructing for A the 'total revenue' curve that indicates the maximum amount of commodity 1 that A can secure through monopolistic discrimination in the sale of any given amount of commodity 2. This is

[4] It is also clear that this line of investigation loses interest in circumstances where market power must be assumed absent.

[5] It is perhaps not obvious under what conditions this apparatus is applicable to the multiproduct business enterprise. I shall consider this matter in Section 3.

[6] In fact, with three countries trading two undifferentiated commodities in the absence of transport costs, one would expect no trading link to exist in competitive equilibrium between one pair of them. If B also exported 2 to C and imported 1, B would implicitly be re-exporting the commodities that it imports from both A and C. To preclude resale in the case of price discrimination of course requires an additional assumption.

equivalent to adding the two offer curves by cumulating small segments of each in order of their maximum slopes, defined as quantities of commodity 1 offered per unit of commodity 2. The process is, of course, analogous to the horizontal aggregation of marginal-revenue curves employed in the partial-equilibrium solution. Once a point has been reached on the steeper (*OC*) offer curve that equals the slope of B's curve at the origin, this aggregation can be done by sliding C's origin along the *OB* curve, keeping the shifting origin at a point whose slope equals the slope of C's curve at the point tracing out the real-total-revenue function (*OMT*). Thus the slope of C's curve at *M*, a point on the envelope function, equals the slope of B's curve at *O'*. Where one of A's trade-indifference curves is tangent to the envelope at *M*, the marginal conditions for maximising A's gains from trade would be satisfied by charging B and C the prices indicated by slopes *OO'* and *O'M* respectively. The higher price is charged to the buyer enjoying the greater average intramarginal surplus.[7]

Note that this envelope total-revenue function will in general lie outside of a collective B–C offer curve aggregated in the way that would describe the trading opportunities if A were to behave either as a pure competitor or a simple monopolist.[8] This is analogous to the distinction between the demand and average-revenue curves made in the partial-equilibrium theory of discriminating monopoly.

A could effect this differential by discriminatory export or import taxes equal to the difference between the slope of a tangent at *M* and the slopes of *OO'* and *O'M* for B and C respectively. This case thus provides answers to the two questions raised in regard to maximising A's gains from trade:

[7] Because the elasticity of an offer curve as generally drawn changes throughout its length, and because position ('intensity of demand') matters as well as elasticity, it is not formally appropriate to describe the disfavoured buyer as possessing the less elastic demand. I shall nonetheless use this expression below as shorthand for the concept of a buyer whose demand for small quantities is 'intense' but whose elasticity of reciprocal demand falls relatively fast as his volume of imports increases. Inelastic stretches of the offer curves are, of course, irrelevant.

[8] This aggregation is shown by Becker [5]. The whole analysis could equally well be carried out in terms of consumption-possibility loci for A [4].

A should choose B as its partner in a trading club and should grant B a preference equal to the difference between slopes OO'

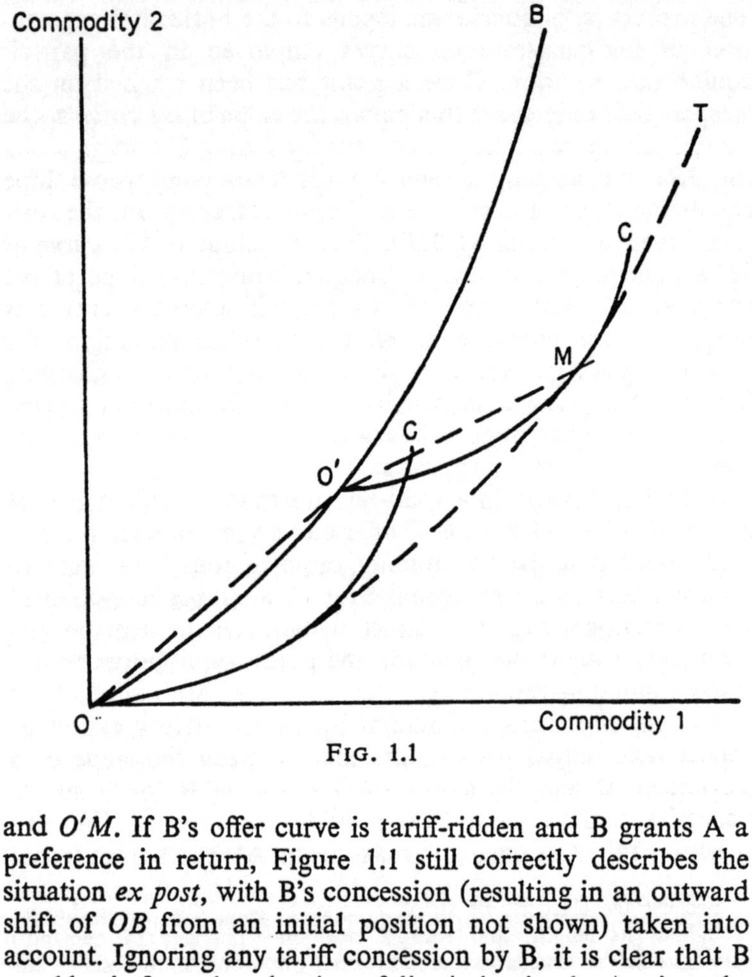

FIG. 1.1

and $O'M$. If B's offer curve is tariff-ridden and B grants A a preference in return, Figure 1.1 still correctly describes the situation *ex post*, with B's concession (resulting in an outward shift of OB from an initial position not shown) taken into account. Ignoring any tariff concession by B, it is clear that B would gain from the adoption of discrimination by A; given the assumption of constant or diminishing returns in A's production structure, B's terms of trade must have improved from an initial non-discriminatory value lying between OO' and $O'M$, permitting B to reach a higher trade-indifference curve at O'. Likewise, A benefits by moving to a trade-indifference curve tangent at M from one that was tangent to a collective B–C offer curve lying uniformly inside *OMT*. A does not benefit, strictly speaking, from the preferential terms of trade offered to B, but rather from the adoption of price discrimination overall. C loses through deterioration of its terms of trade.

Note that the employment of bilateral agreements is incidental to A's unilateral maximisation of welfare through discrimination. That is, what the argument shows is the scope for mutually acceptable trading agreements as vehicles for achieving discrimination. Why such a vehicle is chosen becomes an important but secondary question.[9] It could serve to commit B to preclude resale or otherwise augment A's gains from favouring B; B could bribe a politically reluctant A to undertake discrimination; and so forth. An agreement between A and C is conceivable, but only to formalise C's defeat for lack of a trading alternative. The real question raised by an agreement between A and C, however, is that of the all-or-nothing offer.

1.2 *The role of the all-or-nothing offer*

The all-or-nothing offer, a simple extension of the theory of discriminating monopoly developed in Section 1.1, could readily be embodied in an agreement on the exchange of limited numbers of commodities, as is suggested by references to 'bulk trading' and 'coercive reciprocity' in the trading experience reviewed below. Baldwin [4] has shown how a trading entity capable of inflicting an all-or-nothing offer on a partner can calculate the maximum barter offer that can be forced, at any given terms of trade, and derive therefrom a reciprocal demand curve for the partner showing the set of maximum all-or-nothing offers that would just lie on the margin of acceptability. It can be thought of as a means of extracting the best gross barter terms of trade or the maximum volume of imports attainable for any given quantity of exports.

In general, the same traits make a trader more vulnerable to an all-or-nothing offer as make him a candidate for being the disfavoured partner in simple price discrimination. Figure 1

[9] Some writers on business reciprocity (especially [3, 14]) have raised the question of why barter agreements should be used when the discriminating monopolist can maximise by simply rigging the money price of any product in which he has the requisite market power.

can be taken as showing the process of determining optimal all-or-nothing offers to two trading partners if we suppose that *OB* and *OC* at the outset represent all-or-nothing offer curves. A trading agreement would be central to imposing an all-or-nothing offer on any partner, but its payout would be greater with one who would be disfavoured in a move from simple monopoly to discriminating monopoly. This contrasts to the case of discrimination without an all-or-nothing offer, where a bilateral trading agreement seems most useful to deal with the favoured trader.

At the limit, all-or-nothing offers would improve A's welfare (as against any alternative trading systems) and leave B and C indifferent as against no trade at all. Beyond this it is neither simple nor, for present purposes, useful to go on comparing the all-or-nothing offer to alternative trading situations.

1.3 *Selection of trading partner and distribution of benefits*

The literature on preferential trading has not assumed the discriminating monopolist's rationality in the choice of partners. The presence or absence of this rationality, however, serves usefully to classify the possible distributions of gains and losses from preferential arrangements that it predicts. I wish to develop this point and also to show how the more myopic approach taken by customs-union theory usefully points to the criteria that a rational trader would use in picking a 'good' partner for an agreement.

Figure 1.2[10] describes the same trading situation as Figure 1.1 but does not depict the offer curves faced by A and, instead, concentrates on the divergences for A and B between internal opportunity costs and external price ratios (all taxes or subsidies causing these distortions are assumed to be financed by lump-sum transfers). *OT* is the *initial* world price ratio at which A trades with B and C. Trade is restricted by both A and B, so that their internal opportunity-cost ratios are relatively unfavourable to their respective export goods. This is illustrated by the slopes of tangents at P_A and P_B to trade-indifference curves of A and B respectively. Note that A's initial trade with C is shown by the

[10] Figures 2 and 3 employ the same basic devices and notation as a number of those presented by Kemp [18], whose exposition provides the most convenient point of contact with the literature.

vector $P_B P_A$, indicating the excess of A's offer of two for one over B's offer of one for two at *OT*. Now A and B form a trading club that involves a *small* cut of their trade restrictions in favour of each other. A's original restrictions remain in relation to its trade with C, however. If the preference causes *no* change in A's terms of trade with C (C's offer curve is

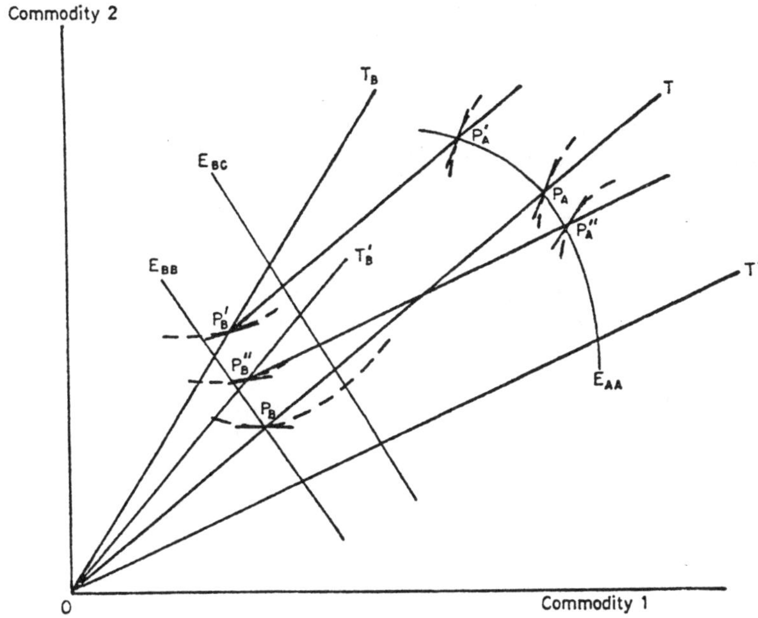

FIG. 1.2

perfectly elastic), it is clear that A will lose from the exchange of preferences. If A continues to trade with C to some extent, A's internal opportunity-cost ratio remains locked to terms of trade *OT*, and the effect of the preferential reduction in A's tariff is to let B trade at prices, indicated by OT_B, that are somewhat more favourable than *OT*. Trade between A and B is now shown by vector OP'_B. Point P'_B serves as a base for A's trading vector with C, this trade continuing at the original terms *OT*. Trade with C carries A to a position of equilibrium at P'_A, placing A on a lower trade-indifference curve than before, B on a higher one, and leaving C's welfare unaffected.

Clearly, this result is consistent with Section 1.1; offering a preference to one trading partner in a 'competitive' market cannot be a profitable unilateral act for the donor. A could benefit from this manouvre, without destroying B's gains, only if the terms of trade OT improve. This requires, of course, that the discrimination favouring B shrinks A's trade with C *and* results in improved terms of trade. Should the preference improve A's external terms of trade to OT, B's gains would be reduced. The preference now improves B's terms of trade with A only to OT'_B; B's trading equilibrium at P''_B still results in a higher welfare level than P_B. But A's trading vector with C, $P''_B P''_A$ (parallel to the new final terms of trade OT'), permits A to enjoy a higher level of welfare at P''_A rather than a lowered one at P'_A.[11]

The conclusions of the preceding two paragraphs are standard in the literature [18, chap. 2; 38, chap. 2]. What I wish to point out is those traits of B's trade-indifference map which make it a relatively attractive entity to be tapped by A for membership in a trading club. A 'myopic criterion' that A might naturally employ is the extent to which a preference for B would expand A–B trade and thereby shrink the volume and improve the terms of A's trade with C. The relevant traits are shown by the Engel curves E_{ij} where i is the country whose Engel curve is shown and j is the country whose prices (initial internal opportunity costs) give rise to the particular curve. Thus E_{BB} is B's Engel curve at B's own initial prices. Also shown is E_{BC}, B's Engel curve at initial world or external prices (I assume for expository convenience that C is a free trader). A preference granted by A to B tends to raise B's income and push B's internal prices toward the initial external terms of trade OT. Figure 2 makes clear that the resulting expansion of A–B trade will be greater the higher is B's income elasticity of demand for imports (the steeper is E_{BB}) and the higher is the marginal rate of substitution in B (the farther does E_{BC} lie from E_{BB} along OT).[12] A's own preference map (slope of E_{AA}) of course also affects the outcome.

[11] There is nothing to preclude the preference improving the terms of trade sufficiently for A that B's benefits from the preference are more than offset by the loss on its basic terms of trade: P''_B lies below P_B.

[12] It is worth recalling that these are trade-indifference curves. They incorporate substitution in production and, without necessarily violating

So far I have neglected the possibility of compensation. A *sufficiently* large improvement in A's terms of trade could leave B worse off, but it would always pay A to bribe B to enter into the arrangement, leaving B on or above the indifference curve at P_B and A at a position preferred to P_A. Other significant roles for compensation will be noted below.

1.4 *Optimal rate of preference and possibilities for compensation*

Section 1.1 indicated the optimal preference for the favoured trading partner from the viewpoint of the discriminating monopolist. That analysis neglected the possibilities of compensation being paid as part of the reciprocal bargain, and took only passing notice of the possible consequences of trade restrictions by the passive partner. Both factors influence the possibilities of mutually beneficial reciprocal arrangements. In contrast to the case of the discriminating monopolist, the theory of customs unions shows that the arrangement maximising the *joint* welfare of A and B as trading-club members is internal free trade coupled with a common 'optimum tariff' against the outside world [18, chap. 8].[13] This solution differs from the result of discriminating monopoly pricing by A in B's favour, and a bribe from B to A would generally be both profitable for B and necessary to induce A to move to the solution that maximises their joint welfare.[14]

As in Section 1.3, however, some useful predictions seem to emerge from more myopic cases in which A's and B's trading club raises their joint welfare without necessarily maximising it.

stability conditions, can encompass increasing returns [22, chap. 5]. Thus, the distance between E_{BB} and E_{BC} along OT might be substantially augmented by a range of increasing returns in B's production-possibility function. (This would raise the chances of a reversal in the pattern of trade between A and B, a possibility not considered here.)

[13] In terms of Figure 1.2, this would require, in the case where the external terms of trade are variable, that the slopes of A's and B's trade-indifference curves be equal at P''_A and P''_B, wherefore B's trade-indifference curve would be tangent to vector OT'_B at P''_B; and that the difference in slopes between P''_A and OT' corresponds to the optimum tariff. That is, the common slope at P''_B and P''_A should equal the slope of C's offer curve at the point of equilibrium. Figure 2 as drawn depicts cases in which A and B have failed to exhaust the possibilities of mutually beneficial preferences.

[14] These conclusions relate to the earlier discussion of compensation and tariff-ridden offer curves by Scitovsky, Johnson and others.

Specifically, I shall explore the arrangement that maximises the gain from preferential trading when actions by the club have no effect on the external terms of trade.[15] This gain is conceptually independent of the gain from improving the external terms of trade, since we can define the optimum rate of internal preference *relative* to the external terms of trade, and thus determine it for those terms which would correspond to the optimum tariff or, alternatively, for any other value of the external terms of trade. The case where the external terms are given pertains not only to circumstances where A and B are relatively small traders. It also serves most usefully to illustrate the case where the prices of goods 1 and 2, and thus the external terms of trade, are fixed by imperfectly collusive arrangements involving A, B, and other parties. The preferential arrangement between A and B in that case becomes a device for one of them to chisel on his collusive agreement without, he hopes, provoking an adverse shift in the market price of his export.

In Figure 1.3 the external terms of trade are given at *OT*; OP_B again represents initial A–B trade, and P_BP_A is A's trading vector with C. In this case no discrimination in favour of B is profitable for A, and a small preference for B would, as before, raise B's welfare while reducing A's. Suppose, however, that B undertakes to bribe A to offer such a preference. Given A's external tariff (and the fixed distortion that it introduces between A's internal opportunity-cost ratio and world prices or C's internal ratio), we can identify the optimum rate of preference for B in A's tariff as the one which would maximise A's welfare subject to the condition that the bribe paid by B just exhausts B's gains from the preference. (That is, B's bribe is the maximum it would pay to secure a given preference.)

As Figure 1.3 shows, this optimum rate of preference would be the one that just offsets the distortion introduced by B's own tariff and aligns B's internal prices with those prevailing in the outside world (*OT*, or C's internal opportunity-cost ratio). E_{BC} is B's Engel curve at these external prices, and the rate of preference just defined would leave B's trading point somewhere

[15] I shall assume throughout that changes in production and consumption in B, when a non-incremental preference changes internal prices, never suffice to extinguish or reverse A's trade with C. Kemp [18] thoroughly explores the conditions under which such changes occur.

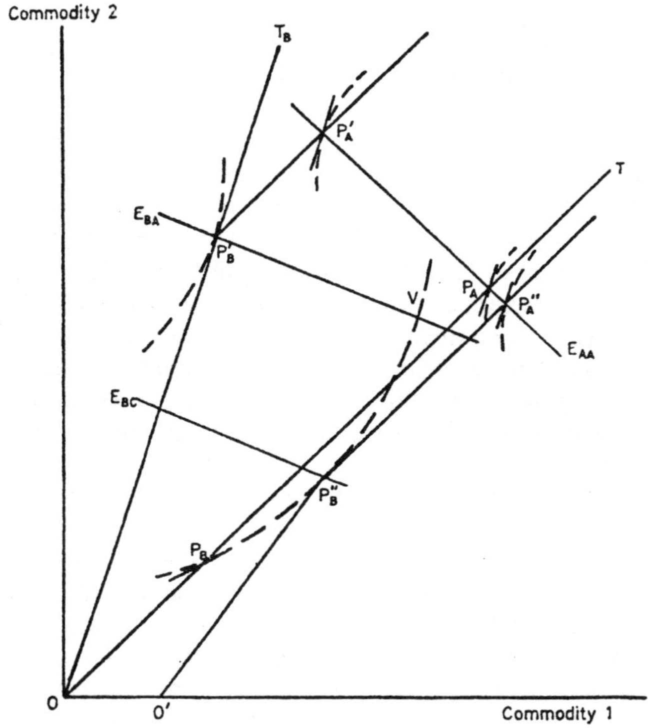

FIG. 1.3

on this line. The maximum that B would pay to A for this preference would be OO' of commodity 1. After this bribe is paid, A trades with B from O' to P''_B, the vector $O'P''_B$ offering to B external prices that lie between world prices (OT) and A's internal prices (slope at P_A). (The size of the bribe is determined by the size of the preference needed to align B's internal prices with world prices OT.) At P''_B B is left on the same trade-indifference curve as at P_B – its welfare just failing to be improved by the preference. A also trades with C at unchanged external prices along $P''_BP''_A$; given these prices it is clear that no rate of preference, leaving B at some other point on its original trade-indifference curve, would permit A so large a gain in welfare. In short, even without gains from discriminating monopoly, a preferential arrangement could be mutually beneficial to the extent that it offsets inefficient tariff protection by one of the partners. Further gains would be available to the club if A also moves to an optimum external tariff, which with fixed external terms of trade would be zero.

Figure 1.3 also allows us to show (following Kemp [18, chap. 4]) that for A and B to go all the way to internal free trade may be inefficient when the external tariff is not optimised. Free trade permits B to trade at A's internal prices along the vector OT_B, whose slope is equal to that at P_A. Trade between A and B would be carried to P'_B, leaving B better off than at P_B; A trades with C at the unchanged external terms of trade along $P'_BP'_A$ and, in the absence of compensation, emerges worse off at P'_A. The question is, could B bribe A to form a free-trade area and thereby improve A's welfare while leaving B no worse off? In the Figure as drawn, the answer is no. At A's internal prices, the maximum bribe that B would pay carries it to V, the intersection of its original trade-indifference curve with the relevant Engel curve E_{BA}. Although this bribe exceeds OO', it would not allow A a net improvement in welfare; A would trade from V along a vector parallel to OT, winding up at a point on E_{AA} that is inferior to P_A.[16] Thus we see that bribes might go either way; A might bribe B to co-operate in discrimination that would improve A's terms of trade (Section 1.3), or alternatively B might bribe A for help in an admittedly circuitous exercise in offsetting the welfare cost of B's own tariff.

In the cases considered in this section, as in Section 1.1, an agreement is not necessary to every preferential arrangement that will raise the welfare of one trader without worsening that of the favoured partner. It becomes necessary when compensation must be paid, and it clearly may be useful in all cases for various incidental purposes. It can help to disguise discrimination, a likely requirement if one or both trading partners take part in imperfect collusive agreements to keep the prices of their export goods above the level of internal opportunity costs. In Figure 1.3, for example, consider the total transaction between A and B involved in reaching trading point P''_B – a bribe by B of OO' followed by trade to P''_B. Taking the exchange as a whole, it appears that B has been afflicted with worse terms of

[16] A free-trade area is not necessarily without net benefit; point V could equally well lie below OT, permitting A to trade to a superior position. The result depends on the shape of B's trade-indifference curve.

trade (a line from O to P''_B would be flatter than OT), yet with a slight reduction in the bribe, B would become better off. As with simple monopolistic discrimination, the possibilities of disguise through reciprocal agreements are further expanded if we note that compensation for some other debt might be thrown into the same package.

1.5 *Predictions from theory of preferential trading*

Besides showing what preferential agreements would be chosen by optimising trading entities, this section has sought to predict the empirical occurrence and weigh the significance of several types of discriminatory arrangements. In framing a study of actual trading agreements, theory will ideally allow us to work backward from the structural traits, form, and content of the agreement to its economic significance. The inventory basically contains three possible types of agreement. Section 1.1 showed the potential uses of agreements to implement monopolistic discrimination, especially as a device for disguising the treatment given to the favoured buyer, securing his co-operation in preventing resale, or perhaps extracting a bribe for the favouritism. The agreement embodying an all-or-nothing offer, noted in Section 1.2, would differ in worsening rather than improving the terms of trade of the 'passive' partner, although either type of agreement should result in an expansion of bilateral trade.

Discriminatory reciprocal trading agreements can also result from the efforts of traders to improve their market positions in the face of constraining collusive agreements on price or other restraints on trade that deter gainful independent action by the trader (Section 1.4). Unlike the types of agreements effecting monopolistic discrimination, this class depends on an initial situation of disequilibrium going deeper than the failure to exploit all profitable discrimination. There is hope of distinguishing this type of 'competitive discrimination'[17] on the basis of its necessary relation to these initial conditions. Making this distinction is important for a correct normative evaluation

[17] This label is only partly satisfactory and hence will be kept in quotation marks. Its sense is that: (*a*) monopoly power for the club members as a bloc is not necessary; (*b*) discrimination can result from defections from collusive or monopolistic agreements.

of trading agreements. As specialists in industrial organisation have long recognised, although a clear case exists against monopolistic forms of discrimination, 'competitive discrimination' may possess redeeming virtues if it serves as a wedge to erode a collusively maintained price or undermine other inefficiencies.

2. Trade Agreements of Developing Countries

Bilateral trading agreements have been used extensively by the developing countries during the past two decades, both among themselves and with the centrally planned economies.[18] These agreements are far from homogeneous in form, running from specific agreements on the exchange of particular commodities (sometimes with compensation or planned imbalance) to general shopping lists that involve on the surface no more than 'a simple expression of mutual friendship and interest' [36, pp. 86–87]. These barter arrangements shade into other types of bilateral dealings among countries, such as the outright state-trading operations of the centrally planned economies and the agreements used by the industrial nations after the Second World War to permit the balanced bilateral expansion of trade in the face of extreme shortages of international reserves.

My procedure will be to suggest a number of hypotheses based on the theoretical analysis of preferential trading and to note how fully the available evidence on these trading agreements seems to confirm them. My aim will be to establish or reject *some* role for the model of discrimination in explaining these agreements, and not to exclude competing hypotheses. The hypothetical alternatives are numerous. Trading agreements could serve as devices for reducing uncertainty, as ways to reduce fluctuations in international reserves and thus reduce

[18] The only systematic survey information seems to be that collected by the UNO Economic Commission for Africa. It uncovered around three hundred agreements drawn between 1955 and 1963, a large minority of them with other African countries, the bulk of the rest with the centrally planned economies. Bilateral trade under these agreements accounts for something approaching a fifth of Africa's total trade [32, pp. 3–11]. Virtually all African countries have concluded at least one such agreement [33, pp. 15–16].

the need for reserves, or as ways of accommodating the administrative necessities of the centrally planned economies. Ideally, empirical evidence could be gathered that would weigh the explanatory force of these hypotheses against the discrimination model. Unfortunately, what is readily available proves quite inadequate for that purpose; the limited descriptive sources lack much of the pertinent information, and only India's experience has been analysed at all extensively [1] [9] [10] [26].

2.1 *Implementing a preferential agreement*

For a trading agreement to give rise to a discriminatory transaction, it must either stipulate the quantities of goods to be exchanged or substitute some institution for the competitive market to settle the terms of the barter. But this does not seem the typical case. All surveys seem to agree that arrangements of the 'shopping list' variety are in the majority.[19] This lack of extensive preplanning is also shown in the wide dispersion of actual trade levels *ex post* around the targets stipulated in the agreements [23, pp. 77–86]. Even the 'shopping list' agreement could give rise to discrimination, however, if it set up some device that permits non-market transactions or balances to develop. One such device is the use of a state-trading institution by the less-developed country. This is clearly not uncommon, either as a general tool of policy or as an agency to implement trading agreements.[20] Another is the periodic review of the state of bilateral balance of trade under the agreement. A central clearing arrangement is frequently used, and the negotiations over bilateral clearing balances obviously could control the terms of the gross barter transaction.

2.2 *Terms of trade under preferential agreements*

For a trading arrangement to result in discrimination, it must lead to terms of trade (net of lump-sum compensation, and measured outside of tariff walls) that differ from those prevailing with non-members of the club. As Sections 1.1, 1.2 and 1.4 show, assessing the *sign* of the difference requires further information about which party is (the more effectively)

[19] See [23, pp. 67–70; 33, p. 15; 36, pp. 86–87].
[20] See [9, p. 62; 34; 35, p. 27].

sequestered from market alternatives and whether an all-or-nothing offer is in force.

Certainly, there is convincing evidence that *some* less-developed countries take deteriorated terms of trade under *some* bilateral arrangements in order to segment the markets for their primary products, and indeed this is one of the publicly stated objectives of these agreements.[21] Sometimes a tariff preference is explicitly involved, although the terms of the General Agreement on Tariffs and Trade discourage this practice [32, p. 47; 33, p. 17]. Some agreements made by the developing countries, especially with the centrally planned economies, seem to yield after the event poorer terms than multilateral trading, although one cannot tell whether this situation was tacitly foreseen by the contracting parties or instead represents an unanticipated result.[22] Still, many analyses suggest that the bulk of transactions under bilateral agreements take place at world market prices, and that even the trade flows handled by state trading corporations may be marked up by similar percentages both ways, so that no significant net distortion results. India's experience, which has been examined in some detail [1; 9; 10; 26, chap. 2, pp. 287–288], is consistent with no net distortions. Furthermore, the significance of discrimination under bilateral arrangements becomes obscure in those cases where the parties both suffer overvalued exchange rates; what appears to be discrimination with particular commodity markets might not be when assessed at a correct shadow price for convertible foreign currency.[23] One can conclude from this evidence only that the terms under some bilateral arrangements are consistent with the implementing of monopolistic discrimination.

2.3 *Discrimination and resale*

For a trading agreement to involve discrimination at least one trader must be able to segment the market for his exports.

[21] See [32, pp. 21, 36–37; 33, pp. 15–16; 35, pp. 28–29].

[22] See [23, pp. 43–44; 32, pp. 61–64; 39, pp. 100–101].

[23] In confirmation of this, bilateral arrangements among countries with inconvertible currencies sometimes exclude trade in commodities with extensive export markets in convertible-currency areas. See [12, p. 349; 30, p. 52; 39, p. 98].

That is, some trait of the product, its characteristics of use, or the structure of transport costs must impose significant restraints on its resale by the favoured buyer. Alternatively, the terms of the agreement may involve a prohibition on resale.

Bilateral trading agreements typically cover primary products or occasionally simple manufactures, not easily susceptible of market segmentation. Thus one would expect evidence of difficulties in preventing resale if discrimination is occurring. Developing countries have complained periodically of resale of their primary products on multilateral markets by the centrally planned economies, confirming the use of agreements by the former group to effect discrimination (Section 2.2). Furthermore, some agreements in fact do preclude re-exports unless specific permission is secured.[24] Since the agreements in question are among nations with inconvertible currencies, they might be serving as an offset to disequilibrium exchange rates.

2.4 *Demand elasticity and choice of partner*

It was noted that the trading partner likely to be favoured by discrimination through a bilateral trading agreement would tend to be one with high income and substitution elasticities for one's export product (Section 1.3). The height of these parameters is a relative matter, of course. Profitable discrimination requires not only that they differ, but also that the exporter bulks large enough as a supplier of the goods in question that these differences can be monopolistically exploited.

Although these predictions could be tested in some detail, I shall settle for reporting impressions from the evidence at hand. The developing countries in most cases enter into trading agreements covering only their principal exports. The nations most active in forging these arrangements seem to be the larger ones, whose exports of individual products are thus more likely to comprise a significant share of world production. Scattered evidence, including a detailed analysis for India, suggests that the relatively low-income countries selected as club members are likely to have higher income elasticities for primary products than the industrial nations. A weaker probabilistic argument

[24] For evidence on these points see [13, pp. 331–332; 23, pp. 40–41, 54–59; 30, pp. 52–54; 32, p. 61; 33, p. 15].

along this line can be made for their price elasticities. The trading of simple manufactures under bilateral agreements by countries such as United Arab Republic seems consistent with this prediction.[25]

2.5 *Preferential trading and debtors' bargaining power*

Practices in the settlement of net balances under bilateral trading agreements are quite various, but debts are not typically cleared up through the transfer of convertible currencies. Furthermore, swing credits are usually extended, so that the club members focus their joint attention on the net balance only at infrequent intervals. Given these practices, theory suggests weakly that a trading partner selected as a buyer whose demand will respond sensitively to a price concession will enjoy some bargaining power when the question arises of settling debit balances that he has built up. (The same holds true no matter what the benefit accruing to the creditor; this prediction supports the discrimination hypothesis only in that the expansion of the creditor's sales matches his hypothetical motive for joining the club.)

Examples are rather common of bilateral creditors making generous concessions when they negotiate terms for clearing up outstanding balances. The debtor's exports may be valued significantly above world prices, or the creditor may settle for commodities in excess of its import quotas or of substandard quality that renders them difficult to sell or utilise.[26]

2.6 *Adverse demand shifts and resort to bilateral trading*

It was argued in Section 1.4 that a preferential trading arrangement can become particularly attractive when external terms of trade are inefficiently out of line with an entity's internal opportunity costs. This would be the case both for small traders restricting their commerce, although unable to improve their terms of trade thereby, and participants in imperfectly collusive price-fixing arrangements who can benefit from selective price concessions even without raising the price to disfavoured buyers. The latter line of argument in particular predicts that interest in preferential trading arrangements would rise when demand for

[25] See [9, pp. 58–60] on India, [32, pp. 51–55] on U.A.R.
[26] See [12, pp. 358–359; 30, p. 52; 39, pp. 100–101].

a particular principal export declines, unless prices are fully flexible.

Many observers note that bilateral trading arrangements arise when countries are facing either deteriorating terms of trade or Balance of Payments difficulties from reductions in the demand for their exports. The worsening terms of trade experienced by many developing countries after the Korean War offered a strong incentive to seek out bilateral arrangements, and they spread rapidly at that time [12, p. 361; 32, pp. 46, 63–64]. Devaluation by an export competitor has caused resort bilateral agreements [32, pp. 30, 41]. The evidence also suggests that distorted price structures encourage the use of agreements when selective price reductions are more attractive than general ones [30, p. 85; 12, pp. 349, 352]. If trading arrangements are used to offset fluctuating sales in multilateral markets, one would expect that trade flows under bilateral agreements would not necessarily be stable themselves, but that they would contribute to the stability of a country's total trade. This result has been noted by those remarking on the failure of bilateral agreements themselves to generate a stable flow of trade [9, pp. 64–65; 35, p. 28].

This evidence does not necessarily point to 'competitive discrimination' undertaken to offset inefficient distortions of trade if we allow that preferential arrangements might result from 'satisficing' behaviour. That is, monopolistic discrimination might be sought only in response to a downturn in the gain from simple monopoly. The uncertainties and administrative costs of bilateral arrangements also might cause countries to pursue them seriously only when their terms of trade worsen, even if discrimination would have been profitable prior to the adverse development. The primacy of 'competitive discrimination' would be shown, however, if we find that countries negotiate bilateral arrangements in response to those concluded by other countries. This defensive behaviour has been occasionally noted [26, p. 194; 30, p. 80].

2.7 *Preferential arrangements and volume of trade*

It is well known that movement of a seller from simple monopoly to a profit-increasing position of discriminating monopoly does not necessarily increase the total quantity sold.

Nonetheless, the agreement with the favoured buyer taken alone should result in an increased volume of trade. Furthermore, since a shift of the terms of trade against the disfavoured buyer seldom seems to coincide with the adoption of a preferential arrangement, one would expect the preference also to result in the short run in increased internal prices and total production of the commodities exported under the agreement.

Once more, causal support exists for both predictions. Very large expansions of bilateral trade following agreements are often noted, although in developing countries this growth could also result because official efforts are necessary to bestir the forging of commercial links. An examination of India's experience confirms the increase of internal prices of exportables associated with the expansion of trade under bilateral arrangements [1; 10; 26, chap. 9].

2.8 *Compensation and extraneous transfers*

If a purpose of trading agreements is to effect clandestine price discrimination, it is possible that bribes might be negotiated as part of the arrangement (Sections 1.3, 1.4). Likewise, there may be advantages in lumping extraneous transfers into the agreements in order to assist in disguising their discriminatory significance.

The information available on trading agreements is too thin to allow developing and testing predictions about the direction of compensation. Still, it is worth noting the evidence that these agreements frequently serve as vehicles for planned transfers or compensations that may or may not be extraneous to the trading agreement. Agreements are used as vehicles for the transfer of foreign aid from the centrally planned economies and between France and her former colonies. The repayment of long-term credits in commodities may be part of an agreement, or alternatively the device may be used to tie foreign aid. Such extraneous matters may be involved as co-operation in air transport and the use of port facilities.[27] Although these instances are consistent with the use of trading agreements for discriminatory purposes, they cannot be said to provide positive evidence.

[27] For evidence see [23, pp. 19–24; 26, chap. 3; 32, pp. 9–10, 16–17, 47–48; 33, pp. 17–18].

2.9 *Summary and evaluation*

Some evidence supports each of a number of predictions about bilateral trading agreements used by the developing countries, drawn from the general-equilibrium theory of preferential arrangements. It is too weak to assert the primacy of this motive behind the agreements, although in a few cases it seems to out-perform other explanations of these agreements where they supply contradictory predictions.[28] I can only offer the usual hope that more detailed information will someday permit the competing explanations to be unravelled more thoroughly. The theory of preferential trading in fact predicts discrimination of several different sorts – monopolistic action with or without all-or-nothing offers, and 'competitive discrimination' to offset inefficient trade interferences or cheat on collusive prices. The evidence here supports the existence of both competitive and monopolistic discrimination without permitting even a qualitative judgement on their respective significance. Little if any evidence confirms the prevalence of the all-or-nothing offer, however much attention it has received in the general literature on state trading.

3. Business Reciprocity Arrangements

Reciprocity arrangements have been common among large business enterprises in certain United States industries at least since the 1920s. They involve a trading agreement between two firms, each of which purchases an input that is an output of the other.[29] As with international trading agreements, the evidence available on the occurrence and effects of business reciprocity is far less than one would wish. Businesses are under less

[28] Agreements with the centrally planned economies are sometimes seen as a method for stabilising the volume and terms of trade of the developing countries. As it is usually put, this argument pertains just to bilateral trade and not to the developing countries' total trade. Thus, one often finds expressions of dismay that this bilateral trade by itself seems anything but stable. On the other hand (Section 2.6), the preference theory predicts with some success that bilaterals would be employed to stabilise total and not bilateral trade.

[29] Agreements involving more than two firms appear not at all uncommon. A may sell B and buy from C, who is also B's customer. For examples, see [29, p. 84]. One survey found 44 per cent of firms engaging in more complex reciprocity arrangements [20, p. 301].

obligation than governments to make their activities known, and the possible illegality of these dealings under the antitrust laws has not helped to loosen executive tongues. Most reciprocity arrangements appear to be informal, as when firm A urges its own purchases of good 1 from B as a reason why B should buy 2 from A, or when A dangles its willingness to start purchasing 1 from B in order to protect or expand its sales of 2.

From the general form of these agreements, it seems clear that they *might* serve to embody the forms of barter discrimination identified in Section 1. The threat to withdraw extant purchases carries the ring of the all-or-nothing offer, and (as we shall see) the model of 'competitive discrimination' (Section 1.4) corresponds closely to the principal explanatory hypothesis evolved by writers on business reciprocity. The relation of the trading entity described by the expository machinery used in Section 1 to the business firm, however, may require explanation. The correspondence is direct if we think of the firm as a multiproduct enterprise purchasing intermediate goods but not necessarily requiring them in fixed proportions to its outputs. It is helpful (though not necessary) to assume that the firm can produce at some cost each of the inputs that it purchases externally (in observed positions of equilibrium). The firm should face declining excess-demand curves for the products it trades, so that its isorevenue contours will possess the same general properties as indifference curves. Divergences arise between internal opportunity costs and external terms of trade because of the use of this market power, which permits firms to impose effectively export taxes on goods they sell; prices diverge from marginal production costs for the output, the input goods, or both. The firm's activities are thus assimilated to the model of trading entities except in regard to determining the scale of production in the sense of total value added. Unlike the national economy, we abjure thinking of the firm as equipped with a fixed endowment of primary factors of production. Since questions of scale enter only incidentally into the hypotheses about reciprocal trading, that non-congruity will cause no trouble.

As in the case of international trading agreements, various explanations for business reciprocity have been offered. The practice is generally agreed to be irrelevant in purely competitive product markets, where at most reciprocity could apply mutual esteem as a device for solving the inessential indeterminacy of bilateral pairing among large numbers of traders. The reduction of uncertainty could (once more) supply an explanation. The most popular model, however, accords with the theory of 'competitive discrimination.'[30] Assume that the sellers of products 1 and 2 each belong to imperfect collusive arrangements that aim to maintain the money prices of the respective products they sell. The relative market price of the two products will then be fixed. If the price lies above marginal cost for the product of which each firm is a net seller, the individual seller will potentially benefit from any device that expands his sales without threatening to shatter the collusive agreement or induce retaliation. (This gain does not depend on the complete success of collusion in maximising joint profits for the selling group as a whole, although it increases with the margin between price and marginal cost.) The exercise of reciprocity, according to the literature, provides one such device for expanding sales. If one of the firm's existing suppliers of good 1 is a reciprocity candidate, the threat to transfer purchases would suffice to make him switch his demand for good 2, and indeed possibly to pay a premium for it. If neither firm is selling to the other at the time reciprocity is arranged, an even wider range of price ratios (lying between their two internal opportunity-cost ratios) and including the market price ratio permit mutually profitable trade.[31]

Relating these oligopolistic circumstances to the case of simple monopolistic discrimination and developing its policy implications will both prove difficult exercises. On the one hand, discrimination may occur; on the other, clandestine chiselling on the collusive agreement could lead to a more efficient general level of prices than if reciprocity were disallowed.

I turn now to the evidence about business reciprocity as a type of general-equilibrium price discrimination. All the caveats

[30] For expositions, see [3; 14; 29; 37, chap. 6].

[31] The cases identified in the two preceding sentences can be related to price ratios indicated in Figure 3. If A is already buying commodity 1 exclusively from B, the range of price ratios permitting mutually profitable reciprocity lies between OT and P_B. These conclusions do not depend on whether the firm produces some of its requirements of the input it buys; if such production takes place, marginal cost should equal the input's initial market price.

from Section 2 will apply: the evidence is decidedly patchwork and it does not serve to discriminate between competing hypotheses.

3.1 *Industry characteristics, firm size and incidence of reciprocity*
If the general equilibrium model of preferential trading plays an important role in explaining business reciprocity, the distribution of reciprocity should vary from industry to industry in association with the traits that make it both possible and profitable. The first of these, obviously enough, is that firms both sell a significant portion of their output as intermediate goods to other firms and buy substantial portions of intermediate inputs; without this condition no reciprocity is possible. It should also be true that seller concentration is reasonably high, so that either discriminating monopoly becomes possible or collusive arrangements are likely to maintain prices significantly above marginal costs. Finally, since reciprocity arrangements no doubt involve fixed costs to the firms that are independent of the volume of business affected, one would expect more bilateral dealings in industries where firms are of large absolute size.

Table 1.1 presents results from what appears to be the only remotely systematic survey of a thousand purchasing agents in what appears to be a fairly representative sample of industries [28]. The industry categories are too broadly drawn to supply more than general indications, but the portion of respondents classifying reciprocity as an important factor in buyer-seller relations matches perfectly against the predicted traits of reciprocity potential and level of seller concentration. The process industries and iron and steel clearly possess a good deal of reciprocity potential, and in the United States most of their subsectors have relatively high levels of seller concentration. Industries such as non-metallic products and construction materials possess moderately high reciprocity potential (columns 5 and 6)[32] but significantly lower seller concentration in many

[32] In evaluating the information in columns 3–6 it is probably appropriate to add the 'don't know' observations to reported values near zero. Qualitative evidence on the pervasiveness of reciprocity makes one doubt that reciprocity potential in excess of 10 per cent could often go unnoticed except in an atomistic industry, and industries of highly competitive structure seem under represented in the sample.

subsectors, and thus show an unsurprising lower incidence of reciprocity (column 1).

Table 1.1 also indicates the role of absolute size in explaining the occurrence of reciprocity. The explanatory power of size

TABLE 1.1. *Extent and Importance of Business Reciprocity Agreements, by Industry and Size of Firm, Based on Survey of Purchasing Agents*

Industry or size of firm (sales)	Reciprocity 'a factor' in buyer-seller relations (%) (1)	Reciprocity increased due to excess capacity (%) (2)	Proportion of sales made to suppliers: Don't know (%) (3)	0–10 (%) (4)	10–30 (%) (5)	over 30 (%) (6)
Miscellaneous non-metallic products	68	50	17	60	13	10
Chemicals, petroleum, other process industries	100	63	16	32	41	11
Iron and steel	100	69	7	23	30	40
Services	45	28	27	42	19	12
Metal fabricators	56	37	9	79	7	5
Construction materials	55	31	6	83	11	0
Electrical	44	41	6	78	12	4
Consumer goods	36	15	27	70	3	0
All industries, by volume of sales ($million):						
less than 10	46	20	8	78	10	4
10–50	62	37	6	68	22	4
over 50	78	52	30	28	22	20
All respondents	51	35	8	74	12	6

Source: Calculated from *Purchasing*, LI, (20 November 1961) 76-77.

no doubt derives from several sources. One is the transaction costs of reciprocity, mentioned above. This would operate without any other differences between large and small firms. The table shows, however, that reciprocity potential is significantly greater for large firms: 42 per cent of purchasing agents in firms selling goods worth over $50 million annually believe that over 10 per cent of sales are made to suppliers, whereas the figure is only 26 per cent for medium-size firms. Finally, numerous studies of market structure show that absolute size and seller concentration (relative size) are highly correlated, so the influence of concentration is also reflected. Other surveys confirm the importance of reciprocity to the large firm; for instance, 60 per cent of the firms on *Fortune's* list of the five hundred largest non-financial corporations employ 'trade-relations men,' the current euphemism for those charged with arranging reciprocity deals [21, p. 180].

3.2 *Excess capacity and persistence of reciprocity*

For a number of reasons mentioned in Section 2.6, a reduction in demand for a trader's output might promote a search for reciprocity arrangements. If the maintenance of sticky collusive market prices is an important condition for reciprocity, as the standard view suggests, falling demand should be reflected in excess capacity and a decline in marginal cost relative to market price. Thus an increase in the resort to reciprocity would be expected during recessions. On the other hand, some observers have marked excess capacity as a necessary condition for reciprocity, implying that it would show little persistence with the return of good times.

The evidence shows clearly that reciprocity tends to increase during recessions. It first drew attention during the depression of the 1930s [11, 20]. The survey summarised in Table 1.1 [28] took place just after the minor recession of 1960–61, and the percentages of respondents noting an increase during the recession (column 2) are not only high but also correlated with the portion viewing reciprocity as a significantly persistent factor. Another survey of purchasing agents [8] found that 43 per cent of them noted an increase in reciprocity during the early 1960s, 26 per cent in the relatively prosperous 1952–1959 period, only 17 per cent during the highly prosperous years 1946–1951. At least one observer suggests that industries with high fixed costs, where excess capacity would tend to widen the gap between price and short-run marginal cost more markedly, are notable for their volume of reciprocal dealings [2, p. 117].

But the amount of reciprocity could fluctuate with excess

capacity while resting on a large permanent base, and this also seems to be the case. In no period since the Second World War have many observers found reciprocity to be levelling off [8, p. 10], and it has been called 'a traditional way of life' in some industries [22, p. 180]. Firms' organisational arrangements for furthering reciprocity are clearly not meant to serve only in foul weather [27, p. 29]. Descriptions of individual reciprocity arrangements show them to be long-lived, and industries' trading patterns sometimes grow ridden with them so that firms obligate themselves to divide up their purchases in complex relation to the distribution of their sales.[33]

3.3 *Reciprocity and constrained pricing*

The link between reciprocity and high seller concentration confirms the relation of reciprocity to discrimination in a general way, but fails to distinguish between the 'monopolistic' and 'competitive' cases (Sections 1.1, 1.2, 1.4). The latter turns on imperfect collusion, the former on the power to discriminate; both tend to rise as we move across the spectrum of industries toward those with higher concentration. The probable significance of 'competitive discrimination' would rise if some evidence associates the practice specifically with defections from collusive prices. Some such evidence does exist.

Price is likely to be most rigid where its minimum value is set by public authority, as in the case of public utilities and common-carrier transportation in the United States. Furthermore, discrimination in the form of selective price-cutting is normally illegal in these sectors. They should, then, be strong prospects for systematic and sustained reciprocity. This prediction is amply confirmed. During the 1930s it was found that purchasing by the United States railroads was riddled with reciprocity, and it paid large buyers of transportation services (such as meat packers) to purchase companies manufacturing railway equipment just for their reciprocity potential.[34] Local public utilities apparently also practice reciprocity heavily [20, pp. 299–300],

[33] See [19; 28, p. 71; 29; 37].

[34] For descriptions, see [29, 37], and also *Reciprocity in Purchasing and Routing*, 188 I.C.C. (1932) 417; and *Waugh Equipment Co.*, 15 F.T.C., (1931) 232.

although their near-monopoly position (compared to railroads) may lend it a different significance. Finally, among unregulated industries selling intermediate or producer goods, one gets the general impression that reciprocity is more common, the more standardised are the goods in question [2, 28]. The high cross-elasticities of demand between competing sellers of such goods inflate their interest in various sorts of collusive pricing arrangements. Reciprocity is likely to prove an attractive way to chisel in these cases because direct price discrimination is hard to conceal, and also potentially vulnerable to legal attack (under the Robinson–Patman Act) even if rivals are unable to retaliate effectively [3, p. 1027].

3.4 *Terms of trade under reciprocal arrangements*

The theory of preferential trading shows that mutually acceptable terms of trade may often lie within limits of some width. If reciprocity were due only to collusive pricing practices, as the standard explanation suggests, reciprocal exchanges would take place solely at market prices and would be free of elements of monopolistic discrimination in this sense. On the other hand, firms might also use reciprocity against disfavoured partners to improve their terms of trade (Section 1.2). This would be possible where the potential partner lacks a way to sustain his current sales at a comparably reduced net profit by any alternative strategy (e.g. a price cut).

The quality of the evidence available on the terms of reciprocity deals is lamentably poor, since businessmen are naturally reluctant to testify on the point. The standard protestation is that reciprocal transactions take place only at market prices, and in the one survey dealing with this point only 18 per cent of managers canvassed would admit using reciprocity to extract prices higher than their competitors' [20, p. 301]. Neutral observers, however, are often sceptical about the degree of adherence to market price. The purchaser's specifications for a given product are not independent of the identity of the seller who may supply it. 'The buyer often makes the low man – he can determine who is going to come in with the low bid, just by making special demands' [21, p. 192]. The amount of ancillary service provided by a seller and aspects of the quality of his product can be varied, even if nominal price is that of 'the market'.[35]

A strong piece of indirect evidence of this forcing of penalty prices via reciprocity is the universal dislike of the practice voiced by purchasing agents, whose proximate objective is to minimise input costs to the firm.[36] If firms possessed monopoly/monopsony power as traders in general equilibrium, discriminatory reciprocity should prove as attractive to them – when the firm is on the winning end – as to the salesmen. On the other hand, if reciprocal trading tends heavily to depend on imperfectly collusive pricing, the sales department will always appear to garner the gains from the firm's favourable reciprocity deals, the purchasing agent to suffer the cost of unfavourable ones inflicted on the firm.

Care must be taken in identifying the gainers and losers from reciprocity. When firm A inflicts reciprocity on firm B, one of its current suppliers, by threatening to divert purchases, the best that B can hope for is to maintain its prior terms of trade, merely by switching its purchases to A. Where the firms have not been trading with each other, however, and both sell in imperfectly collusive markets, the difference between A's internal opportunity-costs and market prices also becomes territory in which the bargain might settle.[31] The firm that initiates the transaction then might appear to be the loser, in terms of market prices, with apparent financial losses (if any) in purchasing more than offset by gains on sales. My general impression is that firms pursue reciprocity mainly along the first of these two routes – rummaging through lists of their current suppliers in search of reciprocity potential.[37]

3.5 *Reciprocity, mergers and diversification*

An indication (though not a measure) of the distortion that reciprocity can create in patterns of economic activity is the

[35] For evidence see [2, p. 122; 20; 29]. Also, some weight can perhaps be given to the *a priori* argument that if B was not purchasing from A at market prices and now does so under 'reciprocity' pressure, the former arrangement must in general have given B better terms of trade in *some* fashion.

[36] See [2, pp. 119–122; 15, p. 100].

[37] The literature on reciprocity suffers from trying to make a false dichotomy between 'coercive reciprocity' and reciprocity involving

diversification that a trading entity might undertake in its mix of products for the purpose of increasing its reciprocity potential. The growth of conglomerate enterprise has had the result, accidental or intended, of greatly increasing possible reciprocal dealings for many firms, and the conglomerate movement has been cited as a reason for the post-war growth of reciprocity.[38] The earlier purchases of railway equipment firms by meat packers were mentioned above. More recently, several mergers attacked by the Federal Trade Commission have involved a large company that makes heavy purchases from other firms acquiring a smaller (and not necessarily successful) company for its reciprocity potential.[39]

3.6 *Business reciprocity, welfare and economic policy*

Reciprocity has been a lively issue in American antitrust policy during the past few years. Mergers have been struck down on the ground of their reciprocity potential where the acquiring firm is a buyer of substantial absolute size in its input markets, and the acquired firm holds a significant share of the market in which it sells.[40] Reciprocity itself does not enjoy a well-defined status at law, but the Antitrust Division has secured consent decrees against several large firms whereby they agree for a period of time to undertake no reciprocity arrangements. In the consent decrees the signatories do not admit their guilt of charges brought under Section 1 of the Sherman Act, so the effect is to create a presumption that systematic reciprocity is illegal without providing any well-defined legal standard.

Because of this situation it seems particularly important to summarise the results of this analysis of the theory and practice of business reciprocity and indicate briefly what sort of economic inefficiency the practice may involve. The evidence

concessions from collusive prices. This results from failure to notice the consequences of imperfect collusion existing in the market for both products, which on the evidence cited here (Sections 3.1–3.3) seems quite likely. Cf. Ferguson [14, pp. 571–573], who admittedly considers what I have called 'competitive reciprocity' to be 'of limited empirical validity'.

[38] For example, [11, p. 851; 21, p. 180].

[39] See [27, p. 28; 29, pp. 78–79; 37, chap. 6].

[40] The volume of commentary on these cases is large. See [6; 14; 16; 37].

suggests that business reciprocity operates primarily as a second-best device for firms engaged in the imperfectly collusive maintenance of their selling prices to effect a preferential price shift. Without any change in collusively maintained prices, it is possible for at least one party to a reciprocal agreement to gain from the expansion of trade on which price exceeds marginal cost. Approximately equal losses will be inflicted on firms from which trade is diverted, so that no net social gain occurs if market prices are unaffected. Where a firm inflicts reciprocity on an existing supplier through an actual or implied threat to withdraw purchases, it gains, the supplier loses, and losses also accrue to the firm(s) from which the supplier's purchases are diverted. A net social loss occurs to the extent that transactions are diverted to a higher-cost supplier. Thus, most reciprocity appears to represent 'competitive discrimination' (Section 1.4) coupled with some use of the all-or-nothing offer (Section 1.2).

In contrast to the trading agreements employed by developing countries, little evidence suggests that business reciprocity is used to effect monopolistic price discrimination (as described in Section 1.1). That is, there is no indication that sellers search out for a reciprocity partner – the sort favoured by a discriminating monopolist – one with (in effect) high price and income-elasticities of demand for the monopolist's export (Section 1.3). There is no evidence of profitable resale or efforts to prevent it (Section 2.3). There is no indication that the expansion of trade through reciprocity assists the active party in effecting discrimination against outside traders, since the usual pattern of the agreement is to improve his terms of trade or leave them unchanged, rather than to worsen them selectively (Section 1.5). The passive party might acquiesce in deteriorated terms of trade, however, with the expectation that he could recoup through discrimination against excluded parties. Whatever its discriminatory significance, 'competitive discrimination' may help to avert general adjustments of collusively restrained market prices that would otherwise occur.

These conclusions can be related briefly to the literature on economic policy toward business reciprocity. There, discussion of the effects of reciprocity has been confused by preoccupation with the effects of 'forestalling' competitors (a matter of some concern under the antitrust laws, especially the Robinson–Patman Act, but little *direct* relevance to economic welfare) and unsuccessful pursuit of the notion that reciprocity somehow serves to increase the leverage of a monopoly position. As recent contributions have correctly argued [3, 14], there is no well-defined sense in which reciprocity directly raises market power. It can decrease efficiency, by coercion of a supplier to shift from a cheaper to a dearer source of supply, however, and it can raise the profitability of a position of market power already held. More attention might be given to this real cost of discrimination, especially in view of the evidence that reciprocity is highly persistent and can distort procurement patterns throughout an industry. Systematic reciprocity of that sort can also contribute to barriers to entry in the sense of raising the incidence of those resulting from any of their conventional sources.[41] To that extent monopoly power may be *indirectly* increased. Sporadic reciprocity might serve the desirable function of other forms of 'price chiselling' in undermining imperfectly collusive pricing arrangements, but the evidence reviewed above provides little empirical hope for a justification along this line. Reciprocity seems typically to be an entrenched and sustained practice, and even sporadic reciprocity may provide firms with a substitute for manoeuvres that would be *more* likely to undermine collusive prices.[42] The case against sustained and systematic reciprocity in a concentrated industry, or against conglomerate mergers that would make such reciprocity possible,[43] seems reasonably sound.

[41] Thus, given some economies of scale, a potential entrant must expect to capture some minimum share of the market before attaining minimum average costs. He will see his chances as reduced if reciprocity precludes detaching present purchases from their old suppliers, and he is locked into the 'pessimistic assumption' of the Sylos-Bain model about the reduction from the ruling price that will be needed to attract extra demand equal to his minimum efficient output; see [24].

[42] The dilemma of the possible virtues of sporadic price discrimination versus the vices of persistent discrimination is familiar in the literature of antitrust.

[43] See [31, pp. 1386–1393].

References

[1] AHUJA, K. 'India's Trade with Eastern Europe – A Comment', *Indian Economic Journal*, IX, (January 1962) 361–5.

[2] AMMER, D. S. 'Realistic Reciprocity', *Harvard Business Review*, XL, (January–February 1962) 116–24.

[3] ANDERSON, J. P. 'Reciprocal Dealing', *Yale Law Journal*, LXXVI, (April 1967) 1020–29.

[4] BALDWIN, R. E. 'Equilibrium in International Trade: a Diagrammatic Analysis', *Quarterly Journal of Economics*, LXII, (November 1948) 748–62.

[5] BECKER, G. S. 'A Note on Multi-Country Trade', *American Economic Review*, XLII, (September 1952) 558–68.

[6] BOCK, B. 'Mergers and Reciprocity', *Conference Board Record*, II, (July 1965) 27–36.

[7] COOPER, C. A. and MASSELL, B. F. 'Toward a General Theory of Customs Unions for Developing Countries', *Journal of Political Economy*, LXXIII, (October 1965) 461–76.

[8] DAUNER, J. R. 'The Attitude of the Purchasing Agent Toward Reciprocity', *Journal of Purchasing*, III, (August 1967) 5–15.

[9] DAVE, S. 'India's Trade Relations with East European Countries, 1952–53 – 1959–60, A Study in Bilateralism', *Indian Economic Journal*, IX, (July 1961) 48–68.

[10] DAVE, S. 'India's Trade with East European Countries – Rejoinder', *Indian Economic Journal*, IX, (April 1962) 479–83.

[11] DEAN, J. 'Economic Aspects of Reciprocity, Competition and Mergers', *Antitrust Bulletin*, VIII, (September–December 1963) 843–52.

[12] DE LOOPER, J. H. C. 'Current Usage of Payments Agreements and Trade Agreements', *I.M.F. Staff Papers*, IV, (August 1955) 339–97.

[13] DE NEUMAN, A. M. ' "Tied" International Trading – the Indonesian Rami Fibre Test Case', *Economic Journal*, LXIV, (June 1954) 324–36.

[14] FERGUSON, J. M. 'Tying Arrangements and Reciprocity:

An Economic Analysis', *Law and Contemporary Problems*, XXX, (summer 1965) 552–80.

[15] FINNEY, F. R. 'Reciprocity and Public Policy', *Antitrust Law and Economics Review*, II, (summer 1969) 97–110.

[16] HALE, G. E. and HALE, R. D. 'Reciprocity under the Antitrust Laws: A Comment', *University of Pennsylvania Law Review*, CXIII, (November 1964) 69–76.

[16a] HENDERSON, A. M. 'A Geometrical Note on Bulk Purchase', *Economica*, XV, (February 1948) 61–9.

[17] JOHNSON, H. G. 'An Economic Theory of Protectionism, Tariff Bargaining, and the Formation of Customs Unions', *Journal of Political Economy*, LXXIII, (June 1965) 256–83.

[18] KEMP, M. C. 'A Contribution to the General Equilibrium Theory of Preferential Trading', *Contributions to Economic Analysis, No. 61*, (Amsterdam: North Holland Publishing Co., 1969).

[19] LEWIS, H. T. 'No Matter What you Call It – It's Still Reciprocity', *Purchasing*, LII, (15 January 1962) 74–5.

[20] LEWIS, H. T. 'The Present Status of Reciprocity as a Sales Policy', *Harvard Business Review*, XVI, (spring 1938) 299–313.

[21] MCCREARY, E. JR, and GUZZARDI, W. JR, 'A Customer is a Company's Best Friend', *Fortune*, LXXI, (June 1965) 180–2.

[22] MEADE, J. E. *A Geometry of International Trade*, (London: George Allen & Unwin, Ltd, 1952).

[23] MIKESELL, R. F. and BEHRMAN, J. N. *Financing Free World Trade with the Sino-Soviet Bloc*, Princeton Studies in International Finance, No. 8, Princeton, N.J., (International Finance Section, Princeton University, 1958).

[24] MODIGLIANI, F. 'New Developments on the Oligopoly Front', *Journal of Political Economy*, LXVI, (June 1958) 215–32.

[25] ROBINSON, J. *The Economics of Imperfect Competition*, (London: Macmillan, 1933).

[26] SEN, S. *India's Bilateral Payments and Trade Agreements, 1947–48 to 1963–64*, (Calcutta: Bookland Private Ltd, 1965).

[27] SIMON, L. S. 'Industrial Reciprocity as a Business

Strategy', *Industrial Management Review*, VII, (spring 1966) 27–39.

[28] SLOANE, L. 'Reciprocity: Where Does the P.A. Stand?', *Purchasing*, LI, (20 November 1961) 70–9.

[29] STOCKING, G. W. and MUELLER, W. F. 'Business Reciprocity and the Size of Firms', *Journal of Business*, XXX, (April 1957) 73–95.

[30] TRUED, M. N. and MIKESELL, R. F. *Postwar Bilateral Payments Agreements*, Princeton Studies in International Finance, No. 4, Princeton, N.J., (International Finance Section, Princeton University, 1955).

[31] TURNER, D. F. 'Conglomerate Mergers and Section 7 of the Clayton Act', *Harvard Law Review*, LXXVIII, (May 1965) 1313–95.

[32] U.N.O. Economic Commission for Africa, *Bilateral Trade and Payments in Africa*, U.N.O. Doc. E/CN 14/STC/24 (1963).

[33] U.N.O. Economic Commission for Africa, *General Review of Activities in Trade and Customs*, U.N.O. Doc. E/CN 14/W.P. 1/3 (1966).

[34] U.N.O. Economic Commission for Asia and the Far East, 'State Trading in Countries of the E.C.A.F.E. Region', *Proceedings of the United Nations Conference on Trade and Development*, New York: United Nations, 1964. Vol. VII, pp. 1–32.

[35] U.N.O. Economic Commission for Asia and the Far East, 'Trade between Developing E.C.A.F.E. Countries and Centrally Planned Economies', *Economic Bulletin for Asia and the Far East*, XV, (June 1964) 16–51.

[36] U.N.O. Economic Commission for Asia and the Far East, 'Trade Liberalization in the E.C.A.F.E. Region', *The Asian Development Bank and Trade Liberalization*, Regional Economic Cooperation Series, No. 2. U.N.O. Doc. E/CN 11/707 (1965).

[37] U.S. Federal Trade Commission, *Economic Report on Corporate Mergers: Staff Report*, in U.S. Senate, Committee on the Judiciary, Subcommittee on Antitrust and Monopoly, *Economic Concentration*, Hearings pursuant to S. Res. 40. Washington: Government Printing Office, 1969. Part 8A.

[38] VANEK, J. *General Equilibrium of International Discrimination: the Case of Customs Unions.* Harvard Economic Studies, Vol. 123 (Cambridge, Mass.: Harvard University Press, 1965).

[39] VERBIT, G. P. *Trade Agreements for Developing Countries* (New York: Columbia University Press, 1969).

[14]

HOW TO HAGGLE AND TO STAY FIRM: BARTER AS HIDDEN PRICE DISCRIMINATION

ELLEN MAGENHEIM and PETER MURRELL*

Barter transactions, conducted openly by established corporations, play an increasingly significant role in the U.S. economy. The model developed here helps explain why firms use barter and yields predictions concerning the circumstances under which barter is likely to occur. It is shown that when two firms barter goods used as inputs, price discrimination occurs. This price discrimination is hidden from the firms' other customers because the real values of the transacted goods to the barterers are different from the accounting prices used in the transaction. Since price discrimination that is observed by potential customers might have an adverse effect on the selling firm's future bargaining power, barter will have value as a means of hiding price discrimination.

I. INTRODUCTION

It is standard in economics to assume that when economic agents are given a choice between trading for goods and trading for cash, they will choose the latter. If a good is received in payment, it must be traded again unless, coincidentally, it is identical to one that would have been purchased for cash. The second trade involves not only transactions costs but uncertainty arising from fluctuations in the value of the traded item. Given the rarity of "coincidence of wants," cash transactions will usually be preferred.

There is evidence, however, that growing numbers of businesses are choosing to barter. The structure of such transactions varies from direct barter between two firms to indirect bartering through exchanges. The significance of barter activity is difficult to estimate because no systematic data collection has been conducted. A study by the U.S. Congress [1982] estimates that barter has been growing at a rate of almost 20 percent a year from the mid-1970s, and will probably sustain a 15 percent growth in the immediate future. According to the International Reciprocal Trade Association [1985], the gross volume of the barter exchange industry has been estimated to be $450 million in 1985, up from $400 million in 1984. Barter Exchange, Inc. [1984] even claims that barter will account for 15 percent of U.S. GNP by 1990.

Two standard features of this rapidly growing form of exchange argue that traditional explanations of barter might not apply. First, the tax laws treat barter as equivalent to cash transactions (see Keller [1982]). Firms engaging in barter, therefore, have the same tax liabilities as would have been the case had they simply undertaken the equivalent cash exchange. Thus, tax consid-

* Swarthmore College and University of Maryland, College Park. We would like to thank Timothy Goodspeed and an anonymous referee for helpful suggestions.

Economic Inquiry
Vol. XXVI, July 1988, 449–459

erations do not influence the desirability of barter.[1] Second, barterers usually choose to exchange at the terms of trade implied by market prices. Examination of membership contracts of commercial barter exchanges supports this assertion. Keller [1982] notes that the contract of Barter Systems International specifies that goods are sold for trade units with each trade unit representing one dollar of the "prevailing price." Barter Exchange, Inc. [1984] states the same policy using the "normal" cash price of a good. Given valuation at market prices, the absence of tax advantages, and costs associated with in-kind payments, one must ask why barter is increasingly common.

This paper demonstrates that barter, at terms of trade equal to market prices, can be in the mutual interest of two parties. The approach focuses on the fact that firms may want to price discriminate, but will want to hide that discrimination in order to maintain a strong bargaining position vis-a-vis other customers. We show that barter enables both parties to a transaction to practice price discrimination, the effective terms of which are hidden from all other economic agents, including the trading partner.

Section II includes a discussion of why the open use of two or more prices might be costly for firms. The conclusion is that firms have an incentive to conceal price discrimination. Section III examines barter as a vehicle for price discrimination using a simple example focusing on a situation in which two firms obtain production inputs in the exchange. Since the exchange of inputs is the prototypal transaction within barter clubs, this example captures the characteristics of an important segment of modern barter. Using the example, barter, at terms of trade equal to market prices, can have three characteristics: price discrimination is present, is mutual, and is hidden. Section IV formalizes the analysis and shows that, if a firm has an opportunity to price discriminate and hide that discrimination, it will do so. The conditions are derived that show when barter, as price discrimination, can be mutually beneficial to two firms. These conditions allow prediction of which firm characteristics are likely to be correlated with barter activity.

II. THE CHOICE OF A PRICING STRATEGY

The usual analyses of price discrimination ignore the costs of deviating from a policy of charging all customers the same price. These costs include damage to the firm's reputation as a tough bargainer and revelation of cost information that can be used to the firm's detriment in future negotiations.

Suppose a firm employs a strategy of haggling in order to force customers to pay their reservation prices. A high price is offered and then lowered until the reservation price is reached. The customer knows a profit-maximizing firm

1. We recognize that tax evasion may be the motivation behind some barter deals, especially those between private individuals for consumption goods. But the analysis focuses on a type of barter for which tax evasion is not likely to be an explanation. We examine barter between established firms—transactions often conducted through barter exchanges. In such transactions, where the cost of the acquired item is tax deductible, the reporting of the transaction may have little consequence for tax liability. Indeed, in the simple examples presented, a firm's tax bill would be independent of the reporting of barter.

will not offer a price lower than marginal cost. By openly haggling, the seller reveals information about its marginal costs. Riley and Zeckhauser [1983] show that when seller commitment to a pricing strategy is possible the gains to haggling (i.e., price discrimination) can be more than offset by the losses generated by encouraging future buyers to refuse purchases at higher prices.[2] To avoid these losses the firm must develop a reputation for charging uniform prices. Such a reputation will deter a firm's customers from trying to obtain better prices. One way this reputation can be built is for the firm to follow a long-term policy that eschews recognizable price discrimination.[3]

Okun [1982, 151] defines reputation as a flow of information from one consumer to the next. Note, then, that if evidence of price discrimination can be suppressed, a firm can maintain its reputation for price uniformity even when it varies the terms of trade among customers. It will be shown that barter allows firms to hide price discrimination from its regular customers. As a result, the benefits of price discrimination can be enjoyed without suffering the costs of losing the reputation for charging uniform prices.

III. THE ELEMENTS OF BARTER

Barter as Implicit Price Discrimination

For reasons made clear below, transactions are examined in which the good acquired through barter is used as an input, substituting for one that would be selected in the absence of barter. Associated with this change in production methods is a change in costs. In this sense, one can think of goods sold for cash and bartered goods as different products: one variety is produced in the normal manner and the other is produced with the bartered input. Thus there exists differentiation both in the mode of production and the terms of sale.

In this section, it is shown that price discrimination can be an important element in barter; this requires a definition of price discrimination appropriate to the present context. When goods produced under identical conditions are sold in different markets, evidence of discrimination is found solely in different prices. When costs differ between markets, however, the definition of price discrimination cannot rest only on price comparisons. One must take into account cost differences, as has been shown in analyses of price behavior in differentiated product markets. Thus, Phlips's [1983, 6] approach is followed in determining whether price discrimination occurs:

2. Stigler [1961, 223–24] presents another reason why uniform prices are desirable:

> From the manufacturer's viewpoint uncertainty concerning his price is clearly disadvantageous. The cost of search is a cost of purchase, and consumption will therefore be smaller, the greater the dispersion of prices and the greater the optimum amount of search. This is presumably one reason . . . why uniform prices are set by sellers of nationally advertised brands: if they have eliminated price variation, they have reduced the cost of the commodity (including search) to the buyer. . . .

3. While there may be immediate gains to discriminating, the firm must consider the long-run implications. According to Okun [1981, 143] ". . . price discrimination among . . . customers would be destructive to long-term relations."

> . . . price discrimination should be defined as implying that two varieties of a commoditiy are sold (by the same seller) to two buyers at different *net* prices, the net price being the price (paid by the buyer) corrected for the cost associated with product differentiation.

However, as Phlips [1983, 7] recognizes, this definition is incomplete. Differences in net prices might result solely from cost differences, rather than from price discrimination. Therefore, Phlips adds a further element:

> When some form of product differentiation . . . is introduced in the analysis, price discrimination typically serves to open *new* markets and thus to increase sales [1983, 19].

That is, the variation in net prices must reflect the price discriminator's efforts to maximize profits by pursuing different strategies in different market segments [Phlips 1983, 7]. To establish that price discrimination exists in barter, therefore, two conditions must hold: that different net prices are charged in different markets and that new markets are opened up in order to increase overall profits.

In order to demonstrate that barter can be a vehicle for price discrimination, consider a simple example. Firm A (firms and the products they produce are denoted by the same letter) faces a downward sloping demand curve:

$$P_A = 32 - Q_A$$

where P_A is the market price of A and Q_A is the quantity sold for cash at the market price. Firm A faces the following production function:

$$Y_A = L_A^{1/2} K_A^{1/2}$$

where Y_A is quantity produced, L_A is the quantity of labor used, the K_A is the quantity of some second factor of production. It is assumed that K is produced in many varieties, but A can use the cheapest type available. The price of labor is 1 and the cheapest variety of K costs 16. Then, the firm has a constant marginal cost of 8 and, if it does not price discriminate, it will produce 12 units and sell A at a price of 20 to make a profit of 144.

Now consider firm B. It produces a commodity that can be used for A's K input, but the price of B is currently 20. Suppose A offers a 1:1 barter deal, which B accepts.[4] (Discussion of why B accepts is postponed.) It is assumed that B is not a regular customer of A, and that B will not resell the unit of A acquired in barter. Y_A will now rise by 1 unit, L_A by 4 units, and the K input by ¼. However, as A has acquired 1 unit of K in the barter, market purchases of K will fall by ¾. Thus, cash revenues remain unchanged and costs fall by 12 (¾ less K must be bought) minus 4 (4 units more of labor). Profits rise by 8.

It is now easy to see that the two conditions comprising Phlips's definition are satisfied by this barter deal. Since A's sales to customers other than B have remained constant, the change in profits must be due to the barter transaction. From A's perspective, the net price to B (price minus cost, which equals the

4. It is assumed that A practices second degree price discrimination but the range of prices is restricted to the market price and the price charged in barter. In reality, a firm would charge a range of implicit barter prices.

change in profits) is 8, which is different from the prevailing net market price for A of 12 (the market price of 20 minus the marginal cost of 8). The barter has raised A's profits; an extra customer has been attracted by offering conditions better than those previously prevailing.

The example has shown that barter can be profitable to A. One can easily imagine conditions in which the transaction is also profitable to B. For example, suppose B faces market and cost conditions similar to those of A. Suppose the good A could be used as B's nonlabor input. Then, B would have profited from barter in exactly the same way as A. Therefore, two firms with market power can both profit from bartering at the rate implied by market prices. The extra profit arises from price discrimination.

Simple intuition shows why the barter can be profitable for both A and B. When price is above marginal cost, inputs are being used in inefficient quantities. If the two firms produce inputs for each other, they can, without changing their use of other inputs, exchange products and consequently raise their combined net physical output. Something for nothing has been created as a consequence of the inefficiency of the original position. Thus, the example does not rest on any peculiarity of the production functions faced by the two firms. Rather, the possibility of mutually beneficial barter arises from the potential gains from trade that must be present in any monopoly equilibrium.

The use of a model in which barterers supply each other with inputs is explained below. Now, however, the plausibility of this construction is addressed. Consider an example of barter between a magazine and a computer company, cited by *CFO* [March 1985]. The computer manufacturer advertises in the magazine, while the magazine uses computers. Each provides an input usable in the other's production process. There are similar products, however, that can play the same role in production. At market prices, each producer purchases inputs from other suppliers. Given the discounts implicit in price discrimination, however, this particular transaction becomes attractive to both partners.

This situation is most likely to occur within industries producing and using differentiated products. The use of a differentiated product as an input provides the flexibility required to make barter feasible and attractive to both the "buyer" and "seller" of the traded good. Returning to the example cited above, the computer company and the magazine prefer not to purchase each other's variety for cash at prevailing market prices. (For example, they may not need some special feature for which other customers are willing to pay.) But, if given those special terms that are implicit in barter, each company will choose to use the other's product.[5]

How Barter Hides Price Discrimination

Riley and Zeckhauser [1983] conclude that a firm having the ability to price discriminate might choose not to do so because of the adverse effect of haggling

5. There are numerous other examples of the type of barter deals described here. See *CFO*, March 1985.

on future bargaining power. However, that conclusion rests on the assumption that a firm's actions are fully observed by prospective customers. If a non-uniform price structure can be hidden, the firm might discriminate. Barter will be shown to hide price discrimination.

Price discrimination occurs when a firm generates greater profits by offering a variety of prices. Discrimination is hidden when the range of prices cannot be detected by customers. In barter, exchange is undertaken at "official" prices: accounting information reveals nothing to other customers. Evidence of price discrimination can be found only in the fact that the true cost of the transaction, the effective price, is lower than the market price. Finding effective prices, however, requires knowledge of the firms' production functions. In our example, one would have to know A's production function to determine the net price charged to B. Not only will these customers be ignorant of the effective prices implicit in the barter, but even B does not know to what extent the net selling price to A is less than market price. Each participant's effective terms of trade are hidden from the other participant.

There are two senses in which price discrimination can be hidden. One is qualitative—the simple fact of its existence. The second is quantitative—the extent to which prices vary between market segments. If discrimination is hidden in the first sense, it must be hidden in the second. But the converse is not true. Thus, we ask whether barter can be advantageous even if price discrimination is not hidden in the first sense.

Open price discrimination reveals information about a firm's costs. Customers charged the higher price know that marginal costs are no greater than their price *minus* the price difference between the two markets. Thus, they obtain quantitative information on marginal costs, which can be used in future bargains. In contrast, when the price difference is hidden, customers paying the higher price learn only that marginal cost is below their price. This fact could already be deduced from the knowledge that the seller has market power.

In barter, the quantitative degree of price discrimination is hidden even from the partner in the exchange. Thus, even if everybody understands that barter implicitly involves price discrimination, it might still be used. By obscuring the effective terms of trade and, thereby, quantitative information on the differences between prices and marginal costs, barter has advantages over standard price discrimination.

The above observations reveal why firms do not openly resell the goods obtained through barter. In reselling, firms will need to offer a lower-than-market price.[6] In offering the bartered good at a lower price, firms reveal information about their marginal costs. This revelation is at odds with the original motivation for undertaking barter.

6. If price discrimination is implicit in A bartering, A will exchange with B only if any resale must occur at below-market price. Such would be the case, for example, if nontransferable warranties were important in the sale of A, or if A could make resale difficult. The example conforms to these cases. The computer company can choose to honor a warranty only with the original owner. The magazine can effectively control the use of its advertising space.

Given both the rarity of "coincidence of wants" and the advantages of hidden price discrimination, this argument predicts the development of institutions which enable firms to undertake multilateral exchanges that disguise price concessions. These institutions will broker exchanges between a variety of firms, none of which knows the effective terms-of-trade received by trading partners. Hence, the barterers will require the brokers to "resell" at prevailing prices. If buyers were forced to pay the market price in cash, however, they would prefer to buy directly from the manufacturer. But if buyers can pay in kind and thereby price discriminate, they might find the "price" offered by the broker attractive.

Our theory, therefore, helps explain why barter exchanges exist. They are a means of combining one advantage of cash exchange with one advantage of barter. First, as in cash exchange, trades are not constrained by the search for a bilateral coincidence of wants.[7] Since many firms can participate in the exchanges, a variety of goods is available. Second, as in bilateral barter, a sale can be accounted at market prices, without those prices implying anything about the true worth of the transaction to the seller. Because of limitations on its use, a "dollar" that can be spent only at a particular barter exchange must be worth less than a dollar of cash. This feature of barter exchanges allows price discrimination to be hidden. No brokerage based on cash exchange at prevailing prices would have this property.

Why the Price Discrimination Must Be Mutual

It has been assumed so far that both firms are able to price discriminate. Given that assumption, both firms profit from trading an additional unit of output through barter. Within the context of the model, barter will occur only if the price discrimination is mutual.

Returning to the previous example, for brevity's sake, B is assumed to have the same demand and production functions as A, even though these firms produce quite different goods. The assumptions that B was not one of A's regular customers and that B could not resell the unit of A obtained allow A to engage in price discrimination. To establish the necessity of mutual price discrimination, let us examine the consequences if these assumptions about A are correct, but the analogous assumptions about B do not hold. (That is, A is able to sell the unit of B at close to market price.)

If A could obtain the market price for the unit of B gained in barter, that price would fall to 19. B's revenues from its regular customers would fall by 12 and its costs by 8. B's total profits would fall from 144 to 140, as a result of the barter. Thus, if B cannot maintain market separation or, indeed, cannot price discriminate for any other reason, the barter transaction would not be consummated at rates of exchange implied by market prices.

Unless barter offers B price discrimination advantages, B will require an exchange on terms better than those implied by market prices. But such terms

7. Firms will want to know which other firms participate in the exchange. They must ensure that none of their high-price customers are participating.

reveal information to other customers about A's marginal costs. A cannot accept such terms. Thus, barter will not proceed if B cannot price discriminate. Mutual price discrimination is necessary for barter.

IV. A MODEL OF PRICE DISCRIMINATION THROUGH BARTER

It has been shown both that price discrimination is intrinsic in barter, and that barter hides price discrimination. The formal model developed next allows identification of the conditions under which firms choose to price discriminate by barter. These conditions, which are framed in terms of simple properties of cost functions and prices, are also used to derive conclusions concerning the types of industries and firms that are most likely to barter.

The derivation of the results is in two steps. The decision to price discriminate is examined first. This step is necessary because, in our view, the decision to barter is effectively a decision to price discriminate. To allow latitude in that decision, it is assumed that discrimination can be costly—that the dual-price structure might become generally known and that, as a result, the firm must give regular customers a lower price. In the second step, the special characteristics of barter are introduced into the model.

The model builds upon the example presented in section III. The firm undertakes a simple form of price discrimination.[8] The firm first finds the single-price monopoly output and then seeks customers who, while unwilling to pay the monopoly price, are willing to pay more than marginal cost.[9] Market 1 is the primary market and the hidden price discrimination occurs in market 2. The firm faces $D_1(q_1)$, the inverse demand curve for the market as a whole; (p_1, q_1) is the price-quantity combination in that market. Once the firm has fixed (p_1, q_1), there will be a set of possible price discriminating transactions. For these transactions, the inverse demand curve is $H(q_1, q_2)$ and (p_2, q_2) is the price-quantity combination. The first argument of $H(.)$ is included because the range of opportunities open to the firm in the secondary market depends upon the equilibrium in the primary market.

Initially the producer considers whether to price discriminate. If this price discrimination is not discovered by customers paying the higher price, the producer will earn profits in excess of the single-price monopoly profits. If it is discovered, customers currently paying the higher price will know that the producer's marginal cost is less than the lower price. The firm will lose the ability to stay firm at the higher price [Riley and Zeckhauser 1983]. If the price discrimination is discovered, the firm will be forced to charge the same lower price to all customers.[10] Hence, an abortive attempt to maintain the

8. We show that the firm will undertake even this highly restrictive form of price discrimination. Then, *a fortiori*, a firm will undertake price discrimination when faced with a more flexible situation.

9. More specifically, the firm finds the monopoly price, taking into account the effect of that price on opportunities for price discrimination.

10. It is assumed that the firm will not be forced to charge the price of the second market; rather, it has to sell at a price lying between the two prices. This assumption is made because it is necessary in the barter model, where the price in the second market does not exist.

secrecy of price discrimination will result in profits lower than the single-price monopoly profits.

The firm's decision depends on a balancing of the gains from successfully hiding price discrimination versus the losses if it is discovered. To formalize the firm's decision, the function $M(q_2)$ is introduced—the probability that customers paying the higher price learn about the lower price. It is assumed, trivially, that $M(0) = 0$ and that $M'(q_2) > 0$. A stronger assumption to be invoked is that $M(q_2)$ is continuously differentiable. In conjunction with the other assumptions, continuity means that there are opportunities for price discrimination that have a small probability of detection. If $C(q_1 + q_2)$ is the cost function, a risk-neutral firm will maximize

$$M(q_2)\,[D(q_1 + q_2)\cdot(q_1 + q_2) - C(q_1 + q_2)] \\ + [1 - M(q_2)][D(q_1)\cdot q_1 + H(q_1, q_2)\cdot q_2 - C(q_1 + q_2)] \quad (1)$$

The only constraint on the firm's actions is that $q_2 \geqq 0$, which when binding indicates that the firm has decided not to discriminate. One can then prove the following.

THEOREM 1. *Maximization of (1) will lead to $q_2 > 0$. The firm will always choose to price discriminate.*[11]

Theorem 1 shows that the modelling of the decision to price discriminate is not restrictive. Thus, when barter is embodied in the analysis, any necessary conditions for the profitability of price discrimination that arise must derive directly from the nature of barter itself, rather than from any peculiarities of the model.

Adapting the model to the specific circumstances surrounding barter, we return to the example of firms A and B: B is a customer in market 2 and q_2 is the amount of A bartered to B. As barterers trade at market prices, one unit of A exchanges for $D(q_1)/P_B$ of B. As before, B is an input into the production of A, although not necessarily one chosen by A under other circumstances. Since B is used to produce A, A's cost function must be modified. Let $C[q_1 + q_2, q_2, D(q_1)/P_B]$ be the total cost[12] of producing $q_1 + q_2$, given that q_2 units of A are to be exchanged for $q_2D(q_1)/P_B$ units of B. Firm A maximizes

$$M(q_2)\{D(q_1 + q_2)\cdot(q_1 + q_2) - C[q_1 + q_2, q_2, D(q_1)/P_B]\} \\ + [1 - M(q_2)]\{D(q_1)\cdot q_1 + D(q_1)\cdot q_2 - C[q_1 + q_2, q_2, D(q_1)/P_B]\} \quad (2)$$

Given the above assumptions, the next theorem can be proved.

THEOREM 2. *If at the non-price-discriminating monopoly equilibrium, market price is greater than the marginal cost of production using the bartered good, a firm will find it profitable to barter.*

Applying theorem 2 to both firms, one obtains conditions for the barter deal to be consummated. Of course, the theorem would be empty if the conditions could not be simultaneously satisfied for both firms. However, the earlier example shows that the conditions are not restrictive. In that example, two

11. Proofs are available, on request, from the authors.

12. The total cost is calculated with good B valued at the market price, P_B.

firms with "normal" production functions and facing "normal" demand curves found a barter deal mutually profitable; theorem 2 holds in the example.

With additional assumptions concerning the comparability of the bartered input and the firm's regular inputs, theorem 2 can be strengthened in an enlightening way. Let us analyze the decisions of firm A. Suppose A usually uses a good K as an input. Goods K and B are indistinguishable for A's purposes. The price of K, P_K, is less than P_B and, before barter, A chooses to use K. Let MC_A be the marginal cost of producing A when K is used—the marginal cost in the pre-barter equilibrium. Then it is easy to prove the next theorem.

THEOREM 3. *Firm A will find it profitable to barter with firm B if*

$$P_A/MC_A > P_B/P_K.$$

Theorem 3 identifies the conditions under which barter is likely to occur. To best understand these conditions, examine each side of the above inequality separately. The fact that barter is more likely the greater is A's market power can be seen from the left-hand side. The right-hand side shows that barter is more probable when a firm can choose between inputs that perform the same function in its production process and that have comparable prices. Of course, for barter to be consummated the equivalent of theorem 3 for B must also be satisfied. One must ask, therefore, whether firm B can have some degree of market power *and*, simultaneously, that goods B and K can be close substitutes from firm A's viewpoint. This simultaneous requirement is entirely plausible if B is part of an industry with highly differentiated products.

Firm B, and the producers of rival products, could have two very different sets of potential customers. The regular buyers of B value highly its special characteristics. B has some degree of market power over these customers. There are also potential customers, such as A, who do not value the particular features of B, but use as an input a product that has the same basic characteristics. If B must avoid haggling, and the customers who value the products' special characteristics are numerically dominant in the market, B might set a high price, using market power over those customers who value B's special characteristics. The price of B will then be well above marginal cost; theorem 3 will be satisfied in the version relevant to B's decisions. At the same time, the price of B may be close to the prices of rival products; theorem 3 will be satisfied in the version relevant to A's decisions.

Given the prevalence of differentiated product industries in modern economies, the conditions of theorem 3 seem unrestrictive. Indeed, the example of the exchange of an advertisement in a magazine for a personal computer conforms exactly to the situation discussed in the previous two paragraphs.

V. CONCLUSIONS

One argument has been developed showing why firms might choose to barter rather than trade for cash. Barter allows firms to avoid a cost of price discrimination: the relevation of information that can be used to the firm's detriment in future bargains. Although the theory does not rely upon the existence of any institutional barriers to trade, the desire to circumvent legal restraints, e.g., the Robinson-Patman Act, might provide a further motive to price discriminate through barter. In such a case all the analysis of the paper applies except that in section II.

The theory also gives one reason why barter exchanges exist. The primary disadvantage of bilateral barter is the cost of finding a partner for the transaction due to the improbability of a coincidence of wants. Participation in an exchange provides the price discrimination advantages of barter while loosening the constraints of finding a coincidence of wants. The model, however, predicts a limit on the growth in the size of these exchanges. To preserve the effectiveness of their price discrimination, firms will want to avoid the possibility of bartering with their regular customers. Thus, barter exchanges must remain small enough for any firm to know that there is only a slight probability that one of its regular customers is a member.

This paper presents a positive analysis of one reason for the existence of barter. It is fitting, however, to end with a comment on welfare implications. The welfare consequences of barter are similar to those of standard price discrimination, but with an added element. In the present case, a firm hides price discrimination by searching for a "buyer" who can supply an input of production. In all likelihood, a cost-minimizing producer would not use this input. Thus, an element of inefficiency in production might be introduced. Weighed against this inefficiency is the fact that barter allows a firm to maintain a uniform price structure, which may reduce consumers' search costs.

REFERENCES

Barter Exchange, Inc. "Press Release," Austin, TX 1984.

CFO. "Bartering: New Twist to an Ancient Trade," March 1985, 48–52.

Keller, Robert I. "The Taxation of Barter Transactions." *Minnesota Law Review*, December 1982, 441–512.

International Reciprocal Trade Association. "Press Release," Washington, DC, 1985.

Okun, Arthur. *Prices and Quantities: A Macroeconomic Analysis*. Washington, DC: Brookings Institution, 1981.

Phlips, Louis. *The Economics of Price Discrimination*. Cambridge: Cambridge University Press, 1983.

Riley, John and Richard Zeckhauser. "Optimal Selling Strategies: When to Haggle, When to Hold Firm." *Quarterly Journal of Economics*, May 1983, 267–89.

Stigler, George J. "The Economics of Information." *Journal of Political Economy*, June 1961, 213–25.

U.S. Congress, 128 Congressional Record, 53060, March 1982, remarks of Senator Baucus.

[15]

The Economic Journal, **102** (*September* 1992), 1171–1183
Printed in Great Britain

COUNTERTRADE TRANSACTIONS: THEORY AND EVIDENCE*

Richard E. Caves and Dalia Marin

Countertrade consists of bilateral agreements (usually) between Western industrial enterprises and government agencies or state-owned enterprises in developing countries (LDCs) and centrally planned economies (CPEs), whereby sales of goods by the western exporter are linked contractually to the exporter's purchases of other goods or services from the countertrade partner.[1] Although 15–20% of international trade may be governed by this type of barter or reciprocity (Hammond, 1990), countertrade has received very little scholarly attention, despite its seeming defiance of the economic presumption that barter is less efficient than money-for-goods transactions. As many descriptive studies show (e.g. Welt, 1984), countertrade consists mainly of barter and counterpurchase transactions that commit the exporter to buy goods from the partner in an amount related to the value of his sale. A special case (not emphasised in this study) is the buyback transaction, whereby the exporter of capital goods takes payment in the flow of output that the partner obtains from those goods (Murrell, 1982; Hennart, 1989).

This paper reports findings from a sample of 230 countertrade agreements. We develop an analytical framework that both explains the mutual attraction of countertrade deals to the parties and predicts the terms of trade in individual transactions. Various statistical tests serve to assess assumptions underlying the model, evaluate various predictions and corollaries, and distinguish between certain competing hypotheses about the motives or effects of countertrade transactions.

I. A FRAMEWORK FOR ANALYSING COUNTERTRADE TRANSACTIONS

Of the many explanations offered for countertrade, the most cogent ones focus on price discrimination by the exporter (Caves, 1974), the avoidance of distorted or sticky prices (Fisher and Harte, 1985, pp. 156–67), and the concealment of information about the quality of the partner's goods (Amann and Marin, 1989). Here we provide a theoretical framework that draws these explanations together and generates testable propositions. We assume the following.

A 1. The profit-maximising exporter quotes a price p_x per unit of output x.

* We are grateful for grants from the Jubiläumsfond of the Austrian National Bank and the Austrian Ministry of Trade and Industry in support of this project's empirical research, and the Division of Research, Harvard Business School, for additional assistance. Roy Mendoza played an important role in initiating this project. We also gratefully acknowledge the excellent research assistance of Angela Köppl, and the cooperation of the many persons who assisted by providing data and answering our questions.

[1] The terms *exporter* and *partner* will be used as shorthand in this paper. It is not fruitful to treat the partners to these barter transactions as if they were symmetrically positioned.

p_x is common knowledge. The market for x is not purely competitive in that buyers regard other offers of x as imperfect substitutes.

A 2. The countertrade partner is a state ministry or enterprise with the responsibility for acquiring importable x and marketing some exportable output c in pursuit of national benefits. Product c is not (normally) exported. The partner knows its quality (and thus its market price p_c^*). This knowledge is private, but quality can be contracted upon and verified at a cost. The partner quotes a price p_c in negotiations; $p_c \geqslant p_c^*$.

A 3. Each party's reservation price is private information. The exporter's reservation value r_x might be its marginal cost or the marginal revenue from an alternative sale. The trading partner's reservation values are v_x, its benefit from consuming the western export, and r_c, its opportunity cost of producing the countertrade good; $p_c > r_c$.

A 4. Because the western exporter is assumed not to be a pure competitor, $p_x > r_x$. Also, $v_x > r_c$ and $v_x > r_x$, but $v_x \gtrless p_x$. A Pareto-improving exchange is therefore feasible.

A 5. A competitive industry of trading houses or brokers can assist the negotiation of countertrade deals, verify qualities of countertrade goods, and locate buyers for goods that do not conform to conventional standards of quality and other attributes.

A 6. The partner is unable to resell the exporter's good even if $v_x < p_x$. This bald assumption, making price discrimination feasible, stands in for the subtle ways in which countertrade facilitates discrimination: (1) partners (CPEs and LDCs) are apt *a priori* to have low reservation prices; (2) countertrade negotiations themselves can expose information on the partner's reservation price; and (3) the effective price paid for the export good is obscure to third parties.

These assumptions suffice to make feasible counterpurchase and barter deals that share the main features of deals actually observed and would dominate any alternative transactions for the parties. The exporter quotes $p_x > r_x$, its reservation value (by A 4). The quantity of x exchange in a countertrade deal is normalised at one unit, sale of which compels the exporter to buy q units of the partner's goods at the quoted price p_c. The market value of these goods (net of the trading firm's charge) is p_c^*. The exporter's net benefit is therefore $B_x = (p_x - r_x) - q(p_c - p_c^*)$. The first term is positive by A 4 and the second may be negative by A 2. If $B_x > 0$ despite $p_c > p_c^*$, the exporter will seek to minimise q in negotiating the countertrade deal.[2]

The partner obtains gross benefit v_x and net benefit $(v_x - p_x)$ from consuming the exporter's good. The deal's value to the partner therefore is $B_c = (v_x - p_x) + q(p_c - r_c)$. The second term is positive by A 3. If so, $B_c > 0$ does not require $v_x > p_x$. Since $p_c > r_c$, the partner bargains to maximise q.[3] With the

[2] If $p_c < p_c^*$ contrary to A 2, the exporter shares the partner's interest in increasing q. We consider the implications of this case below. With $p_c > p_c^*$, a competitive exporter ($p_x = r_x$) will not accept a countertrade deal.

[3] If $p_c < r_c$ contrary to A 3 but $v_x > p_x$, the countertrade partner simply buys x for cash (that is, minimises q).

parties negotiating on q given the parameters, there exists a maximum q^x at which the exporter breaks even and a minimum q^p at which the partner's benefits are non-negative. If $q^x > q^p$ a deal is viable after bargaining over the surplus associated with $q^x - q^p$.[4]

Common knowledge of p_x (A 1) is important for this result. If the counterpartner stipulates q in advance and p_x is private information, the bargaining will focus on p_x rather than q, and a bargaining range can be defined on p_x. Alternatively, if the western exporter can keep p_x private while discovering v_x and r_c, p_x can be quoted to maximise B_x. For the exporter the optimal $p_x \geqslant v_x$, increasing with the partner's benefits from $q(p_c - r_c) > 0$.

Although a countertrade deal can yield net benefits to the participants, the conditions are stringent for it to be the best choice for both parties. Consider their total benefits, $B \equiv B_x + B_c = (v_x - r_x) + q(p_c^* - r_c)$. Although it was shown natural for them to bargain over q given p_x and p_c, the expression for B demonstrates that they share an interest either in maximising q if $p_c^* > r_c$ or setting $q = 0$ if $p_c^* < r_c$. That is, one party or the other has an incentive to renegotiate the deal. If the partner's goods are unprofitable to sell ($p_c^* < r_c$), both parties are better off if they simply negotiate a mutually agreeable p_x and scrap the sale of the countertrade goods.[5] If the countertrade goods are profitable to sell ($p_c^* > r_c$), the partner prefers to untie the quantity sold of the countertrade goods from the purchase of the exporter's good; if locked into the exchange, the partner would be willing to pay a higher p_x in order to expand profitable sales of countertrade goods ($p_c > p_c^* > r_c$). If the counterpartner can discover p_c^* by dealing directly with the trading house, countertrade can still be an advantageous shelter to allow the parties to share the benefits of price discrimination by the exporter.[6] Without price discrimination a countertrade deal is inferior to a marketing agreement between partner and a trading house, whose offer of marketing services (by A 5) cannot be beaten by the exporter.[7]

The terms just defined correspond directly to the terms set in actual countertrade agreements, permitting us to estimate the distribution of benefits. Consider the exporter's benefit function, $B_x = p_x - r_x - q(p_c - p_c^*)$. The empirical counterpart to q is the compensation ratio, the total value (not volume) of purchase obligations assumed by the exporter divided by the value of the initiating export (qp_c/p_x). The term $(p_c - p_c^*)/p_c$ is referred to as the discount ratio. The product of the compensation ratio and the discount ratio is therefore equivalent to the model's $q(p_c - p_c^*)$ normalised by the value of exports, and provides the terms-of-trade measure (i.e. the exporter's concession) to be explained.

The analysis yields these empirical implications.

[4] The break-even minimum q^p is 0 if $v_x > p_x$, $(p_x - v_x)/(p_c - r_c)$ if $v_x < p_x$ and $p_c > r_c$. The break-even maximum q^x for the exporter is $(p_x - r_x)/(p_c - p_c^*)$.

[5] That is, the western exporter can profit by offering a lower p_x in exchange for setting $q = 0$.

[6] Those benefits can be positive if $(v_x - r_x) > 0 > q(p_c^* - r_c)$. Hennart (1989) emphasised the role of transaction costs in determining p_c^*.

[7] This analysis omits the dependence of x_v on the number of units bought and of p_c^* and r_c on q, because the empirical investigation focuses on the occurrence and terms of countertrade deals, not their scales.

(1) The terms of the deal are constrained by various reservation prices. Although these are not observed directly, we can devise proxies for the differences among deals in v_x (relative to p_x), r_x (relative to p_x), and the structural determinants of r_c or p_c relative to p_c^*. These proxies will pick up both long-run and short-run influences on these reservation values. For example, a leading exporter's reservation value should exceed that of a fringe producer with a lesser goodwill asset. Excess capacity or softening market prices should lower a seller's reservation price.

(2) Rich if diverse predictions bear on the parties' competitive positions. The model rules out pure competition in the exporter's market but admits differences in the extent of product differentiation and the exporter's goodwill asset. Although we make no assumption about the goals behind price-setting (p_c) by state organisations, we can still test the hypothesis that the scope for credible values of p_c is limited by competition.

(3) Countertrade deals seem to involve substantial transaction costs of bargaining, verifying the qualities and attributes of the countertrade goods, and locating buyers for nonstandard merchandise. This property has testable implications for (e.g.) the situations of novice and experienced participants.

II. DATA SET AND PRELIMINARY TESTS

In order to test these hypotheses we secured information on a sample of 230 completed countertrade agreements from trading firms and producers in Vienna active in countertrade.[8] An information form soliciting information on 37 aspects of each transaction was developed and pretested (copies are available from Dr Marin). Definitions and concepts were reviewed carefully with each respondent, and answers were checked for consistency and to minimise missing observations. The agreements all took place after 1977, with 67% in 1986 and 1987. Individual parties were not identified, but we know for each the geographic origin, institutional type, and the Standard International Trade Classification (SITC) numbers of the commodities exchanged.

Each respondent was asked to provide information on a representative sample of the deals with which it had been involved. The sample, presumably reflecting the proportions in the parent population, was dominated by counterpurchase transactions (76·5%), with the rest divided between barter (11·3%) and buybacks (12·2%). The goods exchanged are mainly industrial: 87% of the exports and 60% of the partners' goods are classified as SITC 5–7.[9]

Reflecting Vienna's role as intermediary in East–West trade, 86·5% of the countertrade partners were CPEs and members of the Council of Mutual Economic Assistance (CMEA); the remaining 13·5% were LDCs. State agencies were the countertrade partners in 85·2% of cases, with the others divided between state-owned enterprises (9·1%) and private firms (5·7%).

[8] It is desirable to sample both trading firms and exporters handling their own countertrade deals, because the two are apt to differ systematically in size of firm and transaction, access to in-house use of partner goods, and other ways (Welt, 1984, pp. 88–91; Lecraw, 1988).

[9] The properties of our sample seem similar to those of the only other large-scale sample known to us, Jones and Jagoe (1988).

The western partners were industrial firms mostly based in the European Community (27·5%) and other industrial countries (66·8%).

The statistical analysis of the terms of trade in countertrade deals is prefaced by a series of simple tests of association that shed light on the theory and how to proceed with explaining terms of trade.

Terms of Trade Components

We start with components of the terms of trade. The compensation ratio (*CR*) is defined as the value of goods to be purchased or obtained by the exporter divided by the value of the exporter's sale. The discount (*D*) is the markdown (gross of the trading firm's commission) required to market the partner's goods. The product of these variables (*CR*∗*D*) measures the overall rate of markdown or discount accepted by the exporter.

We also obtained the respondent's direct evaluation of the deal's outcome: whether some or all of the gross discount was absorbed by the exporter (*ABSORB* = 1 if yes, 0 otherwise). If the exporter's standard price is known (publicly quoted), the intermediary monitoring the transaction can calculate directly whether *CR*∗*D* involves a significant concession by the exporter.

The proportion of *ABSORB* = 1 observations is important. If countertrade were simply an artifact of non-convertible currencies or arbitrary policies of the partners, and the exporters were pure competitors, no discount should have been absorbed. *CR* and *D* would represent unilateral choices made by the countertrade partners that we have no basis for explaining. In fact, respondents judged that the exporter had absorbed some discount in 52·2% of the transactions, and had not done so in 32·6% (no response in 15·2%). Bussard (1987) also reported absorption in about one-half of his sample. There is room for a bargaining process.

The correlation between *CR* and *D* should reveal something about relative bargaining power. A negative correlation is predicted if the exporter's opportunity-cost restraint (r_x) is fairly tight, so the counterpartner can impose a high *CR* or a p_c generating a high *D*, but not both.[10] *CR* and *D* are in fact uncorrelated (0·02), but only six transactions involve both high *CR* ($\geqslant$ 1·1) and high *D* (> 15%). Apparently most exporters cannot freely adjust their prices to prevent the invasion of their profits by high values of *CR*∗*D*.

Is the deal's value to the exporter related to *ABSORB*? The probability that the exporter gives up some surplus should increase with *CR* and *D*. However, only 40% of exporters were believed to absorb some discount when *CR* $\geqslant$ 1·1, while 65·5% did when *CR* < 1·1; the difference is significant at the 1·5% level. The same pattern appears with respect to *D*; with (the few) cases of *D* $\leqslant$ 0 deleted, the discount was partly absorbed in 57% of cases with *D* > 15%, but in 70% of cases with *D* $\leqslant$ 15%. These data have a consistent interpretation: western exporters elect to accept sales revenues lower than their nominal prices

[10] *D* is a decision variable for the partner for two reasons. The asking price of a state trader is an administered price, in 77% of our sample according to respondents' judgements. Also, the partner commonly sets limits on the exporter's choice of counterpurchase goods and in that way can manipulate the exporter's choices towards or away from those expected to require deep discounts (given their prices).

only within narrow limits. A CPE or LDC organisation that mandates high values of *CR* and/or *D* obtains a deal only if the exporter's asking price is marked up to offset the exaction.[11] The result is consistent with exporters making real sacrifices of their margins within limits of their opportunity costs.

Quality of Partners' Exportables

Industrial goods that partners offer for countertrade are commonly said to fall below conventional western standards in quality, design, or performance, a property that we showed to be theoretically important. The data support this

Table 1

Relation of Countertrade Terms to Qualities of Countertraded Goods

Qualities of goods	Discount % < 10	Discount % ⩾ 10	Discount absorbed Yes	Discount absorbed No
(1) Design of countertraded goods				
Below western standard	27	34	37	15
Equal western standard	40	26	27	30
Not applicable	53	33	49	25
Statistical significance*	10%		5%	
(2) Quality of countertraded goods				
Below average	6	18	12	11
Average	49	39	55	23
Above average	65	37	47	36
Statistical significance	5%		n.s.	
(3) Technical standard of countertraded goods				
Outdated	7	9	12	4
Equal western standard	62	35	51	27
Not applicable	51	49	50	39
Significance level*	n.s.		n.s.	
(4) Effect of existence of exchange for partner's type of goods				
Exchange exists	16	13	22	2
No exchange	29	23	25	26
Significance level	n.s.		1%	

* Chi-squared test performed on the applicable cells only.

hypothesis only in part. With the quality of countertraded goods rated from 'excellent' to 'very poor', only 11% fall below average and 47·5% are rated above average. They falter most commonly in design (27% below western norms, which is almost half those for which design is relevant), occasionally in technical standards (7% were outdated, which is 14% of those to which technical standards are applicable). Furthermore, quality is significantly related to the gross discounts that exporters experienced in disposing of counterpurchase goods (Table 1). Discounts greater than 10% are significantly (10% level) more prevalent when design is below western standard (Table

[11] A confirming pattern appears in the sizes of penalties on exporters for failure to complete their counterpurchases as scheduled. There is a statistically significant tendency for high penalties to be associated with low values of *CR*; that is, high penalties appear in agreements only when there will likely be little to penalise.

1 (1)) or quality below average (Table 1 (2)). The few technically substandard products are not heavily discounted (Table 1 (3)).

Table 1 also includes cross-tabulations with *ABSORB*. Absorption of the discount is more common when design is below standard and technical qualities are outdated (only the former is significant), but not when product quality is low. The pattern is weakly consistent with the hypothesis that partners offering substandard goods have low incomes and reservation prices for western exports, favouring them for price discrimination.

The theoretical model would fail if every commodity, whatever its attributes, could be priced by the market at a negligible transaction cost. Even organised commodity markets price only goods with standard qualities or attributes. The model's assumption about market information structures implies that partner goods traded on organised exchanges obtain better treatment than others, although they still face discounts. Table 1 (4) provides mixed evidence: the existence of an exchange is unrelated to *D*, but exporters are significantly more willing to absorb discounts when the presence of an exchange-determined price reduces uncertainty.

Role of Experience

The repetition of transactions and the role of experience in countertrade hold interest because of (on the one hand) the transaction costs they seem to involve and (on the other) the theoretical implication that parties are unlikely to repeat deals if determination of the qualities of countertrade goods is the only issue. Some exporters engage in countertrade deals often enough to develop their own specialised departments (Lecraw, 1988). Parties to most sampled transactions participate regularly in countertrade: 65·6 % of the exporters, 59·8 % of the partners. Only 14·5 % of exporters and 8·9 % of partners were novices. The prevalence of repeated dealings is consistent with the price-discrimination hypothesis.

Inexperience is costly in that novice and occasional exporters are under-represented in deals with $CR < 1$, while veterans are over-represented (significant at 3 %). No pattern appears for the countertrade partners. Neither group's experience is at all related to *D*. Veteran exporters absorb discounts in 58·7 % of the cases and occasional exporters in 72·2 %, but novices fall in between (61·3 %), and the pattern is not statistically significant. However, novice and occasional partners benefit from the absorption of discounts more often than do regular partners (a weak tendency significant only at 25 %). The only consistent rationale for this pattern is that customers with low reservation values are favoured by low prices.

Role of Short-term Disequilibrium

Although business reciprocity in the United States has been associated with short-run disequilibria with sticky prices and excess capacity, this basis for countertrade seems less plausible for exporters in global industries who offer differentiated products. Only 36 % of the transactions involve export of western goods that are standardised in both quality and design; 22·3 % are standardised in only one dimension, 41·7% in neither. Price inflexibility seems irrelevant to partner goods with impacted values, but countertrade sometimes serves to evade agreements to maintain cartel prices and foreign-exchange disequilibria (Hammond, 1990, pp. 34, 131–2). The data base includes the respondents' judgements about price trends for both parties' goods and whether either party holds excess capacity. Of exporters in rising-price markets, only 25% accepted obligations to purchase goods subject to large discounts ($D \geqslant 10\%$), while 41·1% did in falling-price markets, but the difference is not statistically significant. For the partners' goods, price trends are unrelated to the absorption of discounts. The exporters' excess capacity has no significant effect on *CR* or *D*.

III. DETERMINANTS OF TERMS OF TRADE

The terms of trade, reflected in *CR∗D* and *ABSORB*, are now analysed by means of multiple regression. Many of the predicted influences were mentioned in the preceding section but not competition, on which we now focus. We expect each party's share of the joint surplus in bilateral countertrade bargains to decrease with the closeness of competition that it faces and increase with the competition facing its transaction partner.

Measuring Competition

Respondents judged how much competition each trading party faces: (1) little competition worldwide; (2) little competition nationally, although substantial worldwide; (3) substantial competition both nationally and internationally. Also obtained was each party's rank in the world market: (1) a leading producer; (2) a significant middle enterprise; (3) a follower firm. To describe each party's categories of market structure and competitive position, we designate its status as exporter (*X*) or partner (*P*), its competition level (*C*), and its rank (*R*), while we treat the three tranches of *C* and of *R* as if they were cardinal and have equiproportional effects (*XCR* and *PCR*). Thus $XCR = 6$ denotes either a fringe exporter in an industry concentrated locally but not globally or an intermediate firm in an unconcentrated industry. Parties with low values of *c* of course face little competition and therefore should do better in countertrade deals. Because *CR∗D* represents a concession for the exporter, it should increase with *XC* and decrease with *PC*.

We assume that the value or quality of the goodwill asset that a firm possesses increases with its market share or rank. A superior asset yields the firm a larger (less elastic?) demand at any given price, if the product is differentiated, or a lower level of variable cost. Therefore *CR∗D* should increase with *XR* and decrease with *PR*, if we suppose that seller competition affects the partners (public-sector agencies and firms) and (investor-owned) exporters similarly.

Of the exporters 45·7% faced little competition worldwide, only 16·5% extensive competition both locally and internationally. The partners faced more competition: only 16·5% met little worldwide while 50·4% encountered extensive competition. The same difference appears in parties' market ranks. The status of leading producer was enjoyed by 66·3% of the exporters, 13·9%

of the partners. The status of fringe partner applied to 23·5% of the exporters, 67·8% of the partners. The pattern is consistent with the price-discrimination hypothesis, but also suggests that of the partners too many lacked market power for us to test its effect.

Information on Absorption

How can we utilise the variable *ABSORB*, which indicates when the exporter was judged to absorb some of *D*? If *ABSORB* = 0 accurately identifies cases in which the exporter obtained the same marginal revenue as in non-countertrade sales, such cases should provide no information on the effect of differences in competitive conditions, because either no difference exists or exporters could manipulate an unobservable p_x. Only cases for which *ABSORB* = 1 would contain useful information on competitive forces.

To test this implication we allowed the coefficient of *CR*D* on each regressor to differ between the cases of *ABSORB* = 1 and *ABSORB* = 0. In the event none of the predicted differences appeared, for which we have no explanation. Furthermore, we got nowhere in trying to explain *ABSORB* directly.

Other Influences

The data set allows the testing of the other predicted influences on the terms of trade. Because the tests involved somewhat tedious screening of alternative specifications, we describe the statistical embodiments only of hypotheses that enjoyed some support.

(1) Exporters obtained lower benefits where the partner goods were of low quality or inferior design, indicating the partner's low ability to pay.

(2) Parties with excess capacity or subject to declining market prices obtained poor terms of trade.

(3) Experienced trading partners did better than parties inexperienced in marketing their goods to foreign customers.

(4) Because of information and transaction costs, exporters who could use their partners' goods directly or market them locally obtained better terms.

(5) Product differentiation amplified the effect of limited competition in improving a party's terms.

Regression Results

We report the results piecemeal, starting with competitive conditions. There is little multicollinearity among the regressors, and missing observations on some variables warrant a sequential approach.

We regressed *CR*D* on dummy variables representing combinations of the market-structure and competitive-position classes, grouped to consolidate empty or nearly empty cells. Leading producers in the internationally concentrated industries (1, 1) were the omitted class. In Table 2 almost all signs conform to the hypothesis that a party obtains better terms of trade the more concentrated its industry and the higher its rank, implying positive (negative) coefficients for exporters (partners) in weaker positions and/or more competitive industries. For the exporters the slope coefficients increase as

Table 2

Effect of Number of Competitors and Competitive Position on Outcomes of Countertrade Transactions

Western exporter			Countertrade partner		
Market concentration	Exporter's position	Coefficient	Market concentration	Exporter's position	Coefficient
1	2, 3	7·36**	1	2, 3	−2·67
2	1	−1·89	2	1, 2	−1·53
2	2	1·68	2	3	−3·31
2	3	2·54	3	1, 2	−1·51
3	1	6·02**	3	3	−3·87
3	3	9·22*			

Levels of statistical significance (one-tailed test): * 1 %; ** 5 %. The model's adjusted $R^2 = 0{\cdot}039$, and the relation overall is significant at 6 %.

expected, becoming significant in the most competitive situations. For the partners no such progression is evident, and no coefficient is significant. We then shifted to the variables *XCR* and *PCR*, which treat the ordinal ranks of competition and market position as if they were cardinal variables. In Table 3, equation (3.1), the coefficient of *XCR* but not *PCR* proves statistically significant, and the model's explanatory power increases ($F = 4{\cdot}99$ for equation (3.1), $F = 2{\cdot}23$ for Table 2). If *CR*D* is factored into its components, both regressors significantly affect *CR* (equation 3.2) although neither influences *D*; this contrast is considered subsequently.

We next inquire whether the outcome depends on product differentiation, both as a structural attribute of the types of products exchanged and as ranks or positions of the parties' particular goods. In equation (3.3) the dummy variable $XPDV = 1$ for exporters' goods differentiated vertically by quality, $XPDH = 1$ for goods differentiated horizontally by design, and $XPDVH = 1$ for goods differentiated in both dimensions (0 otherwise). Although no coefficient is statistically significant, the signs suggest that differentiation (especially vertical) improves the exporter's position. In equation (3.4) the coefficients of corresponding dummies indicate that differentiation (especially horizontal) worsens the partners' positions, perhaps due to inferior quality or design of their goods. The database contains three variables that increase with the quality of the partner's goods: $TECH = 1$ for goods meeting western technical standards (0 = substandard); $DESIGN = 1$ for goods meeting western design standards (0 = below standard); *QUAL* increases with product quality (five classes).[12] Regressing *CR*D* or *CR* alone on these variables yields no significant result, but for *D* we obtain equation (3.5). Low-quality goods incur higher discounts (1 % significance). The fact that *D* is related to *QUAL* but not to any other variable suggests that the price of a partner's exportables is typically set at the world price for goods of standard quality and not as a

[12] We also assigned $TECH = 1$ and $DESIGN = 1$ to products for which these attributes are not applicable, so values of 1 indicate all problem-free cases.

Table 3

Determinants of Terms of Trade (and Components) in Countertrade Transactions

Equation number	Regression equation
(3.1)	$CR{*}D = 6.83^{*} + 0.993^{*}\ XCR - 0.252\ PCR$ (3.13) (3.08) (0.89) ($\bar{R}^2 = 0.037$; $F = 4.99^{*}$)
(3.2)	$CR = 83.39^{*} + 5.441^{*}\ XCR - 4.391^{*}\ PCR$ (9.67) (4.25) (3.90) ($\bar{R}^2 = 0.122$; $F = 15.70^{*}$)
(3.3)	$CR{*}D = 8.20^{*} + 1.048^{*}\ XCR - 0.254\ PCR - 2.472\ XPDH - 5.733\ XPDV - 1.919\ XPDVH$ (3.47) (3.19) (0.86) (0.97) (1.50) (0.99) ($\bar{R}^2 = 0.036$; $F = 2.579^{**}$)
(3.4)	$CR{*}D = 8.95^{*} + 0.814^{*}\ XCR - 0.203\ PCR - 5.205^{***}\ PPDH - 3.416\ PPDV - 3.016\ PPDVH$ (3.78) (2.46) (0.70) (1.83) (1.60) (1.26) ($\bar{R}^2 = 0.046$; $F = 3.012^{*}$)
(3.5)	$D = 2.46 + 0.274\ XCR - 0.218\ PCR + 0.727\ DESIGN - 3.482^{*}\ QUAL + 2.076\ TECH$ (0.66) (0.97) (0.65) (0.11) (2.47) 0.55) ($\bar{R}^2 = 0.031$; $F = 2.325^{**}$)
(3.6)	$CR = 87.84^{*} + 3.814^{*}\ XCR - 3.389\ PCR + 18.218^{**}\ XOC + 14.762^{***}\ XNE - 6.203\ POC$ (4.05) (2.58) (2.60) (1.84) 1.31) (0.72) $-\,9.783\ PNE + 3.819\ XPRICE + 3.903\ PPRICE - 13.100\ XCAP$ (0.72) (0.57) (0.67) (1.64) ($\bar{R}^2 = 0.113$; $F = 3.631^{*}$)
(3.7)	$CR{*}D = 6.38^{*} + 0.848^{*}\ XCR - 0.268\ PCR - 1.639\ XPDH - 3.763\ XPDV - 0.429\ XPDVH$ (2.64) (2.60) (0.93) (0.66) (1.00) (0.22) $+\,3.520^{***}\ XEC + 14.353^{*}\ XNIC$ (1.88) (3.59) ($\bar{R}^2 = 0.093$; $F = 4.071^{*}$)
(3.8)	$CR{*}D = 3.97 + 0.629^{**}\ XCR - 0.066\ PCR + 3.304^{***}\ XOC + 2.459\ XNE + 3.116\ XEC$ (1.55) (1.91) (0.23) (1.55) (1.01) (1.60) $+\,14.638^{*}\ XNIC - 3.041\ XUSE + 2.863\ XSLH$ (3.69) (1.51) (1.60) ($\bar{R}^2 = 0.112$; $F = 4.305^{*}$)

Levels of statistical significance: * 1%; ** 5%; *** 10%. Tests are one- or two-tailed as appropriate; see text.

strategic variable in the bargaining process. Consistent with equations (3.1) and (3.2), bargaining must then focus on *CR*, which is hence better explained than *CR∗D*.

The theoretical model assumes that countertrade involves significant transaction costs, and it implies that parties repeat transactions if exporters practise price discrimination, and/or repetition gives rise to learning or abates moral hazard. In equation (3.6) dummies indicate that a party (*X* or *P*) is only an occasional participant in (*OC*) or new entrant to (*NE*) countertrade activities, rather than a regular participant. If veteran participants obtain better outcomes, we expect positive coefficients for *XOC* and *XNE*, negative for *POC* and *PNE*. In equation (3.6) the coefficients of *XOC* and *XNE* are positive and significant (one-tailed tests), the latter at 10%. These coefficients are insignificant if *CR∗D* replaces *CR*.

Equation (3.6) also tests the hypothesis that excess capacity or 'soft' market prices affect a party's benefit. *XCAP* indicates the extent of exporters' excess capacity; *PRICE* indicates goods subject to a rising price trend. If excess capacity and falling prices weaken bargaining power, the coefficients of *XCAP* and *PPRICE* should be positive and of *XPRICE* negative. None is significant and only *PPRICE* takes the right sign.[13]

The effect of experience is probed in another way in equation (3.7), where the region of origin of the exporter is controlled. We know whether the exporter is a European Community enterprise ($XEC = 1$) or from a newly industrialised ($XNIC = 1$) rather than from another western industrial country (mainly Austria, with some United States and Japan). *XNIC* firms should do less well, with competition and product differentiation-controlled. In equation (3.7) the coefficient of *XNIC* is positive as predicted and significant. The coefficient of *XEC* is also positive (though much smaller) and significant at 10% (two-tailed test). These results are unchanged when *XCAP*, *XPRICE*, and *PPRICE* are also controlled.

Equation (3.8) incorporates how the exporter disposed of the partner goods that it received: by using them directly ($XUSE = 1$), selling them mainly in the exporter's national market ($XSLH = 1$), or selling them in other countries (the residual case). In equation (3.8) neither *XUSE*'s nor *XSLH*'s coefficient is significant, but exporters capable of using the partner's goods directly seemed to obtain better deals than those who disposed of them at arm's length; with *D* as the dependent variable, these coefficients are significant at 10 and 5% respectively. Controlling for *DESIGN*, *QUAL*, and *TECH* does not change this result. The negative effect of *XUSE* seems plausible; large western enterprises are probably not efficient users of low-quality inputs. We have no explanation for the positive coefficient of *XSLH*; if anything more heavily discounted goods should go to third markets (developing countries).

IV. CONCLUSIONS

We can reflect on the empirical findings about countertrade in the light of theoretical hypotheses about its bases. Several findings support the price-discrimination model. The exporters possess ample market power to discriminate, and better terms go to novice partners and others with presumed low reservation prices, who should benefit from discrimination. The price-discrimination model is really enveloped, however, by a more general model of countertrade as a device to bargain with an exporter who asks a price higher than its marginal cost. This model is well supported, with the exporters' ability to insist on their asking prices and the partners' ability to demand concessions increasing with each party's market concentration and market dominance. However, the evidence does not associate countertrade with short-run disequilibria in sticky-price markets.

[13] Chi-squared tests show that for both exporters and partners, rising (vs. declining) price trends are associated significantly (10%) with more occasional or new transactions. Rising-price markets attract more novice countertraders.

The hypothesis that countertrade rests on partners' difficulties in marketing goods of non-standard quality or design receives limited support. Some partners' goods do exhibit deficient quality, technical properties, or design. Countertrade can offer some partners least-cost access to western markets, as when the western exporters can use the partner's goods directly. For countertrade to reveal impacted values of partners' goods efficiently, this valuation must be costly however it is done; although that assumption is not tested, countertrade deals themselves evidently involve significant fixed costs. Overall, the discrimination and bargaining model gains more support than the information model, mainly from the extent of repetition of transactions and the importance of learning.

Countertrade has assumed considerable importance in international trade, especially East–West trade. These results ascribe significant explanatory power to a rational-actor model. That explanatory power is not large, however, leaving ample room for the hypotheses that countertrade develops from non-convertible currencies or provides partners only the illusion of benefit. The recent upheaval of political regimes in the main counterpartners and their probable shifts away from centrally planned economies throws the future of countertrade into question. We doubt, however, that the twilight of its importance is at hand.

Harvard University

Institute for Advanced Studies, Vienna

Date of receipt of final typescript: January 1992

References

Amann, E. and Marin, D. (1989). 'Barter in international trade: a rationale.' Working paper no. 257, Institute for Advanced Studies, Vienna.

Bussard, W. A. (1987). 'An overview of CT practices of corporations and individual nations.' In Korth (1987), chap. 2.

Caves, R. E. (1974). 'The economics of reciprocity: theory and evidence on bilateral trading arrangements.' In *International Trade and Finance: Essays in Honour of Jan Tinbergen* (ed. W. Sellekaerts), pp. 17–54. London: Macmillan.

Fisher, B. S. and Harte, K. M. (eds). (1985). *Barter in the World Economy*. New York: Praeger.

Hammond, G. T. (1990). *Countertrade, Offsets, and Barter in International Political Economy*. London: Pinter.

Hennart, J.-F. (1989). 'The transaction cost rationale for countertrade.' *Journal of Law, Economics and Organization*, vol. 5 (spring), pp. 127–53.

Jones, S. F. and Jagoe, A. (1988). *Third World Countertrade: Analysis of 1,350 Deals Involving Developing Countries, 1980–1987*. Newbury, Berks.: Produce Studies Ltd.

Korth, C. M. (ed.). (1987). *International Countertrade*. Westport: Quorum Books.

Lecraw, D. (1988). 'Countertrade: a form of cooperative international business arrangements.' In *Cooperative Strategies in International Business* (ed. F. J. Contractor and P. Lorange), pp. 425–42. Lexington: Lexington Books.

Murrell, P. (1982). 'Product quality, market signalling, and the development of east–west trade.' *Economic Inquiry*, vol. 10 (October), pp. 589–603.

Welt, L. (1984). *Trade without Money: Barter and Countertrade*. New York: Law & Business, Inc., Harcourt Brace Jovanovich.

Part VI
Policy Implications

[16]

COUNTERTRADE AS TRADE CREATION AND TRADE DIVERSION

ABLA M. ABDEL-LATIF and JEFFREY B. NUGENT*

This paper analyzes countertrade as a special case of a customs union in which the countertrade agreement gives rise (as in customs union theory) to both trade-creating and trade-diverting effects. The net effects on welfare are ambiguous. A detailed case study from Egypt and brief examples from other countries illustrate the relevance of this interpretation.

I. INTRODUCTION

Countertrade (CT) grew dramatically in the world economy during the 1970s and 1980s. Common explanations for CT cite national strategies for overcoming foreign exchange and credit constraints and business strategies for creating new markets, reducing the uncertainty of export prices and by-passing the constraints imposed by international price agreements. Other explanations emphasize CT's incentive-compatible features, which overcome the adverse selection and moral hazard problems inherent in the information asymmetries of technology transfer and marketing.

These explanations are not without fault. Mirus and Yeung (1987 and 1992) identify alternative and lower-cost means of pursuing national and business strategies. And the incentive-compatibility argument implies that CT would apply primarily in the case of sophisticated, highly differentiated goods in many different transactions in industries with characteristics favorable to CT. However, evidence shows that CT is applied more frequently to raw materials and simple rather homogeneous goods and services in transactions between single pairs of firms in a variety of industries and products. Most existing theories explain why CT would be more prominent in certain types of countries, sectors, and time periods than in others but generally fail to explain why and how CT is typically confined only to certain partners within sectors, countries, and time periods.

The customs union (CU) theory is a useful alternative perspective on CT. CU theory is useful in explaining why CUs in some cases are trade-creating and therefore welfare-enhancing but in other cases are trade-diverting and hence welfare-reducing. The same principles of trade creation and diversion can explain why CT in some cases is welfare-enhancing but in other cases welfare-reducing even in the same industry, country, and time period. In both CU and CT transactions, the particular trading partners' characteristics are of crucial importance in determining the sign of the net benefits generated.

*Assistant Professor, Department of Economics, American University in Cairo and Professor of Economics, University of Southern California, respectively. This is a revised version of a paper presented at the Western Economic Association International 67th Annual Conference, San Francisco, Calif., July 12, 1992, in a session organized by Professor Nugent. The authors thank Mustapha Nabli for suggestions in the formative stage of this paper, the anonymous referees and Jack Hou for useful comments in the final stage. They also thank the interviewees who gave so generously of their time.

Abbreviations

ACTREE: Arab Company for Transistor Radio and Electronic
CP: Counterpurchase
CT: Countertrade
CU: Customs Union
DC: Developed Country
LDC: Less Developed Country

Section II gives the trade creation and trade diversion analysis of CT. Section III examines a case study from Egypt. Section IV offers conclusions.

II. TRADE CREATING AND TRADE DIVERTING COUNTERTRADE

CT transactions almost invariably are interlinked and take place between specific trading partners, typically between different firms in different industries and countries. Traditional (neoclassical) trade theory holds that the partners in any transaction are essentially anonymous. However, in interlinked transactions generally and in CT transactions particularly, the partners are clearly specified and named. CU theory suggests that partner characteristics potentially are important determinants of the sign and magnitude of transactions' net benefits. In CUs the partners are countries, while in CT they are firms in different countries.

CT can take several different forms. The incentives (or rationale) for each form may vary, at least in relative importance. Some forms might even require (or at least benefit from) certain methods of analysis. Recent CT literature has focused the least analytical attention on perhaps the most important form, counterpurchase (CP) (Hoffmann, 1989). Since other forms of CT such as barter, offset, and buy-back share the characteristics of and rationale for CP, the analysis here also should apply, at least partially, to these other forms. And, since asymmetric information problems are less severe in CP arrangements, in order to simplify and focus on trade creation and diversion, the analysis here abstracts from information asymmetries and general equilibrium considerations.

Consider a simple CP example involving two interlinked transactions, primary and secondary, between two specific firms owned and operated in two different countries, one a developed country (DC) firm and the other a less developed country (LDC) firm. The LDC firm's purchase of a certain intermediate input ("component") from the DC firm is the primary transaction. The DC firm's purchase of another good or service from the LDC firm, which partially or even wholly finances the primary transaction, is the secondary transaction.[1] CP takes place in the following partial equilibrium setting: (i) The market for components in the LDC is competitive. (ii) A rising marginal cost curve characterizes domestic supply. (iii) The LDC firm's derived demand for components is downward-sloping with respect to the components' price. Figure 1 depicts the environment of the primary purchase of components in the LDC. S_d represents the domestic supply curve of other firms in the LDC, D_d the LDC firm's downward-sloping demand for components, and S_{ftt} the cost to that firm of imported components, including tariffs and transaction costs, obtained on the competitive international market. The DC firm is one indistinguishable supplier in that market.

On the other hand, P_f and S_f give the price and supply curve, respectively, of such components in an ideal world without tariffs, other trade barriers, or transaction costs on imported components. Following CU theory, however, the analysis here assumes that the ideal world of zero trade barriers and transaction costs is unattainable and that CP therefore will be a second best (Hoffmann, 1989). As a result, P_{tt} is the price the LDC firm paid for components, S_1 is the quantity of such components the firm purchased from domestic suppliers, and D_1–S_1 is the quantity the firm purchased from foreign suppliers including the DC firm.

1. In the case of buy-back arrangements, the secondary purchase involves a differentiated product produced by the LDC firm itself. In CP arrangements, however, the good involved in the secondary purchase generally is relatively homogeneous and is not produced by the LDC firm (Hoffmann, 1989).

FIGURE 1
LDC Firm's Market for Its Components

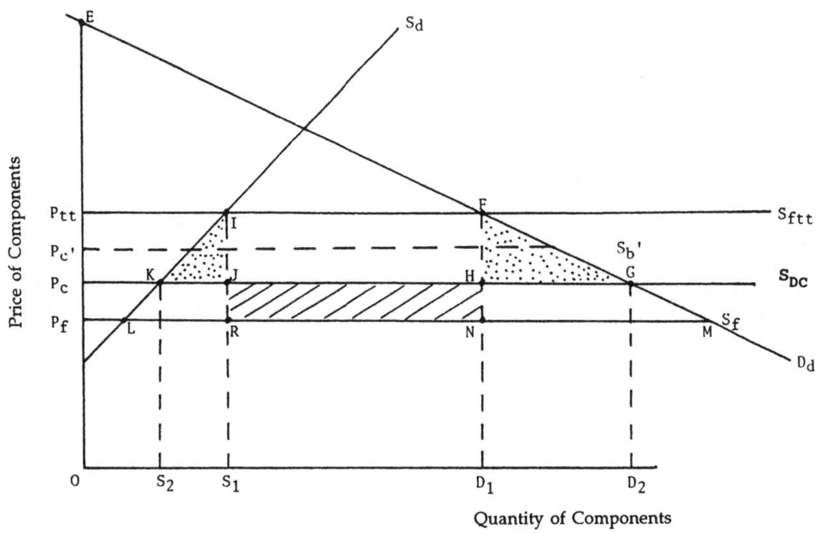

Now consider a CT arrangement whereby the DC firm is willing to supply the LDC firm with components at price P_c if it can do so on an exclusive basis, at least among foreign suppliers. In this case, S_2 would be the quantity purchased from domestic suppliers and (D_2-S_2) the quantity purchased from the DC firm. The LDC firm's consumer (buyer) surplus from countertrading with the DC (triangle EGP_c) considerably exceeds the LDC firm's consumer (buyer) surplus in the absence of CT or in the ideal world of zero transaction costs and trade barriers (triangle EFP_{tt}). This signals the LDC firm's desire to participate in CT with the DC. Part of the LDC firm's gain could result from reductions in tariff payments or in other revenues to the government and from reductions in surplus to the domestic suppliers due to the price decrease of such components from P_{tt} to P_c. Thus, the LDC firm's gain does not necessarily imply that the LDC as a whole would be better off from CT with the DC firm. Indeed, the LDC government's need to protect both its own domestic interests and its nationals' interests explains why it may insist on being a party to the CT contract or on the right to veto the contract. Since P_c and S_{DC} are above P_f and S_f, the CT arrangement imposes a trade diversion cost. However, the CT arrangement also provides a trade creation gain relative to the situation in its absence.

Two quite different and realistic features—tariffs and transaction costs—complicate the analysis. The analysis here first considers the case in which the differences between P_{tt} and P_f and between P_{tt} and P_c are due exclusively to tariffs and then the case in which the differences are due exclusively to transaction costs. Finally, the analysis considers the more complicated case in which the differences between P_{tt} and P_f on the one hand and between P_{tt} and P_c on the other are due to both transaction costs and tariffs.

In the absence of transaction costs, the difference between P_{tt} and P_f would be due entirely to the tariff. As a result, in a partial CU in which the imports of components from the DC firm are exempt from tariffs, P_c and S_{DC} also would exclude tariffs. Comparing the ordinary tariff-distorted equilibrium, in which the price of components is P_{tt}, with the CT-distorted equilibrium, in which P_c is the price of components as in standard CU theory, reveals that (i) the area of trapezoid $P_{tt}IKP_c$ represents an intra-national redistribution from domestic suppliers of components to the LDC firm, (ii) the area of rectangle IFHJ represents another intra-national redistribution from government (tariff revenue) to the LDC firm, (iii) the areas of the dotted triangles KIJ and FGH indicate the net gains to the LDC firm from trade creation (due to the price reduction), and (iv) the hatched area of rectangle JHNR indicates the net loss in government tariff revenue (and in national welfare) due to CT's trade diversion effect.

The comparison unambiguously indicates that (i) the LDC firm gains, (ii) the LDC government loses some tariff revenue, and (iii) LDC domestic suppliers lose some producers' surplus. Additionally, the net benefits or losses of the CT arrangement to the LDC as a whole are ambiguous. Positive net benefits depend on whether or not the areas of the dotted trade creation triangles KIJ and FGH exceed the area of the net trade diversion loss rectangle JHNR.

Next consider the absence of tariffs—in other words, the case in which the difference between S_{ftt} and either S_f or S_{DC} only is due to transaction costs. Presumably, the exclusivity in supply would allow the DC firm to take advantage of economies of scale in transactions and lower its supply price to the LDC firm from S_{ftt} to S_{DC}. The benefits to the LDC firm and the loss in producers' surplus to the domestic components suppliers again would be unambiguous and identical to what they were in the presence of tariffs. In this case, however, no loss in tariff revenue exists, and hence the government revenue is unaffected. However, the rent-seeking and negotiation costs of setting up the arrangement could be quite substantial, In this case, the net benefits of CT to the LDC as a whole would be unambiguously positive and equal to the area of triangles KIJ and FGH plus the area of rectangle IFHJ.

More realistically, the difference between P_{tt} and P_f, on the one hand, and between P_{tt} and P_c, on the other, may be due to both tariffs and transaction costs. Analyzing the net gains of CT to the various parties and to the LDC as a whole is more complex in this case. One must consider the values of P_c and S_{DC} without assuming tariff exemption. However, the analysis is straight-forward and implies that the benefits of CT would lie somewhere in between the two previous cases. In other words, considering both discriminatory tariffs and transaction costs reveals that CT is more likely to be socially beneficial to the LDC than the first case indicates but less likely to be socially beneficial than the second case indicates.

Another interesting case occurs when another firm in the developing country is able to supply the LDC firm with components at price P_c even in the presence of transaction costs and tariffs. This second DC firm is the efficient supplier and introduces another source of trade diversion in CT. This would leave the LDC and the LDC firm with a choice between the second DC component supplier without CT and the original DC partner with CT. In this case, rectangle IFHJ represents a net gain rather than a redistribution from government to the LDC firm. In choosing between the original and the second DC firm, the LDC firm should consider this net gain relative to the net gain from the secondary CT transaction.

CT transactions necessarily are linked. No analysis of CT net benefits and costs can be complete unless it explicitly considers the secondary transaction. Figure 2 presents a parallel analysis for the secondary transaction. Because the LDC firm and the DC firm are linked contractually, the magnitude of the DC firm's demand for the counterpurchased good is positively related to the magnitude of its sales of components to the LDC firm.

One way to capture that relation is to consider the position of S_{LDC} in relation to S_{ftt}. If sales to the LDC firm give the DC firm some advantage—either in transaction costs or in taxes on exports of the exporting country or on DC imports—relative to the transaction cost and tax-inclusive rest-of-world supply curve S_{ftt}, one might expect the S_{LDC} curve to lie below S_{ftt} (see figure 2). For example, the larger the DC firm's exports of components to the LDC firm, the better the DC firm's information might be about the LDC firm and the quality of its export goods. Hence, the lower would be the price (for standard quality) that it would have to pay for these goods (S_{LDC}). Also consider the case in which the DC firm invests its profits from the primary transaction in marketing channels for the LDC firm. This relationship implies that the larger the profits, the greater the expenditures on transaction cost reduction and therefore the lower the position of S_{LDC}. To achieve a similar effect, the exporting LDC could exempt goods under CP agreement from an existing export tax, or the importing country could exempt goods from an existing import duty.

In the initial pre-CT situation without the intermediation of the DC firm, the domestic price for the goods in the DC is P_{tt}. At this price, the quantity that domestic producers supply is S_1, the quantity demanded is D_1, and the quantity imported through traditional channels is D_1–S_1. The difference between P_{tt} and the supply price of firms in the rest of the world, P_f, results from a combination of (i) tariffs in the importing country, (ii) export taxes in the exporting countries, and (iii) transaction costs.

If by any of the aforementioned mechanisms the CT relationship between the LDC firm and the DC firm were to provide DC consumers with access to a lower cost source of the good (S_{LDC}), the price of this good in the DC would drop from P_{tt} to P_c. The effects would include: (i) a reduction in S_d from S_1 to S_2, (ii) a rise in D_d from D_1 to D_2, and (iii) an increase in (D_1–S_1) to (D_2–S_2) as the DC imports more of the semi-finished good from the LDC via the DC firm.

Consider an alternative situation prior to the CP arrangement. The DC might have relied on professional traders when importing the good and could well lack knowledge or experience in the market. The CP requirement that the DC firm import this good could raise the DC's transaction cost of obtaining its imported inputs, suggesting that S_{LDC} might lie above S_{ftt}. For example, S_{LDC}' in figure 1 shows that the trade diversion effects clearly dominate, at least as far as the DC and its firm are concerned.

Even the former case involves some trade diversion. Indeed, the diversion of DC imports from the lowest cost source S_f to the LDC source intermediated by firm DC could make some groups within their respective countries worse off. As a result of CT, DC consumers would benefit unambiguously, but the DC firm could gain or lose and either or both governments could lose tax revenue. As in the primary transaction, the relative magnitude of the trade creation and diversion effects would de-

FIGURE 2
DC Market for the Good Counterpurchased by the DC Firm from the LDC

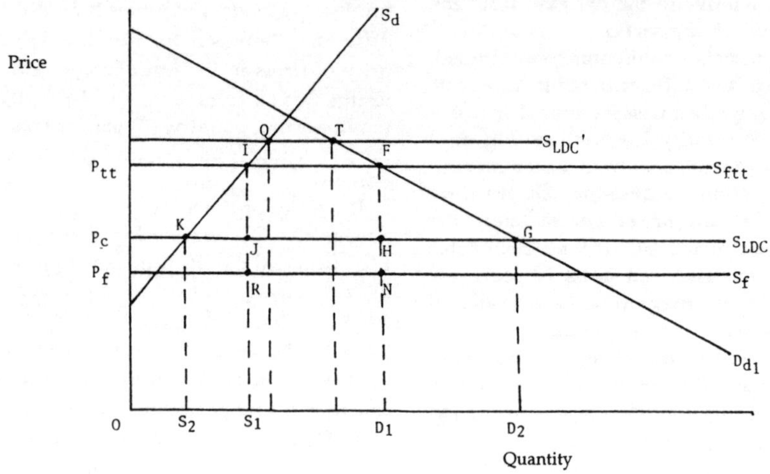

pend on a number of the respective trading partners' characteristics—in particular on the extent to which the difference between P_{tt} and P_c is due to transaction costs, tariffs and export taxes. Once again, the direction (sign) of CT's net social benefits to either country as a whole is theoretically ambiguous and depends on various firm and country characteristics. In essence, these outcomes depend on whether or not CT's trade creation benefits sufficiently compensate for its trade diversion losses.

Calculating CT's net gains for each relevant agent or class of agents in each country involves summing the group-specific effects obtained separately from the primary and secondary transactions.

III. CT CASE STUDY

The analysis here implies that one would have to evaluate each example of CT in general, or of CP in particular, separately and in detail before reaching conclusions concerning the sign and magnitude of the net benefits for either the different parties or the countries as a whole. Since the analysis involves CU theory, one also must demonstrate that real world CT experiences fit into the proposed framework.

Since the details of CT arrangements often are confidential due to commercial or political reasons, demonstrating the model's applicability to a particular case is no easy task.

The analysis here focuses on a CT arrangement between NEC of Japan and the Arab Company for Transistor Radio and Electronic Equipment (ACTREE) of Egypt. This case also involves the Egyptian government, whose approval was required for initiating and annually renewing the agreement. The parties first discussed this arrangement in the early 1980s and formally initiated it in 1987. All parties have renewed and the Egyptian government has reapproved the agreement each year thereafter.

This case is a typical example of CP in that the arrangement is neither a simple spot exchange in kind between two parties of entirely unrelated goods (as in barter) nor an exchange between goods at different stages in the production process (as in offset and buy-back) but rather a clearly interlinked transaction involving exchange of unrelated goods between parties that expect to be related to one another for some time. As in most CP arrangements, the primary transaction involves an intermediate input (TV components) and the secondary transaction a fairly homogeneous product (tourism services). For the six years of the project's existence, Egyptian and world economic conditions have rapidly changed. This case therefore affords insights into such arrangements' dynamic effects and flexibility and robustness under changing environmental conditions. Most important, the primary and secondary transactions are transparent. The analysis thus can examine each separately and obtain relevant information in part through personal interviews.

The agreement calls upon ACTREE to import some components for TV assembly from NEC. NEC-arranged Egyptian tourism exports to Japan partially (but not necessarily entirely) finance the foreign exchange costs to ACTREE. The analysis involves applying the model first to Egypt's ACTREE purchase of components and then to the Japanese consumers' purchase of Egyptian tourism services from NEC.

One important factor contributing to the agreement is the size, growth, and persistence of Egypt's current account deficit. For many years, Egypt maintained a disequilibrium exchange rate backed up by a rather strict and complex foreign exchange rationing system. As a result, firms had difficulty gaining access to the foreign exchange needed to finance imported raw materials, capital goods, and intermediate goods. In financing these deficits, Egypt has relied heavily on emigrant remittances, foreign aid, and other transfers. However, by the mid-1980s the external financing of these deficits had become even more difficult than in the past. This was due to (i) war and economic depression in the Gulf, the region to which most Egyptian workers have migrated and hence the primary source of remittances, (ii) Egypt's decreasing strategic value after the Camp David accords with Israel and the diminution of East-West conflict, and (iii) the rather severe recessions and fiscal crises that most donor countries have experienced in recent years. As a result, an individual firm like ACTREE faced increasing difficulty in financing the foreign exchange requirements of importing components.

ACTREE had been importing components for its TV assembly operations ever since their beginning in 1974. Due to the less than perfect substitutability of various kinds of components in ACTREE's TV assembly lines, the degree to which ACTREE has been able to utilize its productive capacity largely has depended on its ability to gain access to NEC components.

ACTREE purchases its TV components through competitive bidding, but NEC components are more costly than those of comparable quality from Korean and Taiwanese firms. This supports the supposition that the CT partner may not be the lowest cost supplier (see figure 1). ACTREE is not an exporting firm and by the mid-1980s must have faced high and rising transaction costs in gaining access to imported components. This justifies the assumption that the gap between P_{tt} and either P_c or P_f is large. Although ACTREE has to pay import duties on its imported components, whether from NEC or other sources, the CT arrangement with NEC has both trade-creating and trade-diverting effects.

Applying the available information to the model in figure 1, one can see that ACTREE benefits unambiguously from this transaction. It obtains the imported components at transaction costs that are lower and at tariff rates that are no higher than would be the case in the absence of CT. In the two years before the CP agreement with NEC, ACTREE's production was falling. In the five years since the agreement, ACTREE's production increased by more than 60 percent. ACTREE actually pays for its NEC components in Egyptian pounds by reimbursing the local tourist agencies and Egypt Air for their charges for Japanese tourists that NEC brings to Egypt. NEC also benefits unambiguously from this transaction. It is able to sell more of its somewhat higher priced components and hence makes more profit than might be possible in the absence of CT. However, in principle that benefit could be offset by losses incurred in the secondary transaction—that is, in satisfying its requirement to promote Egyptian tourism.

But what about the effects on both the Egyptian government and domestic suppliers of components? Egypt's government suffers no loss in tariff revenue in this transaction. In fact, it might collect slightly more if the quantity of imports were to rise while the tariff rate remained unchanged. However, because Egypt's tariff rate on such components is very low, the increase in tariff revenues relative to the situation without CT is negligible. On the other hand, Egypt's government might well lose tariff revenue in the secondary transaction. Figure 1 shows that at the time the parties initiate the arrangement, the effect on domestic producers of components (S_d) is nil for the precise reason that such producers do not exist. Economies of scale dictate that in the longer run the larger level of production facilitated by CT might encourage domestic component production. Indeed, ACTREE recently has initiated a joint venture with another firm to produce some TV components in Egypt.

One now can apply figure 2 to the secondary transaction—that is, the Japanese imports of Egyptian tourist services through NEC. Several conclusions emerge. First, the assumption that S_{LDC} lies above S_f (and therefore that P_c lies above P_f), implying that NEC would be less efficient than specialized travel firms in promoting Egyptian tourism exports to Japan, is quite reasonable. NEC is a large, high-technology manufacturing firm with no previous experience in the travel industry. Second, the positioning of the S_{LDC} and S_f curves below the S_{ftt} curve (as opposed to above it as in the case of S_{LDC}') also is reasonable. Egyptian tourism came to NEC's attention as a result of its presence in Egypt (learning effects), and NEC's advantage is that its own workers supply one segment of that market. Despite the implicit tax on tourism exports under the complex foreign exchange surrender system then applied in the tourism industry, the analysis here concludes that the CT arrangements yield no saving in either export or import taxes on Egyptian tourism exports to Japan. Third, since by definition Japanese suppliers cannot produce Egyptian tourism services, the S_d curve is irrelevant and could be excluded from the analysis without effect. Eliminating one margin within which trade creation may occur, however, would make trade creation benefits much less likely to outweigh trade diversion losses.

In general, therefore, the secondary CT transaction gives rise to both trade creation and trade diversion. What can one say about the distribution of CT's net benefits (if any) in this transaction? While NEC might have incurred some direct and short-term losses from promoting tourism, these losses are likely to be rather small and more than offset by its gains on the primary transaction.

The Egyptian government appears to incur no loss of implicit export tax revenues from exporting tourism through NEC. Moreover, the NEC-assisted tourism exports are largely "add-on"—that is, additional to existing exports. In practice, the revenues collected indirectly as a result of increased exports and imports under CT represent an increase in revenues to the Egyptian government. Since ACTREE is not directly involved in the secondary transaction, this transaction should not affect ACTREE, which should retain an overall advantage under CT.

But what of the effect on the Egyptian tourism firms? The available data, though by no means definitive, suggests that the tourism firms have not lost and indeed probably have benefitted from CT through NEC. They may have lost slightly due to an implicit 100 percent surrender requirement on the exports through NEC. However, a reduction in the large paperwork burden that the Egyptian government imposes to prevent their underreporting of foreign exchange earnings offsets this loss. More importantly, to the extent that informational externalities exist, CT in tourism may have lowered the cost of subsequent efforts to attract Japanese tourists. Japan sends about 12 million tourists overseas every year and each tourist, on average, spends more per person per day than a tourist from any other country. Thus, the Japanese market is extremely attractive to Egypt. Only a small percentage of Japanese tourists travelled to Egypt before the CT arrangement.

Aggregating the effects of the primary and secondary transactions reveals that both ACTREE and NEC have enjoyed net benefits from CT. NEC has been able to sell more components at higher prices than possible otherwise, and ACTREE has gained assurance of a steady flow of imported components. The fact that both companies have enthusiastically renewed the agreement each year since its inception in 1987 testifies to their derivation of mutual net benefits.

In principle, one or more governments might lose from CT arrangements in which tax exemptions or reductions were granted. However, ACTREE and NEC have no such exemptions or reductions. As a result, neither the Japanese nor Egyptian government has suffered adverse affects.

The analysis here does not include effects on domestic suppliers of the commodities traded in the respective countries since domestic supplies do not exist in this case. The Egyptian tourism sector seems to have benefitted from the secondary transaction—especially Egypt Air, which received almost two-thirds of the entire NEC tourism transaction proceeds. In fact, prior to this CT arrangement Egypt Air's planes on the Tokyo-Cairo route had been flying almost empty.

In the particular case of ACTREE-NEC, the trade creation effects have vastly dominated the trade diversion effects. Why? The reason involves the existence of favorable partner characteristics and other aspects of the institutional setting. NEC may have been a slightly higher cost supplier of components than some alternative suppliers. However, ACTREE used competitive bidding procedures and did not restrict itself to NEC in making procurement decisions. Likewise, because so much Japanese tourism involves employer-sponsored groups, and because NEC and its various affiliates are very large employers, NEC quite easily arranged to send relatively large numbers of tourists to Egypt even though it was not a travel firm. Indeed, this may explain why many other countertrading Japanese firms frequently engaged in tourism (Roscoe, 1986).

Another remarkable observation is that all parties annually renew the arrangement despite the tremendous environmental changes that Egypt in general, and its TV assembly industry in particular, have undergone. The most important change is Egypt's substantial economic policy reforms—in particular, switching from reliance on central planning and import substitution to an increasingly open orientation based on free market forces. By 1991, Egypt had devalued the Egyptian pound and made it freely convertible, allowing it to seek its own value in currency markets and removing any discrepancy between the official exchange rate and the effective price of foreign exchange.

Clearly, these changes have eliminated the transaction cost advantage of NEC components purchased under CT. However, ACTREE believes that attracting more tourists to Egypt yields indirect benefits as the market for ACTREE's TV sets may be slightly larger than otherwise possible. The number of additional Japanese tourists in Egypt has been about 4,000 in a normal year, earning about $8 million, and is expected to rise each year. Moreover, until such time as Egypt irrevocably adheres to its reform course, the arrangement provides insurance to both NEC and ACTREE against possible default on the reform front. While the benefits of maintaining the agreement to the principal parties involved have fallen considerably, the transaction costs of renewing the agreement also are very low. Moreover, these transaction costs already have produced substantial benefits to all parties in addition to the original two.

IV. CONCLUSIONS AND POLICY SUGGESTIONS

Applying trade creation and trade diversion analysis to the ACTREE-NEC case clearly shows that trade creation benefits can outweigh substantially trade diversion losses. By no means, however, does this conclusion imply a general rule.

Indeed, the CT literature is replete with examples of trade diversion costs that are considerably larger than trade creation effects and that dominate them. For example, Hill (1984) cites the widespread use of linkage fees on CT relationships. These fees compensate for the transaction costs involved in accepting a product not in a firm's normal line of activity (instead of convertible currency) as payment for an imported product or service. For Romanian exports received in CT, this fee was 9 percent of their value during the 1960s and 1970s. Another relatively common signal of trade diversion costs in CT is private firms' tendency to encourage their government agencies to ease the problems of receiving as compensation commodities and services with which they are unfamiliar by taking over these marketing activities (Vezariu, 1985, p. 152). Still another sign is the policy recommendation that a market be set up among the foreign CT partners in a particular country where the various partners could exchange various commodities purchased in CT (as in debt swaps). This arrangement enables partners to wind up with commodities that they can market more easily than the commodities they directly receive in CT (OECD, 1985, p. 20).

The ACTREE-NEC case is particularly instructive in identifying ways in which the various CT parties have minimized these trade diversion costs. One way is to participate in agreements (as NEC has done not only in Egypt but also in Turkey) involving compensation in commodities that the enterprise concerned can market at low cost. Another is to use competitive bidding procedures as ACTREE has done. Still another is to avoid exclusivity of source in the contracts and to use relatively short-term contracts with periodic review provisions as both ACTREE and NEC have done.

CT effects are likely to contain both trade-creating and trade-diverting elements, the relative importance of which are likely to vary significantly with partner and country characteristics. As in CU theory, policymakers should evaluate each CT case separately.

REFERENCES

Abdel-Latif, Abla, "The Egyptian Experience with Countertrade: Case Studies," *Journal of World Trade*, 24:5, 1990, 117–134.

Hill, M., *East-West Trade, Industrial Cooperation and Technology Transfer*, Gower, London, 1984.

Hoffmann, Helga, "Countertrade," in *The New Palgrave: A Dictionary of Economics*, Norton, New York, 1989, 85–87.

Mirus, Rolf, and Bernard Yeung, "Countertrade and Foreign Exchange Shortages: A Preliminary Investigation," *Weltwirtschaftliches Archiv*, *123*:3, 1987, 535–544.

Mirus, Rolf, and Bernard Yeung, "Why Countertrade: An Economic Perspective?", Paper presented at the Western Economic Association International 67th Annual Conference, San Francisco, Calif., July 1992.

OECD, *Countertrade: New Developing Country Practices*, Organization for Economic Cooperation and Development, Paris, 1985.

Roscoe, B., "Demonetized Deals," *Far Eastern Economic Review*, August 1986, 48.

Vezariu, Pompiliu, *Countertrade, Barter and Offsets: New Strategies for Profit in International Trade*, McGraw-Hill, New York, 1985.

ASIAN JOURNAL OF ECONOMICS AND SOCIAL STUDIES Vol. 12, No. 2 (1993), 81–96

COUNTERTRADE, LICENSING AND DIRECT FOREIGN INVESTMENT: COMPARATIVE EFFECTS ON LDCS AND MNES

ABLA M. ABDEL-LATIF
Assistant Professor of Economics
The American University in Cairo

and

JEFFREY B. NUGENT*
Professor of Economics
University of Southern California

Countertrade is a form of international trade that has been receiving much attention from the business community but virtually none on the part of economists. The purpose of this paper is to partially fill this gap by applying some theory to countertrade. In particular, partial equilibrium techniques are used to study the comparative effects of countertrade, licensing and direct foreign investment in subsidiaries (DFI) on both developing countries (LDCs) and multinational enterprises (MNEs). The joint decision making between LDCs on the one hand MNEs on the other in choosing among the three available options and the relevance of transaction cost theory is also discussed.

The word "countertrade" has only recently entered the terminology of international trade. It is being used to cover a multitude of particular commercial arrangements with a bewildering array of names, such as counterpurchase, buyback, switch, offsets and others. What they all share is the explicit linking of import and export transactions between the two trade partners.

Growing usage of the word countertrade reflects the rising importance of the activity itself. Almost every week there are reports of some country or company becoming involved in countertrade. Much of the growing activity involves private Western firms in their trade with either Eastern European Countries (EECs) or LDCs).

Despite the growing attention paid by the business community to this method of trade, countertrade is still an unknown subject for economists. The general purpose of this paper is to bring countertrade to the attention of economists. Its main focus, however, is to theoretically model countertrade to be able to determine how it affects the interests of the various parties involved. The two specific questions raised are: (1) What is the effect of countertrade (licensing

*The authors would like to thank Professors Timur Kuran and Ian Novos for helpful comments on an earlier draft of this paper.

with payment in resultant products) on the welfare of an LDC relative to those of either a regular licensing agreement or direct foreign investment (DFI)? (2) How attractive is countertrade for a MNE compared to a regular licensing agreement or DFI?

The starting point of the analysis is a simple model from Bardhan (1982) where the welfare effects of a licensing agreement and a subsidiary on an LDC are compared. Several changes in Bardhan's model are necessary to accommodate countertrade as an alternative. The results of the amended model are used to evaluate the performance of countertrade. Both analytic and simulation techniques are used.

The paper is organized a follows: in section I we attempt to present some background information on countertrade such as its definition, magnitude and its various forms along with the reasons why it is practiced. Section II briefly presents the basic model. Sections III-V cover the countertrade model, its implications for the welfare of both LDCs and MNEs and the joint decision making of the two parties. The conclusions of the countertrade model are presented in section VI.

I. What Is Countertrade?

While because it is new, terminology about the forms of countertrade lacks standardization, a general definition can be provided. According to the US Department of Commerce (1978), a countertrade transaction is one in which a seller provides a buyer with deliveries and contractually agrees to purchase goods from the buyer equal to an agreed-upon percentage of the original sale values.

One problem in assessing countertrade is uncertainty concerning its magnitude. Different sources vary in their measures of the actual number of countries involved in countertrade and the proportion of world trade comprised of countertrade. Estimates of the percentage of countertrade in world trade vary from 5% to 30%, but are as high as 50% in some kinds of trade such as East–West trade.

Most problems of quantification stem from the fact that neither enterprises nor countries record linked bilateral transactions separately in their international accounts and disclosure statements (Welt 1984, Hodara 1984, Verzaria 1985).

A. *The Main Forms of Countertrade*

Using OECD (1985) categorization, countertrade transactions can be divided into two categories: (1) commercial compensation and (2) industrial compensation.

1. *Commercial Compensation*

Commercial compensation typically consists of an obligation, assumed by one party at the time of effecting a sale, to undertake or cause to be undertaken purchases of products generally not related to or derived from the products sold. The purchases do not necessarily have to be made from the same enterprise as that which bought the goods in question. They are generally one-shot operations for small or moderate amounts, typically completed in 2 or 3 years. The fact that the goods involved in the two transactions are not related is the key difference between commercial and industrial compensation.

2. *Industrial Compensation*

Industrial compensation, on the other hand, involves the sale of technology, plant or equipment with a contractual commitment on the part of the seller to purchase a certain quantity of products that are produced by or derived from the original sale. Because these transactions involve setting up entire production facilities, their values can run into hundreds of millions of dollars. The commitment to buy back goods as a proportion of the original sale is typically greater than in the case of commercial compensation, with counterdeliveries often totalling 100% or more of the value of the original sale. Also, the duration of the transaction is typically much longer, even as high as 25 years.

B. *The Motivation for Countertrade*

LDCs and EECs encourage and mandate countertrade in order to reduce their trade imbalances, foster the exports of certain industries targeted for growth, upgrade certain individual sectors through foreign investment, and safeguard their hard currency reserves. Western countries and companies seem to accept countertrade demands in order to achieve sales that otherwise would be impossible and to gain prominence in new markets, thereby enhancing the prospects for future sales (Welt, 1982). In the case of countertrade requirements imposed by industrialized countries, trade imbalances and hard currency reserves are not the issue. Rather, countertrade is demanded in these cases because of (a) the buyer's leverage over individual supplies in industries in which supply exceeds demand, (b) the procurement is large and (c) there are a number of companies bidding for the contract (Welt, 1985). While each group of countries described above imposes countertrade for the same basic reasons, different countries use this unconventional method of trade in differing degrees and different ways.

II. The Basic Model

The model in Bardhan 1982 considers the case of an LDC that has the choice of: (i) producing cars at home in a domestic firm *licensing* the technology from a MNE, from which it also buys the necessary intermediate components, i.e., the familiar case of licensing with tied purchase of inputs, or (ii) producing them at home in a *subsidiary* of a MNE-DFI. Alternatives (i) and (ii) are denoted L and S respectively in subsequent analysis. In the case of S, the import of components involves intrafirm trade, whereas in the case of L it is interfirm.

The desirability of each alternative is evaluated in terms of total national welfare. In the case of S this is the amount of consumer surplus generated in the domestic market for cars, whereas in the case of L it is this consumer surplus plus the profits for the domestic firm. For simplicity, there is no tax or tariff revenue and all profits of the wholly owned subsidiary in the case of S are remitted abroad.

In the case of L, license fees or royalties are ignored since, with tied purchase of components, the price charged for the latter provides enough leverage for the transnational company.

Finally, it is assumed that is in the case of domestic production under S the size of the domestic market is such that it allows the subsidiary of only one transnational company to cater to this market; similarly in the case of L the licensing firm has a monopoly in the domestic car market.

The domestic market for cars is characterized by the following constant-elasticity demand function:

$$Q = P^{-\eta}, \eta > 1 \tag{1}$$

where Q is the amount demanded, P is the price, and η is the (positively defined) price elasticity of demand.

If Q_S and Q_L are the equilibrium quantities of cars produced under S and L, respectively, the expressions for total national benefit are:

$$B_S = \int_0^{Q_S} [P(Q) - P(Q_S)]dQ = \frac{Q_S^{\eta - 1/\eta}}{(\eta - 1)} \tag{2}$$

$$B_L = \left[\int_0^{Q_L} P(Q)dQ \right] - C(Q_L) \tag{3}$$

where B_S is the consumer surplus at quantity Q under S; B_L is the consumers surplus plus the producer profits at quantity Q_L; and $C(Q_L)$ is the cost function associated with production under L. No part of producer profits under S enters the expression for national benefit, since all of it is assumed to be remitted abroad.

Car components m, are assumed to be produced abroad by the MNE at a fixed per-unit cost k. Imported components m and domestic labor l are combined in fixed proportions to produce cars at home, so that

$$Q = \min(m, l) \tag{4}$$

The domestic market equilibrium for Q, characterized by marginal cost equal to marginal revenue, from equation (1), yields.

$$Q_i = \left[\frac{\eta M_i}{(\eta - 1)} \right]^{-\eta}, \quad i = S, L \tag{5}$$

where M_i is marginal cost for regime i.

Under regime S, the subsidiary of the MNE maximizes

$$P(Q_S)Q_S - \omega l - km$$

subject to equation (4), paying domestic labor at the local wage rate ω. The cost function is this case is:

$$C_S(Q_S; k, \omega) = (\omega + k)Q_S \tag{6}$$

Computing marginal cost, M_S, from equation (6) and output Q_S from equation (5), equation (2) are be rewritten as

$$B_S = (\eta - 1)^{-1}\left(\frac{(\eta - 1)}{\eta(\omega + k)}\right)^{\eta - 1} \tag{7}$$

As for the alternative regime L, q_1 is assumed to be the price charged per unit of car components by the MNE. The cost function of the licensing domestic firm is:

$$C_L(Q_L; q_1, \omega) = (\omega + q_1)Q_L \tag{8}$$

Computing marginal cost M_L and putting it into equation (5), one gets $Q_L(q_1)$. The demand for car components, $M(q_1)$, can be computed by using Shephard's lemma, so that

$$m(q_1) = \frac{\partial C_L}{\partial_{q_1}} = Q_L(q_1) \tag{9}$$

The MNE licensor will utilize its monopoly power (derived from the tied purchase of components by the licensee) to fix q_1 at a level which maximizes the former's profit from the sale of components, that is $(q_1 - k)m(q_1)$. From the first order condition we get:

$$q_1 = \frac{(\omega + \eta k)}{(\eta - 1)} \tag{10}$$

Rewriting equation (3), using equations (5), (8) and (10), we get:

$$B_L = \left[\frac{(2\eta - 1)}{(\eta - 1)^2}\right]\left[\frac{(\eta - 1)}{\eta}\right]^{2\eta - 1} (\omega + k)^{1 - \eta} \tag{11}$$

Having derived the expressions for total national benefit under S and L in equations (7) and (11), respectively, in terms of the parameters η, ω, and k, the two regimes are then compared:

$$\frac{B_L}{B_S} = \left(2 - \frac{1}{\eta}\right)\left(1 - \frac{1}{\eta}\right)^{\eta - 1} = f(\eta) \tag{12}$$

In his paper, Bardhan proves that $f(\eta)$ is less than unity for all values of $\eta > 1$; implying that under the conditions stated DFI would contribute more to the national welfare of the host country than a domestic firm licensing the technology (with tied input purchases) from the MNE. The primary reason behind this result is that the distortion caused by monopoly pricing of intermediate goods for downstream producers is avoided by vertical integration by the MNE. So the subsidiary will market cars at a lower price (which generates more consumer surplus) than the licensing domestic firm.

III. The Countertrade Model

In describing the countertrade model, it is important to consider what we are assuming about the external world and the general environment of international trade. If free trade as advocated by GATT were practiced and there were no transaction costs, all countries involved would benefit and unconventional methods of trade like countertrade would not be necessary. However, today's international trade environment is plagued with high and rising transaction costs and barriers to trade. It is in this environment that countertrade arises as an additional alternative and, therefore, it is in this general context that we assess its net benefit or costs.

Countertrade is introduced into the model as LC which stands for licensing with payment in resultant products or more simply licensing with countertrade. It is one form of industrial compensation.

Other than being the fastest growing form of countertrade, industrial compensation is interesting in still another way. Unlike commercial compensation, where the counterpurchased goods are unrelated to the original sale and often hard to dispose of by the DCs, the goods counterpurchased by the DCs under industrial compensation are the products of their own plants or technologies but produced at lower labour costs in LDCs or EECs. This means that it is actually in the interest of the DCs to increase and not decrease the amounts of final products they buy back because they will either use it in their own lines of production, which would mean a cheaper input than if it were produced at home, or sell it in the international market for a profit.

The procedure followed in analyzing countertrade is to repeat the same calculations as in the basic model for alternative LC in the modified model, and then to compare the benefits to the LDC associated with the three alternatives. The market structure, choice of production and demand functions and finally the measure of welfare are assumed to be the same for LC as for the other regimes.

The introduction of the new regime LC into the basic model adds the following:

(a) The industrial compensation requirement that the payment for components is in terms of final output:

$$q_2 m(q_2) = P_2 CT \tag{13}$$

where $q_2 m(q_2)$ is the total value of components imported by the developing country, q_2 being the new price of components to be decided upon by the licensor (MNE) in the same manner as in a regular licensing agreement. CT is the amount of final output, here cars, that the MNE has to purchase from the LDC at a price P_2 per unit so that the equality in equation (13) holds.

In this version of the model P_2 is chosen to be equal to P, the domestic price for cars, which implies that equation (13) can be rewritten as:

$$q_2 m(q_2) = P(Q_{LC}) CT \tag{14}$$

where Q_{LC} is the total amount of production under *LC*. We note that equations (13) and (14) imply that the payment for components by the LDC is made fully in terms of the final output as is typical in industrial compensation.

(b) The expression for the total national welfare of the LDC under countertrade is still consumers' surplus plus producer's profit. However, since the quantity sold in the domestic market under countertrade is less than the total amount of production Q_{LC}, both consumer and producer surpluses have to account for this change. The total national benefit under *LC*, B_{LC}, is given by the expression:

$$B_{LC} = \left[\int_{0}^{Q_{LC} - CT} P(Q)\, dQ \right] - \omega(Q_{LC}) \tag{15}$$

(c) Given the above description of the nature of industrial compensation, the MNE now has another motive besides maximizing its profits on the sale of components to the LDC, namely, to maximize its profits from selling *CT* in the international market. Mathematically, the licensor's decision-making problem becomes:

$$\max\ ((q_2 - k)m(q_2) + (P_1 - P_2)CT) \tag{16}$$

where P_1 is the price at which the MNE sells *CT* in the international market and $(P_1 - P_2)$ represents the profit gained by the MNE on each unit of *CT*.

P_1 is assumed to be equal to γP where $\gamma > 1$, i.e., P_1 is defined to be a price higher than the domestic market at which the MNE buys *CT* from the LDC (result # 4 discusses the other values that γ can take). The expression in equation (16) can then be written as:

$$\max\ ((q_2 - k)m\,(q_2) + (\gamma P - P)CT) \tag{17}$$

Substituting for *CT* from equation (14) and solving for the first order condition of the maximization problem in equation (17), we get:

$$q_2 = \frac{(\gamma\omega + \eta k)}{\gamma(\eta - 1)} \tag{18}$$

where q_2 is the unique feasible solution of the maximization. Using equation (18) we now solve for Q_{LC} and B_{LC}:

$$Q_{LC} = \left[\frac{\eta^2(\omega\gamma + k)}{\gamma(\eta - 1)^2} \right]^{-\eta} \tag{19}$$

$$B_{LC} = \frac{\eta}{\eta - 1}(Q_{LC})^{(\eta - 1)/\eta}(1 - q_2 Q_{LC}^{1/\eta})^{(\eta - 1)/\eta} - \omega Q_{LC} \tag{20}$$

If we move on to evaluating the performance of all three regimes *L*, *S* and *LC* by comparing the expressions in equations (7), (10), (11), (18) and (20), we reach the following results:

Result 1

The price of components under *LC*, q_2, is significantly less than q_1, the price of components under *L* in the basic model. Figure 1 shows the significant difference between q_1 and q_2 for all values of η. The introduction of countertrade helps reduce the distortion caused by monopoly pricing of intermediate goods for downstream producers.

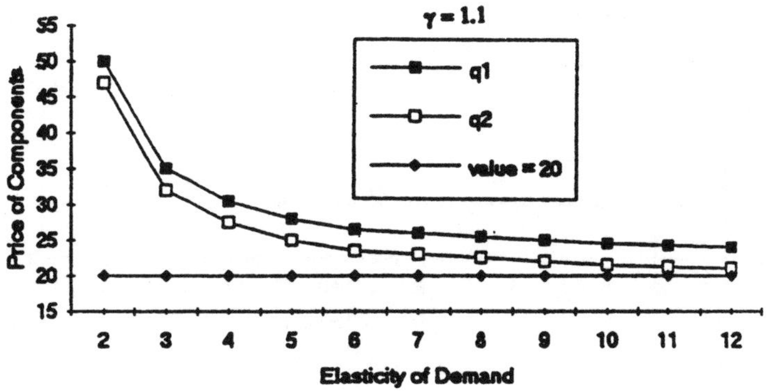

Fig. 1 Relationship between the elasticity of demand and q_1, q_2

The lower price of components under countertrade reflects greater efficiency. It also reflects a change in the attitude of the MNE towards the LDC as it is no longer in the best interest of the MNE to charge the highest price possible for the components. The explicit linking of the import of components to the export of the final output, by making the payment for the components in terms of cars, creates a mutually beneficial relationship between the two parties that discourages exploitation on the part of the MNE even if it were possible.

Result 2

B_{LC} or the national benefit under *LC* is higher than B_L the national benefit under *L*, i.e., *LC* contributes more to the national benefit of the LDC than *L*. This conclusion was reached by calculating the ratio of B_{LC} to B_L from equations (20) and (11) and proving that it is greater than 1. Since it is analytically cumbersome to perform the latter task, computer simulations were used. The ratio B_{LC}/B_L was computed over different ranges of the various parameters: $\gamma = (1.05, 1.1, 1.15)$ and $\eta = (2, 3, \ldots, 16)$ with $\omega = 10$ and $k = 20$.

As shown in Figure 2, B_{LC}/B_L increases as η increases, i.e., the more competitive is the domestic market, the more superior is the countertrade alternative to a regular licensing agreement. From Table 1 we also note that B_{LC}/B_L increases as γ increases, i.e., the more the profit achieved by the MNE per unit of counterpurchased goods, the better the countertrade alternative for the LDC.

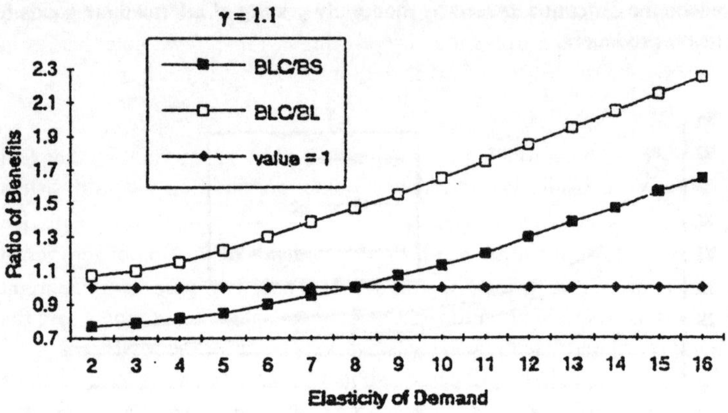

Fig. 2 Relationship between the elasticity of demand and B_{LC}/B_L, B_{LC}/B_S

TABLE 1
RELATIONSHIP BETWEEN B_{LC}/B_L, B_{LC}/B_S, and $\gamma(\eta = 8)$

γ	B_{LC}/B_L	B_{LC}/B_S
1.05	1.11	0.81
1.10	1.37	1.01
1.15	1.68	1.24

Under *LC* there is a gain in both consumer and producer surpluses. If *CT* is larger than the difference between Q_L and Q_{LC}, there will be a loss in consumer surplus that is overcompensated by the gain in producer's profit. The main reason behind the superiority of *LC* is a lower marginal cost (M_{LC}) which implies a larger output and a lower domestic price for the consumers. Both of these result in a larger national welfare despite the fact that less than the total amount produced is consumed locally. As γ increases, q_2 decreases which means an even lower marginal cost. As a result, output is even higher, implying that welfare is higher under *LC*. As η increases, there is a shift to the new demand curve where q_1, q_2, Q_{LC}, Q_L, P_L, and P_{LC} are at lower levels than before.[1] As a result, both B_{LC} and B_L decrease. B_{LC} remains, however, larger than B_L for each level of η and as η increases, B_L decreases faster than B_{LC}; so the ratio B_{LC}/B_L increases and is larger than 1.

Result 3

Following the same procedure explained above, it was found that *LC* is superior to DFI for most values of $\eta(B_{LC}/B_S > 1$ for all $\eta > 8)$. B_{LC}/B_S also

[1]Significant values were found only for values of η between 2 and 11.

increases as η and γ increase (Figure 2 and Table 1 above). The main reason for the superiority of countertrade is a large producer's profit which overcompensates for the loss in consumer surplus due to not using *S*. Finally, we note that, as in Result 2 above, the superiority of *LC* is reinforced by the increase in γ.

Result 4

So far, we have been looking at the situation when $\gamma > 1$ which implies that $P_1 > P_2$. What we consider here are the two other possibilities, $0 < \gamma < 1$. When $0 < \gamma \leq 1$, $P_1 < P_2$ which implies that the MNE makes losses on the countertraded goods. When $\gamma = 1$, on the other hand, $P_1 = P_2$ which is a situation of zero profit (but at the same time zero loss) for the MNE. These two cases are important because they shed some light on the case of commercial compensation where the disposal of the countertraded goods is always a problem for the MNE.

As shown in Figure 3, the price of components under *LC*, q_2, is larger than its counterpart under *L*, q_1, for $0 < \gamma < 1$. The primary reason behind this result is the loss the MNE makes on the countertraded goods because $P_1 < P_2$. To compensate for its loss, the MNE charges the LDC a higher price for the intermediary components. When $\gamma = 1$, on the other hand, $q_2 = q_1$ which means that the countertrade option gives the same results as regular licensing. Since the MNE makes no profit on the countertraded goods, its only concern is the maximization of its profit on the intermediary components which is the same situation as in a regular licensing agreement.

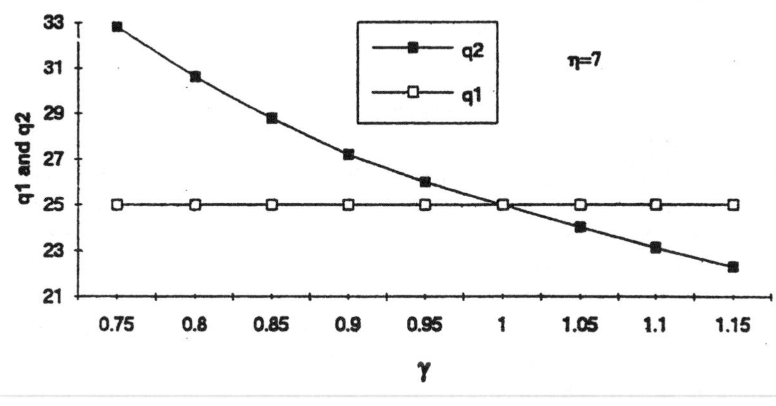

Fig. 3 Relationship between q_1, q_2, and gamma

The relationship between B_{LC}, B_L and B_S also changes as γ changes its values. As shown in Figure 4, $B_{LC}/B_L < 1$ for $0 < \gamma < 1$ which means that countertrade contributes less to the welfare of the LDC than regular licensing does. This result follows directly from the fact that for $0 < \gamma < 1$, the price of components under

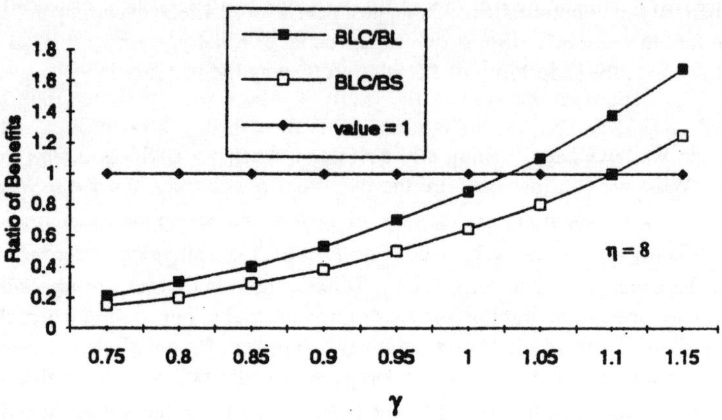

Fig. 4 Relationship between the ratio of benefits and gamma

LC is higher than under *L*. The higher price of components leads to higher costs, lower ouput and lower welfare for the LDC. When the price of components is equal under countertrade and licensing, countertrade still contributes less to the national benefit of the LDC than regular licensing because less than the total output is being consumed at home. As for the comparison between DFI and countertrade, the former alternative was found to be superior to the latter in its contribution to the national benefit of the LDC for $0 < \gamma < 1$. The high costs associated with countertrade make it a less efficient alternative for the LDC.

IV. The Introduction of MNEs into the Countertrade Model

In the previous sections the focus was on how the LDC is affected by countertrade. Shifting the attention to the MNE, however, is extremely important because it allows us to investigate the sweeping but unsubstantiated claim in the literature that Western companies must be coerced into the use of countertrade, resulting in financial losses.

Assuming that the MNE has the option of choosing between countertrade, regular licensing and DFI, we compare profits gained by the MNE in each of these three cases. The alternative that generates larger profits for the MNE would clearly be the more attractive option.

The profits of the MNE under regular licensing, countertrade and DFI are represented by L_1, L_2 and L_3 respectively.

$$L_1 = (q_1 - k)m(q_1) \tag{21}$$

$$L_2 = (q_2 - k)m(q_2) + (P_1 - P_2)CT \tag{22}$$

$$L_3 = PQ_S - C_S(Q_S; k, \omega) \tag{23}$$

L_3 is expressed as the producer's profit on the final output produced Q_s. As explained in Section 2 above, this profit does not go to the LDC; instead it is remitted abroad to the interest of the MNE. L_2 consists of two parts. The first part represents the profit of the MNE on the sale of intermediary components to the LDC. The second part represents the profit it makes when selling *CT* in the international market. L_1, on the other hand, is the expression for profits on the intermediary components. L_2 and L_1 are the same basic expressions that we maximized above to get values for q_2 and q_1. Finally, we note that comparisons between L_1, L_2 and L_3 are conducted by calculating the ratios of any two of these three and comparing them to 1, which is the same procedure followed in comparing regimes from the LDC's point of view.

We first start by comparing countertrade to regular licensing. We compute L_2/L_1, the ratio of profits achieved by the licensor (MNE) under *LC* to its counterpart under *L*, and compare what we get to 1 for various values of η and γ. We start with $\gamma > 1$, or the case of industrial compensation, which is our main interest. From computer simulations in Figure 5 we note that given η and γ, L_2/L_1 is considerably larger than 1. This means that, given any particular level of elasticity of demand in the domestic market, the profits achieved by the MNE under countertrade are always much larger than those achieved by the same licensor under a regular licensing agreement. This is in spite of the fact that as we proved in the previous chapter that the price of intermediary components under *LC* is lower than that under *L* which means the MNE makes less profit per unit of intermediary components under countertrade than under a regular licensing agreement. We also note that as η increases, L_2 and L_1 tend to change at the same rate which leads to a constant ratio.

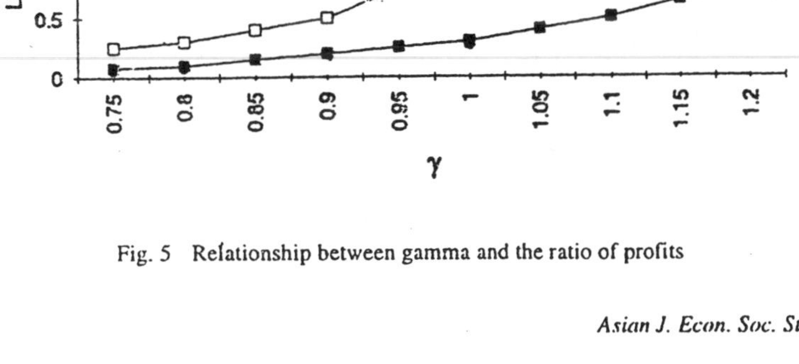

Fig. 5 Relationship between gamma and the ratio of profits

The reason behind this result is that, when $\gamma > 1$, not only does the MNE make profits on the countertraded goods but it also makes higher profits on the components because it charges a lower price which increases demand as explained above.

As η increases, final output decreases which leads to lower levels of profits for both *LC* and *L*. The relationship between *LC* and *L* remains the same, however, as profits under *LC* are larger than those under *L* for each level of η.

If we follow the same procedure described above to compare profits gained by the MNE under the *LC* option (L_2) to their counterpart under $S(L_3)$, as shown in Figure 5 we find that $L_2/L_3 < 1$ for all values of η. DFI generates larger profits for the MNE than countertrade does and is therefore a more attractive option. The main reason behind this result is that Q_S, the final output under the *S* option, is larger than its counterpart under *LC*, Q_{LC}. The large Q_S implies a producer's profit (L_3) that is larger than (L_2) in spite of the low price of components and the profit made on the sale of *CT* in the international market under *LC*. *S* is also superior to regular licensing (*L*). Finally, note that as η increases, L_1, L_2 and L_3 tend to decrease at the same rate which leaves L_2/L_1, L_2/L_3 and L_1/L_3 constant.

When $0 < \gamma \leq 1$, countertrade is the least desirable option for the MNE. As shown in Figure 5 both L_2/L_1 and L_2/L_3 are less than 1. If classified in order of preference for the MNE, DFI would rate first followed by licensing and lastly countertrade. To compensate for its loss on the countertraded goods, the MNE raises the price of components it charges the LDC. A high price of components leads to low demand and ultimately low profits for the MNE.

V. Equilibrium and the Relevance of Transactions Cost Theory

The LDC and the MNE are trying to choose among the three available alternatives *S*, *LC* and *L*. Assuming that both the LDC and the MNE are aware of the forms of agreement that maximize their welfare, an equilibrium is reached when they agree on a specific option. This can happen in two ways: (a) the same regime maximizes the welfare of both the LDC and the MNE and in that case the equilibrium is unique; and (b) when one regime maximizes the welfare of the LDC while a different one maximizes that of the MNE. In the latter case the equilibrium is not unique. Only one equilibrium can prevail, however, and it is in the choice among equilibria that transaction costs play a role.

From the above analysis we note that in the cases of $0 < \gamma < 1$ and $\gamma > 1$ with $\eta < 8$, the interests of the LDC and MNE are in harmony. The *S* regime maximizes the welfare of both parties and is, as a result, the unique equilibrium. The interests of the LDC and MNE are in conflict, however, when $\gamma > 1$ and $\eta > 8$. In that case, there are two equilibria *S* and *LC*, the former being more favourable for the MNE and the latter being more favourable for the LDC. Since there is nothing in the model that favours one equilibrium over the other, factors outside the model would have to determine which one it is going to be.

The choice between equilibria can be analyzed from two different perspectives: the bargaining perspective and the transactions cost perspective. The bargaining framework is the most familiar one for analyzing the relationship between the MNE and the host LDC (Teece, 1986). On one side, the MNE is depicted as having the technology, experience, skills and access to finance and markets that the LDC needs. On the other hand, the LDC is depicted as having the resources, labour force and other factors which can often be configured to provide an attractive investment for the MNE. The assets that each party possesses determine its bargaining power at the negotiating table. The party that is more powerful will use its power to coerce the other party into accepting a form of agreement that is not the most efficient from the latter's point of view. Negotiating power also depends on the special nature of the projects and how badly it is needed by both parties.

If we look at the choice problem in a transactions cost analytical framework, we note that in choosing between *S* and *LC* the LDC and MNE are basically choosing between two forms of contracts. The form of contracts that minimizes the transactions costs is the superior one. While DFI, or *S* in our model, has been known for being a vehicle for the transfer of technology to the LDCs, empirical evidence has proved that there is plenty of room for opportunistic behaviour on the part of both the MNE and the LDC under this form of investment. Several studies (for example Dunning, 1979; Hawkins and Prasad, 1981) have attempted to measure the extent of the technology transfer and benefit to the LDCs through DFI. Most of them came to the conclusion that, by and large, the subsidiaries do not fulfill their promises and tend to exploit local markets rather than benefit them. LDCs often complain the MNEs do not meet their promises of export targets because they find the local market more profitable. At the same time, MNEs complain of opportunistic behaviour on the part of the LDCs. Once the deals are signed and assets, typically hard to withdraw, are deployed by the MNE on the host country soil, the LDC is able to bring pressures to bear for "renegotiations", "adjustments", "surtaxes", "recomputations" and the like—all manifestations of *ex post* transaction costs. From the point of view of the MNE, the LDC begins to cheat on its agreements (Moran, 1974; Mikesell, 1971; Teece, 1986).

If we consider the case of *LC* or countertrade, we find that linking the import of technology by the LDC to the export of products produced by that technology to the MNE tends to reduce the opportunistic behavior by the MNE that is described above. The relationship between the two parties does not end at the sale of technology but extends far beyond which has the effect of guaranteeing that any exploitation on the part of the MNE will be reflected in the quality and pricing of the products it gets back. This situation tends to alter the incentives of the MNE more towards fulfilling its promises to the LDC. At the same time, however, because so much is still unknown about countertrade and there are no universal rules governing it, most studies agree that negotiations are often costly and complicated (e.g., Business International Research Report, 1984).

Which one of the two regimes is superior? The answer really depends on the situation. For instance, an LDC that has favourable previous experience with DFI and dreads the involvement into an unconventional method of trade as countertrade would tend to favour *S* even though it doesn't maximize its welfare. Also, an LDC that is not aware that countertrade maximizes its welfare because of all the conflicting arguments in the business media, the uncertainty of the trade environment and the lack of information on countertrade would also tend to favour DFI. Similarly, a MNE that is well equipped to handle countertrade agreements and that anticipates a long term relationship with this particular LDC would favour countertrade to DFI. Also, a MNE with previous successful experience with countertrade or unsuccessful experience with DFI would prefer *LC* to *S*. In fact, negotiating costs may be so high and so complicated that both sides may choose to avoid them by settling on *L* or regular licensing which is an inferior option for both of them.

It is very unfortunate that we don't have empirical evidence from the car industry to support or refute the conclusions of this model.

VI. Conclusions of the Countertrade Model

The results of our model indicate that countertrade in its industrial compensation form is generally superior to both regular licensing and DFI as far as the welfare of an LDC is concerned, in spite of the fact that less than the total output produced is consumed at home. The main reason behind this result is that the linking of transactions that is the essence of countertrade creates an extended mutually beneficial relationship between the LDC and the MNE which tends to reduce the exploitative power that the MNE is likely to exercise under the other regimes. This result is particularly interesting because it qualifies the conclusions reached in Bardhan's 1982 paper. The mere addition of countertrade (payment for components in terms of final output) to a regular licensing agreement has the effect of boosting the modified licensing to a position superior to alternative *S*.

As far as the MNE is concerned, we conclude that the notion that Western companies always make losses when using countertrade needs to be qualified in more than one way. While DFI seems to achieve more profit for the MNE when compared to countertrade, the latter is superior, in all cases, to a regular licensing agreement despite the fact that the profit the MNE makes per unit of intermediate components is smaller under countertrade than its counterpart in the case of licensing.

Which of the three regimes will actually be agreed upon by the two parties involved is very difficult to determine as it depends on several factors outside the model. Bargaining power and transactions costs would be very relevant. Also important is the accessibility of the two parties involved to the regular channels of trade as this will determine whether or not they will be interested in countertrade in the first place.

In the case of commercial compensation, the other major category of countertrade that was touched upon here, countertrade was found to be inferior to the other two alternatives for both the LDC and the MNE mostly due to the difficulty of disposing of the countertraded goods that is typical under this type of countertrade which leads to the conclusion that commercial compensation should be used cautiously by both sides. It also pinpoints the possible disruption that can arise if commercial compensation is used haphazardly.

Finally, it is important to recognize some limitations of the countertrade model developed in this paper. First, the measure of LDC welfare as consumer surplus plus producer's profit may not be the best measure of welfare. Second, although general equilibrium was considered briefly in the last section, the analysis is only partial equilibrium in character. Third, neither income distribution effects nor taxation and public finance were taken into account in this model. While it is very unfortunate that the results reached here cannot be tested empirically due to lack of data, when such data becomes available, testing should be straightforward.

REFERENCES

Bardhan, P.: Imports, Domestic production and transnational vertical integration: A theoretical note, *Journal of Political Economy*, 90(5) (1982), 1020–1034.

Dunning, J.: Technology exporters and technology transfer controls, TTCS Conference, Seattle (mimeo).

Galbraith, C. and N. Kay: Towards a theory of multinational enterprise, *Journal of Economic Behavior and Organization*, 7 (1986), 3–19.

Hawkins, R. and. A. Prasad (eds.): *Research in International Business and Finance: Technology Transfer and Economic Development*, JAI Press Inc., London, 1981.

Hodara, I.: Countertrade-experiences of some Latin American countries, Geneva UNCTAD, 1984.

Leibenstein, H.: Allocative efficiency versus X-efficiency, *American Economic Review*, 56 (June 1966), 392–415.

Mikesell, R. (ed.): *Foreign Investment in the Petroleum and Mineral Industries: Case Studies in Investor–Host Country Relations*, Johns Hopkins University, Baltimore, 1971.

Moran, T.: *Multinational Corporations and the Politics of Dependence: Copper in Chile*, Princeton University Press, Princeton, N.J., 1974.

OECD: *Countertrade: New Developing Countries Practices*, 1985.

Tecce, D.: Transactions cost economics and the multinational enterprise: An assesment, *Journal of Economic Behavior and Organization*, 7 (1986), 21–45.

US Department of Commerce: *East-West Countertrade Practices*, US Government Printing Office, Washington, 1978.

Verzariu, P.: *Countertrade, Barter and Offset*, McGraw-Hill, New York, 1985.

Welt, L.: *Countertrade Business Practices for Today's World Market*, American Management Association's Publications Division, New York, 1982.

————: *Trade Without Money; Barter and Countertrade*, H.B. Jovanvich Publishers, New York, 1984.

————: Countertrade, *Special Euromoney Report*, 1985.

Williamson, O.: *Markets and Hierarchies: Analysis and Antitrust Implications*, Free Press, New York, 1975.

ELSEVIER Journal of International Economics 40 (1996) 67–84

Journal of INTERNATIONAL ECONOMICS

Mandated countertrade as a strategic commitment

Tore Ellingsen[a,*], Lars A. Stole[b]

[a]*Stockholm School of Economics, Box 6501, S-113 83, Stockholm, Sweden*
[b]*University of Chicago, Graduate School of Business, USA*

Received 1 June 1993, revised 1 March 1995

Abstract

Mandated countertrade is a policy to restrict unilateral imports. A country's government thereby in effect commits domestic firms not to purchase from a foreign trading partner unless there are reciprocal sales. We argue that the policy may be a rational response to fundamental contracting failures, our key assumption being that sellers are incompletely informed about buyers' valuations.

In line with observed practices, the analysis suggests that an optimal mandated countertrade policy will target high mark-up imports and low mark-up exports. Implications for global welfare are ambiguous and depend upon the extent of a double coincidence of wants.

Key words: Mandated countertrade; Trade policy; Asymmetric information

JEL classification: F13; F12

1. Introduction

It is a remarkable fact that barter and other forms of countertrade[1] continue to play a significant role in the world economy.[2] While it is hard to

* Corresponding author. Tel.: 468 736 9260; fax: 468 34 78 18; e-mail: gte@hhs.se.

[1] We do not distinguish between the various forms of countertrade. Offsets, barter, swaps, and buy-backs are some of the many variants of the same fundamental phenomenon. For the purposes of this paper, we will use the terms barter, reciprocal dealing, and countertrade interchangeably.

[2] It is interesting that barter has for so long been seen as an inferior mode of trade. As Jevons, 1875 pointed out, an important function of money is precisely that it facilitates trade in the absence of a "double coincidence of wants." Accordingly, a standard result in modern theories of money is that barter disappears completely in equilibrium.

SSDI 0022-1996(95)01401-2

obtain a precise estimate, we can be fairly sure that at least 10% of world trade involves a two-way flow of goods rather than a simple purchase of goods for money. Some sources such as OECD (1981, OECD, 1985) and UNCTAD (1984) define the practice quite narrowly, but the latter nevertheless estimates that it constitutes 15% of world trade. In a detailed country study of Switzerland, Bürgin (1986) concludes that 13% of its foreign trade takes this form, while the chairman of the American Countertrade Association claimed in a recent interview that countertrade accounts for around 20% of US exports (Fortune, 1992). Based on a variety of sources, including a complete database of publicized deals and a number of interviews, Hveem et al. (1989) put the number at 15–25% of world trade.[3]

Mandated countertrade occurs when unilateral purchases are restricted by a national government. Governments mandate countertrade for their domestic industries by limiting imports which are not accompanied by matching exports. Carter and Gagne (1988) reported that in 1984 countertrade was mandated in some form by 88 countries, and the current number probably runs into three figures. The most powerful policy instrument at a government's disposal is allocation of foreign exchange. The governments of Argentina and Zimbabwe have both required export sales as a condition for allocating currency for imports. Another effective policy is to grant import licenses for certain classes of products only if the purchases are reciprocated; variants of this policy have been used by e.g. Algeria, Argentina, Bolivia, Brazil, Columbia, Costa Rica, India, Indonesia, Korea, Libya, Mexico, Tanzania and Libya.[4] Finally, the policy of requiring counterpurchase for certain public sector imports has been used by Australia, Austria, Israel and Sweden (especially for weapons), among many others. Out of the total volume of countertrade, an informed estimate is that around half is mandated. Walsh (1985) states that most is mandated, but fewer than half of the deals registered by Hveem et al. (1989) involve government mandating.

The data clearly shows that countertrade is not a freak phenomenon. It is sizable and regular enough to demand an explanation. Nonetheless, formal theoretical models of countertrade are still in their infancy. In this paper we shall argue that countertrade could be due to fundamental contracting failures, a position which is shared by an increasing number of observers

[3] Bibliographies of works on countertrade are compiled by Debroy, 1987 and by Zurawicki and Suichmezian, 1991. Some general overviews are Alexandrides and Bowers, 1987 and Hammond, 1990. Information on recent deals can be found in the weekly *Countertrade Outlook* and in the monthly *Trade Finance*.

[4] Sources for this information are Walsh, 1985 and Carey and McLean, 1986. Liesch, 1991 is a recent book on mandated countertrade.

(see e.g. Hennart and Anderson, 1993; Mirus and Yeung, 1993). Specifically, we stress the role of incomplete information at the time of contracting.[5]

As is now well understood, informational asymmetry is one of the main obstacles to efficient trade. The fact that sellers do not usually know exactly the buyers' willingness to pay is taken to explain a number of trading practices. Examples from the literature on optimal selling mechanisms include second-degree price discrimination, bundling, and the form of auction procedures. It seems natural, therefore, to ask whether informational asymmetry can contribute to explain barter as well.

To address the question, we design a very simple model of two countries. In each country there is a domestic producer of some product which is not made in the other country. Due to sellers' market power and their incomplete information, prices are above marginal costs. Hence, there are unrealized gains from trade in both markets. Supposing that the two producers are buyers in each other's market, could barter be a way of exploiting their dual roles to increase trade?

Our first result demonstrates that voluntary (non-mandated) countertrade cannot increase the efficiency of trade. The reason is that if firm i has a low valuation of firm j's product, it rejects barter. Therefore, willingness to barter becomes a signal of a high valuation; in fact only a buyer that would have been willing to purchase in the first place accepts a countertrade agreement! This result serves as a useful benchmark for the examination of government trade policies. The paper's main contribution is to show that mandated countertrade may raise domestic welfare. The intuition goes roughly as follows. Suppose each government cares about the expected surplus of the domestic firm. If country i mandates countertrade, the foreign firm (firm j) knows it cannot make a unilateral sale to firm i. Firm j is therefore willing to accept barter even if its valuation of firm i's product is fairly low (but above its own marginal costs). Hence, even though the domestic firm is prevented from buying, it gets some compensation: essentially, it can choose freely between selling and bartering, depending on is own valuation. From the vantage point of the government, mandating

[5] The role of pre-contractual asymmetric information is also emphasized by Caves and Marin, 1992, who argue that barter could be a form of second-degree price discrimination. In contrast, Chan and Hoy, 1991 and Choi and Maldoom, 1992 emphasize *post-contractual* asymmetric information and the associated difficulty of ensuring correct levels of performance (i.e. moral hazard). Williamson, 1983, Williamson, 1984, Hennart, 1989, and Marin and Schnitzer, 1995, argue that countertrade could be caused by imperfect contract enforcement, the basic idea being that the tying of trades introduces new ways of penalizing non-performance. Finally, Amann and Marin, 1994 claim that countertrade can substitute for missing forwards markets. Neither of these papers studies mandated countertrade.

countertrade is rational whenever the gains from barter outweigh the loss of unilateral imports.

We develop a number of comparative static results. In particular we find that mandated countertrade occurs in equilibrium whenever there is a sufficiently high probability that both firms prefer barter to not trading; in other words, there is a high likelihood of a double coincidence of wants. This result fits the evidence that mandated countertrade is often associated with economies of scale and 'surplus commodities' (see e.g. Outters–Jaeger, 1979; Banks, 1985). Also, asymmetries matter. A low domestic and a high foreign mark-up invite intervention, a result which is consistent with the observations that (i) the export products eligible for countertrade deals are frequently 'non-traditional exports', which do not contribute much to current earnings,[6] and (ii) the import restrictions are typically put on high mark-up items such as weapons, oil, and luxuries (see Walsh, 1985; Carey and McLean, 1986).

Many writers, notably Caves (1974), have remarked on the similarity between international countertrade and reciprocal dealing between domestic firms. Our theory contrasts with much of the literature in that it applies rather specifically to international barter: the mandating of countertrade relies on a credible (non-renegotiable) commitment, and credibility is here ensured by an authority outside the firms (the government).[7] Also, it is rational for the authority to interfere partly because it neglects the welfare of one party (the foreign firm), which seems less likely in a domestic setting.

The paper is outlined as follows. Section 2 introduces the analytical framework. Section 3 presents some preliminary results, in particular that (under our assumptions) non-mandated countertrade is not a viable way of creating trade. Equilibrium trade policies are derived in Section 4. Section 5 concludes.

2. The framework

There are two markets. Each market is served by a single seller.[8] The

[6] The common objection to this view, that low saleability implies an equally low barter value, is thus shown to be incorrect once we leave the world of perfect competition. Drawing a distinction between market value (the profit maximizing price) and profitability, we see that low profit exports can be turned into valuable items of barter, even when the barter transaction is carried out according to market prices.

[7] Of course, there are other mechanisms which may support a credible commitment, notably reputation. Stocking and Mueller, 1957 argues that reciprocal dealing for many years was part of the company policy of DuPont, the large American conglomerate. Possibly DuPont's headquarters were able to play the same role as governments do in our model. For further references to work on domestic reciprocity, consult Ellingsen, 1991.

[8] The assumption of a single seller is inessential to our main results.

sellers are located in separate countries, 1 and 2, and operate under the laws of their respective governments. The seller located in country i is referred to as firm i.

The seller in market 1 is also one of a number of ex ante identical buyers in market 2, and vice versa. (Alternatively, we can think of sellers and buyers as separate firms, but where the seller in market i is located in the same country as one of the buyers in market j.) Each buyer in a market wants exactly one unit of the relevant product. Importantly, each buyer's valuation is private information (it is known to the buyer but not to the seller).

A seller is assumed to have all the bargaining power and thus sets a monopoly price. As is well known, monopoly pricing under incomplete information normally entails an efficiency loss, as the seller will be committed to a price which is higher than the marginal cost and thus typically higher than the lowest possible buyer valuation. This inefficiency is an important ingredient in the present model.

We assume that any buyer can always purchase (anonymously if necessary) at the going market prices. Apart from trading through the market, firms 1 and 2 have an additional option. Since there is a bilateral externality between them, they may try to tie their deals in the two markets. Thus, as an alternative to market transaction the two firms are allowed to barter. For barter to be an interesting option, reselling cannot occur without cost. (With costless reselling, a firm can barter and resell at the monopoly price to another buyer.) For simplicity, we make the stronger assumption that reselling is impossible.[9]

The main focus of the paper is on government mandated countertrade: Each government decides as a matter of long-term policy whether or not to allow unilateral imports. If the government in country i mandates countertrade, it is forbidden for firm i to purchase on market j. Thus, in this case firm i can get hold of firm j's product only through barter.

The timing of events is the following. At $t=1$, cost conditions are observed by all parties and governments decide on their policies. At $t=2$, firms set their market prices. At $t=3$, buyers learn their valuations. Finally, at $t=4$, trade takes place in accordance with the possible countertrade mandates and the pre-existing prices.

What happens at stage 4 when the two firms meet? Clearly, the most efficient trade would come about if they could both agree to sell at marginal cost. However, under a free trade regime this does not seem reasonable. A

[9] Although this is exogenous, it will become clear that by extending the analysis slightly, it is possible to derive prohibitions on reselling as a property of bilateral trading contracts. Moreover, since many bilateral trading agreements severely restrict reselling (see Walsh, 1985; Carey and McLean, 1986), we feel justified in adopting the assumption here.

firm whose valuation of the other's product is low may then earn less from the transaction than if it treats the other as a standard customer at posted prices. For realism, we therefore take it as given that each firm must consent to any bilateral trade agreement. Only firms whose position is thereby improved, relative to trade at market prices, agree to countertrade.

A major modeling decision is what class of countertrade arrangements to consider. We believe we have chosen the simplest possible bargaining model that incorporates the participation constraint alluded to above. Here, either both parties agree to tied trading (barter) or – if one of them rejects it – revert to ordinary market interaction at posted prices (Table 1).

This specification may seem unduly restrictive, but (as we will argue below) allowing for richer trading mechanisms does not substantially affect our results.

We are now ready to introduce our notation and formal assumptions. To avoid unnecessary duplication of expressions, we often state conditions only for firm i. When nothing else is said, the condition then applies for $i = 1,2$, and subscript j reads $j \neq i$. Firm i's unit variable costs are constant, commonly known, and denoted c_i. Firm i's valuation of j's product is denoted v_i and is, as previously mentioned, information private to firm i. (We shall sometimes refer to v_i as firm i's *type*.) The distribution of valuations is common knowledge, and described by an integrable density function $f_i(v)$, with support $V_i = [a_i, b_i]$. Suppose firm i sets the price p. Firm j's demand for i's product is then the probability that v_j exceeds p, i.e.

$$D_j(p) = \int_p^{b_j} f_j(s)\, ds.$$

Firm i's expected profit from selling to firm j at a price of p is $\pi_i = D_j(p)(p - c_i)$, and it is assumed that there is a unique profit maximizing price

$$p_i(c_i) = \arg\max_p D_j(p)(p - c_i).$$

Since the buyers in each market are ex ante identical and the unit variable

Table 1
The market game

Firm 1	Firm 2	
	Accept	Reject
Accept	Barter	Market transaction
Reject	Market transaction	Market transaction

costs are constant, seller i optimally offers the price p_i to the market.[10] The maximum expected profit is denoted as $\pi_i^* = \pi_i(p_i(c_i),c_i)$.

As indicated in Table 1, in the market game firm i can take one of two possible actions. A pure strategy for firm i is thus a one-to-one mapping from the set of types, V_i, into the set of actions, {Accept, Reject}.

Governments decide trade policies. Government i's policy is denoted $T_i \in \{F_i, M_i\}$, where F_i means that country i pursues a free trade policy, and M_i indicates mandated countertrade. In the latter case, country i prohibits unilateral imports; all imports must be tied to exports of similar value. Mandating countertrade entails a direct cost $g_i \geqslant 0$, capturing added administrative costs as well as any punishments imposed by the international community. Apart from g_i, the government only cares about the total expected surplus of the domestic firm. (In addition to the expected profit, π_i, the government thus also considers the potential gain from buying, $v_i - p_j$, and from barter, $v_i - c_i$.) Government i's payoff function (expected utility) is denoted $G_i(T_i, T_j)$, and will be given a precise formulation in Section 4.1. Global welfare is defined as the sum of the two governments' payoffs.

The main objective of the paper is to derive non-cooperative policy equilibria. We focus on pure strategy subgame perfect equilibria in the analysis which follows. In other words, for any policy profile, the governments expect firms to play a (Bayesian) Nash equilibrium in the market game. As it turns out, it is straightforward to characterize the market game equilibria when at least one government intervenes. The analysis is more subtle under the free trade regime.

3. The free trade regime

Suppose that the market game depicted in Table 1 is played by firms which are unrestricted by government intervention, the policy profile (F_1, F_2). It is easy to see that a firm's decision has an impact on the outcome only in the case where the other firm accepts barter.[11] Hence, firm i agrees to barter only if the gain from trade is at least as large as the expected gain

[10] It is well known from the literature on optimal selling mechanisms that, under risk neutrality, an optimal strategy for a seller facing a privately informed buyer is to commit to a fixed price (e.g. Riley and Zeckhauser, 1983).

[11] Thus, both will choose as if the other had already accepted barter, and their beliefs as to whether the other will accept it do not come directly into play. The practical relevance of this observation is, as already indicated, that the simultaneous moves assumption is innocuous. (Excluding weakly dominated strategies, any pure-strategy equilibrium of this particular normal form game is also a sequential equilibrium of any extensive form of the game.) We might as well have assumed that a firm which wants to countertrade takes the initiative by moving first.

from market transaction *given that the other firm is willing to barter*. To express this condition formally, let $\Phi_j = \Pr[v_j \geqslant p_i | A_j]$ be the probability that firm j, having agreed to barter, values its purchase from firm i above market price. The necessary condition for firm i to accept barter can then be written as

$$v_i - c_i \geqslant (p_i - c_i)\Phi_j + \max\{0, v_i - p_j\}, \tag{1}$$

where the left-hand side is the gain from barter and the right-hand side is the expected cost of giving up the market transaction.

A direct consequence of this condition is that if firm i accepts barter when its valuation is $\tilde{v}_i$, then it is rational to accept barter for all $v_i \geqslant \tilde{v}_i$. In seeking the equilibria, we may thus confine attention to the subset of pure strategies which are summarized by such critical values; all types below the critical value rejecting and all types above accepting barter. Formally, let $\underline{v}_i$ be the lowest valuation such that firm i accepts barter. A Bayesian Nash equilibrium of the market game is then completely described as a pair $(\underline{v}_1^*, \underline{v}_2^*)$ such that $\underline{v}_1^*$ is a best reply to $\underline{v}_2^*$ and vice versa.

The probability that firm i will accept barter is clearly $D_i(\underline{v}_i)$. Note that we can write $\Phi_j(p_i, \underline{v}_j) = \Pr[v_j \geqslant p_i | v_j \geqslant \underline{v}_j]$. Since the probability cannot exceed one, we have

$$\Phi_j(p_i, \underline{v}_j) = \min\left\{1, \frac{D_j(p_i)}{D_j(\underline{v}_j)}\right\}.$$

Firm i's best reply mapping, $R(\cdot)$, assigns one or more critical values $\underline{v}_i$ for each $\underline{v}_j$. Using Eq. (1), we have

$$R_i(\underline{v}_j) - c_i = (p_i - c_i)\Phi_j(p_i, \underline{v}_j) + \max\{0, R_i(\underline{v}_j) - p_j\}, \tag{2}$$

or, equivalently,

$$R_i(\underline{v}_j) = \begin{cases} (p_i - c_i)\Phi_j(p_i, \underline{v}_j) + c_i & \text{if } (p_i - c_i)\Phi_j(p_i, \underline{v}_j) + c_i < p_j, \\ [p_j, b_j] & \text{if } (p_i - c_i)\Phi_j(p_i, \underline{v}_j) + c_i = p_j. \end{cases} \tag{3}$$

(To see the equivalence, note from Eq. (2) that a change in regime occurs at the point $\underline{v}_i = p_j$, and that for parameter configurations other than those considered in Eq. (3) firm i should always reject barter.) In the range where $\underline{v}_i \leqslant p_j$ and $\underline{v}_j \leqslant p_i$, we can insert for Φ_i to get

$$R_i(\underline{v}_j) = \frac{(p_i - c_i)D_j(p_i)}{D_j(\underline{v}_j)} + c_i. \tag{4}$$

We are now ready to prove our first result, which says that non-mandated countertrade does not create trade.

Proposition 1. (i) If market prices are identical, i.e. $p_1=p_2=p$, there is a continuum of equilibria, given by all pairs $\{\underline{v}_1,\underline{v}_2\}\in[p,\infty)\times[p,\infty)$. (ii) There are no other equilibria.

The proof is contained in the appendix. Proposition 1 says that the opportunity of barter does not increase trade. Both firms agree to barter only if they would have bought in the marketplace, and then only if market values (prices) are exactly identical. Hence if the firms must bear any administrative costs of arranging barter, we may rule it out altogether.

The intuition behind Proposition 1 is that because a firm with a low valuation has no incentive to barter, its willingness to barter indicates a high valuation. Since each firm influences the outcome only when the other accepts barter, they both act as if they face a high valuation buyer, and are consequently unwilling to barter. We emphasize that the reason why no trade is created is the attractiveness of trading in the market place.[12] To induce barter, trade policies need to make the market place less attractive.

4. Equilibrium trade policies

Having shown that barter does not affect payoffs under the free trade regime, we now study the costs and benefits of mandating countertrade. To simplify the analysis, assume from now on that market prices are identical, i.e. $p_j=p_i=p$.[13] There are four possible policy regimes, and to find the equilibrium regime we first need to define the governments' utilities precisely.

4.1. Governments' payoffs

Recall that the government does not know the valuations of either firm, and cares about the domestic firm's *expected* total benefit. Consider first the free trade regime (F_i,F_j). By Proposition 1, firm i's benefit under the free trade regime is unaffected by the barter option. Hence, the government's expected utility is

[12] A similar 'no trade creation' result appears to hold for any bargaining mechanism, as long as interim individual rationality is imposed and the initial prices are profit maximizing (and hence interim efficient for each party). This result is akin to those of the Maskin and Tirole (1992) analysis of common value mechanism design by an informed principal where interim efficiency implies renegotiation proofness.

[13] Our reason for doing this is to avoid the complications of monetary transfers. If prices are different, a straight barter may be an unconvincing alternative; instead there should be an additional cash payment.

$$G_i(F_i,F_j) = \int_p^{b_i} (v - p)f_i(v)\,dv + \pi_i^*, \tag{5}$$

i.e. the sum of expected 'consumer surplus' and expected profits.

Consider next the regime (M_i,F_j), in which there is one-sided intervention by government i. Firm j is then unable to sell to firm i and hence firm j barters whenever $v_j>c_j$, i.e.

$$\underline{v}_j^*(M_i,F_j) = c_j. \tag{6}$$

Firm i cannot buy, so its best response to $\underline{v}_j = c_j$ is unique and given by Eq. (4),

$$\underline{v}_i^*(M_i,F_j) = \frac{\pi_i^*}{D_j(c_j)} + c_i. \tag{7}$$

Importantly, mandating makes the market option less attractive for the foreign as well as the domestic firm, and hence there is scope for barter. (As $D_j(c_j)<D_j(p)$, it is easily seen that both $\underline{v}_i^*$ and $\underline{v}_j^*$ are smaller than p.) Government i's expected utility now contains three terms; the expected benefit from barter, the expected profit from selling, and the direct costs of mandating:

$$\begin{aligned} G_i(M_i,F_j) &= D_j(c_j) \int_{\underline{v}_i^*(M_i,F_j)}^{b_i} (v - c_i)f_i(v)dv + [1 - D_i(\underline{v}_i^*(M_i,F_j))]\pi_i^* - g_i \\ &= D_j(c_j) \int_{\underline{v}_i^*(M_i,F_j)}^{b_i} [v - \underline{v}_i^*(M_i,F_j)]f_i(v)dv + \pi_i^* - g_i. \end{aligned} \tag{8}$$

The second expression decomposes firm i's expected benefit into the value of the barter option and the expected gain from market interaction.[14]

Suppose instead that country j unilaterally intervenes. Then it is firm i that can't sell. Government i's payoff is therefore the sum of the expected gain from barter and the expected gain from unilateral purchases,

[14] Note that we ignore the case where firm i accepts and firm j rejects barter, as in this case firm j will not buy.

$$G_i(F_i,M_j) = D_j(\underline{v}_j^*(F_i,M_j))\int_{c_i}^{b_i}(v - c_i)f_i(v)\,dv$$

$$+[1 - D_j(\underline{v}_j^*(F_i,M_j))]\int_{p}^{b_i}(v - p)f_i(v)\,dv. \qquad (9)$$

Finally, if both governments intervene, barter represents the only trading opportunity. Firm i thus agrees to barter whenever its valuation exceeds its cost, i.e. $\underline{v}_i^*(M_i,M_j) = c_i$. Government i's expected utility is

$$G_i(M_i,M_j) = D_j(c_j)\int_{c_i}^{b_i}(v - c_i)f_i(v)\,dv - g_i. \qquad (10)$$

Having computed the governments' utilities, we are now in a position to characterize equilibria and social optima. Our basic question is, what characteristics of imports and exports invite mandated countertrade?

4.2. What and when to barter?

The examples cited in the introduction suggest that countertrade policies display regularities with respect to import as well as export characteristics.

We first ask: under what conditions will a country unilaterally mandate countertrade in our model? Subtract Eq. (8) from Eq. (5) and simplify to obtain

$$G_i(M_i,F_j) - G_i(F_i,F_j) = D_j(c_j)\int_{\underline{v}_i^*(M_i,F_j)}^{b_i}[v - \underline{v}_i^*(M_i,F_j)]f_i(v)\,dv - g_i$$

$$-\int_{p}^{b_i}(v - p)f_i(v)\,dv. \qquad (11)$$

Neglecting g_i, the difference is simply the option value of being able to barter, less the lost consumer surplus from being committed not to buy unilaterally. This expression would have been zero if $D_j(c_j)=1$ and $\underline{v}_i^*(M_i,F_j) = p$. However, it follows from Eq. (7) that $\underline{v}_i^*(M_i,F_j) < p$. Hence, we know that there are circumstances in which it pays to mandate countertrade, as well as circumstances in which it does not, or, more precisely:

Proposition 2. Suppose $g^i=0$. Then there exists a number $\delta_i \in (0,1)$ such that, ceteris paribus, it is optimal for country i to mandate countertrade unilaterally if and only if $D_j(c_j) \geqslant \delta_i$.

Corollary 1. For any non-negative g_1 and g_2, there exist pairs (κ_1,κ_2) with $\kappa_1>0$, $\kappa_2>0$ such that if $D_1(c_1)<\kappa_1$ and $D_2(c_2)<\kappa_2$, free trade is a policy equilibrium.

Noting that $\underline{v}_i$ is monotonically decreasing in $D_j(c_j)$, the proof of Proposition 2 is immediate from inspection of Eq. (11). By continuity, it also holds for small costs g_i. The intuition behind Proposition 2 is straightforward. If $D_j(c_j)$ is large, it is likely that firm j accepts barter, and country i has the best of both worlds: it runs little risk that firm j rejects barter, while retaining the opportunity for the domestic firm to reject barter (which is preferable if v_i turns out to be low). On the other hand, if it is unlikely that firm j accepts barter, mandating simply means throwing away consumers' surplus without any offsetting gain. Corollary 1 underscores the importance of a double coincidence of wants: if $D_1(c_1)$ and $D_2(c_2)$ are both sufficiently small, free trade is an equilibrium. (Unfortunately, equally simple conditions for the uniqueness of free trade as an equilibrium cannot be given.)

Proposition 2 highlights the kind of imports which invite restrictions. For example it is tempting for country i to mandate countertrade of imports with high (and sunk) development costs and low variable production costs, the latter being the relevant marginal cost of firm j. The gain from mandating is also affected by the costs and revenues of exports: to see this, keep $D_j(c_y)$ fixed, and recall that the gain from mandating is decreasing in $\underline{v}_i^*(M_i,F_j)$. From Eq. (7), it is readily checked that $\underline{v}_i^*(M_i,F_j)$ is increasing in the profit from selling, π_i^*. Intuitively, the option to barter rather than sell is more valuable when the profit from selling is low. Finally, keeping the profit from selling constant, the gain from barter is decreasing ($\underline{v}_i^*$ is increasing) in the marginal cost, c_i. Here, the explanation is that the barter option is more valuable when the marginal cost is low, as in this case firm i gives up less in the transaction. The above comparative statics can thus be summarized:

Proposition 3. Ceteris paribus, the gain to country i from mandating countertrade is increasing in $D_j(c_j)$ and decreasing in c_i and π_i^*.

Note that the three forces are not independent. The profit π_i depends on the firm's own marginal cost, c_i, as well as on the demand $D_j(\cdot)$. In particular, the marginal cost of the domestic firm affects the gains from mandating in two opposing ways: the direct effect of a higher marginal cost works against mandating, but the effect through the profit from selling works in favor.

So far, we have only considered unilateral deviations from free trade. What about policy equilibria? As it turns out, there are circumstances under which both countries mandate countertrade.

Proposition 4. Suppose $g_1=g_2=0$ and that $D_1(c_1)=D_2(c_2)=1$. Then (M_1,M_2) is the unique policy equilibrium.

We have already shown that M_i is a strict best reply to F_j under these conditions (Proposition 2). That M_i is also a strict best reply to M_j can be seen directly by comparing Eq. (9) and Eq. (10). The reason is obvious. Being unable to sell, it is strictly better to be able purchase at an implicit price equal to the firm's own marginal cost, c_i, than at the price $p>c_i$. In the situation described here, bilateral mandating is also socially optimal; trade is always efficient, and it always occurs. Note that Proposition 4 is not a knife edge result, as each government's utility is continuous in g, D_i and D_j.

Beyond Corollary 1 and Proposition 4 it is hard to give general characterizations of policy equilibria. Do the comparative static results concerning unilateral mandating (Proposition 3) have any relevance (can unilateral mandating occur at all), and if so what is the magnitude of the various effects? Under what conditions is free trade the unique equilibrium? To dig a bit deeper, we shall look at two specific examples.

Example 1: asymmetric characteristics

We first address the question of asymmetric industry characteristics. Let $c_1=0$ and $c_2=2$, let v_1 be uniformly distributed on [0,4] and let v_2 be uniformly distributed on [0,6]. Finally, let $g_1=g_2=g$. These are all the exogenous variables.

The profit maximizing prices are here $p_1=p_2=3$, so market values are identical.[15] Profits are different, though, with $\pi_1^*=3/2$ and $\pi_2^*=1/4$. Notice also that $D_1(c_1)=1$ while $D_2(c_2)=2/3$. Hence, if country 2 mandates countertrade, firm 1 always agrees to barter, but if country 1 mandates countertrade, firm 2 agrees only with probability 2/3. Use Eq. (7) to compute $\underline{v}_1^*(M_1,F_2)=\underline{v}_2^*(F_1,M_2)=9/4$.[16] Manipulating Eq. (5) and Eqs. (8–10), we can compute the governments' payoffs as functions of g in each of the four regimes. The resulting policy game is illustrated in Table 2, with country 1's payoff listed first. From the payoff matrix we can easily find the equilibrium for each value of g. By adding together the payoffs, we can also make a welfare ranking of the policies (Table 3).

[15] To construct uniform examples with identical market prices, simply apply the formula $p_i=(c_i+b_j)/2$.

[16] The equality between $\underline{v}_1^*(M_1,F_2)$ and $\underline{v}_2^*(F_1,M_2)$ is not a pure coincidence. It extends to any pair of uniform distributions of valuations yielding identical prices.

Table 2
Policy game I

	F_2	M_2
F_1	$\frac{13}{8}, 1$	$\frac{83}{64}, \frac{91}{64} - g$
M_1	$\frac{337}{192} - g, \frac{193}{192}$	$\frac{4}{3} - g, \frac{4}{3} - g$

For administrative costs g below 7/192, both countries mandate countertrade. If g is in the interval 7/192, 81/192, i.e. between 1.2% and 14% of the market value, only country 2 mandates countertrade. Finally, if g exceeds 81/192, both countries pursue free trade. Only in this last case do the equilibrium policies coincide with the socially optimal policies.

The example illustrates clearly the role of asymmetries between the two countries. Country 2 has a lot more to gain by intervention than does country 1, and hence is the only country to perform a unilateral intervention. Note that the industry of the intervening country has a considerably lower mark-up than the free trade country. Indeed, this relationship between the mark-ups extends to all situations with uniform distributions of valuations and asymmetric firm characteristics: the firm with the highest mark-up is also less likely to reject barter at marginal cost. Thus the firm with the lowest mark-up has more to gain by mandating countertrade. As we argued in the introduction, some of the factual observations square well with this result.

From the perspective of international regulation of trade policies, the example does not point to an entirely clear-cut conclusion. While mandating of countertrade by country 2 always imposes a negative externality on country 1, there are instances in which the equilibrium is preferable to free trade, and in others the reverse is true.

Table 3
Equilibria and social optima of policy game I

g	Policies	
	Nash equilibrium	Social optimum
$\left[0, \frac{7}{192}\right]$	(M_1, M_2)	(M_1, F_2)
$\left[\frac{7}{192}, \frac{26}{192}\right]$	(F_1, M_2)	(M_1, F_2)
$\left[\frac{26}{192}, \frac{81}{192}\right]$	(F_1, M_2)	(F_1, F_2)
$\left[\frac{81}{192}, \infty\right]$	(F_1, F_2)	(F_1, F_2)

Table 4
Policy game II

	F_2	M_2
F_1	$\frac{3(1-c)^2}{8}, \frac{3(1-c)^2}{8}$	$\frac{(1-c)^2(13-9c)}{32}, \frac{(1-c)^2(17-9c)}{32}$
M_1	$\frac{(1-c)^2(17-9c)}{32}, \frac{(1-c)^2(13-9c)}{32}$	$\frac{(1-c)^3}{2}, \frac{(1-c)^3}{2}$

Example 2: double coincidence of wants

The previous example highlighted the role of asymmetries between the two industries, but kept technology and demand fixed. Our intuition says that mandating countertrade is only profitable if there is a sufficient double coincidence of wants, and so we would like to vary $D_i(c_i)$. We shall confirm the intuition in another simple example, this time with symmetric industries. Let $g=0$. Both firms have marginal cost c and their valuations are drawn from a uniform distribution on the interval [0,1]. The probability of a double coincidence of wants is hence $(1-c)^2$.

Prices are found to be $p_1=p_2=(1+c)/2$. In the case of a unilateral mandate by country i we have $\underline{v}_i(M_i,F_j)=(1+3c)/4$. The payoff matrix for the two governments is then readily computed from Eq. (5), Eq. (8), Eq. (9) and Eq. (10), and is given in Table 4. Clearly the governments' best responses in this policy game depend on the marginal cost, c. Note also that due to the symmetry of the game, there is an even number of asymmetric equilibria (zero or two). Equilibria and social optima are readily derived, and are reported in Table 5.

We already knew from Proposition 4 that a bilateral mandate would be the unique equilibrium for low c. More surprisingly, perhaps, it remains the

Table 5
Equilibria and social optima of policy game II

c	Policies	
	Nash equilibrium	Social optimum
$\left[0,\frac{9}{63}\right]$	(M_i,M_j)	(M_i,M_j)
$\left[\frac{9}{63},\frac{21}{63}\right]$	(M_i,M_j)	(M_i,F_j)
$\left[\frac{21}{63},\frac{27}{63}\right]$	(M_i,M_j)	(F_i,F_j)
$\left[\frac{27}{63},\frac{35}{63}\right]$	(M_i,F_j)	(F_i,F_j)
$\left[\frac{35}{63},1\right]$	(F_i,F_j)	(F_i,F_j)

equilibrium policy as long as the probability of a double coincidence of wants exceeds $(4/7)^2 \approx 32.7\%$. On the other hand, a bilateral mandate is not always an equilibrium. In this example at least, free trade is the unique equilibrium whenever there is a sufficiently low probability of a double coincidence of wants. Possibly, one can build on this result to make predictions about the impact of business cycles on trade policies. Consider a recession. Producers with large stockpiles, or other kinds of excess capacity, also have a low opportunity cost. If their valuation of imports does not fall proportionally, the case for mandating countertrade is made more powerful by the recession.

As in our previous example, there is a tendency towards excessive intervention. Whether that tendency generalizes to all distributions, we do not know. Our conjecture is that there are distributions such that the consumers' surplus is very large relative to the seller's profit, for which there may be too little mandating in equilibrium.[17]

5. Conclusion

We have shown that mandated countertrade may increase the surplus of domestic firms. This could explain why the practice is not limited to underdeveloped countries, tightly regulated economies, or to undemocratic regimes. In our view, the model's most interesting prediction is that countertrade is mandated in order to purchase high mark-up imports in return for low mark-up exports. This implication seems broadly consistent with stylized facts. It can be made subject to rigorous testing, and it does not seem to be implied by any other theory in the literature.

Acknowledgments

Our work has been partially financed by the Swedish Council for Research in the Humanities and the Social Sciences and by the Norwegian Council for Applied Social Science. We are grateful to Drew Fudenberg, Ari Kokko, John Moore, Canice Prendergast, Jean Tirole, and two anonymous referees for helpful comments on earlier drafts. Thanks also to seminar participants at GREMAQ, the Norwegian School of Economics and Business Administration, the Stockholm School of Economics, and the University of Stockholm. Any errors are our own.

[17] At any rate, we would like to play down the welfare implications. The model completely neglects the possibility of *trade diversion* from competitors, which is a main concern of those who oppose countertrade (see Roessler, 1985; Walsh, 1985).

Appendix 1

Proof of Proposition 1

1. Choose any pair $\underline{v}_i$,$\underline{v}_j$ such that $\underline{v}_i \geqslant p_j$ and $\underline{v}_j \geqslant p_i$. It follows that $\Phi_i = \Phi_j = 1$, and it is immediate from Eq. (2) that the pair constitutes an equilibrium if and only if $p_i = p_j$.

2. The proof is by contradiction. Suppose that there was an equilibrium pair with $\underline{v}_j < p_i$. Then $\Phi_j = D_j(p_i)/D_j(\underline{v}_j) < 1$ and Eq. (4) implies that

$$(\underline{v}_i - c_i)D_j(\underline{v}_j) = (p_i - c_i)D_j(p_i). \tag{12}$$

Since $D_j(\underline{v}_j) > D_j(p_i)$, we have $\underline{v}_i < p_i$. Next, recall that p_i is the unique maximizer of $(p_i - c_i)D_j(p_i)$. Since both $\underline{v}_i$ and $\underline{v}_j$ are smaller than p_i, we see from Eq. (12) that $\underline{v}_i > \underline{v}_j$.

There are two main cases to consider. Suppose first that $\underline{v}_i < p_j$, and note that this would be implied by $p_i \leqslant p_j$. It follows that $\Phi_i < 1$ and we can perform the same steps as above to conclude that $\underline{v}_i < \underline{v}_j$, a contradiction. If $\underline{v}_i \geqslant p_j$, then $\Phi_i = 1$, and Eq. (2) reduces to $p_i = p_j$. But as we have seen, $p_i = p_j$ implies $\underline{v}_i < p_j$, another contradiction. □

References

Alexandrides, C.G. and B.L. Bowers, 1987, Countertrade: Practices, strategies, and tactics (Wiley, New York).

Amann, E. and D. Marin, 1994, Risk sharing in international trade: An analysis of countertrade, Journal of Industrial Economics 42, 63–77.

Banks, G., 1985, Constrained markets, 'surplus' commodities and international barter, Kyklos 38, 249–267.

Bürgin, R., 1986, Countertrade: Eine theoretische und empirische Analyse aus der Sicht einer kleinen offenen Volkwirtschaft (Schweiz) (Lang, Bern).

Carey, S.C. and S.A. McLean, 1986, The United States, countertrade and Third World trade, Journal of World Trade Law 20, 441–473.

Carter, J. and J. Gagne, 1988, The dos and don'ts of international countertrade, Sloan Management Review 29, 31–37.

Caves, R., 1974, The economics of reciprocity: Theory and evidence on bilateral trading agreements, in: W. Sellekaerts, ed., International trade and finance (Macmillan, London).

Caves, R. and D. Marin, 1992, Countertrade transactions: Theory and evidence, Economic Journal 102, 1171–1183.

Chan, R. and M. Hoy, 1991, East–West joint ventures and buyback contracts, Journal of International Economics 30, 331–343.

Choi, Chong J. and D. Maldoom, 1992, A simple model of buybacks, Economic Letters 40, 77–82.

Debroy, B., 1987, Bibliography: Countertrade, Foreign Trade Review 21, 363–375.

Ellingsen, T., 1991, A model of countertrade, Working paper EI/3 (STICERD, London School of Economics).
Fortune, 1992, 125, June 29, 25.
Hammond, G., 1990, Countertrade, barter and offsets in the international economy (St. Martin's, New York).
Hennart, J.-F., 1989, The transaction-cost rationale for countertrade, Journal of Law, Economics, and Organization 5, 127–153.
Hennart, J.-F. and E. Anderson, 1993, Countertrade and the minimization of transaction costs, Journal of Law, Economics, and Organization 9, 290-314.
Hveem, H. et al., 1989, Countertrade, the global perspective: The growth of bilateral contracting and its political implications, Oslo Countertrade Project Report No 1.
Jevons, W.S., 1875, Money and the mechanism of exchange (Appleton, London).
Liesch, P.W., 1991, Government mandated countertrade: Deals of arm twisting (Brookfield, Aldershot).
Marin, D. and M. Schnitzer, 1995, Tying trade flows: A theory of countertrade with evidence, American Economic Review, 85, 1047–1064.
Maskin, E. and J. Tirole, 1992, The principal–agent relationship with an informed principal, II: Common values, Econometrica 60, 1–42.
Mirus, R. and B. Yeung, 1993, Why countertrade? An economic perspective, International Trade Journal 7, 409–433.
OECD, 1981, East–West trade: Recent developments in countertrade (OECD, Paris).
OECD, 1985, Countertrade: Developing country practices (OECD, Paris).
Outters-Jaeger, I., 1979, The development impact of barter in developing countries (OECD, Paris).
Riley, J. and R. Zeckhauser, 1983, Optimal selling strategies: When to haggle, when to hold firm, Quarterly Journal of Economics 97, 267–289.
Roessler, F., 1985, Countertrade and the GATT legal system, Journal of World Trade Law 19, 604–614.
Stocking, G.W. and W.F. Mueller, 1957, Business reciprocity and the size of firms, Journal of Business 30, 73–95.
UNCTAD, 1984, Trade and development report (United Nations, Geneva).
Walsh, J.I., 1985, The effect on third countries of mandated countertrade, Journal of World Trade Law 19, 592–603.
Williamson, O.E., 1983, Credible commitments: Using hostages to support exchange, American Economic Review 73, 519–540.
Williamson, O.E., 1984, Credible commitments: Further remarks, American Economic Review 74, 488–490.
Zurawicki, L. and L. Suichmezian, 1991, Global countertrade: An annotated bibliography, in: Research and information guides in business, industrial, and economic institutions, Vol. 5 (Garland, New York).

Part VII
Managerial Aspects

[19]

Journal of Marketing Management, 1992, **8**, 335–349

C. W. Neale, D. Shipley★ and P. Sercu†

University of Bradford, UK, ★Trinity College, Eire and †Katholieke Universiteit Leuven, Belgium

Motives for and the Management of Countertrade in Domestic Markets

The emergence and persistence of modern countertrade (CT) is attributed to many factors including circumventing credit and foreign exchange problems, surmounting barriers to otherwise closed markets, hiding price cuts or simply exporters' need to remain competitive. Because CT arrangements comprise bundles of buying, selling and financing contracts, explaining why firms conduct CT requires explanation of why a package deal is preferred to a set of component contracts. Examination of domestic CT stripped of "international ramifications" reveals the inherent rationale for CT as a desire to hide price discounts and to overcome cash shortages. Questionnaire data obtained from UK and Canadian firms broadly support this. If CT is worth undertaking, it requires effective management. The paper concludes by discussing the implications of CT for marketing strategy and planning.

Introduction

Countertrade (CT) is the generic term used to describe a range of transaction methods in which goods and services are traded as complete or partial payment for other goods and services. Estimates of the share of total global trade accounted for by CT vary widely from about 5% to as much as 40% (e.g. Banks 1984; Economist Intelligence Unit 1985; Ford 1986; Mirus and Yeung 1986). Most observers agree that the incidence of CT has grown considerably and consistently since the late 1970s and that even on conservative estimates, it now represents many billions of dollars annually. Accordingly, CT is increasingly recognized as an important focus for attention by companies, academics and government officials (e.g. OECD 1981; International Trade Commission 1986; DTI 1988).

Valuable insights into the various forms of CT have been offered elsewhere (e.g. Khoury 1984; Huszagh and Barksdale 1986; Cho 1987; Hennart 1990) and some discussion is presented below. However, previous studies of CT have largely focused on its international trade context. Domestic CT, known to exist both in North America and the UK (Shipley and Neale 1988; Healey 1989), has been largely neglected and further analysis would be of value to academics, managers and public policy makers.

This paper has two primary aims. The first is to examine why firms choose to participate in CT rather than in conventional transactions in their domestic markets. Data relating to the benefits and problems of domestic CT as perceived by UK and Canadian participants are presented. If companies are to maximize the

Address for correspondence: C. W. Neale, University of Bradford, Management Centre, Emm Lane, Bradford BD9 4JL, UK. Tel: 0274–733466. Fax: 0274–546866.

0267–257X/92/040335+15 $08.00/0

benefits of domestic CT, they need to apply effective strategic principles to managing it. Accordingly, the second main aim is to present appropriate strategic management recommendations for domestic countertraders.

Explanations for Countertrade

The literature discusses many motives for the existence of CT. CT may help governments of importing countries to avoid balance of payments problems and to maintain employment in key sectors by controlling the products allowable as exchange. Morover, CT enables importing companies to circumvent hard currency and credit difficulties; to access Western markets more easily by penetrating marketing channels and overcoming other entry barriers such as adverse country-of-origin stereotypes and high distribution costs; and to disguise dumping, to offload low quality products and to shift goods in world excess supply (Weigand 1980; Kaikati 1981; Yoffie 1984; Nykryn 1985; Okoroafo 1988; Jones 1990). Accepting demands for CT enables the Western exporter to gain volume when sales are sluggish so as to fill out under-utilized capacity and meet contribution targets.

Thus, in conventional analysis, CT is at least partly viewed as a response to environmental adversity. Moreover, in this analysis, CT is treated as a "second-best" alternative to conventional trading, which is considered less bothersome, more liquid and more certain. But this is overly negative. Other observers have argued that Western exporters should exploit the adversity-driven demands of importers to improve both short-term and long-term positioning (Shipley and Neale 1988; Menzler-Hokkanen 1989). The protracted nature of CT negotiations facilitates long-term relationship-building and, by appeasing customers when their needs for CT are most acute, Western firms can establish loyalty and so beat or pre-empt rivals in the long-term. Accordingly, Western exporters are urged to be proactive in seeking out CT opportunities rather than treating them as a last resort mode of trading.

One argument against this is that CT is a highly risky business. But when has exporting been anything other than risky? Moreover, much or all of the CT risk has been alleviated with the development of a global countertrade service infrastructure (Palia 1990). There is now a plethora of service firms offering specialist banking, brokerage, legal, insurance and marketing capabilities to the proactive countertrader (Carter and Gagne 1988). Moreover, many companies such as ICI, Rothmans, General Motors and Ford have developed specialist CT departments to internalize the appropriate competence.

Some proponents of CT have argued that it can be a preferential mechanism to conventional transacting. Mirus and Yeung (1986) consider barter more efficient than the same transaction conducted in terms of money if it saves search and transactions costs. They see CT as an exchange of bundled goods and services according to competitive advantage: the exporter receives a product plus reduced uncertainty regarding future market access, while the importer receives a bundle of product and service benefits. The exporter benefits whenever the gain (net of marketing costs) from the goods accepted plus the long term benefit of more certain market access exceeds the cost of its exports. In this respect, CT is a rational response to uncertainty and differential transaction costs.

CT can also generate economies of time since it enables exporters to avoid delays resulting from currency rationing regimes by an importer's government. Kogut (1986) depicts CT as a form of internalization whereby large diversified multinational corporations can source raw materials and components via CT if the terms surpass the stated offers met from current vendors. This company-to-company trade meets the needs of each counterparty and saves on distribution costs, achieving better terms of trade than in the open market.

Parsons (1985) distinguishes between barter ("contemporaneous exchange of commodities") and other CT forms where each leg of the transaction may be executed at separate times. These offers "involve complex contracts over long time horizons which represent solutions to difficult problems of uncertainty and trade over time". For example, he sees counterpurchase as a device for the forward selling of commodities where no organized forward or future market exists, while buybacks are "efficient agency contracts which bind the original equipment purchasing country against various dangers of which the supplier is either aware or over which it may exercise influence" (Parsons 1985).

Such contributions are ingenious and insightful, but they tend to overlook the need to explain why CT "packages" involving serious transaction costs of drafting and implementation appear preferable to a set of independent contracts.

International CT Packages

Sercu (1990) proposes that any of the various CT methods can be synthesized into package deals of standard trade and financing arrangements. This may be illustrated by analysing the sort of a compensation deal conducted between a "Western Exporter" and an "Eastern European importing agency", as described by Raemy-Dirks (1986). Like pure barter, where the direct exchange of two unpriced goods is usually carried out on trust, without introducing bank guarantees or letters of credit, compensation involves exchange by means of single contract. Each flow of goods is, however, valued in monetary units and is reflected in principle in a counterflow of finance.

The financial flow may consist of the clearing of claims and does not necessarily require a transfer of foreign exchange. Indeed, most such deals are arranged precisely to avoid foreign currency transfers. Payment for the primary delivery is allowed on credit by the supplier, whose claim for payment is registered in a clearing account in the Eastern European country and will be liquidated by the counter-delivery. Thus, the claim for repayment of the credit is cancelled by the delivery.

A Western delivery may not always take place first. It is also possible to make a prior purchase in the customer country. When the exporter has found compensation goods available from his buyer, he can either take them himself or, if a right of assignment has been agreed, sell them to a trader at a reduced price, thus paying a CT premium. Both deliveries can now be carried out. The trader pays the exporter the value of the goods less the CT premium, while an internal clearing arrangement might apply between the exporter and importer. If the goods cannot be delivered simultaneously, the counterparty may issue a guarantee of delivery, for example, a performance bond issued or guaranteed by a bank. Less commonly, a letter of credit may be issued. If the contract involves full compensation, the internal clearing mechanism is redundant.

The Equivalent Package Deal

Replicating this form of compensation deal as an "orthodox" transaction would require three individual contracts: (i) an export contract between the two principals, (ii) an import-financing contract such as a bank loan, (iii) a "forward" export contract signed by the importer in which the proceeds of the forward sale are used to service the import-financing loan. Clearly, each of the contracts could stand alone, as is generally the case in conventional trade. Some of the signatories might play a part in more than one contract, albeit without necessarily affecting the independence of the contracts. For example, in standard trade, the counterparty in the forward export contract generally is a third party (e.g. a trader), but the buyer could also double as the supplier of imported goods. Financing could be provided by a bank, but also by the exporter. As a package, these contracts form a perfect substitute for a compensation deal, at least, in the absence of default risk. To deal with this, various standard risk-shifting techniques could be used in each of these (independent) component contracts. Some of these risk-shifting contracts might actually lead to dual roles for some of the parties in two or more contracts. For instance, if the forward contract is signed not between the importer and a trader, but between the importer and the exporter who then unloads the goods via a trader, the risk of non-delivery is shifted from the trader to the exporter to guarantee the loan and thus assume the default risk. But the same redistribution of risk is achieved if the bank loan is extended not to the importer (who would then pay the exporter), but directly to the exporter. In both examples, there is a net gain if the exporter is in a better position to ascertain the risks than the trader or the bank. Otherwise, there seems to be no obvious reason to shift the risk. An alternative risk-redistribution mechanism could involve a scheme that ensured that the proceeds of the forward sale were actually used to amortise the loan.

Finally, risks of non-delivery are present in all transactions, but they are usually shifted via bank guarantees, such as letters of credit.

Bundling in Other Forms of CT

Packaging elements can also be found in other forms of CT.

(a) A *buy-back deal* can be replicated by an import contract for plant and equipment, a loan to finance the import contract and a sub-contracting scheme whereby the buyer of the equipment sells forward part of the plant's output. Here, the single forward deal is replaced by a long-term, sub-contracting arrangement, essentially a series of forward contracts. Again, the counterparty of the sub-contracting deal could be the original supplier of the equipment and, to guarantee the servicing of the loan, the bank could insist that the latter party guarantees the loan, or equivalently takes out the loan itself.

(b) A *counterpurchase agreement* is distinguished by its forward export contract containing a delivery option to the exporter (who can select from a list of available goods), plus a limited timing option. These options also have counterparts in many futures contracts (Parsons 1985; Mirus and Yeung 1986).

(c) *Switchtrade* makes the forward contract (with delivery option) transferable, a distinction similar to that between forward and futures contracts.

Most, if not all, CT techniques are merely combinations of standard contracts (imports, import-financing and forward-type exports, plus risk-shifting arrangements). A CT contract, beyond simply being a device for trading without cash, is a deal where imports, secured loan and exports form part of one package. Thus many of the advantages claimed for CT are:

either advantages of trade *per se* (earning money to pay for import of goods or technology, creating employment etc.),
or advantages from selling (forward) to a middleman such as a trader, a distributor, or a Western producer of similar goods, rather than directly marketing the goods (easier access to distribution channels, marketing expertise, etc.),
or advantages of forward contracts or long-term subcontracting deals (redistribution of risks).

Likewise, the net attractions of a buy-back deal are merely the advantages of any turnkey and technology-transfer contract less the problems of any long-term subcontracting deal such as price risk, delivery risk, risk of creating a competitor, etc. To explain CT, we need not explain why firms or agencies wish to buy inputs, wish to sell to a middleman, or desire forward-type contracts. Rather, we have to explain why package deals are preferred over separate deals. If packages offered no specific advantages, there would be no incentive to tie and interlink the three contracts (plus their secondary risk-shifting contracts) into one complex deal.

Countertrade as a Response to Market Imperfection

Kogut (1986) and Mirus and Yeung (1986, 1991) argued that bundled transactions are a response to the sort of market imperfections endemic in centrally-planned economies and some other less-developed countries, where the market system is not well established.

Many economic transactions involve information asymmetry involving goods which have quality and/or effort dimensions often only fully observable to suppliers, for example marketing and distribution services. Information asymmetry encourages the supplier to shirk by over-stating and under-supplying the unobservable characteristics. In addition, there is the issue of protecting property rights where some of the goods and services traded are information-based. Their value reduces as their degree of dissemination increases and as the information is appropriated (Mirus and Yeung 1991).

In market economies, principal-agent problems can be solved by ownership of the distribution channels, i.e. internalization through foreign direct investment to incorporate buyer and seller within the same enterprise. A second way of solving these problems is by explicit contracting, for example, to stipulate that returns are conditional on performance.

In non-market economies, where, for example, ownership is either very restricted or excessively costly, such measures are of dubious effectiveness. In addition, they require a legal system capable of enforcing laws in an unambiguous, impartial fashion. Without such a legal system, ownership rights are difficult to protect and explicit contracts can be violated without serious legal repercussions.

Mirus and Yeung (1991) suggest that in such conditions, a bundled CT transaction is a useful device for dealing with principal-agent and property rights problems. In a CT deal, the foreign party "finds that its compensation depends entirely on its efforts to identify and successfully sell exportable local goods", and thus has no incentive to shirk. Nor is the foreign party likely to demand re-negotiation of the price for supplying marketing services. It has already made full delivery of the bundled deal—to threaten to stop the marketing services would damage the foreign partner more than the local party. Further, "the arrangement ensures that the foreign party's rights in marketing are not easily appropriated by the local party". In short, in non-market economies, or in trading transactions with them, CT is a rational form of contracting to deal with agency problems and the protection of property rights (Mirus and Yeung 1991).

However valid this analysis may be for dealing with non-market economies, it fails to explain the prevalence of CT *between* already developed nations, or CT *within* already developed nations. The former case is conducted mainly through offset arrangements, usually in defence contracts, where the importer insists that the product should incorporate a specified local content (Liesch 1988). This is usually due to the importing government wishing to enhance politico-economic objectives such as employment or regional development of industry. However, CT arrangements between firms *within* already-developed economies require separate explanation.

Package Deals in Domestic CT

A common argument favouring international CT is lack of foreign exchange reserves. Its "domestic" analogue is a severe liquidity crisis suffered by at least one of the CT firms. For example, a cash-strapped newspaper or broadcasting company might prefer to exchange advertising slots in exchange for vital inputs such as printing paper or video equipment for which it cannot pay cash. One advantage is speed. A standard, open-account sale (with immediate payment) of the same advertising space to a third party should always be possible if a sufficient discount is offered, but "immediate" payment often really means payment within, say, 10 days, to which mail float and bank float have to be added, delays that might be very costly. In contrast, the CT deal would not require any cash outflow for these vital inputs.

Alternatively, an "immediate" bank loan might be arranged on the strength of a standard sales contract, but the bank would have to be convinced that the sales contract is genuine and (almost) risk-free and then a contract would have to be drafted that ensures that the bank will obtain sufficient of the sales proceeds to liquidate the loan. All this may create costs and unacceptable delay compared with the CT option. Finally, even if an open contract really generated immediate cash, the idea of selling advertising space at an explicit and open discount may not appeal to the firm, whereas a CT deal could conceal a price-cut.

The relative benefits of the CT solution are probably circumstance-specific. If package deals were universally more efficient they would predominate, which is by no means the case even in international trade. Tying sales to purchases represents a return to the dark (moneyless) ages, when a hungry blacksmith had to find a farmer whose horse needed a new shoe. Avoiding all this is what money and markets are meant for. Even if acceptable goods have been identified, the bundling of three basic contracts plus all accessory, risk-shifting contracts into one mega-contract still implies enormous complications. In general, therefore, tied and inter-linked contracts must be more costly to draft, monitor and implement than standard, independent contracts. Conversely, the advantage of CT in the cash-shortage case should only arise because of exceptional financial distress costs that do not apply under normal trading circumstances.

The "hidden discount" aspect of the preceding argument prompts a second potential rationale for CT, the desire to camouflage part of a business agreement. In CT, prices need not be made explicit in the contract. Even for financial reporting purposes, there are ample opportunities and incentives to use offsetting misrepresentations of the true costs and proceeds. Firms might prefer to conceal a discount which, if made explicit, might set a precedent invoked by other customers, may fall foul of anti-dumping or fair trading practices legislation, or may start a price war. There may also exist a mutual desire to inflate sales.

Many other "international" explanations, however, hardly apply to domestic CT. Circumventing cartel agreements such as OPEC, for instance, would rarely be relevant. Political or psychological motives, such as getting away with poor quality without having openly to accept a low price or fooling voters with offset agreements in arms and aviation deals, would not be convincing in the domestic case where the parties are corporations rather than government officials.

Some other alleged advantages of international CT can be dismissed out of hand in the case of domestic CT, e.g. belief in planning ideology, for instance, would be unusual, if both parties in the CT contract were Western firms! Also, a belief in CT as a way to prise open new markets, using the stick-and-carrot policy of "no sales without purchases", would not be important to most Western firms. In domestic CT, information asymmetries are far less important and monitoring costs lower, while problems of marketing expertise can easily be dealt with using standard intermediate franchising contracts and sub-contracting arrangements. Economies in terms of agency costs and contracting costs, in the case of buy-back deals, are based on asymmetric information about the value of technology and would, therefore, rarely apply to domestic CT where buy-back is uncommon. Creating or preserving trade and employment are advantages of trade *per se*, and can be obtained by other means. They have little to do with the essence of CT, namely, the packaging of immediate or future exports with secured finance for imports. Similar comments apply to risk-shifting. A severe shortage of cash or a desire to stabilize production may explain why some traders may want to sell goods forward or why firms may be interested in long-term sales contracts or sub-contracting deals. Yet it does not explain why firms choose the tortuous solution of tying export, import and financing contracts into a single package deal.

To sum up, the rationale for CT within a developed economy is

(i) a need to inflate sales or to gain hidden price reductions on either side of the contract and/or
(ii) the benefits of a rapid solution to financial distress.

The main disadvantages, apart from those inherent in forward contracts or sub-contracting deals, are complexity and cost. It is difficult to envisage more convincing pros and cons.

Methodology and Data

Empirical evidence pertaining to domestic CT is very scarce. However, comparative data on both inter- and intra-national CT have been generated by Neale and Shipley (1988) in the UK and by Neale, Shipley and Dodds (1991) in Canada. These studies did not specifically attempt to examine why companies participate in CT. Rather, they sought perceptions concerning the advantages and problems of CT. It is reasonable to expect, however, that these factors provide some insight into the motives for countertrading.

The UK data were collected in 1985 by means of a mail survey of Marketing Directors of "The Times 1,000" largest firms. The questionnaire sought information about the level of participation in CT, the geographical regions of customer countries and the effects of countertrading. Standard response-building techniques were utilized although budget restrictions precluded more than a single mailing. The research instrument contained questions seeking both factual and attitudinal answers. The latter related to the benefits and problems of CT and the reasons for increasing CT participation.

A pilot survey was conducted prior to the Canadian survey to identify necessary wording changes in the questionnaire, resulting in several amendments. The final document was mailed in Winter 1987–8 to the Vice Presidents of Marketing of the companies listed in the "Financial Post 500" largest firms. The response-building techniques and single mailout were replicated from the UK study.

Low response rates were not unexpected in both surveys owing to the quasi-clandestine aspects of CT. CT participants are generally unwilling to "broadcast" their involvement. However, the response compares well with most other studies. In the UK, there were 217 (22%) usable responses. Of these, 160 companies (74%) carried out no CT, 35 (16%) were active in international CT and 22 firms (10%) undertook domestic CT. None of the UK firms conducted CT in both market categories.

In Canada, 135 usable responses were received (27%). Among these, 103 firms (76%) did not countertrade, 18 firms (13%) engaged in international CT, 12 firms (9%) engaged in intra-national CT and three firms (2%) undertook CT in both arenas. There were thus 15 Canadian firms (11%) with domestic CT experience. The total responses contained 57 UK companies (26%) and 33 Canadian firms (24%) with some form of CT experience. There is no significant difference in these response rates or in sample composition ($\chi^2 = 0$).

Results

(i) Benefits of CT

Respondents' perceptions concerning the benefits derived from domestic CT are displayed in Table 1. This shows both the ranking of particular benefits and the measures attached to them, based on a five-point Likert scale. This reveals considerable similarity among the perceptions of the two samples (rank correlation coefficient = +54%). The three most highly-ranked benefits in both samples concern increased competitiveness, increased volume and fuller capacity use while the benefit ranked fifth in both samples concerns entry into difficult markets. These are powerful advantages. However, from a broad perspective, they are benefits that would accrue from investing to build successfully a differential advantage of any nature. This raises the original theoretical issue: why should firms choose to use CT as the means for winning business?

Table 1. Benefits from domestic CT

	UK (n = 22)		*Canada* (n = 15)	
	Mean	*Rank*	*Mean*	*Rank*
Increases company competitiveness	2·82	1	3·06	3
Increases sales volume	2·77	2	3·40	2
Allows fuller use of productive capacity	2·36	3	3·60	1
Overcomes credit difficulties	2·32	4	1·87	7
Allows entry into difficult markets	2·14	5	2·66	5
Provides source of attractive inputs	2·13	6	2·74	4
Allows disposal of declining products	1·96	7	2·13	6

Means are based on responses to questions based on a 5-point Likert scale where 1 = "not a benefit" ranging through to 5 = "a benefit of utmost importance".
Rank correlation coefficient between UK and Canadian samples = +0·54.

One explanation is that CT *is* used as a way to implement secret price cuts without the risk of spoiling the broader or long-term market. Some support for this obtains in the much lower mean scores recorded by both samples for "allows disposal of declining products" as a CT benefit. If the object was to shift obsolete or otherwise declining products, firms could announce price reductions overtly without fear of spoiling long-term sales or opening a price war.

Further support for CT as a medium for secret price cutting is implicit in the benefit "provides attractive source of inputs". In this case, however, the benefit is best expressed from the customer's perspective. It is difficult to conceptualize how CT can provide more attractive sources unless "attractiveness" is provided in terms of lower prices or preferential benefits. In either case, the CT customer not only secures a sale, but also obtains better value for money, which is, effectively, a price reduction.

The second proposed motive for engaging in domestic CT is to alleviate financial difficulties. In this context, "overcomes credit difficulties" was the fourth-ranking benefit among the UK respondents although it is perceived as the least important advantage among the Canadian firms. The UK result is difficult to explain since it is unlikely that many of the UK's largest 1,000 firms would have suffered in financial distress during the prosperous mid-1980s. The bi-national disparity may be explained, however, by differences in prevailing interest rates, which tended to be at higher levels in the UK. Notwithstanding, the UK result is consistent with the theoretical proposition described.

(ii) Problems of CT

The rankings and scores for the perceived problems of domestic CT are presented in Table 2. This reveals less similarity across the two samples and a correspond-

Table 2. Problems of domestic CT

	UK (n = 22)		Canada (n = 15)	
	Mean	*Rank*	*Mean*	*Rank*
Firm has no "in-house use" for goods offered	2·59	1	1·86	6
Complex negotiations	2·32	2	2·27	2=
Difficult to resell goods offered by customers	2·27	3	1·80	7=
Customers' negotiating strength	2·22	4	2·00	4=
Time consuming negotiations	2·18	5	2·27	2=
Problems over "pricing"	2·04	6	2·60	1
Increases costs	1·86	7	1·80	7=
Customer becomes potential competitor	1·77	8	1·54	9
General increase in uncertainty	1·68	9	1·53	10
Need for costly brokerage facilities	1·50	10	2·00	4=

For explanation of mean see Table 1.
Rank correlation coefficient between UK and Canadian samples = +0·39.

ingly lower rank correlation (+39%). The variables ranked first and third by the UK firms, but only sixth and seventh by the Canadians, both concern the perennial difficulty of how to use or dispose of products received. The findings suggest that the Canadian companies are more discerning in the selection of goods receivable and/or more effective at marketing them. Both sets of firms rank three types of negotiation difficulties among the five most important problems. This indicates the inescapable difficulties of packaging multiple contracts into a single bundle. This suggests that CT must confer countervailing advantages, which are not available in conventional modes of trade.

Both samples attach a measure of some importance to "problems over pricing". This is unlikely to reflect the historical difficulty of trying to decide how many sheep are worth a cow, which is easily resolved with the use of a currency numeraire. It is more likely that the problems arise in deciding the level of covert price discounting, particularly if one party becomes overly ambitious. This difficulty is likely to be exacerbated by the cited problems of "need for costly brokerage facilities" and "increases costs". The Canadians rank the former problem more highly than the UK firms. It may be, therefore, that fewer Canadians have internalized the brokerage function, which some UK countertraders are known to have done (Neale and Shipley 1990).

"Customer becomes potential competitor" is given little importance by either sample. This is most likely to be a serious problem in the buy-back variant of CT (Weigand 1980), in which few of the respondents engage domestically. Finally, low mean importance was assigned to "general increase in uncertainty". Given that the existence of uncertainty is evident in some of the other problems cited, the inference is that the perceived importance of the uncertainty is subjugated by the promise of the benefits that domestic CT confers.

Managerial Imperatives for Effective Countertrading

It is clear that participants in domestic CT can gain useful benefits, but encounter considerable problems. The incidence of domestic CT in the USA has increased by some 15% per annum during recent years (Healey 1989) and similar trends might be expected in Britain and elsewhere. To maximize the likelihood of success, participants will need to build top management commitment to CT success and to adopt a strategic approach to its management.

Top management support is required to inspire an appropriate CT culture within the company. CT should not be treated casually as a marketing frill. It is too risky to enter into in a half-hearted manner or without adequate resource provision (Carter and Gagne 1988). Top management responsibilities should demonstrate enthusiasm for CT, to communicate the benefits and pitfalls, to influence the choice of strategy and to allocate sufficient budgets, manpower and time to ensure that an effective organization is in place.

The second prerequisite for profitable CT is the achievement of a tight strategic fit between, respectively, conditions prevailing in the CT environment, the CT strategy and the company's CT organization. Without the triangular strategic fit illustrated in Figure 1, failure beckons.

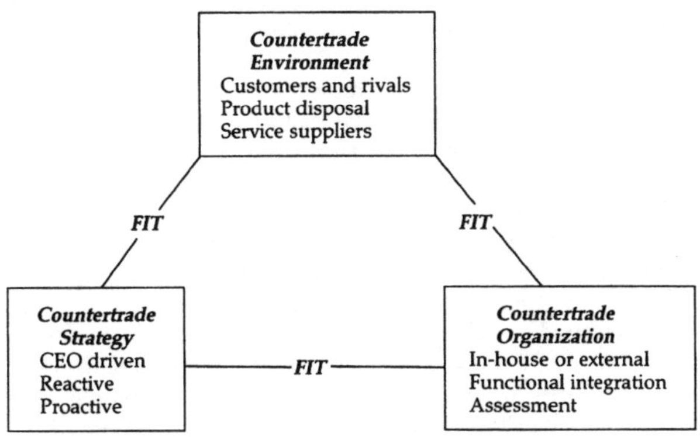

Figure 1. ***Strategic countertrade imperatives***

The first element in strategic planning for CT is to achieve deep understanding of conditions in the CT enviroment. Research needs to begin with actual and potential customers. Who are they, what are their specific needs in terms of products and CT methods? What segmentation patterns exist? How are customers organized for CT and what is their reputation, reliability, credit status and negotiating style? A key issue concerns the exchange products on offer. Do they meet required specifications and quality levels and can they be profitably resold or absorbed into production processes internally? Another important requirement is to gain full knowledge of specialist CT service suppliers. What advice and expertise is available from brokers, agents, resellers, lawyers and financial specialists, and how will utilization of these affect cost and effectiveness? Also, who are the existing and potential competitors for CT business? What are their strategies? How can they be beaten? Although offering CT terms can be a means for achieving company differential advantage, its CT offering must be more attractive than that of rivals to ensure differential advantage in the CT business itself.

The second keystone in the strategic CT triangle is the choice of strategy. The general dimensions of strategy formulation, such as strategic objectives, focus, segmentation and positioning, are similar for any mode of trade. However, another dimension of strategy selection concerns the choice between a reactive or a proactive strategy. The former is a cautious, risk-averse approach founded on fear of CT problems and infamy surrounding the numerous "nightmare" experiences that occurred before the development of the CT service industry. The reactive approach does not incorporate active search for CT opportunities. Rather, it merely consists of passive acquiescence to customer demands for CT terms when refusal would result in lost sales. CT is treated as a "second-best" or last resort. This approach can be viable, but only if the participant utilizes the expertise of the specialist service suppliers. Without these, reactive participation enhances the risks of failure, since reluctant and/or infrequent CT players are unlikely to internalize the necessary expertise. Moreover, the absence of search inevitably involves losing CT opportunities and the benefits these could provide.

Conversely, a proactive CT strategy embodies determined scanning for profitable CT opportunities. Adherents recognize the risks, but endeavour to minimize them and maximize the advantages by building relevant competence into an effective organization. Moreover, frequent CT involvement generates scale and experience economies. It also creates a reputation for willingness to participate that attracts repeat business from proactive customers and builds a network of contacts for profitable product disposal. In summary, a proactive strategy increases CT effectiveness and profitability.

The third element of the strategic triangle, effective organization, is critical to CT success. Three key organizational principles apply. First, there is a need for a clearly-defined chief co-ordinator of CT activity to provide accountability, authority and leadership. Second, since all CT deals involve some unique characteristics, flexibility is required so that relevant expertise can be incorporated to meet specific needs. Third, since CT involves many complex dimensions, the organization needs to include personnel drawn from several functions. Depending on the particular circumstances of a particular deal, there may be important roles for specialists from finance, legal, technical, production, quality control, distribution and sales as well as marketing.

What constitutes the most appropriate organization for a particular company under specific conditions, depends on numerous factors. Prominent among these are objectives and available resources; the scope and frequency of CT involvement; customer characteristics, needs, exchange products and location; contract complexity, size, cost and risks; competitive conditions and the company's own strategy. Infrequent or novice countertraders who lack adequate competences, need to recruit relevant service suppliers externally. This raises the costs, may dilute confidentiality and keeps the customer at arm's length. However, it also ensures relevant skills, increases objectivity and improves product disposal probabilities. Among proactive and frequent countertraders, the development of specialist in-house competences and systems is justified by scale economies, closeness to the customer, increased control, greater flexibility and closer confidentiality. Depending on conditions, the scope of an internal CT organization ranges from a small team of specialists to a dedicated CT department or division such as those of ICI or General Motors. Nevertheless, even proactive participants need to employ external facilitators as needs arise.

The composition of the negotiating team is a major determinant of CT profitability. Negotiations are complex, time-consuming and costly. Moreover, they normally involve fierce bargaining, often with highly professional, trained, tough and sophisticated specialists on the customer's team. Moreover, negotiations often disintegrate prior to completion. Accordingly, the team should comprise trained multi-disciplinary specialists with freedom to abort rather than accept unfavourable terms. Notwithstanding these difficulties, the lengthy negotiations can produce highly profitable contracts and cement close personal relationships among negotiators leading to longer-term repeat business.

Finally, effective evaluation and control mechanisms are essential features of the CT organization. Evaluation criteria need to be established for each deal as well as for the long-term programme. Responsibility for comparing these against performance and control implementation lies with senior CT management. Periodic CT audits are required by long-term repeat countertraders to identify environmental movements, organizational weaknesses and necessity for strategy adaptation.

Summary and Conclusions

This study endeavours to explain why, in their domestic trade, companies elect to engage in the highly complex "package deals", which CT entails, instead of simpler, conventional modes of trading. Many of the motives given for CT participation are either specific to international trade or benefits that can be obtained in any form of trade. When CT is examined in the context of domestic trade, most of the international influences can be discounted. It is posited here that intra-national CT is undertaken for two reasons. First, to administer secret price reductions and, second, to avoid short-term credit problems. Conclusions from the empirical research reported are tentative owing to the potential for small numbers bias. Nevertheless, support for both of the motives is found among the UK and Canadian samples studied.

The incidence of domestic CT is unknown since the subject has received only very limited empirical attention. However, there is reason to believe that the incidence may grow (Healey 1989). To exploit the benefits of this expected growth, companies need to apply sound strategic principles. Relevant guidelines were presented in the preceding section. To enhance further academic understanding, further research is required. In particular, case analysis as well as large sample quantitative research into the motives, effects, management and organization of domestic CT would provide stimulating findings.

Acknowledgements

The authors would like to acknowledge both the helpful comments of Rolf Mirus and also the extent to which they have drawn on his work with B. Yeung in the third section of the paper. Many thanks are also due to Colin Dodds who organized the collection of the Canadian data.

References

Banks, G. (1984), "The economics and politics of countertrade", *The World Economy*, **6**, No. 2, pp. 159–182.

Carter, J. R. and Gagne, J. (1988), "The do's and don'ts of international countertrade", *Sloan Management Review*, **29**, No. 3, pp. 31–37.

Cho, K. O. (1987), "Using countertrade as a competitive marketing tool", *Management International Review*, **27**, No. 1, pp. 50–57.

Department of Trade and Industry (1988), *Countertrade: A Guide for Exporters*, London, DTI.

Economist Intelligence Unit (1985), *North–South Countertrade*, Special Report No. 174, London.

Ford, J. G. (1986) "Report on Countertrade", presented to The Commission on External Relations of the European Parliament. (P.E. Doc. A 2–117/86).

Healey, N. (1989), "Two pigs for a personal computer", *Management Today*, October, pp. 116–118.

Hennart, J.-F. (1990), "Some empirical dimensions of countertrade", *Journal of International Business Studies*, **21**, No. 2, pp. 243–270.

Huszagh, S. M. and Barksdale, H. (1986), "International barter and countertrade: an exploratory study", *Journal of the Academy of Marketing Science*, **14**, No. 1, pp. 21–28.

International Trade Commission (1985), *Assessment of the Effects of Barter and Countertrade Transactions on US Industries*, Washington, D.C. US International Trade Commission, October.

Jones, S. F. (1990), *North–South Countertrade: Barter and Reciprocal Trade with Developing Countries*, Economist Intelligence Unit Special Report No. 194, London.

Kaikati, J. (1981), "The international barter boom: Perspective and challenges", *Journal of International Marketing*, **1**, pp. 29–38.

Khoury, J. (1984), "Countertrade: forms, motives pitfalls and negotiation requisites", *Journal of Business Research*, **2**, No. 2, pp. 47–62.

Kogut, B. (1986), "On designing contracts to guarantee enforcibility: theory and evidence from East–West trade", *Journal of International Business Studies*, **17**, No. 2, pp. 47–62.

Liesch, R. W. (1988), *Government-Mandated Countertrade: The Economics of the Australian Government Offsets Program*, Unpublished PhD Thesis, Brisbane, University of Queensland.

Menzler-Hokkanen, I. (1989), "Countertrade arrangements in international trade: a tool for creating competitive advantage?' *Scandinavian Journal of Management*, **5**, No. 2, pp. 5–22.

Mirus, R. and Yeung, B. (1986), "Economic incentives for countertrade", *Journal of International Business Studies*, 27, No. 3, pp. 27–39.

Mirus, R. and Yeung, B. (1991), *Countertrade—what have we learned?* (Paper presented at the International Trade and Finance Association Conference, Marseilles.

Neale, C. W. and Shipley, D. (1988), "Effects of countertrade-divergent perceptions between practitioners and non-participants", *Journal of Management Studies*, **25**, No. 1, pp. 57–72.

Neale, C. W. and Shipley, D. (1990), "Empirical insights into British countertrade with Eastern bloc countries", *International Marketing Review*, **7**, No. 1, pp. 15–31.

Neale, C. W., Shipley, D. and Dodds, J. C. (1991), "Aspects of countertrade involvement by British and Canadian exporters: a comparative study", *Management International Review*, **31**, No. 1, pp. 19–35.

Nykryn, J. (1985), "Combining import deals with export activities". In: *East–West*

Trade and Finance in the World Economy. (Ed) Saunders, C. T. (London), Macmillan, pp. 253–264.

OECD (1981), *East–West Trade: Recent Developments in Countertrade?*, Paris, OECD.

Okoroafo, S. C. (1988), "Determinants of LDC—mandated countertrade", *International Marketing Review*, **5**, No. 1, pp. 17–24.

Palia, A. P. (1990), "Worldwide network of countertrade services", *Industrial Marketing Management*, **19**, No. 1, pp. 69–76.

Parsons, J. E. (1985), *A Theory of Countertrade Financing of International Business*, Sloan School of Management, Working Paper WP1632–85.

Raemy-Dirks, C. (1986), "Countertrade: linked purchases in international trade". In: *Trade Financing*. (Ed) Gmur, C. J. (London), Euromoney Publications, pp. 17–27.

Sercu, P. (1990), *Pros and Cons of Countertrade: A Critical Note*, European Institute for Advanced Studies in Management, Working Paper 90–07.

Shipley, D. and Neale, C. W. (1988), "Countertrade: reactive or proactive?" *Journal of Business Research*, **16**, No. 3, pp. 327–335.

Weigand, R. (1980), "Barters and buy-backs: let Western firms beware", *Business Horizons*, **23**, No. 3, pp. 54–61.

Yoffie, D. B. (1984), "Profiting from countertrade", *Harvard Business Review*, **62**, May/June, pp. 8–16.

Buy-Back and Technology Transfer — Some Theoretical Considerations

Rolf Mirus
University of Alberta

Bernard Yeung*
University of Alberta

Abstract
Transferring technology to an economy characterized by tight government controls and/or central planning is problematic because the lack of competition in goods markets and inadequacies in the markets for workers and managers combine to weaken the incentive structure and reduce the information flow. After examining these issues from the viewpoint of the supplier of technology this paper develops a number of hypotheses which suggest that buy-back may be a helpful means to alleviate the resulting difficulties.

Résumé
Les transferts de technologie à une économie caractérisée par des contrôles gouvernementaux serrés et/ou par la planification centralisée sont problématiques parce que l'absence de concurrence sur les marchés des produits manufacturés s'ajoute aux insuffisances des marchés tant pour le personnel que pour la direction pour affaiblir le système des primes de rendement et ralentir la diffusion de l'information. Après avoir examiné ces questions du point de vue de celui qui fournit la technologie, ce papier émet un certain nombre d'hypothèses qui suggèrent que le rachat (buy-back) pourrait être un moyen utile d'alléger les difficultés qui en résultent.

INTRODUCTION

Buy-back is usually carried out between a firm in a developed economy and an enterprise in a less developed country with a state-controlled economy; the former provides capital and technology[1] to the latter and takes a significant portion of its compensation in the form of output the capital and technology help to produce. The exchange usually stretches over a lengthy period of time. The provision of capital and technology may take several years during which a manufacturing plant is constructed. The stream of output taken back may span many years after production begins. The capital and technology supplier participates actively in both the initial plant construction and the later manufacturing phases, supplying on-going skill transfer, supervision and maintenance. However, the capital and technology supplier usually has no substantive and lasting ownership control of the manufacturing facilities and the transferred technology. The business relation between the two parties is like a combination of licensing, turn-key project and management contract; it is also similar to a terminal joint venture. The significant activity, however, is the technology transfer undertaken.[2]

Conducting technology transfer to centrally planned economies and/or to less developed economies with active government involvement can be highly problematic. These economies are often characterized by state-owned monopolies, price and wage controls, a non-convertible currency, and foreign exchange controls. Business entities usually have little autonomy as employment and input allocations are largely determined by the state. The prime responsibility of management is frequently to meet production targets. Consequently, efficiency-seeking behavior is much less pronounced than in Western economies and useful market intelligence, as well as economic data, is also severely limited.[3] These adverse business conditions are formidable obstacles to successful technology transfer. In this paper we argue that buy-back, under the circumstances, may be a means — and not necessarily the best — of promoting the successful transfer of technology. While our findings are preliminary and in need of empirical verification they serve the purpose of stimulating research on the strategic aspects of buy-back.

* Professor and Associate Professor of International Business, Faculty of Business, University of Alberta, Edmonton, Alberta, Canada, T6G 2R6. We would like to acknowledge financial support from the Doug Muir Fund and helpful suggestions of Jean-François Hennart, Mansour Javidan and Gilbert Reschenthaler, as well as three anonymous reviewers. Bernard Yeung also acknowledges the support of the Royal Bank's International Business Fellowship (87-88). Earlier versions of this paper were presented at the ASAC Toronto Conference, June 1987 and the Conference of the European International Business Association, Antwerp, December 1987.

A SIMPLE CASE — ILLUSTRATION

We include the following synopsis of a pertinent case study to highlight some but not all of the notions we will formulate more fully in this paper.

During 1986 a Canadian engineering services company not previously engaged in international business heard of an opportunity to develop a turn-key chemical plant in China. After some initial contacts it was learned that product buy-back was stipulated as part of the payment. With the help of a project management company experienced in Asia negotiations were expedited and a contract was signed in December 1986. This contract was subsequently renegotiated to better suit the parties' needs; in the meantime it served to cement their relationship.

Our interviews with the key Canadian manager suggest that the buy-back feature was critical in concluding this deal. The major reason was that the foreign exchange allotted to the Chinese customer — an amount unknown to the Canadian side until "unearthed" through the help of Hong Kong agents — was inadequate to allow for positive profits. The alternative of obtaining an increase in the foreign exchange allocation, while not out of the question, was judged unlikely in the foreseeable future.

For the Chinese customer, a fine chemical factory, a more efficient way to produce ethylene diamine for the growing domestic market was a priority. Yet it was their first involvement with a Western supplier and the Canadian technology was new. They were therefore interested in a contract that protected them from the risks of a below-par performance of the new plant when using locally available feedstocks.

The resultant contract then included a performance clause in the buy-back portion. For example, should the plant turn out to be only 90% as efficient as claimed by the Canadians, the final price would be reduced by 10%. Such penalties (bonuses) assured the Chinese side that they would not have to seek additional government funds to fulfil the contract. It also gave the Canadian firm a minimum cash price and a performance incentive.

In the view of the Canadian management, the inclusion of buy-back in the contract therefore had three effects:

1. The negotiations were speeded up by avoiding delays from additional requests for foreign exchange.
2. The plant design was better adapted to accommodate Chinese feedstocks.
3. The very best employees were sent to China for assembly, supervision and start-up training.

In consequence, we argue below that buy-back, under the circumstances, may be a means to facilitate technology transfer.[4] Our discussion pertains to the negotiation phase, the planning and implementation, the monitoring of the performance of expatriates conducting the transfer, the possibility of nurturing a future competitor, and issues regarding the reputation of the local production force.

BUY-BACK EXPEDITES NEGOTIATION

At the negotiation table, difficulties arise in several ways. First, most of the major items in the transactions being negotiated are not frequently and competitively traded, at least not in the local markets. Their terms of exchange are then bargaining subjects; the bargaining is driven by subjective evaluation based on private information not commonly shared and objective benchmarks such as market prices are absent.[5] As a result disagreement is probable. The transferring firm and the locals may disagree about the productivity of their respective inputs, the relative importance of their contributions, and the valuation of the output. Also, less market orientation means that local managers put less emphasis on the quality of technology (Kogut, 1986, p. 51) so that their valuation of any particular technology would likely be different from that of a Western firm.

Second, foreign exchange is an issue. The local firm may not currently have any and may not be confident of receiving an allocation in the future. Its own valuation of foreign exchange may be far above that indicated by the official rate; at the same time the authorities dislike outlays of scarce foreign exchange. The local firm is then reluctant to offer payment in foreign currency and, even if it does, its offer may not appear reasonable when converted at the official rate.

Third, due to the prevalence of price and exchange controls, the transferor would likely demand a risk premium or hedging arrangements which the transferee might find unjustified because from his point of view the risks are less, and are not very damaging. Finally, the emphasis on quantitative production targets leads the local managers to demand rigid quantity commitments in production volume and forward sales.

Buy-back means to exchange in terms of goods rather than money.[6] Offering to do so would alleviate the above problems for several reasons.[7] First, an assessment of the terms of the exchange is more direct. The transferor can directly use world-market prices to assess the compensation. Also, he does not need to worry about exchange rates of currencies. The transferee can directly apply its shadow prices to assess the terms of the exchange without worrying about the discrepancy between the real and nominal values of prices. Second, this mode of exchange avoids disbursement of scarce foreign currency and is therefore appealing to local enterprises. Third, this form of exchange is a natural resolution to price and capital controls and the associated risks. Exchanging in terms of goods is like employing commodity hedges and, hence, both the transferor and the transferee reduce their exposure to price and foreign exchange controls as well as risks. Local price and exchange controls are not applicable to this portion of the contract.[8] Finally, given their familiarity with quotas and targets, the local managers will find the quantity stipulation and forward sales nature of buy-back attractive.[9]

The above arguments lead to the following hypotheses, all of them subject to the condition that other things are equal:

H1. In technology transfer projects the time spent on negotiation is less when buy-back is involved than when a standard contract denominated in convertible currency is concluded.

H2. In technology transfer projects the risk premium the transferor charges due to price and exchange controls is less with buy-back than with standard contracts.

H3. In technology transfer projects the transferee's valuation of a technology is higher with buy-back than with standard contracts.

BUY-BACK FACILITATES THE ACTUAL TRANSFER

At the planning and implementation level the transferor would find two obstacles to an optimal technology transfer.[10] First, the local managers would probably make insufficient efforts to search for and appropriately adapt a suitable foreign technology. They do not face much competitive pressure and a strong relation between reward and profit-performance is absent. Moreover, the local reward system tends to heavily penalize mistakes and to distrust initiatives. Consequently, the local managers would be inclined to import foreign technology as is, rather than to search for and to introduce improvements.[11]

Second, the local managers would probably not be inclined to commit themselves to long production runs and repeated technology transfer which are means to attain economies of scale in technology transfer. From Teece (1977) we learn that there are economies of scale in technology transfer which can be exploited through long production runs and repeated interaction. However, to the local managers a long production run involves substantial pre-committed inputs and forward sales and it consequently entails more risks. Given the emphasis on meeting quotas and the tendency of the reward system to penalize mistakes, they would be very reluctant to commit themselves to long production runs. Reinforcing this hesitation are their doubts about the foreign transferor's commitment to a thorough transfer and their fear that the transferor would behave in a scheming manner after a long term contract is signed.

An important cause of the first problem is the lack of information search which is, in turn, caused by the lack of competition and the sub-optimal incentive structure skewed towards penalizing mistakes. Buy-back, by its very nature, makes use of this feature and induces information search. In a buy-back arrangement, the local manager is obligated to deliver a significant quantity of output to the technology supplier. If the obligation is not fulfilled, a 'mistake' is perceived to be made and the local manager will be penalized. To avoid penalties, the local manager, before and after concluding a buy-back arrangement, would pay careful attention to the production capacity of the technology, the labor productivity, the future allocation of inputs and local economic targets.[12] The technology transferor, too, would search for this type of information because of the need to ascertain commensurate compensation for his supplies. These information search activities will certainly lead to more extensive local adaptation of the foreign technology.[13]

The second problem is that long production runs and repeated transfer, the two means of exploiting the economies of scale in technology transfer, are usually foregone as a result of the risk aversion of local managers. Again, the buy-back feature helps. First, it likely extends production runs because of the addition of buy-back quantities to local demand. Second, it gives the local management confidence that the transferor has a keen interest in the success of the project since now the return on his own resource is at stake. The local manager is then more willing to engage in long production runs. Third, in order to fulfil the buy-back commitments, participants from both parties have a common interest to work in close and repeated mutual consultation.[14] Consequently, the benefits of economies of scale in transferring technology can be reaped.

The above discussion leads to the following hypotheses, again subject to the ceteris paribus clause:

H4. In technology transfer projects the imported technology is more suitably adapted to the local conditions (e.g. the capital-labor intensity is closer to the local norm) when buy-back is involved than when a standard monetary contract is concluded.

H5. In technology transfer projects the production run is longer when buy-back is involved than when it is not.

H6. In technology transfer projects the frequency of information exchanges between the transferor and the transferee is higher with buy-back than with a standard contract.

BUY-BACK AS A MONITORING DEVICE ELICITING EXPATRIATES' EFFORT

When the transfer is on-stream, the transferor would have difficulty in supervising its expatriates' effort in conducting the transfer because the local managerial atmosphere is permissive and without an adequate monitoring system.[15]

The transferring firm would find it very difficult, if not impossible, to judge whether its expatriates are working well even if there are good results. Without a benchmark standard and credible accounting, it is difficult to attribute the results to the various causes: the local competitors may be too inefficient, the local inputs may be too inexpensive, the transferred technology may be intrinsically very valuable, or the expatriates may have indeed performed well. If there are poor results, the transferring firm would have similar difficulties in delineating its expatriates' share of blame among the many confounding factors. The permissiveness of the local market for managers thus spills over: the expatriates might be more inclined to shirk.

Buy-back is taking a significant portion of the output back and that gives the transferring firm first-hand information on the results of the technology transfer including the rate of production, the quality control of output, the timeliness of delivery, the packaging, etc. Buy-back then serves as a monitoring device and exerts pressure on expatriates to perform. This method is more effective, albeit more cumbersome and costly, than stipulating direct exports. The results on direct exports are subject to additional confounding factors, some of which are determined by local market conditions. Because of the characteristics of the local economy, the results on direct exports would become very noisy signals. Also, there may not be any benchmark for comparison, especially when the transferee does not have genuine local competitors. Accordingly, the following hypothesis is advanced.

H7. In technology transfer projects the transferor has more information on the efforts of expatriates and is more satisfied with their efforts when buy-back is involved than when it is not, ceteris paribus.

BUY-BACK AS A SIGNAL FOR SUCCESSFUL TECHNOLOGY TRANSFER

Additional problems for the transferring firm may be caused by absenteeism, low productivity and unsatisfactory workmanship of the local labor force.[16] Even if the transferor has the ability to overcome these deficiencies, it would still find conveying this message difficult. The resulting low expectations regarding the success of the transfer diminish the value of its technology in the eyes of the local partner.

If a firm is indeed confident that it can overcome these difficulties, it will want to signal this ability to the market, lest it suffer a loss as a result of the reputation problem. Buy-back may be such a signal, conveying the message that the quality of the output is high and the firm is able to overcome the obstacles to a successful transfer of technology. (This 'signalling' idea was first raised in Murrell (1982).) In a buy-back deal the supplier's compensation depends significantly on the value of the output produced with the technology. The value of the output, in turn, depends on the success of the technology transferred. Buy-back may also create other important types of dependence; for example,the transferor may depend on the timely delivery of the stream of output. Accepting buy-back as a significant part of the compensation, the transferor shows confidence in succeeding in the technology transfer project. This gesture would then have the effect of raising the expected value of the output and, therefore, the value of the technology.

An issue which has been overlooked in this connection and therefore worthy of note is that this signalling effect exists only if the signal is credible, that is, firms which cannot overcome the obstacles to a successful technology transfer would not be interested in conducting buy-back. This credibility aspect implies that buy-back is not a universal means to overcome the reputation problem. It also says that the ex post value of the transferred technology is verifiably higher than usual when buy-back is actually conducted. Finally, we note that experienced firms with past success would not need to resort to the buy-back signal.

The above discussion leads to the following testable hypotheses:

H8. Of two similar technology packages transferred into state-controlled economies the one with buy-back commands a higher value, both ex ante and, on average, ex post.[17]

H9. In conducting technology transfer, more experienced firms with a good record in technology transfer are less eager to offer buy-back than less experienced firms without a record.

BUY-BACK AS A TACTIC TO REDUCE FUTURE COMPETITION FROM THE TRANSFEREE

A final worry of the transferor is that the transferee will become a competitor in the future. As is well known, in the economies we are discussing the transferor does not have any meaningful ownership control of the technology and the manufacturing facilities which the technology helps to construct. Equipped with an advanced technology and inexpensive local inputs, the transferee may become a competitor to be reckoned with.

Buy-back can be a strategic move to reduce the possibility that the transferee successfully invades the transferor's markets in the future. The buy-back clause first allows the transferee to export readily without significantly learning international marketing of its own output. In comparison with a standard contract less learning occurs about the nature of the destination markets. At the same time, in the presence of capacity constraints and diminishing returns, the transferee obviously has less capacity for and a higher marginal cost of exports after making the buy-back payments. It then has less incentive to search for additional export markets on its own. With reduced search for additional export sales, the transferee has less knowledge about international marketing and export growth is adversely affected. At the very least, the benefits of acquiring international marketing knowledge are delayed. Consequently, it is less likely that the transferee can successfully invade the transferor's export markets in the future. In this sense, buy-back is a strategic move to reduce the probability of nurturing a future competitor. This line of reasoning suggests the following hypothesis for empirical investigation:[18]

H10. In technology transfer projects, the fraction of output exported by the transferee (other than that purchased back by the transferor) is less when buy-back is involved than with a standard contract; the difference between the fractions exported in these two cases increases over time as transferees not facing buy-back become more experienced in direct international sales.

CONCLUSION

This paper has examined buy-back in the context of technology transfer. After pointing out the difficulties of conducting technology transfer in planned economies, it suggests that buy-back serves to mitigate them and it introduces testable hypotheses.

Our arguments help explain the often overlooked phenomenon that buy-back was rather common in East-West technology transfer in the seventies, i.e., some time before other forms of countertrade gained popularity.[19] They are presented here to stimulate further research into this important aspect of international business. At the same time we *stress* that a technology transferor should not necessarily stipulate buy-back. In particular, the potential benefit of buy-back in facilitating technology transfer will have to be weighed against the high transaction costs typically involved in this form of contracting.

The need for empirical follow-up to the notions developed in this paper cannot be over-emphasized. Data availability is a major obstacle. While it is possible to test a few of the hypotheses using available micro-economic and industrial data (e.g. Murrell (1982)), we believe that data quality and sample size represent very severe constraints. The testing of some hypotheses (e.g. H1, 2 and 8) would actually require proprietory data. Moreover, some of the suggested hypotheses (e.g. H6, 7 and 9) cannot be tested using industrial or economic data. We therefore believe that a survey approach is required to test most of our ideas.[20] To design such a survey will necessitate several in-depth case studies that allow for the effects of firm size, nature of technology and product, and differences in the recipient environment. While such work is now underway, the complexity of the task should not be underestimated.

NOTES

1 The term 'technology' refers not just to production technology but also to management technology.

2 Buy-back contracts are part of the emerging literature on countertrade, examples of which are Murrell (1982), Kogut (1986), Khoury (1984), Mirus and Yeung (1986) and Lecraw (1987, a.). Murrell (1982, p. 590) maintains that buy-back is an important form of countertrade and so does Walsh (1984). "East-West Trade-Recent Developments in Countertrade" (O.E.C.D., 1981, p. 32) estimated that buy-back contracts between 1969 and 1980 were worth $30 to $48 billion of Western exports and $35 to $42 billion of Western imports from the East. The Economist (Oct. 5, 1985, p. 21) comments that buy-back is common in East-West trade.

3 This description applies to Eastern bloc countries, socialist countries in Asia, and, to a lesser extent, to some less developed countries. For a more thorough discussion of systemic factors causing low efficiency under central planning and management, see Gomulka and Nove (1984), especially p. 35-37.

4 As indicated above buy-back is not necessarily the best way to transfer technology. Indeed the project manager in the situation described suggested that the company would not always be willing to engage in a buy-back transaction. We certainly do not intend to suggest that buy-back is superior to reliance on markets.

5 Even when relevant local market prices exist, they may be subject to so much government interference that their nominal and real values diverge significantly. The extent of this divergence is subjectively evaluated. As a result it often turns out to be a source of dispute.

6 We, of course, do not mean that money is not involved at all. Rather, we mean to emphasize that a very significant portion of the exchange is conducted in terms of goods.

7 We do not imply that offering to exchange in terms of goods can resolve all the problems during negotiations. Rather, our contention is that doing so can resolve some of the problems so that an agreement becomes more probable and can be more quickly reached.

8 Just as in standard contracts the risk of non-payments remains for the transferor.

9 The O.E.C.D. (1981) reports that East European sources view buy-back similarly: it corresponds to the needs of the centralized planning system by providing stable data, by stabilizing economic fluctuations to some extent, and by making available the distribution and marketing network of the West (p. 14). Also, there is a claim that buy-back may be a way of avoiding accusations of dumping in a protectionist environment (p. 15).

10 From Morley and Smith (1977) and Lecraw (1979) we learn that technology transfer would be more sub-optimally performed (i) the more costly information is, (ii) the higher the degree of uncertainty, (iii) the more risk averse managers are, (iv) the less competitive the economy, and (v) the more freedom managers have to engage in non-profit-maximizing behavior. (Both Morley and Smith (1977) and Lecraw (1979) concentrate on factor employment in their discussion of the sub-optimality in technology transfer. We take the liberty to apply their insights more generally.) These conditions likely exist to a greater or lesser extent in the recipient countries. Many types of x-inefficiency are expected to exist. We only mention those we think can be helped by buy-back.

11 For a more thorough discussion and empirical corroboration, see Lecraw (1979). Note that our argument also applies to the expatriates from the transferor's side.

12 It is worth pointing out that attainment of pecuniary targets is easy to 'fake' using creative accounting while to do so for quantitative targets in buy-back is more difficult. Consequently, less search for the type of information mentioned in the text will be conducted when pecuniary targets are imposed instead. The incentive effect of buy-back is lessened when long lead times are required and reinforced by the relatively low job mobility in the recipient countries.

13 We hasten to point out that buy-back is seen as a second-best arrangement- it is desirable because of the existence of sub-optimality in the incentive and organizational structure in the local markets. This point applies also to the next argument and to the discussion in the 'monitoring' sub-section.

14 Similar ideas were advanced as far back as 1974. McMillan and St. Charles (1974) maintained that joint ventures (a business relationship not dissimilar to buy-back) offer the best assurance to Eastern partners that the Western associate will provide production technology, managerial expertise and marketing assistance on a continuing basis.

15 There are two reasons for the absence of an effective system to monitor managerial performance related to economic efficiency. (i) Economic efficiency is hard to scrutinize because prices are not a good representation of value and because the accounting systems in these countries tend to be underdeveloped. (ii) The lack of competitive and value-maximizing investment behavior results in underdevelopment of screening devices to identify inefficient managers.

16 In the economy we are discussing, a worker ordinarily cannot be dismissed by management, and promotion is often based on political performance, relationships with people, and seniority. Wages are fixed by the state and may bear little relation to job performance and to the economic value of the goods and services workers produce.

17 For an indicator of value, we suggest using Tobin's q, i.e., market value/ replacement cost.

[18] As pointed out by one referee, the transferee gains a guaranteed market which lowers the discount rate applicable to future cash flows from the investment in marketing, knowledge and the like. While this should increase the willingness to make such investments, it also slows down the acquisition of international marketing skills.

[19] The O.E.C.D. (1981) estimated that during 1969-1980 there were 290 firm East-West buy-back arrangements with a total value of between $30 and $48 billion. The bumper year was 1976 (pp. 28-32, as well as Tables 1 and 2). See also Zaleski and Wienert (1980), pp. 96-110 and Tables A-33 to A-39, pp. 364-385.

[20] For a good and recent example see Lecraw (1987), b.

REFERENCES

Davidson, William H. and Donald G. McFetridge, (1985) "Key Characteristic in the Choice of International Technology Transfer Mode", *Journal of International Business Studies*, Vol. 16, No. 2, Summer: 5-21.

Gomulka, Stanislaw and Alec Nove, (1984) *East-West Technology Transfer: I-Contribution to Eastern Growth: An Econometric Evaluation*, O.E.C.D. Paris.

Khoury, Sarkis J., (1984) "Countertrade: Forms, Motives, Pitfalls, and Negotiation Requisites", *Journal of Business Research*, Vol. 12 257-270.

Kogut, Bruce, (1986) "On Designing Contracts to Guarantee Enforceability: Evidence from East-West Trade", *Journal of International Business Studies*, Vol. 17, No. 1, Spring: 47-62.

Lecraw, Donald, (1979) "Choice of Technology in Low-Wage Countries: A Non-Neoclassical Approach", *Quarterly Journal of Economics*, Vol. 43, No. 3, Nov.: 631-654.

———, (1987,a) "Countertrade as a Form of International Cooperative Arrangement", in Farok J. Contractor and Peter Lorange (eds.) *Cooperative Strategies in International Business* (Lexington, Mass.): Lexington Books, D.C. Heath & Co.

———, (1987,b) "The Economics and Management of Countertrade: Theory and Evidence", Mimeo, University of Western Ontario.

Mirus, Rolf and Bernard Yeung, (1986) "Economic Incentives for Countertrade", *Journal of International Business Studies*, Vol. 17, No. 13, Fall: 27-39.

McMillan, C.H. and D.P. St. Charles, (1974) "Joint Ventures in East Europe: A Three-Country Comparison", the Canadian Economic Policy Committee, C.D. Howe Research Institute, Canada.

Morley, Samual A. and Gordon Smith, (1977) "Limited Search and the Technology Choices of Multinational Firms in Brazil", *Quarterly Journal of Economics*, Vol. 41, No. 2, May: 263-287.

Murrell, Peter, (1982) "Product Quality, Market Signalling and the Development of East-West Trade", *Economic Inquiry*, Vol. 20, No. 4, Oct.: 589-603.

O.E.C.D., (1981) East-West Trade-Recent Developments in Countertrade", Paris.

Teece, David J., (1977) "Technology Transfer by Multinational Firms: the Resource Cost of Transferring Technology Know-How", *Economic Journal*, Vol. 87, June: 242-261.

White, Lawrence J., (1976) "Appropriate Technology, X-Inefficiency, and A Competitive Environment: Some Evidence from Pakistan", *Quarterly Journal of Economics*, Vol. 40, Nov.: 575-589.

White, Lawrence J., (1978) "The Evidence on Appropriate Factor Proportions for Manufacturing in Less Developed Countries: A Survey", *Economic Development and Cultural Change*, Vol. 27: 27-60.

Williamson, Oliver E., (1979) "Transaction-Cost Economics: The Governance of Contractual Relations", *Journal of Law and Economics*, Vol. 22, No. 2, October: 233-261.

Zaleski, Eugene and Helgard Wienert, (1980) "*Technology Transfer Between East and West*", O.E.C.D., Paris.

Part VIII
Domestic Barter in the Absence of Credible Fiat Money

[21]

The Transition from Barter to Fiat Money

By JOSEPH A. RITTER*

How did it become possible to exchange apparently valueless pieces of paper for goods? This paper provides an equilibrium account of the transition between barter and fiat-money regimes. The explanation relies on the intervention of a self-interested government which must be able to promise credibly to limit the issue of money. To achieve credibility, the government must offset the benefits of seigniorage by internalizing some of the macroeconomic externalities generated by the issue of fiat money. The government's patience and the extent of its involvement in the economy are key determinants of whether the transition can be accomplished. (*JEL* E42)

> "The Mongol IlKhans in Persia, impressed by the use of paper money by their suzerain in China, decided to use the same device themselves. Technical advisers were sent from Peking, and an elaborate organization was set up. The Persians, however, had not been accustomed to the use of paper currency by several hundred years of gradual developments. They simply refused to believe that these nicely printed pieces of paper were worth anything, and the experiment was a failure."
>
> —Gordon Tullock (1957)

How did it become possible to exchange apparently valueless pieces of paper—fiat money—for goods, and why did it take so long for pure fiat money to become prevalent, given the obvious benefits to its issuers? The juxtaposition of these questions at first seems paradoxical. This paper argues that the answers to these two questions are fundamentally linked. The first question has occupied monetary theorists for decades, though much of modern monetary theory has avoided it in favor of one that is closely related but more easily answered: Can an artificial economy be structured in a reasonable way so that there are equilibria in which an apparently worthless commodity has a positive price? The second puzzle has received little attention, though on reflection it is striking that widespread use of purely fiat money is a 20th-century development (Milton Friedman and Anna J. Schwartz, 1986), since the idea and physical implementation are simple.

This paper presents an explicit solution to the first puzzle in a simple artificial economy. In formal terms I ask whether there is an equilibrium transition path between a barter equilibrium and a steady-state monetary equilibrium. The paper also suggests a possible solution to the second, less widely considered puzzle. The answer suggested here is that the money issuer or government must attain a critical level of "credibility" before the transition can take place.

Most economists would probably relate a stylized "history of money" something like the following. As specialization caused problems in coordinating trade, societies naturally settled upon certain commodities, usually metals, as media of exchange. Later, the minting of a certain quantity of a metal into coin acted as a signal of the quantity and purity of the metal. The signals of standardization needed credibility, and the process of standardization was therefore frequently undertaken by governments who had established a reputation for some degree of honesty (which they frequently exploited). From coinage, which was commodity money

*Research Department, The Federal Reserve Bank of St. Louis, P.O. Box 442, St. Louis, MO 63116. I thank Joe Haubrich, Dale Stahl, Charles Swanson, David Wheelock, Leslie Young, and the referees for helpful suggestions and discussions. This paper represents the views of the author and not necessarily those of the Federal Reserve Bank of St. Louis or the Federal Reserve System.

in most senses, it was a relatively small step to substitute the use of paper representing contracts between the bearer and a bank or government. The contract specified payment on demand of a fixed quantity of a commodity (or coin).

From time to time, particularly during periods of crisis, governments suspended convertibility of paper currency (i.e., they reneged on the contract). Why did the currency continue to have value (though it frequently depreciated relative to goods) during such episodes? The obvious answer to this question focuses on the belief that convertibility would soon be restored.[1] While it is an easy matter to verify whether coinage has been debased, it is not easy to verify a government's good intentions or lack thereof. Therefore the government must have already established credibility in some way *before* the episode of inconvertibility so that economic actors have some reason to believe that the suspension is temporary.

The next stage is troubling for monetary theory, though hints of the trouble have already arisen above. Relatively recently in historical terms, governments have renounced even the intention of restoring convertibility of their currencies. Individuals are expected to accept intrinsically worthless pieces of paper, fiat money, in exchange for goods and services. These pieces of paper no longer represent any contract, and there is no expectation that they will in the future. Paradoxically, they continue to be an acceptable medium of exchange. How can such a situation be supported? Obviously, one requirement is that the supply of paper money be limited. The question of the government's credibility again arises, but the government has the conflicting motive of seigniorage. "Credibility" in this context must mean that individuals believe that the government will not attempt to exploit this source of seigniorage to the point where money becomes worthless.

There are, of course, many possible sources of such credibility.[2] Political scientists would point to notions of the legitimacy and stability of the government. Sociologists might imagine a tacit social pact between the government and citizens. Economists are, of course, always inclined to pursue the implications of agents' rational self-interest.

Without denying the importance of other motivations, I follow the latter course and ask under what conditions a policy of limiting the supply of fiat money will be incentive-compatible, given the government's explicit objectives. In the specific model used here, credibility is bestowed upon the government as a consequence of its size and patience. Before a critical size is reached, the government cannot credibly limit its money issue, so the money it issues is worthless. Similarly, if the government is too impatient for seigniorage revenue, its money is worthless. This extends and formalizes a similar argument by Friedman (1959)[3] and follows in the spirit of Friedman and Schwartz's later call for a public-choice perspective on monetary policy. I argue therefore that the transition from a barter economy to a monetary economy can be formally understood as the result of a self-interested intervention by a government which is large relative to the economy.

Section I outlines the model and the barter equilibrium that is assumed to exist

[1] It could be argued that suspension was a well-understood contingency in the contract, but the point is not important in the present context. Michael D. Bordo and Finn E. Kydland (1992) discuss the role of the gold standard as such a contingent rule.

[2] It is possible, of course, to supplement what I am calling credibility with legal restrictions. There are many historical examples of government attempts to use laws to enforce the use of debased or inflated currency. They have usually been unsuccessful in the short run and always unsuccessful in the long run. Since legal restrictions have a long history and fiat money, for the most part, a short one, they have apparently been notably unsuccessful in establishing fiat-money regimes. Also, see footnote 18.

[3] "...[S]ome external limit must be placed on the volume of a fiduciary currency in order to maintain its value. Competition does not provide an effective limit, since the value of the promise to pay, if the currency is to remain fiduciary, must be kept higher than the cost of producing additional units. The production of a fiduciary currency is, as it were, a technical monopoly, and hence, there is no presumption in favor of the private market as there is when competition is feasible" (p. 7).

in the absence of money. Section II describes steady-state monetary equilibria. The proposition that no monetary equilibrium can exist when rational individuals issue money is established in Section III. Section IV demonstrates that coordinated action by a group of agents which is large relative to the economy—a government—can, if certain conditions are met, allow the economy to circumvent problems which prevent existence of a monetary equilibrium when individuals issue money. The artificial economy described here undergoes a transition directly from barter to a fiat-money equilibrium. However, the analysis also sheds light on the historical question of why fiat money had only a sporadic existence until recently, despite obvious advantages to its issuers. Section V discusses this issue in detail in light of the results in Section IV.

I. The Model and Barter Equilibrium

Fiat money is troubling for textbook Walrasian theory because the theory predicts that it will not have value. This is not surprising given the metaphor of a central Walrasian auctioneer who instantaneously reconciles all excess demands in the economy. It is necessary to alter the model in a fundamental way to admit the possibility that a commodity which does not directly produce utility for any agent will have a positive price. In the most well-known such alteration, the overlapping-generations model, money's ability to facilitate current transactions plays no role; instead it makes possible otherwise impossible intergenerational transactions. Other major approaches, cash-in-advance constraints and inclusion of real balances in the utility function, appeal only indirectly to the ability of money to facilitate transactions, but this aspect is kept in the background for simplicity.[4] Thus none of the standard models is appropriate for the study of a monetary transition.

Recently, Nobuhiro Kiyotaki and Randall Wright (1991, 1993) have constructed search models along the lines of Peter Diamond (1982) in which a fixed stock of fiat money can have positive value in a steady-state equilibrium because it allows agents to circumvent the famous problem of the double coincidence of wants. They show that such a monetary equilibrium is quite robust to changes in the environment, including the presence of assets that dominate money in rate of return.[5] The model used here follows in this vein.

The economy consists of an infinite number of agents who live forever. Each agent is periodically endowed with one indivisible unit of one of J different market goods ($J \geq 2$) and derives utility from only one of the J goods and from a nonmarket good. For convenience below, define $x \equiv 1/J$. Agents are uniformly distributed over the J^2 possible types of agents, and the marginal distributions of endowment type and consumption-good type are independent. All agents must trade in order to consume any market good, including those who consume the good with which they are endowed.[6]

In each period, agents decide whether to attempt to trade. If they do not, they consume one unit of the nonmarket good. Each agent who does enter the market is randomly matched with another agent, and they decide whether they wish to trade. If an agent concludes a trade in which he acquires the type of good from which he derives utility, he consumes it immediately and receives a new endowment at the start of the next period.[7] Otherwise he consumes nothing. The holdings of either goods or money (defined below) by agents who do

[4]Robert C. Feenstra (1986) and Dean Croushore (1993) show that money in the utility-function models can be derived from a more primitive shopping technology which *assumes* that real balances make shopping more efficient.

[5]Diamond (1984) also introduces money into a search-theoretic framework in which all transactions are required to use money.

[6]This assumption reduces algebraic clutter considerably without altering the model in any important way. Kiyotaki and Wright (1993) explicitly relax this assumption in their Appendix A.

[7]The "unemployed" state in Diamond's (1982) model in which agents wait for production opportunities is not central here, so it is collapsed.

not attempt to trade or do not successfully trade are unchanged. Thus agents will always have exactly one unit of either money or a market good at the start of the next period.

At time t the expected lifetime utility of an agent is given by

$$V_t = E_t\left\{\sum_{\tau=t}^{\infty} \beta^{\tau} C_{\tau}\right\}$$

where $\beta \in (0,1)$ is a discount factor and

$$C_\tau = \begin{cases} U & \text{if the consumer obtains his market consumption good at time } \tau \\ A & \text{if the consumer consumes the nonmarket good at time } \tau \text{ (autarky)} \\ 0 & \text{otherwise.} \end{cases}$$

The expectation is conditional on the state of the economy and the holdings of the agent at time t.

Money is defined to be an additional commodity which is freely available in indivisible units to any agent at any time. However it may be uniquely differentiated by the issuing agent or group of agents (i.e., counterfeiting is not possible). No agent derives utility directly from money. Money can be issued or goods consumed while an agent carries money or goods, but each agent can carry over only one unit of either goods or money to the next period. As in Kiyotaki and Wright's (1989, 1991, 1993) work, this means that money, if it is used, serves primarily as a medium of exchange and only trivially as a unit of account, since relative prices are constrained by the technology to be either 0 or 1.

Assume initially that there is no money. I will say that a barter equilibrium exists if each agent prefers to attempt trade given that other agents attempt trade. Let V^{B} be the expected utility of an agent in a barter equilibrium. No time subscript is necessary at this point because an agent always goes to the market holding goods and faces the same distribution of potential trading partners. Define b as the probability of meeting another agent with whom barter is possible, that is, the probability an agent of type jk (endowed with j, consumes k) meets an agent of type kj. In a barter equilibrium $b = x^2$ where $x \equiv 1/J$. In a barter equilibrium an agent will successfully trade and get payoff U in the current period with probability b. He returns to the market to play the same game in the following period whether he gets the payoff or not. Thus the following equation determines V^{B}:

$$V^{\mathrm{B}} = b(U + \beta V^{\mathrm{B}}) + (1-b)\beta V^{\mathrm{B}}.$$

This gives

$$V^{\mathrm{B}} = \frac{bU}{1-\beta}.$$

Given that all other agents barter, the agent's Bellman equation is

$$V = \max\{bU + \beta V, A + \beta V\}$$

with the maximization performed over the choice of autarky or barter. I assume that $Ux^2 > A$ so that barter is preferred in every period and $V = V^{\mathrm{B}}$. Consequently, a barter equilibrium exists.

II. Steady-State Monetary Equilibria

A useful starting point in the study of money in this model is to assume an exogenously determined money stock and to ask what conditions allow a steady-state monetary equilibrium to exist. This provides a point of reference with earlier search models (Kiyotaki and Wright, 1991, 1993) and a useful analytical base for the study of equilibria other than steady states. Since the economy is (eventually) to be studied outside steady states, the definition of a monetary equilibrium allows for the explicit treatment of subgames that start in a given period.

Definition: A *monetary equilibrium* (at t) is a sequence of money supplies $\{M_\tau\}_{\tau=t}^{\infty}$ and actions and expectations by agents, such that, given the actions and expectations of all other agents, (i) at least one agent attempts to trade in $\tau \geq t$ and (ii) each agent who trades accepts money in exchange for goods in $\tau \geq t$.

Assume for the moment that there is a constant money supply M, measured as the fraction of the population holding money. How the current money supply M may have gotten into circulation is the central focus of the paper and will be addressed subsequently. Let $V^{M}(M)$ and $V^{G}(M)$ be the expected lifetime utilities of trading agents holding money or goods, respectively, in a monetary equilibrium with a constant money supply M. Let p_t be the probability per period that an agent holding money will be able to *purchase* his consumption good using money, and let s_t be the probability that an agent holding a good will be able to *sell* it for money. In a steady-state monetary equilibrium the constant transition probabilities are $b=(1-M)x^2$, $p=(1-M)x$, and $s=Mx$.[8] The symmetry of the model guarantees that no agent will be made better off by trading either goods or money for a good that he does not consume; these transition probabilities do not depend on the commodity held or desired. This eliminates the usual reasons for the emergence of a particular commodity money. Robert A. Jones (1976), Kiyotaki and Wright (1989), and Seonghwan Oh (1989) construct models in which commodity money arises endogenously.

If a steady-state equilibrium exists with money supply M, the expected lifetime utilities of agents holding money and goods are given by

$$(1)\quad V^{G}(M)=b[U+\beta V^{G}(M)]+s\beta V^{M}(M) + (1-b-s)\beta V^{G}(M)$$

$$(2)\quad V^{M}(M)=p[U+\beta V^{G}(M)] + (1-p)\beta V^{M}(M).$$

These equations imply

$$(3)\quad V^{G}(M) = (1-M)\left[1+\frac{\beta M(1-x)}{1-\beta(1-x)}\right]V^{B}$$

and a similar expression for $V^{M}(M)$. It will be useful later to notice that while $V^{G}(M)$ and $V^{M}(M)$ are quadratic in M, their difference is linear in M:

$$(4)\quad V^{M}(M)-V^{G}(M) = \frac{p-b}{1-\beta(1-p-s)}U=(1-M)\psi$$

where $\psi>0$ depends only on U, x (or J), and β.

The conditions under which a steady-state monetary equilibrium exists are characterized by the following proposition.

PROPOSITION 1: *If the money supply is fixed at M from t onward, there is an $\bar{M}<1$ such that a monetary equilibrium exists at t if and only if $M \leq \bar{M}$.*

PROOF:

In the case of constant money supply it is sufficient to show that for an appropriate $\bar{M}$: (i) goods-holders will enter the market when $M \leq \bar{M}$ and will not enter when $M > \bar{M}$ and (ii) money-holders will enter the market whenever goods-holders choose to enter. (They obviously do not enter when goods-holders do not.)

Since the economy is in a steady state, it is sufficient for part (i) to show that it is not optimal to consume the reservation good in the current period, that is,

$$V^{G}(M) > A+\beta V^{G}(M)$$

[8]The probability p, for example, is the product of the probability $(1-M)$ that the agent will meet someone holding goods times the probability x that the agent will meet someone who is endowed with the good he consumes. These formulas become more complicated in later sections, but I keep the same b, p, s notation for barter, purchase, and sale probabilities.

if and only if $M < \overline{M}$ for some $\overline{M}$. Since $V^{G}(M)$ is quadratic and concave in M, greater than $A/(1-\beta)$ when $M=0$, and equal to zero when $M=1$, it follows that an appropriate $\overline{M}$ exists.

Part (ii) requires that

$$V^{M}(M) \geq A + \beta V^{M}(M).$$

if $M < \overline{M}$. This follows from the fact that $V^{M}(M) > V^{G}(M) > A/(1-\beta)$ by (4) and part (i) of the proof.

The intuition behind Proposition 1 is simple: When an equilibrium exists, agents accept money because other agents accept money, but as the money supply increases, it becomes easier to trade goods for money but harder to trade money for goods. Thus if the proportion of the population holding money is too high, on average it takes too long to find goods for market activity to be worthwhile, so autarky is preferred. This phenomenon is just a specialized version of "too much money chasing too few goods" in a stylized model where inflation cannot occur.

III. Laissez-Faire Money

Can a monetary equilibrium be generated by the actions of rational individuals issuing money? An agent holding goods who meets someone with whom he cannot barter, but who is holding his consumption good, will always have an incentive to issue money. Not surprisingly, this causes any potential monetary equilibrium to collapse because too much money is issued. Since individual decisions do not result in "the social contrivance of money," this provides a role for the institution—a government—which is introduced in the next section.

PROPOSITION 2: *There is no monetary equilibrium in which agents issue money individually.*

PROOF:

There are two varieties of potential equilibria to be considered. Either all agents issue undifferentiated money, or agents accept differentiated money issued by a fraction α of all agents. The first is formally equivalent to the second when $\alpha = 1$, so no distinction need be maintained. An agent of type jk carrying good j who meets an agent of type ki carrying good k with $i \neq j$ issues money if he is in the subset of agents whose money is accepted since this results in a utility gain of U. The difference equation that governs the evolution of the money supply under this process is:

$$(5) \qquad M_{t+1} = M_t + \alpha m_t(1-M_t)$$

where $m_t = (1-M_t)x(1-x)$ is the probability that an agent carrying goods will wish to issue money.[9] The last term in (5) is the proportion of agents carrying goods $(1-M_t)$ who can issue valuable money (α) and who will meet an agent carrying the good they wish to consume, but with whom barter is not possible (m_t). Clearly M_t converges to 1. As M_t converges to 1, m_t, p_t, and b_t each converge to 0. Since the agents consume only if one of the corresponding events occurs, utility of both goods and money-holders converges to 0 as well. Since utility of $A/(1-\beta)$ can be obtained in the reservation activity, at some time goods-holders must cease to enter the market, and money becomes worthless. The well-known backward-induction argument implies that it could not have had value in any previous period.

Proposition 2 can be interpreted as the consequence of a kind of coordination failure: the average agent would be better off with a positive amount of money in circulation,[10] yet because individuals do not consider the aggregate externality they impose by issuing money, this outcome is not supported by individual rationality. Thus valued money cannot arise endogenously with-

[9] This probability m_t later becomes more complicated, but, as for b, p, and s, I will keep the same notation for analogous quantities.

[10] If $2\beta(1-x) > 1$, *every* agent would be made unambiguously better off by the introduction of at least a small amount of money.

out adding more structure to the model. Since the model (which is essentially the same in this respect as Kiyotaki and Wright's [1991] model) contains no mechanism for attaining the steady-state equilibrium, it is incomplete in an important sense. The way in which the model is completed has important implications for existence of a monetary equilibrium and the welfare of agents in the equilibrium.

IV. Government Money

The previous sections showed that while in principle a monetary equilibrium can exist in this economy when there is a small enough fixed money supply, individuals' self-interest cannot accomplish the transition from barter equilibrium to a steady-state monetary equilibrium. This section introduces a government which provides a mechanism that allows the transition to occur.

The government is formally modeled as a coalition of otherwise unremarkable agents.[11] This is not intended as a definitive model of government, but only as a vehicle to give substance to two crucial aspects of the problem which would otherwise be too ill-defined to allow progress: the government's objectives and the notion of credibility. Indeed, there is no theoretical reason why this coalition should be called a government; it serves none of the other functions usually associated with a government. There is no theoretical reason, for example, why this could not represent a large bank whose goal is to maximize the private gains from issuing notes. Friedman and Schwartz (1986 p. 45) report, however, that they "do not know...of any example of the private production of purely inconvertible fiduciary moneys." Moreover, given the obvious benefits of fiat money, it is hardly surprising that governments have given themselves legal monopolies in its production.

To be specific, I assume that, for reasons outside the scope of the model, a coalition of agents exists encompassing a fraction $\alpha > 0$ of the population and uniformly distributed over the J^2 types. This coalition is called "the government." Only one such coalition forms.[12] Such a monopoly might arise for historical or political reasons, and seigniorage would provide one strong incentive to establish and maintain it. The structure and objectives of the government are known to all agents. There is nothing special about the interaction of these agents with the rest of the economy except that they can issue money which is identified with the government and that they act in concert. The government does not levy taxes, and it does not have a monopoly on a particular good. It has, however, the ability to limit the issue of money by individual members. This ability to act collectively to limit money issue (i.e., as a monolithic entity) distinguishes the government from the fraction α of the population hypothesized in the proof of Proposition 2. The fact that the government is large in relation to the rest of the economy suggests that it may have an incentive to limit the amount of money issued by the coalition so that a monetary equilibrium will not collapse.

Naturally, this is a very narrow view of the nature and function of government, but it has at least two benefits. First, its symmetry makes it technically tractable. Second, it gives the government no advantage in the issue of money other than the ability of the coalition members to act collectively or, equivalently, its size (it can be treated as a single agent). In particular, the government has no comparative advantage in the sale or purchase of a particular subset of goods. It

[11] S. Rao Aiyagari and Neil Wallace (1993) use a similar construct to study the effects of government intervention on welfare and uniqueness of equilibrium in a search-theoretic model of money.

[12] Though the government is formally modeled as a coalition of agents, the term I have chosen for this coalition emphasizes that it should be regarded here as a single monolithic political entity whose formation is outside the scope of this paper. An interesting alternative would be to study an equilibrium in which both the number and size of coalitions were allowed to be endogenous as an attempt to understand why there are different national monies.

will become apparent below that size endows the government with a limited kind of credibility. The structure imposed thus emphasizes that it is size (credibility) alone which allows the government to overcome the coordination failure which otherwise prevents the establishment of a monetary equilibrium in this economy.

At the time the government becomes active in monetary affairs ($t = 0$), the economy is still in a barter equilibrium since, as shown in the previous section, a monetary equilibrium cannot be established without it. The government chooses a monetary policy which maximizes the expected welfare of a representative member. *Ex ante* all members are identical except that they hold and consume different goods, so this policy also maximizes individual members' expected utility. Since the government's size and composition are exogenously determined, I do not address the issues surrounding internal incentives; with respect to the issuing of money, the government coalition *by assumption* acts collectively.

The government chooses a sequence of values of μ_t, the proportion of its members permitted to issue money, with money-issuing licenses allocated randomly if $0 < \mu_t < 1$. An agent with a license to issue money will wish to do so if he is not already holding money and meets a trader who has a good he wishes to purchase but with whom barter is impossible.[13] Proposition 3 characterizes the shape of the optimal money-supply path and greatly simplifies later analysis.

PROPOSITION 3: *The government's optimal path of M_t will follow*

$$M_{t+1} = M_t + \mu_t \alpha m_t (1 - M_t)$$

with

$$(6) \qquad \mu_t = \begin{cases} 1 & t < T \\ 0 \le \mu_t \le 1 & t = T \\ 0 & t > T \end{cases}$$

for some finite $T \ge 0$. In other words, the government prefers to increase the money supply from zero to a steady-state value M as rapidly as possible. Moreover, $0 \le M \le \overline{M}$.

PROOF:

In this model, seigniorage is the additional consumption that results from the ability to consume sooner than if it were not possible to issue money. Therefore since $\beta < 1$, it is optimal to issue money as soon as possible.[14] The fact that $M \le \overline{M}$ follows from the fact that a steady-state monetary equilibrium exists only if the money supply is less than or equal to $\overline{M}$.

Thus the optimal monetary policy is a transition path of finite length to a steady-state monetary equilibrium. Proposition 3 does not provide any reason to think that $M > 0$ is feasible for the government (that traders will accept money), only that, if it is feasible, money is issued as rapidly as possible. Along the transition path, individual members of the coalition are permitted to issue money at will until the last period of the transition path when only a fraction of the members may issue money. In period T, licenses to issue money are randomly awarded only to the fraction of the coalition's members required to reach the money-supply target. Thus if m_t is the probability that a coalition member will want to issue money, the probability μ_t of a coalition member being permitted to issue money is set so that $M_{t+1} - M_t = \alpha \mu_t m_t (1 - M_t)$.

A. *Monetary Equilibria with Binding Precommitment*

When precommitment is possible, Proposition 3 allows the government's planning

[13] The member of the government would be indifferent between barter and money issue, but the trading partner would not be. I assume therefore that if barter is possible it takes place.

[14] If agents were risk-averse, there would be an incentive to spread out the benefits of issuing money over a longer period.

problem to be reduced to choice of a steady-state money supply M:

$$(7)\quad \max_{M} W_0(M) = \sum_{t=0}^{\infty} \beta^t [M_t p_t + (1 - M_t) \times (b_t + \mu_t m_t)] U$$

subject to

$$M_{t+1} = M_t + \mu_t \alpha m_t (1 - M_t)$$

with μ_t defined as in Proposition 3 ($\mu_t = 1$ before M_t reaches M and $\mu_t = 0$ after). Denote the solution to (7) by M^*. A natural conjecture at this point is that the government by virtue of its size has an incentive to limit money issue sufficiently that a monetary equilibrium can exist. This conjecture turns out to be correct. The proof requires the following lemma, whose proof is conceptually straightforward but algebraically tedious and therefore presented in the Appendix.

LEMMA 1: *Along any path of the money supply which satisfies Proposition 3, goods-holders and money-holders will prefer market activity to the reservation activity.*

PROPOSITION 4: *When the government can irrevocably commit itself to a monetary policy, the money-supply path induced by solving (7) is a monetary equilibrium.*

PROOF:

It is sufficient to show that the solution to (7) is characterized by $M^* \leq \overline{M}$ since Lemma 1 guarantees that agents will be willing to attempt trade at any point along the transition path. Since $M^* > \overline{M}$ results in valueless money, the value to the government of such a strategy would be $W_0(M^*) = V^{\mathrm{B}}$; the barter equilibrium would persist. It may be easily verified, however, that $(1 - M)V^{\mathrm{G}}(M) + MV^{\mathrm{M}}(M)$ has a positive derivative at $M = 0$, so given that $V^{\mathrm{G}}(0) = V^{\mathrm{B}}$, it is apparent that there is at least one $M > 0$ to which the government could commit itself that would make it better off.

B. *Monetary Equilibria without Precommitment*

The ability to precommit is equivalent to an assumption that the government is unable to issue money once it reaches the money supply that solves (7). If this assumption is relaxed, the nature of the game played between the government and the public is more complicated, because the government's plan may be dynamically inconsistent.

Consider a monetary equilibrium in the model with precommitment. In the subgame that begins in period $T+1$ the money supply is constant at M^*. If precommitment is not possible, it is necessary to determine whether a constant money supply M^* that solves (7) is a Nash equilibrium of this subgame. If M^* is an equilibrium of the subgame, Lemma 1 will then guarantee that the entire path is a monetary equilibrium; that is, the solution to (7) is subgame perfect. By construction M^* is the best value less than $\overline{M}$ and therefore is the government's best option among the class described by Proposition 3. However, the government has another choice: once M^* is achieved, drive the economy back to barter by issuing more money. This is a perfect-foresight model, so in the absence of precommitment this option must not be preferred by the government if money is to have value. Proposition 5 adds the condition required for a monetary equilibrium without precommitment.

PROPOSITION 5: *In the absence of binding precommitment, the path for the money supply induced by solving (7) is a monetary equilibrium if and only if the solution M^* satisfies*

$$(8)\quad V^{\mathrm{B}} \leq W^* \equiv (1 - M^*)V^{\mathrm{G}}(M^*) + M^* V^{\mathrm{M}}(M^*).$$

PROOF:

Since M^* solves (7), rational agents foresee that only the prospect of driving the

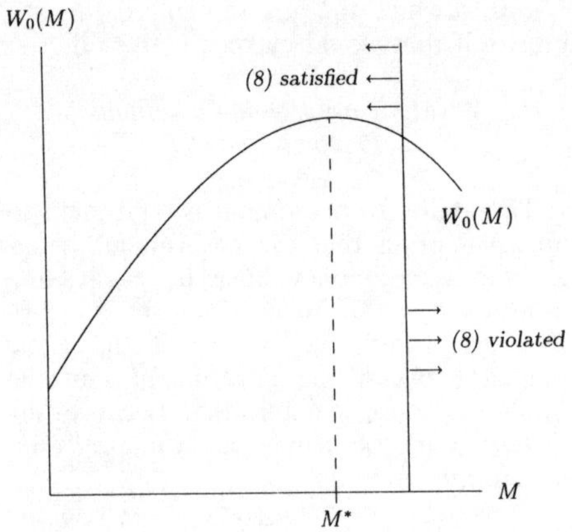

FIGURE 1. MONETARY EQUILIBRIUM EXISTS

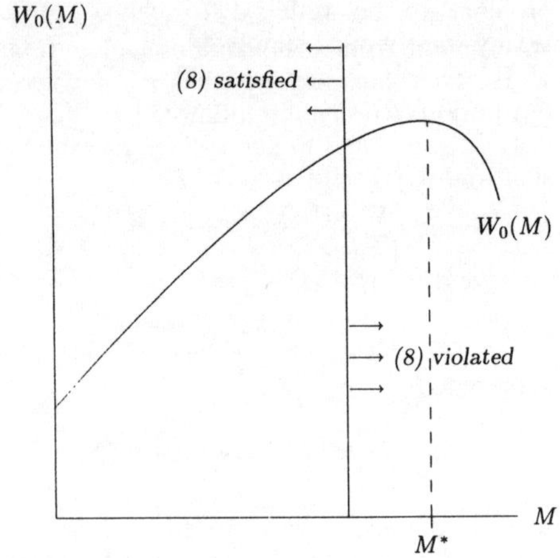

FIGURE 2. MONETARY EQUILIBRIUM DOES NOT EXIST

economy back to barter might induce the government to issue more money. Therefore this is the only kind of deviation from the proposed Nash equilibrium (of the subgame) that must be considered. If the government does issue more money, traders will no longer accept money, since it will ultimately be worthless. W^* is the subgame utility of the government if it does not issue more money. Suppose first that $W^* < V^{\mathrm{B}}$. Since money becomes worthless immediately (so there is no transition path), the government achieves subgame utility V^{B}, and as $W^* < V^{\mathrm{B}}$, the government prefers this outcome. Hence M^* is not a Nash equilibrium of the subgame, and no monetary equilibrium exists. Suppose instead that $W^* > V^{\mathrm{B}}$. For the same reasons, there would be no transition path if the government chose to issue more money, so again the government achieves V^{B} by issuing additional money. Now, however, the government has no incentive to deviate from the proposed equilibrium. In this case, Lemma 1 guarantees that the money-supply path is a monetary equilibrium.

Figure 1 shows an example of a monetary equilibrium at M^*. Along the vertical line, (8) is satisfied with equality. Figure 2 illustrates a case in which the monetary equilibrium does not exist. If binding precommitment were possible, the government would choose to issue M^*, but this choice is not dynamically consistent; traders will realize that once the money supply is M^*, it is in the government's interest to force the economy back to barter by making money worthless.

Proposition 5 provides only implicit answers to the questions posed in the Introduction. More explicit statements require a closer examination of the behavior of the solution to (7) as parameter values vary. A necessary condition for $M^* \leq \bar{M}$ to be optimal is that the government does not have an incentive to issue a small additional amount of money. The appropriate derivative is somewhat more complicated than it would be for a simple comparison of steady states. Suppose that M^* is reached at T. Starting from a baseline with $M_T = M_{T+1} = M_{T+2} = \cdots = M$, does the government wish to increase the money supply during period T? This would change $M_{T+1}, M_{T+2}, \ldots$, but not M_T. The appropriate necessary condition is

$$\frac{\partial W_T(M_T, M_{T+1}, M_{T+1}, \ldots)}{\partial M_{T+1}} = 0$$

where the derivative is evaluated at $M_T =$

$M_{T+1} = M^*$, where W_T is the welfare of the government from the standpoint of period T. By exploiting the fact that W_T involves one period of transition followed by a steady state, it is possible to get an explicit expression to differentiate:

$$\begin{aligned} W_T(&M_T, M_{T+1}, M_{T+1}, \ldots) \\ &= M_T W_T^{\mathrm{M}}(M_T, M_{T+1}, M_{T+1}, \ldots) \\ &\quad + (1 - M_T) W_T^{\mathrm{G}}(M_T, M_{T+1}, M_{T+1}, \ldots) \\ &= M_T\big[p_T U + p_T \beta V^{\mathrm{G}}(M_{T+1}) \\ &\qquad + (1 - p_T)\beta V^{\mathrm{M}}(M_{T+1})\big] \\ &\quad + (1 - M_T)\big[(b_T + \mu_T m_T)U \\ &\qquad + s_T \beta V^{\mathrm{M}}(M_{T+1}) \\ &\qquad + (1 - s_T)\beta V^{\mathrm{G}}(M_{T+1})\big] \\ &= \left[M_t p_T + (1 - M_T) b_T + \frac{1}{\alpha}(M_{T+1} - M_T)\right] U \\ &\quad + \beta V^{\mathrm{G}}(M_{T+1}) \\ &\quad - M_{T+1}\beta\big[V^{\mathrm{G}}(M_{T+1}) - V^{\mathrm{M}}(M_{T+1})\big] \end{aligned}$$

where $W_T^{\mathrm{M}}(\cdot)$ and $W_T^{\mathrm{G}}(\cdot)$ are the expected utilities of coalition members holding money and goods, respectively, at time T. (These differ from the utilities of nonmembers because of the possibility of seigniorage.) The last equality makes use of the facts that $\mu_t m_t = (M_{T+1} - M_t)/[\alpha(1 - M_t)]$ and $s_t = xM_t + \alpha\mu_t m_t$ since the probability of a goods-holder meeting the appropriate kind of money-holder is xM_t, and the probability that he will meet a coalition member who wants to and is allowed to issue money is $\alpha\mu_t m_t$. Performing the differentiation and letting ψ be the same constant defined in (4), the necessary condition is:[15]

$$0 = \frac{1}{\alpha} U + \beta V^{\mathrm{G}\prime}(M) + \beta\psi(1 - 2M).$$

Solving the equation for M yields

$$(9)\quad M^* = \frac{1}{2}\left(\frac{1-2x}{1-x}\right) + \frac{1}{2\alpha}\left(\frac{1}{x(1-x)}\right)\left(\frac{1-\beta}{\beta}\right).$$

Condition (8) is satisfied with equality at $(1-2x)/(1-x) = (J-2)/(J-1)$, where J is the number of goods. According to Proposition 5, an equilibrium exists if and only if $M^* < (J-2)/(J-1)$. Therefore, combining (8) and (9), an equilibrium exists if and only if the parameters α and β lie in the region

$$(10)\qquad \beta \geq \frac{1}{1 + \alpha\left(\frac{J-2}{J^2}\right)}.$$

with $\alpha \leq 1$ and $\beta \leq 1$ as usual. This relationship is shown in Figure 3.[16]

Proposition 6 highlights two particularly interesting applications of (10) which are apparent from Figure 3.

PROPOSITION 6: *(i) For $J > 2$ there is a $\beta_{\min} \in (0, 1)$ such that an equilibrium does not exist for any α if $\beta < \beta_{\min}$. (ii) Given $J > 2$ and $\beta \in [\beta_{\min}, 1)$, there is an $\alpha_{\min}(\beta) \in (0, 1]$ such that an equilibrium exists if and only if $\alpha \geq \alpha_{\min}(\beta)$. (An equilibrium does not exist for $J = 2$.)*

Impatience increases the value of the short-term payoff of seigniorage relative to steady-state payoffs with the result that a government is more likely to desire a money supply that violates (8). Thus even when α is large, an equilibrium exists only for high values of β (low rates of time preference).

[15] It is easily verified that this is a maximum.

[16] Written in terms of the rate of time preference ρ, the boundary is linear; $\rho \leq \alpha(J-2)/J^2$.

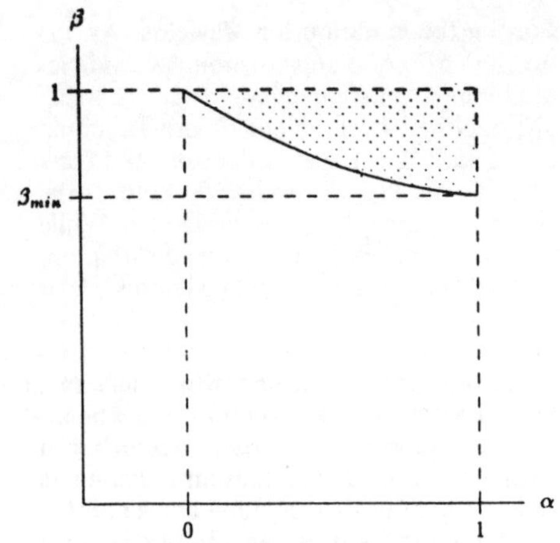

FIGURE 3. MONETARY EQUILIBRIUM EXISTS FOR PARAMETERS IN STIPPLED REGION

Proposition 6 suggests an answer to the second question posed in the Introduction. Whether the government has enough credibility in this economy to issue fiat money is determined by the interplay of its impatience (β) and its size (α). If the government is too impatient, it cannot credibly promise to restrict the money supply, so its currency will have no value regardless of its size [part (i)]. Even if the rate of time preference is low, the steady-state money supply desired by a government that is smaller than $\alpha_{\min}(\beta)$ still does not satisfy the time-consistency constraint (8) [part (ii)]. Since the government cannot credibly limit the money supply, agents will not accept its money. The more general lesson is clear: individuals must believe that the lure of additional seigniorage is offset by some other interest before they will accept unbacked currency. In this paper the internalization of macroeconomic externalities generated by issuing money provides the offsetting interest; the government recognizes that its steady-state utility will be measurably lower if it issues more money.

Even in the restrictive framework developed in this paper, it is not difficult to imagine why fiat currency was a relatively late development. The discount factor plays a powerful role in the model. If the government is too eager to extract resources via seigniorage, other considerations do not even come into play. The absence of effective tax-collection systems, especially when it is a consequence of political instability, can be plausibly interpreted in this way, since the government would be forced to exploit the printing press if it were available. However, a low rate of time preference is not by itself a sufficient condition for existence of an equilibrium. In addition the government must internalize a sufficiently large share of the aggregate externality generated by issuing money. For a strictly self-interested government like the one analyzed, this requirement translates into size, but if, for example, the government were motivated to maximize the expected utility of all agents, its objective function would internalize the externality entirely.

It can be shown that the first term on the right-hand side of (9) is the value of M that maximizes steady-state welfare. Note that the monetary policy that maximizes social welfare is obtained when $\alpha = 1$ (i.e., when the government is the grand coalition and maximizes the welfare of the representative citizen). Equation (9) then contains two important and intuitively appealing welfare implications of this model. First, because society values seigniorage, the socially optimal monetary policy leads to a steady-state money supply that is higher than that which maximizes steady-state welfare. Kiyotaki and Wright (1993), for example, derive the latter. Second, it is obvious from (9) that when $\alpha < 1$, the government will issue more than the socially optimal quantity of money if an equilibrium exists; it does not fully internalize the aggregate externality generated by issuing money but captures all social gains from seigniorage. This is really just a weaker version of the problem, which leads to absence of an equilibrium if α is too small and appears to be a robust implication of a public-choice approach to money.

V. Discussion

The direct transition from barter to fiat money modeled in this paper appears at first glance to be counterfactual in two ways.

The historical evolution of money is generally thought to proceed from barter to commodity money to fiat money, and the transition has been punctuated by many reversals. The theoretical results should, therefore, be interpreted in light of the following observations about the relationship between reality and the theory.

First, a commodity-money regime is really nothing more than a barter equilibrium that is asymmetric in the sense that a particular good is universally acceptable. As Karl Menger (1892), Jones (1976), Kiyotaki and Wright (1989), and Oh (1989) have argued, the transition from barter to commodity money can be understood as a natural outgrowth of individual interests in the exchange process. Fiat-money equilibria, on the other hand, seem very unlikely to arise in such a way. Indeed Proposition 2 demonstrates that, in the present model at least, they are impossible.[17] When the transition to fiat money occurs one faces a puzzle: how does a situation arise in which people willingly accept an item with zero fundamental value in exchange for goods? It seems reasonable that at least some aspects of the answer may be shared by transitions from both symmetric and asymmetric barter.

Second, the irregular transition and the long delay before the appearance of pure fiat money could be interpreted as a symptom of the uncertainty surrounding a fiat-money equilibrium. In the real world, individuals lack perfect foresight, so they face a signal-extraction problem: how to weigh the government's promises to restrict the amount of unbacked currency. A new government may have a "honeymoon period," which it can perhaps extend by a period of conservative monetary policy and by legal restrictions on the use of other monies, but when the government attempts to exploit this source of revenue, perhaps because of changing preferences or circumstances, evidence accumulates against it, and agents' valuation of the currency changes. As the government repudiates its promises, individuals repudiate its currency.[18]

Third, the development of private banking resulted in the use of deposits and bank notes as media of exchange before the widespread appearance of fiat money. While this is a crucial facet of the overall development of modern payments systems, it is important to recognize that private bank notes and deposits represent claims on an underlying monetary standard.[19] Therefore, the same question (once removed) arises for bank money: how did it become possible to exchange claims on apparently valueless pieces of paper—fiat money—for goods?

These consideration would complicate a formal model but do not diminish the central thrust of this paper: a transition to unbacked money can be accomplished, even in a perfect-foresight economy, if and only if the government has some means of making credible its promise to restrict the use of the printing press.

[17] Benjamin Klein (1974) comes to the opposite conclusion, but in a model in which competitive money-issuing firms are able to precommit to a particular money-supply path.

[18] A fascinating example of a punctuated transition to fiat money can be found in the monetary history of ancient China. The Chinese were apparently the first to invent paper money and to make it inconvertible. Tullock (1957) and Lien-sheng Yang (1952) describe the repetition over several hundred years of a cycle in which fiat money became almost worthless through "the use of inflation for budgetary purposes" (Tullock, 1957 p. 395) and was eventually replaced by new money issued by a new dynasty. Chinese governments experimented with a number of techniques to support and promote the use of fiat money by constraining either themselves or the public, but as Tullock notes, "Any effect they may have had, however, was more than canceled out by the activities of the government mint" (p. 399), and "the use of paper money was, in each case, eventually abandoned" (p. 396). Ultimately, after this repeated failure, the Ming dynasty in the 15th century A.D. quit trying to issue fiat money.

[19] To the extent that banks hold only fractional reserves of the prevailing currency or coin, these claims may be risky and therefore not perfect substitutes for currency, but the banks' liability is not limited to reserves. In the absence of deposit insurance, market perception that assets are not sufficient to cover liabilities causes a run on the bank.

VI. Conclusion

This paper provides an equilibrium account of the transition between barter and fiat-money regimes. The explanation relies on the intervention of a self-interested (though not necessarily nonaltruistic) government which must be able to promise credibly to limit the issue of money. In the model used here, a government achieves this credibility by internalizing some of the macroeconomic externalities generated by the use of fiat money, thus offsetting the benefits of seigniorage. The key determinants of the government's ability to issue fiat money are the government's patience for revenue and the extent of the government's involvement in the economy, both of which could take a long time to mature. The paper thus provides, simultaneously, an account of the transition to fiat money and a possible explanation for its delayed appearance. These questions have previously received almost no attention in monetary theory.

Appendix

PROOF OF LEMMA 1:

The proof of Lemma 1 proceeds by using backward induction to demonstrate that $V_t^{\mathrm{G}}(M_t, \ldots, M_{T-1}, M, M, \ldots)$ and $V_t^{\mathrm{M}}(M_t, \ldots, M_{T-1}, M, M, \ldots)$, the time-$t$ expected utilities of goods- and money-holders who attempt trade given that other agents attempt trade, are in fact the maximum attainable utilities for agents holding goods and money, respectively. In other words it will not be optimal in any period t to deviate from the strategy of attempting to trade. The arguments to V_t^{G} and V_t^{M} are suppressed subsequently.

Two strictly algebraic results are established first. The non-steady-state counterparts of (1) and (2) are:

$$V_t^{\mathrm{G}} = b_t U + s_t \beta (V_{t+1}^{\mathrm{M}} - V_{t+1}^{\mathrm{G}}) + \beta V_{t+1}^{\mathrm{G}}$$

$$V_t^{\mathrm{M}} = p_t U - p_t \beta (V_{t+1}^{\mathrm{M}} - V_{t+1}^{\mathrm{G}}) + \beta V_{t+1}^{\mathrm{M}}.$$

Subtracting, substituting recursively, and

$$\begin{aligned}
\text{(A1)}\quad V_t^{\mathrm{M}} - V_t^{\mathrm{G}} &= (p_t - b_t)U + (1 - p_t - s_t)\beta(V_{t+1}^{\mathrm{M}} - V_{t+1}^{\mathrm{G}}) \\
&= (p_t - b_t)U + (1 - p_t - s_t)\beta\{(p_{t+1} - b_{t+1})U \\
&\quad + (1 - p_{t+1} - s_{t+1})\beta[(p_{t+2} - b_{t+2})U + \cdots \\
&\quad + (1 - p_{T-1} - s_{T-1})\beta(V^{\mathrm{M}}(M) - V^{\mathrm{G}}(M))]\cdots\} \\
&= (p_t - b_t)U + (1 - p_t - s_t)\beta\Bigg\{(p_{t+1} - b_{t+1})U \\
&\quad + (1 - p_{t+1} - s_{t+1})\beta\Bigg[(p_{t+2} - b_{t+2})U + \cdots \\
&\quad + (1 - p_{T-1} - s_{T-1})\beta\Bigg((p - b)U \sum_{q=0}^{\infty} [\beta(1 - p - s)]^q\Bigg)\Bigg]\cdots\Bigg\}
\end{aligned}$$

applying Proposition 3, one obtains equation (A1), at the bottom of the preceding page, where b, p, and s are the respective steady-state transition probabilities (as in Section II) and where the last equality is obtained using (4). Noting that $p-b \leq p_{t+i}-b_{t+i}$ for $t+i \leq T$ and $1-p_t-s_t \leq 1-p_{t+j}-s_{t+j}$ for $j \geq 1$, then,

$$\text{(A2)} \quad V_t^{\mathrm{M}} - V_t^{\mathrm{G}} > (p-b)U \sum_{j=0}^{\infty} [\beta(1-p_t-s_t)]^j = \frac{(p-b)U}{1-\beta(1-p_t-s_t)} = \frac{(1-M)x(1-x)U}{1-\beta(1-x)[1-\alpha x(1-M_t)]}.$$

Noting that $p_t - b_t \geq p_{t+i} - b_{t+i}$ for $i > 0$ and $1-p-s \geq 1-p_{t+i}-s_{t+i}$ for $t+i \leq T$,

$$\text{(A3)} \quad V_t^{\mathrm{M}} - V_t^{\mathrm{G}} < \frac{(p_t-b_t)U}{1-\beta(1-p-s)} = (1-M_t)\psi.$$

Turning now to the main argument, recall that money supply M is reached in period T. Since $M \leq \overline{M}$, Proposition 1 guarantees that it is optimal for both goods- and money-holders to trade in T. Thus $V^{\mathrm{G}}(M)$ and $V^{\mathrm{M}}(M)$ are the maximum utilities unattainable at T.

As an inductive hypothesis, assume that in $t+1 \leq T$, V_{t+1}^{G} and V_{t+1}^{M} are the maximum attainable utilities for agents who are not part of the government. The Bellman equation at t for a goods-holder not part of the government is

$$V_t = \max\{A + \beta V_{t+1}^{\mathrm{G}}, V_t^{\mathrm{G}}\}$$

where the maximization is over the choice of whether to attempt trade or to consume the reservation good.

Clearly a goods-holder attempts trade if

$$G_t^{\mathrm{G}} \equiv b_t U + s_t \beta (V_{t+1}^{\mathrm{M}} - V_{t+1}^{\mathrm{G}}) > A.$$

Using (A2), one obtains equation (A4), below. Then, defining $\bar{b}$ and $\bar{s}$ as the respective steady-state transition probabilities when $M = \overline{M}$,

$$\begin{aligned} G_t^{\mathrm{G}} - A &> b_t U + xM_t\beta(1-\overline{M})\psi - [\bar{b}U + \bar{s}\beta(1-\overline{M})\psi] \\ &= (1-M_t-1+\overline{M})x^2U + (M_t-\overline{M})\beta(1-\overline{M})\psi \\ &= (\overline{M}-M_t)[x^2U - x\beta(1-\overline{M})\psi] \\ &= (\overline{M}-M_t)\frac{1}{\overline{M}}[\overline{M}x^2U - (A-\bar{b}U)] \\ &= (\overline{M}-M_t)\frac{1}{\overline{M}}[x^2U - A] \\ &> 0. \end{aligned}$$

$$\begin{aligned} \text{(A4)} \quad G_t^{\mathrm{G}} &> b_t U + s_t\beta\frac{(1-M)x(1-x)U}{1-\beta(1-x)[1-\alpha x(1-M_t)]} \\ &= b_tU + \beta(1-M)x(1-x)U\frac{M_t x + \alpha x(1-x)(1-M_t)}{1-\beta(1-x)+\beta\alpha x(1-x)(1-M_t)} \\ &> b_tU + \beta(1-M)x(1-x)U\frac{M_t x}{1-\beta(1-x)} \\ &= b_tU + xM_t\beta(1-M)\psi \\ &> b_tU + xM_t\beta(1-\overline{M})\psi \end{aligned}$$

Thus V_t^{G} is the maximum utility at t of a trader holding goods.

The Bellman equation for a money-holder not in the government is

$$V_t = \max\{A + \beta V_{t+1}^{\mathrm{M}}, V_t^{\mathrm{M}}\}$$

where again the maximization is performed over the actions of attempting trade and consuming the reservation good. The money-holder chooses to attempt trade if

$$G_t^{\mathrm{M}} \equiv p_t U - p_t \beta (V_{t+1}^{\mathrm{M}} - V_{t+1}^{\mathrm{G}}) > A.$$

Using (A3),

$$G_t^{\mathrm{M}} > p_t U + (1 - M_{t+1})\psi$$

$$> p_{t+1} U + (1 - M_{t+1})\psi.$$

The last quantity is the gain to money-holders from trade in a steady-state equilibrium with money supply $M_{t+1} < \overline{M}$ and is therefore greater than A.

Finally observe that members of the government are always at least as well off as nonmembers.

REFERENCES

Aiyagari, S. Rao, and Wallace, Neil. "Government Transactions, Policy, and the Medium of Exchange." Federal Reserve Bank of Minneapolis Working Paper No. 516, 1993.

Bordo, Michael D. and Kydland, Finn E. "The Gold Standard as a Rule." Federal Reserve Bank of Cleveland Working Paper No. 9205, 1992.

Croushore, Dean. "Money in the Utility Function: Functional Equivalence to a Shopping-Time Model." *Journal of Macroeconomics*, Winter 1993, *15*(1), pp. 175–82.

Diamond, Peter. "Aggregate Demand Management in Search Equilibrium." *Journal of Political Economy*, October 1982, *90*(5), pp. 881–94.

______. "Money in Search Equilibrium." *Econometrica*, January 1984, *52*(1), pp. 1–20.

Feenstra, Robert C. "Functional Equivalence Between Liquidity Costs and the Utility of Money." *Journal of Monetary Economics*, March 1986, *17*(2), pp. 271–91.

Friedman, Milton. *A program for monetary stability*. New York: Fordham University Press, 1959.

Friedman, Milton and Schwartz, Anna J. "Has Government Any Role in Money?" *Journal of Monetary Economics*, January 1986, *17*(1), pp. 37–62.

Jones, Robert A. "The Origin and Development of Media of Exchange." *Journal of Political Economy*, August 1976, *84*(4), pp. 757–75.

Kiyotaki, Nobuhiro and Wright, Randall. "On Money as a Medium of Exchange." *Journal of Political Economy*, August 1989, *97*(4), pp. 927–54.

______. "A Contribution to the Pure Theory of Money." *Journal of Economic Theory*, April 1991, *53*(2), pp. 215–35.

______. "A Search-Theoretic Approach to Monetary Economics." *American Economic Review*, March 1993, *83*(1), pp. 63–77.

Klein, Benjamin. "The Competitive Supply of Money." *Journal of Money, Credit, and Banking*, November 1974, *6*(4), pp. 423–53.

Menger, Karl. "On the Origin of Money." *Economic Journal*, June 1892, *2*(6), pp. 239–55.

Oh, Seonghwan. "A Theory of a Generally Acceptable Medium of Exchange and Barter." *Journal of Monetary Economics*, January 1989, *23*(1), pp. 101–19.

Tullock, Gordon. "Paper Money—A Cycle in Cathay." *Economic History Review*, Second series, April 1957, *9*(3), pp. 393–407.

Yang, Lien-sheng. *Money and credit in China: A short history*. Cambridge, MA: Harvard University Press, 1952.

[22]

Barter and Monetary Exchange Under Private Information

By STEVE WILLIAMSON AND RANDALL WRIGHT*

We develop a model of production and exchange with uncertainty concerning the quality of commodities and study the role of fiat money in ameliorating frictions caused by private information. The model is specified so that, without private information, only high-quality commodities are produced, and there is no welfare gain from using money. With private information, there can be equilibria (and sometimes multiple equilibria) where low-quality commodities are produced, and money can increase welfare. Money works by promoting useful production and exchange. In efficient monetary equilibria, agents adopt strategies that increase the probability of acquiring high-quality output. (*JEL* E40, D82, D83)

> "To barter is to exchange goods for other goods rather than money. This was common in early days. Presumably, however, the deal was not always fair. Barter is from the old French *barater*—to cheat!"
>
> [Mike Atchison, 1991 p. 23]

This paper develops a model of production and exchange under private information concerning the quality of commodities. Qualitative uncertainty and the impediments it presents to exchange have been important elements of the economics of information at least since the contribution of George A. Akerlof (1970). In the spirit of his model, we assume that inferior-quality commodities—"lemons"—are cheaper to produce but less desirable for consumption. Since it is not always possible for consumers to discern the quality of every commodity they may have occasion to desire, there is an incentive for sellers to produce low-quality output and attempt to cheat uninformed buyers. Buyers therefore face a risky decision every time they cannot identify a commodity's quality. We construct a model that captures these ideas and use it to study exchange both with and without fiat money, defined as an intrinsically worthless but universally recognizable medium of exchange.

Many traditional discussions of money have emphasized its function as a medium of exchange and especially its role in overcoming the "double coincidence of wants problem" with pure barter (W. Stanley Jevons, 1875). The focus is often on the intrinsic properties of objects that make them more or less natural media of exchange, including properties such as a relatively low storage or exchange cost and a relatively high cost of producing the object privately, such as counterfeiting or digging precious metals out of the ground (Karl Menger, 1892). Recently, some of these ideas have been formalized using search-theoretic equilibrium models of the exchange process (see e.g., Nobuhiro Kiyotaki and Wright, 1989, 1991, 1993) (see Joseph M. Ostroy and Ross M. Starr [1990] for a

*Williamson: Department of Economics, University of Iowa, Iowa City, IA 52242; Wright: Department of Economics, University of Pennsylvania, Philadelphia, PA 19104, and Federal Reserve Bank of Minneapolis, 250 Marquette Avenue, Minneapolis, MN 55480. We thank Peter Diamond, Mark Gertler, Gary Gorton, Tom Sargent, Neil Wallace, and seminar participants at Bonn, British Columbia, Chicago, Iowa, Cornell, Carnegie Mellon, Penn, Simon Fraser, Texas-Austin, Texas A&M, Rice, Western Ontario, and the Federal Reserve Bank of Minneapolis for their input. Two anonymous referees also made suggestions that improved the paper significantly. Alberto Trejos provided research assistance. Financial support from the Lynde and Harry Bradley Foundation, the University of Pennsylvania Research Foundation, and the National Science Foundation is gratefully acknowledged. The views expressed here are those of the authors and not necessarily those of the Federal Reserve System or the Federal Reserve Bank of Minneapolis.

survey of earlier related work). In these models money can arise endogenously as a medium of exchange, leading to reductions in the search and transactions costs associated with direct barter.

Traditional discussions have also argued that, in addition to helping to reduce the double-coincidence problem, money is important in mitigating frictions associated with moral hazard or adverse selection. These frictions can be impediments to exchange when agents have limited opportunities for enforcing contracts and there is private information concerning the quality of goods or the intentions of agents to honor private claims.[1] Armen A. Alchian (1977 p. 139) has gone so far as to argue that overcoming the double-coincidence problem is at most a minor part of what money accomplishes, and private information is the principal friction underlying the institution of monetary exchange:

> "It is not the absence of double coincidence of wants, nor the costs of searching out the market of potential buyers and sellers of various goods nor of record keeping, but the costliness of information about the attributes of goods available for exchange that induces the use of money in an exchange economy."

The basic framework adopted here is related to the search-theoretic literature, in the sense that agents meet randomly in pairs over time, they carry unit inventories (consisting here of either good-quality commodities, bad-quality commodities, or fiat currency), and they trade if and only if it is mutually agreeable. However, we abstract from the double-coincidence problem by assuming that all commodities of a given quality provide the same utility to all consumers. This makes pure barter easy and means that there is no welfare-improving role for money without private information. We then add the assumption that sometimes an individual may be unable to recognize the quality of commodities that are for sale. As compared to models based on the double-coincidence friction, now buyers have to decide whether or not to purchase commodities of unknown quality, and sellers have to choose the quality of their output. This leads to some different implications and different interpretations of the role of fiat money.[2]

We begin by studying nonmonetary equilibria, where fiat currency does not circulate. In this case, private information may or may not lead to agents producing low-quality commodities and trying to pass them off on uninformed consumers. If the private-information problem is not too severe, there will exist an equilibrium where only high-quality output is produced; if it is more severe, some low-quality output will necessarily be produced; and if it is severe

[1]General discussions are contained in Karl Brunner and Allan H. Meltzer (1971) and Armen A. Alchian (1977). Models where money helps ameliorate lemons problems in the exchange of goods are constructed by Robert G. King and Charles I. Plosser (1986) and Dan Bernhardt and Merwan Engineer (1987). Scott Freeman (1985) and S. Rao Aiyagari (1989) consider models with private information concerning the quality of assets. Other papers in which private information in credit markets expands the role for fiat currency include Bruce Smith (1986), Saquib Jafarey and Peter Rupert (1992), and Williamson (1992). Robert M. Townsend (1989) studies a model in which private information leads to a role for money as a record-keeping device. These models are all very different from what will be presented here. Abhijit V. Banerjee and Eric S. Maskin (1991) have written a paper with qualitative uncertainty that is similar to ours in spirit. However, they try to keep markets as close to Walrasian as possible, and they impose informational frictions by assuming that there are some commodities that certain agents are simply not allowed to acquire. In contrast, we adopt a search-theoretic approach with bilateral exchange and allow our traders to attempt to acquire all commodities, even though they might face the possibility of getting "ripped off." In combination with some other technical differences, this leads us to focus on different issues and to derive different results.

[2]According to one commentator, the double-coincidence problem occurs when you need a taxi, all you have is one of your recent research papers, and you cannot find a cabby who wants it. In the model to be presented here, all cabbies want research paper, but unfortunately, some of them cannot recognize good monetary theory. On the other hand, they can all recognize money.

enough, the only equilibrium is one where no high-quality output is produced. For given parameter values, sometimes multiple Pareto-ranked equilibria coexist. This illustrates an externality or strategic complementarity inherent in the exchange process that, to our knowledge, has not been discussed in the previous literature: the production of better-quality output on average increases gains from trade, which then encourages every individual to produce better-quality output.

We then introduce generally recognizable fiat currency. It is shown that it is possible for an active (nondegenerate) monetary equilibrium to exist when the only nonmonetary equilibrium is degenerate. Furthermore, even when active nonmonetary equilibria exist, there may also exist monetary equilibria that entail higher welfare. Since use of money does not improve welfare without private information, given that we assume away the double-coincidence problem, it must therefore help to ameliorate the information problem. In fact, the use of money leads to agents adopting trading strategies that increase the probability of high-quality output being exchanged. In a monetary economy, the sellers of high-quality commodities have the luxury of demanding payment in cash, for example, which can generate positive incentive effects on other traders and producers.

Although there can exist several qualitatively different types of monetary equilibria, the ones that tend to do best in terms of welfare are those in which agents refuse to trade good-quality commodities for commodities whose quality they cannot recognize. This effectively imposes a "cash-in-advance" constraint on the producers of bad commodities, in that they must sell their output for money before trading for a consumption good. Given this, individuals are more willing to bear the cost of producing high quality in order to avoid cash-in-advance. The reason that agents buying with money are more willing to take a chance on something they cannot recognize than agents buying with their own high-quality commodities is that the former have a greater chance of getting high quality in return. That is, because money is universally recognizable, while commodities are not, sellers of high-quality output are more willing to trade if payment is in cash than if one tries to barter.

From another perspective, the fact that agents are willing to give up high-quality commodities for a universally recognizable money means that it can have value in exchange even though it has no value in consumption. In a monetary equilibrium, the probability of executing a trade is greater and the expected time until a trade is executed is shorter when one has currency rather than a commodity for sale. Although we make assumptions that essentially fix the price in any exchange to be either 1 or 0 (i.e., agents either swap inventories one-for-one or do not trade at all), the exchange value of various objects is determined by the expected time it takes to execute a successful transaction starting with these objects. Our emphasis on the time it takes to trade an object at a given price (its *liquidity*), rather than the relative price at which it can be sold instantaneously, is shared with many search-theoretic monetary models.

In practice, qualitative uncertainty in a market can be reflected in both the amount of time required to sell a particular good and in the price one receives for it. In Akerlof (1970), low average quality is reflected in a low market price, but his model completely abstracts from the idea that uncertainty makes goods more difficult to buy and sell and thereby increases search and other transaction costs. The model considered here is a polar opposite to Akerlof's, in the sense that price is not affected at all by the presence of differentially informed agents, but the amount of time it takes to buy and sell is. The fact that we abstract from price effects does not mean that they are uninteresting or unimportant, only that we wish to focus on another aspect of the frictions created by qualitative uncertainty. The model presented below is well suited to the study of how uncertainty affects the time required to buy and sell goods and is also a natural model within which to consider the role of fiat money.[3]

The paper is organized as follows. Section I presents the basic framework, and Section II analyzes the complete-information case as a benchmark. Section III considers nonmonetary equilibria with private information, and Section IV considers monetary equilibria. Section V concludes with some general comments and possible extensions.

I. The Basic Model

Time is discrete and continues forever. There is a continuum of homogeneous, infinite-lived agents, whose population is normalized to 1. There are three objects that may potentially be traded in this economy: a good-quality commodity, a bad-quality commodity, and money.[4] Both good and bad commodities can be produced by all agents, with the cost in terms of disutility to producing one unit of the good commodity equal to $\gamma > 0$ and the cost to producing the bad commodity equal to 0. All objects (money and commodities) are indivisible, freely disposable, and storable at zero cost, but only one unit at a time. This implies that agents' inventories always consist of at most one unit of one object—either a good commodity, a bad commodity, or money. Consumption of either money or a bad commodity yields zero utility. Consumption of one unit of a good commodity yields utility $u > 0$ if it was produced by someone else, while consumption of one's own output yields zero utility.[5]

Money cannot be produced by any private individual. At the beginning of the initial period, a fraction M of the agents in the economy are chosen at random, and each is endowed with one unit of cash. They may either keep it or dispose of it. Then, any agent without money can produce. In each succeeding period agents meet pairwise and at random and decide whether or not to trade. Trade always entails a one-for-one swap of inventories, since objects are indivisible (which allows us to ignore bargaining), and takes place if and only if it is mutually agreeable. There are no private credit arrangements, since agents who meet in one period will meet again in another period with probability zero. Agents holding (good or bad) commodities are called *commodity traders*, while agents holding money are called *money traders*. Let p be the proportion of commodity traders holding commodities that are good (and $1-p$ the proportion holding commodities that are bad).

Money is always identifiable. In any meeting between an agent and a commodity trader, however, there is a probability $\theta \leq 1$ that the former recognizes the quality of the latter's commodity.[6] This probability is independent across commodity traders when they meet. Agents do not know whether

[3]Although the first-generation search-theoretic monetary models neglected prices almost entirely, bilateral bargaining has been introduced explicitly into the framework in recent papers by Shouyong Shi (1992) and Alberto Trejos and Wright (1992). We think this model, with prices fixed and all of the effect of qualitative uncertainty occurring via changes in the time required to execute a trade, is complicated and interesting enough that we have not yet attempted to combine bargaining, private information, and money.

[4]To motivate the analysis of private information, it may help to imagine a large number of differentiated commodities. However, since consumers will derive the same utility from every commodity, holding quality fixed, we can proceed as though there is a single consumption good.

[5]The assumption that agents derive no utility from the consumption of their own produce is an easy way to generate gains from trade and is common in search-based models of exchange (see e.g., Peter A. Diamond, 1982, 1984; Kiyotaki and Wright, 1991, 1993); it can be relaxed in a generalized version of the model. The assumption that agents cannot consume their own output or endowment is also used in many cash-in-advance models (see e.g., Robert E. Lucas, 1980).

[6]As suggested above, this is meant to capture the fact that in modern economies with many commodities it is typically not possible to identify the quality of everything one may need. For example, one consumer may be well informed concerning clothing but ignorant when it comes to electronics, while another is an expert in electronics but cannot tell Armani from K-Mart. Nonetheless, there are times when the former needs to purchase a stereo or the latter a suit of clothes.

other agents recognize their commodities and do not know anything about other agents' histories. When two traders meet, they simply inspect each other's inventories and simultaneously announce whether or not they wish to trade. If both announce "trade" then they swap inventories and separate, whereupon the quality of each object is revealed if it was previously unknown. A trader then has the option of consuming the object, disposing of it, or storing it until the next period. If the object is consumed or disposed the agent can instantaneously produce a new commodity of either good or bad quality at the associated cost.

Agents choose production, consumption, disposal, and trading strategies in order to maximize the expected discounted utility of consumption net of production costs. In doing so, they take as given the strategies of others and the probabilities of meeting agents holding particular inventories. We look for stationary Nash equilibria in which the strategies and meeting probabilities are time-invariant and expectations are rational. The meeting probabilities are summarized by m, the probability of meeting a money trader, and p, the fraction of commodity traders holding high-quality commodities. If no one disposes of money then $m = M$, where M is the initial endowment of the stuff; if some agents dispose of money then we can have $m < M$. We confine attention mainly to what we call *active* (or nondegenerate) equilibria, where at least some good commodities are produced and consumed, and utility is strictly positive.[7]

II. Complete Information

As a benchmark, in this section we consider the case of $\theta = 1$ so that there is no private information. Let V_j denote the *payoff* or *value function* at the end of a period for an agent holding object j, where $j = \text{g}$, b, or m denotes a good commodity, a bad commodity, or money, respectively. Let $r > 0$ be the (common) discount rate. Let $W = \max(V_{\text{g}} - \gamma, V_{\text{b}})$ represent the value function for an agent with nothing in inventory, who is deciding which quality commodity to produce. By definition, in any active equilibrium at least some production of the good commodity must occur, which implies $p > 0$ and $W = V_{\text{g}} - \gamma \geq V_{\text{b}}$. We begin with nonmonetary equilibria, in which money is never accepted in trade. In an active nonmonetary equilibrium, anyone initially endowed with fiat money disposes of it, which means $m = 0$.

Suppose an active equilibrium exists, so that $V_{\text{g}} - \gamma > 0$. Then it is not hard to see that when a trader meets someone with a good commodity he will want to trade, and when he meets someone with a bad commodity he will not want to trade. Hence, traders with bad commodities can never trade for good commodities, which implies that no bad commodities are produced and $p = 1$ in any active equilibrium without private information. Thus, if an active nonmonetary equilibrium exists, every agent produces a good commodity in the initial period, and each period thereafter he meets, trades, consumes, and produces another good commodity. To verify that this in fact constitutes an equilibrium we need to check that an agent has no incentive to deviate from this strategy when everyone else is following it; in other words, we need to check that it is a fixed point of the best-response correspondence.

We make extensive use of a fundamental principle of dynamic programming known as the *unimprovability criterion*.[8] To apply this, first note that the payoff to an individual from producing a good commodity, given

[7]There will always exist degenerate equilibria; for example, if no trades are ever accepted then agents may as well not produce any good commodities, which is an equilibrium generating zero utility.

[8]A candidate policy is called *unimprovable* (more accurately, unimprovable in a single step) if the payoff from using it cannot be increased by deviating to a different decision at a single date and then reverting back to the candidate policy for the rest of time. Obviously a payoff-maximizing policy is unimprovable; it is also true that an unimprovable policy is payoff-maximizing as long as the instantaneous return function is bounded below (see David M. Kreps, 1990).

the candidate equilibrium strategy, is $V_g - \gamma$, where

$$(1) \qquad rV_g = u - \gamma.$$

This and the more complicated expressions for payoff functions that appear later are special cases of general results in Appendix A. If the individual deviates by producing a bad commodity, tries to trade (without success, since $\theta = 1$), and then reverts next period to producing a good commodity, his payoff is V_b, where

$$(2) \qquad rV_b = V_g - \gamma - V_b.$$

Equations (1) and (2) imply that $V_g - \gamma \geq V_b$ if and only if

$$(3) \qquad u \geq (1+r)\gamma.$$

We conclude that when others are producing only good commodities the individual strategy of producing only good commodities is unimprovable, and therefore a best response and therefore an equilibrium, if and only if (3) holds.[9] Let Z denote welfare, defined as the expected utility of the representative agent in the initial period *before* the endowment of money is distributed and production takes place. In the unique active nonmonetary equilibrium $Z = Z^*$, where Z^* satisfies

$$(4) \qquad rZ^* = u - (1+r)\gamma.$$

Except for the borderline case where (3) holds at equality, (4) implies $Z^* > 0$ whenever this equilibrium exists, and it strictly Pareto-dominates an inactive equilibrium.

We now consider monetary equilibria, in which fiat currency is accepted in at least some exchanges. In this economy, one can show that money is either always accepted or never accepted in exchange (see below), and so we concentrate on the case of *pure* monetary equilibria in which money is accepted with probability 1. For money to be accepted in exchange for a good commodity we require $V_m \geq V_g$, which implies $V_m > V_g - \gamma$; therefore no one ever disposes of currency, and $m = M$. As above, for an active equilibrium we require $V_g - \gamma \geq V_b$, and no agent with a good commodity trades for a bad commodity. The fact that no trader ever accepts bad commodities implies $p = 1$, exactly as in the nonmonetary case. It only remains to check that if others are accepting money and producing good commodities then this strategy is a best response for an individual.

To this end, note that the payoff functions for agents with either good commodities or money, given the candidate strategy, satisfy the following conditions:

$$(5) \qquad rV_g = (1-M)(u-\gamma) + M(V_m - V_g)$$

$$(6) \qquad rV_m = (1-M)(u-\gamma) + (1-M)(V_g - V_m).$$

These imply that $V_m = V_g$, and so a deviation from the candidate strategy by not accepting money does not improve one's payoff. Further, a deviation by producing a bad commodity yields V_b, where V_b again satisfies (2). This does not improve one's payoff if and only if $V_g - \gamma \geq V_b$, which holds if and only if

$$(7) \qquad M \leq 1 - r\gamma/(u-\gamma).$$

By the unimprovability criterion, accepting money and producing only good commodities is a best response and therefore an equilibrium if and only if (7) is satisfied.

This equilibrium exists for some $M > 0$ if and only if $u > (1+r)\gamma$. By (4), this is the same as the condition for the existence of the active nonmonetary equilibrium. Hence, whenever the active monetary equilibrium exists, so does the active nonmonetary equilibrium, and we claim the latter is Pareto superior. In the monetary equilibrium, expected utility is $Z = MV_m + (1-M)(V_g - \gamma)$,

[9] This is the unique active equilibrium, where an active equilibrium is defined as one generating positive utility. There is also an equilibrium where $0 < p < 1$ and $V_g - \gamma = V_b = 0$, but we call it degenerate.

which simplifies to

$$(8) \qquad rZ = (1-M)[u-(1+r)\gamma].$$

This is decreasing in M, and $M = 0$ implies $Z = Z^*$, where Z^* is welfare in the nonmonetary equilibrium. Thus, the welfare-maximizing value of M is zero here. This should not be too surprising—things have been rigged so that money has no role without private information.[10]

It may be helpful to compare the present model with the one in Kiyotaki and Wright (1993), which is very similar when $\theta = 1$, except that it includes a double-coincidence problem. In particular, there is a number x, with $0 < x < 1$, such that x equals the probability that an agent selected at random accepts a given commodity and also equals the probability that a commodity selected at random is accepted by a given agent. Smaller values of x make barter more difficult. In the present model $x = 1$, so that (at least when $\theta = 1$) barter is trivial. For $x \in (0,1)$ there exist exactly three active equilibria: a nonmonetary equilibrium where money is never accepted, a pure monetary equilibrium where money is accepted with probability 1, and a mixed monetary equilibrium where money is accepted with probability x. We set $x = 1$ here, so the latter two cases coalesce, and there is no equilibrium where money is accepted with a probability strictly between 0 and 1.

For a general value of $x \in [0,1]$, the payoff functions in pure monetary equilibrium satisfy

$$(9) \qquad rV_g = (1-M)x^2(u-\gamma) + Mx(V_m - V_g)$$

$$(10) \qquad rV_m = (1-M)x(u-\gamma) + (1-M)x(V_g - V_m)$$

which should be compared with (5) and (6). Note that barter requires a double coincidence, which occurs with probability x^2, while a cash purchase requires a single coincidence, which occurs with probability x. Welfare is given by

$$(11) \qquad rZ = (1-M)[Mx + (1-M)x^2](u-\gamma) - (1-M)\gamma r.$$

If x is small enough, then Z is increasing in M at $M = 0$, and consequently the welfare-maximizing value of M is strictly positive.

When barter is sufficiently difficult, there is a role for fiat money even without private information. We set $x = 1$ in this paper in order to remove the double-coincidence friction entirely and focus on qualitative uncertainty. If money is going to have a welfare-improving role in what follows, it will be exclusively due to the presence of private information.

III. Private Information: Nonmonetary Equilibria

We now assume that $\theta < 1$, so that in some meetings agents are not able to identify the quality of a commodity in a potential trading partner's inventory. Agents may try to take advantage of a lower cost to producing bad commodities with the hope of being able to pass them off on uninformed consumers, which means p may potentially be less than 1. However, p cannot be zero in any active equilibrium, by definition, since this would yield zero utility. We also restrict attention for now to nonmonetary equilibria, where $m = 0$.

As in the previous section, two commodity traders who meet and recognize each other's inventories as good quality will al-

[10] As a technical aside, we could have followed Aiyagari and Neil Wallace (1991, 1992) and considered a slightly different setup in which agents cannot produce until they consume. This implies that those initially endowed with money never produce in nonmonetary equilibrium, although they are still a part of the meeting technology (i.e., agents with commodities still have a probability M of meeting a money trader every period). Under these assumptions, money traders are better off in the monetary equilibrium, and commodity traders are indifferent, and so *ex ante* welfare is higher. However, it remains the case that Z is decreasing in M.

ways want to trade. Also, an agent with a bad commodity is willing to trade at every opportunity, since at worst he gets another bad commodity in return. The only nontrivial decisions concern whether to produce good- or bad-quality output, and whether to accept or reject a commodity of unrecognized quality when you are currently holding a good commodity yourself. Let Σ denote the probability with which an agent believes that other traders with good commodities will accept commodities of unrecognized quality, and let σ be an individual's best response. Observe that we must have $\Sigma > 0$ in any active equilibrium.[11]

The best-response problem is now described by the following equations (again, formal derivations are contained in Appendix A):

$$(12)\quad rV_g = \theta p[\theta + (1-\theta)\Sigma](u + W - V_g)$$

$$+ (1-\theta)\max_{\sigma} \sigma\{p[\theta + (1-\theta)\Sigma](u + W - V_g)$$

$$+ (1-p)(W - V_g)\}$$

$$(13)\quad rV_b = p(1-\theta)\Sigma(u + W - V_b).$$

Equation (12) sets the flow return to holding a good commodity, rV_g, equal to the sum of two terms. The first term is the probability that the individual meets someone with a good commodity he can identify, θp, multiplied by the probability the other agent is willing to trade, $\theta + (1-\theta)\Sigma$, multiplied by the gain from trading, $u + W - V_g$. The second term is the probability that the individual meets someone with something he cannot identify, $1-\theta$, multiplied by the gain from choosing the acceptance probability σ. Similarly, (13) sets the return to holding a bad commodity, rV_b, equal to the probability that the individual meets someone with a good commodity who is uniformed but still willing to trade, $p(1-\theta)\Sigma$, multiplied by the gain from trading.

An equilibrium now consists of values for p and Σ with the following properties. First, $V_g - \gamma > V_b$ implies $p = 1$ and $p < 1$ implies $V_g - \gamma = V_b$ (recall that p can be less than 1 but cannot be 0). Second, given p, $\sigma = \Sigma$ must solve the maximization problem in (12). There are potentially three types of equilibria. A type-a equilibrium has $p = 1$, which implies $\Sigma = 1$; in this case, no bad commodities are ever produced, and therefore traders always accept commodities even when they cannot recognize them. A type-b equilibrium has $0 < p < 1$ and $\Sigma = 1$; in this case, some bad commodities are produced, but traders still always accept commodities even when they cannot recognize them. A type-c equilibrium has $0 < p < 1$ and $0 < \Sigma < 1$; in this case some bad commodities are produced, and traders randomize between accepting and rejecting commodities they cannot recognize. We take up each case in turn.

First consider a type-a equilibrium, with $p = \Sigma = 1$. In such an equilibrium, if it exists, private information is not a problem in the sense that the outcome is the same as when $\theta = 1$. This might still be an equilibrium, even if $\theta < 1$, because agents might be disciplined into producing only good commodities by the possibility of having bad commodities rejected; that is, the reduction in cost may not be worth the required increase in the time it takes to sell low-quality output. This requires $V_g - \gamma \geq V_b$. Using the unimprovability criterion, we insert $p = \Sigma = \sigma = 1$ into (12) and (13) and rearrange to find that $V_g - \gamma \geq V_b$ if and only if $\theta u \geq (1+r)\gamma$. We conclude that a type-a equilibrium exists if and only if $\theta \geq \theta_1$, where

$$(14)\quad \theta_1 = (1+r)\gamma/u.$$

Now consider a type-b equilibrium with $0 < p < 1$ and $\Sigma = 1$. If $V_g - \gamma = V_b$, then unimprovability implies that it is a best response to produce a good commodity with

[11] The proof is immediate: if $\Sigma = 0$ then unrecognized commodities are never accepted, and so bad commodities are never produced; but then consumers should accept unrecognized commodities, contradicting $\Sigma = 0$.

an arbitrary probability.[12] After substitution of $\sigma = \Sigma = 1$ into (12) and (13), $V_g - \gamma = V_b$ can be solved for

$$(15) \qquad p = \frac{\gamma(1-\theta+r)}{\theta(u-\gamma)} = p_b.$$

Notice that $p_b > 0$, and $p_b < 1$ if and only if $\theta > \theta_1$, where θ_1 is defined in (14). We therefore need only check that $\sigma = 1$ is also a best response. If we insert $W = V_g - \gamma$ and $\Sigma = 1$ into (12), $\sigma = 1$ is a best response if and only if $pu - \gamma \geq 0$. By (15), this holds if and only if $\theta \leq \theta_2$, where

$$(16) \qquad \theta_2 = (1+r)u/(2u-\gamma).$$

Hence, equilibrium b exists if and only if $\theta_1 < \theta \leq \theta_2$.

Finally, consider a type-c equilibrium, with $0 < p < 1$ and $0 < \sigma < 1$. Any $p \in [0,1]$ is a best response if $V_g - \gamma = V_b$, and any $\sigma \in [0,1]$ is a best response if an individual is indifferent between accepting and rejecting an unrecognized commodity. By virtue of (12), the latter requires

$$(17) \quad p = \frac{\gamma}{\gamma + [\theta + (1-\theta)\Sigma](u-\gamma)} = \pi(\Sigma).$$

Notice that $0 < \pi(\Sigma) < 1$ for all $\Sigma \geq 0$. Using $p = \pi(\Sigma)$, we now can solve for the value of Σ that yields $V_g - \gamma = V_b$:

$$(18) \quad \Sigma_c = \frac{\theta(u-\gamma) + (1-\theta)\gamma - (1-\theta+r)[\gamma + \theta(u-\gamma)]}{(1-\theta)[\gamma + (1-\theta+r)(u-\gamma)]}.$$

For future reference, let $p_c = \pi(\Sigma_c)$. One can show that $0 < \Sigma_c < 1$, and therefore equilibrium c exists, if and only if $\theta_3 < \theta < \theta_2$, where θ_2 is defined in (16) and θ_3 is defined by

$$(19) \quad \theta_3 = 0.5r + \frac{0.5}{u-\gamma}\sqrt{r^2(u-\gamma)^2 + 4r\gamma(u-\gamma)}.$$

The above analysis indicates that the set of equilibria depends on θ relative to three critical values, θ_1, θ_2, and θ_3, which themselves depend on the other parameters. Figure 1 graphs θ_1, θ_2, and θ_3 as functions of r for given but arbitrary values of u and γ. Notice that there exist three values of r, with $0 < r_1 < r_2 < r_3$, such that the following is true. For $r < r_1$ we have $\theta_3 < \theta_1 < \theta_2$; in this case, equilibrium c is the unique active equilibrium for $\theta \in (\theta_3, \theta_1)$, equilibria a, b, and c coexist for $\theta \in (\theta_1, \theta_2)$, and equilibrium a is the unique active equilibrium for $\theta \in (\theta_2, 1)$. For $r_1 < r < r_2$ we have $\theta_1 < \theta_3 < \theta_2$; in this case, equilibria a and b exist for $\theta \in (\theta_1, \theta_3)$, all three coexist for $\theta \in (\theta_3, \theta_2)$, and equilibrium a is the unique active equilibrium for $\theta \in (\theta_2, 1)$. Finally, for $r_2 < r < r_3$ we have $\theta_1 < 1 < \theta_2 < \theta_3$; in this case, equilibria a and b coexist for $\theta \in (\theta_1, 1)$, while equilibrium c does not exist for any θ. We always assume $r < r_3$ from now on, which is equivalent to assuming that the active equilibrium exists when $\theta = 1$.

The following general observations can be made. First, there are always values of θ less than 1 such that equilibrium a exists. This means that a little private information can always be introduced and the "first best" outcome will still be an equilibrium. Second, there are always values of θ close to 0 such that no active equilibrium exists. This means that enough private information can be introduced so that all economic activity shuts down. Third, there are always values of θ such that multiple equilibria coexist. Finally, notice that equilibrium c is the only possible equilibrium where θ is very low, and its existence depends on a low value of r. Equilibrium c has the greatest chance of surviving when the private-information problem is severe because $\Sigma < 1$ imposes the greatest discipline on producers of bad commodities: not only do they have to meet uninformed agents, the latter also have to be willing to take a chance, which

[12] By use of an appropriate law of large numbers for continuum economies (see Harold Uhlig, 1987), the proportion of agents with good commodities is equal to the probability with which the average agent produces a good commodity. Alternatively, we can simply impose that a fraction p of the agents always produce good commodities while the rest always produce bad commodities, since both are best responses.

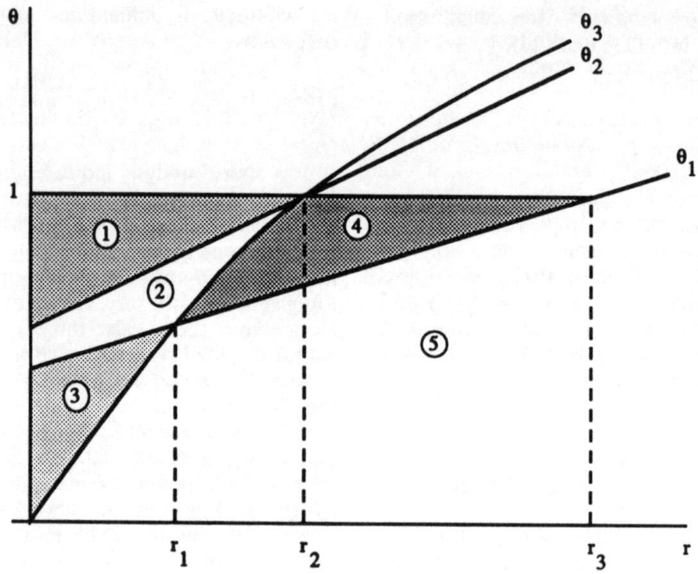

FIGURE 1. θ_1, θ_2, AND θ_3 AS FUNCTIONS OF r

Notes: Region 1, equilibrium a exists; region 2, equilibria a, b, and c exist; region 3, equilibrium c exists; region 4, equilibria a and b exist; region 5, no active equilibrium exists.

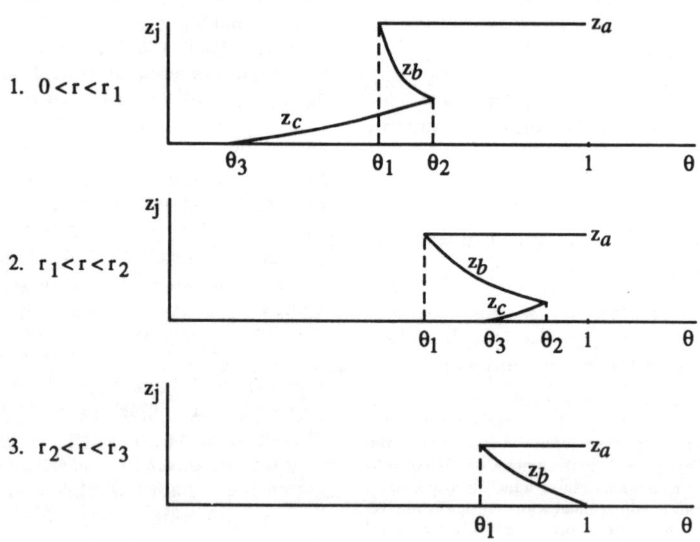

FIGURE 2. WELFARE IN EQUILIBRIA a, b, AND c AS FUNCTIONS OF θ

occurs with probability Σ. Low values of Σ reduce the incentive to produce bad commodities, which would otherwise be great when θ is small.[13]

We now demonstrate that when multiple equilibria coexist they can be Pareto-ranked. Let Z_j be welfare in equilibrium j, where $j = \text{a, b, or c}$. Straightforward algebra implies that Z_j can be written as

$$(20)\quad rZ_j = p_j[\theta + (1-\theta)\Sigma_j](u-\gamma) - (1-p_j)(1-\theta)\gamma - r\gamma.$$

As $p_a = \Sigma_a = 1$, welfare is greatest in equilibrium a and, of course, $Z_a = Z^*$ where Z^* is welfare in the nonmonetary equilibrium with $\theta = 1$. Since $\Sigma_c < \Sigma_b = 1$, and since it is also possible to show that $p_c < p_b < 1$, it is immediate from (20) that $Z_c < Z_b < Z_a$. In Figure 2 we plot welfare in equilibria a, b, and c as functions of θ, for all values of θ for which they exist. Three cases are shown, corresponding to values of r in each of the three intervals described by Figure 1.

The multiplicity of Pareto-ranked equilibria is due to a *strategic complementarity* (see Russell Cooper and Andrew John, 1988). When more agents produce high-quality output, there is a direct effect that increases the value of producing both good and bad commodities, with the value of producing a good commodity increasing by more provided that the probability of "getting caught" with a bad commodity, θ, is in the appropriate range. There is also an indirect effect. If more good commodities are produced, then an unidentified commodity is more likely to be acceptable, which encourages the production of lemons. If θ is in the appropriate range, given the other parameters, the direct effect dominates; then a strategic complementarity exists and leads to multiple equilibria, as shown in regions 2 and 4 of Figure 1. If θ is too high or too low, however, there is an overwhelming tendency to end up in equilibrium a or c; this leads to uniqueness, as shown in regions 1 and 3.[14]

IV. Private Information: Monetary Equilibria

In this section, we demonstrate that with private information there can exist active monetary equilibria under circumstances in which the only nonmonetary equilibrium is degenerate, and that even if an active nonmonetary equilibrium exists there may also exist a monetary equilibrium that entails higher welfare. We also demonstrate that several different types of monetary equilibria are possible, although we give conditions under which a unique outcome exists. We also interpret the mechanism by which the use of money mitigates the private-information problem, and discuss some welfare implications.

We restrict attention to equilibria with $0 < p < 1$. One can show that there exists a monetary equilibrium with $p = 1$ if and only if $\theta \geq \theta_4$, where $\theta_4 = (1+r)\gamma/[(1-M)u + M\gamma]$.[15] Since $\theta_4 > \theta_1$, whenever this equilibrium exists there also exists an active nonmonetary equilibrium with $p = 1$, and the

[13]The existence of equilibrium c depends on the willingness of agents with good commodities sometimes to forgo a trade for something that they cannot recognize in favor of waiting to trade later for something that they can recognize. This willingness to wait depends on the discount rate being sufficiently low, which explains the role of r in the discussion. Similar results obtain in other private-information models. For example, in Townsend's (1982) environment, optimal allocations exhibit intertemporal links which are absent in the corresponding optimal allocations under full information, due to the fact that under private information agents may have incentives to make apparently inferior trades in the present in order to gain something for the future.

[14]Welfare does not depend on θ in equilibrium a, is decreasing in θ in equilibrium b, and is increasing in θ in equilibrium c. In this sense equilibrium b seems perverse: welfare is higher the greater the private-information problem. This results from the fact that the fraction of high-quality goods, p_b, depends negatively on θ in this equilibrium, as can be seen from (15). Of course, in the presence of multiplicity it is typical for some equilibria to have counterintuitive comparative-static properties.

[15]Equivalently, a monetary equilibrium with $p = 1$ exists if and only if $M < 1 - (1-\theta+r)\gamma/(u-\gamma)$. This generalizes the necessary and sufficient condition for the existence of a monetary equilibrium when $\theta = 1$, given in (7).

latter generates greater welfare. Thus, if money is to have a welfare-enhancing role in this economy, it cannot *completely* alleviate the private-information problem by driving out *all* bad commodities. Since $0<p<1$, in what follows, $V_g-\gamma=V_b$. We also restrict attention to equilibria where money is universally accepted, which implies that $V_m \geq V_g$. In contrast to the situation with $\theta=1$, when $\theta<1$ there may well exist mixed monetary equilibria where money is sometimes but not universally accepted. However, it can be shown that if such an equilibrium exists then there also exists a nonmonetary equilibrium that yields higher welfare (details are available from the authors upon request). Since we are interested in equilibria where the use of money potentially leads to an increase in welfare, we do not pursue mixed monetary equilibria here.

Denote the probabilities that good commodity traders and money traders accept commodities that they cannot recognize by Σ and Ω, respectively. Then the best-response problem is described by (again, see Appendix A):

$$(21)\quad rV_g=(1-M)\theta p[\theta+(1-\theta)\Sigma](u-\gamma) + M[\theta+(1-\theta)\Omega](V_m-V_g) + (1-M)(1-\theta) \times \max_{\sigma} \sigma\{p[\theta+(1-\theta)\Sigma] \times(u-\gamma)-(1-p)\gamma\}$$

$$(22)\quad rV_b=(1-M)p(1-\theta)\Sigma u + M(1-\theta)\Omega(V_m-V_b)$$

$$(23)\quad rV_m=(1-M)\theta p(u-\gamma+V_g-V_m) + (1-M)(1-\theta) \times \max_{\omega} \omega\{p(u-\gamma+V_g-V_m) + (1-p)(-\gamma+V_g-V_m)\}.$$

Equation (21) sets the return to holding a good commodity equal to the sum of three terms. The first term is the probability that the agent meets a commodity trader with a good commodity he recognizes, $(1-M)\theta p$, multipled by the probability that the other agent is willing to trade, $\theta+(1-\theta)\Sigma$, multiplied by $u-\gamma$. The second term is the probability that the agent meets a money trader who is willing to trade, $M[\theta+(1-\theta)\Omega]$, multiplied by V_m-V_g. The final term is the probability that the agent meets a commodity trader with something he cannot recognize, $(1-M)(1-\theta)$, multiplied by the gain from choosing σ. Equations (22) and (23) have similar interpretations.

TABLE 1—CANDIDATE MONETARY EQUILIBRIA

Σ	$\Omega=0$	$\Omega=\Phi$	$\Omega=1$
0	N	P	P
Φ	P	P	P
1	D	D	D

Key: N, monetary equilibrium does not exist; D, dominated by nonmonetary equilibrium; P, money potentially improves welfare.

Several different types of equilibria are possible, depending on whether Ω and Σ are elements of {0}, {1}, or Φ, where Φ denotes the open interval (0,1). The set of possibilities is shown in Table 1. We give each case a label in terms of (Σ,Ω): for instance, equilibrium (0,0) has $\Sigma=\Omega=0$, equilibrium $(0,\Phi)$ has $\Sigma=0$ and $0<\Omega<1$, and so on. There could never exist a (0,0) equilibrium with $p<1$, since someone has to accept commodities of unrecognized quality in order for bad commodities to be produced. Furthermore, it may be shown that whenever there exists an equilibrium with $\Sigma=1$ there also exists a nonmonetary equilibrium which implies a higher level of welfare (details are available from the authors upon request). This leaves us with exactly five candidate equilibria in Table 1 that have the potential to Pareto-dominate active nonmonetary equilibria: $(0,\Phi)$, $(0,1)$, $(\Phi,0)$, (Φ,Φ), and $(\Phi,1)$.

Because there are several qualitatively different types of equilibria and some of them are not amenable to closed-form solutions, we do not attempt a complete analytical characterization, as we provided for nonmonetary equilibria in the previous section. Below we will describe the set of equilibria numerically for certain parameter values. However, we begin with a case in which analytical results are fairly tractable: the equilibrium with $(\Sigma,\Omega)=(0,\Phi)$. This case is important because there is a region of parameter space, characterized by low values of θ, in which this equilibrium exists, none of the other candidate monetary equilibria exist, and the only nonmonetary equilibrium is degenerate.[16]

When $(\Sigma,\Omega)=(0,\Phi)$, $0<\Omega<1$ implies that the final term in (23) vanishes. Then, since $\Sigma=0$, (21)–(23) simplify to

$$rV_{\mathrm{g}}=(1-M)\theta^2p(u-\gamma)+M[\theta+(1-\theta)\Omega](V_{\mathrm{m}}-V_{\mathrm{g}}) \tag{24}$$

$$rV_{\mathrm{b}}=M(1-\theta)\Omega(V_{\mathrm{m}}-V_{\mathrm{b}}) \tag{25}$$

$$rV_{\mathrm{m}}=(1-M)\theta p(u-\gamma+V_{\mathrm{g}}-V_{\mathrm{m}}). \tag{26}$$

To verify that $(0,\Phi)$ is an equilibrium, we need to find values for p and Ω in $(0,1)$ with the following properties:[17]

$$V_{\mathrm{m}}-V_{\mathrm{g}}\geq 0 \tag{27}$$

(so that accepting money is a best response);

$$V_{\mathrm{g}}-\gamma=V_{\mathrm{b}} \tag{28}$$

(so that $0<p<1$ is a best response);

$$p\theta(u-\gamma)-(1-p)\gamma\leq 0 \tag{29}$$

(so that $\sigma=0$ is a best response); and

$$pu-\gamma+V_{\mathrm{g}}-V_{\mathrm{m}}=0 \tag{30}$$

(so that $0<\omega<1$ is a best response).

In Appendix B we show that, as long as r is not too large given u, γ, and θ, these conditions will be satisfied, and hence the $(0,\Phi)$ equilibrium will exist, for all M in an interval $(\underline{M},\overline{M})$ where $0<\underline{M}<\overline{M}<1$. As stated above, in a region of parameter space with low values of θ, this equilibrium exists, none of the other monetary equilibria in Table 1 exist, and the only nonmonetary equilibrium is the degenerate one that yields $Z=0$. The $(0,\Phi)$ monetary equilibrium yields $Z>0$, and therefore it Pareto-dominates the only (inactive) nonmonetary equilibrium. This illustrates how the introduction of fiat currency can improve welfare by allowing the existence of an active monetary equilibrium when the private-information problem is so severe that economic activity would otherwise shut down.

How is it that the use of fiat money reduces the information problem in this case? First, an agent with a good commodity who is confronted with an offer of an unrecognized commodity has the luxury of rejecting the offer and demanding either cash or a good that can be recognized. If the probability p is low, it is advantageous to incur the waiting cost and hold out for either money or something that can be recognized, rather than taking a chance. Moreover, the $(\Sigma,\Omega)=(0,\Phi)$ strategy imposes the greatest amount of discipline on the producers of bad commodities. Since $\Sigma=0$, bad-commodity holders can never trade directly for a good commodity. They must trade first for money, which is possible since $\Omega>0$ (although not automatic since $\Omega<1$), and then use this money to make a purchase. This effectively subjects

[16] Since the only nonmonetary equilibrium is degenerate, this region is contained in region 5 in Figure 1. In particular, at the point where $u=2\gamma$ and $r=0.01$ the situation is as depicted in the first panel of Figure 2, with $\theta_3=0.11$, $\theta_1=0.505$, and $\theta_2=0.673$. For $\theta=0.10$, no active nonmonetary equilibrium exists, and one can show numerically that equilibrium $(0,\Phi)$ exists at least for some M, while no other candidate monetary equilibrium exists for any value of M. An appropriate appeal to continuity guarantees that the situation will be qualitatively similar in an open neighborhood of this point.

[17] Notice how we exploit the unimprovability criterion here. Since at each instant in time the agent only needs to make a single decision (accept or reject money, produce a good or a bad commodity, etc.), we can demonstrate that a given strategy is a best response by showing that the agent's payoff cannot be increased by deviating from this strategy at any single decision point. We do not also have to show that the agent's payoff cannot be improved by combinations of deviations (e.g., stop accepting money and simultaneously start producing only bad commodities, etc.).

bad-commodity traders to a cash-in-advance constraint, while good-commodity holders can also trade for cash but additionally can barter directly whenever they meet another good-commodity trader and both recognize the other's inventories.[18]

This suggests that it is *socially* desirable to subject bad-commodity traders to cash-in-advance—but how is it also *individually* optimal? There seems to be a paradox here. In order for money to be accepted we require $V_m \geq V_g$; yet at the same time money traders are more willing than commodity traders to trade for something that they cannot recognize. The resolution of this apparent paradox is that a money trader has a greater probability than a commodity trader of receiving high quality in an exchange opportunity. In general, the probability that trading money for an unrecognized commodity yields a good commodity is p, while the probability that trading a commodity for an unrecognized commodity yields a good commodity is only $p[\theta+(1-\theta)\Sigma]$. Since money is universally recognizable, you have a greater chance of getting high quality when you offer money rather than another commodity. Therefore you are more likely to take a chance on something you cannot recognize when you have money, even though $V_m \geq V_g$.

Again, the $(0,\Phi)$ equilibrium exists uniquely when θ is small. If θ becomes larger and the private-information problem becomes less severe, then other equilibria may appear. For $u = 2\gamma$ and $r = 0.01$, when $\theta = 0.10$, for example, $(0,\Phi)$ is the only active equilibrium; but when we increase θ to 0.20 all five of our candidate monetary equilibria exist for some values of M, as does a unique active nonmonetary equilibrium which is of type c. Figure 3 shows equilibrium welfare for a range of values of M for each of the equilibria when they exist. All of the monetary equilibria exist and dominate the nonmonetary equilibrium for some values of M.

At the risk of taking liberty with conventional usage, we call the value of M that maximizes welfare across all equilibria the *optimal quantity of money*. Then the *optimal monetary equilibrium* is the one that yields the highest welfare at the optimal quantity of money. As seen in Figure 3, in this example the optimal monetary equilibrium is $(\Sigma,\Omega)=(0,\Phi)$, the one we previously analyzed analytically. For a range of parameter values that we examined, the optimal monetary equilibrium was either of the type $(0,\Phi)$ or $(0,1)$ (the latter being a limiting case of the former). Both of these equilibria impose discipline on the producers of bad commodities by effectively subjecting them to a cash-in-advance constraint.[19]

We computed the optimal quantity of money for a range of values for θ. One perhaps surprising finding is that the optimal quantity of money is not monotonic in θ. For low values of θ, the optimal monetary equilibrium is of type $(0,\Phi)$, and the optimal quantity of money falls with θ. For higher values of θ, the optimal monetary equilibrium is of type $(0,1)$, and the optimal quantity of money rises with θ. For sufficiently high values of θ the optimal quantity of money is zero, since there exists a type-a nonmonetary equilibrium. Our calculations also reveal that p, the fraction of commodities that are good-quality, can be lower in the optimal monetary equilibrium than in the nonmonetary equilibrium, and that $(1-M)p$, the fraction of all traders holding

[18]There is always *some* barter in any active equilibrium. If an agent has a good commodity, the probability of a direct exchange for another good commodity is bounded below by $(1-M)p\theta^2$.

[19]It might be thought that a more natural equilibrium would involve $\Omega = 0$ (money traders never accept commodities they do not recognize), which imposes discipline on the producers of bad commodities by forcing them to barter directly and by not allowing them to sell their goods for cash. As seen in Figure 3, an equilibrium with $(\Sigma,\Omega)=(\Phi,0)$ exists and dominates the nonmonetary equilibrium for some values of M, but it can be dominated by other monetary equilibria. Direct barter is not particularly difficult in this environment, and therefore, forcing producers of bad commodities to barter directly does not impose a very effective discipline on them. It is more effective to force them to use money, since this requires making two trades instead of one and increases the expected time required to acquire a consumption good.

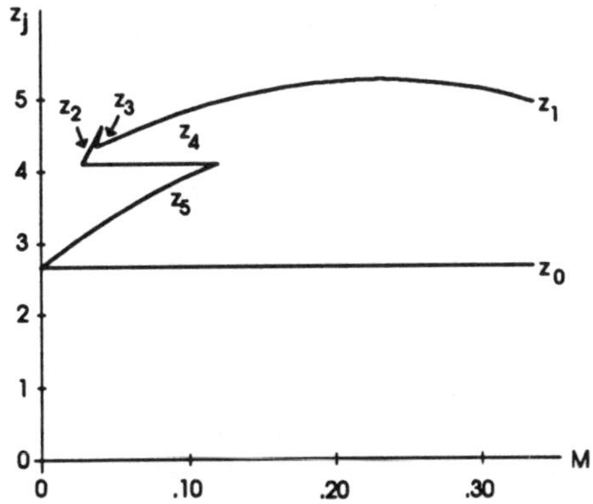

FIGURE 3. EQUILIBRIUM WELFARE FOR A RANGE OF VALUES OF M

Notes: z_0, welfare in nonmonetary equilibrium; z_1, welfare in $(0,\Phi)$ equilibrium; z_2, welfare in $(\Phi,1)$ equilibrium; z_3, welfare in $(0,1)$ equilibrium; z_4, welfare in (Φ,Φ) equilibrium; z_5, welfare in $(\Phi,0)$ equilibrium.

good commodities, can be higher or lower. However, the *probability of acquiring a good commodity* each period was always highest in the optimal monetary equilibrium. Money works by promoting useful exchange, in the sense that it not only can lead to more transactions, as in existing search models, but it also leads to the exchange of more high-quality output.

We close this section with a caveat. In the interest of tractability, it has been assumed throughout that agents carry either one unit of money or one real commodity, but not both simultaneously. This means that we have had to restrict attention to a very particular type of monetary intervention: a change in the initial endowment of M, such that when we increase the number of agents endowed with money we simultaneously reduce the number with real commodities. Not only is this a somewhat special experiment, it means that increasing M always tends to reduce welfare to a certain extent. What is interesting is that, despite this restriction and despite the assumption that there is no double-coincidence problem, the introduction of some fiat money can be welfare-improving when there is private information. The point is that it is harder, not easier, for money to have a welfare-improving role under our assumptions, and therefore it is all the more striking that such a role has been shown to exist.

At the same time, the results have an interpretation in terms of "real-world" policy issues. Since fiat money is universally recognizable and acceptable, buying with cash conveys an obvious *liquidity* advantage over attempting to barter in the equilibria with private information. The variable M measures the fraction of the population with liquid assets, and an increase in M affects average liquidity by increasing the fraction of traders with the universally acceptable asset. To the extent that policymakers have some control over the amount of liquidity in the system, in the sense of the ratio of traders with more liquid assets to traders with less liquid assets, this is a relevant issue. What has been shown is that increasing liquidity can increase welfare in the presence of private information, even under extreme assumptions that are not otherwise conducive to an efficiency role for money or liquidity.

V. Conclusion

This paper has analyzed a model of production and exchange under private information, abstracting from the double-coincidence problem in order to isolate the impact of informational frictions. Our framework is related to Akerlof's (1970) model of qualitative uncertainty, but it is also very different, as we abstract from the impact of differentially informed agents on price and study the impact on the time it takes to buy and sell. With no private information, there is a nonmonetary equilibrium in which all agents produce good-quality commodities, trade, and consume every period. There is no role for money, in the sense that a monetary equilibrium may exist but it is Pareto dominated by the nonmonetary equilibrium. With a little private information, the complete-information outcome can still be supported as an equilibrium, but as the private-information problem becomes severe other equilibria emerge with production of bad commodities. For some parameter values there exist multiple Pareto-ranked nonmonetary equilibria.

The strategic complementarity behind the multiplicity seems different from those that have been discussed in related models in the literature. For instance, in Diamond (1982, 1984), the existence of multiple Pareto-ranked equilibria results from increasing returns to scale in the meeting technology and suggests that policy interventions which promote search and production might be beneficial. In Kiyotaki and Wright (1991, 1993), the existence of multiple Pareto-ranked equilibria results from a coordination problem in the social choice of media of exchange and suggests that the government may have some role in helping to influence this choice. Here the results suggest that a welfare-improving direct intervention might take the form of monitoring production or trade to ensure quality. However, a central point of the paper is that welfare can potentially be improved through a more indirect and presumably less costly means: the introduction and maintenance of a generally recognizable currency.

When the private-information problem is severe, the introduction of fiat currency can lead to active equilibria when the only nonmonetary equilibrium is degenerate. In this case, there can be no economic activity without money. Even when active nonmonetary equilibria exist, the introduction of fiat money can improve welfare. However, money never completely alleviates the private-information problem, since welfare is always lower in the optimal monetary equilibrium than in the first-best outcome. Any monetary equilibrium that dominates an active nonmonetary equilibrium has the property that some bad-quality commodities are produced and traded. Money does not drive out all bad commodities. Rather, it allows agents to adopt trading strategies that ultimately increase the probability of acquiring high quality. Attempting to buy with money rather than barter increases the probability that what is obtained will be high quality, precisely because the seller recognizes money but might not recognize another commodity.

The model also illustrates another fundamentally important property of fiat money. Notice that bad commodities are very similar to money in the sense that they are perfectly durable objects with zero consumption value and can be produced at zero cost; hence, one might conjecture that bad commodities could serve as a medium of exchange. There is a critical difference between fiat money and bad commodities, however: the former cannot be produced privately. If bad commodities are to be accepted in exchange by holders of good commodities, we require $V_b \geq V_g$; but if any good commodities are to be produced at all, we require $V_g - \gamma \geq V_b$. Hence, if bad commodities are accepted as a medium of exchange no one will ever produce good commodities. Either bad commodities will have to cease being media of exchange or the economy will be stuck in an inactive equilibrium.

The important characteristics of money clearly include durability and recognizability; but it is also critical that money cannot be produced privately at too low a cost. There can exist equilibria with privately produced money if the cost of producing it is sufficiently high. Suppose there is some intrinsically worthless and perfectly recognizable and durable object—a precious metal, say—that can be produced privately at a cost per unit that exceeds the cost of producing a good commodity. There will be equilibria where some agents produce the precious metal and others produce commodities, with the amount of privately produced money endogenous. As Milton Friedman (1960) has pointed out, however, it is socially preferable to adopt a fiat currency which can be produced costlessly as long as private production or counterfeiting can be controlled, since this avoids the initial cost of mining the precious metal.

Several extensions come to mind. An ambitious project would be to incorporate bilateral bargaining theory into the framework in order to endogenize the price level, as is done in Shi (1992) or Trejos and Wright (1992) in search models of money without the (possibly severe) complication of private information.[20] In terms of privately produced money, one could imagine introducing a variety of objects with different degrees of recognizability and asking whether more recognizable ones necessarily arise endogenously as media of exchange; our guess is that the answer may be no. One could allow agents to differ in their ability to recognize quality, or allow agents to invest in information, or in some other way make θ endogenous. Potentially, a role could be derived for specialized traders or other types of intermediaries.

Concerning intermediaries, although the environment as currently specified rules out credit, the potential superiority of fiat money can be interpreted as suggesting that a monetary system with publicly provided currency dominates one with private currency created by a laissez-faire banking system. There is a body of research supporting the notion that movement toward laissez-faire banking would be socially desirable (see the discussion in Williamson [1992]), although there are also arguments to the effect that legal restrictions on the issue of private money might be beneficial (see Bernhardt and Engineer, 1991; Williamson, 1992). Our model provides support for the latter, more traditional, position: that private note provision under laissez-faire banking is undesirable. Of course, this discussion is only meant to be suggestive, and there are many details that need to be considered. We relegate further exploration of these topics to future work.

Appendix A

Here we derive equations (21)–(23) describing the best-response problem for an agent in a monetary equilibrium with private information. The best-response problem in a nonmonetary equilibrium or without private information is a special case, derived by setting $M=0$ or $\theta=1$. To reduce notation, let

$$\lambda_1 = M[\theta+(1-\theta)\Omega]$$

be the probability of meeting a money trader who is willing to trade; let

$$\lambda_2 = (1-M)\theta p[\theta+(1-\theta)\Sigma]$$

be the probability of meeting a commodity trader with a good commodity that can be recognized who is willing to trade; let

$$\lambda_3 = (1-M)(1-\theta)$$

be the probability of meeting a commodity trader with a commodity that cannot be recognized; and let

$$\Delta = [\theta+(1-\theta)\Sigma]$$

be the probability that an agent with a good commodity is willing to trade.

Consider an agent with a good commodity. Bellman's equation of dynamic programming says that V_g satisfies

$$\text{(A1)}\quad V_g = \frac{1}{1+r}\max_{\sigma}\{\lambda_1 V_m + \lambda_2(u+W) + \lambda_3\sigma p\Delta(u+W) + \lambda_3\sigma(1-p)W + [\lambda_3\sigma p(1-\Delta) + \lambda_3(1-\sigma) + (1-\lambda_1-\lambda_2-\lambda_3)]V_g\}.$$

[20] It is possible that using bargaining theory to determine prices may not affect the results qualitatively. Suppose you are reluctant to buy something because you think it might be a lemon. Then any offer by the seller to reduce the price may only increase your belief that it is a lemon. Hence, take-it-or-leave-it offers at a fixed price could be a feature of some equilibria. On the other hand, it may be worth introducing bargaining to see how average price is affected by private information and the introduction of money.

Simplification yields

$$\text{(A2)}\quad rV_g = \lambda_1(V_m - V_g) + \lambda_2(u + W - V_g) + \lambda_3 \max_{\sigma} \sigma\{p\Delta(u + W - V_g) + (1-p)(W - V_g)\}.$$

Upon substitution of $W = V_g - \gamma$, λ_j, and Δ, (A2) reduces to (21). The derivations of (22) and (23) are very similar and are therefore omitted.

Appendix B

Here we show that $(0, \Phi)$ is a monetary equilibrium for all M in a nondegenerate interval $(\underline{M}, \overline{M})$, as long as r is not too big given u, γ, and θ. First, note that (30) implies $V_m - V_g = pu - \gamma$. Using this and subtracting (24) from (26) we find

$$\text{(B1)}\quad M(pu-\gamma)(1-\theta)\Omega = (1-M)\theta(1-\theta)p(u-\gamma) - [r + (1-M)\theta p + \theta M](pu - \gamma).$$

Now using (28) and subtracting (25) from (24), we find

$$\text{(B2)}\quad M\gamma(1-\theta)\Omega = M\theta(pu-\gamma) + (1-M)\theta^2 p(u-\gamma) + r\gamma.$$

Solving (B1) and (B2), we find

$$\text{(B3)}\quad p = \frac{\gamma}{\gamma + (u-\gamma)[\theta + (1-\theta)M]}$$

$$\text{(B4)}\quad \Omega = \frac{(1-M)\theta(u-\gamma)[\theta + (1-\theta)M] - rK}{(1-\theta)MK}$$

where $K = \gamma + (u-\gamma)[\theta + (1-\theta)M]$.

Equilibrium conditions (28) and (30) are satisfied by construction (we used them to solve for p and Ω). Simple algebra implies

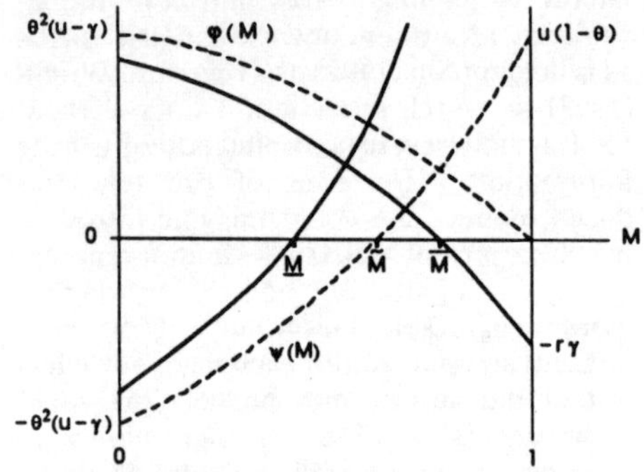

Figure B1. The Functions φ and ψ

Note: The dashed curves depict the functions for $r = 0$; as r increases, the functions shift, as indicated by the solid curves.

that (27) and (29) hold for all parameter values. Clearly, (B3) implies that $0 < p < 1$. Therefore, all that remains to check in order to verify that $(0, \Phi)$ is an equilibrium is the condition $0 < \Omega < 1$. Equation (B4) implies that $\Omega > 0$ if and only if $\varphi(M) > 0$ and that $\Omega < 1$ if and only if $\psi(M) > 0$, where

$$\text{(B5)}\quad \varphi(M) = -\theta(1-\theta)(u-\gamma)M^2 + [(1-\theta)(\theta - r) - \theta^2](u-\gamma)M + C$$

$$\text{(B6)}\quad \psi(M) = (1-\theta)(u-\gamma)M^2 + [(1-\theta)\gamma + (r - \theta r + \theta^2)(u-\gamma)]M - C$$

and $C = \theta(u-\gamma)(\theta - r) - r\gamma$. The functions φ and ψ are shown for the case $r = 0$ as the dashed curves in Figure B1, and both are positive if and only if M is in the nondegenerate interval $(\tilde{M}, 1)$. As r increases, the functions shift as indicated by the solid curves. We conclude that, as long as r is not too large given u, γ, and θ, there will exist a nondegenerate interval $(\underline{M}, \overline{M})$, where $0 < \underline{M} < \overline{M} < 1$, such that the equilibrium $(\Sigma, \underline{\Omega}) = (0, \Phi)$ exists if and only if $M \in (\underline{M}, \overline{M})$.

REFERENCES

Aiyagari, S. Rao. "Gresham's Law in a Lemons Market for Assets." *Canadian Journal of Economics*, August 1989, *22*(3), pp. 686–97.

Aiyagari, S. Rao and Wallace, Neil. "Existence of Steady States with Positive Consumption in the Kiyotaki-Wright Model." *Review of Economic Studies*, October 1991, *58*(5), pp. 901–16.

______. "Fiat Money in the Kyotaki-Wright Model." *Economic Theory*, 1992, *2*(4), pp. 447–64.

Akerlof, George, A. "The Market for 'Lemons': Qualitative Uncertainty and the Market Mechanism." *Quarterly Journal of Economics*, August 1970, *84*(3), pp. 488–500.

Alchian, Armen A. "Why Money?" *Journal of Money, Credit, and Banking*, February 1977, Part 2, *9*(1), pp. 133–40.

Atchison, Mike. *Word for word*. New York: Plume, 1991.

Banerjee, Abhijit V. and Maskin, Eric S. "A Walrasian Theory of Barter and Money: I." Mimeo, Harvard University, 1991.

Bernhardt, Dan and Engineer, Merwan. "An Adverse Selection Theory of Money." Working paper, Queen's University, 1987.

______. "Money, Barter, and the Optimality of Legal Restrictions." *Journal of Political Economy*, August 1991, *99*(4), pp. 743–73.

Brunner, Karl and Meltzer, Allan H. "The Uses of Money: Money in the Theory of an Exchange Economy." *American Economic Review*, December 1971, *61*(5), pp. 784–805.

Cooper, Russell and John, Andrew. "Coordinating Coordination Failures in Keynesian Models." *Quarterly Journal of Economics*, August 1988, *103*(3), pp. 441–64.

Diamond, Peter A. "Aggregate Demand Management in Search Equilibrium." *Journal of Political Economy*, October 1982, *90*(5), pp. 881–94.

______. "Money in Search Equilibrium." *Econometrica*, January 1984, *52*(1), pp. 1–20.

Freeman, Scott. "Transactions Costs and the Optimal Quantity of Money." *Journal of Political Economy*, February 1985, *93*(1), pp. 146–57.

Friedman, Milton. *A program for monetary stability*. New York: Fordham University Press, 1959.

Jafarey, Saquib and Rupert, Peter. "An Equilibrium Model of Cash-in-Advance with Private Information." Mimeo, State University of New York-Buffalo, 1992.

Jevons, W. Stanley. *Money and the mechanism of exchange*. London: Appleton, 1875.

King, Robert G. and Plosser, Charles I. "Money as the Mechanism of Exchange." *Journal of Monetary Economics*, January 1986, *17*(1), pp. 93–115.

Kiyotaki, Nobuhiro and Wright, Randall. "On Money as a Medium of Exchange." *Journal of Political Economy*, August 1989, *97*(4), pp. 927–54.

______. "A Contribution to the Pure Theory of Money." *Journal of Economic Theory*, April 1991, *53*(2), pp. 215–35.

______. "A Search-Theoretic Approach to Monetary Economics," *American Economic Review*, March 1993, *83*(1), pp. 63–77.

Kreps, David M. *A course in microeconomic theory*. Princeton, NJ: Princeton University Press, 1990.

Lucas, Robert E., Jr. "Equilibrium in a Pure Currency Economy," in John H. Kareken and Neil Wallace, eds., *Models of monetary economies*. Minneapolis: Federal Reserve Bank of Minneapolis, 1980, pp. 131–45.

Menger, Karl. "On the Origin of Money." *Economic Journal*, June 1892, *2*, 239–55.

Ostroy, Joseph M. and Starr, Ross M. "The Transactions Role of Money," in Benjamin M. Friedman and Frank H. Hahn, eds., *Handbook of monetary economics*, Vol. 1. Amsterdam: North-Holland, 1990, pp. 3–62.

Shi, Shouyong. "Money and Prices: A Model of Search and Bargaining." Unpublished manuscript, University of Windsor, 1992.

Smith, Bruce. "Limited Information, Money, and Competitive Equilibrium." *Canadian Journal of Economics*, November 1986, *19*(4), pp. 780–97.

Townsend, Robert M. "Optimal Multiperiod Contracts and the Gain from Enduring Relationships Under Private Information." *Journal of Political Economy*, December 1982, *90*(6), pp. 1166–86.

_____. "Currency and Credit in a Private Information Economy." *Journal of Political Economy*, December 1989, *97*(6), pp. 1323–44.

Trejos, Alberto and Wright, Randall. "Search, Bargaining, Money and Prices." Unpublished manuscript, University of Pennsylvania, 1992.

Uhlig, Harold. "A Law of Large Numbers for Large Economies." Research Department Working Paper No. 342, Federal Reserve Bank of Minneapolis, 1987.

Williamson, Steve. "Laissez-Faire Banking and Circulating Media of Exchange." *Journal of Financial Intermediation*, June 1992, *2*(2), pp. 134–67.

Part IX
Conclusion

[23]

WHY COUNTERTRADE? AN ECONOMIC PERSPECTIVE

Rolf Mirus
Bernard Yeung

Countertrade is a peculiar form of transaction allegedly popular in less developed countries and in centrally planned economies. It attracted much interest in the past decade. As the landscape of economic systems drastically changed recently, one wonders what the fate of countertrade will become. In this article we review various motivations for countertrade. We argue that the validity of many popular explanations is suspect. We contend that countertrade exemplifies bundled market transactions, a phenomenon generally observed when transaction difficulties are encountered. The bundling is a contractual arrangement that alleviates the market-for-lemons problem, the principal-agency problems, difficulties in the protection of property rights, and time-inconsistency problems. Bundled transactions will remain as long as the transaction difficulties exist. Terminology may change, but the economic do not.

* * * * *

I. INTRODUCTION

During the last 15 years the phenomenon of countertrade has received the attention of both those involved in international business transactions and those who analyze the practices in this field. In the process the awareness and the understanding of the various operational aspects of different

---

Rolf Mirus is on the faculty of business at University of Alberta, Edmonton, Canada.

Bernard Yeung is on the faculty of the School of Business at the University of Michigan.

types of countertrade, as well as the motivations behind them, have increased dramatically. Countertrade has become the generic term to describe a set of cross-border contracts that link a seller's exports to imports from the buyer, and researchers have begun to adduce empirical evidence on its extent and geographic distribution.

Countertrade often takes place in less developed economies and in centrally planned economies. It is then often associated with policy objectives in these economies like dealing with foreign exchange shortages and promotion of exports. As the landscape of economic systems has changed drastically in recent years, one wonders what the fate of countertrade will become. In this article we review some proposed motivations for countertrade. We argue that the validity of many popular motivations is questionable. We contend that countertrade exemplifies bundled market transactions, a phenomenon generally observed when transaction difficulties are encountered. The bundling is a contractual arrangement that alleviates the market-for-lemons problem, the principal-agency problems, difficulties in the protection of property rights, and time-inconsistency problems. Bundled transactions will remain as long as they reduce existing transaction difficulties.

In the next section we discuss the various forms of countertrade and why countertrade is peculiar relative to usual market transactions. In addition, the observed pattern of countertrade is highlighted. In the third section we critically evaluate some alleged relationships between countertrade and policy objectives. In Section IV we discuss the role of countertrade as a device for dealing with market imperfections stemming from information asymmetry and opportunistic behavior. In the concluding section we present our view regarding the future of countertrade.

II. NATURE OF COUNTERTRADE, FREQUENCY, AND DISTRIBUTION

Countertrade has become a generic term for transactions that are reciprocal in nature. The terminology employed today can be traced to the pre-

World War II (WWII) years when normal trade relations were breaking down. Following German hyperinflation, competitive devaluations and protectionism meant a global collapse in trade and in international financial and banking markets. Unwilling to see Germany cut off from its traditional raw materials supplies in the Balkans, the Reichsbank agreed to the establishment of a clearing system that settled only net positions—and only once a year—a measure that permitted traditional trade flows between Germany and the Balkans to continue. These arrangements were called *Kompensationsgeschaeft* (compensation trade), a term attributed to the then-President of the Reichsbank. Another term used in the context of such bilateral clearing operations was *Gegengeschaft*, which literally translates to "countertrade."[1] During and after WWII, when financial markets were in disarray, Britain used similar bilateral arrangements, as did Western Europe when setting up the European Payments Union. Subsequently the communist countries copied such clearing systems and used them among themselves and also in trade with neighboring countries like Finland. Conceptually, all these arrangements are trade credit accounts between familiar trading partners exchanging unrelated goods.

In the 1970s and 1980s countertrade was different from the old practice although some similarities remained. Current countertrade partners are not necessarily familiar partners and goods exchanged are sometimes vertically related. Current countertrade can be categorized as follows [see, for instance, Mirus and Yeung (1986) and Lecraw (1988, p. 426)]:

Barter: The direct exchange of goods and services, which is completed in a short period of time, e.g., an exchange of $200 million of frozen lambs from New Zealand for Iran crude oil (Khoury, 1984).

Counterpurchase: The assumption by an exporter of a transferable obligation through a separate but linked contract to accept as full or partial payment goods and services from the importer or import-

[1]See Robert V. Roosa, "Countertrade in the World Economy" in Pringle (1985).

ing country. The contract is usually stipulated to be fulfilled within a given period of time, e.g., 5 years, and the goods or services received in return are usually prespecified in a list and are subject to availability and changes made by the original importing country. In essence, then, counterpurchase is an intertemporal direct exchange of goods and services. For example, in 1977 Volkswagen sold 10,000 cars to the former East Germany and agreed to purchase goods from a list set up by the East Germans over the next 2 years, up to the value of the cars sold to East Germany (Hennart, 1989).

Buyback: An agreement by an exporter of plant and equipment to take back in the future part of the output produced by these goods as full or partial payment. The important difference between counterpurchase and buyback is that in buyback the goods and services taken back are tied to the original goods exported whereas that is not the case in counterpurchase. Another important difference is that a buyback deal usually stretches over a longer period of time (as long as 15 or 20 years) than a counterpurchase deal. For instances, the Xerox Corporation sold to the Peoples Republic of China the plant and technology for the production of low-volume photocopying machines, and contractually committed to repurchase a very large portion of the photocopy machines produced in the Chinese plant (Kortian, 1988).

Offset: Requirements placed on the exporters by the importer or importing country to produce part of the product or source parts, or to assemble the product in the importing country.

From the outset, we would like to argue that offsets do not represent a new practice; they are equivalent to "content protection," which is a well-known part of strategic trade policies implemented by developed countries. For instance, 60% domestic content requirement is an integral part of the old Canada–U.S. Auto Pact. This view finds support in some of the results of Hennart (1990, pp. 256–257, tables 2 and 3), which show that offsets are predominantly a developed country phenomenon. Offsets can be analyzed in terms of traditional international trade theories.[2] Because offsets are characterized by a different analytical content and less often involve an implicit contractual relationship between trading firms, we exclude them from our subsequent discussion in order to maintain our focus.

The intriguing features common to barter, counterpurchase, and buyback is "bundling": the exchanges of goods and services are bundled together (the exchanges are implemented either concurrently or intertemporally). In normal market transactions buying and selling of goods and services is unbundled, an arrangement made possible by the use of money and the "market" as an institution. Thus, an individual can sell goods and services to obtain monetary income and can then use the income for other desired goods and services. Such unbundling greatly facilitates transactions and allows more efficient economic exchanges.

There are several presumed advantages in unbundling transactions. First, transactions, when unbundled, can be carried out without a double coincidence of wants. Thus, more transactions can be carried out and search costs are lower. Second, unbundling and the reliance on money facilitate the intertemporal allocation of exchange activities. By unbundling one can choose to consume and to work at different times. The cost of storing the fruits of one's efforts is much reduced by using money, resulting in more freedom and opportunities to make better use of one's resources. Third, unbundling transactions through market mediation leads to the use

---

[2]Offset has the purpose of protecting domestic value-added and hopefully also stimulating domestic industrialization. For the policy to make sense, the domestic content requirement has to be binding. Once it is binding, it has the effect of increasing a good's production cost and thus reduces its international competitiveness. Therefore, the immediate effect of content protection is that it artificially increases the employment of domestic resources, but the effect is somewhat mitigated by the loss of sales due to higher production cost. In the long run, the binding nature of domestic content protection will induce firms to invest more in the productivity of foreign inputs than in domestic inputs. Yet the implication of this result must be evaluated together with the possibility of increasing returns to scale in industrialization. The higher employment of domestic inputs may lead to more technology transfer and may also have an independent spillover industrialization effect.

of money as a unit of account. The calculation of economic benefits and costs is greatly facilitated. As it turns out, in market economies most transactions are unbundled.

While countertrade does not represent an extreme form of bundling, and money as a unit of account is not totally bypassed—in many countertrade deals only a fraction of the initial purchase is paid for in goods and services—the question remains why a significant part of the buying and selling of goods and services should be bundled together. To provide an answer, it is necessary to understand the environment within which countertrade transactions take place. This is essentially the line of thought advanced independently by Kogut (1986, pp. 49–56) and Mirus and Yeung (1986, pp. 28–29).

The impression one gets is that bundled trade, i.e., countertrade, takes place where the market institution is imperfect. This is verified by some of the data: Hennart (1990, tables 5–7) shows that buyback takes place almost uniquely in trade between centrally planned economies and developed economies. Counterpurchase takes place between developed economies and centrally planned economies, OPEC countries, and some middle-income economies.[3] Finally, middle-income economies barter with developed economies or middle-income economies. Some very sophisticated trading states like Hong Kong, Singapore, and Taiwan are included in the middle-income group in Hennart's (1990) sample. Bartering or counterpurchasing with these states is not different from dealing with developed economies. Hence, countertrade can be said to generally take place between mature market economies and economies with a less sophisticated market system.[4] While this picture of countertrade is sketchy, it provides the background against which the issues under review can be addressed.

---

[3]The classification used by Hennart (1990) includes many Latin-American countries in the middle-income group.

[4]Hennart (1990, tables 9–11) also shows that food and raw materials, including fuel, are the common items in barter while manufacturing goods are for counterpurchase.

III. COUNTERTRADE AND ALLEGED POLICY OBJECTIVES

We begin by investigating the relationship between countertrade and some alleged policy effects. There are five such effects:

1. Countertrade is a means to exercise a nation's market power.
2. Countertrade is implemented because it helps a country to deal with foreign exchange shortages.
3. Countertrade can be used to promote exports.
4. Countertrade can be used to reduce uncertainty regarding export receipts.
5. Countertrade is used to bypass an international price agreement like, for example, that of OPEC.

(1) Is countertrade a means to exercise a nation's market power?

As far as we know, Banks (1984) was the first to voice disagreement with this policy objective. Most centrally planned economies and economies in less developed countries are too small to have any significant market power. On world markets, they are more likely to be a price taker than to face an imperfectly elastic offer curve. Moreover, even if they had market power, the way to exploit their market power would be to levy the optimal tariff rather than to countertrade, which is more cumbersome and does not generate direct tariff revenue. Hence, countertrade can hardly be a means to exploit a nation's market power. If it were administered for such policy objective, it would be nothing more than a mistake awaiting correction.

(2) Does countertrade help to resolve foreign exchange shortages?

While it is often said that countertrade is used to conserve foreign exchange reserves, a direct analysis of the alleged relationship is rare.[5] To analyze the relationship, it is necessary to clarify the meaning of *foreign exchange shortages.* There are two plausible interpretations of the term. The

[5]Objections, however, have been raised. See, for instances, Banks (1984).

first is that a country's currency is fixed at too high a price and the government is running out of reserves to defend the exchange rate. The second is that a country is running out of foreign exchange and credit to buy the additional imports it desires. The two interpretations are, of course, not mutually exclusive.

The first interpretation is a balance-of-payments issue. Making use of the definition of the current account, Mirus and Yeung (1987) show that countertrade can help the balance of payments of a country only if it has the effect of improving the country's income. Hence, if bundled trade creates efficiency, countertrade does help the balance of payments. Their more detailed analysis can be simplified by resorting to the monetary approach to the balance of payments. According to this approach, the balance of payments is equal to the change in the demand for domestic money minus the change in the supply of money created by monetary authorities. The change in the demand for money is positively related to income growth and inversely related to the opportunity cost of holding money. While countertrade is unlikely to affect domestic money creation, it can affect the change in the demand for money by changing income and the opportunity costs of holding money. For example, if countertrade is efficiency enhancing, it stimulates income growth and thus helps to improve a country's balance of payments. Moreover, if the efficiency gain leads to a lower inflation rate and thus a lower opportunity cost of holding money, the demand for money will also grow causing a further improvement in the balance of payments.

The upshot of the analysis is that if countertrade indeed improves the balance of payments, it is due to its effect on economic efficiency, not because it avoids using foreign exchange in buying imports. At the risk of reading too much into policymakers' intentions, one would question whether efficiency improvement is on their mind when mandating countertrade. Moreover, one would also have to ask whether there are not less cumbersome policy measures that would have the same impact on the balance of payments. In the next section we shall see that under some circumstances countertrade is indeed efficiency improving. But when that is the case, countertrade is chosen voluntarily and needs no policy restrictions to materialize.

The second interpretation of foreign exchange shortages is also analyzed by Mirus and Yeung (1987). The question is whether a country suffering from foreign exchange shortages and being denied new hard currency loans can use countertrade to raise its import consumption. Countertrade can be viewed as using future exports to finance current imports. Seen in this light, there is no compelling reason to believe that countertrade can increase current imports beyond what a well-functioning capital market would allow.

A possibility exists, however, that mandating countertrade represents an attempt to circumvent austerity provisions imposed on heavily indebted countries. Creditors may insist on earmarking a portion of the country's export earnings for debt service. Hence these creditors closely monitor import spending. This can be viewed as a situation whereby a part of the normal export earnings is subject to an austerity "tax." If countertrade export earnings are not included as normal export earnings, the austerity tax is bypassed. In consequence countertrade can be used to increase one's imports. A country that suffers from a severe austerity tax and has a high desire for additional imports may opt for countertrade even if it is inefficient (i.e., the country's goods are sold for less in the form of countertrade than in normal money-mediated transactions). The result is that countertrade can increase a country's imports. Because this result depends on a loophole in austerity measures imposed by creditors, it is unlikely to persist.

(3) Can countertrade promote exports?

Apparently, countertrade can be used to promote exports. Mirus and Yeung (1986) advance the argument that barter and counterpurchase deals can be seen as sales of domestic goods for bundles of foreign goods and marketing services provided by one and the same foreign firm. The marketing services are identifying and promoting exportable domestic goods. The exchange makes use of the comparative advantage of a foreign firm in marketing and reduces the domestic producer's market making and search costs. Presumably, then, exports are expanded. However, when foreign firms' marketing skills are used, the domestic producers do not acquire much market knowledge. Using countertrade to promote or stimulate exports is a short-cut that saves marketing cost on the one hand but sacrifices learning on the other. This strategy may thus have undesirable long-run implications.[6] In any case, if export promotion is the underlying reason for countertrade, we would expect countertrade activities to decline over time as a nation's exports establish a foothold in the world market.

In some countries where a part of hard currencies earnings has to be submitted to the central government, countertrade may also promote exports. The submission of hard currency earnings to a central government is equivalent to a tax on exports. In some of these countries, countertrade is an openly or tacitly sanctioned means to bypass the export tax. Because countertrade allows an exporter in these countries to get a higher after-tax price, it promotes exports. However, countertrade will not promote exports beyond what they would have been in the absence of the export tax. The export promotion effect of countertrade is thus more apparent than real. Moreover, recent economic liberalization in many countertrading nations renders this motivation for countertrade obsolete.

(4) Can countertrade be used to reduce uncertainties in prices of exports?

One can argue that countertrade is a form of forward selling of exports with the forward price determined by the current price of imports. Hence, countertrade reduces uncertainties in prices of future exports. Recently, it was argued (Dixit, 1989; Ingersoll and Ross, 1992) that the opportunity to invest is an option. The value of waiting rather than exercising the option decreases as uncertainties decrease. Reducing uncertainties then reduces the withholding of investment. Thus, if countertrade indeed reduces uncertainties in export prices, it prompts more undertaking of investment opportunities.

Does countertrade indeed reduce uncertainties in export prices? Casson

[6]In essence, that is why Mirus and Yeung (1986, p. 36, H5) suggest that countertrade is used to sell occasional surplus items with a low probability of recurrence.

and Chukujama (1988) argue that there are no obvious reasons why forward claims have to be marketed through countertrade. They (p. 10) suggest that "although forward selling is an element in both counterpurchase and barter, it is really only in the special case of long-term barter deals between two distrustful parties seeking a simple mechanism of indexation that the superiority of countertrade over conventional forward trading is apparent."

The forward sales nature of countertrade is not self-evident, nor is the advantage of such forward sales.[7] Because countertrade deals are bundled transaction of exports for imports, the proceeds from a countertrade forward sale are immediately spent on imports. Hence, a countertrade forward sale is bundled with a loan to finance current imports that will be repaid by future receipts from the original forward sale. The foreign countertrade partner would, of course, have the incentive to call for the delivery of domestic countertrade goods as early as possible (in order to have a higher gain in terms of the interest rate on the loan). At the same time, when the delivery of domestic countertrade goods is called, the actual quantity delivered and thus the actual interest earned will depend on the current purchasing power of the original countertrade credit earned by the foreign countertrading partner at the outset. The foreign creditor will call for delivery when the benefit of early delivery exceeds the benefit of waiting for a higher purchasing power of the original countertrade credit.

The point here is that the apparent reduction of uncertainties in export prices comes at the cost of granting a put option of exports with a zero

---

[7]Chin (1992) presents an interesting analysis of the strategic advantage embedded in the forward-selling feature in countertrade. Her model involves a two-stage, three-firm game whereby the firms have identical constant marginal cost and a fixed downward sloping linear market demand. The advantage of forward selling in her model is similar to that of capacity commitment. She contends that for a firm attempting forward selling "the countertrade commit is better than a simple forward contract because it is legally tied to an import contract that is carried out immediately. . . . Countertrade provides more observability and more credibility than a simple forward contract" (p. 7). Her opinion coincides with our ideas in the next section.

exercise price. The above suggests that one kind of uncertainty is replaced by another. It is thus not obvious that countertrade reduces uncertainties.

(2) Is countertrade used to bypass international price agreements?

The answer to this question appears affirmative, and it seems to be quite straightforward. Hennart (1990) provides the circumstantial evidence that OPEC countries are actively involved in bartering and counter-purchasing with developed countries, presumably for the purpose of bypassing the OPEC price agreement on oil. Yet it is puzzling why it should take such a cumbersome arrangement to bypass price agreements. There must be less expensive methods, like creative accounting and billing practices, that can also bypass price agreements. The impression one gets is that while countertrade indeed is useful for bypassing international price agreements, it is likely not conducted solely for this purpose. If it were, it should be displaced by some better approaches as time goes by.

Overall, our conclusion is that the relationship between countertrade and many of the "alleged" policy objectives is rather tenuous, perhaps with the possible exception of the "export promotion" objective. Moreover, countertrade does not seem to be the only policy to achieve the desired objectives (if it ever is effective), and it is likely not the best policy. There are two implications from this conclusion. First, countertrade as a tool for the alleged policy objectives is of questionable value. Because it is unlikely to be effective, it will lose appeal and will be gradually replaced by better policies. Second, countertrade must have derived its importance because of economic benefits other than those intended by policymakers.

IV. COUNTERTRADE AS BUNDLED TRANSACTIONS

The implication that countertrade derives its importance because of its economic benefits is worthy of further exploration. The economic incentives for countertrade were first explored by Kogut (1986) and Mirus and Yeung (1986) and formally analyzed by Kortian (1988). Their common theme is that bundled transactions represent a response to market imperfections that are often found in centrally planned economies and some developing countries. In the words of Mirus and Yeung (1986, p. 29), "in these economies, a competitive price system, pure profit motive, and private ownership of the means of production are often absent. . . . [F]oreign investors face many restrictions and a lack of information about the business environment." Simply put, the market, as an institution, is not well established in these economies. The following explores why bundled transactions are useful in such an environment *but are less so in more developed market economies.*

Many economic transactions involve goods and services that are characterized by information asymmetry. These goods and services have quality and/or effort dimensions that are often observable only to suppliers. Examples include the production effort, the quality of marketing services, of the production technology, and of capital goods that need follow-up services and related technology transfer. The information asymmetry gives suppliers an incentive to overstate the unobservable dimension and the buyers the reason to doubt the stated level of the unobservable dimension. A "market-for-lemons" problem (Akerlof, 1970) thus exists. The information asymmetry also gives suppliers an incentive to undersupply the unobservable dimension, a situation known as a principal-agency problem.[8]

Associated with the information asymmetry phenomenon is the issue of the protection of property rights. Some of the goods and services just referred to may be information-based. Their value varies inversely with the degree of dispersion of the information: if the information is appropriated by others its value is reduced. Hence, it is important to the original supplier that these property rights not be appropriated by the buyer.

Another transactional difficulty arises from the fact that many economic transactions extend over time. Due to physical laws, a machine can only produce a limited amount of output per unit of time. Without taking the accumulated value of output flows over several periods, many machines are not worth building. Also due to physical laws, many productions proj-

[8]For a more extensive discussion, see Mirus and Yeung (1986).

ects are putty-clay in nature. To supply a flow of goods and services, specific investments need to be made, and it may take a long time to complete the investment. Yet once the investment is made, the resources are sunk and cannot be switched to other uses without incurring prohibitively high costs.

The above implies that the buyer of a flow of goods and services has some monopsonistic power over the supplier once production comes "on-stream." The significant lead time between investing to become a supplier and the actual delivery of supply also means that the seller has some monopolistic power over the buyer once production starts. The reason is that it takes time and is costly for the buyer to switch to another seller. This bilateral relationship implies the potential for time-inconsistent behavior—the buyer or the seller, or both, will have incentives to exercise bargaining power once the packaged transaction involving flows of goods and services has gone beyond the initial phase. They may seek renegotiation of prices and/or quantities in their favor. This is known as a time-inconsistency problem.[9]

The time-inconsistency problem also exists in a forward purchase of the services of intangible assets like marketing skills and technological support. These services are based on proprietary information. Yet their provision leads to leakage of this information, hence to a reduction of its value. A current buyer of these services will then have the incentive to renege on a previous price agreement and to renegotiate for a lower price of the services. On the other hand, it can also happen that the buyer needs to make investments that are difficult to reverse. For instance, the buyer may invest in production facilities, the productivity of which depends on the continued supply of marketing services. The supplier of these services may then have an incentive to renege on a previous sales agreement and to renegotiate for a higher price.

In market economies there are two common ways to deal with the

---

[9]The above discussion is essentially taken from Mirus and Yeung (1986).

problems referred to, namely, the market-for-lemons problem, the principal-agency problem, the protection-of-property-rights problem, and the time-inconsistency problem. The first way is through ownership. Internalization, the well-known concept underlying foreign direct investment, is a way of overcoming these problems. When the buyer and the seller are both within the same firm, all three aforementioned problems disappear. Vertical integration is another example of using ownership to overcome the problems. In the current context, there is little analytical difference between vertical integration and foreign direct investment.

The other way to address the problems is through contracting. For example, a contractual guarantee is often a signaling device to resolve the market-for-lemons problem. To deal with agency problems, a compensation contract can stipulate that returns be conditional on performance. Licensing agreements usually contain restrictions that prohibit the appropriation of property rights. Many long-term contracts also contain penalty clauses that discourage attempts to renegotiate ex post.

In central planning economies and many less developed countries the effectiveness of these approaches to address transaction problems is questionable. First, in these environments ownership tends to be either very restricted or prohibitively costly. Second, the above measures, in order to be effective, require a judicial system that is unambiguous, impartial, and capable of actually enforcing the laws. As such a judicial system is rarely found in these countries, enforcement of guarantees is not certain. Also, ownership rights are not protected and explicit contracts can be violated without serious legal consequences. Third, in these economies, because of the lack of competition and restraints on profit-seeking behavior, information flow is often inadequate, so much so that the information necessary for writing and enforcing long-term monetary contracts may not be available.

Under these circumstances countertrade, as a bundled transaction, turns out to be a useful device. As will be discussed below, countertrade addresses the problems of lemons, agency, time-inconsistency, and property rights. In so doing countertrade facilitates transactions.

Barter and Counterpurchase

In barter and counterpurchase, a foreign firm delivers its goods in exchange for some domestic goods that it chooses from a predetermined list and which it either has to use itself or can find a third party buyer for. As suggested by Mirus and Yeung (1986) and later by Hennart (1989), this is equivalent to exchanging domestic goods for bundled foreign goods and marketing services provided by one and the same foreign firm. The marketing services include the identification of potential exports and actual exporting of domestic goods. Since the full benefit of the efforts goes to the foreign party, the bundling eliminates the foreign party's incentive to shirk in searching for and actually selling exportable domestic goods on the world market.[10] It also eliminates the foreign party's incentive to overstate the value of its marketing services.

In barter and counterpurchase the time-inconsistency problem is mitigated by the arrangement that the foreign party delivers goods to the domestic party first. Indeed, it is against the delivered goods and services that the foreign party is given credit for counterpurchasing. Stopping the marketing services, the foreign party hurts itself more than the local party. The predelivered goods and services then serve as a performance bond that reduces the foreign party's incentive, and bargaining power, to demand ex-post renegotiation of the price for its marketing services. The foreign party's delivery of goods and services then represents a precommitment measure that makes its promise to market domestic goods more credible than otherwise would be the case.

---

[10]The implication of bundling on agency behavior is only implicitly discussed in Mirus and Yeung (1986, p. 36). Hennart (1989) makes the implicit point explicit. While Mirus and Yeung emphasize only the identification of export opportunities, Hennart's argument is based on the usual motivation to vertically integrate production and distribution. Countertrade is then seen as a means to deal with ownership constraints. In a free market without ownership constraint, the integration of production and distribution is not an obvious choice when raw materials, food, and simple manufacturing goods, as opposed to sophisticated manufacturing goods, are involved. And the former are the most frequently bartered/counterpurchased goods. Hence, the motivation for vertical integration is not obvious.

The local party appears to be better able to change the terms of the transaction in its favor by withholding more easily exportable goods. Yet there is no reason to suspect that the foreign party is not aware of this possibility in advance. In our view the service bundled into a counterpurchase arrangement is not the continuous marketing of readily exportable goods but actually the foreign party's effort to identify viable foreign sales of local goods that are not yet known to be exportable. Thus, the local firm's ex-post exclusion of easy-to-export items from counterpurchasing should not be seen as a violation but as an intended aspect of a counterpurchase contract.

Finally, the counterpurchase arrangement ensures that the foreign party's property rights in marketing are not easily appropriated by the local party. The reason for this is that the local party is not involved in marketing activities like market initiation and development. Fundamentally, transfer of marketing skills is not called for in barter and counterpurchase.[11]

Buyback

In buyback transactions, the bundling of the purchase of capital goods/technology with the selling back of the subsequent output first addresses the market-for-lemons problem. The bundling is a signal: the capital goods and technology sold are so valuable that the supplier itself is willing

[11]The counterpurchase case reported in Abdel-Latif and Nugent (1992) provides an excellent illustration of our points. They report that the Arab Company for Transistor Radio and Electronic Equipment (ACTREE) of Egypt has been buying TV components since 1987 from NEC of Japan, which in turn exports a "tour to Egypt for Japanese." NEC collects yen from Japanese tourists whose touring expenses in Egypt are paid by ACTREE in Egyptian pounds. The yen NEC collected will be credited toward ACTREE's purchase of TV components. In essence, NEC supplies both TV components and marketing services to Egypt. (Note that previously Egypt was not a tourist attraction to the Japanese.) It is the sole beneficiary of its marketing effort and thus will not undersupply its marketing services. Because NEC bundles its TV components with its marketing services, it is paid a premium for its TV components above the price of similar Taiwanese or Korean products. While Egyptian tourist companies learn more about Japanese tourists in entertaining those NEC attracted, they were not directly involved in marketing the Egyptian tourist attractions to Japanese at the beginning.

to accept the subsequent output as a part of the payment for the original capital and technology (Murrell, 1982). It also signals that the transferor is confident of the success of the transfer (Mirus and Yeung, 1989). Such a signal overcomes the market-for-lemons problem associated with information asymmetry in capital goods and technology. Thus the truly high-quality capital and technology package succeeds in attracting a more appropriate price. A signaling equilibrium is a separating equilibrium that does not always exist. The implication is that buy-back as a signaling device does not always work.

Second, buyback addresses the agency behavior of the supplier of the capital goods. When a significant portion of the capital/technology supplier's receipts consists of the subsequent output produced with the capital/technology delivered, then the supplier's revenue depends on the success of the capital goods and the related technology transfer and maintenance services in production. Therefore the supplier has less incentive to shirk on efforts.[12] The supplier will be more dedicated in the provision of services, maintenance, and general technology transfer.[13]

Moreover, if the quality (hence, the value) of the output and the quality of the capital goods and the technology transferred are positively related, the quantity of output contracted to be taken back becomes a control mechanism that can affect the quality of the capital goods and technology transferred. For example, if output quantity and quality are substitutes, a restriction on the quantity taken back induces the supplier to deliver high-quality capital goods and technology that produce high-quality output.

The bundled trade in buyback also reduces the ability of the involved parties to demand contract renegotiation. The incentive to renegotiate stems from the fact that the output produced by the traded capital

---

[12]Kortian (1988) captures the point in a formal model.

[13]The discussion focuses on the foreign party's shirking behavior. Agency behavior on the part of the local party is less important. The local inputs are usually raw materials and unskilled labor. Their contribution is easier to monitor. Later, we shall discuss the usual financial arrangement in buyback that reduces local parties' agency behavior. Also, we shall discuss the practical benefit of buyback in reducing local managers' inefficient behavior.

goods/technology is often a specific intermediate good used by their seller. Due to the putty-clay nature of this kind of project, the buyer and the seller of the capital goods are characterized by the bilateral relationship referred to earlier regarding the subsequent flows of goods produced: Both the seller and the buyer of a capital goods/technology package are interested in renegotiating their original agreement to their respective advantage. The time-inconsistency problem arises.

Bundling together the exchange of the original capital goods/technology for the subsequent output and the peculiar financial arrangement involved combine to reduce the incentive for both the seller and the buyer of the capital goods/technology to demand ex-post renegotiation of their terms of trade. The peculiar financial arrangement in buyback is as follows[14]: The local party in a buyback deal usually needs to raise on its own a loan to partly pay for the capital goods at various stages of the project. The foreign party actually will make monetary payment for the flows of output it takes back. The proceeds will then be used to pay back the loan the capital/technology recipient raised earlier.

From the supplier's perspective, the initial transfer of capital goods and technology to the buyer firm is priced at a deep discount. The buyback goods are bought later at such a price that there is enough consumer surplus to compensate for the discount. The effect of the arrangement is that it increases the potential loss to the capital and technology supplier if renegotiation breaks down. In addition to the usual damage from the nonshipment of expected buyback goods (which are often intermediate input for further processing), the supplier cannot recoup the original discount granted when selling the capital goods/technology.

From the perspective of the capital goods/technology buyer, a breakdown of the buyback deal will leave it with no receipts from the expected sales of buyback goods and the obligation to pay off the loan it has raised to make the payment for the imported capital goods/technology. It may then

[14]See also Hennart (1989).

face liquidity problems, higher refinancing costs, and even financial distress. These unpleasant consequences reduce the local party's incentive and bargaining power to renegotiate the price of the output flows. It also reduces the buyer's incentive to shirk in producing the buyback goods because of the direct economic benefits it receives when a buyback transaction is completed smoothly.

In a buyback deal, the capital supplier, because it is the proper owner of the subsequent output, will have legitimate rights to monitor the operation and the general use of the capital and technology delivered. These rights provide the capital supplier the opportunity to closely monitor the recipient's behavior, with the result that the former's property rights are better protected.

In addition, buyback seems to provide some practical advantages in managerial control. One advantage derives from the fact that the forward quantity target can be used as a benchmark for success. When the stipulated buyback quantity is not met by output volume, the local management has to admit failure. In most centrally planned economies and in some less developed countries performance of local production units is defined in terms of meeting quantity targets. Meeting such a target is sometimes the only performance measure, especially as profit figures tend to be less meaningful in these economies. Local managers thus find that countertrade deals have a familiar "ring" they can identify with. Indeed, they may know better how to achieve success measured by output volume than to achieve success measured by unreliable profit figures. Also, the quantity target is likely a more useful means to elicit local management's effort than is profit for the reason that meeting a production quota takes real effort while profit figures can be created with relative ease in economies without an objective accounting system.

A second advantage stems from the fact that the buyback output is an effective means to monitor the efforts of its employees involved in the transfer. In economies with little competition and a permissive managerial environment, the transferring firm would find it difficult to judge the performance of those employees who are conducting the transfer. If profit is good, it can be due to the intrinsic advantage of the capital and technology transferred, the lack of competition, the fact that local inputs are just too inexpensive, and/or the employees' performance. Poor profits can also be difficult to attribute to employees because of all the confounding factors. Taking a significant portion of output back offers first-hand evidence on the employees' performance with respect to quality control, timeliness of delivery, packaging, etc. These are useful additional pieces of information to have in evaluating the performance of expatriates.

In summary, countertrade as a bundled transaction represents an incentive-compatible contract that deals with the market-for-lemons problem, agency behavior, time-inconsistency, and the difficulties in protecting property rights. It is a rational economic device to facilitate transactions when ownership is costly and also when ordinary contracts are not very effective. In the case of buyback, countertrade is also a means to mitigate difficulties in managerial control caused by grossly imperfect local managerial labor market.

V. CONCLUSIONS

More than a decade has passed since countertrade began to receive serious attention. It is therefore appropriate to ask what we have learned from studying the phenomenon. The first important lesson is that the relationship between countertrade and the alleged policy objectives is somewhat tenuous. To us the more useful avenue of analysis is the study of the economic motivations for countertrade.

Countertrade is much more popular in centrally planned economies and in less developed countries. As these economies lack mature and competitive markets, this location specificity sheds light on the role of countertrade. In such an environment countertrade can be viewed as a rational form of contracting to deal with transaction difficulties. As well, countertrade possibly leads to the additional practical advantages in managerial control in the midst of grossly imperfect managerial labor markets.

The practical advantages exist due to the peculiar environment within which countertrade usually takes place. They quite likely disappear when the environment changes—as is happening now in many countries. Restructuring, i.e., privatization and the development of markets in Eastern Europe and elsewhere, may therefore mean that the environment within which countertrade usually takes place is changing so as to reduce its frequency. Reduced ownership restrictions are likely to shift the organizational forms toward joint ventures and wholly owned production facilities. Improved knowledge, experience, and legal enforcement of contractual obligations will likely mean increasing prevalence of longer term and more sophisticated explicit transaction contracts.[15]

However, the usefulness of bundled transactions to deal with information asymmetry and transaction difficulties is unlikely to vanish. Usually these problems are resolved by ownership integration and explicit long-term contracts. But ownership is not necessarily desirable, and there are situations where integration will cause diseconomies in management and other agency costs (Ethier & Horn, 1990). Explicit contracting may be prohibitively difficult when the transaction is so complicated that monitoring and enforcement become costly. A bundled transaction is possibly a viable resolution of such transaction difficulties.

Indeed, bundled transactions are not unknown in market economies. For instance, Masten and Snyder (1990) report that in the shoe industry the United Shoe Machinery Corporation used a bundled form of transaction in supplying shoe-making machines to users. The company supplied shoe-making machines to users under long-term contracts taking returns that were dependent on the flow of output. The bundled transaction was very similar to countertrade. Masten and Snyder explain the observation in exactly the same terms as researchers do in explaining countertrade.

[15]There may be some political pressure for the restructuring countries to resort to countertrade. Many of these countries are suffering from payment imbalances and/or international credit problems. Politicians may use countertrade to hide imports from the watchful eyes of monitors, as we discussed in Section III, for the purpose of smoothing out the costs of austerity (Sercu, 1990).

Sadly, empirical research on countertrade is very difficult. Information on most countertrade deals is proprietary in nature. Hence, the lack of publicly available data likely will prohibit empirical examination of the analytical microeconomic results on countertrade. The lack of reliable macrodata will also make the examination of the macroeconomic policy analysis difficult.[16] However, if we are willing to accept that the essence of countertrade is bundling and expand our probing to all bundled transactions, we may have a better chance to empirically examine their usefulness in overcoming transaction difficulties.

REFERENCES

Abdel-Letif, Abal M., and Jeffrey B. Nugent, "Countertrade as Trade Creation and Trade Diversion: Theory and Case Study Illustration," Paper presented to the Session on Countertrade and Aid at the 67th WEA International conference, San Francisco, July 12, 1992.

Akerlof, George, "The Market for Lemons: Qualitative Uncertainty and the Market Mechanism," *Quarterly Journal of Economics,* Vol. 84, 1970, pp. 488–500.

Banks, Gary, "The Economics and Politics of Countertrade," *The World Economy,* Vol. 4, 1984, pp. 159–182.

Casson, Mark, and Francis Chukujama, "Countertrade: Theory and Evidence," mimeo, University of Reading, 1988.

Chin, Judith C., "Strategic Leadership Aspects of Countertrade," mimeo, Department of Economics, Tufts University, June 1992.

Dixit, Avinash, "Entry and Exit Decisions Under Uncertainty," *Journal of Political Economy,* Vol. 97, No. 3, June 1989, pp. 620–638.

Ethier, Wilfred J., and Henrik Horn, "Managerial Control of International Firms and Patterns of Direct Investment," *Journal of International Economics,* Vol. 28, 1990, pp. 25–45.

[16]Some recent empirical work includes that of Casson and Chukujama (1988), Lecraw (1989), and Hennart (1990).

Hennart, Jean-Francois, "The Transaction-Cost Rationale for Countertrade," *Journal of Law, Economics, and Organization*, Vol. 5, No. 1, Spring 1989, pp. 127–153.

Hennart, Jean-Francois, "Some Empirical Dimensions of Countertrade," *Journal of International Business Studies*, Vol. 21, No. 2, 1990, pp. 243–270.

Ingersoll, Jonathan E., Jr., and Stephen A. Ross, "Waiting to Invest: Investment and Uncertainty," *Journal of Business*, Vol. 65, No. 1, Jan. 1992, pp. 1–30.

Khoury, Sarkis J., "Countertrade: Forms, Motives, Pitfalls, and Negotiation Requisites," *Journal of Business Research*, Vol. 12, No. 1, 1984, pp. 257–270.

Kogut, Bruce, "On Designing Contracts to Guarantee Enforceability: Theory and Evidence from East–West Trade," *Journal of International Business Studies*, Vol. 17, No. 1, Spring 1986, pp. 47–62.

Kortian, Tro, "Theoretical Formalization of a Countertrade Transaction: Asymmetric Information, Moral Hazard, and Optimal Buy-Back Contractual Arrangements in International Trade," mimeo, Department of Economics, University of Pennsylvania, October 1988.

Lecraw, Donald, "Countertrade: A Form of Cooperative International Business Arrangement," in F. Contractor and P. Lorange (Eds.), *Cooperative Strategies in International Business*, D.C. Heath, Lexington, MA, 1988.

Lecraw, Donald, "The Management of Countertrade: Factors Influencing Success," *Journal of International Business*, Vol. 20, No. 1, Spring 1989, pp. 41–60.

Masten, Scott, E., and Edward A. Snyder, "United States v. United Shoe Machinery Corporation," mimeo, University of Michigan, 1990.

Mirus, Rolf, and Bernard Yeung, "Economic Incentives for Countertrade," *Journal of International Business Studies*, Vol. 17, No. 3, Fall 1986, pp. 27–39.

Mirus, Rolf, and Bernard Yeung, "Countertrade and Foreign Exchange

Shortages: A Preliminary Investigation," *Weltwirtschaftliches Archiv,* Vol. 123, No. 3, 1987, pp. 535–544.

Mirus, Rolf, and Bernard Yeung, "Buy-Back and Technology Transfer—Some Theoretical Considerations," *Canadian Journal of Administrative Sciences,* Vol. 6, No. 3, Sept. 1989, pp. 31–36.

Murrell, Peter, "Product Quality, Market Signalling and the Development of East-West Trade," *Economic Inquiry,* Vol. 20, 1982, pp. 589–603.

Pringle, Robert (Ed.), *Countertrade in the World Economy,* Group of Thirty, New York, 1985.

Sercu, Piet, "Pros and Cons of Countertrade: A Critical Note," Katholieke Universiteit Leuven, Bedrijfs economische Verhandeling No. 9003, 1990.

Name Index

The International Library of Critical Writings in Economics

1. Multinational Corporations
   Mark Casson
2. The Economics of Innovation
   Christopher Freeman
3. Entrepreneurship
   Mark Casson
4. International Investment
   Peter J. Buckley
5. Game Theory in Economics
   Ariel Rubinstein
6. The History of Economic Thought
   Mark Blaug
7. Monetary Theory
   Thomas Mayer
8. Joint Production of Commodities
   Neri Salvadori and Ian Steedman
9. Industrial Organization
   Oliver E. Williamson
10. Growth Theory
    (Volumes I, II and III)
    R. Becker and E. Burmeister
11. Microeconomics: Theoretical and Applied (Volumes I, II and III)
    Robert E. Kuenne
12. The Economics of Health
    (Volumes I and II)
    A.J. Culyer
13. Recent Developments in Macroeconomics
    (Volumes I, II and III)
    Edmund S. Phelps
14. Urban and Regional Economics
    Paul C. Cheshire and Alan W. Evans
15. Modern Public Finance
    (Volumes I and II)
    A.B. Atkinson
16. Exchange Rate Economics
    (Volumes I and II)
    Ronald MacDonald and Mark P. Taylor
17. The Economic Value of Education: Studies in the Economics of Education
    Mark Blaug
18. Development Economics
    (Volumes I, II, III and IV)
    Deepak Lal
19. The New Classical Macroeconomics
    (Volumes I, II and III)
    Kevin D. Hoover
20. The Economics of the Environment
    Wallace E. Oates
21. Post Keynesian Theory of Growth and Distribution
    Carlo Panico and Neri Salvadori
22. Dynamic Labor Demand and Adjustment Costs
    Giorgio Galeazzi and Daniel S. Hamermesh
23. The Philosophy and Methodology of Economics (Volumes I, II and III)
    Bruce J. Caldwell
24. Public Choice Theory
    (Volumes I, II and III)
    Charles K. Rowley
25. Evolutionary Economics
    Ulrich Witt
26. Economics and Psychology
    Shlomo Maital and Sharone L. Maital
27. Social Choice Theory
    (Volumes I, II and III)
    Charles K. Rowley
28. Non-Linear Dynamics in Economic Theory
    Marc Jarsulic
29. Recent Developments in Experimental Economics
    (Volumes I and II)
    John D. Hey and Graham Loomes

30. Monopoly and Competition Policy (Volumes I and II)
F.M. Scherer
31. The Economics of Technical Change
Edwin Mansfield and Elizabeth Mansfield
32. The Economics of Exhaustible Resources
Geoffrey Heal
33. The Economics of Institutions
Geoffrey M. Hodgson
34. The Economics of Transport (Volumes I and II)
Herbert Mohring
35. Implicit Contract Theory
Sherwin Rosen
36. Foundations of Analytical Marxism (Volumes I and II)
John E. Roemer
37. The Economics of Product Differentiation (Volumes I and II)
Jacques-François Thisse and George Norman
38. Economic Growth in Theory and Practice: A Kaldorian Perspective
John E. King
39. Markets and Socialism
Alec Nove and Ian D. Thatcher
40. Recent Developments in the Economics of Education
Elchanan Cohn and Geraint Johnes
41. The Theory of Inflation
Michael Parkin
42. The Economics of Location (Volumes I, II and III)
Melvin L. Greenhut and George Norman
43. Financial Intermediaries
Mervyn K. Lewis
44. The Political Economy of Privatization and Deregulation
Elizabeth E. Bailey and Janet Rothenberg Pack
45. Gender and Economics
Jane Humphries
46. Macroeconomics and Imperfect Competition
Jean-Pascal Bénassy
47. Labor Economics (Volumes I, II, III and IV)
Orley C. Ashenfelter and Kevin F. Hallock
48. The Economics of Altruism
Stefano Zamagni
49. The Economic Analysis of Rent Seeking
Robert D. Tollison and Roger D. Congleton
50. Economics and Biology
Geoffrey M. Hodgson
51. The Economics of Ageing
John Creedy
52. Fiscal and Monetary Policy (Volumes I and II)
Thomas Mayer and Steven M. Sheffrin
53. The Economics of Information (Volumes I and II)
David K. Levine and Steven A. Lippman
54. Transaction Cost Economics (Volumes I and II)
Oliver E. Williamson and Scott E. Masten
55. Agricultural Economics
George H. Peters
56. International Debt (Volumes I and II)
Graham Bird and P. Nicholas Snowden
57. Economics and Discrimination (Volumes I and II)
William A. Darity, Jr
58. Business Cycle Theory
Finn E. Kydland
59. International Trade (Volumes I and II)
J. Peter Neary
60. The Money Supply in the Economic Process
Marco Musella and Carlo Panico

61. Small Firms and Economic Growth (Volumes I and II)
Zoltan J. Acs
62. Producer Cooperatives and Labor-Managed Systems (Volumes I and II)
David L. Prychitko and Jaroslav Vanek
63. Ethics and Economics (Volumes I and II)
Alan P. Hamlin
64. The Economics of the Family
Nancy Folbre
65. The Economics of Training (Volumes I and II)
Orley C. Ashenfelter and Robert J. LaLonde
66. Chaos Theory in Economics: Methods, Models and Evidence
W. Davis Dechert
67. General Equilibrium Theory (Volumes I, II and III)
Gérard Debreu
68. Economic Growth: Theory and Evidence (Volumes I and II)
Gene M. Grossman
69. Long Wave Theory
Christopher Freeman
70. The Economics of Communication and Information
Donald M. Lamberton
71. The Foundations of Public Finance (Volumes I and II)
Peter Jackson
72. The Theory of the Firm
Mark Casson
73. The Economics of Uncertainty (Volumes I and II)
John D. Hey
74. The Economics of Global Warming
Tom Tietenberg
75. The Development of Ecological Economics
Robert Costanza, Charles Perrings and Cutler Cleveland
76. Economic Growth in the Long Run: A History of Empirical Evidence (Volumes I, II and III)
Bart van Ark
77. The Economics of Productivity (Volumes I and II)
Edward N. Wolff
78. The Economics of Population: Key Modern Writings (Volumes I and II)
Julian L. Simon
79. Political Business Cycles
Bruno S. Frey
80. Cultural Economics: The Arts, the Heritage and the Media Industries (Volumes I and II)
Ruth Towse
81. Law and Economics (Volumes I, II and III)
Richard A. Posner and Francesco Parisi
82. Independent Central Banks and Economic Performance
Sylvester Eijffinger
83. Culture, Social Norms and Economics (Volumes I and II)
Mark Casson
84. Industrial Policy and Competitive Advantage (Volumes I, II and III)
David B. Audretsch
85. The Economics of Housing (Volumes I and II)
John M. Quigley
86. Economic Demography (Volumes I and II)
T. Paul Schultz
87. Trade and the Environment: Economic, Legal and Policy Perspectives
Alan M. Rugman and John J. Kirton with Julie A. Soloway
88. The Economics of Fiscal Federalism and Local Finance
Wallace E. Oates
89. Price Theory and its Applications
Bernard Saffran and F.M. Scherer

90. Women in the Labor Market (Volumes I and II)
Marianne A. Ferber
91. Market Process Theories (Volumes I and II)
Peter Boettke and David Prychitko
92. Input–Output Analysis (Volumes I, II and III)
Heinz Kurz, Erik Dietzenbacher and Christian Lager
93. Mathematical Economics (Volumes I, II and III)
Graciela Chichilnisky
94. The Foundations of Regulatory Economics (Volumes I, II and III)
Robert B. Ekelund, Jr.
95. The Economics of Marketing
Martin Carter, Mark Casson and Vivek Suneja
96. Service Industries in the Global Economy (Volumes I and II)
J.R. Bryson and P.W. Daniels
97. Economic Justice (Volumes I and II)
Giorgio Brosio and Harold M. Hochman
98. Foreign Exchange Intervention: Objectives and Effectiveness
Sylvester C.W. Eijffinger
99. Economic Anthropology
Stephen Gudeman
100. Consumer Theory
Kelvin Lancaster
101. The Economics of Famine
Jean Drèze
102. Microeconomic Theories of Imperfect Competition
Jean J. Gabszewicz and Jacques-François Thisse
103. The Economics of Executive Compensation (Volumes I and II)
Kevin F. Hallock and Kevin J. Murphy
104. The Foundations of Long Wave Theory (Volumes I and II)
Francisco Louçã and Jan Reijnders
105. The Economics of Commodity Markets
David Greenaway and C.W. Morgan
106. Corporate Governance (Volumes I, II, III and IV)
Kevin Keasey, Steve Thompson and Mike Wright
107. Economic Welfare: Concepts and Measurement (Volumes I and II)
John Creedy
108. Economic Forecasting
Terence C. Mills
109. Recent Developments in Game Theory
Eric S. Maskin
110. The Economics of Increasing Returns
Geoffrey Heal
111. The Economics of Corruption and Illegal Markets (Volumes I, II and III)
Gianluca Fiorentini and Stefano Zamagni
112. The Economics of Price Discrimination
George Norman
113. The Economic Theory of Auctions (Volumes I and II)
Paul Klemperer
114. The Economics of Regional Policy
Harvey W. Armstrong and Jim Taylor
115. Economic Integration and International Trade
Carsten Kowalczyk
116. The Political Economy of Science, Technology and Innovation
Ben Martin and Paul Nightingale
117. The Economics of Science and Innovation (Volumes I and II)
Paula E. Stephan and David B. Audretsch
118. Innovation, Evolution of Industry and Economic Growth (Volumes I, II and III)
David B. Audretsch and Steven Klepper

119. The Economics of Energy (Volumes I and II) *Paul Stevens*
120. Privatisation in Developing Countries (Volumes I and II) *Paul Cook and Colin Kirkpatrick*
121. The Economics of Tourism (Volumes I and II) *Clem Tisdell*
122. The Economics of Unemployment (Volumes I, II, III and IV) *P.N. Junankar*
123. Privatisation and Corporate Performance *David Parker*
124. Income Distribution (Volumes I, II and III) *Michael Sattinger*
125. International Finance (Volumes I and II) *Robert Z. Aliber*
126. Welfare Economics (Volumes I, II and III) *William J. Baumol and Charles A. Wilson*
127. The Theory of Trade Policy Reform *Carsten Kowalczyk*
128. The Economics of Defence (Volumes I, II and III) *Keith Hartley and Todd Sandler*
129. The Economics of Property Rights (Volumes I and II) *Svetozar Pejovich*
130. Gender and Development: Theoretical, Empirical and Practical Approaches (Volumes I and II) *Lourdes Benería with Savitri Bisnath*
131. The Economics of Politics (Volumes I and II) *Dennis C. Mueller*
132. Economic Theory and the Welfare State (Volumes I, II and III) *Nicholas Barr*
133. The Regulation and Supervision of Banks (Volumes I, II, III and IV) *Maximilian J.B. Hall*
134. The Political Economy of Monetary Union *Paul De Grauwe*
135. The Economics of Sport (Volumes I and II) *Andrew Zimbalist*
136. The Economics of Advertising *Kyle Bagwell*
137. Regulation, Economics and the Law *Anthony I. Ogus*
138. The Economics of Barter and Countertrade *Rolf Mirus and Bernard Yeung*
139. The Economics of Technology Transfer *Sanjaya Lall*

Future titles will include:

The Political Economy of Development
Amitava Krishna Dutt

Public Procurement
Sue Arrowsmith and Keith Hartley

The Economics of Intellectual Property
Ruth Towse and R.W. Holzhauer

Forecasting Financial Markets
Terence C. Mills

New Developments in Exchange Rate Economics
Lucio Sarno and Mark P. Taylor

The Economics of Migration
Klaus F. Zimmermann and Thomas Bauer

Speculation and Financial Markets
Mark P. Taylor and Liam Gallagher

Macroeconomics and the Environment
Mohan Munasinghe

The Economics of Language
Donald M. Lamberton

The Economics of Poverty and Inequality
Frank A. Cowell

The Economics of Structural Change
Harald Hagemann, Michael Landesmann and Roberto Scazzieri

The Economics of Labor Unions
Alison Booth

Path Dependence
Paul David

The Economics of Crime
Isaac Ehrlich

The Economics of Organisation and Bureaucracy
Peter Jackson

The Economics of Business Strategy
John Kay

Alternative Theories of the Firm
Richard Langlois, Paul Robertson and Tony F. Yu

New Institutional Economics
Claude Ménard

Forms of Capitalism: Comparative Institutional Analyses
Ugo Pagano and Ernesto Screpanti

The International Economic Institutions of the Twentieth Century
David Greenaway and Robert C. Hine

The Economics of the Mass Media
Glenn Withers

International Financial Integration
Sylvester C.W. Eijffinger

The Economics of Budget Deficits
Charles Rowley, William F. Shughart and Robert D. Tollison

The Economics of Contracts
Lars A. Stole

Comparative Law and Economics
Gerrit de Geest and Roger Van Den Bergh

Cost-Benefit Analysis
Arnold C. Harberger and Glenn P. Jenkins

The Economics of Networks
Michael Katz and Carl Shapiro

The Economics of Free Trade
Robert W. Staiger

Happiness in Economics
Richard A. Easterlin

Cognitive Economics
Massima Egidi and Salvatore Rizzello

The Economics of Conflict
Keith Hartley and Todd Sandler

Long Term Trends and Business Cycles
Terence C. Mills